CINCINNATI

LLE • Lexington

Perryville

RICHMOND

• Appomattox • Petersburg

XVILLE

Greensboro • • Durham
Raleigh

CHARLOTTE • Goldsboro

HATTANOOGA Wilmington

alton

ATLANTA

AUGUSTA CHARLESTON

SAVANNAH

Atlantic

Ocean

CO

0   50   100   150

SCALE OF MILES

THE ARMY OF TENNESSEE

GENERAL JOSEPH E. JOHNSTON

THE ARMY
OF
TENNESSEE

BY

STANLEY F. HORN

UNIVERSITY OF OKLAHOMA PRESS

NORMAN

Books by STANLEY F. HORN

The Boys' Life of Robert E. Lee
(NEW YORK, 1935)

The Hermitage, Home of Old Hickory
(RICHMOND, 1938)

Invisible Empire
(NEW YORK, 1939)

This Fascinating Lumber Business
(INDIANAPOLIS, 1943)

Gallant Rebel: The Fabulous Cruise of the C.S.S. Shenandoah
(BRUNSWICK, N.J., 1947)

The Robert E. Lee Reader
(INDIANAPOLIS, 1949)

The Army of Tennessee
(INDIANAPOLIS, 1941; NORMAN, 1953)

Library of Congress Card Catalog Number 53-5478

TABLE OF CONTENTS

LIST OF ILLUSTRATIONS

LIST OF ILLUSTRATIONS—Continued

LIST OF MAPS

THE ARMY OF TENNESSEE

FOREWORD

AN ARMY is not merely a large aggregation of men with guns in their hands. To make an army you must have men and you must have guns, but there is an additional, intangible ingredient which is the deciding factor in its success or failure. An army has a personality. It has a character of its own, totally aside from the character of the individuals who compose it. That character, to be sure, is derived in large measure from the qualities of those individuals. A band of enthusiastic volunteers, fired with patriotism, is manifestly better material for an army than a herd of sullen conscripts. But as the inert iron bar is transformed into the flashing Damascus blade by an elusive tempering force, so may an army be transformed by the spirit of its commander.

"The Army of Northern Virginia," one poetic commentator has said, "carried the Southern Confederacy on its bayonets for four long years." That is true—at least it is true of the Southern Confederacy in Virginia. But all of the War Between the States was not fought in Virginia. There was another Confederate army, strangely neglected by most historians of the war—the Army of Tennessee. It, too, carried the fortunes of the Confederacy on its bayonets no less valiantly than its more famous sister army in Virginia. With stubborn bravery it faced the armies of stout Midwesterners under such leaders as Grant and Sherman and Thomas, and it matched them blow for blow.

The Army of Tennessee, however, labored under the crippling disadvantage of shifting and inexpert leadership, a hardship which is conspicuously noticeable in comparison with the great good fortune of the Army of Northern Virginia. The latter had the incomparable advantage of being led continuously by one man, and that man one of the greatest military figures of all time. Robert E. Lee was at its head from early in 1862 to its last sad day at Appomattox. All its battles were fought under his skillful guidance. The men in the ranks and the officers who commanded them had the cumulative benefits of his wise and successful leadership. They had gained from experience a proper faith in him which lent reflected brilliance to their own efforts.

No such advantage was enjoyed by the Army of Tennessee. There was no fault to be found with the valor of the men who composed it. But its history is one long, tragic story of changing commanders, of bickering and wrangling among its leaders, of victories whose fruits were not gathered, of defeats which by a slight turn of fortune's wheel might have been signal victories—a discouraging succession of disappointments and might-have-beens. It fought under all these blighting handicaps for nearly four years without losing heart. It suffered at Nashville, in December 1864, the most devastating defeat administered to any army in the whole history of the war; but, undaunted, it gathered its ragged and hungry survivors together and pushed forward again to fight one more successful battle before the final surrender.

"There is not a sadder story of this war," wrote one bitter and disgusted commentator, "than the history of this army, struggling heroically not only to overcome its enemies but to bear up under the misfortune of its leadership."[1] It is indeed a sad story, but it is a story that has never been written. The biographies or the personal memoirs of the various ill-starred commanders provide an account of the part they played in the army's career, but a continuing story of the army itself has never been set down. In no one narrative is there to be found an account of its Via Dolorosa, stretching from Shiloh's bloody field to the final furling of its ragged flags at Durham Station in North Carolina.

This, then, is an effort to tell that story. It is the story of the Confederacy's military activities between the Appalachians and the Mississippi River. During the latter years of the war after the Federals had gained control of the river, those Confederate States lying west of it were set up as the "Trans-Mississippi Department," which was administered almost as a separate government. There will be no attempt to recount the history of the Trans-Mississippi Department; it affords material for a volume in itself. But to the extent that it is necessary to provide a background of understanding will be mentioned incidentally those corollary military activities beyond the great river that affected the fortunes of this army. Its own peculiar sphere of action was great enough. It left its bloody footprints on the soil of Tennessee, Kentucky, Mississippi, Georgia, Alabama, South Carolina and North Carolina; it fought and marched over more territory than any other organized body of Confederate troops—an area approximately 300 by 600 miles—and it carried its battle flag to the very banks of the Ohio River.

The most painstaking effort has been made to have all statistical information as nearly accurate as possible. Figures as to the numbers engaged and the losses in the various battles and campaigns are derived from the *Official Records*[2] and from Livermore's *Numbers and Losses in the Civil War in America*. Frequently, however, exact statistics are not available, owing to the incomplete nature of the records and confusion in the use of such vague and loose terms as "effectives," "present for duty," etc. Adding to the difficulties of the conscientious student and writer has been the destruction of part of the Confederate archives, so that some much-desired information is not available at all. Often the commanders of armies themselves had only an approximate idea of their forces, being unable to get accurate reports from their subordinates. Many of the official reports are incomplete, conflicting as to facts and vague in details. One Confederate brigadier, it is said, paid no attention to time as marked by the standard chronometers but measured the flight of the hours by his meals. "I expect to leave here right after breakfast," a typical report would read, "and get there by dinner-time; but if I don't make it by then I'll surely be there in time for supper." Such informal and colloquial communications were shocking to the graduates of the Military Academy at West Point; but the tedious paper work of the army was obnoxious to these lawyers, planters, bankers, politicians and storekeepers now wearing the uniforms of colonels, brigadiers and major generals. "I joined this army to fight, not write," one of them spat out disgustedly when rebuked for not making his reports regularly—and of such was the Army of Tennessee.

ADDENDUM—1968

MORE THAN ONE HUNDRED YEARS have passed since the end of the Civil War, and historians are still searching for new facts and making new interpretations of the old. Particularly gratifying to me has been the increasing recognition by historical writers of the vitally important part played by the Army of Tennessee during the four years of conflict.

One of the by-products of this increased interest in the exploits of that army was a renewed demand for *The Army of Tennessee*, which had been out of print for some time. Thus the publishers have issued this new printing of the book.

During the twenty-seven years since *The Army of Tennessee* was originally published, there have been no developments which would necessitate or justify substantial changes in the text. There might be amplifications, of course, of some of the events and activities which are here treated only briefly. It does not seem to be either necessary or desirable, however, to expand for the mere purpose of expansion.

A few obvious typographical errors have been corrected, and the present edition is believed to be factually and typographically correct, providing what it was originally intended to be: a reliable one-volume account of the valuable contribution made by this valorous and long-suffering army to the cause of the Southern Confederacy.

S. F. H.

Nashville, Tennessee
February 29, 1968

CHAPTER I

THE WESTERN BORDER STATES

1. THE OPENING STRATEGY

THE military strategy of the Southern Confederacy in the early days of 1861 was primarily defensive. "All we want is to be let alone," President Jefferson Davis said plaintively in his first message to the Confederate Congress in April, and at that time this was essentially the attitude of the fledgling army of which he was the titular commander in chief. Later on there was a change to the actively aggressive as Lee burst across the Potomac into Maryland and Pennsylvania. But the army which was being so feverishly organized during the infant republic's early days was, it was generally understood, designed to fight at home—if it fought at all. It would take its stand on its own side of the border separating the seceded states from their late sisters, there to await and repel any attempt at invasion by an armed force. Many of the Southern people, indeed, labored under the delusive belief that this was all that would be necessary, that the Yankees would be willing to let the seceded states go in peace if they showed that they were prepared to resist invasion. Subsequent events proved this sanguine view to be unfounded.

In the eastern theater of war—that is, in Virginia—the pursuit of a defensive plan did not involve any particularly complex problems. The Potomac River formed a visible, traditional and clearly understood geographical division between the North and the South. When blue-clad troops crossed the Potomac into Virginia, invasion would become a reality, and the Confederate soldiers were expected to act accordingly. Elsewhere, however, the frontier was not so clearly established, and it was not long before unforeseen complications developed.

In that part of the country west of the Appalachian mountains—in 1861 still referred to as "the West"—there were confusing political and geographical factors. The provisional government of the Confederate States of America was formally organized at Montgomery early in February 1861, but for several months it was by no means clear just where the northern frontier of the Confederacy would finally be. The secession of

15

Virginia soon clarified this point in the East, but until Tennessee seceded in June the southern line of that state was the northern border of the Confederate territory in that sector, and it was not until Arkansas seceded in May that the Confederate boundary west of the Mississippi River was advanced from northern Louisiana to southern Missouri.

Missouri and Kentucky were doubtful states—doubtful but with very strong Southern inclinations—and the struggle for political mastery of these border states was one of the most exciting and important chapters of the early history of the war. Their great political and military importance was recognized by both sides from the very first. Kentucky in the Confederacy would advance the northern boundary line to the formidable barrier of the Ohio River. If Missouri became a Confederate state, it would flank a large part of the western border of the loyal state of Illinois, constituting a constant threat.

Moreover, as the grand strategy of the war unfolded, it became more and more apparent to every military observer that the Confederacy's left flank was its most vulnerable point. Indeed, the military collapse of the Confederate cause was accomplished in the end by a turning of this left flank. Such a turning movement would have been difficult, if not impossible, had Missouri and Kentucky been allied with the Confederate cause. With the Confederates occupying such important strategic points as St. Louis, Louisville and Paducah, they undoubtedly would have continued to hold the Mississippi River throughout the war; and control of that river, involving also the retention of the important port of New Orleans, might easily have changed the whole complexion of the conflict.

Considering all these things, therefore, the supreme importance of the activities in Missouri and Kentucky in the early days of the war is immediately apparent. In fact, without some knowledge of what went on in these two border states in the early months of 1861, it is impossible to have a proper understanding of the fundamental strategy of the forces operating in the western sector of the Southern Confederacy.

2. MISSOURI

It was in Missouri that the war in the western theater first manifested itself in tangible form. Missouri, generally speaking, was strongly pro-Southern and Democratic in its traditions and its politics. In the election of 1860 the state gave Lincoln only 17,017 votes to 146,420 for his combined opponents. At the same time there was a sharp division of senti-

ment among the people as to the wisdom or expediency of secession, with
probably a majority in favor of remaining in the Union.

As to the advisability of secession there was no question in the resolute mind of Claiborne F. Jackson, the governor. He was a full-fledged
pro-Southern secessionist. He denounced Lincoln's call for troops in
April 1861, as "illegal, unconstitutional and revolutionary in its object;
inhuman and diabolical." "Not one man," he said to Lincoln defiantly,
"will the State of Missouri furnish to carry on such an unholy crusade."
In this view he was strongly supported by the lieutenant governor,
Thomas C. Reynolds, and by a large part of the state legislature. There
had been a state convention held in February 1861, which adopted resolutions against separation from the Union; but Jackson still considered secession as the state's proper course and resolutely bent his efforts in that
direction.

Missouri had been a veritable cockpit of prewar tumult and disorder.
There had been constant turbulence and strife along the border between
Missouri on the one side and Kansas and Iowa on the other, where a fire-
and-tow state of savage hostility existed between the slaveholders and the
abolitionists. This feeling had spread from the border throughout Missouri and was intensified after Lincoln's election in November. Between
then and his inauguration the following March, there was a swelling tide
of friction between the opposing schools of thought, which reached its
high point in St. Louis.

Here Francis P. Blair, Jr., youngest son of a well-known father, was an
active, untiring Union man who added to his zeal a gift for diplomatic
and tactful relations which earned the respect even of those who opposed
him politically. Blair was determined that Missouri should not secede,
and he rallied the Union sympathizers of St. Louis into a compact, determined minority organization which was highly effective against the disorganized majority of secessionists. The friction in St. Louis just at this
time was aggravated by local elections in which national issues played a
leading part. The Union men organized themselves into "Wide Awake"
societies which found their counterpart in the "Minute Men" organizations of the pro-Southerners. The Wide-Awakes held torchlight parades
and broke up secession meetings. The Minute Men rallied 1,000 members, drilled and armed, who vowed their willingness to fight for the
Southern cause. They boldly flew a secession flag from their headquarters
in the old Berthold mansion at Fifth and Pine.

Jackson and Reynolds, for their part, worked with frantic zeal, leaving
nothing undone to bring about Missouri's withdrawal from the Union

and adhesion to the Southern Confederacy. In furtherance of his secession designs, Governor Jackson on April 22, following up his defiant rejection of Lincoln's requisition for troops, issued a call for a meeting of the state legislature in Jefferson City on May 2 and ordered the militia of the state to assemble in their respective military districts on May 3.

It was an open secret that Jackson was particularly anxious to seize, in the name of the state of Missouri, the arms and munitions stored in the United States arsenal at St. Louis. This was a rich prize: 60,000 Enfield and Springfield rifles; 1,500,000 ball cartridges; 90,000 pounds of gunpowder; several siege guns and fieldpieces; machinery and other munitions. The Confederacy could have used that material to good advantage. When the state militia brigade under General Daniel M. Frost, a West Point graduate, assembled in St. Louis in response to the Governor's call, the Union men were greatly alarmed by the show of force. They immediately interpreted it as the initial step in a move to seize the arsenal; and they speedily frustrated any such attempt by moving most of the arms across the river into Illinois for safekeeping.

General Frost's militia forces were thus left in a helpless state. They were practically without arms and now had little prospect of getting any. Governor Jackson met this emergency by sending two emissaries to request aid of the Confederate President, Jefferson Davis, at Montgomery. These agents readily enlisted the President's support. They went on from Montgomery to New Orleans and arranged for the shipment of munitions from Baton Rouge where the United States arsenal had just been seized by the Confederates. Although to allay suspicion the cases of rifles, etc., were crated and marked "marble," and a howitzer and a mortar were packed in sugar hogsheads, the watchful Blair and his friends found out about it as soon as the arms reached St. Louis, and they were correspondingly alarmed.

While Governor Jackson was thus busying himself, the Union leaders had not been inactive. Blair had arranged for the organization of a Committee of Safety to look after Union interests in St. Louis, and they secretly raised and drilled a strong force of "Home Guards." While General William S. Harney was at this time commander of the Department of the West, with headquarters in St. Louis, Blair and his warm-blooded friends did not consider him sufficiently aggressive in suppressing the secession movement. They therefore succeeded in having a company of U. S. Army regulars hurried to St. Louis under the command of Captain Nathaniel Lyon, Harney being called to Washington on some pretext. During his absence Lyon was the ranking military representative of the

United States, and his violent anti-secession sentiments, his zeal and his loyalty to the old flag were sufficient to satisfy Blair or anybody else. Blair and Lyon made an excellent team—earnest, energetic, resourceful and indefatigable. To their efforts may be largely attributed the fact that Missouri did not actually become one of the states of the Southern Confederacy.[1]

The immediate object of Lyon's interest when he reached St. Louis was the militia force under General Frost gathered at Camp Jackson. The Governor of the state, of course, was fully within his rights in assembling these state troops there, and Lyon had no legal right to take exception to their presence. He regarded them, however, as a menace to the maintenance of the Federal authority, and he was determined to disperse them. Lyon was not the type to be deterred by any considerations of legality; lack of numbers was all that caused him to hold his hand. This difficulty was removed when Blair's Home Guards were mustered into the United States service, giving Lyon a force of about 7,000 men. With this number at his command he felt strong enough to take action against Camp Jackson.

Displaying an unexpected flair for the theatrical, he reconnoitered the militia camp himself, disguised in feminine attire with his red whiskers concealed behind a veil while he rode demurely in a light open carriage driven by a colored coachman.[2] Apparently he was just an innocent old lady out for an airing, but his gimlet-sharp blue eyes missed nothing as he drove up and down the streets of the camp—streets which, significantly enough, bore such names as "Beauregard" and "Jeff Davis." After sizing up the strength and position of the militia camp, Lyon returned, divested himself of his skirts and got down to business.

A hasty conference with Blair and the Committee of Safety resulted in a decision to move on the militiamen at once. The next day, May 10, the Federal forces marched out, surrounded the camp and demanded its surrender. Frost, seeing the hopelessness of his position, promptly capitulated, and there was no bloodshed—except for some innocent bystanders and some soldiers who were killed when Lyon's troops had a clash with the citizens as the prisoners were being marched through town.

Among the sight-seeing civilians whose safety was menaced by the soldiers' gunfire during this clash was a peaceable citizen, Mr. William Tecumseh Sherman, president of the street railway company. Mr. Sherman, accompanied by his little boy, Willie, had gone out to see the prisoners marched in. He had recently resigned his position as superintendent of the State Seminary of Learning and Military Academy at Alexandria,

---

20 THE ARMY OF TENNESSEE

Louisiana, had just accepted the civilian job in St. Louis and had decided to take no part in the war which was so plainly imminent. Another inconspicuous person who was there and witnessed the street fighting was a shabby-looking ex-army officer named U. S. Grant. Grant at this time had no official connection with the armed forces of the nation. Purely in a civilian capacity, he was helping the Governor of Illinois muster in some volunteer regiments in the southern part of the state and had come across the river to St. Louis for a casual visit while waiting for one of the regiments to assemble.

The seizure of the state militia by the Federal troops, of course, created a sensation throughout Missouri. Spurred by this overt act, the legislature, still in session in Jefferson City, promptly clothed Governor Jackson with supreme military authority. They enacted what was called the "Military Bill," specifically authorizing the Governor to organize the armed force of the state and providing him with an appropriation of $3,000,000 for the purpose. Thus encouraged, Jackson energetically proceeded with plans to raise more troops and resist any effort to compel Missouri to stay in the Union.

The day after the capture of Camp Jackson General Harney returned to St. Louis and resumed active command of his department. He did not approve of Lyon's audacious action against the state militia, and there ensued a bitter and intense rivalry between the adherents of the moderate Harney on the one side and the fire-eating followers of Lyon and Blair on the other. Both factions sent delegations to Washington to tell their sides of the story to Lincoln. Meanwhile St. Louis seethed with excitement.

It is a curiously interesting commentary on the confusion of these disordered times to observe that while Harney was being denounced as a pro-Rebel by the extreme Unionists, he was at the same time being excoriated by a Southern paper for his "vile, illegitimate and unauthorized assumption of power."[3] The same paper from which these words are quoted expressed deep sympathy for Missouri, saying that "steps will ultimately be taken to drive from her border the pestiferous band of barbarians who are every day nursing the treason which the apostate Harney has hatched."

While the "pestiferous band of barbarians" wrangled, Governor Jackson lost no time in proceeding with the organization of the state militia under the Military Bill. He divided the state into nine military districts, appointing a brigadier general to each, and put all the new troops under the command of Sterling Price, who was given the rank of major general. Price was ex-governor of the state, had acquired some military experience as a commander of volunteers in the Mexican War and had been a strong pro-Union man before Lincoln's call for troops. He immediately maneuvered General Harney into a military agreement by which Price was recognized as "having by commission full authority over the militia of the State of Missouri" and instructed "to direct the whole power of the state officers to maintain order within the state." Harney agreed not "to make military movements which might otherwise create excitements and jealousies."[4] The effect was to leave Governor Jackson and General Price virtually in complete control, except for St. Louis which was firmly held by the United States troops, so that Missouri, though technically still within the Union, was then in actuality an active ally of the Confederate government.

While Jackson was perfecting his plans, Blair's and Lyon's influential friends in Washington had contrived to have Harney relieved as commander of the Department of the West and succeeded by Lyon, with the rank of brigadier general. The dismissal of Harney was accomplished in a singularly irregular manner: The order was issued by Secretary Cameron on May 16 and entrusted to Blair to be delivered to General Harney "in case the people's interest required it."[5] Blair (Lyon's friend and Harney's enemy) stood the strain of carrying the dismissal order for two weeks but on May 30 he delivered it to Harney, and Lyon was in the saddle.

Governor Jackson and Price went to St. Louis on June 11, under a safeguard, and held a long conference with Lyon and Blair in the Planters Hotel. Jackson proposed to proclaim Missouri's neutrality, disband the Home Guards and forbid the sending of any more United States troops into the state. Lyon, on the other hand, demanded the disbandment of the militia, giving the Federal government full military control of Missouri. No agreement being possible, Jackson and Price returned to Jefferson City, and the Governor next day issued a proclamation to the people charging that the Federal government was "energetically hastening the execution of their bloody and revolutionary schemes for the inauguration of civil war in your midst" and calling 50,000 militia into active service to "drive out unanimously the invaders who have dared to desecrate the soil your labors have made fruitful."[6] Having sounded this tocsin, he withdrew to Boonville, fifty miles up the river, and planned to make a stand there in case of attack.

Plodding old General Scott in Washington was keeping an eye on the stormy proceedings in Missouri and was greatly disturbed by the developments. He was himself a strong Unionist of unquestionable loyalty, but he did not have any very great confidence in the judgment of the rash and flashy Lyon, and subordinated him to McClellan by the simple expedient

of extending McClellan's department to include Missouri. This was a
bitter blow to Lyon and his friends. Nor was it particularly welcomed by
McClellan himself, who, thoroughly occupied with his campaign in
western Virginia, admitted that he knew very little about affairs in Missouri and hardly felt capable of directing the campaign there. Lyon did
not sulk in his tent, however, and despite the clipping of his wings moved
promptly to occupy Jefferson City and pursue Jackson and Price and whatever militia forces they were able to assemble. They had burned the railroad bridges between St. Louis and Jefferson City, but Lyon loaded his
troops on steamboats and landed at Jefferson City on the fifteenth,
proceeding in the direction of Boonville when he found that the militia
were gathering there.

The Governor's call for volunteers had resulted in the assembly at
Boonville of a motley crowd of about 800 Missourians of pro-Southern
sympathies, entirely disorganized and inadequately armed. Furthermore,
they lost the benefit of Sterling Price's leadership when he was taken sick
and had to be carried to Lexington. Left under the command of Colonel
John S. Marmaduke,[7] they were able to put up but scant resistance to the
advance of Lyon's well-drilled and well-equipped regulars, with batteries
of artillery, but they held off the attacking force for an hour and a half
before they scattered in retreat. Although it was hardly a real contest, the
honors of the battle at Boonville, such as it was, went completely to the
Union forces.

This engagement, viewed in the light of later battles, was little more
than a paltry crossroads skirmish, but at the time it was of tremendous
moral importance. It virtually ended the effective civil administration of
Governor Jackson, who from then on was hardly more than a fugitive,
with his prestige very badly damaged.[8] The Union leaders now held the
state capital, and they hastily called a state convention on July 22, at
which the Military Bill was repealed and the state offices declared vacant.
A provisional state government, with the blessing of the Washington
authorities, was set up at St. Louis with Hamilton R. Gamble as governor,
and Gamble at once declared his unconditional adherence to the Union.

After his rout of the militia at Boonville, Lyon planned a concentration of his available forces at Springfield in southwestern Missouri, in-
tending to make this his base and hold the Confederates south of the
Arkansas line. Before moving on Boonville he had detached two regiments under Colonel Franz Sigel and sent them down into the southwest
for the purpose of cutting off its militia which was assembling under
General Rains. Sigel, however, was not successful in this design. He

encountered Rains and about 4,000 of the militia forces at Carthage on July 5 and was roughly handled. The Missourians outnumbered the troops under Sigel and trounced them soundly. This affair, coming as it did at a time when battles were a novelty, was dignified with the name of the "Battle of Carthage," and described by the press as "an obstinate, desperate affair between General Rains and the St. Louis Dutch, continuing from eleven o'clock in the morning until dark."[9] The true nature of the encounter was more accurately indicated by the same paper's report of the casualties. "The Missourians lost 8 killed; the Dutch lost a large number." The fact was that Sigel made a very poor showing and was glad to get away with what was left of his two regiments and return to Lyon's camp. In addition to Sigel's, other regiments joined Lyon at Springfield, until he soon had assembled a force of about 8,000. He made active efforts to recruit his command and to obtain reinforcements from other points, but the news of the Confederate victory at Manassas on July 21 chilled the ardor of the Missouri Unionists and recruiting lagged.

Price meanwhile had recovered sufficiently from his illness to be taken in an ambulance to Cowskin Prairie near Cassville where by the end of July he had assembled about 6,000 or 8,000 pro-Southerners. Approximately half of them were armed with shotguns, fowling pieces or even flintlocks, but several thousand had no weapons at all. Aside from arms, they were pitifully deficient in equipment. They had no tents, no uniforms, no canteens, no quartermaster stores, no forage for their horses. They had somehow acquired eight cannon, but they had no shells—a deficiency which they supplied by using smooth stones, chains and iron rods for missiles. Feeding the men and their horses was a pressing problem. So, on the whole, Price's "army" was of decidedly doubtful value as an effective military force.[10]

There were gathering at the same time in northwestern Arkansas, near Bentonville, some Confederate troops under General Ben McCulloch— a fairly well armed and disciplined small army of 4,000 infantry, 2,000 cavalry and two batteries of artillery.[11] Price importuned McCulloch to advance and join him and give battle to Lyon, but McCulloch, under the Confederate policy of not sending troops into states which were not in the Confederacy, demurred. Furthermore, McCulloch professed something close to contempt for the military prowess of Price and his Missourians and evinced a notable lack of enthusiasm about co-operating with them. Price, however, eventually induced McCulloch to join him by promising to waive his own superior rank and permit McCulloch to command the entire army after they had joined forces.

Affectionately called "Old Pap" by his soldiers, Price bore the more imposing official title of "Major General of Militia, serving with Confederate Troops." Strictly speaking, he outranked McCulloch. The Missourians thought he far eclipsed McCulloch in military skill, and one of his admiring staff said, "He had won more battles in Mexico than McCulloch had ever witnessed."[12] But he was unselfishly anxious to deal Lyon a blow if it could be done, and he gladly turned over the command to McCulloch in exchange for his co-operation.

McCulloch's rank was only that of brigadier general, but he commanded all the Confederate troops in the vicinity, gathered from the states of Arkansas, Texas and Louisiana. He was a man of about forty years of age and was generally considered a good, practical soldier. He had held the rank of major in the United States Army, had served in the Mexican War, had been a Texas Ranger and had been engaged in Indian fighting. He had little patience with official red tape, but was a strict disciplinarian, and, above all, insisted that his men must be crack rifle shots and must take good care of their arms. He saw to it that rations and forage were provided for troops and horses. His soldiers regarded him highly. He was himself an excellent horseman and an experienced and able leader of rangers or irregular cavalry. One highly un-military characteristic of his was a repugnance to being annoyed with prisoners. Those captured by him were promptly disarmed and paroled after he had threatened to hang them on the nearest tree if they again fell into his hands without having been first exchanged. "I'd rather fight them than feed them" was his laconic explanation of this singular policy.[13]

While all these preparations for battle were going on in southwest Missouri, Lincoln and Cameron at Washington decided on another change in the army organization. It was so obviously impractical for McClellan (or anybody else) in Virginia to direct a campaign on the Missouri-Arkansas border, that General John C. Frémont was ordered to St. Louis to command a newly established "Department of Missouri," comprising the states of Missouri, Kansas, Illinois and Kentucky.

Frémont was a pompous,[14] showy, self-satisfied army officer whose fame depended largely on his explorations in the West, where he had won the title of "The Pathfinder." He had also the political prestige of having been the Republican Party's first candidate for President in 1856, and he had an ambitious and influential wife, the former Jessie Benton, daughter of U. S. Senator Thomas H. Benton. He never displayed any particular military ability at any time in any circumstances. One of Lyon's supporters said later that "Frémont's arrival in St. Louis was a national disaster."[15] Although it was hardly so catastrophic as that, it is a fact that Frémont never did render any signal service to the Union cause there or elsewhere. Lyon, for his part, did not relish the surrender of his autonomy, but he seemed to be animated by a genuinely patriotic fervor and he went ahead vigorously with his campaign.

When Frémont took command in St. Louis on July 25 he arrived at what must have appeared to him a most unpropitious moment. The pro-Southern element in the city, which embraced a large part of the population, was jubilant over the recent smashing Confederate victory at Manassas, and the Union sympathizers were correspondingly subdued. One St. Louis paper of abolition sentiments[16] bluntly suggested that Lincoln "propose overtures of peace and thus put a stop to this bloody and unnatural war." Southern papers on the other hand were emphatic in pointing out the dangers of a premature peace,[17] and there were disquieting rumors of an imminent Confederate military offensive against the southern Missouri border. Upon his arrival Frémont was told, and believed, that the Confederates had 50,000 men massed on the Arkansas frontier—25,000 under Price menacing Lyon at Springfield, 12,000 under Pillow marching on Cairo, 5,000 under General Jeff Thompson approaching Cape Girardeau, and Hardee with 5,000 at Pocahontas aiming at Ironton.[18]

These figures were liberally exaggerated, but it was a fact that the Confederates were indeed planning to wrest Missouri from the Union by aggressive action. The plan was so nebulous and unorganized, however, that it soon came to an abortive end.

The principal obstacle to the success of the proposed Confederate campaign was the absence of one commanding administrative head in military affairs and the impossibility of bringing about any effective co-operation between the numerous independent commands in the field. The available Missouri forces consisted of Price's hard-pressed, half-organized rabble in the southwestern part of the state—of indeterminate numbers but probably amounting close to 10,000—and about 2,000 militia under General Jeff Thompson resting uneasily at Bloomfield. The regular Confederate forces along the Arkansas border were under three independent commanders, each reporting directly to Richmond and none under any obligation to co-operate with any of the others except voluntarily. McCulloch, as has been explained, was in northwestern Arkansas with 6,000 or 7,000 men; he was willing to co-operate with Price, provided he was given command of the combined forces. General William J. Hardee was at Pocahontas, commanding "that portion of

Arkansas lying west of the White and Black Rivers and north of the Arkansas River to the Missouri line"—but nobody seemed to know exactly how many men he had with him or just what he planned to do.

General Leonidas Polk, at Memphis, was entrusted with the defense of the Mississippi River. Governor Jackson went to him and urged him to initiate a movement into Missouri. Jackson professed to be "quite sanguine of redeeming his state from the thraldom of the Lincoln despotism"[19] and went on to say that Price and McCulloch had 25,000 or 30,000 men; 100,000 could be raised in Missouri if arms were available. Inspired by this enthusiastic misinformation, Polk on July 23 ordered 6,000 Tennessee troops under General Gideon J. Pillow to cross the river from Tennessee to New Madrid and expect to be joined there by 3,000 Missouri troops. His plan was for Pillow and Hardee to effect a junction at Ironton, then capture St. Louis and move up the Missouri River, "raising the Missourians as they go."[20] McCulloch, meanwhile, was to advance on Lyon, defeat him and put him to flight. Pillow and Hardee would cut off Lyon's retreat and capture his force, then move across into Illinois and take Cairo in the rear.

To meet this threatened Confederate thrust, Frémont was none too well prepared. Aside from Lyon's army at Springfield, he had about 4,000 men under his immediate command at St. Louis. General John Pope had five regiments in the state north of the Missouri River, but to keep the Confederate sentiment subdued there quite occupied his time. General Prentiss had eight regiments at Cairo, but six of them were three-months recruits whose term of enlistment had just about expired—and they were not thought likely to re-enlist, as their pay was past due.

Frémont sent frantic telegrams in all directions pleading for reinforcements—to Washington, to Kansas, to California, to Texas and New Mexico—but none were forthcoming. Meanwhile, tormented with the persistent rumors of the threatened advance of the great horde of Confederates supposed to be gathering all along the Arkansas border, he undertook to perfect his defensive and offensive plans.

His basic idea (a thoroughly sound one) was that the possession of the immediate valley of the Mississippi River "would hold the country by the heart," as he expressed it.[21] He was anxious to re-establish a firm hold on the state of Missouri, only because possession of it was essential to his plan, "of which the great object was the descent of the Mississippi River." The immediate cause of his anxiety was the small disintegrating garrison at Cairo, for he rightfully considered Cairo the key to the success of any southward operations on the river. He concentrated on this to the neglect of other activities in his department, and Lyon, down in the far corner of the state, felt that he was forgotten and slighted.

Frémont would have been spared a part of his worries if he had known how haltingly the Confederate plan of invasion was proceeding. The lack of unified command made itself felt before the campaign started. Hardee at Pocahontas was an experienced soldier—a graduate of West Point and later Commandant there, a veteran of the Mexican War and author of a famous *System of Tactics*. He did not appear to be in a co-operative mood, or, at any rate, was apparently unable to co-operate with anybody. Price asked him to move on Rolla, the terminus of the Southwestern Railroad in Missouri, and create a diversion there while Price and McCulloch were engaging Lyon. Hardee replied on July 27 that it was impossible for him to move his command from Pocahontas; the Arkansas state forces were just then going through the red-taped process of being formally transferred to the Confederate Army, and he had actually under his command only 2,300 men, whom he described as "badly organized, badly equipped and wanting in discipline and instruc-tion."[22] Ten days later, however, he did move 1,250 men up to Greenville, Missouri, and reported that he was ready to co-operate with General Pillow and General Jeff Thompson. Rough and ready General Thompson seemed ready to co-operate with anybody. On July 30 he wrote Pillow:

"I am working for the cause and am willing to work in any kind of harness and in any part of the team—just so you do not tie me behind the wagon."[23]

Pillow and Hardee found it impossible to agree on a plan of operation; and while each was finding fault with the ideas of the other, Frémont, on August 1, with 3,800 of the men he had in St. Louis hastened to the relief of Cairo. Cape Girardeau and Bird's Point opposite Cairo were occupied and fortified. This display of activity effectually bluffed off Pillow's creeping advance, and he soon recrossed his troops into Tennes-see. Frémont then adopted a defensive program which consisted of the fortification of Cape Girardeau and the three Missouri towns—Ironton, Rolla and Jefferson City—which were the termini of the railroad lines leading out of St. Louis. On the twenty-fourth of August he started work on the construction of thirty-eight mortar boats and two gunboats to operate on the rivers. U. S. Grant, who had been commissioned colonel of one of the Illinois regiments he drilled, had recently been promoted to the rank of brigadier general and Frémont now assigned him to the command of southeastern Missouri, with headquarters at Cairo. On September 8 Frémont wrote President Lincoln an outline of the elaborate plan of operation he had evolved.[24]

The last vestige of hope for an organized Confederate advance into Missouri was destroyed when Polk received word from McCulloch early in August that he was back in Arkansas after having advanced into Missouri and won a Pyrrhic victory over the Federals under Lyon at Wilson's Creek.

After effecting the combination of the Confederate and Missouri forces near Cassville, McCulloch had moved forward in the direction of Springfield with his army of close to 11,000. Arrived at Wilson's Creek, eight miles from Springfield, he established his camp and began to lay his plans for an attack on the town. The assault was set for the night of August 9, and the movement of the troops actually started. A threat of rain stopped it, the marching orders were countermanded, and the troops re-established their camp and resumed their interrupted slumber without troubling themselves to put out their pickets again. The next morning about daybreak they were themselves assailed suddenly by Lyon's forces, advancing from Springfield in a surprise attack which resulted in a hotly contested battle of surprising ferocity. The intense combat lasted for four or five hours and was said to have been the hardest four hours' fighting that up to that time had ever taken place on the American continent.[25] A seasoned officer referred to it in later years as "one of the stubbornest and bloodiest battles of the war,"[26] and another called it "the severest battle since Waterloo."[27] The Confederate loss was about 1,200 and the Federal 1,300.

McCulloch's command of approximately 11,000 was little more than an unorganized band of raw recruits, armed with patriotism and clothed in enthusiasm. Probably not more than 7,000 actually took part in the battle. Even so, they outnumbered Lyon's force of 6,000, though the Federal force included 1,200 regulars and several batteries of regular artillery.

Lyon moved to the attack in two columns, and the battle was begun by an assault on the Confederate rear by General Sigel. This was a complete surprise and at first successful, but Sigel was finally routed and driven from the field with the loss of his colors and his artillery. He retreated so precipitately that he did not stop until he had got back to Springfield. Lyon, attacking in the front, also surprised the careless Confederates and at first forced them back. They rallied, however, and there soon ensued a fierce man-to-man encounter in the course of which General Lyon was killed. Demoralized by this loss, the Federals forfeited the initiative and at length retreated from the field. The Confederates, although technically victorious and outnumbering their vanquished foe, found their ammunition exhausted and were otherwise so disorganized by the affray that they were unable to make any immediate pursuit, permitting the Union force to retire unmolested in broad daylight. The retreat was so hurried, however, that they left their dead on the field, including the body of General Lyon, which McCulloch sent through the lines in an ambulance under a flag of truce.

The Federals fell back to Springfield and thence to Rolla. McCulloch, the battle over, was ordered by the finicky Richmond authorities to leave Missouri and return to the legal Confederate soil of Arkansas. The Missourians under Price slowly followed the retreating Federals and established themselves at Springfield. Here they unexpectedly came again into possession of the body of General Lyon, for the retreating Federals in their haste had left it in its coffin in the courthouse. Price ordered Lyon's burial with military honors. A few days later the remains were disinterred and turned over to the general's brother who came through the lines under a flag of truce with a letter from Frémont. Price was visibly nettled at Frémont's addressing him as "Mr." Sterling Price,[28] instead of using his military title, but that did not prevent him from doing the proper thing.

The Battle of Wilson's Creek (or Oak Hill, as it was sometimes called by the Confederates) was the first real purposeful encounter between the Northern and Southern armed forces in the West, and the battle attracted widespread attention out of all proportion to its actual importance. The victory, such as it was, was heralded with joy throughout the Confederacy. Jefferson Davis mentioned it exultingly in a Message to Congress as another evidence of the superiority of the Confederate arms. But it had no important result.

The retreat of McCulloch's army to Arkansas left Price in a precariously dubious and uncomfortable position at Springfield. He was now in the attitude of being openly at warfare with the United States force, but, at the same time, his troops were not a part of the Confederate Army nor did he hold a Confederate commission. And Missouri was still one of the United States.

Nothing could be done about the status of the state until the legislature would meet in Neosho, though the anomalous position of Price and his men was recognized and steps taken to rectify it. Immediately after the Battle of Wilson's Creek, Governor Jackson sent his personal aide, Colonel Snead, to Richmond to explain the condition of affairs and to obtain the co-operation of the Confederate States by negotiating an alliance with the Richmond government. Such a treaty was made between Missouri and the Confederate States of America, and within the next few months two regiments of infantry, one of cavalry and two batteries of artillery had been mustered into the Confederate service from Missouri.

The Confederate sympathizers in Missouri now clamored for Price to put his troops into action and move northward to the Missouri River, but Price hesitated for more reasons than one. Aside from the inadequacy of his numbers, he was hampered by a shortage of munitions. Though he had garnered 3,000 new rifles as his very welcome share of the spoils of Wilson's Creek, there was a continuing scarcity of the raw materials of warfare—powder and ammunition. The Missouri forces were largely self-sustaining even in such basic materials as these, and the ammunition used in the rifles and cannon at Wilson's Creek had been to a great extent handmade in camp. Artillerymen made their own sabots for the cannon balls and sewed up the charges of powder in homemade flannel bags. Bullet molds were whittled out of split blocks of wood, and the balls run from native lead.[29]

Under such conditions of meager preparedness, Price was naturally hesitant about launching an aggressive campaign. As the clamor for his advance continued, however, he decided not to wait for the supply of ammunition he was hoping to receive from the South, and on August 25 set out on a march northward toward Lexington on the Missouri, which was held by a small Federal force, the "Irish Brigade" under Colonel Mulligan. Price diverged sufficiently to the westward from his direct line of march to make a Sunday raid on Fort Scott, Kansas, where some eighty mules were seized before the garrison, surprised at their worship, could lay down their hymn books and grab up their rifles. There was also a minor but successful brush with the Jayhawkers of Lane and Montgomery near Fort Scott.

Price shambled along in leisurely fashion to Lexington, arriving there on September 11 with a column which had been steadily and materially enlarged by enthusiastic recruits, but which was sorely lacking in drill, discipline, accouterment and supplies. It could hardly be called an army, but was picturesquely and fairly described by one observer as "a shifting and tumultuous throng of from 5,000 to 15,000 men." Despite its lack of effective organization, it greatly outnumbered the garrison under Colonel Mulligan, which was entrenched on the campus of Masonic College where, it soon developed, there was a fatal shortage of drinking water.

Price was crippled by being almost completely out of percussion caps, though he expected a new supply by special messenger at any moment. He therefore took his time about investing the city, not pushing the siege for nearly a week after he arrived. Frémont in St. Louis took no effective steps to help the beleaguered Mulligan who had been ordered to stay there until he was relieved or reinforced. A small body of regulars under General Sturgis was indeed ordered out from Fort Leavenworth to his relief, but Price sent cavalry under General Slack across the river to meet them, and at the first clash Sturgis retreated, leaving his tents and baggage in Slack's possession. Frémont also attempted to take some of the pressure off Mulligan by ordering General James Lane to make a "demonstration" along the Kansas-Missouri border with his notorious Jayhawkers, the familiar name of the Kansas militia in the United States service. Lane was a member of the United States Senate from Kansas who had been seized with the military fever.

There had been hostility and violent disorder on the Kansas border throughout the fall and winter of 1860, and now there sprang up bands of marauders, like those of Jennison, Quantrill, the Youngers, et al., which killed and plundered more or less indiscriminately. Lane gladly acted on Frémont's official authorization for a raid into Missouri. He swooped down on the village of Morristown near the state line and burned it, and swept a wide swath of pillage, arson and murder of private citizens through a belt of Missouri territory six miles wide and fifteen miles long. But this, it turned out, was too late to afford any relief to Mulligan.[30]

At Lexington a small supply of the precious percussion caps had finally reached Price on September 14,[31] and he moved at last to attack the beleaguered Mulligan. In closing in on the city he made use of a novel expedient—a sort of rolling breastworks, composed of water-soaked bales of hemp which the advancing men trundled along in front of them—and this was about the only notable feature of the affair which resulted in the surrender of the thirsty and outnumbered garrison to his men "after 52 hours of continuous firing."[32] Colonel Mulligan wept at the very thought of surrendering. Some of his cavalrymen in their chagrin shot their horses rather than see them fall into the hands of the Rebels. Price, who had adopted McCulloch's system, paroled all the prisoners, but he carried away with him plenty of booty—wagons, teams, ammunition, 5 cannon, 3,000 muskets, 750 horses, $100,000 worth of commissary stores, and the great seal of the state of Missouri which Mulligan had taken from the capitol at Jefferson City. He also recovered from Colonel Mulligan the stupendous sum of $985,000 in money ($165,000 of it gold and the balance greenbacks) which Mulligan's predecessor at Lexington had seized from the state bank—to prevent its falling into Price's hands, he said. When it did thus fall into his hands, Price counted it carefully and, amazingly, restored the whole sum to the bank![33]

Governor Jackson had joined Price while he waited before Lexington. When Mulligan finally surrendered, he issued a proclamation on September 21 reciting that Federal troops had invaded the state, that "war now exists between the State of Missouri and the Federal Government, and a state of war is incompatible with the continuance of our union with the government." He therefore called for a meeting of the state legislature in extraordinary session, in Neosho on October 21, "for the purpose of giving to the people of Missouri an opportunity of determining whether it be proper now to dissolve the constitutional bond which binds us to the United States when all other bonds are broken."

After his capture and occupation of Lexington, Price did not tarry there long. He was still plagued by the shortage of percussion caps, having only two rounds on hand, and so on October 2 he marched out of Lexington and retired into southwestern Missouri. Here he was joined by McCulloch, who advanced into Missouri from Arkansas with his regular Confederate force. Eventually, on October 15, the two armies took up a position at Neosho where the legislature was to assemble in a few days. Meanwhile, as soon as Price retired from Lexington, Lane and his Jayhawkers staged a raid into the country south of there which had been left in a defenseless position by Price's retreat. They burned and sacked the village of Osceola.

Frémont at about this juncture showed signs of sudden interest in affairs in the Southwest. He published an order establishing a Missouri army of 35,000 men, allocated in five divisions under Generals Pope, McKinstry, Hunter, Sigel and Ashboth. These officers were ordered to advance with their commands and concentrate at Springfield, where he himself would take general command. The concentration was effected in such a sluggish and dilatory way as to suggest an unwillingness on the part of some of his subordinates to co-operate with Frémont, but at last they all assembled. Frémont unfolded to them his grandiose plan of campaign—to advance on the combined forces of Price and McCulloch, wherever they might be, to fight and defeat them; then move on Memphis, engage Albert Sidney Johnston's and Hardee's forces separately and, after defeating them in detail, seize the Mississippi River and capture New Orleans, neatly splitting the Confederacy in two. Hunter punctured this dream by unexpectedly and dramatically pulling out of his pocket an order from the War Department authorizing him to relieve Frémont and take charge of the Missouri army.

Frémont, it seems, had become intoxicated with the glory of his own power and prestige. On August 28 he had electrified the whole nation by issuing a proclamation of martial law in Missouri, declaring that any citizen-soldier caught with arms in his hands would be summarily executed, and also proclaiming freedom for the slaves of all persons engaged in the rebellion against the United States.[34] This precipitate action shocked even President Lincoln, who was busily engaged in an effort to appease the slaveholding state of Kentucky and keep her within the Union, and who was not ready for any premature talk of emancipation. He promptly ordered Frémont's proclamation withdrawn, and from then on Frémont's star declined and his days were numbered. In disposing of him, Lincoln again resorted to the irregular and unorthodox process of entrusting the order to the prospective successor, to be delivered at discretion. The first inkling Frémont had of his dismissal was when Hunter handed him the President's letter at Springfield.

The next day, after the crestfallen Frémont had departed, Hunter held a council of war and read to the assembled generals a letter from President Lincoln advising the abandonment of the campaign, although leaving it to Hunter's discretion. The generals strongly recommended advancing on the enemy, but Hunter exercised the discretion permitted him and decided to retire, which he did on November 2.

Hunter's tenure of office was short. On November 9 General Halleck was made commander of a new Department of Missouri, to include that part of Kentucky west of the Cumberland River. He promptly placed Pope in charge of what was designated as the Central Missouri District. During the month of December Generals Pope and Prentiss effectually established the Federal supremacy in central and northern Missouri, although Price still maintained his domain in the southwestern part of the state.

Meanwhile, the Missouri legislature had assembled at Neosho on September 21, and, once assembled, lost little time in getting to work. Governor Jackson sent it a message in which he spoke of the hostilities in the state and specifically recommended an ordinance of secession, an act of union with the Confederate States, and any necessary accompanying legislation.

The legislature duly passed the act of secession. Senators and Representatives were elected to represent Missouri in the Confederate Congress, and the issuance of state bonds was authorized. Missouri was formally accepted into the Confederate States by the Richmond Congress on November 28, 1861, and the Senators and Representatives were admitted to their seats when they got to the capital.

Missouri was thus technically recognized as a member of the Confederate States of America and was represented by a star in her flag, but the connection was on a vague and unsatisfactory basis. Governor Jackson and President Davis clashed almost at once. The President urged the Governor to tender the state troops to the Confederate government in order that they might be organized into brigades and divisions, receive general officers, and be "relieved from the anomalous position they now occupy, as militia of the Confederate States without being a part of their organized army."[35] Jackson replied with a recitation of the sufferings of the Missouri militia, charging neglect by the authorities at Richmond. This nettled Davis, who wrote Jackson a typically acid letter:

"We want muster rolls, and you send me only your reasons why the Missouri volunteers may not be willing to enter the service of the Confederate States and contribute to make up the army which is needed to defend Missouri."

Eventually Price was commissioned a major general, and his army was mustered into the Confederate service and fought valiantly throughout the war. Governor Jackson and President Davis remained at loggerheads, however, and Jackson's unpopularity in Richmond's official circles was reflected onto General Price. A revealing entry in a current diary said:

"General Price of Missouri is too popular and there is a determination on the part of the West Pointers to kill him off. I fear he will gain no more victories."[36]

The continued presence of Price's armed forces in Missouri was an increasingly irritating thorn in the flesh of the Unionists, especially after he and his men became the standard-bearers of the Stars and Bars. It therefore was deemed a matter of major importance to drive him from the state. Late in December General Samuel R. Curtis was sent to take charge of Federals concentrating at Rolla, some 12,000 to 15,000 men, and a month later he launched a movement in the direction of Springfield, where Price was camped. Price went into Arkansas where he again made contact with McCulloch who had taken up winter quarters near Cross Hollows. Curtis followed Price as far into Arkansas as Fayetteville. Then he fell back and established a line on Sugar Creek a short distance north of the town at Pea Ridge, near the Missouri line.

The mutual distrust existing between Price and McCulloch obviously having made it difficult or impossible for them to work together, and the need for effective leadership in that theater of war being apparent, General Albert Sidney Johnston, the Confederate commander in the West, on January 15, had appointed General Earl Van Dorn to command west of the Mississippi. He was given full charge of operations in Missouri, Arkansas, the Indian Territory and Louisiana as far south as the Red River, with authority to recruit in Texas.

Earl Van Dorn was a native of Mississippi and a graduate of West Point, having been appointed to the Academy by President Andrew Jackson. He served with considerable distinction in the Mexican War, and later was engaged in various encounters with the Indians in the West. He was a captain in the famous 2nd Regiment of United States Cavalry, of which Albert Sidney Johnston was colonel; Robert E. Lee, lieutenant colonel; W. J. Hardee and George H. Thomas, majors, with several lesser officers who later became generals in the Federal or Confederate service, such as Kirby Smith, Stoneman and Hood. When Mississippi seceded in January 1861, Van Dorn resigned from the United States Army and was appointed a brigadier general in the Mississippi state forces, of which Jefferson Davis was major general. When Davis was elected President of the Confederate States, Van Dorn succeeded him as major general of the Mississippi troops. He soon resigned this commission to accept one as a colonel in the regular army of the Confederate States, and was assigned to service in Texas. He proceeded to Galveston, where he assembled a force of volunteers, captured three United States steamships, including the famous *Star of the West*,[37] and captured also a force of United States regulars at Indianola—all the Federal troops then in Texas. For this exploit he was acclaimed a hero throughout the South and tendered a ball and banquet at San Antonio. On the other hand, he was denounced as a pirate by a Lincoln proclamation, and a fire-eating Northern newspaper offered a reward of $5,000 for his head— a great honor, since the same paper's bid for the head of General Beauregard was only $3,000!

In September 1861, following his successful Texas expedition, Van Dorn was ordered to Virginia, where he was raised to the rank of major general and put to work organizing the cavalry to operate in that state.

He was going along with this work satisfactorily when the necessity for a new commander west of the Mississippi arose, and he was chosen for this service.

Van Dorn lost no time proceeding to Arkansas, where he assumed command on January 19. On his arrival at Pocahontas, where he meant to make his headquarters, he immediately began to lay elaborate plans for a thrust into Missouri, with the object of capturing St. Louis and moving aggressively into Illinois. Price was then at Springfield, where General McIntosh, with McCulloch's infantry, and General Albert Pike with his command were ordered to join him. McCulloch with his mounted men was to meet Van Dorn at Pocahontas, and a call for reinforcements was sent to the Governors of Texas, Louisiana and Arkansas. By the last of March, Van Dorn thought, he would have 18,000 men and Price 15,000. His plan of campaign was for them to unite at some point in Missouri north of Ironton and move in strength on St. Louis, which he confidently expected to take.

But Price, as we have seen, assailed by Curtis, retired from Springfield into Arkansas. There his old friction with McCulloch again asserted itself and Van Dorn got urgent letters from both generals asking him to come to northwest Arkansas and take command in person. He hastened to do it, riding more than 200 miles on horseback in four days. He telegraphed ahead to stop all retrograde movements and get ready to advance, and when he arrived at Fayetteville on March 3, he took immediate charge of operations. He ordered General Albert Pike to join him with his force of 3,000, including 1,000 Indians, and moved at once on Curtis, still camped on Sugar Creek at Pea Ridge, near Bentonville.

The Battle of Pea Ridge, or Elkhorn Tavern as it was also called, began on the morning of March 6, with Van Dorn commanding about 14,000 men and Curtis nearly as many. The Confederate force was divided into two corps under McCulloch and Price. Van Dorn separated them, leaving McCulloch's army as his right wing before the enemy, while with Price's corps, constituting the left wing, he made a detour and got in the Federals' rear. Here he had the full advantage of such benefits as accrue from that strategic position, but his two wings were seven miles apart, with big mountains between them, and practically out of contact throughout the battle. Curtis placed his lines back to back, each reinforcing the other as the exigencies of the battle demanded. In this peculiar fashion the battle was fought, the action extending over two days.

McCulloch's corps met with especially warm resistance when it

advanced to the attack, and McCulloch himself was killed by a Federal
sharpshooter. His second in command, General McIntosh, also was
killed and the next ranking officer, Colonel Hebert of the 3rd Louisiana,
was captured. The Confederate forces on this front, deprived of effective
leadership and without orders, faltered and fell back in confusion, leaving
Curtis' entire army free to give battle to Price. The demoralized remnants of McCulloch's corps made their way eventually to a junction
with Price, but not until the battle was over the next day. News of the
disaster to his right wing finally made its way to Van Dorn, but undis-
mayed he vigorously pressed the attack by Price's men and drove the
Federals back steadily until close of day. During the night, however,
Curtis reorganized and in the morning moved to the attack.

Owing to the peculiar style of the battle, each army had got itself
astride the other's line of communications, a situation particularly embarrassing to Van Dorn, as the Federals were between him and his
ammunition trains, and his rations and supply of ammunition for both
rifles and cannon were almost exhausted. When he was attacked on the
morning of the eighth, therefore, Van Dorn began a retreat toward Van
Buren, maintaining a brisk rear-guard action through the morning.

In his report to the Secretary of War, Van Dorn tried to put the
best light possible on the outcome of the Battle of Pea Ridge:

"Although I did not, as I had hoped, capture or destroy the enemy's
army, I have inflicted upon it a heavy blow, and compelled him to fall
back into Missouri; this he did about the 16th inst."

The Federals, however, claimed Pea Ridge as a victory for their arms,
as it undoubtedly was. Certainly it frustrated the Confederate plans for
an invasion of Missouri, whereas, if Van Dorn had been successful in
capturing or smashing Curtis' forces, he would have had the way clear
for a sweep to St. Louis. The Confederate loss in the battle was 1,300;
the Union loss 1,350.

As a matter of fact, the Battle of Pea Ridge virtually ended the war in
Missouri. The Confederates were never again able to invade the state in
force, though it was ravaged by the more-or-less irregular raids of Shelby
and Porter and was, for the duration of the war, afflicted with the incur-
sions of guerrillas under Quantrill[38] and others of his sort who professed
allegiance first to one side and then the other.

Pea Ridge was notable for this outstanding feature: it was the first
engagement, and also about the last, in which the Indian regiments played

a part. The Indians did not take to the discipline and drilling of the regulars, and they did not like to fight outside their own territory. They went back to the Indian Territory after the battle, and, though they retained their organization throughout the war and carried on some desultory fighting, they were not a decisive factor.[39]

Immediately after the Battle of Pea Ridge, Van Dorn withdrew the shattered and demoralized remnants of his command to encampment on the Frog Bayou road near Van Buren, where they were reorganized into an effective, compact fighting force of 16,000 men which he officially designated the "Army of the West." General Halleck, meanwhile, was planning a concentration of all the Federal forces in the West on the Tennessee and Mississippi Rivers for a thrust at the Confederate vitals. Following Pea Ridge, he had ordered Curtis not to advance any farther into Arkansas but to join in the concentration on the Mississippi. Concerned by this Federal activity, the Confederate authorities instructed Van Dorn to take his army within supporting distance of the defenses of the Mississippi. This gave him a chance to renew his dream of an attack on St. Louis. On March 17 he wrote General Albert Sidney Johnston that he expected to give battle to the enemy near New Madrid and would then march on the city.[40] But he had hardly started his army from Van Buren before he was suddenly ordered, on March 23, to take it to Memphis as quickly as possible and join Johnston and Beauregard in their pending movements which culminated in the Battle of Shiloh. So on to Little Rock he went and to Des Arc on the White River, where after numerous difficulties and delays he finally arranged for steamboat transportation for his men and arrived in Memphis on April 18—nearly two weeks after Shiloh had been fought.

3. KENTUCKY

In 1861 Kentucky's attitude toward secession was strangely indecisive, wavering and inconsistent;—particularly strange, considering the state's strong traditional adherence to the principle of states' rights and what might have been expected to be its natural course of sympathy and helpfulness toward the other Southern states. The famous Kentucky Resolutions of 1798 expounded the Jeffersonian concept of the relation of the states to the Federal government; in fact, it later developed, the resolutions were written by Thomas Jefferson himself. These principles were reaffirmed by resolutions adopted in 1799, and Kentucky had never receded from her strongly iterated position that "the several states composing the United States of America are not united on the principle of unlimited submission to their general government."

The political influence of Henry Clay was still the most potent in Kentucky, however, and the pro-Southern sentiment, although probably preponderant, lacked aggressive leadership. John C. Breckinridge and Simon Bolivar Buckner, the outstanding exponents of the states' rights school, could not or would not take the lead in espousing actual secession. The Union forces, even though in the minority, were effectively organized and vigorously active. Out of this strange state of affairs grew the incredibly naïve effort to maintain an impossible neutrality in the nascent war between the North and the South.

The situation in Kentucky at this time is well described by William Preston Johnston:

"Everything tended to fasten the Federal authority on the people of Kentucky. The established government, even when regarded as a tyranny, has mighty advantages. In Kentucky the Union seemed panoplied; and, as lingering superstition paralyzes the arm of the recent convert who would cast down the idols of ancient gods, conviction of duty could not rouse the people to action till the time for action had passed, and chains were on every limb. The state government had been elected by the state rights party; but the Legislature suffered from all the dissensions which had produced the schisms in that opposition which had lately been vanquished by the solid minority that elected Lincoln. Under the urgent advice of veteran leaders, like Guthrie and Crittenden, entreating time for compromise, the trimmers and waverers got possession of the government and of the public confidence. It seemed so much better to trust those that promised peace than men who called for armament, expenditure and action!"[41]

This reference to "the solid minority that elected Lincoln" was a particularly apt allusion in Kentucky—the state of Lincoln's birth. In the Presidential election in November 1860, Kentucky cast 145,862 votes, of which Lincoln received only 1,366. The electoral votes of the state went to Bell and Everett, of the Constitutional Union Party, who received 66,016 popular votes.

It is not surprising to observe, therefore, that Lincoln's call for troops, following the fall of Fort Sumter, instantly developed a strong show of pro-Southern sentiment in the state. Governor Beriah Magoffin, after the fashion of the Governors of other Southern states, resented the President's call and replied defiantly: "I say emphatically: Kentucky will furnish no troops for the wicked purpose of subduing her sister Southern states." A large part of the population of Kentucky echoed and applauded these sentiments, and the optimistic Cotton States were encouraged to expect that Kentucky would join them in setting up the Southern Confederacy.

The state legislature had met in extra session in January 1861 and resolved:

"That we protest against the use of force or coercion by the General Government against the seceded states as unwise and inexpedient and tending to the destruction of our common country."

Furthermore, the Governor was instructed by the legislature to reply to certain bellicose resolutions which had been addressed to Kentucky by Northern legislatures:

"That when those states should send armed forces to the South for the purpose indicated in said resolutions, the people of Kentucky, uniting with their brethren of the South, will, as one man, resist such invasion of the soil of the South at all hazards and to the last extremity."

The secessionists were not able to muster a majority in the legislature, however; and by a vote of 48 to 47 a resolution was carried declaring for the maintenance of the state's neutrality.

Lincoln's call for troops not only aroused the resentment of the pro-Southern Kentuckians and the defiant refusal of the Governor; it also prompted a meeting of Union sympathizers in Louisville at which a straddling resolution was adopted:

"That, as we oppose the call of the President for volunteers for the purpose of coercing the seceded states, so we oppose the raising of troops in this state to co-operate with the Southern Confederacy; that the present duty of Kentucky is to maintain her present independent position, taking sides not with the Administration nor with the seceding states, but with the Union against them both, declaring her soil to be sacred from the hostile tread of either and, if necessary, to make the declaration good with her strong right arm."

Just how this could be done no one attempted to explain, but all Kentucky seemed hypnotized by the fatuous dream of a miraculous, peaceful neutrality to be somehow achieved between the battle lines of the sections then girding themselves for a bloody struggle.

On April 24 Governor Magoffin called an extra session of the legislature to meet in May, emphasizing the need for the state to place itself in "a complete position for defense." When the legislature met, it officially and formally approved the Governor's action in refusing to furnish troops in response to Lincoln's call. It resolved:

"That this state and the citizens thereof should take no part in the civil war now waged, except as mediators and friends to the belligerent parties and that Kentucky should, during the contest, occupy the position of strict neutrality."

In accordance with this resolution the Governor issued an official proclamation of neutrality, and on May 24, before adjourning, the legislature disposed of the question of secession by resolving that:

"Kentucky will not sever her connection with the national Government, nor take up arms for either belligerent party; but arm herself for the preservation of peace within her borders."

The Unionists in the legislature had managed to pass a law requiring the State Guard to take the oath of allegiance to the United States as well as to the state of Kentucky, and this later on proved helpful to them.

This State Guard of Kentucky was a more potent and important body of troops than most such organizations. At its head was Simon Bolivar Buckner, a graduate of West Point and former instructor there, and a veteran of the Mexican War in which he was wounded and promoted for gallantry. He had resigned from the army in 1855 and settled in Louisville in 1858. With nothing more arduous to occupy his time than the management of his wife's estate, he undertook the organization of the militia as a sort of hobby. Under his excellent leadership, as inspector general with the rank of major general, he developed it into a well-drilled, compact body of from 10,000 to 12,000 uniformed, armed state troops, which boasted a military effectiveness unequaled by any organized soldiery in the whole country except the regular United States Army. Buckner himself was a states' rights Democrat in politics, and the men composing the State Guard were generally of pro-Southern views; nevertheless he leaned backward in abstaining from use of his position or force to advance his own political beliefs in the crisis. Some of the more enthusiastic of the Southern sympathizers left Kentucky, went South and enlisted in the Confederate Army. Just over the Tennessee state line near

Clarksville, Camp Boone was established as a rallying point for pro-Confederate Kentuckians.

Meanwhile, the Union adherents in Kentucky were not idle in a military way. Soon after Lincoln's call for volunteers two bodies of troops known as the 1st and 2nd Kentucky Regiments were recruited and mustered across the river in Ohio, near Cincinnati. In June, Lovel H. Rosseau set up Camp Joe Holt in Indiana opposite Louisville and began to organize the Louisville Legion. Then in July, growing bolder, Camp Dick Robinson was set up near the state capital, Frankfort, in the central part of Kentucky, and here 2,000 Federals were assembled under the direction of William Nelson. He was a bushy-haired, bearded giant of a man, towering four inches above six feet and weighing 300 pounds. He rose to the rank of major general in the Union Army and was known to his men as "Bull" Nelson for his blustering, overbearing manner.[42] A native of Kentucky, he was an officer of the United States Navy, and during the spring of 1861 he spent a good deal of time in the state as a sort of unofficial observer for President Lincoln. At his suggestion, Lincoln sent him 10,000 muskets, and with these the Union Home Guards were later armed.[43]

In the circumstances, as was not unnatural, Kentucky's professed neutrality was generally regarded as a sham; both North and South were suspicious of the real intent. The impossibility of any genuine neutrality in such an explosive situation was generally recognized by all thinking people. While it was conceivable that a state might avail itself of the supposed right of secession, withdraw from the Union and assert its independent sovereignty, it was a manifest absurdity for a state to remain in the United States during a war in which the Union was at stake and still refuse to take part. It was no wonder, therefore, that both sides manifested grave suspicion of Kentucky's real motives and purposes.

So long as Tennessee remained within the Union the question of what to do about Kentucky was not such a serious one, except as a nice, abstract problem in political theory. But when Tennessee in June 1861 seceded from the Union and cast her lot with the Confederacy, then the Kentucky question became acute. It was a particularly pertinent question, of course, in Tennessee. A mass meeting was held in Nashville in August for the announced purpose of considering the relations of the two states. In addressing this meeting Andrew Ewing, a prominent Tennessean, declared:

"The policy of the Lincoln administration seems to be to provoke a struggle on the borders of Kentucky and Tennessee, probably for the purpose of diverting our forces from Virginia. Our people are anxious to avoid this conflict, and have assembled to-day to say to the people of Kentucky: 'If this war is to come, Kentucky must make it. We are friendly and desire to remain so, only asking of Kentucky, if she can not go with us, that she maintain her neutrality inviolate and not permit the formation of Federal camps in her territory and the transmission of Federal soldiers, arms and munitions across her territory to invade Tennessee.' "[44]

Northern critics hotly denounced Kentucky's neutrality as nothing more than a device of the secessionists for holding the Tennessee border safe from invasion. As a matter of fact, short of its actual secession, nothing would have suited the Confederates better than for Kentucky to be able actually to maintain a position of real neutrality and serve as a buffer state between the Ohio River and the Kentucky-Tennessee state line which there constituted the Confederacy's northern frontier. The Southerners, however, were laboring under no delusions. They recognized Kentucky's neutrality as practically impossible, no matter what her intent, and the prevalent inclination in the South was to regard her action as one of perfidy and treachery.

The declaration of neutrality, contended one strongly Confederate paper in Nashville, "was adopted hypocritically and treacherously to deceive the Confederate States and allow the despot, Lincoln, to cover Kentucky soil with his mercenaries and from that cover to invade Tennessee."[45] The South as a whole took that view.

Whether or not this was a correct view, it soon began to look as though that were the way it was going to work out in practice. As soon as the neutrality proclamation was issued in May, Buckner was sent to Washington to inform President Lincoln of the state's position. He returned with the report that Lincoln had agreed to observe this neutrality— although the President later denied any such agreement. General Buckner went also to Cincinnati to lay the matter officially before General George B. McClellan, the Federal commander there. He came away with the impression that McClellan had agreed to respect Kentucky's desire to remain neutral, although subsequently McClellan insisted he had made no such commitment. At any rate, Buckner advised Governor Magoffin that McClellan had, and in Tennessee made a similar report to Governor Isham G. Harris. He urged Governor Harris, in view of the Federal government's supposed concurrence, to observe Kentucky's neutrality and to prevent any movement, across the border, of Tennessee armed forces, which were at that moment technically independent, not yet having been formally transferred to the Confederacy.

Governor Harris agreed to the convention, although when Buckner arrived in Nashville he was just on the verge of sending a detachment of Tennessee troops, under General Pillow, to Columbus, Kentucky, on the Mississippi River. The inhabitants of Columbus were strongly Southern in sympathy and had petitioned Governor Harris to send a force to occupy their town and protect it from what they thought a threatened invasion by Federal troops from Cairo. At Buckner's behest, Harris withheld Pillow from occupying Columbus, and to allay the citizens' fears Buckner sent to the town six companies of the Kentucky State Guard under Colonel Lloyd Tilghman. Some color to Federal recognition of the principle of neutrality was given when Major Robert Anderson, the hero of Fort Sumter, though designated as commander of the "Department of Kentucky," was ordered to maintain his headquarters at Cincinnati.

As the summer wore on, it began to be increasingly apparent to everybody that the status quo in Kentucky could not be preserved. Buckner, in particular, felt that he was in a compromising position, as his own sympathies were openly and undeniably Southern; hence on July 20 he resigned his commission at head of the State Guard and withdrew to Tennessee. Soon after his resignation, although an effort was made to hold it together, the Guard was disbanded and its arms and munitions were turned over to the pro-Union Home Guard.

On the first of September the Federal government threw off any pretense of recognizing neutrality and took active steps toward occupation. Major Anderson moved his headquarters from Cincinnati to Louisville. Nelson, who had been working more or less under cover, came out in the open, was commissioned a brigadier general and authorized to organize at Maysville, Kentucky, a force to operate in the eastern part of the state. The troops at Camp Dick Robinson were placed under the command of Brigadier General George H. Thomas. There were signs of an impending shift of troops from Cairo to Columbus. In fact, Frémont's letter to Grant assigning him to the command of the forces in southeast Missouri stated that it was his intention to occupy Columbus.

Holding back no longer in deference to Kentucky's neutral avowals, Major General Leonidas Polk moved up swiftly from his encampment at Union City in Tennessee and seized Columbus on September 4. He just barely got there ahead of Grant, for the latter was preparing to grab it on the following day.[46] Forestalled at Columbus, Grant occupied Paducah for the Federals. Both sides had crossed the Rubicon. Kentucky's neutrality was a punctured bubble. Polk issued a proclamation declaring it had become a military necessity for the Confederates to occupy Columbus, "the Federal Government having, in defiance of the wishes of the people of Kentucky, disregarded their neutrality by establishing camps and depots of arms and by organizing military companies within their territory, and by constructing a military work on the Missouri shore, immediately opposite to and commanding Columbus, evidently intended to cover the landing of troops for the seizure of that town."[47]

General Polk at once communicated to Governor Magoffin the reasons for his action and offered to withdraw if the Federal troops would do so simultaneously, both agreeing not to occupy any point in Kentucky in the future. Governor Harris immediately appointed a board of commissioners[48] to call on Governor Magoffin "in an effort to preserve friendly relations between the states of Kentucky and Tennessee and to prevent, if in their power, social estrangement and war between the people of the two states."[49] The commissioners reached Frankfort on the ninth, delivered the message from Harris to Magoffin and told him that Harris had instructed Polk to withdraw but Polk had refused, persisting in his refusal even after Harris had had the Confederate Secretary of War, LeRoy P. Walker, order him out of the state. Polk reiterated that holding his position at Columbus was a military necessity and that retiring from it "would be attended with the loss of many lives." The question was appealed to President Davis, who promptly decided that "the necessity justifies the action." Polk stayed in Kentucky.[50]

President Davis in his message to the Confederate Congress on November 18, 1861, said:

"Finding that the Confederate States were about to be invaded through Kentucky, and that her people, after being deceived into a mistaken security, were unarmed and in danger of being subjugated by the Federal force, our armies were marched into that state to repel the enemy and prevent their occupation of certain strategic points which would have given them great advantages in the contest—a step which was justified not only by the necessities of self-defense on the part of the Confederate States, but also by a desire to aid the people of Kentucky."[51]

Magoffin, now thoroughly bewildered by the web in which he and his state had become entangled, sent a message to the legislature urging a resolution that would require North and South alike to keep out of Kentucky and in good faith respect its neutrality. This position was supported by the leading Frankfort paper in a strong editorial:

"Do we intend to maintain our neutrality in good faith? If we do, shall we suffer either belligerent to remain on our soil? Our opinion is emphatically that the Legislature should require both sides to withdraw."[52]

The legislature, however, was now strongly under the influence of the pro-Unionists. It showed its loyalty by passing a law making enlistment under the Confederate flag a misdemeanor and the invasion of Kentucky by Confederate troops a felony, with heavy penalties for both. Instead of following Magoffin's suggestion, it passed a resolution calling on the Confederate troops to get out—but not mentioning the Union invaders. Magoffin vetoed this one-sided protest, but pressure was brought to bear on him and on the thirteenth he issued a proclamation stating that "Kentucky expects the Confederate or Tennessee troops to be withdrawn from her soil unconditionally." Polk, of course, disregarded the demand based on this new one-way neutrality and held his ground at Columbus. Kentucky within a few days formally declared its allegiance to the Union.

Later, on November 18, there was held at Russellville (within that southern part of the state occupied by the Confederates) a "Sovereignty Convention" which passed an ordinance of secession, elected G. W. Johnson governor, chose other state officials, and sent commissioners to Richmond to represent the state. In December the Confederate Congress voted to admit Kentucky and throughout the war the state had Representatives and Senators who were elected by the vote of the Kentucky soldiers in the Confederate armies.

CHAPTER II

TENNESSEE GIRDS FOR WAR

A POPULAR, cynical witticism in the state during the war reckoned that "Tennessee never seceded; Isham G. Harris seceded and carried Tennessee along with him." Making proper allowance for the use of exaggeration for emphasis, that presents a fairly accurate picture. Governor Harris was beyond any question the dominating personality in Tennessee in 1861— and her most aggressive and determined secessionist.

A majority of Tennesseans had at first viewed with reluctance the prospect of separation from the Union. When the proposal to call a secession convention was submitted to popular vote soon after South Carolina had gone out, it was decisively rejected by 91,803 to 24,749. Pro-Southern sentiment, however, increased. Meetings of Southern sympathizers were addressed by fire-eating orators. The newspapers clamored for secession. The actual beginning of hostilities quickly brought matters to a head. The issue of the Memphis Appeal[1] carrying on account of the fall of Fort Sumter also contained a news item about a meeting of "the friends of Southern freedom," held the preceding evening "at early gaslight," at which Lincoln and his effort to reinforce Sumter were violently denounced. To leave no doubt of its own sentiments, the *Appeal* carried at its masthead a woodcut of the Confederate flag, above a realistic picture of a cannon belching volumes of smoke from muzzle and touchhole.

Other papers were equally belligerent in their pro-Southern expressions, and the secession sentiments were raised to the boiling point by Lincoln's call for troops. Fiery Governor Harris answered Lincoln with characteristic vigor. "Tennessee will not furnish a single man for coercion, but fifty thousand if necessary for the defense of our rights or those of our Southern brothers." The Governor's bold defiance was applauded and supported by most of the people. As soon as the legislature could be convened it voted to submit to the electorate a "declaration of independence" from the United States. Aside from East Tennessee where the population, then and throughout the war, remained preponderantly Unionist in sentiment, the overwhelming majority quickly turned to favor separation from the Union and alliance with the Southern Confederacy. The formal

47

ordinance of secession was not submitted to a vote until June 10, 1861, when it was carried by 108,511 to 47,338. In the meantime Governor Harris had proceeded as vigorously with his mobilization of resources as though secession were an accomplished fact. Volunteer military organizations had blossomed spontaneously throughout Tennessee. They had drilled and paraded and been presented with silk Confederate flags. Drums had beat and fifes shrilled in the streets. Bands had played the *Bonnie Blue Flag* and *Dixie*. The people were ready to fight.[2]

As authorized by the legislature, Governor Harris on May 7 entered into a military league with the Confederate States of America and two days later named a full staff of officers for the state's military forces.[3] He appointed also a Financial and Military Board[4] which took over the difficult task of co-ordinating the work of mobilization and handled it effectively until August when the Tennessee troops were finally transferred to the authority of the Confederate States. Meanwhile, the Governor had placed the state soldiers and military operations under the command of General Gideon J. Pillow, and, recognizing the supreme importance of the Mississippi River, had stationed him in Memphis where he could give his personal attention to developing the defenses of the river.

A West Point graduate and a veteran of the Mexican War, General Pillow was Tennessee's outstanding military figure. He took over his new duties with alacrity and enthusiasm. With the limited resources at his command, he undertook the organization of the troops and the construction of defensive positions. It was immediately obvious that the Mississippi River constituted an open and inviting highway for the invasion of the South; consequently any defensive plan must contemplate the blocking of that river to invaders. Pillow placed two batteries at Memphis and started the construction of a fortification called Fort Wright at Randolph, a small town sixty-five miles north of Memphis, and a more ambitious work a few miles farther north which was later named Fort Pillow. It was located on what was called the First Chickasaw Bluff, at the lower end of a big horseshoe bend—a very strong position. Fortifications were begun also on Island No. 10 in the Mississippi, just off the extreme northwestern corner of the state.

On July 4, 1861, Pillow was superseded by General Leonidas Polk of the Confederate Army, who was assigned to the command of what was known as Department No. 2, with headquarters at Memphis, his territory embracing West Tennessee, northern Mississippi and Alabama, eastern Arkansas and northern Louisiana.

General Polk was a strange product of the times—a graduate of West

Point who had resigned from the army soon after his graduation to study for the ministry, then had risen in the Episcopal Church to be the Bishop of Louisiana. In June 1861, Bishop Polk had gone to Virginia in his clerical capacity to visit the Louisiana troops. A former resident of Tennessee, he stopped for a visit in that state on his way to Virginia, and Governor Harris asked him to see President Davis in Richmond and impress on him the very great importance of effectively speeding up the defenses of the Mississippi Valley. Bishop Polk and President Davis had been schoolmates at West Point and were old friends. Polk's roommate at the Academy had been Albert Sidney Johnston, and when Polk called on Davis he urged him to give Johnston the Mississippi Valley job. But Johnston was not then available. He was still on his way east from California, where he had resigned his commission in the United States Army. The situation on the Mississippi demanded immediate attention. Davis, to Polk's surprise, asked him to assume this command—at least until Johnston's arrival. After considerable deliberation and parley, Polk accepted a commission as major general in the Confederate Army and returned to Tennessee to resume his practice of the military arts.

Northern critics professed to be horrified at the spectacle of a bishop of the Church laying aside his vestments to don a soldier's uniform, but the people of the South greeted the appointment with enthusiasm. A Memphis paper commented editorially:

"Bishop Polk has devoted the flower of his talent and life to the service of that God that he now draws his sword to defend. Like Jephthah, Gideon and David, he is marshaling his legions to fight the battle of the Lord, even Israel's God, the Lord of Hosts! All hail to our intrepid and wise chief, who has chosen to sanctify the western division of the Confederate army by the miter above the girdles and stars!"[5]

Polk did not resign his bishopric, considering his service in the Confederate Army as only temporary. "I feel," he said, "like a man who has dropped his business when his house is on fire, to put it out; for, as soon as the war is over, I will return to my sacred calling."[6]

He had a full appreciation of the importance of his post.[7] When he arrived in Memphis and assumed command on July 13 he fell to work at once in an energetic effort to mobilize his forces and perfect his defenses. The Tennessee state troops had not yet been transferred to the Confederate service, but this technicality was overcome by the Governor's authorization for them to serve under General Polk's orders.

One of the first things the Bishop-General did was to take steps to meet the serious problem presented by the disaffection in East Tennessee. On his way from Richmond to Memphis he made a firsthand appraisal of the touch-and-go nature of conditions there. The people had been strongly opposed to secession. Even after the state had officially and legally seceded, they showed a strong disinclination to accept the decision of the majority of their fellow Tennesseans. Such influential and eloquent leaders of the district as Andrew Johnson and W. G. ("Parson") Brownlow helped promote this disaffection among the Unionists, and the feeling ran so high that there was even talk of a secession from Tennessee. Small squads of East Tennesseans slipped through the mountain passes into Kentucky every night, and among those who stayed at home there were organized armed companies who drilled secretly and longed for an opportunity to strike a blow at the Confederates.

After seeing the alarming state of affairs there, Polk stopped in Nashville for a conference with Governor Harris and other loyal adherents of the Confederacy. Then he telegraphed the Richmond authorities urging the vital importance of sending to East Tennessee a strong body of Confederate troops under an able commander. His telegram included a recommendation of Felix K. Zollicoffer for commander.

Zollicoffer was a former Nashville editor and member of Congress, a man of great attainments in his profession and very popular in the state. Aside from a brief period of service in the Florida war, however, he was totally lacking in military experience, and he had no formal training in that art.[8] It is difficult to see why, as was later claimed by General Polk's biographer, "many of his contemporaries believed . . . that he was the ablest military commander whom the State of Tennessee at that time gave to the cause of the Confederacy."[9] Zollicoffer was a valiant, magnetic, patriotic man, but as a commanding officer he was in a role for which he was unfitted. He was simply not a soldier—by training or by instinct. Polk, however, regarded the situation in East Tennessee as one which called for the talents of a diplomat as much as those of a military genius. He was decidedly relieved when Zollicoffer was commissioned brigadier general and sent off to Knoxville with a motley force of raw recruits, numbering some 3,000 or 4,000.

With this problem behind him, General Polk now felt able to concentrate on the defenses of the Mississippi and the situation in Missouri, both of which called for promptest consideration. Work on the fortifications at Fort Pillow and Island No. 10 was pressed, although it was problematical how he could get the heavy guns needed for them. Island No. 10 was the northernmost of the river defenses. Polk had it manned within a month after his arrival in Memphis, although only six guns were available for the batteries. He considered it inevitable, however, that Kentucky's sham neutrality would soon be abandoned; and, from the first, he looked upon Columbus, Kentucky, as the natural key to the Confederate defense of the river. Aside from its position on the Mississippi, Columbus was the northern terminus of the Mobile & Ohio Railroad at that time; hence its strategic importance was such that Polk was frankly determined to secure it "at all hazards."[10] One of his first moves was to order General Clark to come up from Corinth, Mississippi, with the two regiments under his command, and camp at Union City in Tennessee, close to the Kentucky border, where he could pounce on Columbus as soon as a plausible excuse presented itself.

While engaged with these problems on the east bank he was attempting also to co-ordinate the forces west of the river in an organized movement into Missouri. When he failed because he could not get independent commanders to pool their efforts, General Polk, on August 29, recommended to President Davis that the Confederate operations "be combined from west to east across the Mississippi Valley and placed under the direction of one head." Again he nominated Albert Sidney Johnston. "The success of our campaign in this valley may depend upon such an arrangement," he said.[11]

The President's reply was an order extending Polk's command to include Arkansas and all Missouri. But it was now too late to breathe life again into the collapsed Missouri campaign. By this time Polk had both eyes on Columbus, because of the suspicious and threatening movements of Federal troops in its vicinity. General Grant at Cairo on September 2 had dispatched a land and naval force to occupy Belmont, Missouri, straight across the river from Columbus. Polk considered this a sufficiently overt act to justify taking possession of Columbus, which he promptly did, as mentioned in the preceding chapter. Clark's troops were set in motion from Union City on September 3, and got there within twenty-four hours. They were joined by Pillow's men who recrossed the river from New Madrid, where they were replaced by General Jeff Thompson's Missourians.

The commander was now fairly well satisfied with his strategic dispositions. As described by his son:

"General Polk's plan for the defense of the river was this: Columbus, the advanced and most important point, was to be most thoroughly fortified. The lines in the rear, covering the batteries commanding the river, were to be so constructed as to permit of their being held by a fraction of his force, the larger portion remaining free to operate in the open field. Island No. 10 was to be fortified as a reserve to Columbus; New Madrid to be fortified so as to prevent the enemy getting possession of the Missouri shore at that point, and thus obstructing river navigation below No. 10; while Fort Pillow was to form the last stronghold in the chain."[12]

Polk's correspondence with Governor Magoffin after his occupation of Columbus was still in progress when the complexion of the whole war in the West was changed by Albert Sidney Johnston's long-awaited arrival in Richmond, where he was greeted with the greatest possible enthusiasm.

If there was any one thing on which everybody seemed agreed in 1861 it was that Albert Sidney Johnston was the Number One soldier of the continent. When General Polk was urging on Jefferson Davis the appointment of a single commander in the West he suggested only two names: Albert Sidney Johnston and Robert E. Lee—and of the two Johnston was his first choice. President Davis, in after years, said: "I hoped and expected that I had others who would prove generals; but I knew I had one, and that was Sidney Johnston." That this was sincerely his opinion was evidenced by the fact that in rating his officers accorded the rank of full general, he placed Johnston first on the active list.[13] When a committee of citizens of Memphis went to Richmond to urge a supreme commander for all the operations in the West, it was Johnston to whom they gave the preference. The people of the South felt that they had gained the strength of an additional army when he joined the Confederacy, and, when he died at Shiloh, they felt (and they still feel) an almost unanimous conviction that his loss was the greatest single blow suffered by the cause. Jefferson Davis expressed this feeling after the war: "When he fell, I realized that our strongest pillar had been broken."[14] There are many Southerners today who agree with him that Johnston was "the greatest soldier, the ablest man, civil or military, Confederate or Federal, then living."[15]

Johnston's outstanding and incomparable military merit has become axiomatic, and to question the legend now is sheer audacity. Through a perspective of eighty years, however, it is hard to find the basis for this almost unchallenged opinion that he was the supremely qualified soldier, that his death was an irremediable catastrophe.[16]

In 1861 Albert Sidney Johnston was fifty-eight years old, but a man of strong physique, commanding presence and magnetic personality. His career in the United States Army had been entirely creditable, but not conspicuously brilliant. He graduated from West Point at the age of twenty-three. He was married three years later, and when his wife died in 1835 he resigned from the army. But a life of inaction was incompatible with his nature and in a few months he was off to join the Texans in their fight for freedom. Winning the confidence of Sam Houston, he served as commander in chief of the army after Texas had won her independence and later became the young republic's secretary of war. He took an active part in various battles and negotiations with the Indians, but resigned in 1840 after a falling out with Houston. He returned to his home state, Kentucky, where he married again in 1843; then he went back to Texas, bought a plantation and settled down in his new home as a cotton planter. When the Mexican War broke out in 1846 Johnston took up arms again as colonel of a Texas regiment, but his command of six-months volunteers disbanded before they saw action and left him again a civilian. For a time he served at Monterey as an inspector general of volunteers under General Butler. Although recommended by Old Rough and Ready for appointment as a brigadier general, he did not get it. He went home to his Texas ranch and took no further part in the war. When General Taylor became President in 1849 he made Johnston a paymaster in the United States Army, with the rank of major—a humdrum job that lasted six years. His break came while Jefferson Davis was Secretary of War under Franklin Pierce. Two new cavalry regiments had been created. Johnston's name was put forward to command one of them, and Davis liked the idea. So, in March 1855, he became colonel of the 2nd Cavalry—with Robert E. Lee as his lieutenant colonel and William J. Hardee and George H. Thomas as his majors. Even by then his reputation as a soldier seemed firmly established. General Scott is quoted as saying that he regarded his appointment as "a Godsend to the Army and to the country."[17]

Johnston's regiment was mustered in at Jefferson Barracks, St. Louis, and marched to the frontier of Texas where it was stationed and served, fighting the Indians, for the next two years. When the Mormon disorders broke out in Utah in 1857, he headed the United States troops sent to quell them. This duty accomplished, he returned to the East in the summer of 1860, with the brevet rank of brigadier general. In December he was appointed to the command of the Pacific Coast, with headquarters at Fort Alcatraz, San Francisco. When Texas seceded he promptly resigned his commission, and was succeeded by General Sumner on April 25, 1861.

There was an inclination at that time to suspect Johnston of a melodramatic conspiracy to seize California and turn it over to the Confederates. It was a baseless and hysterical suspicion. Montgomery Blair is authority for the statement that President Lincoln sent Johnston a major general's commission, in the hope that he would remain in the United States Army.[18] Before the commission could reach San Francisco, Johnston had started for Texas by the route over the desert, accompanied by a group of pro-Southerners—eight other resigned Army officers and twenty-five civilians. They left California late in June and had a painful journey across the sandy wastes—2,000 miles of Arizona, New Mexico and Texas under the midsummer sun, through the hostile Apache country and in constant danger of interception by some troop of Federal soldiers. At last they got to New Orleans. Johnston went on immediately to Richmond, where on September 5 he offered his sword to the Confederacy.

His trip north had been a continuous ovation, with groups of admirers gathering at the railroad stations to hail him and with confidence everywhere expressed in his great ability. "Noble, gallant man!" exclaimed one rapturous editor, "the compeer of Davis, Beauregard, [Joseph E.] Johnston and Lee."[19] Davis was delighted when Albert Sidney Johnston put in his appearance at the White House of the Confederacy. He lost no time debating what should be done with the great man. And when he straightway dispatched him to his difficult post, Johnston bore the imposing title of "General Commanding the Western Department of the Army of the Confederate States of America."

CHAPTER III

ALBERT SIDNEY JOHNSTON IN COMMAND

EXPERIENCED soldier that he was, Albert Sidney Johnston must have been appalled when he contemplated the immense tasks confronting him, the inadequate means at his disposal. The line he was supposed to hold extended from the mountains of eastern Kentucky and Tennessee westward across the Mississippi River to the Kansas boundary. To defend the sector between the mountains and the Mississippi he found barely 20,000 men, and these poorly armed and equipped.

He had been empowered by President Davis to make the final decision whether Kentucky should be officially occupied by the Confederate troops or Polk's men withdrawn and the state's pseudo-neutrality respected. It did not take the practical soldier long to make up his mind. On his way to Nashville he stopped off at Knoxville and instructed Zollicoffer to move the very next day to occupy Cumberland Gap in Kentucky.[1] Just as soon as he got to Nashville on September 14, he commissioned Simon Bolivar Buckner a brigadier general[2] in the Confederate Army and started him out for Bowling Green, Kentucky.[3] Buckner arrived there in time to receive within his lines a distinguished fugitive—John C. Breckinridge of Lexington, whose arrest had been ordered by the Federal authorities because of his outspoken pro-Southern sentiments. Breckinridge had been Vice-President of the United States under Buchanan, and in that capacity had presided over the joint session of the House and Senate which declared Abraham Lincoln elected President. He himself had polled 850,000 votes for President in 1860 as the candidate of the Southern wing of the Democratic Party, and had just been elected to the United States Senate from Kentucky. But he resented the invasion of his state by the United States troops, and declared in an address to an assemblage of Kentuckians at Bowling Green: "To defend your birthright and mine, I exchange with proud satisfaction a term of six years in the Senate of the United States for the musket of a soldier."[4]

When General Johnston went to the state capitol to confer with Governor Harris he was accorded a tremendous ovation by admiring and vociferous citizens gathered on the grounds. He was forced to make them

55

a short speech, which began with the significant words: "Fellow-soldiers—
I call you *soldiers*, because you all belong to the reserve corps."[5] A Nashville paper commented editorially:

"This was a well-timed remark and showed that, as a military man, he
knew what was coming. The South will need all of her force. Every able-
bodied man may as well make up his mind to it, and that soon."[6]

The crowds at Nashville cheered lustily; the newspapers of the state
exulted at the prospects for success opened up by his presence. When his
appointment was announced a Memphis paper had said:

"General Johnston will come among us . . . with a prestige already
clustering about his reputation which will inspire our army with a degree
of unbounded confidence and zealous enthusiasm which, as yet, they have
failed to experience. The advent of General Johnston will give a new
impetus to military movements in the Mississippi Valley, we believe,
which will soon be developed in tangible results at once brilliant, scientific
and satisfactory."[7]

A few days later the same paper said of him, after he had assumed
command in Tennessee:

"His every act, movement and order mark the man as possessing all
the qualities of a wise, discreet and brave general."[8]

It was gratifying, no doubt, to be such an inspiration, but General
Johnston knew that it would take something more than "unbounded
confidence and zealous enthusiasm" to turn back the Federals then gathering for a thrust at the vitals of the South.

When Buckner moved from Nashville to Bowling Green with 4,000
troops he took with him every armed man available in that sector. Zollicoffer had taken 4,000 men to Cumberland Gap. Polk had about 11,000
at Columbus. And that was the sum total of the force at Johnston's command to hold the whole Tennessee-Kentucky border. To be sure, there
were a few straggling regiments at various concentration camps in Tennessee which had not been trained or for which there were no arms.
Every available armed man was put across the Kentucky border by Johnston within a week after his arrival in Nashville in an effort to make the
greatest possible display of his limited strength. Although his immediate
strategy was entirely defensive, he strove to create the impression of an

impending offensive, and he heightened this by making showy if aimless demonstrations with cavalry troops at various scattered points, which gave the appearance of widespread activity.

The fact remains, however, that he could really maintain little more than a 400-mile skirmish line, resting on three widely separated points. His aide-de-camp, Colonel Munford, was not far wrong when he said after the war: "To those who ask why so able a man lost Kentucky and Tennessee, and seemed to fail, four words will answer, namely: *He had no army.*"[9]

Military critics differ as to whether Johnston made the best possible use of his limited facilities. There is no gainsaying that his line across the state of Kentucky left much to be desired from many standpoints, military and otherwise. But its location was limited and governed by practical conditions which are well explained by his son and biographer, William Preston Johnston:

"In determining his line of operations, General Johnston had to consider the geography of the theatre of war, the political complexion of the population, and the strength and disposition of the forces opposed to him. Each of these conditions was of such a character as to put him at a disadvantage. . . . As Columbus and the Cumberland Mountains had become the extremities of the Confederate line by force of natural conditions, so Bowling Green, likewise, became its salient. . . . Any point in advance of Bowling Green [was] unsafe; while Bowling Green itself, situated on the turnpike, railroad and river, was a good position for defense. . . . The line was not all that could be wished; it ran through an unfriendly or lukewarm population, and it was pierced by two great rivers [the Tennessee and Cumberland] whose mouths were in the possession of the enemy; but every other line had equal or greater disadvantages. In war, as elsewhere, we must take things as we find them, not as we would have them."[10]

Nobody realized better than General Johnston the great weakness of his position, the tragic paucity and unpreparedness of his forces, and the pressing need to augment them. Indeed, he recognized the desperate nature of his deficiencies instantly. No sooner was he in Nashville than he sent two personal emissaries to the Governors of Alabama and Georgia asking them for arms which, he understood, they had available. He also wrote urgently to President Davis, pointing out his need for men. None of his pleas brought results. In this instance, as in others, the Confederacy was hoist on its own petard of states' rights. "Our own coast is threatened with invasion by the Federal forces," wrote Governor Moore of Alabama—although this supposed threat was purely imaginary. "It is utterly impossible for me to comply with your request," said Governor Brown of Georgia, always the obstructionist. General Bragg at Pensacola wrote: "Our extreme southern country has been stripped of both arms and men." And Davis, head of this new republic founded on the sovereignty of the states, was unable to order anything done. As his son bitterly comments, General Johnston "lacked nothing except men, munitions of war and the means of obtaining them. He had the right to ask for anything, and the state executives had the power to withhold everything."[11]

Particularly embarrassing was the scarcity of weapons with which to supply the men rallying to the Confederate colors. The pitiful inadequacy and obsolescence of the arms are indicated by his requisition of additional gunflints to be used in the flintlock muskets which a large part of his soldiers were using. A flintlock was still a passably serviceable weapon for shooting squirrels in fair weather, but it was useless in the rain—and it was scarcely a match for the modern breech-loading rifles, and even repeaters, with which the Federals were supplied. Governor Harris issued an impassioned appeal to the people to bring in rifles and shotguns and pistols to be purchased by the state and turned over to the soldiers, expressing a determination to exhaust all resources "before the foot of the invader shall pollute the soil of Tennessee." But this appeal did not produce many firearms.

Scarcity of arms was the all-shadowing problem of the whole Confederacy at this time; Johnston's plight was not unique. "We could bring into the field and maintain with ease 500,000 men, were arms and munitions sufficiently abundant," said the Confederate Secretary of War.[12] The Richmond authorities were scouring the markets of Europe for guns, but they were hard to find—and harder to deliver at a Southern port. The Secretary of War eventually sent Johnston 1,000 Enfield rifles which had been brought into Savannah by a blockade runner from Bermuda,[13] and later 3,650 more. But Johnston's lack of small arms was never relieved, and many of his men remained entirely unarmed right up to the Battle of Shiloh.

His efforts to increase his man power were equally discouraging. As promptly as possible he drew the able Hardee with his small force from its idle position in the swamps of northeastern Arkansas and had them join Buckner at Bowling Green. The combination was designated the "Army of Central Kentucky," and Hardee was promoted to major general and commander. The Richmond government ordered Terry's Texas Rangers to report to Johnston, and this gave him another capable and well-trained regiment, although Terry's men were dismounted when they arrived and had to be supplied with horses.

When assigned to the West, Johnston had been authorized by the President "to call for troops from Arkansas, Tennessee and such portion of Mississippi as may be within the limits of your command."[14] Accordingly, on September 21, he called on the Governors for 50,000 men— 30,000 from Tennessee and 10,000 each from Arkansas and Mississippi, specifying that the Arkansas troops were to be sent to General McCulloch and used in the defense of their own state. They were slow in replying to this requisition, and the mobilization of the additional forces was given a setback when Secretary Benjamin notified Johnston that the government, for reasons of economy, had decided to accept no more twelve-months volunteers and ordered him to disband all those already recruited and unarmed. The Secretary rebuked him for calling on the Governor of Mississippi for reinforcements without first consulting the War Department; there was some technical or political reason against it. Before being notified of this inhibition, Governor Pettus of Mississippi had already furnished four regiments. Now that Mississippi was shut off and the Arkansas recruits had been assigned to McCulloch, Johnston was left with only Tennessee to strengthen his army. By Christmas Day that state had come through with 15,000 men and had a total of fifty regiments in the field. General Polk induced General Lovell at New Orleans as a personal favor to lend him two regiments for a few weeks, and early in January the Richmond government sent Floyd's and Maney's brigades from Virginia.

Nevertheless, it was painfully obvious that the Confederate authorities at Richmond had no conception of the gravity of the crisis impending in Tennessee. The Davis government, to be sure, was faced with many difficulties and many complex problems, not the least of which were political. The Federals were gathering a big army in Washington under McClellan to carry out the "On to Richmond" idea, and, for political reasons, it was deemed advisable to subordinate everything else to the protection of the Confederate capital. Fear of alienating the Governors of the Gulf states made President Davis unwilling to take troops away from them to aid Johnston in Tennessee. But, as one competent critic has said, "It was the error of the Administration not to have perceived that the defense of Tennessee was vital, and that it was in more immediate peril even than Virginia—that a stab in the back is as fatal as one in the breast."[15]

E. A. Pollard, the fiery Richmond editor, is not always a reliable source of information when he is speaking of Jefferson Davis, for whom he entertained an active dislike, but he accurately sums up this state of affairs:

"Our situation in Kentucky was one of extreme weakness and entirely at the mercy of the enemy, if he had not been imposed upon by false representations of the number of our forces at Bowling Green. . . . Our own people were as much imposed upon as were the enemy with respect to the real strength of General Johnston's forces, and while they were conjecturing the brilliant results of an advance movement, the fact was that inevitable disasters might have been known by the government to have been in store for the Southern cause in Kentucky and Tennessee, and to be awaiting only the development of a crisis. The utter inadequacy of General Johnston's forces was known to the government. The authorities at Richmond appeared to hope for results without the legitimate means of acquiring them; to look for relief from vague and undefined sources; and to await, with dull expectation, what was next to happen. While the government remained in this blank disposition, events marched onward."[16]

These are bitter words, but they closely approximate the truth.

In a last effort to arouse the Richmond authorities to the gravity of the situation, General Johnston on January 9 sent a personal messenger, Colonel St. John R. Liddell of General Hardee's staff, with letters to Secretary Benjamin and to President Davis, and an urgent oral message to the President.[17] Liddell relates that he found Mr. Davis in a "disturbed and careworn" frame of mind. When he had finished reading Johnston's letter he exclaimed irritably: "My God! Why did General Johnston send you to me for arms and reinforcements when he must know that I have neither? He has plenty of men in Tennessee, and they must have arms of some kind—shotguns, rifles, even pikes could be used. . . . Where am I to get arms or men?" Liddell was not abashed by the President's irritation. He suggested that troops might be spared to Johnston from points less immediately threatened, but Davis petulantly objected that he could not strip those places of their defenses. Then Liddell presented an appealing picture of his commander's necessities. It was entirely unavailing. At last he shut the White House door behind him and went out into Richmond's snowy streets with this chilly parting message: "Tell my friend, General Johnston, that I can do nothing for him, that he must rely on his own resources."[18]

How extremely limited were those resources is well known. Aside from men and munitions, the transportation conditions and facilities also were more favorable to the Federal invaders. Steamboats were the principal mode of travel and were of particular importance because so much of the Federal advance was to be along the waterways. Unfortunately for the Confederates, it developed that most of the steamboats on the Mississippi and its tributaries were Northern-owned, and when the war broke out the Northern owners promptly withdrew them to the safety of the Ohio and the Mississippi above Cairo. The scarcity of steamboats is shown by the fact that there were only three serviceable boats left at Nashville on the Cumberland. Boat yards for construction and repair were largely nonexistent. It was practically impossible to build gunboats to match the ironclads the Federals were constructing for use on the rivers.

The railroad facilities at Johnston's command were also limited. There was a direct line from Louisville, through Bowling Green, to Nashville, and there was a line from Bowling Green to Memphis. Columbus in western Kentucky on the Mississippi was the northern terminus of the Mobile & Ohio, which ran southward through Humboldt and Jackson in Tennessee and Corinth in Mississippi to Mobile. It crossed the Louisville-Memphis line at Humboldt and at Corinth it crossed the Memphis & Charleston, which ran from Memphis to Chattanooga through Corinth, Tuscumbia, Decatur and Stevenson, Alabama. The Nashville & Chattanooga Railroad ran from Nashville southeast to Chattanooga via Stevenson, and there made connection with the Western & Atlantic for Atlanta. At the outbreak of the war it stretched westward from Nashville only about twenty miles to Kingston Springs. After the Federals occupied Nashville they extended this line to Johnsonville on the Tennessee River, to make connection with the steamboats. The rolling stock on all these railroads and the tracks, too, soon fell into a sad state of disrepair. Facilities and materials for maintenance and replacement were virtually unobtainable.

Johnston's military force was tremendously outnumbered at every point. He had three separate armies holding his line: Polk on the left at Columbus, Hardee in the center at Bowling Green and its environs, and Zollicoffer on the right at Cumberland Ford. Polk had about 10,000 or 11,000 against Grant's 20,000 to 25,000 at Cairo; Hardee's total force of about 25,000 was opposed by twice that number under Sherman (and later Buell); and Zollicoffer's 4,000 were facing Thomas with 8,000 or 10,000. In addition, Johnston had skeleton garrisons in the incomplete works of Fort Henry and Fort Donelson under Brigadier General Lloyd

Tilghman, two or three regiments at Hopkinsville under General Alcorn (most of them down with the measles),[19] and a few roving cavalry companies watching the roads and fords. These last included some loosely organized troopers under a little-known Kentucky captain named John H. Morgan,[20] and others under a certain Tennessee civilian, Colonel Nathan Bedford Forrest.

Within a few days after his arrival at Nashville General Johnston went to Columbus to join his old-time West Point friend and roommate, General Polk, who was superintending the erection of fortifications and continuing his feverish efforts to strengthen and supply his little army. Johnston's presence at Columbus was hailed by the press as the inauguration of "a new and better era" in the prosecution of the war.

"Though but a single week has elapsed since he assumed active control of affairs," said a Memphis paper, "a masterly vigor has suddenly imposed itself into military operations throughout the Mississippi Valley that is gratifying to the highest degree. . . . We venture to say that in no section of the Confederacy are the movements of the troops being conducted with more secrecy, judgment and despatch, or defenses being prosecuted with more energy and skill."[21]

Under direction of Johnston and Polk the work on the fortifications proceeded steadily. Soon the face of the bluff rising above the little town bristled with tier after tier of heavy guns. Early in October Johnston heard from Buckner at Bowling Green that the Federals were advancing in his direction. So he transferred his personal headquarters to that point and reorganized the army there into two divisions under Buckner and Hardee, with himself in chief command. Hardee's division was thrown out before Bowling Green about eighteen miles, close to Munfordville on Green River. Johnston attempted that show of bustling activity all along his thin front which he hoped would give the enemy an exaggerated idea of his strength and be construed as a threat of attack. Fortunately for him, it had just exactly that desired effect. While Johnston was fervently praying that Sherman would not advance until he got more men and guns, Sherman, who credited him with about twice as many men as he really had, thought it great luck that the supposedly superior force did not swoop down and capture Louisville.[22]

CHAPTER IV

THE FIRST BATTLES

IF GENERAL JOHNSTON had remained at Columbus just a few days longer he would have had the privilege of personal participation in the first battle fought on his front. True, it was not much of a battle compared with the more sanguinary contests with which the soldiers were later to become all too familiar, but the Battle of Belmont, fought just across the river from Columbus, attracted an attention at the time out of proportion to the numbers engaged and its effect on the status quo.

In a way, it was a comedy of errors. It was based on misapprehensions, featured with fumbling mismanagement and devoid of results—except sacrifice and suffering, the dead and wounded on both sides. Historically it is chiefly worthy of note as the first battle in which General U. S. Grant was engaged—and his most generous critics admit that his military fame would be insecure if its rested only on this engagement.

Grant was a West Point graduate, but he had been out of the army since 1854. He had taken part in the Mexican War, where, as he tells in his *Memoirs*,[1] he was assigned to the Quartermaster Corps and saw little actual fighting. He frankly admits his embarrassment when he was called to command an Illinois regiment in 1861 and realized that he did not know enough about tactics to drill it properly. The fact that he had been a regular army officer, however, automatically recommended him to command one of the new volunteer regiments, and, with trained officers as scarce as they were, he was soon promoted to brigadier general. For battlefield experience, then, Grant at Belmont was about on a par with the greenest volunteer officer, and he showed all the nervous ineptitude of the tyro.

Just why the Battle of Belmont was fought at all it not quite clear. In his official report Grant says:

"The object of the expedition was to prevent the enemy from sending out reinforcements to Price's army in Missouri, and also from cutting off columns that I had been directed to send out from this place [Cairo] and Cape Girardeau in pursuit of Jeff Thompson."

If this were indeed the object, it was based entirely on a misconception. No reinforcements were going forward to Price, nor was there any movement to cut off the Federal columns sent out against General Thompson. Thompson had no force in the field, and any Federals after him were on a wild-goose chase.

As a matter of fact, Grant's attack on Belmont seems to have been more or less of an afterthought, growing out of what started as nothing more than a demonstration on Columbus. He left Cairo on the evening of November 6 with about 3,000 men on six steamboat transports, accompanied by two gunboats, the *Tyler* and the *Lexington*. Simultaneously, General C. F. Smith at Paducah marched in the direction of Columbus with 2,000 men.

Grant states in his *Memoirs*: "I had no orders which contemplated an attack by the National troops, nor did I intend anything of the kind when I started out"; and he says later on that it was not until the morning of the seventh that he "speedily resolved to . . . capture Belmont, break up the camp and return."[2] On the other hand, there is some evidence that he had previously thought of making his own headquarters there. At any rate, before leaving Cairo, he had sent a dispatch to Colonel Oglesby in northeast Arkansas ordering him to march toward New Madrid on the Mississippi and "communicate with me at Belmont."

Belmont was a shabby, straggling settlement of three houses and a steamboat landing on the Missouri bank of the Mississippi, just across from Columbus. Here Polk had set an observation camp consisting of one regiment of infantry under Colonel Tappan, a battery of artillery and a small cavalry force. It was partially protected by an abatis, but the soldiers had not yet learned the value of breastworks. The location was so unhealthful that more than half Tappan's force were on the sick list. The camp was of no military importance, merely an outpost of the strongly fortified position across the river at Columbus.

Grant landed his column on the Missouri side three miles above Belmont at about eight o'clock on the morning of the seventh, the point of debarkation being concealed from the camp by timber. He advanced immediately, the gunboats dropping down the river to engage the Confederate batteries at Columbus. As soon as he learned of Grant's movements, General Polk sent Pillow across to Belmont with four regiments. Pillow marched them and the small garrison out in front of the protecting abatis and hastily prepared to meet Grant's advancing column. The fighting began about 10:30 A.M.

The Battle of Belmont was a military engagement in its simplest and most elementary form—two approximately equal bodies of infantry fighting in parallel facing lines. The troops on both sides were mostly raw and inexperienced, under fire for the first time, but they fought bravely and resolutely, the tide of battle wavering from side to side. First one and then the other would charge and retire, but gradually the Federals pressed the Confederates back to the river bank and occupied their camp.

The Mississippi was at its seasonal low stage, with the water level several feet below the high and almost vertical secondary banks. The fleeing Confederates took refuge on the lower shelf where they were temporarily protected from the fire of the Federals. At this point when the day seemed hopelessly lost and the Confederates might easily have been trapped and captured, a regiment of reinforcements from Columbus checked the impetuous drive of Grant's victorious men—and then the elated Federals stopped to enjoy the fruits of victory. Grant says disgustedly:

"The moment the camp was reached our men laid down their arms and commenced rummaging the tents to pick up trophies. Some of the higher officers were little better than the privates. They galloped about from one cluster of men to another, and at every halt delivered a short eulogy upon the Union cause and the achievements of the command."[3]

Meanwhile the troops under Pillow were scurrying up the river bank. More reinforcements had come over from Columbus under General B. F. Cheatham, whom General Polk accompanied in person. The big Whitworth rifled gun[4] at Columbus began to rake the captured Confederate camp site with a deadly plunging bombardment. Grant ordered the camp set on fire to end the plundering and started a hurried return to his transports. With his own fresh regiments and Pillow's hastily reorganized men, Polk fell on Grant's flank. The withdrawal became a pell-mell retreat. The fleeing Federals cast aside their rifles and colors and the spoils of battle as they ran. Even a large number of the wounded were abandoned. So great was the haste and confusion that one regiment, separated from the others, was forgotten by the transports, and escaped only with great difficulty. Grant himself narrowly missed being left on the bank as the boats frantically made off.[5]

In his official report he represents the expedition as a success, inasmuch as it accomplished his purposes (whatever they were) and in a letter to his father he says unequivocally: "The victory was most complete."[6] In his *Memoirs*, however, he admits that "Belmont was severely criticized in the North as a wholly unnecessary battle, barren of results or the possibility of them from the beginning."[7] The Confederates regarded the battle as a brilliant victory and it was so celebrated throughout the South.

As for the valor of the men engaged in the Battle of Belmont, the gracious tribute of a Confederate commentator is fair to all:

"Whatever other comment may be made, or lesson drawn from it, its story is highly honorable to the individual courage, tenacity and intelligence of the American soldier. Those western troops who, fighting forward among fallen timber, broke through a Confederate line not much weaker than their own, were no ordinary men. The shattered and routed Southerners who, after an hour's interval, were ready to join in an irresistible charge that reversed the fortunes of the day, evinced the spirit that made them famous on so many fields. Federal and Confederate alike may look back and feel that there was nothing to be ashamed of in the fighting at Belmont."[8]

After the battle there were several meetings of Confederate and Federal officers on flag-of-truce boats in the river to discuss the exchange of prisoners and other official matters. Many of them had been at West Point and in the old army together; the war was too young for those asperities which developed later, and the meetings became pleasant, convivial affairs. A current Nashville newspaper story tells how "the officers, both Federal and Confederate, mingled with each other, drank champagne together, told anecdotes and incidents of the late battle, complimenting each other upon the heroism and bravery displayed on both sides, and altogether had a most delightful time."[9] On one occasion, General Cheatham drew General Grant into a spirited discussion of horse racing, in which both were interested, and when Cheatham jovially suggested that they settle the war by a horse race on shore, Grant said he wished they could. As a group were engaged in a festive round of champagne, an Illinois colonel, N. B. Buford, proposed a toast which he said they could all drink: "To George Washington, the Father of his Country," to which General-Bishop Polk roguishly added "—and the first rebel," as they emptied their glasses amid shouts of friendly laughter.

The next activity on Johnston's front was at the extreme other end of his attenuated line. This right wing was growing important, since the Federal forces in eastern Kentucky were being urged to move into East Tennessee to relieve the Unionists there.

The Federals were commanded by General George H. Thomas, a

trained and competent regular army officer, destined to prove one of the more capable leaders on the Northern side. In his operations in this, his first serious command, he gave evidence of that skill which was later to bring him renown.

Zollicoffer, having fortified the mountain passes, had been ordered by Johnston to leave a few men at Cumberland Gap and with the rest move westward to a position that would protect both the Jamestown and Jacksboro roads. Thus the approaches from central Kentucky both to East Tennessee and to Nashville would be commanded, as it was not certain just which way the Federals might come. Johnston meant Zollicoffer to stay on observation until reinforced or joined to the main army. There were no direct telegraph wires, and the condition of the roads made communication by courier slow and difficult. Messages between the two generals were sometimes three or four days in transmittal. The uncertain state of affairs was a constant source of uneasiness.

Zollicoffer's first brush with the Federals was in the latter part of October when he encountered General Thomas' vanguard, under General Schoepf, at Wild Cat Mountain near Rockcastle River. In numbers involved and strategic results this engagement was unimportant, although Zollicoffer's men were forced to fall back to Cumberland Ford with a sad loss of "face." Later he drove Schoepf out in a panicky retreat that came to be known as "the Wild Cat Stampede" and the tarnished prestige was in some measure restored.

There was another clash early in January at Prestonburg in the northeastern corner of Kentucky, where about 1,600 Confederates under General Humphrey Marshall[10] were attacked by Colonel James A. Garfield with about 2,000 Federals. The official reports of Marshall and Garfield are so widely at variance it is difficult to realize they both are describing the same engagement. Each claimed a crushing victory, each to have driven the other in confusion from the battlefield. As a matter of fact, both did retreat after the encounter, but as Garfield retreated fifteen miles and Marshall only seven, the Confederates felt more amply justified in claiming victory! . . . But this was mere byplay. The opposing forces of Thomas and Zollicoffer were the important factors.

Zollicoffer's eventual undoing was born of his own brave but ill-advised aggressiveness. Just to stay passively on observation was not congenial to a man of his dynamic nature. He had been feeling his way forward into Kentucky during November until he reached Mill Springs on the south bank of the Cumberland. From this coign of vantage he could watch the movements of his adversary. Johnston thought he should go no farther and said so. But his mingled zeal and inexperience led him into a fatal tactical error, precipitated a battle both unnecessary and disastrous that shattered the Confederate force and cost his own life. Instead of keeping safely to the south side of the river, as sound judgment dictated and as Johnston had pointedly suggested, Zollicoffer laboriously moved his men across the stream and made his camp at Beech Grove. Here he was in a precarious position, with the river at his back and the enemy under Thomas only a short distance before him—a state of affairs by all tradition bad.

Evidences of his lack of military experience had not gone unnoticed in Richmond, and President Davis at this juncture assigned General George B. Crittenden to command the district.[11] He made his headquarters at Knoxville on November 24. As soon as he heard that Zollicoffer had crossed the Cumberland he sent a courier with orders to cross back at once. When, however, he went to Zollicoffer's camp early in January to take personal command, he found to his dismay that this had not been done. Zollicoffer naïvely explained that he thought the position on the north side of the river preferable and had decided to stay there until they could talk it over. As Thomas was now moving forward to attack the Confederates, Crittenden made a virtue of necessity and prepared to defend himself in his camp.

The Federals were divided into two bodies of troops. Thomas himself accompanied the column aiming directly at the Confederate camp. Schoepf's division was in camp near Somerset on the north bank of Fishing Creek, a small stream flowing into the Cumberland just a few miles north of the Confederate position.

By January 18 Thomas had got within six miles of the Confederate lines and encamped at Logan's Cross Roads. Obviously a clash was imminent. A steady, heavy rain fell throughout the day, and this made Crittenden suddenly change his plans from defensive to offensive. The rain, he reasoned, would swell Fishing Creek to such proportions as to make it temporarily impossible for Schoepf to join Thomas; so he might apply the old military principle of smashing an enemy in detail. He called a council of war and laid before his two brigadiers—Zollicoffer and Carroll—a plan to surprise Thomas in his camp. The officers unanimously concurred. The advance began at midnight of the eighteenth.

The march through the pouring rain and pitch-black darkness was a nightmare. The sleepy, miserable men stumbled along blindly. The guns bogged in the mire. The rain beat down in torrents as men and horses strained and struggled to extricate them. So great was the confusion and delay that the advance guard did not reach the Federal pickets until after daybreak, and the surprise was now of course impossible. All the same Crittenden went on with his plan of battle, and the attack was delivered by Zollicoffer's brigade, although only two of his regiments were on the scene, the others being strung out along the muddy road for a mile or more.

Thomas' men were just beginning to crawl out of their tents for roll call. They fell back under Zollicoffer's initial onset. Then as the regiments formed and came up into position they stiffened their defense. They were admirably drilled and disciplined, in numbers about equal to Crittenden's command, and provided a brave and stubborn opposition. The Confederates were cold, hungry and exhausted from their all-night march through rain and mud. To add to their miseries, the rain had ruined the flintlock rifles with which so many of the Tennessee regiments were outfitted, and these had to be sent to the rear. At the height of the battle the Confederates suffered a blow which climaxed their troubles and proved the turning point of the engagement. Brave to the point of rashness, and conspicuous in a white rubber raincoat, Zollicoffer had ridden far ahead of his troops right up to the enemy. He was so near-sighted that he mistook a mounted Federal officer, Colonel S. S. Fry, for one of his own men and was in the act of giving him an order when Fry fired at him point-blank and put a fatal bullet through his breast.[12]

However scant may have been his grasp of military science, Zollicoffer was the idol of his men. The news of his death brought paralyzing confusion to the ranks of his already disheartened brigade. They broke into flight. Crittenden had his full column up and in action, but the retreat of Zollicoffer's men turned the tide. The entire Confederate force began to give ground. Soon they were in rapid retreat to their former camp, and, by the time the Federals replenished their ammunition and took up the chase, they had made good their escape.

On the night of the nineteenth the demoralized remnants of Crittenden's army crossed to the southern side of the Cumberland on a wheezy little stern-wheel steamboat. In their desperate panic they left behind their artillery, their wagons, their horses, their supplies, their dead and wounded—including Zollicoffer. The wild retreat carried them far into Tennessee. What was left of them finally camped at Chestnut Mound, about eighty miles from Nashville.

The defeat of Crittenden's army was complete and crushing. In fact, it almost ceased to be an army. Discouraged soldiers deserted by scores, and their excited stories of the disaster to the Confederate arms spread dismay throughout the whole region. But for a sudden change in the Federal plan of campaign, Thomas might have marched into East Tennessee and taken it all without much trouble.

This was the first serious reverse suffered by the Confederates since the war had started, and the Southern people were staggered. As soon as they recovered from the stunning shock, their wounded pride sought a scapegoat—and straightway found one in Crittenden. The vilification heaped on him by the newspapers went to the utmost extreme. No words were too bitter. Typical was the comment of a Nashville paper:

"But for the deplorable fact that General Crittenden of Kentucky (who is, we regret to say, generally regarded as a common drunkard) had been made the superior in command of the lamented Zollicoffer, the devoted hearts of Southern patriots might not to-day be lacerated and overwhelmed with grief almost insupportable."[13]

The Nashville editor charged that Crittenden at the time of battle was "in an almost beastly state of intoxication," and, warming to the theme, said that an investigation would doubtless "connect with Crittenden's crime of drunkenness the greater sins of treason, treachery and cowardice." Much was made of the fact that his brother was a general in the Union Army; it was freely insinuated that his own sympathies were really on the other side. According to one newspaper story—false of course—a messenger had been captured carrying plans of the Confederate camp from Crittenden to Thomas.

Within a few weeks the hysterical abuse began to die down. A charitable Memphis paper deplored the fact that the commander had been accused of treason, for which there was no better foundation than "the creative imaginations of the cowardly poltroons who fled in consternation and dismay from the battlefield"[14]—but it was still insisted that he was a "besotted inebriate" and should be removed. Jefferson Davis officially exonerated him, but after a little while the unfortunate Fishing Creek commander was permitted to resign and go to Texas.

CHAPTER V

THE DEFENSE OF TENNESSEE

WITH the exception of the battle of Fishing Creek (also called Mill Springs, or Logan's Cross Roads) the winter of 1861-62 was inactive for Johnston's army, though the Federal forces were obviously making elaborate arrangements for some sort of concerted action, presumably awaiting only the coming of spring.

Jefferson Davis, in a letter to a Mississippi Congressman, had predicted that the South would find it necessary to make better preparations. The North, he said, would soon replace its "holiday soldiers" and "pathfinders" (a thrust at Frémont) with "men of education and experience in war."[1] The accuracy of this forecast was shown when, late in 1861, there was a shake-up in the Federal command. On November 1 General McClellan took General Scott's place as commander of all the armies. One of his first acts was to put General H. W. Halleck over the Department of the West in place of General Hunter, who had temporarily succeeded Frémont. Two weeks later General Don Carlos Buell supplanted Sherman in command of the Department of the Ohio. Sherman had asked that his army be increased to 60,000 men, and had vouchsafed the view that for a victorious advance into the South 200,000 would eventually be required. This was considered such a wildly extravagant estimate that serious fears as to his sanity were entertained, and it was thought advisable to relieve him of his command until these doubts could be resolved.[2] Buell's domain in Kentucky extended westward only to the Cumberland River. Beyond that Halleck was in charge. The two officers were entirely independent of each other, subject only to orders from McClellan in Washington.

Besides these changes in official assignments, the North was evidently astir. Gunboats were building on the Ohio River. Along the Louisville & Nashville Railroad, as far south as Munfordville on Green River, supplies were being accumulated and troops concentrated. General Johnston was aware of what was going on, but could do nothing to interfere. All his efforts to increase his small and scattered force were still unavailing. He saw nothing to do but wait for spring and meet the advance

71

as best he could with the means at his disposal. Meanwhile he played his game of "bluff" in a skillful and convincing manner which deceived many, North and South. J. B. Jones in Richmond, to be sure, was writing in his diary:

"The Northern papers give the most extravagant numbers to an army in Kentucky. Some estimates are as high as 150,000. I know, and Mr. Benjamin knows, that General Johnston has not exceeding 29,000 men."[3]

But all Southerners were not so discerning, and at this same time the sanguine editor of the Memphis *Appeal* was fatuously boasting:

"General Johnston . . . has had large accessions to his army from various quarters. . . . He will go and hunt the enemy if the latter delays his attack very much longer."

The "large accessions" to General Johnston's army existed only in the imagination of this optimistic editor, but now at last the situation in the West received a little more attention from the Richmond authorities. The stunning defeat at Fishing Creek had aroused them from their Micawberism and suddenly riveted their attention on the Tennessee-Kentucky front. Before, their eyes had been so focused on the defense of Richmond they had almost overlooked the needs beyond the mountains. Senators and Representatives from those Western states became insistent, and the Military Committee of Congress realized that something must be done to relieve the widespread apprehension.

The clear call was for more men and more guns, but this kind of help was—or seemed to be—out of the question. The supply of guns was still pitifully inadequate. A lull in recruiting had cut down the number of available new soldiers. President Davis, for political reasons, was unable or unwilling to insist on the transfer of troops from less threatened points in the South. Some gesture of helpfulness had to be made, however, so finally as a result of the deliberations of members of Congress and their conferences with President Davis and Secretary Benjamin, it was decided to transfer General Beauregard from Virginia to the Mississippi Valley. His immediate command would include the forces of General Polk at Columbus, within the department of General Albert Sidney Johnston.

For both military and psychological reasons the move seemed good. Pierre Gustave Toutant Beauregard was at the moment the outstanding

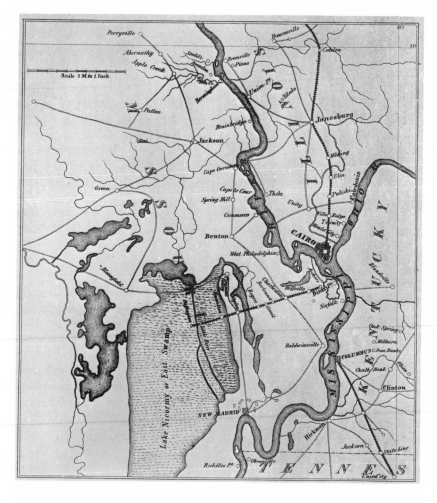

Contemporary map of the seat of war in southern Missouri in 1861.

Centreville
Jan.? 29th 1862

My dear General,
I have just received the enclosed letter, much to my regret. I have been hoping that the views of the War Department might be changed.

Your transfer from this army is a great loss to it. a very great loss to me. the troops you have formed regard you as their general. & My confidence in you makes me feel weakened by our separation. You will take with you my best wishes. The best is that you may have fair opportunities. You know how to use them.

Very truly yours
J. E. Johnston

Genl Beauregard.

Original letter from Joseph F. Johnston to Beauregard expressing regret at Beauregard's transfer from Virginia to the army in Tennessee.

military hero of the Confederacy. A Louisianian of French descent, forty-three years of age, he was an experienced soldier. The outbreak of war found him Superintendent at West Point, where he had graduated. He had commanded the force that fired the first shot of the war on Fort Sumter. He had commanded the army in Virginia that bore the brunt of the Battle of Manassas before General Joseph E. Johnston came up. In the Southern mind he was the "Hero of Sumter," the "Hero of Manassas," the personification of victorious militancy. That he was a military genius of the first water was accepted without question. It was not unreasonable to assume that his coming to the West would help restore morale. Also Davis and Benjamin probably found it a politic means of killing two birds with one stone. Beauregard had been at loggerheads with them over seniority of rank, and also because of some objectionable features of his report of the Battle of Manassas. If this wrangle could be ended and, at the same time, the defensive forces of the great valley strengthened, it would prove an admirable solution of both difficulties. Beauregard might be the round peg to fit exactly into the round hole of Western defense.

The general himself viewed the proposed transfer with less enthusiasm. He was patriotic, but he was also intensely vain and ambitious for personal renown, and his instinct told him that the Virginia scene would offer greater opportunities for fame. Pressure was brought to bear on him, however, by Colonel Roger A. Pryor, the member of the Military Committee who carried on the negotiations. Pryor emphasized the chance for notable service to the Confederacy, the inspiration Beauregard's name would give the West, the gravity of the crisis. Furthermore, he told Beauregard that the Confederate Army in Johnston's department totaled 70,000 men—40,000 directly under Johnston and 30,000 with Polk at Columbus.

Beauregard accepted this estimate with a grain of salt. If Johnston had such strength, why had he remained so long quiescent? But at length he told Colonel Pryor he would accept the transfer under three conditions: "First, that the Army of the West should consist of the effective force stated by him [Pryor] or, if not, should be sufficiently reinforced to enable him [Beauregard] to assume the offensive immediately upon his arrival in the Mississippi Valley; second, that he should take with him his personal and general staff and, if he required them, ten or twelve experienced officers from the Army of the Potomac [later styled the Army of Northern Virginia]—none above the rank of colonel—some of whom were to be promoted to be brigadier and major generals, the others to receive staff appointments; and, third, that he should return to the command of his own army in Virginia as soon as his services could be dispensed with in the West and, if possible, in time for the spring campaign."[4] Pryor assured him that these conditions would be met,[5] so, still reluctantly, Beauregard set out for his new field of endeavor and arrived at Johnston's headquarters in Bowling Green on February 4.

The first shock of disillusionment came when General Johnston revealed to him that the whole Confederate Army in his department numbered not more than 45,000 men of all arms and conditions.[6] As Beauregard's biographer expresses it:

"This fearful disparity between the actual effectiveness of General Johnston's command and the fanciful figures which, by authority of the Secretary of War, Colonel Pryor had given him, struck General Beauregard with amazement."[7]

Dismayed by the thought of this insufficient force arrayed against more than 100,000 Federals, Beauregard saw the utter impossibility of an offensive and the extreme difficulty of even an effective defense against the advance up the Tennessee which General Johnston was expecting at any time. Johnston added to his discomfiture by remarking that he had little confidence in the works on the Tennessee and Cumberland. They were "tolerably well fortified," he said, but he expressed doubt of their ability to withstand a determined attack.[8]

This apprehension was thoroughly well founded. Through a seemingly unavoidable combination of circumstances, the fortifications had never received the undivided, sustained attention of any one capable person. As they stood in February 1862, they represented the combined judgment and misjudgment, attention and inattention, of a variety of Confederate officers—some competent and some not notably so.

From the very first days of the war in the West, one of the things most apparent to all observers on both sides was that the Tennessee and Cumberland Rivers offered an inviting double pathway to the heart of the Confederacy.[9] The former has its headwaters in the mountains of East Tennessee, whence it flows south in a big bend through northern Alabama, touches the northeastern corner of Mississippi, and then runs north through western Tennessee and Kentucky to the Ohio. The Cumberland rises in eastern Kentucky, curves in a wide sweep through Middle Tennessee to where Nashville stands on its southern bank, thence flows northwest to its confluence with the Ohio. Smithland at the mouth of the Cumberland is only twelve miles from Paducah at the mouth of the Tennessee. Such is the odd geological formation that during their course through western Tennessee and Kentucky the two rivers flow almost due north, while the Mississippi, about a hundred miles away, pursues a roughly parallel channel due south. Small wonder that General Johnston felt the deepest anxiety when he thought of these rivers penetrating his line. The Tennessee could carry an invading Northern army into north Alabama as far as Florence just below Muscle Shoals and into control of the important Memphis & Charleston Railroad.[10] The Cumberland could lead them straight to Nashville, the capital of Tennessee, a city the Confederacy could ill afford to lose.

Nashville was the largest and most important city south of the Ohio River, with the exception of New Orleans, and occupied an important strategic position. Besides being on the Cumberland River, it had railroads leading north to Louisville, south to Decatur, southeast to Chattanooga and Atlanta, and west toward Johnsonville on the Tennessee. Since the outbreak of the war it had been converted into a giant arsenal and depot of supplies. Its warehouses were bursting with food and clothing accumulated by the Commissary and Quartermaster Departments. A quickly constructed plant was manufacturing 100,000 percussion caps a day; it had supplied the caps for the Battle of Manassas. The Nashville Plow Works, reversing the biblical formula, was manufacturing sabers; other plants made muskets, saddles, harness and knapsacks. Looms were turning out thousands of yards of gray jeans, and nimble fingers were sewing them into uniforms for the soldiers. Two local foundries were now casting cannon, and one of them was turning out rifled guns. The highly valued rifling machine had been made from plans obtained by a spy sent to a Northern arsenal after the beginning of the war.[11]

The importance of the Cumberland and Tennessee Rivers had not escaped the notice of Governor Harris. One of the first things he did after his state seceded was to order the construction of forts on the rivers to control them and repel invaders. Selection of the best possible location for the forts·was delegated to General Daniel S. Donelson, a West Point graduate—and, incidentally, a nephew of General Andrew Jackson's wife. The only limitation on his choice was that they should be as far north (down the rivers) as possible, but must be within the borders of Tennessee, since Kentucky was at that time maintaining the figment of neutrality. Donelson reported that the strongest point on the Cumberland was a high bluff on the west bank a mile below the village of Dover.

Dover was forty miles from the river's mouth, and, aside from its communication by river, was connected with Nashville, seventy-five miles away, by a road passing through Charlotte. In General Donelson's judgment there was no particularly good location on the Tennessee within the borders of the state, but he selected a point on the east bank, almost due west of the chosen site on the Cumberland and about twelve miles from it, as being the best available.

Accordingly, with some misgivings, the places selected were ordered fortified. The one on the Cumberland at Dover was named in honor of General Donelson; that on the Tennessee was called Fort Henry for Gustavus A. Henry, Confederate Senator from Tennessee. The surveys were entrusted to a competent civil engineer, Adna Anderson, assisted by W. F. Foster (later General A. P. Stewart's chief engineer), and they started work on May 10. Mr. Anderson chose for the site of the fort on the Tennessee a point just opposite the mouth of the Big Sandy River, but this location was shifted five miles farther down to Kirkman's old landing by Major Bushrod R. Johnson when on May 28 he was appointed chief engineer of the Tennessee troops. At the Tennessee River there is an offset in the Kentucky-Tennessee state line, the line west of the river being several miles south of the line east. By reason of this offset the western bank opposite Fort Henry was Kentucky soil—which was then regarded as inviolate. To Colonel A. Heiman and his regiment, the 10th Tennessee, were assigned the task of building Fort Henry, and they made such progress that they were able to mount the first gun as early as July.[12]

Fort Henry got all the attention at first and the site of Fort Donelson was quite neglected, but in October Colonel R. W. McGavock with three companies of Tennessee troops was sent to Dover, and he signed communications as "Commanding at Fort Donelson." Work on the fortifications still languished, however, and Senator Henry (who was keeping an eager eye out) wrote General Polk apprehensively that only these 300 men, with four guns, stood between the Ohio River and Nashville. "There is no part of the whole West," he said, "so exposed as the Valley of the Cumberland." He stressed the importance of defending the rolling mills in this valley which were manufacturing iron for the Confederacy.[13]

As soon as General Johnston was assigned to the West and arrived on the scene, he saw that both river forts must be put under a competent commander who would aggressively push them to completion. In early October he asked that Major A. P. Stewart be appointed a brigadier for this purpose, but Secretary Benjamin named a Kentuckian, Lloyd

Tilghman, instead. Tilghman assumed duty on November 17. He was dilatory, and by February 1 the forts were still only partially built. Their garrisons, however, had been strengthened; he had 5,700 troops—3,400 at Fort Henry and 2,300 at Fort Donelson.

The sites selected and the method of fortification may or may not have been the best possible under the difficult conditions prevailing. At any rate they were subjected to most unrestrained criticism, especially by the officers who later commanded—and surrendered—them. General Tilghman, speaking of Fort Henry, referred to "its wretched military position" and "its unfortunate location. . . . The history of military engineering records no parallel to this case." General Floyd was equally emphatic about Fort Donelson in his official report:

"It was ill conceived, badly executed and still worse located. I consider the place illy chosen, out of position, and entirely indefensible by any reinforcements which could be brought there to its support."

Nor were these merely the afterthoughts of defeated commanders. Criticism was plentiful from the very first. In September General Johnston had sent an engineer officer, Lieutenant Dixon, to examine the positions and report. In Dixon's opinion Fort Henry was not situated most favorably but he acknowledged that it was a strong work. Instead of abandoning it and re-locating at another point he recommended that it be completed and that other fortifications be built on the high ground right across the river, where neutrality was no longer an obstacle. Fort Donelson, Dixon reported, might also have been better located, but, in the circumstances, it would be better to retain it, too, and strengthen it with outworks against its landward approaches. Although handicapped by a lack of tools and labor, Dixon undertook the job of building up the breastworks and planned and executed a system of obstructions in the river below the fort. Barges loaded with stone were sunk in the channel and heavy iron chains were stretched from bank to bank under the water—impediments that lost effectiveness when the river rose above them.

Soon after construction was started on Fort Henry in September, Governor Harris commissioned Captain Jesse Taylor, a trained naval artillerist, to take command of the guns already mounted. His practiced eye told him at once that it was not in the right place—"on the east bank of the river in a bottom commanded by high hills rising on either side of the river," and he promptly reported this to the state authorities. Their tart response was that it had been located by competent engineers, with a strong hint between the lines that Taylor should attend to his guns and not question the judgment of his superiors. His further observations, however, strengthened his conviction that the fort was a trap; its highest point was far below high-water mark, and would be flooded by an ordinary spring rise. He said as much to General Polk at Columbus, by whom he was referred to General Johnston, and Johnston sent Major J. F. Gilmer, his recently appointed chief engineer, to investigate. As a result of Gilmer's inspection it was decided not to change the site but to put up immediately another fortification (called Fort Heiman) at a high point on the opposite (Kentucky) side of the river commanding Fort Henry— a work which had previously been authorized but never carried out.[14]

Johnston urged on Gilmer the necessity of fortifying Nashville and the river between Nashville and Fort Donelson, establishing what he styled "a line of the Cumberland" as a defensive position if it became necessary to fall back from Bowling Green. Gilmer agreed, but despite their most earnest efforts this work languished. The need of fortifying Nashville was laughed at; Gilmer was derided as "Johnston's dirt digger."[15] Labor was scarce and, although repeated appeals were made for the hire or loan of slaves, the completion of the vital defensive works on the rivers proceeded at snail-like pace.

Johnston learned late in January, on the eve of Grant's advance up the Tennessee, that work on Fort Heiman had hardly begun, and that Tilghman was still debating with himself whether it was too late to build it. When this news was brought to him he displayed great agitation. "It is most extraordinary—I ordered General Polk four months ago to at once construct those works; and now, with the enemy on us, nothing of importance has been done. It is most extraordinary."[16] He telegraphed Tilghman: "Occupy and intrench the heights opposite Fort Henry. Do not lose a moment. Work all night."[17] He ordered Gilmer, now a lieutenant colonel, again to Fort Henry to inspect the work and do whatever was necessary. Gilmer met Tilghman there on the thirty-first; but it was hard to do what needed to be done in the little time left.

Johnston's analysis of all the signs led him to the conclusion that Halleck would attempt to turn his left with an advance up the Tennessee, while Buell exerted pressure on Bowling Green. So he used his utmost endeavors to make the river forts stronger. In response to his insistent requests for help from Richmond, a brigade under General John B. Floyd had been sent to him, consisting of four Virginia regiments and one from Mississippi. On January 20 he dispatched this brigade and part of

Buckner's to Russellville, Kentucky, to strengthen Fort Donelson. At about the same time, General Pillow was placed in command at Clarksville, Tennessee, within helping distance of the fort. But it was still glaringly clear that Fort Henry and Fort Donelson were chinks in the Confederate armor. Johnston spent more than one sleepless night over them.

CHAPTER VI

THE FALL OF THE FORTS

1. THE FIRST ATTACK

ON JANUARY 22 General Johnston wrote a blunt and candid letter to Adjutant General Cooper in Richmond, telling of Zollicoffer's defeat and predicting that the Federals would try to capture Nashville by taking Forts Henry and Donelson. He explained his desperately precarious position, with only 14,000 men under his immediate command facing Buell's 40,000, with his right wing crushed through the Fishing Creek disaster, and with the probability that the river forts would fall before the impending attack. Earnestly he pleaded again for reinforcements:

"If force can not be spared from other army corps," he said, "the country must now be roused to make the greatest effort that it will be called upon to make during the war. No matter what the sacrifice may be, it must be made, and without loss of time. Our people do not comprehend the magnitude of the danger that threatens. . . . All the resources of the Confederacy are now needed for the defense of Tennessee."[1]

But this outspoken letter failed to stir the authorities from their apathy. They resumed their preoccupation with affairs in Virginia, their dreaming of European intervention—and the Federals kept on building the juggernaut which was to crush the Confederates' left wing.

The earliest threatening gesture had come toward the middle of October when the gunboat *Conestoga* made its way up the Tennessee on a reconnaisance and threw a few shells at Fort Henry to develop the location and range of the Confederate guns. During the ensuing winter the *Conestoga*, accompanied by the *Lexington*, made frequent appearances below Fort Henry, firing a few shells and then retiring.

In January, as a diversion in favor of Thomas in eastern Kentucky, there was a reconnaissance in force by both infantry and gunboats. McClernand marched overland from Cairo with 6,000 men to menace Columbus; C. F. Smith with two brigades moved down into western

Kentucky from Paducah, threatening Fort Henry and all the Kentucky country between the fort and Columbus; Admiral Foote in his gunboats steamed up the Tennessee in concert with Smith.

The water in the river at this time was barely deep enough to float the gunboats, but the season of the rises was approaching and enough had been learned of the Confederate weakness for Grant to telegraph Halleck at St. Louis on January 28: "With permission, I will take Fort Henry on the Tennessee and establish and hold a large camp there." Foote backed him up with a similar telegram. Halleck gave his consent. On February 2 the start up the river from Cairo was made: Grant with 17,000 troops in transports and Foote with seven gunboats. Since there had been heavy rains, the river was now at a high stage and still rising, so that the gunboats could operate at greatest efficiency.

Fort Henry was a solidly constructed earthwork fortification, with five bastions. Nine guns faced the river and five were on the land side. A little way from the fortification landward, infantry entrenchments had been thrown up on a rise of ground, protecting it against attack from that direction and also commanding the road to Fort Donelson. The only favorable feature of the location was that the fort stood at a slight bend in the river, with a view straight north for several miles.

It was on the morning of the fourth of February that the lookout in Fort Henry, peering downriver through the mists, discerned the fleet of gunboats approaching, and behind them what looked like an endless stream of transports. The plumes of their black smoke marked the course of the river as far as eye could see. Torpedoes had been placed in the river by the Confederates. The men on the boats saw them and fished them out. The gunboats arrayed themselves in formation about three miles below the fort and began to shell the Confederate position, while the transports discharged their blue-clad cargo on the east bank at Bailey's Ferry. Grant himself was with the troops on this side, but 6,000 under C. F. Smith were detached to the west bank to take Fort Heiman—which Smith found unfinished and unoccupied. In late afternoon of the fifth when the troops had all disembarked, the gunboats moved in closer to renew their fire. Not until then did the Confederate guns answer. After a few rounds the gunboats dropped downstream and the action ceased for the day.

Tilghman was not in the fort at the time of this first attack. On the night of the third he had gone with Colonel Gilmer to inspect Fort Donelson, leaving Colonel Heiman in command. The next morning

Tilghman heard the ominous boom of the Fort Henry guns but, with notable lack of enterprise, did nothing till a message from Colonel Heiman in midafternoon told him the Federals were landing. Tilghman and Gilmer got back to Fort Henry about midnight. On the fifth, they hurried their preparations. The troops were placed behind the breastworks on the landward side. Tilghman sent Johnston a semi-cheery message: "My force is in good spirits but badly armed"—a masterpiece of understatement. As a matter of fact, the men were armed with shotguns and fowling pieces! Even the 10th Tennessee, described as "the best equipped regiment of the command," was provided with old flintlock "Tower of London" muskets which had been used by the militia under Andrew Jackson in the War of 1812![2]

Tilghman's telegram expressed his determination to "hold my position to the last," though asking for reinforcements. At midnight he wired again, "I must have reinforcements and with well-drilled troops. The green men with me are well-nigh worthless. More of them would be in my way. The high water threatens us seriously." In fact, the river was rising so rapidly it was an open question whether the garrison would be visited first by the water or by the enemy.

Tilghman seems to have lost his resolution right after sending his last telegram to General Johnston that night. Hardly had it gone when he called a conference of his leading officers, and successful resistance to the overwhelming force of the enemy seeming impossible, surrender was decided on. Tilghman was against giving up the troops as well as the fort. He ordered them to prepare to march at once to Fort Donelson.

Left at the fort was a sacrifice garrison to man the guns—Lieutenant Watts of Company B, 1st Tennessee Artillery, with fifty-four men, together with Captain Taylor. They were ordered to hold the fort for at least an hour the morning of the sixth to enable the troops under Colonel Heiman to make good their escape. Tilghman accompanied his fleeing men until he saw them well on their way, then heroically and unselfishly returned to Fort Henry to share the fate of Watts's men.

That morning the fleet of seven gunboats advanced up the river in line of battle from their anchorage behind Panther Island.[3] Of the fort's total of nine guns on the river side, only two—a rifled gun and a columbiad —could damage the gunboats' armor. Captain Taylor assigned one of the gunboats to each of his guns. The eager gunners opened accurate fire as soon as the vessels came within range. An early shot disabled the Essex with a shell through her boiler. Most of the fire from the smaller ordnance, however, rattled harmlessly off the ironclads, while their guns showered metal on the fort. The discomfiture of the little garrison was soon increased by a series of untoward accidents: the big rifled gun burst, disabling its crew and others near it; the columbiad became spiked with its own priming wire and could not be repaired; two of the 32-pounders were put out of action by the fire from the gunboats; two other guns exhausted their ammunition. The battery was reduced to four effective pieces, and the man power so cut down that General Tilghman himself was serving as a gunner. With odds of four to fifty-four, the only question was how long the Confederates could hold out. After more than two hours of resistance, during which the fort took a terrific battering, the colors were lowered and Tilghman sorrowfully surrendered to Flag-Officer Foote. The river had risen so high that when Foote's officer approached to receive the surrender his cutter could sail right through the sally port.

While all this was going on, General Grant's infantrymen still floundered around in the muddy bottoms. They had no part in the capture, but occupied the fort late in the afternoon. Grant telegraphed the news to Halleck, who notified President Lincoln, and the Northern states went wild with joy as newspaper extras screamed "FORT HENRY HAS FALLEN!"

2. FORT DONELSON'S FALL

When he heard of the surrender of Fort Henry, Johnston made what arrangements were possible to prepare Fort Donelson for the assault which was logically expected to follow. First was the detail of supplying a commander, for the troops were left without a head now that Tilghman had started on his way to a Northern prison. Brigadier General Bushrod R. Johnson was named on February 6. The next day Pillow with all the troops under him at Clarksville was ordered to move to Donelson and assume command. Johnston had no great faith in the impregnability of Fort Donelson. He told Pillow to hold it as long as he could, then evacuate it and march to Nashville by way of Charlotte. General Clark at Hopkinsville with 2,000 men and Floyd with his brigade at Russellville were to concentrate at Clarksville, and though Floyd might use his own judgment when he got there, it was indicated to him that he also should move to the support of Donelson.

Pillow, at the fort on the ninth, went to work energetically, aiming especially at restoring the confidence of the troops, sadly shaken by the Fort Henry surrender and the legend of terrible invincibility which the quick success of the gunboats had created. He was ably assisted by Colonel Gilmer, who applied himself to strengthening the defenses.

At a bend of the river, Fort Donelson stood on a hill the highest point of which was a hundred feet above water level, and, like Fort Henry, gave a view for several miles to the north—the direction from which a gunboat attack must come. Facing the river were two well-placed batteries, aggregating thirteen guns. At the top of the bluff was a big rifled gun and two carronades. Halfway down the hillside toward the river was the lower battery of one ten-inch columbiad and eight smoothbore 32-pounders, all protected by earthworks. The summit was crowned by the fort itself—an irregular bastioned earthwork enclosing about fifteen acres, within which were rows of rude log huts built by Tilghman's original garrison.

The fort was intended primarily for field supports for the water batteries and commanded them at close musket range. It was not designed for nor adapted to defense from the landward side, as no attack had been originally expected there. The country on this side was exceptionally rugged and difficult—a chain of densely wooded ridges, intersected by deep gullies and ravines, many of which were now filled with backwater, interfering with troop maneuvers and also impeding communication. To remedy the weakness on this side, Colonel Gilmer had improvised a system of rifle pits along a series of ridges to the west and back of the fort, following the crest of the high ground irregularly to the southward, curving back across the Charlotte road to the river above Dover. The town was thus enclosed entirely within the Confederate lines. The commanding generals established their headquarters at the Dover Inn close by the steamboat landing. At the time Fort Henry fell, the rifle pits were only about one-third finished, and Colonel Gilmer had to hustle to get them into defensible shape. He strengthened the water batteries by narrowing the embrasures with sandbags and completing the mounting of the guns.

Just to the north of the hill Hickman's Creek flows into the river. It was so filled with backwater that it made an impassable barrier. South of the fort Indian Creek, also swollen, intersected the terrain and almost completely isolated the right wing of the Confederate line. Farther south, just above the town and outside the works, Lick Creek flowed into the Cumberland. The space enclosed within the Confederate defenses fronted about a mile on the river. The rifle pits, due to their irregularity, extended for nearly three miles, at a distance from the river varying from a quarter to three quarters of a mile.

From Clarksville, Floyd moved on to Cumberland City on the river sixteen miles above (that is, south of) Fort Donelson, where the railroad diverged from the south bank. He conceived the idea that the principal stand should be made there, and after a conference with Buckner proposed to withdraw Buckner's troops from the fort to Cumberland City. Pillow, who believed in making the fight for the river at the fort, refused to let Buckner out to join Floyd. He appealed to Johnston at Bowling Green for support and, going by steamboat to Cumberland City, found Floyd ready to come on in as Johnston had now ordered him to. His force arrived during the early morning hours of the thirteenth. By reason of his senior rank, Floyd assumed command—the fifth commander of the fort within one week.

Johnston was beginning to see the handwriting on the wall. Nashville had not been fortified; the fight to hold it must be made at Fort Donelson. He realized that Bowling Green was no longer tenable; the troops there must fall back on Nashville. He had called a council of war with Generals Beauregard and Hardee. The former favored a concentration of all the troops at Fort Donelson, there to force a decisive battle with Grant. Johnston was unwilling to abandon the railroad and highway between Bowling Green and Nashville completely, on the score that his main object should be to gain time to remove the ammunition and provisions gathered at Bowling Green, and the immense stores of food and supplies which (against his own advice) had been piled up at Clarksville and Nashville by the Confederate Commissary and Quartermaster Departments. Furthermore, he felt that his responsibilities were too great to risk destruction of his army if he let it get penned in between Grant and Buell.

At a meeting held on February 7 in General Beauregard's quarters at the Covington House in Bowling Green,[4] the three generals agreed that preparations should be made for Hardee's army to go from Bowling Green to Nashville "in rear of the Cumberland River." Also, that, since the fall of Fort Henry had given the enemy control of the Tennessee and therefore separated the army at Bowling Green from the army at Columbus (to whose command Beauregard had been assigned), the two must thenceforth "act independently of each other until they can again be brought together." The position at Columbus had become precarious. "The main body" of troops there were to be withdrawn to Humboldt, Tennessee, leaving only "a sufficient garrison . . . for the purpose of making a desperate defense of the river at that point." Island No. 10 and Fort Pillow on the Mississippi were to be "defended to the last extremity." This agreement on policy was reduced to a written memorandum, which was signed by Beauregard and Hardee.

Admit all his strategic difficulties, still if the facts are considered deliberately and dispassionately, the conclusion seems inescapable that in this crisis Johnston did not display the judgment which we would be justified in expecting of his supposed genius. It was painfully obvious that, scattered as they were, his meager forces could not resist such an attack as the superior Federal power could bring against him. Equally obvious, this long-feared attack was at hand; the crisis must be faced at last.

Unquestionably he was actuated by the loftiest motive of devotion to the Southern cause. Unquestionably he had very little to work with. But he acted with an excess of caution. This was no time for caution. It was a time for courage and audacity—and audacity does not seem to have been one of his outstanding qualities. He saw Buell's great threatening army lowering at him in Kentucky, and knew that only his little force at Bowling Green stood between it and Nashville. Away to his left he saw his scanty garrison at Columbus, and knew it was all that blocked the way to Northern conquest of the Mississippi. He looked at that narrow neck between Forts Henry and Donelson, and knew they were the only barriers to penetration of the vitals of the South.

One thing was plain: he could not possibly defend all three of these points against a sustained, well-manned attack. The indicated defensive step was to concentrate his fighting power quickly and boldly at some one point, and there attempt to deliver a crushing blow against a segment of the enemy. Beauregard thought a concentration at Fort Donelson might bring a superior force to bear against Grant, able to hurl him back and perhaps destroy his army. For this Hardee's 14,000 men would have to be withdrawn from Bowling Green. But why not? They were no more an obstacle to Buell's 40,000 than an observation garrison would be, if Buell really decided to advance. But these 14,000, added to the troops already gathering at Donelson, would give the Confederate arms just what every commander seeks—a superior force against an isolated detachment. Indeed, Fort Donelson seemed the logical place to make a stand in strength, for if it fell, Bowling Green and Columbus would almost automatically follow. But if Grant could be crushed at the fort, Buell would be forced to fall back and defend the Ohio.

True, there was a possibility that such a concentration would be unsuccessful, though now it does not seem a probability. Grant's full force did not arrive at Donelson until the morning of the thirteenth. By that time Johnston might have been there with 30,000 against 15,000. So he could have attacked with a decisive superiority as Grant came up, instead of letting him deploy and take position unopposed. Best of all, it would have brought the Confederate fighting forces at this critical point directly under the guiding hand of the commanding general, who could make instant decisions, and not leave them to the divided counsels of the bickering and incompetent subordinates under whom they finally took the field.

If Johnston fully appreciated the importance of the fight to be made at Fort Donelson and the tragic consequences of a defeat—and he did— it is hard to understand why he did not hasten up and assume command,[5] even though he thought a concentration there unwise. Apart from the benefit of his presence at the scene of the battle, was it not the proper place for the commander of an army whose fate was at stake in pitched battle? Could not the uncontested retreat of Hardee's division from Bowling Green have been managed by Hardee himself without Johnston's being on hand? Do history's pages record a similar picture of a commanding general marching leisurely off with a retreating column while near by the greater portion of the army girds for a life-and-death battle under inefficient and inexperienced underlings?

Grant, in announcing to Halleck the capture of Fort Henry, had said confidently: "I shall take and destroy Fort Donelson on the 8th and return to Fort Henry." But the steadily rising river flooded the low ground, the roads were under water for a space of two miles from the fort, and he could not carry out his schedule. The day after the fort fell, with his staff and a part of a cavalry regiment he personally reconnoitered within a mile of the Donelson works. With unconcealed contempt for his adversaries, he says in his *Memoirs* that he had known Pillow in Mexico and felt confident that it would be perfectly safe to "march up within gunshot of any entrenchments he was given to hold. . . . I knew that Floyd was in command, but he was no soldier and I judged that he would yield to Pillow's pretensions."[6] This keen analysis of his opponents' weaknesses, however, was necessarily based on knowledge after the event, for, as a matter of fact, neither Pillow nor Floyd was in the fort on the eighth.

His movement on Fort Donelson did not start until the eleventh, when it began under McClernand. Grant followed with the main body on the twelfth, leaving General Lew Wallace with 2,500 men to hold Fort Henry. Foote and the gunboats started on the eleventh—down the Tennessee to Paducah, up the Ohio twelve miles, and then forty miles up the Cumberland. He was accompanied by transports carrying six regiments of reinforcements who had arrived at Fort Henry just as Grant was preparing to set out. At Paducah the convoy picked up eight more transports loaded with troops—10,000 additional soldiers for Grant.

After he got out of the low ground near the Tennessee, Grant's march was without difficulty. The sun was shining, the weather unseasonably warm and balmy, and the men, inspired by the easy victory over Fort Henry, stepped briskly along the sandy road, confident and in high spirits. The retreating Confederates had left no rear guard. The roads had not been obstructed. When McClernand's men got about two miles from the Donelson entrenchments they encountered a detachment of cavalry under Forrest that slowed them down for a while. That was all. Grant invested the fort at his leisure, the Confederates apparently being too preoccupied and too demoralized to interfere.

Characteristic of the nip-and-tuck nature of things at Fort Donelson is the fact that on the morning of the thirteenth, as Grant was deploying his men for their opening attack, General Floyd was just arriving at the Dover landing and hurrying his troops into position behind the breastworks. The Confederates were arrayed in two divisions. The right wing, stretching from Hickman's Creek to Indian Creek and immediately protecting the water batteries, was entrusted to General Buckner. Across the wide expanse of swollen Indian Creek and curving beyond the precious road to Charlotte was the left wing under Pillow, with Bushrod R. Johnson second in command. McClernand's division, when it arrived before the Confederate works on the night of the twelfth, took position on the extreme right, facing Pillow. General C. F. Smith[7] occupied the left, his left on Hickman's Creek. When Foote's convoy of transports came along, the 10,000 reinforcements were placed in the center under General Lew Wallace, who had been called up with the garrison left behind at Fort Henry. Grant's total army, not counting the men on the gunboats, was about 27,000; Floyd's is placed at less than 15,000.

During the night of the twelfth the Federals had placed batteries on the crests facing the Confederate lines and posted a regiment of sharpshooters in advanced position. Early next morning these sharpshooters, supported by brisk artillery fire, began to harass the Confederates who were still working on their entrenchments. About noon McClernand made a sudden and determined infantry attack on Pillow's right. It was driven off, though gallantly and persistently sustained, the artillery on both sides taking active part in the fighting. Smith launched an attack on Buckner's lines in the afternoon, but this also was repulsed. In the course of the morning the Carondelet, first of Foote's flotilla, arrived on the river front and began firing on the water batteries, throwing no less than 158 missiles into the open works. The batteries had just been completed and manned, and the artillerists were so inexperienced they had to be taught how to handle the big guns. They were in the midst of the instruction drill when the *Carondelet* rudely interrupted.[8] Nevertheless, they returned the fire with spirit, and soon a 128-pound shot from the big columbiad made a direct hit, disabled the gunboat's machinery and sent her away crippled.[9]

The weather, a large factor in the story of Fort Donelson, stayed mild and fair through the morning, but during the afternoon there was a sudden change. A slow, cold drizzle developed into a steady, pelting downpour of sleety rain. The temperature dived to a low of 10° that night, and an icy gale swooped down from the north, transforming the rain into a roaring blizzard of sleet and snow.

The annals of both armies set this down as a night of horrid suffering. The freezing north wind drove stinging snow spitefully against blue and gray alike. The lines were so close together that fear of the unsleeping sharpshooters' deadly aim made fires impossible. The thinly clad Confederates huddled miserably in their shallow trenches. Across the hollows, the Northern troops suffered equally, for they had improvidently thrown aside their overcoats and blankets on the gay march from Fort Henry, deceived by the treacherous mildness.

Miserable as they were, the two armies kept up their firing the whole bitter night long, and the roar of the storm was pierced by booming of artillery and crackle of musketry. The suffering was one of the ghastliest chapters of the war. Artillery the day before had set the woods afire. The helpless wounded, trapped between the lines, were cruelly tortured— many of them to a frightful death. Then, with the coming of darkness, those who had escaped death by burning were exposed to the danger of death from freezing. Feeble, agonizing cries for help rang out through the blackness of the storm, but no help could come while the crests of the ridges blazed with the fire from the sharpshooters and the fieldpieces. War that night was truly hell—a bloody, freezing hell on earth.

When day broke on the fourteenth, the ground was covered with two inches of snow, a blanket of pure white—except where it was splotched with red. The biting northern wind still swept the battlefield. The fitful fighting of the night died down. The half-frozen Confederates seemed paralyzed into inaction by the cold. Grant was occupied with the readjustment of his lines, getting the reinforcements that had come with Foote's convoy properly placed in the center. But for occasional scattered and ineffective firing there was little action by the land forces, but on the water side of the beleaguered fort a different story was told.

The whole flotilla arrived that morning, and early in the afternoon Foote struck. Encouraged by his easy success at Fort Henry, he confidently planned to drive straight at the water batteries, silence them with the superior fire of his ironclads, pass up the river and then enfilade the faces of the fort with broadsides. The gunboats opened from a range of a mile and a half as they steamed up the river and advanced until they were within 150 yards of the land batteries. The Confederate guns were bravely manned and efficiently officered. The fate of the defenders of Fort Henry did not affect the confidence of the Donelson artillerists, who had learned their lesson quickly. They faced the furious fire with a coolness and courage which aroused the admiration even of their enemies. Their ten light guns had little effect on the armor of the gunboats, but their columbiad and rifled gun were formidable weapons in capable hands. With these two big guns they hammered the ironclads destructively, the steady rain on the plates reverberating along the Cumberland bluffs and across the hills like the sound from a great forge. Shell and solid shot penetrated the armor, and decks were slippery with blood. The pilot wheel of Foote's flagship, the St. Louis, was carried away by a direct hit. Other machinery took a terrific battering. The St. Louis alone was riddled with fifty-seven hits, Foote himself being wounded twice, but it fared no worse than the others. One after another the gunboats were disabled by the cyclone of fire from the Confederate batteries.

At last, after fighting more than an hour, Foote, bleeding from his wounds, with tears in his eyes, gave the order to withdraw, and the crippled fleet dropped down the river out of range. His loss in killed and wounded was fifty-four. The Confederates, miraculously, had not a man killed, and the batteries were uninjured, although the breastworks had been almost totally blown away by the salvos.

Colonel Forrest had viewed the engagement, purely as a spectator, from near by on the river bank where he had ridden with his second in command, Major D. C. Kelley. In his official report he paid a deserved tribute to the gallantry displayed by both sides: "No one could do justice in description to the attack or the defense. More determination could not have been exhibited by the attacking party, while more coolness and bravery never were manifested than were seen in our artillerists." As he watched, Forrest grew excitedly apprehensive over the outcome, seeing the apparently irresistible avalanche of shot and shell from the gunboats. Turning to Major Kelley, a former minister,[10] he cried: "Parson, for God's sake pray! Nothing but God Almighty can save that fort!"[11]

Similar fears were felt by Floyd, who, in the midst of the bombardment, telegraphed Johnston about the onslaught: "The fort can not hold out twenty minutes."[12]

He was indeed in a difficult position and an unfortunate frame of mind. He was not a trained soldier. His only military experience had been in some inconclusive and unsuccessful engagements in West Virginia early in the war. He had not the least familiarity with the task of holding a fortified position like Donelson. He undertook its defense reluctantly, and was half-whipped when he marched his men behind the breastworks. Moreover, he was of an indecisive disposition, and this natural vacillation was intensified by the conflicting advice he received from his two associates—the hopeful, confident Pillow, and the cautious Buckner, who was convinced of the hopelessness of their job. Nor were harmonious relations improved by the fact that Buckner and Pillow were personal enemies, still nursing an old feud from the Mexican War.

Before the gunboats began their bombardment that morning, Floyd had called a council of war, at which it was unanimously voted to evacuate. It was known that Grant would that day receive reinforcements (exaggeratedly estimated at from 30,000 to 50,000), and they thought it would be wisdom to make an immediate attack on his extreme right in an effort to seize the road leading to Charlotte and thus open up the way for a withdrawal of the army to Nashville. The attack was to be made by Pillow's massed division. About noon his men were ordered out of the trenches and into formation in the open ground to the rear and left of their occupied line. Buckner's division was to cover the withdrawal, should the sortie prove successful, and he was preparing for the movement when he got word early in the afternoon that it had been deferred. Pillow had decided it was too late in the day.[13]

That night Floyd again called his generals into council. The decisive victory over the gunboats had not, in his mind, outweighed the menace of the reinforcements which had been filing into Grant's lines. Stubbornly pessimistic, he still thought it impossible to hold the fort with less than 50,000 men. Again he proposed that they try to force their way out to Nashville by the Charlotte road; again there was unanimous agreement. They would march at dawn.

Through the bitter cold night the Confederates worked tirelessly at realignment. Over the icy roads, through the snow and frozen mud, the men and guns were pulled out of the advanced trenches and assembled in new positions on the left. The noise they made, strangely enough, was not heard by Grant's men shivering in their encampments close by, and there was every reason to believe the sally would prove a total surprise, as planned.

Pillow was ready to advance at daybreak, Saturday the fifteenth. His men were massed against McClernand's right, with Forrest and his cavalry covering the extreme left of the attacking column. Buckner had left a lone regiment of 450 men to hold the rifle pits and taken his assigned position in support of Pillow to attack the right of the Federal center.

Pillow moved promptly on schedule at 5 A.M., but when McClernand's main line was reached, the alert and well-disciplined bluecoats were found arrayed in line of battle, ready for the assault. Despite their hardy resistance, they were pushed back. They slightly outnumbered Pillow's force, but the charging Confederates never relaxed the impetus of attack and rolled McClernand steadily before them.[14] McClernand, after trying for three hours to stem the tide, at eight o'clock sent a courier to General Lew Wallace on his left asking for aid. Wallace was unable to comply, because his hands were strangely tied by the positive orders of General Grant who, it now developed, was not on the scene.[15]

Early in the morning Grant had left his headquarters and gone to visit Captain Foote on his flagship, leaving behind him definite instructions to each of his division comanders not to move from position without his explicit consent. When Wallace sent to headquarters for permission to lend McClernand the help he needed there was no one to give it. Wallace ventured on his own responsibility to send one brigade, but this was by no means enough. The pressure of Pillow's relentless attack pushed McClernand into complete and precipitate retreat, driving him for two miles onto Wallace's right. Now Wallace, fighting in self-defense, joined vigorously in the battle. But even the combined divisions were not strong enough to stay the impetuous onset. Pillow's resistless advance continued, with Buckner joining in on the flank, and by early afternoon the Confederates had achieved the end sought by the sortie: the Charlotte road was completely in their control, and McClernand's and Wallace's men were retreating in confusion, crying, "All's lost! Save yourselves!"[16]

At this point Pillow would seem to have had only two possible courses. The first and more obvious was to follow the original plan and effect the escape of the army to Nashville. The entire right wing of the Union force was thoroughly stampeded and nothing stood in his way. If he did not do that, his only alternative was to pursue the defeated enemy vigorously. There was some chance that, following up the successes of the morning, he could cripple or annihilate the demoralized Federals, especially as they were still under the disadvantage of having their commander absent.

But Pillow adopted neither of these courses. Instead, after pausing to send an absurdly vainglorious telegram to Johnston—"On the honor of a soldier, the day is ours!"—he ordered the whole army back to their positions in the works. Buckner raised strong objection. He questioned Pillow's authority either to change the plan of battle or to give him orders. While they wrangled, Floyd arrived on the scene. Buckner laid the matter before him. Floyd agreed that the original plan should be pursued and told Buckner to stay where he was. But when he consulted Pillow, he characteristically reversed himself and ordered all the men— Buckner included—back to the fort.

Meanwhile, Grant had at last returned to the battlefield. Apprised of the successful break-through of the Confederates on his right, he concluded accurately that the concentration on their left must have undermanned their right. He ordered Smith's division to attack it, and also ordered his right wing to retake the positions lost to Pillow. By this time Pillow was on his way back to his original line and Grant's advancing column merely followed the withdrawing Confederates. Smith's men resolutely and bravely plowed through the obstructions before the Confederate right, now occupied by the single regiment left there in the morning. By the time Buckner and his division had made their way over the muddy and circuitous roads and got within sight of their old stamping ground, they had the chagrin of seeing that hapless regiment take to its heels before Smith's onslaught. They tried strenuously to oust Smith's division from their own former position and when that failed took possession of a hill overlooking it. Skillfully placing his artillery where it would do the most damage, Buckner stopped the Federal advance for the day.

Night fell with all the troops in or near their original posts—all those not left dead and mangled in the snowy underbrush where the armies had struggled since dawn. Floyd and Pillow—self-hypnotized by some strange delusion—telegraphed Johnston that they had won a great victory. Buckner's pessimism was as excessive as their enthusiasm. In his official report he says:

"I regarded the position of the army as desperate, and that the attempt to extricate it by another battle, in the suffering and exhausted condition of the troops, was almost hopeless. The troops had been worn down with watching, with labor, with fighting. Many of them were frosted by the intensity of the cold; all of them were suffering and exhausted by their incessant labors. There had been no regular issue of rations for a number of days, and scarcely any means of cooking.[17] Their ammunition was nearly expended. We were completely invested by a force fully four times the strength of our own." Of his own situation, he added: "My right was already turned, a portion of my intrenchments in the enemy's possession; they were in a position successfully to assail my position and the water batteries; and . . . I could not resist the assault which would be made at daylight by a vastly superior force."

It was a dismally dramatic scene that Saturday night when Floyd and Pillow and Buckner with their aides gathered in Floyd's headquarters in the little Dover Inn on the river bank to discuss their next step. Buckner and Pillow plunged into acrimonious controversy over the miscarriage of the battle plans. Buckner insisted that the object of the morning's sortie had been gained when possession of the Charlotte road was won and that the army should have proceeded to march on to Nashville. Pillow claimed that the agreed plan had been for the men to return to the encampment for their equipment and then withdraw under cover of night. He proposed that this should now be done. But it was objected that this was no longer possible, that the Federals had cut off both means of escape—the road to Charlotte and the river road to Cumberland City and Clarksville. Scouts reported the river road, where it crossed Lick Creek, under three feet of water and therefore impassable to infantry. They had seen fires burning on the hillsides, indicating that the enemy's right overlapped the roads.

Forrest expected nothing but a resumption of the fighting the next morning and, exhausted by his day's exertions, had gone to bed early. About midnight he was awakened by a messenger and summoned to Floyd's headquarters where he found to his amazement that the generals were discussing surrender. He put up a vigorous protest. He did not believe the roads were closed. As late as nine o'clock he had reports that the enemy had not reoccupied the lines on their extreme right. The fires observed, he suggested, were McClernand's former campfires, the embers of which had been fanned by the wind or else been rekindled by stragglers. He urged Floyd to march his men out, offering to cover the retreat with his horse, and "guaranteed that the Federal cavalry would not bother the rear of the infantry."[18] But his protestations went unheeded. The generals were convinced the roads were closed and would not be persuaded otherwise.

Buckner expressed the view, and Floyd finally seemed to agree with him, that there was nothing to do but surrender. Pillow shrank from the thought and offered an alternative. Two steamboats had been sent to Clarksville with the wounded and the prisoners; one or both of them would be back at daybreak. Why not try to hold the fort for at least one more day and during that day use the steamboats to ferry the soldiers across to safety? But Buckner was adamant. The enemy would surely attack at dawn, he said, and he could not hold his ground for thirty minutes. Could they not cut their way out through the enemy's lines, even though completely encircled? Pillow asked. But Buckner said that it would cost the lives of three-fourths of their men; anyhow they were so exhausted they could not march ten miles supposing they made good their escape from the fort. The medical director gave his opinion that it would probably be fatal to most of the soldiers if they tried to wade out across Lick Creek, even if there were no opposition from the enemy.

The more they debated their plight, the more hopeless Buckner convinced them it was. The troops penned up in the fort, he said, were worn out, miserable and dispirited—so unutterably weary that some had fallen asleep on their feet under fire. The besieging army was known to exceed them in numbers, and the superiority was supposed to be even greater than it actually was. In the end Buckner's despondent persistence prevailed. Reluctantly it was agreed that surrender was inevitable and should be made before daybreak to avoid further sacrifices of life.

At this juncture the generals fell into an unseemly squabble. Who should shoulder the burden of the actual surrender? Floyd said emphatically that he would suffer any fate before he would fall into enemy hands. He announced his determination to escape and take his brigade with him.[19] Pillow doggedly insisted that, personally, he would never surrender. Buckner was nettled at the attitude of his superiors and austerely intimated that they were founded on considerations which should not influence a commander. He said that if he were in command he would surrender the army and share its fate himself. Thereupon Floyd said quickly: "If I place you in command, will you allow me to draw out my brigade?"

Buckner answered: "Yes, if you do so before the enemy acts upon my communication."

Floyd without hesitation turned to Pillow, his next in command. "General Pillow, I turn over the command to you." Pillow formally passed it on to Buckner, and Buckner straightway "sent for a bugler, pen, ink and paper, and opened the negotiations for surrender."[20] Forrest, meanwhile, had asked for and received permission to take out his cavalry through the backwaters and was making his preparations.

One of the steamboats, the *General Anderson*, arrived, as expected, at daybreak, ironically bringing 400 reinforcements just in time to be included in the surrender. Floyd presumed on his authority to commandeer the boat, and immediately began loading two of his Virginia regiments on it to be ferried across the river. His Mississippi regiment was assigned the duty of guarding the landing to hold off other would-be fugitives while the Virginians were embarking, with the understanding that they would be included among the escapees. When the boat returned from its trip across the river, however, the other two Virginia regiments were taken aboard, followed by Floyd and his staff. Buckner notified Floyd that the message of surrender had been sent to Grant and that the steamboat must make off without further delay. So it puffed away with Floyd, his staff and his Virginia troops, leaving the Mississippi regiment forlornly on the landing—to their great and clamorous disappointment.[21] Pillow and his staff, accompanied by Gilmer, had meanwhile got across the river on an abandoned scow that somebody had found somewhere.

The troops in the fort had rested through the night and awoke expecting a renewal of the fight. When they heard they were to be surrendered they expressed such immediate and unanimous dissatisfaction that the bugler with the flag of truce had a hard time getting to the front line where he could signal the enemy. Visions of the horrors of a Northern prison imbued many with a desperate determination to escape, which carried them through the icy water or through the surrounding woods to safety. Besides the 3,000 or more who got away on the steamboats, Forrest led his cavalry through the backwaters,[22] with nearly every horse carrying double—a jubilant infantryman clinging behind the rider. The gunners cut their horses out of their harness and rode off through the water. Some simply walked through the lines and made off. In the confusion and disorganization after the actual surrender Sunday morning there was a good deal of this, with discipline in both armies relaxed to the vanishing point. General Bushrod R. Johnson, not having been reported or enrolled as a prisoner, was among those to take advantage of the situation and walked unchallenged through the Federal lines. He later reported that "many of the men and officers commenced to leave Fort Donelson as soon as they heard of the proposed surrender. . . . I have not learned that a single one who attempted to escape met with any obstacle." In all, several thousands of the defenders made their escape in one way or another. The exact number made prisoner was never officially announced. Estimates run all the way from 5,000 to 12,000; it was probably somewhere near 7,000 or 8,000.

The duty of surrendering the fort which had devolved on Buckner involved problems as uncertain as they were unpleasant. So far, there had been no such capitulation of an armed Confederate force in the field. There was still some question what terms might be offered by a Federal commander to men who had been officially denounced as guilty of treason. Buckner felt he was fortunate in having Grant to deal with, not only an old West Point and Mexican War associate and friend, but one under considerable personal obligation to him. Grant had been stationed in Oregon in 1854 when he was permitted to resign from the army rather than face court-martial for habitual intoxication. In straitened circumstances, he had borrowed money for his passage to New York, and when he arrived there a few weeks later he was almost destitute. His financial affairs reached a crisis when his hotel refused him further credit for room or board and even seized his baggage. In this emergency he had appealed to his old friend Captain Buckner, then in New York, and Buckner had restored his credit at the hotel, had his baggage released and tided him over until he was able to collect some money from a creditor, pay his bills and go home to Missouri.

All this passed through Buckner's mind as he penned his note to Grant asking for an armistice to discuss terms of surrender. Surely his old friend had not forgotten his help in time of need and would make the humiliating procedure as painless as possible. But Grant's reply gave no sign of recollection or consideration. It was curt and to the point: "No terms, except unconditional and immediate surrender, can be expected. I propose to move immediately upon your works." Buckner had no alternative but to submit. In his answer, however, he characterized the victor's terms as "ungenerous and unchivalric," these words, he later said, being deliberately chosen to indicate to Grant his surprise and disappointment that a former friend should be unwilling to ease the burden of his chagrin and humiliation.[23]

Despite the brusque tone of his demand, Grant when he arrived at Buckner's headquarters to proceed with the actual surrender was, to use Buckner's words, "very kind and civil and polite." Buckner remarked that if he had been in command of the fort from the first Grant would never have got so close without opposition; whereupon, as Grant tells it, "I told him that if he had been in command I should not have tried in the same way I did."[24] He added facetiously that Pillow need not have been so anxious to escape. "If I had captured him, I would have turned him loose. I would rather have him in command of you fellows than as a prisoner."[25]

Grant had not entirely forgotten Buckner's material aid. Just before Buckner started off dejectedly on his trip to prison, he diffidently offered him a loan if he needed money, but Buckner, although appreciating the courtesy, declined.[26]

A by-product—and a redeeming one—of the Fort Donelson disaster was the rise of the star of Nathan Bedford Forrest. Although but the commander of a regiment, he had already attracted attention as a cavalry leader of unusual dash and enterprise. It was his unconquerable spirit at Fort Donelson, so sharply in contrast with some of his superiors, that first brought him sharply into the public eye as a man worth watching. Forrest was a native Tennessean, had spent his youth and early manhood in Mississippi, and at the outbreak of the war was a planter and a prosperous business man of Memphis, dealing principally in slaves. He had had the benefit of very little formal education, but was possessed of strong will, determination and a magnetic personality, the capacities of a born leader. He lacked a few weeks of being forty years old when the war started, but he at once enlisted in a Tennessee regiment and was prepared to serve as a private when Governor Harris asked him to raise a regiment of calvary. This he soon did, equipping it with saddles and pistols bought with his own money, and was promptly in the field. With no military training, no previous contact with military affairs, he immediately displayed signs of that inborn talent for the art of war which advanced him in time to the rank of lieutenant general in the Confederate service and made his name a terror to the Federals.

Forrest summed up his basic principles of tactics in one sentence: "I just took the short cut and got there first with the most men"[27]—a succinct declaration which is still sound, although repetition by those who would overemphasize his lack of education has distorted it into the absurdly impossible jargon: "I gits thar fustest with the mostest men." He was, in the words of those who followed him, "a natural-born fighter." As they splashed through the cold backwaters out of fallen Fort Donelson, Forrest and his men were riding their way into a place in history that has been equaled by few of the great cavalry commanders of all time.

CHAPTER VII

TO FIGHT ANOTHER DAY

1. NASHVILLE ABANDONED

ON THE eighth of February General Johnston had officially notified the Secretary of War in Richmond[1] that, because of the loss of Fort Henry and his fears for Fort Donelson, he had the day before ordered Hardee to evacuate Bowling Green and retreat to Nashville, sixty-five miles away. Hardee had fallen to work at once, and the evacuation of the main body of the troops was accomplished by the thirteenth, although Hardee himself did not leave until the next day. All the siege guns and other military stores were removed southward by railroad, but a very large accumulation of commissary and quartermaster's stores could not be moved and was burned. The bridges across the Barren River also were burned, and when Buell's advance guard learned of the evacuation and reached the north bank on the morning of the fourteenth, all they could do was to throw a few futile shells across the river at the town.

Movement of troops out of Bowling Green had begun on the eleventh. The downpour of rain and snow and the sub-freezing weather found the whole 14,000 strung out along the muddy road to Nashville. The health of the men at Bowling Green during the early winter had been exceptionally good, with only 500 in the hospital when the evacuation was ordered. Now the retreating army's battle with the elements was more destructive than any clash at arms. Many froze to death as they camped by night on the way; thousands more were overcome by exhaustion or disease engendered by exposure; and by the time the jaded army reached Nashville no less than 5,400 of its 14,000 were under doctor's care or had been left ill in the homes of hospitable people.

General Johnston, in advance of Hardee's retreating division, had reached Nashville from Bowling Green on the morning of the fifteenth and made his headquarters in Edgefield, then a separate town directly across from the capital on the north side of the Cumberland. At midnight he had received Floyd's and Pillow's exultant telegrams announcing "a victory complete and glorious" at Fort Donelson,[2] and he lay down to sleep feeling comparative ease after several days' anxiety. But before day-break he had been aroused by a messenger with another telegram from Donelson—this one bearing the surprising and heartbreaking news of the decision to surrender.

The enormously tragic portent of the fort's capitulation was instantly clear. Johnston had feared just such an eventuality, though the sanguine wires from Donelson had temporarily allayed his apprehensions. It meant the collapse of his whole line, the loss of the Confederacy's narrow foot-hold in Kentucky, the overrunning of a large part of Tennessee by the blue invaders. The unfortified and indefensible city of Nashville must, of course, be surrendered. With no fortifications left on the river, there was no way to stand off the gunboats which could now come sweeping up without opposition. Hardee's force, reduced to less than 10,000 by sick-ness and straggling, was totally unequal to stopping either Buell or Grant, much less both of them.

Crossing over to Nashville early in the morning of Sunday, the six-teenth, Johnston found the city gleefully celebrating the supposed glori-ous victory of the preceding day. The boastful claims had been hastily printed in newspaper "extras," and the people were wildly jubilant. When the general informed Governor Harris of the fort's fall, and the news leaked out to the public, there was a sickening revulsion of feeling, the pendulum swinging the full arc from elation to gloom. Excitement spread through the city, which straightway became electric with rumors: Buell with 35,000 men was even then within twenty-five miles; a fleet of Yankee gunboats had already passed Clarksville and Nashville would be shelled by the combined guns of the fleet and the army by 3 P.M.; Gover-nor Harris had ordered the women and children to leave the city before it was bombarded and destroyed!

None of these rumors was true, for the soldiers and the gunboats were still far away, but by constant repetition they gained all the overpowering strength of truth until Nashville was in a perfect frenzy of terror. Fear even penetrated the churches, and the excited congregations were hastily dismissed so they might lose no time getting out of town before the bom-bardment began. The people were beside themselves with panic.

One eye-witness, an officer in Johnston's army, has left a graphic pic-ture of the stampede:

"Some wept at the thought of abandoning the city to a fate which they esteemed as dreadful as utter destruction; and many, infuriated, loudly advocated burning it to the ground, that the enemy might have nothing of it but its ashes. . . . When the excitement and fury were at the highest pitch, and officers and privates were alike influenced by it, it seemed as if the bonds of discipline would be cast off altogether. Crowds of soldiers were mingled with the citizens, who thronged the streets all night; and yells, curses, shots rang on all sides. In some houses the women were pale and sobbing, and in others there was even merriment, as if in defiance of the worst."[3]

A complicating factor in the panic was that while so large a part of the citizens were terrified at the thought of a battle to be fought in or near the city, there was another more belligerent part just as wildly aroused when they heard it would not be defended. A noisy mob of them gathered outside the house in which Johnston was staying. The lusty, loud-mouthed inebriate who acted as their leader mounted the steps, banged on the door and shouted: "We have come to demand of our generals whether they intend to fight for us or not. We have a right to know whether they are going to fight for us, or intend abandoning us and our wives and children to the enemy. We will force them to tell us!"[4] The crowd, like a Greek chorus, howled its approbation. Members of the general's staff buttered them with assuaging words and finally induced them to disperse.

All through the terrible, turbulent Sabbath the terror-stricken men, women and children surged through Nashville's streets. Some just wandered aimlessly from one place to another, eagerly catching the latest rumor and passing it on. Others, more practical-minded, loaded their possessions onto wagons and into carriages for a hasty departure. Those who had no private vehicles crowded to the railroad stations and jammed the departing trains; men even clung precariously to the tops of the coaches as they pulled out. Johnston had advised Governor Harris to remove the state archives, and a special train left in the afternoon carrying the Governor and other officials with their precious records to the safety of Memphis. This official exodus added to the fears of the people. Banks and business houses removed their specie and other valuables. The roads and streets were choked with departing wagons, trucks, drays—any form of wheeled vehicle was in demand, at rates of hire which soared to twenty-five dollars an hour.

During the early part of the day the vanguard of Hardee's retreating army arrived and limped wearily through the packed and muddy streets, adding their bit to the panic as straggling soldiers joined the mobs milling about the town and told fearsome stories of the hordes of bloodthirsty

Yankees hot on their tracks. In the afternoon Mayor Cheatham obtained from Johnston assurance that he would make no stand to defend the city, and in the evening the Mayor, in a speech to the people assembled in the Public Square, promised them the city would not be subjected to the hazard of battle. He urged them to quiet their fears and stay home. He promised to go out and meet the advancing Federals himself and surrender Nashville peacefully. Then he sowed the seed of trouble by promising to distribute among the citizens all the provisions in the Confederate warehouses that could not be moved to safety.

When there were still no signs of the gunboats or of Buell's troops Monday morning, the panic somewhat subsided, although the stores and post office were closed, and business, including the publication of newspapers, was suspended. Hardee's army still poured depressingly through the town on the way to their temporary encampment on the Murfreesboro pike, churning the mud into quagmire as the cursing drivers lashed the struggling horses of the artillery and wagon trains. The steamboat from Fort Donelson arrived early carrying Floyd and his men—and General Pillow, who had been picked up at Clarksville.

The promised distribution of the surplus army stores had begun that morning. The crowds seeking a share of the spoils quickly degenerated into plundering mobs who defied control and, instead of waiting for what was given them, decided to take what they wanted by force. The first thing Floyd saw as he landed at the wharf was a gang of hoodlums looting a steamboat loaded with meat for the army. And this was typical of what was going on at other places.

When Floyd and Pillow arrived, Johnston wasted no time in criticism or recrimination over the loss of Fort Donelson, but dispatched the latter with 2,500 men to Chattanooga to help hold East Tennessee, and assigned to Floyd the job of restoring order in Nashville.[5] He himself moved on to Murfreesboro with Hardee's army, first burning two unfinished gunboats that were being built at the wharf. Floyd designated the 1st Missouri Infantry to police duty, assisted by Morgan's cavalry. On Tuesday, when Colonel Forrest and his troopers clattered into town on their long ride from Fort Donelson, Floyd turned over to them the restoration of law and order and salvaging as much as possible from the army warehouses for the use of the army itself.

Ever the capable organizer and executive, Forrest tackled this task with energy and ability, and soon began to straighten out the chaotic conditions. His first thought was to remove the stores to a place of safety. Every form of conveyance in the city and surrounding country was com-

GENERAL ALBERT SIDNEY JOHNSTON

General Pierre Gustave Toutant Beauregard

mandeered. No less than 250,000 pounds of bacon, 600 boxes of army clothing and hundreds of wagonloads of flour and other stores and provisions were hauled to the railroad stations and loaded on trains for Chattanooga and Decatur. The precious rifling machine was taken from the gun foundry and sent to Atlanta, along with other ordnance machinery. Forty wagonloads of ammunition were carried a few miles out of town and dumped, then later taken farther south while the Federals were occupying the city.

The difficulty of the duty imposed on Forrest can hardly be exaggerated. When he arrived all the officers of the Quartermaster's and Commissary Departments, with one lone exception, had fled the city, and the plunderers were having things pretty much their own way. He appealed to the mobsters on patriotic grounds to disperse, but when his pleas failed he led his cavalrymen into their midst, beating down the ringleaders with the flat of his saber and forcing them to stop their pillaging. A particularly recalcitrant mob which assembled Friday in front of the big warehouse on the Public Square he scattered with a fire-hose. All that day and Saturday he worked like a beaver to save all the army stores he could. Saturday evening, two of the bridges on the south-bound railroad to Chattanooga washed out and work on that line had to be discontinued.

At a conference of the army and civic authorities on Tuesday morning it had been decided that the suspension bridge and the railroad bridge leading northward across the Cumberland at Nashville must be destroyed as a matter of military necessity. The citizens lifted a loud protest, but the army leaders were consumed with the idea that Buell and his army would arrive at any minute. Although it had been definitely decided not to defend Nashville, by some strange logic it was deemed essential to destroy the bridges as a means of keeping the Yankees out of the city which was to be surrendered to them. So on Tuesday night the railroad bridge was burned and the suspension bridge's big cables were cut, thus isolating the city from the northern side of the river—and, incidentally, causing the citizens a great deal of unnecessary trouble.

The first scouts of Buell's army did not appear in Edgefield until Sunday, February 23. The general himself got there with the advance of his main force Monday evening, and Mayor Cheatham crossed over and surrendered the city to him. Tuesday morning it was formally occupied. A gunboat, shepherding several transports loaded with soldiers,[6] steamed up the river. It tied up on the Edgefield side and trained its guns menacingly on Nashville, while the troops unloaded gleefully at the wharf. The rear guard of Confederate cavalry were still patrolling the streets but prudently retired as the conquering bluecoats, with bands blaring *Yankee Doodle* and *Hail Columbia*, paraded triumphantly to the state capitol. This they seized in the name of the United States Government and hoisted the Stars and Stripes over the cupola,[7] as the news of the conquest went flashing over the telegraph wires to the North. It was a great day for Northern arms. Nashville was the first large Confederate city captured. The happy smiles of the soldiers of occupation were reflected in the faces of the officials at Washington and all the people. The Union Army had gained its first firm foothold on Southern soil.

As soon as Tennesseans and Southerners generally had recovered from the swift succession of shocks caused by the loss of Fort Henry, Fort Donelson and Nashville, they broke out in a volcanic uproar of indignation and faultfinding. There was wholesale condemnation of Floyd and Pillow for abandoning their command, but the chief storm of abuse centered on Johnston—the erstwhile hero and toast of the state. Now he was reviled on every side as stupid, incompetent and even corrupt. President Davis was denounced for his stubbornness in keeping such a nincompoop in charge. Public confidence in General Johnston was so far gone that some new recruits made it a condition of enlistment that they should not be called on to serve under him. The papers forgot that just a few weeks ago they had been heaping unstinted praise on him as "possessing all the qualities of a wise, discreet and brave general." He had failed to keep the invading Yankees out of Tennessee, so off with his head! The Memphis *Appeal*, for example, said bluntly that he had been outgeneraled by Buell and "the fact is too palpable for denial" that his blunders had transferred the war from Kentucky to Tennessee.[8] Ironically enough, a few days later the same paper reprinted the comment of the New York *Herald* on the fall of Fort Donelson. The *Herald* was laboring under the temporary delusion that the bag had included Johnston himself; it described him as "the craftiest general in the rebel host" and his supposed capture as "more significant than would be the capture of half a dozen Beauregards."

Southern press and public did not share this Northern paper's estimate of Johnston's capabilities. The agitation against him spread. President Davis was besieged with letters and protests and demands. Members of the Tennessee delegation in the Confederate Congress presented a petition demanding that he be relieved of command. A leading Tennessean frantically and redundantly telegraphed: "Nothing but your presence can save Tennessee. General Johnston's army is demoralized.

Your presence will reassure it, and will save Tennessee. Nothing else can.
For God's sake come!" One prominent army officer from Mississippi
wired: "If Johnston and Hardee are not removed, the army is demoralized.
President Davis must come here and take the field." Hardee was pro-
claiming that Johnston's military leadership had been greatly overrated.
Even Colonel Mackall, Johnston's own chief of staff, concurred.[9] A
member of Congress[10] telegraphed the President hysterically denouncing
Johnston as guilty of greater errors of omission and commission than "any
other general who ever preceded him in any country," and he too urged
Davis to go to Tennessee and take command of the army. He concluded:
"If your presence is impossible, for God's sake give immediate command
to Beauregard, Bragg or Breckinridge, or all will be irretrievably lost."[11]

A delegation of prominent Tennesseans went to Richmond to beseech
Davis to send somebody, anybody, to relieve Johnston! The President,
irritated, dismissed them. "If Sidney Johnston is not a general, we had
better give up the war for we have no general."[12] He steadfastly refused
to be swayed by all the clamor. With typically thoughtful consideration,
Robert E. Lee took time to write Johnston a kind and friendly letter of
sympathy and confidence.[13]

Johnston himself in a letter to Davis echoed the suggestion that the
President come out for a visit. His presence would "encourage my troops,
inspire the people and augment the army." He went further and volunteered the unselfish observation: "Were you to assume command, it
would afford me the most unfeigned pleasure, and every energy would be
exerted to help you to victory and the country to independence."[14]

It should be borne in mind that these references to Davis' taking
command were no mere idle attempts to flatter the chief executive. His
background was distinctly military: he had graduated from West Point
and served in the regular army; he had commanded a Mississippi regiment
in the Mexican War; and he had served four years as Secretary of War
under Franklin Pierce. Many people (including himself) placed a high
valuation on his military talents; and, if it had been left to his own choice,
he would probably have preferred a place in the field to the President's
chair. So convinced was he of his own military genius that his various
Secretaries of War were hardly more than puppets. He did not hesitate
to go around them in handing out suggestions and orders to the commanders in the field.

All the tornado of censure and abuse General Johnston met in silence,
unperturbed. He displayed that serenity and nobility of character which
had won him so many admirers in happier times. Urged to make a public

defense, he said: "I can not correspond with the people. What the people want is a battle and a victory. That is the best explanation I can make."[15] Later he wrote President Davis: "I observed silence, as it seemed to me the best way to serve the cause and the country," inasmuch as any justification would reveal to the enemy the inadequacy of his force and his resources. This letter, a model of detachment, ended: "The test of merit in my profession, with the people, is success. It is a hard rule, but I think it right. If I join this corps to the forces of Beauregard (I confess a hazardous experiment) then those who are now declaiming against me will be without argument."[16]

But the criticism did not all come from the undiscerning and volatile public. The House of Representatives, its pride wounded, appointed a special committee: "To inquire into the military disasters at Fort Henry and Fort Donelson and the surrender of Nashville into the hands of the enemy," and the halls of the capitol at Richmond rang with denunciations of Johnston, Floyd and Pillow. Unwilling to take snap judgment, Johnston had received Floyd and Pillow without rebuke when they fled to Nashville, and had forwarded their official reports to the government without comment. The President was not inclined to view their behavior so leniently. He wrote Secretary Benjamin on March 11 that their reports were unsatisfactory and gave an aspect to the surrender which he hoped they might alter by supplementary statements. In the absence of such explanations, he instructed the Secretary to order Johnston "to relieve both of those officers from command, and to indicate to them that information is wanted as to their failure to give timely notice of the insufficiency of the garrison to repel the attack, and their failure to attempt to save the army by evacuating the post when it was found to be untenable, and especially why they abandoned the command, and by what means their escape was effected; further to state upon what principle was a selection made of certain troops, being certain regiments of the senior General's brigade, to whose use the transportation on hand should be appropriated."[17]

The unhappy generals were accordingly suspended by Albert Sidney Johnston. After full investigation, Floyd was officially censured and dismissed from the army. Pillow's suspension was in due course lifted and he was restored to duty, but the inquiry found him guilty of "grave errors of judgment in the military operations which resulted in the surrender of the army."[18] He resented this deeply, and said so in a bitter correspondence with Benjamin that lasted over several months. He was never relieved of the odium nor was he ever restored to any active responsible command commensurate with his training and experience. He finally resigned in protest.

2. PREPARING TO STRIKE

The dispersed and disorganized Confederate forces in Tennessee were in a desperately dangerous position. Johnston at Murfreesboro with Hardee's "Army of the Center" was separated by more than 300 miles from Polk's army at Columbus, whose command was about to be assumed by Beauregard. Johnston's 17,000 were menaced by Buell at Nashville. Indeed, Buell seemed to have it in his power to dash after them and crush them almost at will, or at least drive in a wedge that would prevent their joining Beauregard. Grant, astride the Tennessee River with 30,000 confident troops steadily being reinforced, could by moving promptly either turn and take Columbus in the rear or, what was more dreaded, advance quickly by the river into north Alabama or Mississippi and seize the Memphis & Charleston Railroad, described by General L. P. Walker as "the vertebrae of the Confederacy."[19] Such a move would not only keep Johnston and Beauregard apart but would drive a fatal blade deep into the heart of the Confederate States.

The strategy indicated for the Confederates seemed plain enough—a prompt concentration of their divided columns at some strategic point. Johnston immediately undertook it, selecting Corinth in northern Mississippi as the place of rendezvous. After the war (and after Johnston was dead), Beauregard claimed that the joining of forces at Corinth was his idea and that it was only at his insistent urging Johnston adopted it. He represents that Johnston was retreating from Nashville more or less aimlessly and vaguely southward, with no particular purpose in view, and that he sent a personal messenger who, not without difficulty, convinced Johnston of the advisability of joining him at Corinth and offering battle to the enemy.

After all the evidence has been carefully sifted, however, and varying statements and recollections have been weighed against one another, it seems clear that Johnston in retreating from Nashville had no other ultimate objective than a concentration of all his available force (including the men under Beauregard's command) south of the Tennessee River, there to turn and contest the Federal advance. True, he kept his own counsel and was perfectly willing for the enemy to believe he was falling back to Chattanooga, but it is now fairly certain that he had the concentration at Corinth in his mind all the while.[20]

He could hardly have overlooked the advantages of Corinth as a log-

ical place to concentrate—a railroad junction, and close enough to the
big bend of the Tennessee River to be a convenient base against any
hostile irruption from the river banks for many miles. Its suitability
doubtless appealed to Beauregard also, but Johnston had recognized from
the very first that the line of the Cumberland would be hard to defend
and that he might have to fall behind the Tennessee to make a final stand.
To prepare himself for the contingency he had had all this country
mapped by his engineers, and there is ample evidence that he had considered its potentialities long before Beauregard called them to his notice.
In fact, one of his officers, Colonel Frank Schaller, makes the amazing,
the almost incredible statement that in January, while looking at his
engineers' map Johnston had put his finger on a crossroads marked
"Shiloh Church" and said: "Here the great battle of the Southwest
will be fought."[21] Beauregard dismisses this as a product of Colonel
Schaller's too vivid imagination, and it does seem hard to believe, but
without it the testimony is convincing. As early as February 27 (just two
days after the Federals occupied Nashville) Johnston wrote Secretary
Benjamin: "I will move this corps of the army . . . toward the left bank
of the Tennessee, crossing the river near Decatur, in order to enable me
to cooperate or unite with General Beauregard."[22] And when Colonel
Liddell was sent by Johnston to President Davis in January with a personal plea for reinforcements he told Davis flatly that Johnston expected
soon to be attacked and, unless reinforced, would be "compelled to fall
back . . . to the Memphis & Charleston Railroad on the line of the Tennessee River."[23] Further evidence in this direction is supplied by the
fact that, in November 1861, Johnston had his chief commissary officer,
Major Jackson, accumulate large depots of supplies at Corinth and at
Holly Springs, Mississippi.[24] Whoever thought of it first, once concentration at Corinth was decided on, Johnston took prompt and vigorous
steps to bring together there the greatest possible number of men. His
strategy was based on the assumption that the enemy would not be content to rest idly on the Tennessee and the Cumberland. The rivers were
valuable only as avenues for invading and occupying the country. The
occupation could not be achieved until they left the rivers behind and
marched into the interior. Grant, it was correctly guessed, would strike for
the Memphis & Charleston line. It was assumed, with equal accuracy,
that Buell's army would be ordered to join him. Johnston's plan was to
assemble his maximum force at Corinth as swiftly as possible, strike and
destroy Grant before he could be joined by Buell, and then turn on
Buell—the sound strategy of striking the enemy's fractions in detail.

He wasted little time on reorganization at Murfreesboro. On February 28 he began his march southward through Shelbyville and Fayetteville to Decatur, Alabama, on the south bank of the Tennessee. The renewal of the retreat deepened the soldiers' dejection. The dispirited army sloshed along, its progress hampered at every step by steady rain, swollen streams, washed-out bridges and hub-deep mud. On March 18 Johnston wrote President Davis that his passage of the river at Decatur was almost accomplished and the head of his column was already at Corinth. By the twenty-fifth the last of Hardee's division had reached the rendezvous and was in position. Crittenden's division of about 5,000 men was halted at Burnsville and Iuka on the railroad to the east.[25] Johnston himself got to Corinth on the twenty-second. Beauregard arrived in time for the meeting.

The two generals had had their last conference at Nashville on February 15, when it was agreed that Beauregard should take over in the Columbus sector; also that the main force at Columbus should be withdrawn, with the War Department's approval, and all Beauregard's troops held in readiness in West Tennessee to oppose whatever movement the Federals might make toward Memphis and north Mississippi, now that they controlled the Tennessee.

Beauregard had left Nashville by rail on the fifteenth for Decatur, spent the night, and gone on by the Memphis & Charleston to Corinth where it crossed the Mobile & Ohio. Unfamiliar with the territory, he shrewdly confined his travel to the daylight hours, so that he might inspect the topography. At Corinth he heard the disturbing, but not unexpected, news of the loss of Fort Donelson, and wired Johnston for instructions. "You must now act as seems best to you," he was told. "The separation of our armies is for the present complete."[26]

Beauregard found a special train awaiting him through the courtesy of the Mobile & Ohio officials, and on the morning of the seventeenth left Corinth for Columbus. He felt ill, so ill that when the train reached Jackson he had to get off.[27] He rested there and made it his headquarters. He telegraphed General Polk at Columbus to come and confer with him, told him he must take charge of the army until his own health permitted active work again.

Beauregard was joined at Jackson not only by Polk but by his own adjutant, Colonel Thomas Jordan, and his chief engineer, Captain D. B. Harris, both of whom had been sent ahead to Columbus to inspect the fort and the surrounding country. After a thorough discussion—Polk wanted to keep at Columbus enough of a garrison to dispute the passage of the Federal gunboats—it was decided to abandon that "Gibraltar of the West" and establish a new line.

This line, as tentatively fixed by Beauregard and his engineers, was interstate in its nature, reaching from northwestern Alabama to southeastern Missouri, touching also Kentucky and Mississippi and stretching across the whole width of Tennessee. It had its right at Corinth, with a strong body of advanced troops at Iuka and a small force at Tuscumbia protecting the railroad communications eastward. From Corinth it extended up through Jackson, Humboldt and Union City in Tennessee to its new left at Island No. 10 in the Mississippi and the near-by town of New Madrid on the Missouri side of the river, with cavalry patrols in southwestern Kentucky. Probably never before were so few troops spread out over such a long, thin line. But the Mobile & Ohio was within the line in West Tennessee and made possible a quick concentration to meet any Federal advance from the west side of the Tennessee. As an added precaution against an incursion, squadrons of cavalry with light artillery patrolled the bank to watch for boats and prevent a surprise landing.[28]

Beauregard's idea was that the Mississippi could be better defended at Island No. 10 and New Madrid than at Columbus; also that they would require smaller forces and so release a large part of the big Columbus garrison for service in the field. Polk strongly disagreed with this appraisal. He felt that Columbus, even with a reduced force, was the most defensible point by reason of its gun power. He argued that to abandon the fort at that time, following so closely on the reverses at Fishing Creek, Fort Donelson and Nashville, would have a depressing psychological effect, while a determined maintenance would be a tonic to drooping spirits. He offered to undertake the defense with even 5,000 or 6,000 men, less than Beauregard planned to station at Island No. 10 and New Madrid. But Beauregard's mind was made up and all argument could not sway him. Columbus must be abandoned.

As a matter of fact, defense at New Madrid presented a difficult and complex problem because of the river's capricious course. Flowing southward forty miles from Columbus, the Mississippi, just at the point where it is interesected by the Kentucky-Tennessee state line, suddenly doubles back in a big twin bend shaped like a reversed S. At the southern toe of the first bend, in the middle of the river and commanding from its end an unobstructed view upstream for several miles, lies Island No. 10. Ten miles farther down but to the northwest by the compass, at the northern toe of the next twist (known as Madrid Bend), is the town of New Madrid, Missouri, then weakly protected with three forts mounting seven guns each and held by a garrison of two Arkansas regiments under Colonel Gantt. About 180 miles farther south by the river's meanderings, on the Tennessee side, was Fort Pillow. It had been elaborately planned but never finished. Beauregard's engineers were instructed to complete the works on a contracted basis so that they could be held by 3,000 men instead of the 10,000 for which they were originally intended.

To Polk was given the unwelcome duty of withdrawing from Columbus not only the troops but all the stores and ordnance he had so laboriously assembled. He accomplished this with the greatest possible secrecy, working mainly at night, and kept the watchful enemy in such ignorance that they had no inkling of the evacuation until he was gone. No less than 140 guns had been mounted at Columbus. He got them away without losing one. The heaviest were taken downriver to the works on Island No. 10, others to the batteries on the Tennessee side opposite the island, and still others to New Madrid, where land defenses were built besides the batteries bearing on the river.

General J. P. McCown was assigned command of the forces around Madrid Bend; A. P. Stewart and his brigade were placed in New Madrid, making a total of 7,000 men there and at Island No. 10. The rest of the Columbus garrison, nearly 10,000 men, under General Polk, were stationed at Humboldt, an important railroad junction, where the troops could be moved to either Memphis or Corinth as necessity might dictate.

Not till March 5 did Beauregard assume active command of the department but meanwhile he was not idle. Despite the handicap of his illness, he was calling for everything he could think of to strengthen his position and his forces. He sent letters and telegrams and personal emissaries to Richmond and to the Governors of Mississippi, Louisiana, Alabama and Tennessee, expressing his "profound anxiety" and appealing for support. He promised if reinforced to take the offensive and even held out the glittering hope of capturing Cairo, Paducah and St. Louis.[29] In his zeal he overlooked no possible means of advancing the cause. It was at this time that he issued his celebrated appeal to "the planters of the Mississippi Valley" to contribute their plantation bells to the army to be melted up and used for casting cannon. This appeal was the subject of much patriotic poetry in the South, but it elicited from the brimstone-tipped pen of George D. Prentice a caustic comment in the Louisville Courier:

"The rebels can afford to give up all their church bells, cow bells and dinner bells to Beauregard, for they never go to church now, their cows have all been taken by foraging parties, and they have no dinner to be summoned to."[30]

Beauregard's cry for bells met with enthusiastic response, but his efforts to get help from the Governors were somewhat less fruitful. Colonel Liddell, when he approached Governor Moore of Louisiana, was particularly exasperated at that haughty official's dogged and sulky independence. Perceiving that the prompt addition of Van Dorn's and Price's commands from west of the river might well provide the balance of power in the next contest with the enemy in Tennessee, he wanted Moore to wire Jefferson Davis suggesting that the steamboats lying at New Orleans wharves would be ample to bring the trans-Mississippi reinforcements quickly to Johnston's aid. The Governor flatly refused. When Liddell turned to the Governor's friend and adviser, Attorney General Moise, he was told that the Governor had been snubbed by President Davis and "would not subject himself to any further indignities from that quarter."

Astonished at such a petty attitude in such a crisis, Liddel impulsively exclaimed: "I would take a thousand snubbings to save the cause."

Moise shook his head. "Well, the Governor will not, and it is useless to talk further about it."

So the steamboats stayed at the levee, Van Dorn's army waited in Arkansas for transportation, and Johnston waited at Corinth for Van Dorn.

One of the telegrams sent by Beauregard from Jackson was fraught with gravest import for the embryonic Army of Tennessee and for the whole Confederacy. This was the wire to General Cooper at Richmond, stating that he was in despair about his health, and asking that General Braxton Bragg be sent out at once from Pensacola. "When well, I will serve under him," said Beauregard, "rather than not have him here." The warmth of his words indicates his high esteem for Bragg, and this feeling was general in the South—though destined to be sharply reversed.

Braxton Bragg was a soldier of West Point training, with no little practical experience, and much was expected of him when he cast his lot with the Confederacy. He was born in North Carolina in 1817, and upon his graduation from the Military Academy in 1837 took part in the Seminole War in Florida. In the Mexican War he served as an artillery captain under General Zachary Taylor, and his name became a household word from Taylor's reported order at the battle of Buena Vista: "A little more grape, Captain Bragg." (Bragg himself said that Taylor's actual words were "Captain, give them hell!")[31] He was lieutenant colonel under Albert Sidney Johnston on the expedition to Utah, but resigned from the army in 1856 and was commissioner of swamp lands of Louisiana when the war started. He entered the Confederate service as a brigadier general and was assigned to the command of Pensacola, Florida, being promoted to the rank of major general early in 1862. While at Pensacola he displayed an unusual ability as an organizer, specializing in drill and discipline. The troops he trained were celebrated for their efficiency. They regarded him, however, as a hard taskmaster and too much a stickler for formality, red tape and precise conformity with all rules and regulations.

General Grant had served with Bragg in the Mexican War. In his *Memoirs* he speaks of him as "a remarkably intelligent and well-informed man, professionally and otherwise. He was also thoroughly upright. But he was possessed of an irascible temper and was naturally disputatious. A man of the highest moral character and the most correct habits, yet in the old army he was in frequent trouble. As a subordinate he was always on the lookout to catch his commanding officer infringing upon his prerogatives; as a post commander he was equally vigilant to detect the slightest neglect, even of the most trivial order."[32]

Grant relates an anecdote which, though doubtless apocryphal, is illustrative of Bragg's reputation as a martinet.

"On one occasion," he says, "when stationed at a post of several companies, commanded by a field-officer, he was himself commanding one of the companies and at the same time acting as post quartermaster and commissary. He was first lieutenant at the time, but his captain was detached on other duty. As commander of the company he made a requisition upon the quartermaster—himself—for something he wanted. As quartermaster he declined to fill the requisition, and indorsed on the back of it his reasons for so doing. As company commander he responded to this, urging that his requisition called for nothing but what he was entitled to, and that it was the duty of the quartermaster to fill it. As quartermaster he still persisted that he was right. In this condition of affairs Bragg referred the whole matter to the commanding officer of the post. The latter, when he saw the nature of the matter referred, exclaimed: 'My God, Mr. Bragg, you have quarreled with every officer in the army, and now you are quarreling with yourself!' "[33]

Indeed, Braxton Bragg was a strange and unfortunate mixture. Nearly all observers, on both sides, give him credit for the highest moral character and for skill in planning and carrying out some military maneuvers, but his execution of his own plans was hampered by an innate vagueness of purpose, and his unpopularity with practically everyone he encountered greatly diminished his effectiveness. In his defense it should be said that he was the victim of a painful and distressing chronic ailment—migraine, or sick headache—and he was often ill from other causes during his campaigning. "He was frequently in the saddle when the more appropriate place for him would have been in bed," wrote an officer in his army who was no great admirer. "This infirmity caused him to be irritable, often harsh, and this alienated from him the affection and enthusiasm of his troops, and he was never without serious friction with some, and at times all, of his corps commanders."[34]

Recognition of Bragg's genuine patriotism and unselfish devotion to the Southern cause is general. Perhaps none of his subordinate commanders had more reason for antagonism than General Polk, a feeling which was naturally reflected in Polk's son, but in his biography of his father that son says generously:

"In spite of General Bragg's conspicuous failure as a commander of an army in the field, and his evident inability to accept and face the ill results of his own official acts, yet in all matters touching his private duty to the cause of the South he was unselfishness itself. No man loved it better, no man gave it more devoted service, none laid his all upon its altar more ungrudgingly, and no one would have laid down his life for it more cheerfully."[35]

Beauregard's application for Bragg's transfer from Pensacola to Tennessee was referred by the War Department to Bragg himself with permission to use his own discretion. He sent a personal emissary to Johnston to confer with him on his army and its necessities. When this messenger returned he reported the state of affairs in Tennessee in such alarming terms that Bragg immediately decided the cause could best be served by temporarily abandoning Pensacola and transferring his force of about 10,000 men to Corinth. He joined Beauregard in Jackson early in March and was at once given authority to issue orders in Beauregard's name for his department.

The troops he brought up from Pensacola and Mobile were well-drilled and reliable, but the others now placed under his command were mostly raw recruits. He referred to them disparagingly as "the mob we have, miscalled soldiers."[36] But within a month his stern discipline had whipped them into better shape, and in a letter to his wife he spoke proudly of their improvement.

Beside this new strength, Beauregard was reinforced by General Ruggles from New Orleans with 5,000 men. Operating on the railroad in the neighborhood of Corinth, there were some 3,000 more under Generals Chalmers and Walker. All these, with the forces under Polk, gave Beauregard a total command of about 23,000 (not including the garrisons at New Madrid and Island No. 10) when he joined Johnston at Corinth late in March. General Van Dorn had been ordered to bring his army of 20,000 from Arkansas but he was delayed by lack of transportation and arrived too late to take part in the ensuing battle.

Meanwhile, fortunately for the Confederate plans, the Federals had been behaving with inexplicable deliberation and want of enterprise. Halleck was now in command of all their forces in the West—Buell east of the Tennessee; Grant between the Tennessee and the Mississippi; Curtis in southwestern Missouri—but for all his enlarged powers he seemed hesitant and uncertain. He was a really remarkable character, a strange mixture of ability and inability. He was a native of New York state, born in 1815. After his graduation from West Point in 1839, he was an assistant professor at the Academy. The government sent him on a military tour of Europe. In 1846 he published a book entitled *Elements of Military Art and Science* which was highly esteemed in army circles. During the Mexican War he was stationed in California, where he did not see much active service but developed skill in civil administration. He resigned from the army in 1854 and took up the practice of law, in which he showed great proficiency, but when the war started in 1861 he returned to the service and was commissioned a major general. When he was assigned to the supreme command in the West, after the fall of Fort Henry, his administrative ability served to straighten out the tangles left by some of his predecessors, but his clumsy and confused manipulation of his forces showed he could write better than he could fight.

Buell had approached Nashville with the extremity of caution. Even after occupying the undefended city, he was consumed with fear that the fleeing Johnston might suddenly turn on him. Johnston's retreat was skillfully covered by his cavalry, notably that under Captain John H. Morgan, and Buell could not learn much about the location and movements of the main body.

After the capture of Fort Donelson, Grant through some vagary went off on an unauthorized and unnecessary trip to Nashville. He soon found himself in disfavor as a result and "virtually in arrest and without a command," as he expresses it.[37] Halleck was surprised and irritated when he discovered his absence from his post. Nashville was quite outside his department. On March 1 Halleck had telegraphed Grant to move his army up the Tennessee River, but Grant was not there to get the message. Some anonymous person wrote Halleck that he was off on a spree. Halleck, giving this some credence despite its anonymity, on March 3 wired General McClellan in Washington that he had not heard from Grant in a week. "He left his command without my authority and went to Nashville," Halleck continued. "I can get no returns or reports of any kind from him. I am tired and worn out by this neglect and inefficiency." He passed on the rumor that "Grant has resumed his former bad habits"—a polite euphemism. McClellan was too occupied with his own troubles in the East to worry overmuch about the misconduct of some backwoods commander. He impatiently wired back that generals must observe discipline as well as private soldiers. "Do not hesitate to arrest him at once if the good of the service requires it," he said. So Halleck wired Grant to turn over his command to General C. F. Smith, ending plaintively: "Why do you not obey my orders?"

Halleck in St. Louis was thoroughly out of touch with what was going on in the field. On March 4 he telegraphed Buell that the Confederates were concentrating at New Madrid, he was sending 20,000 men against them, and Grant had gone up the Tennessee to destroy railroad connections at Corinth, Jackson and Humboldt. None of this was true. The Confederates were not concentrating at New Madrid. Grant had not gone up the river. As a matter of fact, the movement up the Tennessee did not get under way until March 10—and then under General Smith. Smith made Savannah on the east bank his headquarters, stationed Lew Wallace's division as an outpost at Crump's Landing on the west bank about three miles up, dispatched General Sherman on an expedition farther on to land somewhere near Eastport and make a lodgment on the Memphis & Charleston Railroad. Sherman had succeeded in convincing the Federal authorities that he was not insane, and Halleck, with thinly disguised misgivings, had restored him to active service and made him a division commander.

Sherman left Savannah on March 14, went ashore at the mouth of Yellow Creek on the west side near the Mississippi state line, and late that night started a cavalry force, supported by artillery and infantry armed with crowbars, picks and axes, on a march to Burnsville nineteen miles away to tear up the railroad track. The weather interfered. The spring rains were pouring down. After they had gone a few miles, the streams were found so swollen as to be almost impassable. The guns could hardly be pulled through. Men and horses were drowned in the attempt. So the foray was abandoned and the entire force—drenched and mud-bespattered—returned to the transports. Then they crept a few miles up to Indian Creek, within sight of a Confederate redoubt at Chickasaw, but found the landing covered by water. In fact, the entire west bank was soon submerged, from Chickasaw north to Pittsburg Landing, the water having risen fifteen feet in twenty-four hours. So Sherman, thwarted, steamed down to make camp at Pittsburg Landing.

Pittsburg Landing is on the west bank about nine miles above (south of) Savannah and about five miles north of the village of Hamburg. Here a steep bluff rises to about a hundred feet, at its highest point, above the river's low-water level. It was regarded as an exceptionally good steamboat landing, the high ground providing a storage space for merchandise far above the danger of flood at any time. Two roads ran to Corinth, twenty-two miles away, and, although not so close as Hamburg, it was the favored place to unload steamboat cargoes destined for that center.

On the way up the river Sherman had made note of Pittsburg Landing and the high ground adjacent and had been favorably struck by it. He sent back a message to General Smith recommending that a division be stationed there while he was upriver. Hurlbut and his force were awaiting him in transports when he returned. With his eye still on that important Memphis & Charleston Railroad, Sherman on the seventeenth moved his cavalry out in the direction of Corinth "for a strong reconnaisance, if possible to be converted into an attack."[38] He was stopped, however, near Monterey, a village about ten miles from the Landing, where he encountered Confederate cavalry. So he gave up all idea of attack and fell back to his camp.[39] The expedition was barren of results. Sherman did learn from the people that "trains were bringing large masses of men from every direction into Corinth," but the great significance of this information he seems not to have grasped. He reported to General Smith at Savannah that "every road and path is occupied by the enemy's cavalry" and that he was convinced he could not reach the railroad without a considerable engagement—which had been expressly forbidden by General Halleck.

Sherman recommended that the Federal force be concentrated at Pittsburg Landing as a base of operations; he was "strongly impressed with the importance of the position, both for its land advantages and its strategic position. . . . The ground itself admits of easy defense by a small command, and yet affords admirable camping ground for a hundred thousand men."[40] In a letter to General John A. Rawlins, Grant's aide, he describes it as a "magnificent plain for camping and drilling, and a military point of great strength."

His recommendation led to a concentration of the entire Federal force at this point. The divisions of Prentiss, McClernand and Smith[41] were moved up from Savannah. Grant, who had now been restored to his command of the whole army, kept a small garrison at Savannah where he maintained his own headquarters, presumably to await the arrival of Buell, who was now marching with 25,000 men from Nashville to join up.

The divisions at Pittsburg were rather peculiarly and carelessly arrayed, apparently with no thought of possible need for defense against attack, but at least they had a picket line extended over a semicircle of about three miles. Sherman's division was camped in a line that crossed the Corinth road at the little log-cabin meetinghouse called Shiloh Church. Here the general set up his tent and established headquarters— and thus unconsciously fixed both the place and the name of one of the bloodiest battles of the war, a battle destined to shock the whole world by its heavy losses. McClernand was slightly to Sherman's rear and Prentiss to his left. Farther back were the divisions of Hurlbut and Prentiss (now under W. H. L. Wallace). Stuart's brigade of Sherman's division was placed on the far left at Lick Creek, with a wide gap between his right and Prentiss' left. This space, Sherman explained later, was intended to be occupied by Buell's forces when they came up; apparently he was unaware that Grant had changed his plans and ordered Buell to go into camp at Hamburg, south of the creek.

General Sherman's estimate of the position at Shiloh was well-founded, but the very factors that in his opinion made it easy to defend gave it also the aspects of a trap. From the high river bank the land stretched back for five miles in a sort of wrinkled plateau, broken by a few ravines, but with ample level ground for camp sites. Except for occasional farms of from sixty to seventy-five acres in plowed ground and pasture, the country was densely wooded, with heavy brush beneath the trees. Pittsburg Landing—a warehouse and post office, with one or two dependent cabins—was located about midway between the mouths of Snake Creek to the north and Lick Creek to the south. These streams were five or six miles apart at the river, but the distance narrowed to three miles or less at the point where the Federal camps stretched roughly from Lick Creek to Owl Creek, a southern branch of Snake Creek. The terrain was thus of general quadrilateral shape, with the river to the east, the creeks to the north and south. The Federal camps faced the open

country toward Corinth to the southwest, with a swampy tributary of
Owl Creek along the immediate front of Sherman on the right. The
country was cut up with roads—some of them county highways, some
mere wagon tracks through the woods. Two roads ran from Corinth
to Pittsburg Landing. Two led north across Snake Creek to Crump's
Landing. Crossroads through the woods in all directions made a perfect
maze. Near the river bank were deep gullies, now filled with backwater,
and all the intersecting ravines were boggy from wet-weather springs and
streams.

The concentration of the Federals at Pittsburg Landing did not go
unnoticed by Beauregard's scouts. He shifted his forces accordingly.
Bragg was already at Corinth organizing the reinforcements as they came
in. Now Polk also was ordered to move there with Clark's division, leaving
a division under General B. F. Cheatham at Bethel to guard against any
sudden movement of the enemy westward from Pittsburg or Crump's
Landings. It was at this juncture that Johnston and his wing arrived.
Steps were immediately taken for the reorganization of the combined
forces into a cohesive unit, for it was agreed by Johnston and Beauregard
that arrangements should be perfected with the least possible delay
to strike a blow at Grant's army before he could be joined by Buell's
slowly advancing column.

This reorganization now became what was officially designated the
"Army of Mississippi." It consisted of four groups called "corps,"
although they were numerically hardly more than normal divisions.[42]
Polk commanded the First Corps, four brigades, 9,136 men. The Second,
under Bragg, was the largest—six brigades, 13,589 men. The Third,
under Hardee, numbered 6,789 in three brigades. And in the Reserve
Corps there were three brigades, 6,439 men, under General Crittenden,
who was to be replaced on March 31 by John C. Breckinridge.[43] Johnston
made Bragg his chief of staff, and, surprisingly, tendered Beauregard
command of the whole army in the impending battle.

Why he did this is by no means clear. He left no personal account
of his action and motives. His son has this to say:

"Though General Beauregard declined the offer, he evidently mis-
interpreted its spirit and intention. He imagined it was a confession of
inadequacy for the duty, in which case he ought to have accepted it.
The truth was that, coming into this district which he had assigned to
Beauregard, Johnston felt disinclined to deprive him of any reputation
he might acquire from a victory. He had not the slightest idea, however,

of abdicating the supreme command, and said to friends who remonstrated with him: 'I will be there to see that all goes right.' He was willing to yield to another the glory, if thereby anything was added to the chance of victory. The offer was rather quixotic, but characteristic."[44]

General Beauregard's account of the episode gives a somewhat different impression.

"To my surprise," he writes, "General Johnston, with much emotion, informed me that it was his purpose to turn over to me the command of the entire force being assembled at Corinth, and thereafter confine himself to the duties of department commander, with his headquarters either at Memphis or Holly Springs, in Mississippi. This course, as he explained, he felt called upon to take in order to restore confidence to the people and even the army, so greatly impaired by reason of recent disasters. Thoroughly understanding and appreciating his motives (and about these and his words there could be no possible misinterpretation), I declined as altogether unnecessary the unselfish tender of his command, but agreed, after some further exchange of views touching the military situation, to draw up a plan for the organization of our forces and, as second in command, to supervise the task of organization."[45]

It is difficult, at this late day, to establish the real explanation. One finds it hard to believe that Johnston would carry courtesy and chivalry to such an extreme or shirk leadership at the critical moment. No one ever acused him of lacking courage, moral or physical. He had shown fullest confidence in his ability to lead troops in battle. To relinquish command when he had at last assembled a good-sized army with which to face the enemy on something like even terms—this seemingly was the last thing that would have occurred to him. It is possible that, despite his outward calm, the savage criticism over Fort Donelson and Nashville had undermined his confidence or induced a morbidity that prompted an impulsive act of renunciation. At any rate he seems not to have insisted on his offer once Beauregard refused it, so it may have been nothing more than a perfunctory gesture which Beauregard magnified into an admission of weakness.

Johnston gave no other sign of hesitation, but jumped into preparations for battle. "We two together will do our best to secure success," he told Beauregard.[46] The order of organization on the new basis was published on March 29.

All was now in readiness for the collision with Grant's army in its camp around Shiloh Church. If Johnston delayed, it was because he hoped each day that Van Dorn's army of 20,000 would come from Arkansas. At the same time, he knew he must strike before Buell joined Grant and he anxiously watched Buell through his scouts. The fuse that set off the blast was lighted when Cheatham at Bethel sent word to Polk the night of April 2 that he was menaced by Lew Wallace's force advancing from Crump's Landing. It developed later that this was a mere reconnaissance, but the Confederates did not know it at the time. It might be a movement in strength on Memphis, they thought; it might mean almost anything. Polk sent Cheatham's message on to Beauregard. Beauregard turned it over to Jordan, now adjutant general, and told him to take it to Johnston. Johnston and Jordan together took it to Bragg's headquarters for conference. Whatever Wallace was up to, all agreed the time had come to attack Grant without further delay, especially as the scouts now reported Buell drawing close to Savannah.

As soon as the decision was reached, no time was lost putting the machinery in motion. Colonel Jordan went to work at once in General Bragg's bedroom writing up the preliminary instructions for the corps commanders. They were delivered to Polk and Hardee in person by 1:30 A.M. and at the same time wired to Breckinridge at Burnsville. The generals were told to "hold their commands in hand, ready to advance upon the enemy in the morning by 6 A.M. with three days' cooked rations in haversacks, 100 rounds of ammunition for small arms, and 200 rounds for field-pieces."

Beauregard sat up in bed all night making penciled notes on handy scraps of paper to regulate in detail the march from Corinth on Pittsburg Landing.[47] These notes were given to Jordan who used them in composing the official orders to be issued in General Johnston's name after discussion with him. Making enough copies would take Jordan several hours. While he was at work Johnston and Beauregard explained them orally to the three corps commanders present—that was by 10 A.M. They were to have their troops in motion over the roads prescribed by noon, without waiting for the formal written orders.

The moment so long expected by both Johnston and Beauregard had at last arrived.

CHAPTER VIII

SHILOH

THE Battle of Shiloh was something unique. Its outcome was disappointing to both sides, though both claimed the victory. It gave rise to more intense and sustained controversy between supporters of rival leaders on both sides than any other battle.

In the North Grant and Sherman were violently assailed for being surprised by the Confederates the first morning and for not pursuing them the next afternoon. Some of Grant's critics even went so far as to contend seriously that he was party to a deep-laid conspiracy to prolong the war for political purposes. They insisted that his handling of the battle was so grossly at fault it could not have been due to mere ineptitude but must have been due to something more sinister.[1] Grant freely indulged in sharp and open criticism of associates and subordinates. For his reflections on General Lew Wallace he was forced twenty years later to make belated apology. Buell alleged that Sherman deliberately prevaricated in his account of Shiloh and even charged that he had conspired with Grant to change the official map of the field to cover up their errors.

On the Southern side, there was an almost universal belief that nothing but the death of Albert Sidney Johnston prevented the capture or annihilation of the Federal army on the first day. The prevailing feeling even now is that when he fell Johnston had a great victory within his grasp, and that Beauregard, suddenly thrust into command, threw it away. Beauregard through the rest of his life tried to defend himself, but the South would not listen. It had made up its mind about Shiloh and did not want to change. Johnston was the martyred hero, Beauregard the scapegoat.

The story of Shiloh, as written by both sides, is peppered with ifs and punctuated with question marks. Why wasn't Grant present when his army was attacked? Why wasn't Sherman more alert and watchful? Did Grant slow down Buell's march from Nashville and delay his arrival at Savannah? Would the Federal army have been destroyed if Buell had not arrived when he did? Why did it take the Confederate army so long

122

to get from its camps to the battlefield? Did Beauregard stop the fighting too soon on the evening of the first day? What would Johnston have done if he had lived? Could Van Dorn have moved his army to Corinth in time for the battle? Would his 20,000 men have given the needed power to clinch the victory?

It was twenty-two miles from Corinth to Pittsburg Landing, and marching an army of close to 40,000 untrained men that distance over narrow dirt roads required no slight degree of skill. But Beauregard's scouts had studied the country thoroughly, providing him with rough but fairly accurate maps of its roads and topographical features, and he could prepare detailed and specific instructions for the movement of the assembled troops into a line of battle confronting the Federal camps. Of the two roads from Corinth to the Landing, one passed northward, swinging to the east, and was known locally as the Ridge or Bark Road. The other started east, then ran north through the settlement at Monterey and joined the Ridge Road four or five miles out from the Landing. From Monterey two roads led generally northward to Purdy and Savannah, both intersecting the Ridge Road. At one crossroad was the home of a family named Michie, and "Michie's [or Mickey's] House" became a landmark in the advance to the battle.

Beauregard's orders for the morning of April 3 provided that Hardee's corps should go out of Corinth by the Ridge Road, bivouac that night at Michie's, march on the next day to within sight of Grant's lines, and then deploy for action with his left on Owl Creek and his right extending toward Lick Creek. Bragg's corps was to assemble at Monterey and then pass over to the Ridge Road by the two available highways, camp in the neighborhood of Michie's and next day take position as the second line of battle a thousand yards behind Hardee's corps. Polk had only one division (Clark's) of his corps at Corinth; he was ordered to follow Hardee's line of march to Michie's, an hour in his rear. His other division, Cheatham's, at Bethel, was to hold its position there if attacked; otherwise to assemble at Purdy and march to a junction with Polk on the battlefield, forming a third line on the left. Breckinridge, with the reserve, was to move from Burnsville to Monterey as soon as Bragg's corps was well out of the way, and then to get up by the best available route.

Beauregard's plan was designed to bring the army into action in somewhat unusual fashion—the first two corps (Hardee's and Bragg's) arrayed in single parallel lines, one behind the other, with Polk supporting the left and Breckinridge the right. The more orthodox style of attack was for each corps to face the enemy on a designated part of the front. By some military experts Beauregard has been criticized for not following it. He explains that Hardee's men were used in the first line to secure unity of action because they were accustomed to marching together; that Bragg's troops, not being trained to march by brigades, were likely to be most effective if following and supporting Hardee; and that Johnston had agreed to the formation—but of this there seems considerable doubt. Johnston outlined his plan briefly in a telegram to President Davis on the third:

"Confederate forces—forty thousand—ordered forward to offer battle near Pittsburg. . . . Beauregard second in command, Polk the left, Bragg the center, Hardee the right, Breckinridge the reserve."

Davis charged that Beauregard changed Johnston's original plan without advising Johnston of it until it was too late for him to do anything. How seriously the plan of attack contributed to the confusion of the forces on the battlefield is a moot point—just another of the many in this Pandora's box of a battle.

The intent was to have the army up and in line of battle by the evening of the fourth, with the attack scheduled for delivery at daybreak. It did not seem unreasonable to suppose that it could travel twenty-two miles in two days. There seemed plenty of time and plenty of room for everybody to move without interference or confusion. Students of history like to speculate on what might have been the outcome if the attack had actually been made on the morning of the fifth as planned instead of being delayed a whole day as it was.[2] In the absence of Buell, who did not join Grant on the field until the night of the sixth, could Grant's army have been crushed? Would this have been the turning point of the war, with the victorious Confederates brushing Buell aside and sweeping north to the Ohio? If——

History, however, is recorded by facts, not by ifs, and the facts are that delay and disorder dogged the army in its advance to the battlefield. The burden of responsibility for the mishandling of the march has never been accurately placed, perhaps is impossible to place. Beauregard blamed Polk. Polk indignantly shifted the blame to Hardee. Hardee pointed his finger at Bragg. Polk, indeed, appears blameless. He had but one division of 4,500 men to get ready and he was ready early in the morning of the third. But he had been ordered to move only behind Hardee, and since Hardee did not start until long after noon, he could not march until nearly dark. Still, there was nothing fatal in this delay. For all his late start, Hardee was at Michie's on the morning of the fourth, only eight miles from Pittsburg Landing and not more than four from the point where he was to spread his line of battle. But before he could get into position Bragg ordered him to hold up. Bragg's advance had been hampered, and he needed time to shorten the space between his corps and Hardee's if he was to form line immediately in Hardee's rear. Polk again waited for Hardee, Hardee waited for Bragg, and Bragg fumed about the bad roads, insufficient transportation badly managed, ignorant guides and "the usual delay of a first move of new troops."

Bragg's points were well taken. The whole army was composed mostly of the rawest of raw recruits. Aside from the handful who had been engaged in the Battle of Belmont, few had ever heard a gun fired in anger, and, with the exception of Hardee's men, they had had little or no experience in long marches. It was strange country to all of them. The unfamiliar roads were soon churned into rivers of mud by the wagons and guns as the April rains beat down. A clumsy distribution of the forces into various corps had given Bragg an unwieldy body of men— three times as many as Polk and nearly twice as many as Hardee. Granting these difficulties, it does seem that the skilled and experienced Bragg might have moved more rapidly than he did, but the fact is that it required all day of the fourth for him to travel the six miles from Monterey to Michie's. So it was not until the afternoon of the fifth that all the various troops were in their prescribed positions—just a day later than had been planned.

And the day was too far spent for immediate attack. A council of the commanding generals was held in the middle of the road close behind Hardee's lines. Beauregard was furious at the delay. One imprudent brigade had made a reconnaissance with artillery and Beauregard was sure it would disclose their presence to the Federals and make surprise impossible. "Now they will be intrenched to their eyes," he predicted. He sulkily advised that the attack be abandoned and the army returned to Corinth. But Johnston, having put his hand to the plow, would not look back. Exercising the authority of his supreme command, he vetoed Beauregard's suggestion by the simple announcement: "We shall attack at daylight tomorrow." Turning to one of his staff officers, he added: "I would fight them if they were a million. They can present no greater front between those two creeks than we can, and the more men they crowd in there, the worse we can make it for them."[3]

The men lay under arms in the open woods that night, blessed with calm, clear weather—a pleasant change from the violent storm of the night before and the steady rains that had drenched them as they struggled along the muddy roads and kept them miserably awake beneath the dripping trees. Sunday dawned clear and balmy. They knew that in a few minutes they were to be tossed into the cauldron of their first battle, but they were confident.[4] After all their reverses and retreats they had now turned and taken the offensive. Their waning faith in Johnston was restored. And, besides Johnston, they had Beauregard and Bragg. At Hardee's suggestion Beauregard, in his red cap, rode up and down before Hardee's line to give them a sight of the hero of Sumter and Manassas— after modestly insisting that there be no cheering. Johnston himself was superbly confident. "To-night," he said, as he mounted for the front, "we will water our horses in the Tennessee River!"[5]

There proved to be no ground for Beauregard's fear that the Federals had learned of the Confederate advance and would be alert. In after years both Grant and Sherman indignantly, vehemently and repeatedly denied that they were surprised, but their vehemence and indignation does not alter the fact that the attack at daylight on Sunday, April 6, very clearly caught them completely unawares. Grant was not even on the field.

Sherman was on the ground and, in Grant's absence, in active command of the Federal forces. That he must have been incredibly negligent of the most ordinary precautions is indicated by Johnston's being able to bring an army of nearly 40,000 men unmolested into line of battle within a mile and a half of his camp. He had indeed heard the rash artillery firing of the too spirited reconnaissance on the fourth, and had ridden forward to see what was going on. An officer involved in the brush galloped up and told him breathlessly that he had met the van of Beauregard's army and that Beauregard was advancing to attack them. Sherman dismissed this scoffingly. "Beauregard is not such a fool," he said, "as to leave his base of operations and attack us in ours."[6] He did not even bother to keep out cavalry patrols, those essential antennae of an army in the presence of an enemy. That day he wrote to Grant: "I do not apprehend anything like an attack on our position." But on that very day immediately before him Johnston's 40,000 were being deployed in ambush in the woods with as much deliberation as though marshalling for review. So close were the lines that Beauregard, hearing drums beat

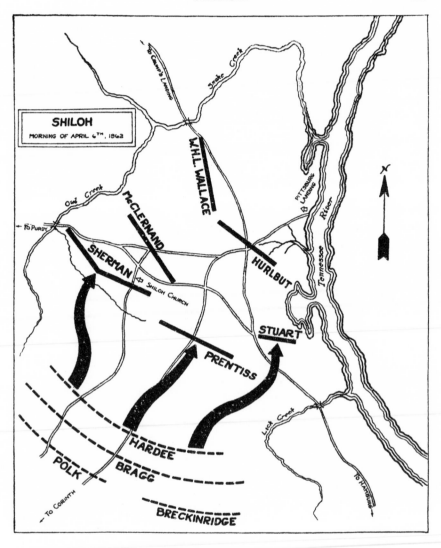

in the evening, sent a staff officer "to suppress such thoughtless and imprudent sounds," and was astonished when the officer reported that they could not be stopped, because they were coming from the Yankee camps![7]

Grant, who still maintained headquarters at Savannah, nine miles away and across the river, was equally complacent and careless. On the fifth he wrote to Halleck that the Confederates had close to 80,000 men at

Corinth but that "I have scarcely the faintest idea of an attack (general one) being made upon us." Consistent with this, the Federal troops were not arrayed in effective line of battle, but scattered more or less indiscriminately over the campground. There had been not the slightest attempt to strengthen the position by breastworks or otherwise. When Nelson arrived at Savannah well in the lead of Buell's troops, Grant visited his camp Saturday afternoon and told Colonel Jacob Ammen, commanding the 10th Brigade, that he would send boats for them "Monday or Tuesday or some time early in the week. . . . There will be no fight at Pittsburg Landing; we will have to go to Corinth where the rebels are fortified."[8] As late as Sunday morning, when the opening volleys were heard in Savannah, he still seemed unable to comprehend that the enemy had sought him out. Even then he made no arrangements to hurry Nelson's brigades to the battlefield by steamboat (which he could have done in half an hour), but instructed them to march south on the east bank of the river to a point opposite Pittsburg Landing and wait to be ferried across.

If Grant and Sherman were oblivious to the imminence of attack, there was one Federal officer who was more alert. Colonel Peabody, commanding the 1st Brigade of Prentiss' division, was vaguely apprehensive that the picket skirmishing of the past few days had more serious meaning than Sherman thought. Something sinister, he felt, something threatening, must be out there in those tangled woods. Unable to sleep, he rose before daybreak on Sunday and led three companies of the 25th Missouri along the Corinth road to see what they could see. Feeling their way cautiously along, they encountered the stealthy advance of Hardee's thin skirmish line. Thinking it a mere outpost, they attacked with spirit, but soon found themselves faced by Shaver's brigade of Hindman's division. Thus the battle was precipitated. The venturesome Federals were soon driven back, and the Confederates swarmed out of the woods into Prentiss' camp with an explosive onslaught that swept everything before it.

A vivid description of that first charge of Hardee's line has been left us by one who became internationally distinguished but was then only a callow young private in Hindman's command. Henry M. Stanley,[9] through a romantic combination of circumstances, was clerking in a country store at Cypress Bend in Arkansas at the outbreak of the war. An unattached youth of twenty, he had joined the Confederate Army, and he found himself that bright April morning lying in the grass beneath the flowering dogwoods, his flintlock musket in his hand, ready to spring to the charge when ordered. While he waited there, tingling with excitement and some little apprehension, he plucked a small bunch of wild violets and placed them in his cap as a talisman. Violets are the flowers of peace; maybe the Yankees won't shoot me if they see me wearing them, he reflected in boyish innocence. Of such innocents, inexperienced in the brutal ways of war, were both those armies composed. They had not known man's inhumanity to man; they had not yet seen their fellows sprawled in the awkward postures of sudden death.

Young Stanley's dreaming was interrupted by the sudden clash of the skirmishers and the strange patter of bullets in the dead leaves of the scrub oaks. When the bugle blew the charge, "we surged forward," Stanley writes.

"We trampled recklessly over the grass and young sprouts. Beams of sunlight stole athwart our course. The sun was up above the horizon. Just then we . . . overtook the skirmishers, who had been engaged in exploring our front. We passed beyond them. Nothing now stood between us and the enemy. 'There they are,' was no sooner uttered than we cracked into them with leveled muskets. 'Aim low, men,' commanded Captain Smith.[10] I tried hard to see some living thing to shoot at, for it appeared absurd to be blazing away at shadows. But, still advancing, firing as we moved, I at last saw a little row of globes of pearly smoke streaked with crimson, breaking out with spurtive quickness from a long row of bluey figures in front; and simultaneously there broke upon our ears an appalling crash of sound, the series of fusillades following one another with startling suddenness, which suggested to my somewhat moidered senses a mountain upheaved, with huge rocks tumbling and thundering down a slope, and the echoes rumbling and receding through space. Again and again those loud and quick explosions were repeated, seemingly with increased violence, until they rose to the highest pitch of fury and in unbroken continuity. All the world seemed involved in one tremendous ruin."[11]

That bright little cameo of action was being reproduced along a front of more than three miles as the whole Confederate army swept forward, waking the echoes with their screeching Rebel yell. General Johnston's plan of battle, as announced to the troops on April 3, set forth his essential tactics: "Every effort should be made to turn the left flank of the enemy, so as to cut off his line of retreat to the Tennessee River and

throw him back on Owl Creek, where he will be forced to surrender."
The exact location of the Federal lines was not known in advance and the
Confederates soon found they had to drive back Prentiss and Sherman
before they could get at Stuart on the left flank.

Hindman's division, moving along the ridge, was the center of their
front line, the pivot on which the turning movement operated. Prentiss,
who received the full fury of the first attack, put up a spirited defense,
but by seven or eight o'clock Hardee's men were in full possession of his
camps. The half-eaten breakfasts on the mess-tables, the abandoned
stores, flags and ammunition proved the completeness of the surprise. The
brigade on the extreme left of the Confederate front line was commanded
by Pat Cleburne, later to shine as one of the army's brightest stars. He
had a marshy hollow to cross that delayed him in getting in contact with
Sherman's front, which was obliqued from his line of advance. Sherman's
men had been aroused by the tumult of the attack on Prentiss and were
arrayed in line of battle by the time Cleburne delivered his assault about
eight o'clock. The first attack was thrown back, but, supported by the
second line, Cleburne pressed forward again, and Sherman, although
reinforced by McClernand, was driven from his camp. Meanwhile,
Chalmers' brigade from Bragg's line had been brought up on the right
wing and was slowly pressing Stuart back.

Displaying rare valor and hardihood but dubious discretion, General
Johnston was active along the right front, urging the men on and leading
them himself when there was any sign of faltering. Beauregard looked
after the left and the reserve. He made his headquarters at Shiloh Church
after Sherman fell back. By now the two armies were meshed in a fury
of combat. The thickets were noisy with the blazing clamor of near
100,000 muskets, the thunder of 200 guns. The impetus of the initial
attack gave the Confederates an advantage. Under the persistent battering
of their fierce assault the Federals yielded ground steadily all along the
line. They rallied from time to time, where opportunity offered in a
copse or on a rise of ground, but again the screeching Confederates
would surge forward, again the harassed bluecoats would fall back.
Sherman and McClernand, pushed toward Owl Creek and the river,
and Prentiss, forced to retreat under the steady pressure on his front, were
given a welcome measure of relief when the fresh divisions of W. H. L.
Wallace and Hurlbut moved up and helped establish a new line about
ten in the morning.

By midday the Federal line had completely changed its position to a
shortened and retracted front. Chalmers had swept down the north bank

of Lick Creek and, turning, had driven Stuart northward along the bank
of the Tennessee, critically endangering the Federal left. Sherman and
Prentiss had been pressed back until the line was now a mile or more in
the rear of its original position, on a shorter arc, and running roughly
northwest and southeast.

At last Grant was on the field. He had been spending his nights at
Savannah, and was eating his breakfast there that morning when sounds
of heavy firing came from the direction of Pittsburg Landing up the
river. The story goes that he was lifting his coffee cup to his lips when
he heard the first burst of firing, and that he set the cup down untasted so
eager he was to hasten to the scene. At any rate, he jumped aboard
the *Tigress*, a dispatch boat which had steam up, and put out toward the
sound of battle. On the way upriver he ran in close enough to Crump's
Landing to speak to Lew Wallace, who had heard the firing too and was
waiting on the bank to see Grant when he passed. Still uncertain what
was up, Grant told Wallace to "get his troops in line ready to execute
any orders he might receive." Wallace replied that his men were ready
and under arms. Leaving him in uncertainty and suspense, Grant hurried
on to Pittsburg Landing, debarked and visited the battlefield. When
Buell got to the Landing early in the afternoon he found Grant once
more aboard the *Tigress* and the river bank swarming with stragglers and
terrified fugitives from the battle front. Grant had sent him word he
had been engaged since early morning defending himself against an army
of 100,000. "If you will get upon the field, leaving all your baggage on
the east bank of the river, it will be a move to our advantage and possibly
save the day to us." A note of exigency, of apprehension, almost of panic
sounds in that message, but twenty-five years later Grant wrote, with
calm assurance: "There was no hour during the day when I doubted the
eventual defeat of the enemy."

Beauregard's plan of attack by parallel corps did not work out so well
in practice. By the middle of the forenoon all the Confederate troops
were tangled together in the first line, with the organizations of corps,
divisions and brigades badly broken. The corps commanders had read-
justed their positions of command: Hardee was now operating on the
left against Sherman; Polk on Hardee's right was in front of McClernand;
Bragg directed the attack on the Federal center, and Breckinridge, on the
right, pushed on against the Federal left in an effort to carry out Johnston's design to drive it up the Tennessee into Snake Creek.

About this time the Confederate attack, hitherto resistless, struck a
snag. Wallace's and Hurlbut's divisions, together with what was left of

Prentiss' shattered force, on the Federal left center, had stumbled on an almost impregnable position. Along the crest of a ridge an old, abandoned road had left a shallow depression, a natural rifle pit, shielded by a heavy growth of blackberry bushes, underbrush and small trees. From the protection of this fortuitous stronghold the steadfast defenders poured out such a merciless cascade of musketry and artillery fire as to whelm each Confederate line that tried to advance. "It's a hornets' nest!" they cried, as they reeled back under the blistering fire, and as the "Hornets' Nest" it is known to history. Grant owed much to the Hornets' Nest that day. But for its gallant and sustained resistance his whole army might well have been destroyed or captured in the early afternoon. It slowed the velocity of the Confederates' momentum and changed the face of things.

For seven or eight hours of almost incessant and bloody fighting the defense of the Hornets' Nest was maintained. Brigade after brigade plunged across the open field and up the brushy slope before it, only to be thrown back. At length, close to six o'clock in the evening, it was turned by combined flank and frontal attacks, supported by blasts of massed artillery. The rush of the charging columns was so impetuous that, before he could make off, Prentiss was surrounded and captured, along with about 2,500 of his command. His division was erased, W. H. L. Wallace was killed, but the sacrifice was not in vain—Grant's army was saved.

While the Hornets' Nest was being so valiantly defended, Grant had taken advantage of the respite to work out a final new line for the day— a very much shorter line. Its left rested on the high bluff above the landing itself, just north of the mouth of Dill's Creek; it curved westward to the Hamburg-Savannah road and with this road went north to the swampy border of Snake Creek which protected the right flank. The left was supported by two gunboats, now shelling the field.

It was during the attack on the Hornets' Nest that the Confederates suffered the loss of their commander—a blow which many Southerners thought then (and many still think) cost the cause the battle and perhaps the war. General Johnston at the time was on the right with Breckinridge's corps, facing Hurlbut's division. He perceived the imperative necessity for breaking the stubborn defense, and when the badly punished troops showed some hesitation about making another attack, he told Breckinridge to order the advance and impetuously volunteered to lead it himself. His sword was in its scabbard. In his right hand he clutched a little tin cup he had picked up while passing through the captured

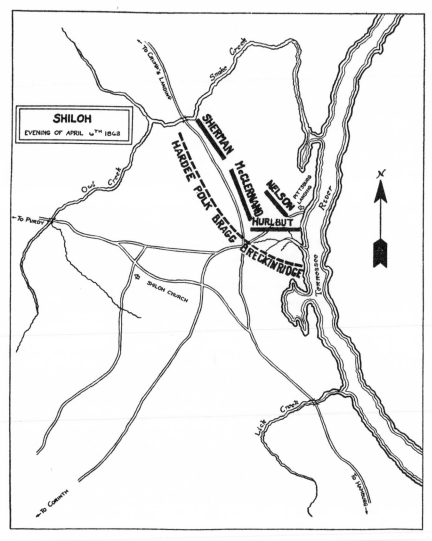

Federal camps, saying lightly it would be his share of the battle spoils.
Waving it above his head as though it were an emblem of authority,
he galloped ahead to the charge, and stayed with the men till they had
gained a foothold on a ridge.[12]

The position won, Johnston passed to the rear, uninjured by the
shower of bullets through which he had passed. He laughingly displayed
to one of his aides the sole of his boot which had been cut in two by a

Minié ball. "They almost tripped me up that time," he said gaily as he rode behind the line. Then, within two or three minutes, a stray shot from some desultory firing struck him in the back of the right thigh, a few inches above the knee, severing the artery. It was a wound which, given instant medical attention—even the first-aid treatment of an improvised tourniquet—need not have been fatal. But Dr. D. W. Yandell, his personal surgeon, was not with him at this moment of all moments. Johnston had asked him to look after a group of wounded prisoners, and he had not yet returned from this mission of mercy. In fact, the General seems not to have been attended by any of his staff when he was struck. All had been sent off on official errands. Governor Harris, on his way back from delivering an order to continue the advance, found him alone, seated on his horse, pale and swaying dizzily in the saddle.

"General, are you wounded?" Harris cried anxiously.

"Yes, and I fear seriously," Johnston replied with characteristic calm, as his reins slipped feebly from his hand. Hastily putting his left arm around his tottering chief, and holding the reins of both mounts in the other hand, Harris guided the horses to a protected depression behind the line and lifted the now unconscious body to the ground. Frantically he tore open the general's blouse and shirt, searched for the wound, could find no wound. Puzzled, he examined the body more closely. He saw the boot overflowing with blood, and at last he found that clean little hole drilled through the back of the leg. But then it was too late. Albert Sidney Johnston was dead. It was 2:30 P.M.

General Beauregard was notified at once, but, contrary to the legend, he did not immediately, in helpless panic, order a cessation of hostilities. On the contrary, he behaved like a soldier, ordered the news concealed from the men,[13] and without flurry assumed responsibility of full command. The fighting went on through the afternoon, the Federals falling back steadily toward the Landing. The order to cease firing was not given until six o'clock—perhaps even later.

Another popular fable has it that at the time of Johnston's death Beauregard was ill in bed in his ambulance, but abundant testimony shows he was on his horse on the battlefield all day long, advancing his headquarters as the lines advanced, and actively in touch with the movement of the troops and the progress of the battle.[14]

The effect of General Johnston's death on the outcome of the battle is a question debated, sometimes with great heat, over the years. What he might have done had he been spared must, of course, remain a matter of conjecture. It is doubtful, however, if he could have materially changed the issue on Sunday. It was after his death that the Hornets' Nest was forced and Prentiss and his men were captured, and that decided advances were made elsewhere in the field. Indeed, a battalion of Mississippi cavalry late in the afternoon swept so far around the Federal flank as to reach the river and actually water their horses in the stream as Johnston had predicted in the morning. The assault was by no means abandoned when he fell. Rather, Beauregard appears to have done just about everything humanly possible during the few hours of daylight that were left.

True, there was something lacking in the control of the Confederate attack, an absence of essential cohesion—but this was as noticeable before Johnston died as it was afterward. It was due chiefly to the utter inexperience of most of the men and many of the subordinate officers. In his comment on the battle General Jordan points to a vital weakness of conduct:

"After the combat was at its height, about meridian, those superior officers who should have been occupied with the concentration and continuous projection of their troops in heavy masses upon the shattered Federal divisions, were at the very front and 'perilous edge' of the battle, leading forward regiments, perchance brigades, into action, with great individual intrepidity and doing a great deal, no doubt, by their personal example to impel small bodies forward. But, meanwhile, to their rear were left the masses of their respective commands, without direction, and thus precious time was lost. The Confederates were not kept continuously massed and employed, either in corps or divisions; mere piecemeal onsets were the general method of fighting after 12 o'clock, with this consequence: Sherman was enabled to make several obstinate, powerful stands, by which he protracted the battle some hours. Had the corps been held well in hand, massed and pressed continuously upon the tottering, demoralized foe . . . the battle assuredly would have been closed at latest by mid-day."[15]

But General Jordan was writing after a lapse of years, with all the advantage of retrospect. It is easy enough to see faults when you are looking backward. Whether Johnston's living on would have corrected the faults he mentions is another matter.

There is no gainsaying that by nightfall Sunday Grant's army was thoroughly whipped and largely disintegrated. If time and other condi-

tions had permitted a continuation of the Confederate pressure, it seems
entirely reasonable to believe that it would have been captured or destroyed. Little resistance was left in it.

General Nelson arrived on the west side of the Tennessee at five
o'clock.

"I found," he says, "cowering under the river bank from seven to ten
thousand men, frantic with fright and utterly demoralized, who received
my gallant division with cries 'We are whipped!' 'Cut to pieces!,' etc.
They were insensible to shame and sarcasm, for I tried both; and, indignant of such poltroonery, I asked permission to fire on the knaves."[16]

Colonel Ammen[17] relates in his diary that while crossing the river
with his brigade late in the afternoon he saw it full of soldiers—officers
as well as men—in small boats and swimming, desperately striving to
reach the safety of the east bank. At the Landing, he says, "the space
between the top of the bank and the river, up and down a half mile
or more, was crowded with men. . . . Such looks of terror, such confusion,
I never saw before and do not wish to see again."

Every observer makes similar report. But most of the poor soldiers,
it should be said in their defense, were unseasoned and inexperienced,
many of them under fire for the first time. This was as true of the
Confederates as of the Federals. There were straggling and confusion
in the Confederate rear also. Some lagged behind to plunder the captured
camps; some simply ran away in fright at their first smell of powder.
Easy enough to say that they should have been whipped up into the
first lines—but the frailty of the flesh cannot be disregarded as a military
factor. Beauregard's conduct of the latter hours of Sunday's battle can
be justly weighed only in the light of the material he had to work with—
the man power and the time available. From that angle, it is hard to
see how Johnston—or anyone else—could have done much more. The
Confederates at Shiloh were not the victims of Beauregard's ineptitude
or sloth. They succumbed to Grant's two stalwart allies—night and
Buell.

The last determined stand of the Federals was made on the extreme
left of their latest, shortened line. Here, on the high ground north of
Dill's Branch, Colonel J. D. Webster of Grant's staff had hastily arrayed
a heavy battery of reserve artillery in a glowering semicircle around the
crest, and had gathered to its support a motley band of stragglers and

fugitives, later augmented and replaced by Nelson's fresh and eager troops. The brigades of Chalmers and Jackson, when at last released from the bloody siege of the Hornets' Nest, were sent against this battery. To approach it they had to get across a deep ravine, partly filled with back-water. At this very moment the advance brigades of Buell's army landed and rushed into position. The Confederate attack was repulsed. Jackson's ammunition was exhausted. While he went in search of aid, the order to withdraw the assault was received. This was the last Confederate thrust of the day.

General Beauregard's order to cease firing was not given, he states, until it grew clear that the troops were too disorganized[18] and exhausted for further effective fighting. Thousands were straggling in the captured camps, where the abundance of food, clothing and firearms tempted the resolution of the most ardent. Those still at the front were worn out with a day of constant struggle, after a night of hard marching through rain and mud. Surely the Confederate army at this hour was at a mini-mum of competence.

By Beauregard's orders the troops fell back Sunday night to the line of the captured camps, where they made their bivouacs. As many as could took refuge in the tents from the rain which started soon after dark. They feasted on the bountiful provisions from the Yankee com-missary and exchanged their flintlocks and smoothbore muskets for the Enfields left behind by the fleeing bluecoats. Beauregard himself, along with Bragg, made headquarters for the night in Sherman's own tent near Shiloh Church. There he received the corps and division commanders who called for orders. "All," he says, "evinced and expressed much satis-faction with the results, while no one was heard to express or suggest that more might have been achieved had the battle been prolonged. All seemed to believe that our troops had accomplished as much as could have been hoped for."[19]

Through his mouthpiece, Colonel Roman,[20] he enlarges on the reasons for gratification.

"The results, indeed, were great and encouraging. A half-disciplined army, poorly equipped and appointed, had assailed an opposing army larger in numbers, nearly half of which was composed of seasoned troops, provided with the best and most abundant armament and supplies, arrayed besides on familiar ground, chosen by its own leaders. That army had steadily been driven back to its last stronghold, a great part of it routed and demoralized; its tents, baggage, subsistence and hospital stores captured, together with thirty stands of colors, fully sixty field-pieces, many thousand small arms and accoutrements, and ammunition enough for another day's battle. General Beauregard's promise that the Confederates should sleep in the enemy's camps was fulfilled."[21]

Indeed the army had done well. If some omnipotent referee had then and there stepped in and stopped the engagement as of Sunday night, the decision must have been awarded to the Confederates. But the battle was not over. Grant was reeling from the punishment he had taken, but, with what was left of his army, he was still on the field. He must be reckoned with next day. Beauregard's army, though victorious, was reduced in numbers and badly disorganized. He must pull it together, get it ready for more fighting Monday. In the rain and darkness nothing could be done that night to straighten out the confusion. But the corps commanders were ordered to assemble their men and be ready "to take the offensive at break of day."[22]

Beauregard had Jordan get off a telegram to Richmond announcing a "complete victory, driving the enemy from every position," on the strength of which President Davis issued a prematurely exultant message to the Confederate Congress.

Beauregard went to sleep in Sherman's bed with a confidence unwarranted. The victim of a sadly inexpert intelligence service, he had received a telegram from Colonel Helm, a cavalry commander in northern Alabama, stating positively that Buell's army was not on the march to join Grant but near Decatur! Adjutant General Jordan was playing host to the distinguished prisoner, General Prentiss. They slept together on a bed improvised from a stack of captured tents and blankets, making snug bivouac as the rain beat down outside. Prentiss accepted his plight in philosophical good humor and discussed things without reticence.

"You gentlemen have had your way to-day," he said to Jordan with a laugh, "but it will be very different to-morrow. You'll see! Buell will effect a junction with Grant to-night, and we'll turn the tables on you in the morning."

Jordan scoffed and waved Helm's reassuring telegram. "You'll see," Prentiss repeated.[23]

If others slept, the indefatigable Forrest was astir. In one of the captured tents he had found a stock of blue army overcoats. He dressed a dozen of his troopers in them, and sent them to reconnoiter within the Federal lines. They penetrated boldly to the Landing, came back with the report that heavy reinforcements were being landed from the steamboats, but that everything was in such disorder a quick, determined attack might push them all into the river. Forrest, ever quick to seize an occasion, hustled to find a corps commander for orders, came upon Hardee and related the findings of his scouts. With typical directness he volunteered that the Confederates should pursue one of two courses: either they should launch an immediate attack or else withdraw and avoid an unequal contest with the fresh troops in the morning. If they waited and fought the next day, he said, they would surely be "whipped like hell." Hardee referred him to Beauregard. Failing to find him in the rainy blackness, he went back to his camp and again sent the scouts out. They saw continued reinforcements at the Landing. Once more he reported the facts to Hardee, but it was now two o'clock, and Hardee gave him perfunctory orders to go back to his regiment, "keep up a vigilant, strong picket-line and report all hostile movements."[24] Forrest fumed and fretted until dawn.

Not more than 20,000 Confederate troops could be mustered into line for a renewal of the fighting Monday morning. At least 6,500 men had been killed, wounded and captured on Sunday, and fully as many more had straggled. Those remaining on the field were almost hopelessly entangled. The regiments of Bragg's, Hardee's and Breckinridge's corps had turned in for the night without order in the captured camps or wherever they could find food. Polk, misunderstanding the orders, had marched back with Cheatham's division to the Confederate camp of Saturday night, a mile and a half beyond Shiloh Church. But Beauregard whipped his lines into some sort of shape as quickly as he could. Hardee was stationed on the extreme right, in command of Jackson's and Chalmers' brigades of Bragg's corps; Breckinridge was on Hardee's left; Bragg took position on the left wing, commanding the other brigades of his own corps, along with Clark's division of Polk's; and when Polk belatedly arrived on the field with Cheatham's division he moved into place between Breckinridge and Bragg.

As morning broke, the slumbers of General Jordan and his genial prisoner, Prentiss, were disturbed by rattle of musketry down toward the river, followed by booming of field artillery.

"There is Buell!" Prentiss exclaimed gleefully. "Didn't I tell you so?"[25]

Grant's battered divisions had been reinforced during the night not only by Buell's army but by Lew Wallace's fresh division of more than 5,000 men. Wallace had at last got his orders from Grant on Sunday— to gather up his brigades, scattered along the Purdy road from Crump's to Stony Lonesome, and march them to the field. At that, the orders were not altogether clear. Wallace was unfamiliar with the tangles of swampy roads, nor did he know exactly where the shifting right wing of Sherman's line might be found. After marching and countermarching the greater part of the day on the north side of Snake Creek, he arrived at the Landing late in the evening, too late to have any part in the day's fighting. But he was a very welcome addition to the Federal forces that Monday morning. He took position on the right flank.

Forrest's pickets and skirmish line on the extreme Confederate right received the shock of the Federals' opening attack by Nelson's fresh division. The defense was so spirited that Nelson was at first forced to fall back. Reinforced, he advanced again, and the tide of battle flowed back and forth in this quarter throughout the morning, with the pressure of the Federal divisions gradually making Hardee yield ground. By ten o'clock Bragg on the left was being similarly pressed by Lew Wallace and Sherman. He was reinforced with some makeshift outfits of stragglers and managed to weather the attack, even repelling the Federals by a counterstroke. Polk with Cheatham's division had got into position in the center in the nick of time to meet McCook's charge about ten-thirty, which was handsomely repulsed.[26] But the élan of the previous day was missing.

Badly battered as were Grant's survivors from the Sunday battle, infusion of the man power of Buell and Lew Wallace re-invigorated them. The Confederates had no such stimulant. They had indeed been wistfully longing for some such timely assistance. Van Dorn with his 20,000 veterans of the Missouri and Arkansas campaign was on the way. They might providentially reach the field in time. Up to the last minute of the fighting Beauregard was hopefully watching for them. In the course of the second day he had a thrill when he saw through the woods a body of troops who seemed to be dressed in white coats. At first he thought they were Federals, but when he saw they were fighting on the Confederate side, the sanguine thought flashed through his mind that the strangely clad soldiers might be the vanguard of the reinforcements. Van Dorn's troops were Westerners; there was no telling what outlandish uniform they might be wearing. But an aide reported that it was the Orleans Guard[27] battalion from New Orleans. They had come on the field right in the midst of the fighting dressed in their peacetime parade uniform of blue. The Confederates, who took every blue coat for a target, began to shoot at them. So they hastily turned their coats inside out, exposing the white linings.[28] Beauregard's last hope of help was dashed. Van Dorn had not come. The battle had to be finished with what was left of those who had started it the day before.

To all outward appearances, those veterans of the first day were doing very well. They held their ground, were never forced back of the line they had assumed last night. Beauregard still kept his post at Sherman's former headquarters at Shiloh Church. There were counterattacks along the line. But there was something in the air that second day which seemed to shadow the consciousness of all—officers and men alike—a feeling that they had shot their bolt, that they could not hope to drive the strengthened Federal army from the field.

Governor Harris, who had joined Beauregard's staff after Johnston's death, was one of the first to sense this. He cautiously mentioned it to Jordan early in the afternoon, asking if there was not risk in staying so long on the field as to make safe withdrawal impossible. Jordan agreed. He tells how he went to Beauregard and posed this question:

"General, do you not think our troops are very much in the condition of a lump of sugar thoroughly soaked with water—yet preserving its original shape, though ready to dissolve? Would it not be judicious to get away with what we have?"

Beauregard had been thinking along the same lines. "I intend to withdraw in a few moments," was his laconic reply. Calling members of his staff, he sent them off with orders to the corps commanders to prepare for the retreat.[29]

There was nothing precipitate or disorderly about it. General Jordan gathered up a few broken organizations of infantry and artillery and posted them on the ridge just south of Shiloh Church facing the Federal front. While he kept up a heavy gunfire, the entire army withdrew. The commands fell back in regular succession from the left, and by four o'clock the last had retired. At this time, Jordan says, not a Federal soldier was in sight. He leisurely followed the retreating army down the Corinth road, stopping to load his caissons with the precious rifles and muskets garnered from the field. The army camped that night on the ground they had occupied the morning of the sixth. Breckinridge as a rear guard was posted on the Corinth road about four miles from the Landing to guard against the expected pursuit—but this precaution proved needless.

The Federals, indeed, seemed quite content to see the Confederates

leave the field and bring the fierce fighting to a close. There is an old
military maxim: "Build bridges of gold for a retreating foe," and Grant
seemed to feel that way about it. "The roads were almost impassable,"
he explains. "I wanted to pursue, but had not the heart to order the
men who had fought desperately for two days, lying in the mud and
rain whenever not fighting, and I did not feel disposed to positively
order Buell, or any part of his command, to pursue."[30] Sherman in his
official report said: "At the time of recovering our camps (about four
o'clock P.M.) our men were so fatigued that we could not follow the
retreating masses of the enemy."

In a letter to his wife, General Polk summed it up: "The enemy was
badly whipped the first day and we ought, from the advantage gained,
to have captured his whole force. We would have done so if we had
had an hour more of daylight. The battle of the day following was a
drawn fight. We left them and they did not follow us."[31]

An eye-witness has left a graphic account of that withdrawal to
Corinth:

"The retreating host wound along a narrow and almost impassable
road, extending some seven or eight miles in length. Here was a long
line of wagons loaded with wounded, piled in like bags of grain, groaning
and cursing, while the mules plunged on in mud and water belly-deep,
the water sometimes coming into the wagons. Next came a straggling
regiment of infantry pressing on past the train of wagons, then a stretcher
borne upon the shoulders of four men, carrying a wounded officer, then
soldiers staggering along, with an arm broken and hanging down or with
other fearful wounds which were enough to destroy life. And, to add
to the horrors of the scene, the elements of heaven marshaled their forces
—a fitting accompaniment of the tempest of human desolation and pas-
sion which was raging. A cold, drizzling rain commenced about nightfall,
and soon came harder and faster, then turned to pitiless blinding hail.
This storm raged with unrelenting violence for three hours. I passed
long wagon trains filled with wounded and dying soldiers, without even a
blanket to shield them from the driving sleet and hail, which fell in
stones as large as partridge eggs, until it lay on the ground two inches
deep."[32]

The next morning when Sherman made a feeble show of pursuit by
marching out a few miles, Breckinridge let loose at him the twin thunder-
bolts of Forrest's and Morgan's cavalry and he gave it up in a jiffy. In
his tent again, he wrote up his report, ending: "Our troops being fagged

out by two days' hard fighting, exposure and privation, I ordered them back to their camps, where they now are."

Breckinridge camped at Michie's for three days waiting to see what would turn up, but the Federals showed no further signs of activity. So he broke camp and rejoined the army at Corinth. The Battle of Shiloh was over.

The losses from this engagement were terrific. The grand total of Confederate loss was 10,699—killed, 1,728; wounded, 8,012; missing, 959. The Federal loss was 13,047—killed, 1,754; wounded, 8,408; captured or missing, 2,885.[33] Besides General Johnston there were distinguished casualties on the Confederate side—General A. H. Gladden, who was killed early in the first day, and George W. Johnston, the Provisional Governor of Kentucky, who had been acting as a volunteer aide on Johnston's staff and who was shot while serving as a private in a Kentucky company.

The effective strength of the total Confederate force, as shown by the field strength of April 3, was 38,773, including the cavalry.[34] Grant's strength the first day was 39,895 "present for duty." The 5,000 men from Crump's Landing under Lew Wallace[35] and Buell's army of about 25,000 comprised his reinforcements for the second day.

CHAPTER IX

RETREAT AND ADVANCE

1. The Retreat

The loss of 10,000 men at Shiloh was a heavy blow to the Confederate Army, particularly as it followed so closely the surrender of the 10,000 at Fort Donelson. These losses were striking at the most vulnerable spot— man power. And even while the campaign was in progress the Confederacy was meeting another sharp thrust at this same Achilles' heel.

During all his activities preparatory to the concentration at Shiloh, Beauregard had been looking anxiously over his left shoulder at the exposed and undermanned positions at Madrid Bend. General McCown in charge of the defenses in this quarter—at New Madrid and on Island No. 10—had an aggregate of about 8,500 men of all arms. Before being assigned to the command, McCown had been called to Jackson and told in person by Beauregard that they could not send him any reinforcements; he must make the best defense with what he had, with whatever assistance might be rendered by the eight makeshift gunboats Commodore Hollins had brought up from New Orleans. But McCown was of a weak and timorous nature, poorly suited to last-ditch duty.

Simultaneous with and parallel to the movement of Generals Grant and Buell to Pittsburg Landing, Halleck had sent General Pope down the west side of the Mississippi in Missouri with 25,000 men, equipped with four heavy siege guns and other artillery. He appeared before New Madrid on March 3, but he skirmished around in that neighborhood for a week or more before delivering his real attack on the twelfth. McCown, who had been plaguing Beauregard with wailing complaints and fervid appeals, was quickly and easily convinced that there was no use trying to hold out against Pope's superior power. Though the importance of holding on to the last extremity had been so strongly impressed on him, he evacuated New Madrid in a hurry the night of the thirteenth. Part of the garrison was transferred to Island No. 10, the rest moved across the river to the Tennessee side. Beauregard described it witheringly as "the poorest defense made by any fortified post during the whole course of the war."[1]

144

Trying to make the best of it, Beauregard ordered that all unmounted guns, supplies and boats be brought to Fort Pillow, which was accomplished under McCown's direction. General Walker was left in charge of Island No. 10 and Madrid Bend. General McCown continued to manifest the same nervousness he had shown from the start and on March 31 Beauregard replaced him with General Mackall, who had been commissioned for the purpose.

Mackall could not do much to better things at Island No. 10, a highly vulnerable point. The Federal gunboats under Commodore Foote steamed down the river and poured into the mud fortifications a bombardment of explosive thirteen-inch shells which after a long siege reduced the island to a watery shambles. Meanwhile Pope had crossed his army over to the rear of the Bend. And the outcome was that on April 7 General Mackall was forced to surrender with some 7,000 men. The gloomy news reached Beauregard on his return to Corinth from Shiloh.

The fall of Island No. 10 was a disaster of no mean proportions. It broke another link in the chain of Mississippi River defenses. It was a sad blow to Southern morale, already weakened by the recent losses and defeats. Furthermore, and by no means of least importance, it seriously reduced the man power of the Confederate forces, taking those 7,000 off to Northern prisons—and as many muskets sorely needed by Beauregard.

That general could not stop to cry over spilled milk. He had every reason to expect an early advance of the Federal army from Pittsburg Landing, and his first and most pressing problem was to place Corinth in some sort of defensive state. Bragg's engineers had laid out a new line of works about three miles before the town. It stretched from the Memphis & Charleston Railroad on the right across the Mobile & Ohio on the left, immediately in the rear of a small creek. Hardee was stationed on the right of this line, Bragg in the center, and Polk's force, on the left, stretched across the Mobile & Ohio tracks into some woods where his left flank rested. Van Dorn, accompanied by Price, had finally arrived with his veterans from Arkansas, and he was posted on high ground to the right and rear of Hardee, commanding the approaches to the line from that flank. Breckinridge formed a reserve behind the town. The cavalry was on the flanks. Beauregard's total force—the survivors of Shiloh plus Van Dorn's and Price's men—now numbered close to 50,000.

Beauregard had his faults, but want of energy was not one of them. He was not content to rest passively in his position at Corinth and wait to be attacked, but promptly organized counter-diversions. The little he had seen of Captain John H. Morgan in the retreat from Shiloh had been enough to reveal a great innate talent to his practiced eye. He determined to make use of it. Morgan was promoted to the rank of colonel, authorized to raise his battalion to a regiment or a brigade, given a war bag of $15,000, and sent off to harass the enemy in Middle Tennessee and Kentucky—a mission which he carried out brilliantly during the succeeding months.

Another projected byplay did not prove so successful. Two regiments of cavalry under Colonels Claiborne and Jackson were ordered to assemble at Trenton, Tennessee, and under command of Claiborne to make a swift dash through western Kentucky and seize Paducah, which was held by only a small garrison. Claiborne was told to spread the report that he was the advance guard of Van Dorn's army, going to seize the mouth of the Tennessee River and cut off the retreat of the Yankees who were about to be attacked by Beauregard in front; also to give out that General Price with his army had crossed the Tennessee and was marching on Nashville. This expedition failed—due to "the notorious incapacity of the officer in command," as Beauregard disgustedly expressed it. He also suggested to General Cooper at Richmond that Kirby Smith move swiftly from East Tennessee in a sudden attack on Nashville—but nothing came of this.

These various gestures could be considered only as diversions. Beauregard's principal source of anxiety must be Halleck's large and steadily growing army which immediately confronted him. It had been Halleck's original program, once his leisurely concentration at Pittsburg Landing was effected, to go there himself from St. Louis and in person lead it against Corinth—the assumption being that the Confederates would obligingly wait to be hit. He had planned to leave St. Louis on April 7. The surprise attack by Johnston and Beauregard on the morning of the sixth temporarily upset his arrangements, but immediately after the Battle of Shiloh he came on to the Landing and assumed active command of the army and the campaign. Halleck, who mistrusted or disliked Grant, was not pleased with the way he had fought the battle and had no idea of leaving the army in his charge. The ultimate victory at Shiloh, however, had made Grant a popular hero. Halleck was afraid to dismiss him outright; so he neatly shelved him by the simple process of naming him "second in command"—with no active duties. "Grant was substantially left out," says Sherman, "with no clear, well-defined command or authority. . . . He felt deeply the indignity, if not insult, heaped upon him."[2]

The army formerly commanded directly by Grant, now called the

"Army of the Tennessee,"[3] was assigned to General George H. Thomas and placed on the right of Halleck's line. The center was occupied by the "Army of the Ohio" under General Buell. And the left was given over to the "Army of the Mississippi" under General John Pope. Pope had been called from his triumphs on the Mississippi, where he was just about to lay siege to Fort Pillow. With his army of about 20,000 he landed on the bank of the Tennessee at Hamburg, advanced and took up a position behind Seven Mile Creek—so called because it was seven miles from the river. Other reinforcements were hurried to Halleck from the Middle Western states. Soon he had gathered together an army whose numbers he placed at 125,000—the greatest single army assembled at one place under one commander during the entire war.

One result of the Battle of Shiloh had been to give each of the participating armies a wholesome respect for the fighting qualities of the other. After taking charge, Halleck did not exactly display impetuosity about going after Beauregard. Pope, flushed with his victories at New Madrid and Island No. 10, was disposed to be more aggressive. He was a commander of some ability, though excessively self-satisfied and bombastic.[4] Acting on his own initiative, he moved forward boldly and established an advanced force at the village of Farmington, only about four miles from Corinth. There he was definitely separated from Buell on his right by a swampy creek. Beauregard determined early in May to take advantage of his isolated position and try to wipe him out before he could be reinforced.

Careful plans were made for the contemplated assault on May 9. Ruggles of Bragg's corps was to advance along the Farmington road and assail Pope directly in front, while Van Dorn was to swing around and get on his left flank. But Van Dorn did not get into action; the attack by Ruggles, though successful, was not supported; and Pope, instead of being smashed, was merely pushed back to his former camp on Seven Mile Creek. Beauregard reported that Van Dorn had been misled by his guides; but Hardee, who was with Van Dorn, says:

"The troops were brought to the point designated in the plan of battle, but the approaches to the enemy's position were not such as were contemplated by General Beauregard. . . . The plan of battle was a very good plan of battle, but the topography of the country in which it was to be fought would not permit its execution."[5]

Pope advanced to Farmington again on May 18, and Beauregard once more laid plans to cut him off from the main Federal body. Elaborate preparations were made for the expected battle. Bragg again marched to the front on the twenty-third, but "unexpected obstacles, topographical and otherwise," delayed Van Dorn for twelve hours from getting into his assigned position on Pope's flank. By that time the co-operative movement had become impossible. Again the attempt to trap Pope had to be abandoned. Considerable skirmishing went on between the lines for several days—General Price was particularly active on the Confederate right[6]—but nothing in the nature of a decisive engagement occurred.

Meanwhile Halleck, having started on April 29, was creeping along toward Corinth. With a remarkable excess of caution, in laughable contrast to the indifference shown before Shiloh, the troops entrenched themselves every night after the day's march, and by this tedious process spent the whole month of May in covering the fifteen miles between Shiloh and the neighborhood of Corinth—doubtless the very slowest uncontested advance ever recorded of any army. Fortunate indeed for the Confederates that Halleck moved with such timid deliberation! Had he displayed the confidence and alacrity justified by his superior force, he might well have surrounded and captured Beauregard's army.[7]

That general was all too well aware of the hole he was in, a bad situation made worse by the alarming amount and rapid increase of sickness in his army. Proper care of the sick was difficult, or rather impossible, because the hospitals and private homes were already jammed to overflowing with the wounded from Shiloh.

Shiloh had been the first great battle in this section of the country. Its impact on a people happily unfamiliar with war and its bloody consequences was terrific. Citizens of Corinth were horrified at the ghastly spectacle as the trains of army wagons lumbered in from the battlefield, dripping blood from their heaped-up piles of groaning, suffering wounded. They faced with dismay the unfamiliar problem of caring for them. No less than 5,000 wounded soldiers, Confederate and Federal, were dumped into the little town, totally unprepared for such an abnormal demand on its hospitalization capacities. Maimed and suffering men lay everywhere—on porches, on sidewalks, on platforms of railroad stations. Doctors and nurses were scarce, but those available rolled up their sleeves and worked at their terrible task until they dropped in their tracks from want of sleep, bloody from their ministrations.

An anguished call went out for more surgeons and more nurses—to a South where the supply of both was tragically insufficient. Patriotic women left their homes in Mississippi and Alabama, inspired by the memory of Florence Nightingale, and went to Corinth to tend the sick and wounded, their numbers eked out by soldiers detailed from the ranks. Most of the doctors were already with the armies, but medical students— or any claiming the slightest knowledge of anatomy or medicine—were rushed into service as surgeons, and there were wholesale—and bungling— amputations of arms and legs in a desperate effort to save cases from the gangrene that had set in during days of inattention. Means of antiseptic treatment were lacking, tetanus was common and eight out of ten of the amputations resulted in death. Erysipelas was widespread among the wounded. Sanitary precautions were not taken; the water supply was not only inadequate but soon contaminated. The men drank the polluted water and an epidemic of typhoid fever broke out. Dysentery was an almost universal complaint. There was a measles epidemic to give variety. Soon Corinth became one vast ward, with 18,000 of the soldiers on the sick list. The sinister yellow flag of the hospital corps fluttered over hotels, public buildings, homes, schools and churches—wherever a sick or wounded man could be laid full length on the floor.

Aside from all this disaster due to what Beauregard described as "the natural unhealthfulness of the place," he was having trouble too over feeding his army; hunger and malnutrition were added to the other physical complaints. Heatedly he telegraphed General Cooper at Richmond: "The false views of administration—to say the least—of Colonel Northrup[8] will starve out this army unless I make other arrangements, which I have done."[9] The actual munitions of war—rifles and cannon and gunpowder—were also scarce. For these he was dependent largely on the factories and warehouses at Atlanta, Augusta and other points in the Southeast with which he was connected by the slender thread of railroad from Corinth to Chattanooga and from Chattanooga to Atlanta.

Recognizing the importance of this railroad to the Confederates, the Federal General Mitchel in Middle Tennessee conceived the bold idea of sending a party of his soldiers, dressed in citizen's clothes, into Georgia to burn the bridges on the state-owned Western & Atlantic Railroad south of Chattanooga. Twenty-two daredevils volunteered for this suicidal adventure. Under the leadership of James J. Andrews, they made their way in disguise to Marietta, twenty miles north of Atlanta. Here, in small groups, they boarded a train as passengers. When it stopped at the Big Shanty station for breakfast they seized the engine and three cars and started north on their wild project. The conductor was Captain W. A. Fuller, who took it as a personal affront that anybody should steal his train. Enraged at their audacity, he hiked out after them on foot, accompanied by two of the train crew. They grabbed a handcar from a section gang, then commandeered an industrial locomotive, finally took over a regular freight locomotive. All the time they pressed hotly after the fast-flying raiders on the stolen engine. The story of "The General," as the engine was called, is an epic of daring enterprise matched by indefatigable pursuit. Captain Fuller and his party, now augmented by volunteers, at last overtook the raiders and forced them to abandon "The General"[10] a few miles south of Chattanooga near Graysville. They captured the whole lot. Eight of them, including Andrews, were executed; eight escaped from detention and six were exchanged.

Corinth was an important strategic point, but an exceptionally poor place for a large army to encamp for any length of time. Beauregard had recognized this from the first, and the probability that it would have to be abandoned—although he dreaded the psychological effect of another retreat. The snail's pace of Halleck's army at last brought it to the very outskirts of Corinth. The great force closely invested the Confederate works. On the twenty-eighth a vigorous demonstration began all along the line, with heavy cannonading throughout the day. Now Beauregard had to do something.

Several days before, on May 25, Beauregard had called a conference of his generals at which the situation was thoroughly canvassed. General Hardee submitted a written statement.[11] It began: "The situation at Corinth requires that we should attack the enemy at once, or await his attack, or evacuate the place," and proceeded to demonstrate logically that the last course was the only one to pursue. The possibility of an attack he dismissed as out of the question, owing to the disparity in numbers—to attack Halleck in his entrenchments "would probably inflict on us and the Confederacy a fatal blow." He thought Beauregard could repel any attack, but manifestly no attack was intended; Halleck would most likely bombard them in their camp until they were forced either to make sorties or else evacuate under fire. On the other hand, Hardee contended, it was still possible to retire in good order, without the hazard of a sortie or partial battle. He summed up: "The enemy every day grows stronger on our flanks, and menaces more and more our communications. If he effects his designs, we must fight at every disadvantage or retreat disastrously." Beauregard and the other generals could not answer these pessimistic views. Plans were made for immediate withdrawal.

Opinions may and do differ over the necessity for this retreat, but all authorities and commentators agree that it was accomplished in an extraordinarily skillful manner. To avoid panic and disaffection among the men, the report was spread through the ranks that an immediate advance was intended. Under cover of this the sick and wounded, the heavy baggage and camp equipment were moved to various points southward on the Mobile & Ohio Railroad, along which line the retreat was to be made. Careful plans were made also to remove the guns and ammunition promptly when the retreat actually began. Details of the troop movement were carefully worked out and reduced to writing. To avoid error, the commanders were assembled in Beauregard's headquarters and each was made to repeat his understanding of his special duties in the presence of the others until they had all mastered their parts. The scrupulous particularity went to the point of instructions to the cavalry of the rear guard to take down all mile posts and finger boards as a means of delaying the pursuit by bewildering the pursuers.

The retreat began on the night of May 29, the wagon trains and the first troops moving out at 11 P.M. By 1 A.M. the whole army was under way, the corps proceeding with prearranged regularity—first Van Dorn, then Bragg, Hardee and Polk in order, with Breckinridge again serving as rear guard. The movement was completely concealed from the enemy by a variety of devices. A single band played retreat, tattoo and taps along the Confederate line, shifting from place to place. The campfires were left burning brightly all along the front. "Quaker" guns, made of logs of wood, and dummy sentinels were arranged along the breastworks, providing realistic silhouettes against the light of the campfires. "Deserters" to the enemy camp gave the confidential information that Beauregard was preparing for an attack the next day. Enough drummers were left in the front lines to beat reveille though the only ears to hear it were the enemy's. But the supreme deception was accomplished by running an empty train of cars back and forth on the Memphis & Charleston tracks through the night. The troops had been told to cheer loudly every time it stopped, to give the impression reinforcements were coming in. Similarly, trains carrying the supplies southward on the M. & O. departed in silence, but were hailed as they came back empty. The ruse was so successful that Pope at 10 P.M. sent Halleck an apprehensive message:

"The enemy are reinforcing heavily in my front and left. The cars are running constantly, and the cheering is immense every time they unload in front of me. I have no doubt, from all appearances, that I shall be attacked in heavy force at daylight."[12]

But at daylight of the thirtieth the Confederate army was out of the trenches and well on its way to the rear. Seven trains loaded with provisions and supplies were, through some error, delayed in Corinth that morning until after the bridges and the road had been destroyed. These trains had to be burned. When the smoke gave Halleck the news of the retreat, he found nothing before him but an abandoned camp and an abandoned city. The entire population, except two hardy families, had fled. Only a handful of deserters skulked in the camp.

In anticipation of the possibility of a retreat, Beauregard had had the country to his rear thoroughly examined for a healthful, defensible location and decided upon Tupelo, fifty-two miles south. He fell back with deliberation and halted for a time behind the Tuscumbia River, only six miles from Corinth, to give battle if pursued. But there was no immediate pursuit—one good reason being that Halleck had only the vaguest idea of the direction of the retreat.[13] He thought at first Beauregard might have moved to Grand Junction, Tennessee, between Corinth and Memphis. While Halleck's scouts were picking up the scent, Beauregard marched from the Tuscumbia to Rienzi and Booneville, then on to Baldwyn. Here another line was established and held until June 7, and Tupelo was reached on the ninth.

When the Federals finally made out where Beauregard was headed, a brigade of Pope's cavalry was sent after him. It swept down to Booneville, destroyed a trainload of ammunition and supplies stalled there by some mismanagement, and captured about 200 of the Confederate wounded. Pope's wishful imagination magnified this into an affair of great proportions. He sent word to Halleck that he had captured 10,000 prisoners and 15,000 stand of arms, and this brag the trustful Halleck—to his later intense embarrassment—incorporated in a triumphant telegram to President Lincoln.

As a matter of fact, the affair at Booneville was of very little military importance, but it uncovered for the Federals the hitherto hidden talents of one who was to figure most prominently in the activities of the Northern Army. Philip H. Sheridan was a graduate of West Point, but had made little progress in the year he had been with the army. He had seen service in Missouri as a captain of infantry, but was later attached to Halleck's staff in St. Louis as a quartermaster, in which capacity he came with Halleck to Pittsburg Landing. While the army was there, the colonel of the 2nd Michigan Cavalry was promoted, leaving a vacancy. The Governor of Michigan came down to confer with Halleck about his successor, and Halleck, more or less at random—since Sheridan had never been in the cavalry—recommended his young quartermaster. He received his appointment on May 27 and within forty-eight hours was off on his first cavalry raid.

Beauregard, reporting his retreat to Richmond, said that "by the evacuation the plan of campaign of the enemy was utterly foiled, his delay of seven weeks and vast expenditures were of little value, and he has reached Corinth to find it a barren locality, which he must abandon as wholly worthless for his purposes." President Davis was not inclined to accept this optimistic view.[14] Aside from its direct and visible results, the withdrawal had corollary effects far-reaching in significance. One of its inescapable immediate consequences was that it rendered Fort Pillow untenable. On June 1, General Villepigue, in accordance with instructions from Beauregard, removed the garrison to Grenada, Mississippi. On the sixth, after a sharp but one-sided naval battle in the Mississippi River, Memphis also was surrendered. The Federal gunboats and transports now had the free run of the Mississippi as far south as Vicksburg. New Orleans, inadequately defended by poorly manned forts on the Mississippi, was soon captured. Vicksburg was left the only Confederate stronghold on the Mississippi, the only obstacle in the way of the Federals' uninterrupted navigation of the river from its source to the Gulf.

Naturally all this was most disturbing to Davis. General Cooper wired Beauregard crisply on the twelfth: "The President has been expecting a communication explaining your last movement. It has not yet arrived." Then, without awaiting a reply, the President on the fourteenth sent his aide. Colonel W. P. Johnston (Albert Sidney Johnston's son), to call on Beauregard with a list of written interrogatories about the retreat and a demand for specific answers to pointed questions.

"I desire to know what were the circumstances and purposes of the retreat from the Memphis & Charleston Railroad to the position now occupied," said Question No. 1 of the catechism; and this was typical of the coldly formal and unfriendly nature of all the questions. Like a salvo of artillery fire, they were fired at the general:

2. "What is the plan for future operations, and whether an advance of the army is contemplated, and what prospect there is of a recovery of the territory which has been yielded?

3. "Why was it not deemed advisable to occupy the hills north and east of Corinth, and could not a stronger line than that around Corinth have been then selected?

4. "What was the cause of the sickness at Camp Corinth? Would it have been avoided by occupying the higher grounds in front? Has it been corrected by retiring to the present position?

5. "Was it at no time practicable to have cut the enemy's line of communication, so as to compel him to abandon the Tennessee River or to permit us to re-occupy Nashville?

6. "What means were employed after the fall of Island No. 10 to prevent the descent of the Mississippi River by the enemy's gunboats? What dispositions were made to defend Memphis, and what was the cause of the failure to preserve that most important of our lines of communication?

7. "What loss of troops, stores, or arms occurred at the time of the retreat from Corinth?"[15]

Beauregard sensed the hostility back of these questions; they constituted a quizzing such as no other Confederate commander was subjected to, either before or after. They were some time reaching him but when they did he answered them fully and in a respectful manner.

Colonel Johnston had been instructed by President Davis "to inspect the troops, to make due inquiry into their organization, their supplies of quartermaster's, commissary and ordnance stores, camp equipage, messing, general administration, including the regularity of all issues and the condition of the troops, especially as to their comfort and the measures taken to preserve their health." He made a comprehensive examination and report. He also recounted in detail a conversation in which General Beauregard said that "if any shadow of doubt rested in the mind of the Executive as to the propriety of the movement in retreat he would ask for a court of inquiry. He was willing to repose his reputation on this movement, and considered it equivalent to a brilliant victory, considering the relative condition and numbers of the two contending armies."

Before Colonel Johnston had this talk with Beauregard on the twentieth, another crisis in the Davis-Beauregard feud had been precipitated—and settled—by telegraph. The general's health had continued very poor. When once he was convinced that Halleck did not mean to pursue and attack him at Tupelo, he began arrangements for a long-deferred leave of absence to recuperate. When he had arrived at Jackson, three months before, his medical director, Dr. Brodie, and his medical inspector, Dr. Choppin, had urged him to rest, for "a total cessation from the duties of command" was necessary to restore his shattered nervous system and to afford him relief from his chronic inflammation of the tonsils and pharynx and from the after-effects of jaundice. At that time Beauregard had persisted in the performance of his duties. Now that he had his army safely ensconced at Tupelo his doctors again insisted on the leave of absence. So, armed with their formal medical certificate of disability, he decided on a vacation at Bladon Springs, a famous watering place on the Tombigbee River, about seventy-five miles north of Mobile.

He seems to have had a veritable genius for getting involved in offi-

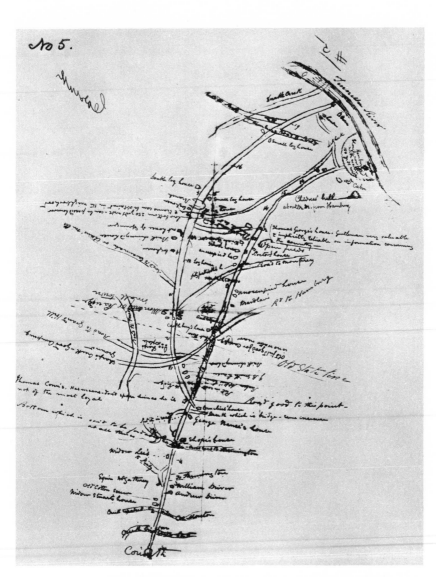

Rough map (made in the field) of the country between Corinth and Pittsburgh Landing, provided Beauregard by one of his scouts.

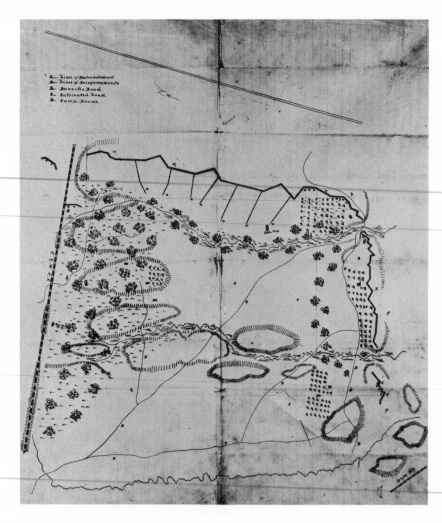

General Beauregard's personal map of the fortifications at Corinth, showing the entrenchments, battery positions, roads, hills and railroads.

cial misunderstandings. By coincidence it happened that on the very day he was arranging to transfer his command temporarily to General Bragg, the next officer in rank, Bragg received a telegram direct from President Davis to go to Vicksburg and relieve General Lovell. Apart from its interference with his private plans, Beauregard, naturally enough, resented this direct communication of orders to one of his subordinates. He immediately informed the Richmond authorities why it was impossible for Bragg to leave Tupelo then. He was taking only "a short rest," he said, and expected to be back to assume the offensive as soon as the forces were sufficiently organized. Receiving no reply, he wired Cooper again the next day, reiterating the necessity for his resting "a week or ten days"—long enough to restore "my shattered health"—and mentioning that he would go to Bladon Springs by way of Mobile. Then he went through with the transfer to Bragg and on the seventeenth left for Mobile to inspect the defenses under General Forney before beginning his vacation. It was there that Colonel Johnston saw him.

Bragg, on friendly terms with both Beauregard and Davis, realized that he was caught in a cross fire. On Beauregard's departure he prudently telegraphed Richmond for instructions. The President seized eagerly on the pretext that Beauregard had deserted his place without authority from Richmond and wired Bragg on the twentieth assigning him permanently to the command of the department[16] in Beauregard's stead. Van Dorn in place of Bragg was ordered to Vicksburg to replace Lovell, taking with him Breckinridge's troops. Beauregard's only official notification of being relieved was a curt note from the Secretary of War enclosing a copy of the President's telegram to Bragg. Genuinely embarrassed by the unexpected development, Bragg repeated to Beauregard by wire the instructions he had received, adding: "I envy you, and am almost in despair." Beauregard answered: "I can not congratulate you, but am happy for the change," and offered Bragg the use of his staff.

Beauregard had the highest regard for Bragg. In fact, the first telegram he had sent to Richmond after the Battle of Shiloh had concluded with this sentence: "I earnestly and urgently recommend Major General Bragg for immediate appointment to General A. S. Johnston's place," and President Davis willingly enough raised Bragg to full general, the sixth such appointment to that rank. Beauregard had no ill-feeling toward his successor, but was exceedingly bitter over the way he had been removed. He had been reluctant to leave Virginia and go west, but, having helped build up the army, he felt a growing regard for it. Not only did he want to remain its leader, but he took the warmest interest in its operations.

Though deposed he corresponded with Bragg about the best methods of campaign and in course submitted to General Cooper, with whom he continued friendly, a plan that aimed at the capture and occupation of Louisville and Cincinnati.

When he had recovered his health and was once more ready for active service he was given command of South Carolina and Georgia, replacing General Pemberton[17]—a palpable reduction in prestige. Some sixty members of the Confederate Congress joined in a petition to Davis to restore him and went in person to urge it. But the President had made up his mind. He would not do it "if the whole world united in the petition," he told the delegation. So Beauregard went to Charleston. Bragg despairingly made his plans.

2. THE ADVANCE

Certainly Bragg's task was no bed of roses. There was open disaffection in the ranks, unconcealed antipathy for the new commanding general. It had started at Corinth, out of the complications arising from the expiration of the terms of service of those who had enlisted for twelve months. The Conscription Act had been recently passed, by which the men whose terms expired were subject to immediate and forcible draft. These men had all volunteered originally from patriotic motives and most of them were perfectly willing to carry on as a matter of principle, but they wanted a breathing spell long enough at least for a visit back home. The authorities showed no inclination to indulge in any leniency. Bragg had been especially severe. When one regiment of Tennessee volunteers insisted on its right to go home at the expiration of its term of enlistment, he brought up a battery of artillery and forced them back into the service[18]— not the most diplomatic way of handling the high-spirited individualists who composed this army. Such harshness, of course, created intense resentment. There were numerous desertions—or absences without leave. But Bragg did not abate his stern regime. Deserters, when captured, were shot, and the men were lined up to witness the executions.

Years later a Tennessee private wrote:

"None of General Bragg's soldiers ever loved him. They had no faith in his ability as a general. He was looked upon as a merciless tyrant. The soldiers were very scantily fed. Bragg never was a good feeder. Rations with us were always scarce. . . . We were crushed. Bragg, so the soldiers thought, was the machine that did it. Bragg was the great autocrat. . . . He loved to crush the spirit of his men. The more of a hangdog look they had about them the better was General Bragg pleased. Not a single soldier in the whole army ever loved or respected him."[19]

This represents the extreme view of the more dissident personnel but, to a modified extent, was fairly typical of all Bragg's soldiers—and many of his officers. There was complete absence of that devotion and blind confidence which characterized the feeling of Robert E. Lee's men for him and which later was shown by this Army of Tennessee for Joe Johnston. On Bragg's behalf it may be said that the army was unquestionably in sad need of stricter discipline than had prevailed before he joined it. He was entirely right in insisting on drill, the recognition of authority and a strict observance of military rules and laws, but he would have attained better results by exercising tact and diplomacy. In many cases his stern application of discipline verged on brutality. When the retreat from Corinth started, not a few of his own men—and some of the conscripts from the other corps—took the chance to desert and go home. His severity had gained for him the name of tyrant throughout the army. No wonder morale slumped when he was raised to the high command.

Bragg took over on June 27. His first official act was to issue a turgid address to the troops, "the brave men of Shiloh and Elkhorn," in which he emphasized the advantages of discipline—a sore subject. He called attention to the need for aggressive steps against "an insolent but wary foe," and promised "a few more days of needful preparation and organization and I shall give your banners to the breeze." He would lead them to "additional honors to those you have already won on other fields." He ended grimly: "But be prepared to undergo privation and labor with cheerfulness and alacrity."

Bragg's inheritance was one great tangle of difficulties. Subsistence for the army was still a pressing problem, rendered no less acute by the chronic inefficiency of the Commissary General at Richmond. Transportation was another bottleneck. Bragg urged the government at Richmond to give financial assistance to the railroads in his territory by which they might amplify their facilities and expedite his movements. A small but important vexation was the sudden insistence of the Postoffice Department on complete charge of the telegraph wires, heretofore operated, as military necessities, by the military forces. Bragg opposed it as detrimental to the army's efficiency, but Davis upheld his Postmaster General. The result was that Bragg's dispatches were so delayed or lost that he ordered the mail instead of the telegraph used in army communication.

But his most pressing problem was the scarcity of good officers. After the transfer of Van Dorn, Breckinridge and Hindman, he complained to General Cooper that Hardee was the only competent major general he had left, Polk having been relieved of his corps and named second in command of the entire force. He minced no words over his subordinates' shortcomings. Ordered to send McCown and his division to East Tennessee, he warned Kirby Smith of McCown's "want of capacity and nerve for a separate, responsible command." He said New Madrid had been lost because of "his errors and want of decision and firmness. . . . I implore you not to trust him with any important position." Naming names, Bragg in a communication to Cooper listed Major Generals Crittenden, McCown and Cheatham and Brigadier Generals Carroll, Trapier and Hawes as "in my judgment, unsuited for their responsible positions." He complained that the caliber of his officers was inferior.

"The elective feature of the conscript law," he said, "has driven from the service the best who remained, and to a great extent has demoralized the troops. So many of our general officers have been absent, wounded or sick that it has been quite difficult to keep up any organization, especially as the whole number attached was short of the real wants of the service. Many recommendations made were not ratified, and some general officers appointed or promoted without recommendations from this quarter are only incumbrances and would be better out of the way."

Another disturbing feature of this was the fact that a large number of the regiments were only skeletons, with few enlisted men on the rolls but complete regimental organizations, giving a total of officers entirely out of proportion to the number of men officered. Nor was this by any means a minor matter. It is hard to imagine a greater obstacle to an army's success than a scarcity of competent officers and a plethora of indifferent ones. Bragg suggested remedies, but Cooper was slow to act. The trouble was, indeed, basic in the army's plan of organization, and almost defied successful solution.

With all these administrative difficulties, however, the health and general spirits of the army picked up promptly at Tupelo. The water supply was better, the weather improved, the men were comfortably quartered and supplied with new clothes, and, best of all, were free from the constant alarums and skirmishing and artillery fire to which they had been subjected at Corinth. Bragg's skill as an organizer made itself felt. The army at Tupelo, despite its antagonistic attitude toward its commander, was molded into a relatively efficient, well-trained fighting unit, ready to take the field—as soon as he could decide where it should be aimed. That was a question.

Clearly it was free from any danger of attack. The Federal army, it was plain, had no idea of advancing into the interior of Mississippi. The War Department at Washington had sent Halleck a congratulatory telegram praising him for his "brilliant and successful" movement on Corinth, but his officers and soldiers began asking what actual benefits were derived from it. Grant, though admitting that it was a place of some strategic importance, thought its possession "barren in every other particular." This feeling crept into the consciousness of Halleck and the higher-ups at Washington. Corinth had been captured. A stupendous Federal army was lodged in the heart of the mid-South. What next? The army was far from its source of supplies, and the maintenance of such a huge body of troops in the enemy's country was no light matter. Farther advance into Mississippi to attack the Confederates at Tupelo required more dash and audacity than Halleck possessed. Some form of action must be taken, however. No doubt about that. This big army could not be allowed to vegetate at Corinth. To encamp there indefinitely was as impractical for Halleck as it had been for Beauregard.

So, within ten days after his bloodless conquest of the city, Halleck began to break up the army he had assembled with so much labor and trouble. On June 10 Grant and Buell were restored to the independent command of their armies and Pope was transferred to Virginia to try his hand against Lee, who had just defeated McClellan in the Seven Days fighting around Richmond. Buell was ordered on the eleventh back across the Tennessee River to occupy East Tennessee, repairing the Memphis & Charleston Railroad as he went. Halleck remained with Grant to hold the line of that road across northern Mississippi.

Buell's advance in the direction of Chattanooga was slow and cautious, and delayed to carry out his order to repair the railroad. He reached Huntsville by the end of the month, but it was not until the middle of July that he got to Stevenson, in a position to menace Chattanooga, which was apparently his objective—if at that time he had a distinct objective. Halleck's dispatches at first spoke of occupying East Tennessee, but later he was writing Buell about a possible march into North Georgia and perhaps to Atlanta. At any rate Buell's presence in the neighborhood of Chattanooga was a definite threat to the South. General Edmund Kirby Smith, in command of the Confederate forces in East Tennessee, on July 20 telegraphed Bragg at Tupelo that Buell had gone so far it seemed a propitious time to move against him. Bragg had been contemplating something of the sort as soon as he might ascertain the nature of the Federals' plans. He took action the very day after he got this telegram. Hardee with his army of 34,000 effectives was ordered to Chattanooga "with the least delay practicable," the artillery, cavalry and wagon trains to march across country and the infantry to go by rail via Mobile, Montgomery and Atlanta. The old Army of the West, numbering about 16,000, which Van Dorn had brought across from Arkansas, was left in Mississippi under General Sterling Price to confront Grant now commanding in that sector. Halleck had been called to Washington on the eleventh to assume supreme Federal command. As one unfriendly Northern critic acidly commented:

"Halleck's demonstrated unfitness for his position induced the administration to find a higher position for him. . . . Unable to command successfully one army, he was ordered to Washington to command all the armies."[20]

On the twenty-third Bragg advised General Cooper that he meant "to strike an effective blow through Middle Tennessee, gaining the enemy's rear, cutting off his supplies and dividing his forces so as to encounter him in detail." Since he still regarded Beauregard with the deference due his former superior, he wrote to him also outlining his plan of campaign and inviting his criticism. At Chattanooga, he told Beauregard, he hoped to join Hardee's force with Kirby Smith's 20,000 and take the offensive against Buell. Meanwhile he would throw General Joe Wheeler's cavalry forward in West Tennessee toward Grand Junction, and General Frank C. Armstrong's cavalry in north Alabama toward Tuscumbia, thus concealing his movement to Chattanooga until he was actually in front of Buell. "Our cavalry is paving the way for me in Middle Tennessee and Kentucky," he said.[21]

This was no perfunctory compliment. The energy of Morgan and Forrest, foreshadowing their later greatness, had hampered and bewildered Buell to such a point as almost to paralyze his force. Beauregard, from his temporary exile at Bladon Springs, wrote to Bragg:

"I am happy to see that my two lieutenants, Morgan and Forrest, are doing such good service in Kentucky and Tennessee. When I appointed them I thought they would leave their mark wherever they passed."

Morgan had been on the warpath since early in the month, when he started out from Knoxville with about 800 men to harass the Federal forces and lines of communication east and north of Nashville. Crossing the Cumberland River at Celina on the eighth they dashed into Kentucky, quickly defeated a battalion of Pennsylvania cavalry at Tompkinsville, capturing their commander, and moved on to Glasgow where they camped on the line of communications between Louisville and Nashville. The news of this audacious raid created such alarm throughout Kentucky, and so far as Cincinnati, that frenzied appeals for help were telegraphed to Washington. Even placid President Lincoln was aroused to wire Halleck at Corinth: "They are having a panic in Kentucky. Please look to it." And there was good reason for alarm. Morgan dashed on to Lebanon, to Harrodsburg, to the very outskirts of Lexington and Frankfort, the state capital. He spent July galloping about in the rich Bluegrass, capturing and destroying supplies, damaging railroads, eluding or defeating the fragmentary forces sent to catch him. By the first of August, when he was back in Tennessee, he had marched over a thousand miles in twenty-four days, had captured and paroled 1,200 prisoners, and had lost in killed and wounded less than a hundred men.

Forrest had been no less active. One of Beauregard's last official acts had been to recommend him for promotion to brigadier general and dispatch him to Tennessee to lead cavalry regiments of Colonels Wharton, Adams and Scott.[22] On July 6 he had left Chattanooga with about 1,000 men, headed for Middle Tennessee. Buell had his eye on McMinnville as a strategic point between Chattanooga and Nashville and had collected at Murfreesboro a brigade of 1,750 men to occupy it. On the thirteenth Forrest swooped down on Murfreesboro and captured the entire force, including all its officers and its commander, General T. L. Crittenden, together with stores valued at almost a million dollars. Buell ordered Nelson out from Nashville to retake Murfreesboro and McMinnville. Thereupon Forrest appeared in Nelson's rear on the railroad and destroyed two of the bridges between him and Nashville.[23] He got so close to Nashville[24] that Governor Andrew Johnson grew panicky and magnified the raid into an attempt to capture the city. He urged that it be fortified and that the citizens be compelled to furnish the labor and materials, saying, "The rebels must be made to feel the burden of their own deeds."

Morgan went on the rampage again north of Nashville and early in August captured Gallatin[25] and its garrison. Most important, he destroyed several bridges and the tunnel through which the railroad passed near Gallatin, and this shut off supplies from Louisville for several months. Buell sent a squadron of cavalry under General R. W. Johnson to drive him out of Tennessee, but Morgan met it at Hartsville, defeated and dispersed it, captured General Johnson and seventy-five other prisoners.

With all this going on in his rear, no wonder General Buell paused at Stevenson and resorted to alert watchfulness. He knew something was up but he did not know what. He awaited developments.

CHAPTER X

THE INVASION OF KENTUCKY

1. The Forward Move

WHILE Buell paused before Chattanooga, hampered by perplexities, Bragg's course still bristled with complications. He was now contemplating operations in a section officially under the jurisdiction of General Edmund Kirby Smith. General Smith was a seasoned soldier, a graduate of West Point. He resigned from the United States Army in Texas in March 1861. His first service in the Confederacy was with the army in Virginia, but in February 1862 he was given command of the "Department of East Tennessee, North Georgia and Northwest Carolina" with the rank of major general, headquarters at Knoxville.

By virtue of Bragg's rank he would automatically be over Kirby Smith when their forces were combined, but in the meantime military etiquette demanded a conference between two independent commanders for a correlation of their activities in the pending campaign. Bragg arrived in Chattanooga on July 29; the next day Kirby Smith came down from Knoxville and they made plans for co-operation. Someone has said that in the lexicon of war there should be no such word as "co-operation," that in any military operation one poor general is better than two good ones, and the events of the next few weeks seem to bear this out. Kirby Smith readily enough recognized Bragg's superior rank and was willing to operate under his direction.[1] But Bragg, conscious of being in Kirby Smith's official territory, did not like to display too much authority. At their Chattanooga meeting they did agree on what Bragg described as "measures of mutual support and effective co-operation,"[2] and there is no question but that each made an honest attempt to carry them out. As earnest in his sincere desire for their combined success, Bragg lent his fellow general a division under General Pat Cleburne; Kirby Smith accepted Bragg's suggestions unreservedly. All the same, there were two autonomous commands, under two independent commanders, operating in the same campaign—an awkward state of affairs under the best of conditions—and it is no great marvel that a fatal sort of muddling uncertainty marked what followed.

162

The agreed-on plan, as reported by Bragg to General Cooper on August 1,[3] was for Kirby Smith to move at once from Knoxville against General George W. Morgan's[4] Federal forces at Cumberland Gap, while Bragg waited at Chattanooga for the rest of his trains to come up. If Kirby Smith succeeded at Cumberland Gap, Bragg said, they would then join and go into Middle Tennessee "with the fairest prospect of cutting off General Buell."

From the correspondence and reports it seems plain that at the outset Bragg had no idea of launching an expedition into Kentucky. His whole concern was the redemption of Middle Tennessee, the driving out of Buell. Kirby Smith writes that "Bragg proposed operating in Middle Tennessee, with Nashville for his objective point."[5] In Bragg's letter to Beauregard and in his early communications to General Cooper at Richmond there is no mention of Kentucky. Middle Tennessee is expressly named the objective. The first thought of a Kentucky campaign is indicated in Bragg's letter to Kirby Smith of August 10:

"It will be a week yet before I can commence crossing the river, and information I hope to receive will determine which route I shall take— to Nashville or Lexington. My inclination is now to the latter. . . . Van Dorn and Price will advance simultaneously with us from Mississippi on West Tennessee, and I trust we may all unite in Ohio."[6]

The next day he outlined his plans to General Price:

"As soon as my transportation comes up, we shall move into Middle Tennessee and, taking the enemy's rear, strike Nashville or, perhaps, leaving that to the left, strike for Lexington and Cincinnati, both of which are entirely unprotected."

Kirby Smith started forward from Knoxville on August 14, with a division under General Churchill and the division under General Cleburne which had just been sent by Bragg. Morgan's position at Cumberland Gap was such as to make a direct assault impracticable. So Kirby Smith decided on a turning movement. To General C. L. Stevenson with 9,000 men he gave the immediate task of investing Cumberland Gap and watching Morgan, while he himself with about the same number crossed the Cumberland Mountains several miles to the south at Big Creek Gap, preceded by a scouting force of cavalry under Colonel John S. Scott.

The weather was hot, the roads were rough, water was scarce. To cap it all, the men outmarched their wagon trains and for nearly a week were without food except what they could gather by the way—not much in this mountainous region. Some salt (a very precious commodity) was captured at Barboursville, and this helped to make palatable the raw apples and roasting ears which they foraged from neighboring farms. "I've just found out that CSA stands for 'Corn, Salt and Apples,' " a wag cried out.[7] The joke spread down the column; the men laughed, hitched up their belts and marched on through the deep dust.

On the twenty-ninth the army crossed the last mountain range, Big Hill, and saw spread out before them the beautiful, lush bluegrass region of Kentucky. Late that afternoon Scott's cavalry encountered Federals near Richmond. Kirby Smith straightway announced he would attack next morning. The Federal force was under General Nelson and amounted to more than 6,000, but they were mostly raw recruits who had been hurriedly collected and rushed out from Louisville as soon as Buell heard of the projected invasion.

At daylight on the thirtieth the Confederates moved forward to the attack, the division under General Cleburne leading. Here Cleburne first demonstrated his capacity for command by laying the ground for a signal victory before he was removed from the field late in the afternoon with a painful wound in the cheek.[8] The engagement at Richmond was warmly contested, lasting all day. Though Nelson was outnumbered and outclassed, he put up a stubborn fight, making three separate stands as the Confederates steadily pressed him back. But Cleburne managed his men so skillfully that by the end of the day Nelson's army had been completely whipped. As a fighting unit it was effectually destroyed, those not killed or captured taking refuge in flight. Nelson's official report of his own casualties was 206 killed, 844 wounded and 4,303 captured. He lost also all his wagon trains and supplies, nine pieces of artillery, 10,000 stand of small arms. The Confederate loss was 78 killed, 372 wounded and 1 missing.

With practically all organized opposition thus removed, Kirby Smith swept on to Lexington, where he remained in virtual control of Central Kentucky through the entire month of September, while his cavalry raided northward to the immediate environs of Louisville, and even to Covington, across the river from Cincinnati.

He occupied Frankfort with 1,500 cavalry, and the officers of the state government fled to Louisville, whither all the state archives and funds had already been transferred. Panic prevailed in Cincinnati. Business was suspended and citizens were impressed to build breastworks. An uprising of Southern sympathizers was feared. General Lew Wallace was hurried in to take command of the city, where he decreed martial law. On the very day of Kirby Smith's victory at Richmond, Lee administered a stinging defeat to Pope at Second Manassas and now was crossing the Potomac—perhaps for a direct assault on Washington. Dismay and despair spread through the North. Grave fears were entertained for the preservation of the Union. Bragg hardly exaggerated in an official address to his army: "The enemy is in full retreat, with consternation and demoralization devastating his ranks."

Kirby Smith's success making Cumberland Gap untenable, General Morgan evacuated it on September 17 and retreated to the Ohio River above Cincinnati. General Humphrey Marshall, marching with 3,000 men into Kentucky from Virginia through Pound Gap, was ordered to intercept the fleeing Federals and hold them until Stevenson could overtake them. But Marshall did not get there in time, and, although General John H. Morgan interposed his cavalry and slowed down the retreat, he could not stop his Federal namesake, who made good his escape.

While Kirby Smith was moving forward from Knoxville, Bragg was completing the reorganization of his army at Chattanooga. It was now formed into two wings, the right under Polk, the left under Hardee. The total force on August 27 was reported as 27,816 officers and men. General Buckner, who had been in prison at Fort Warren for five months, was exchanged on July 28 and went to Richmond, where he was notified of his promotion to the rank of major general. General Lee expressed some desire to have him serve in the Army of Northern Virginia, but he was regarded as belonging to the Western forces and was ordered to report to General Bragg.[9] Buckner joined Bragg at Chattanooga and was assigned to duty under General Hardee.

Bragg was anxious to have Breckinridge and his division accompany him on his campaign, recognizing his great political and moral inflence in Kentucky. On August 8 he said to him in a jovial letter:

"My army has promised to make me military governor of Ohio in ninety days [Seward's time for crushing the rebellion], and as they can not do this without passing your home, I have thought you would like to have an escort to visit your family."[10]

In more serious vein he assured Breckinridge that he wanted him and as many men as Van Dorn could spare—or wanted him alone if he could not bring any men. Hardee backed this up by telegraphing that he had a division for him to lead if he would come.[11]

Breckinridge telegraphed back: "Reserve that division for me."[12]

On the twenty-seventh Bragg wired again urging him to hurry. But Breckinridge was delayed on the way and it was not until October 3 that he finally reached Knoxville with about 2,500 men from the Trans-Mississippi. These he joined with the 4,000 there, and a few days later he was reinforced by 2,000 exchanged prisoners. But it was too late then to help Bragg.

Bragg had crossed the river at Chattanooga on August 28 and begun his forward march—although his destination was still rather vague and largely dependent on developments. The soldiers were buoyant and in good spirits. Many of them were from Tennessee and Kentucky and while they were at Chattanooga had been visited frequently by members of their families bringing boxes and baskets of supplies, clothing and home-cooked food. Now they were on the march through their homeland and some soldier was sure to have kinfolk in every community. The rank and file were feasted on turkeys, chickens, fresh eggs and buttermilk—and not infrequently some of the unregenerate could smell out a moonshine still in one of the mountain coves. It was a pleasant march.

Buell had a much larger army than Bragg (variously estimated in different official reports at from 45,000 to 59,309), but he had a wholesome respect for his opponent's ability, and he went cautiously about interposing himself between Bragg and Nashville. His position in August, when Bragg started out, had its right at Stevenson, its center at Decherd on the Nashville & Chattanooga Railroad, and its left at McMinnville, with the Tennessee River, Walden's Ridge, the Sequatchie River and part of the Cumberland Mountains between him and Bragg. He had a strong force at Altamont, but Wheeler drove them out when Bragg started forward. Buell then ordered a concentration at Murfreesboro, having previously shifted his personal headquarters successively from Stevenson to Decherd to McMinnville. When he got to Murfreesboro he received the disquieting news of Nelson's crushing defeat at Richmond. So he marched the whole army on to Nashville and prepared to defend it against the attack he thought was coming.

As early as August 6 Buell had ordered his engineers to throw up fortifications around the city, defending the roads and bridges. He told them: "See Governor Johnson[13] and, if he approves, devise some defenses also around the Capitol." Governor Johnson did approve—he was decidedly nervous about his own safety as well as Nashville's—and the capitol was barricaded with breastworks of cotton bales and a palisade of cedar posts, bristling with cannon. From behind this protection, Andy

Johnson breathed fiery imprecations on the dastardly Rebels, vowed he would defend the capitol with his heart's blood, would never be taken out of it alive by the conquering Rebels even if the city were captured, etc., etc.

Meanwhile Bragg was coming north as fast as he could up the Sequatchie Valley through Pikeville to Sparta, and on to Carthage and Gainesboro on the Cumberland River. On the march he too heard of Nelson's destruction by Kirby Smith, who wrote urging him "to move into Kentucky and, effecting a junction with my command and holding Buell's communications, to give battle to him with superior forces and with certainty of success."[14] Bragg apparently was taken by this advice. He started on a direct march into Kentucky where, he said, he hoped to join Kirby Smith and gain such a decisive victory over the Federal forces as would encourage the pro-Southern Kentuckians to enlist under the Confederate banner and give him strength for further conquest.

Bragg's immediate destination was Glasgow, about forty miles east of Bowling Green, where he arrived on September 13 and halted for two days to consolidate his force, rest and gather foodstuffs. Straightway he issued a flamboyant proclamation to the citizens of the state, whom he presumed to be eagerly awaiting the arrival of the Confederates.

"Kentuckians," said his proclamation,[15] "I have entered your state with the Confederate Army of the West, and offer you an opportunity to free yourselves from the tyranny of a despotic ruler. We come not as conquerors or despoilers, but to restore to you the liberties of which you have been deprived by a cruel and relentless foe. We come to guarantee to all the sanctity of their homes and altars, to punish with a rod of iron the despoilers of your peace, and to avenge the cowardly insults to your women. . . . I shall enforce a rigid discipline and shall protect all in their persons and property."[16] He concluded: "Kentuckians, we have come with joyous hopes. Let us not depart in sorrow, as we shall if we find you wedded in your choice to your present lot. If you prefer Federal rule, show it by your frowns and we shall return whence we came. If you choose rather to come within the folds of our brotherhood, then cheer us with the smiles of your women and lend your willing hands to secure you in your heritage of liberty."[17]

The response to this grandiloquence was dismally disappointing. Contrary to expectations, the yeomanry of Kentucky showed little enthusiasm about enlisting under the Southern banner. Kirby Smith managed to recruit about a brigade in the Bluegrass, but Bragg's accretions were almost nil. "The people here have too many fat cattle and are too well off to fight," Bragg said crossly to his aide, Colonel Urquhart. This unresponsiveness was particularly exasperating just now inasmuch as, for the first time, the Confederates could arm several thousand new troops— if they had them—thanks to the recent captures. In fact, when Bragg later retreated from Kentucky he had with him 20,000 more rifles than he had when he came—but they were packed away in the ammunition trains instead of carried on the shoulders of sturdy Kentucky recruits where he had hoped to see them.

It did not take Buell long to sense the crystallization of Bragg's plans for the Kentucky invasion. He set out for Louisville with most of his army, leaving Thomas with three divisions to hold Nashville. In a few days he ordered Thomas to come along with his own division, and that left General Negley with only 6,000 at the city. On the fourteenth the Federal vanguard arrived at Bowling Green. Munfordville, fifty miles north, was held by a garrison of some 4,000 men under Colonel Wilder, stationed in a fort on the south side of Green River at the end of the railroad bridge. Buell's plan was to march to Munfordville promptly from Bowling Green and join up with Wilder, but Wheeler's cavalry, ever active, checked him north of Bowling Green and held him there for a time. Learning of Bragg's presence at Glasgow, he moved that way tentatively as though to offer battle. Bragg showed no inclination to accept the challenge, and Buell did not press it. Meanwhile, one of Bragg's foremost brigades, under Chalmers, had made an unauthorized and unwise attack on the Munfordville fort and been sharply repulsed. On the fifteenth Bragg ordered his whole army to advance on Munford-ville. The next day, after crossing Polk's corps to the north of the river, he invested the town and its defending fortification.

The Federals at Munfordville were doomed, caught between the pincers of Hardee on the one side and Polk on the other, with Forrest's cavalry thrown across the rear to prevent escape. Bragg on the seventeenth formally demanded of Colonel Wilder the surrender of the garrison, in-forming him that this overwhelming investment made capitulation in-evitable. Wilder was an Indiana industrialist with no military experience whatever. He did not like the idea of surrendering—but could see noth-ing else to do. Finally he adopted the unorthodox (but probably sensible) expedient of going under a flag of truce to General Buckner's headquarters and asking his advice. He explained his ignorance, said he had been told Buckner was not only a trained soldier but a gentleman who would not deceive him. If his position was hopeless, he explained, he did not want to sacrifice the lives of any of his men in a useless defense. On the other hand, he did not want to be stampeded into a surrender which a more experienced commander might not consider necessary. He was willing to leave it to Buckner—as one gentleman to another. Buckner, taken aback by this naïveté, declined to advise his trusting enemy. That's not the way wars are fought, he told Wilder. He did go so far as to tell him that he ought to try to defend the fort as long as possible if he thought that thereby he might help Buell. But he assured him that his little command was encircled by Bragg's whole army with a hundred pieces of artillery in a commanding position where they could batter his defenses into dust. Wilder asked politely if he might be permitted to inspect the beleaguering forces and count the cannon.[18] Buckner in his most gentlemanly manner consented to this; and Wilder, convinced by ocular demonstration, said sadly: "I believe I'll surrender." So Buckner took him to Bragg, and Wilder gave up the fort and its entire garrison, together with all its artillery and stores and 5,000 stand of small arms.[19]

In announcing this capture to General Cooper at Richmond, Bragg concluded:

"My admiration and love for my army can not be expressed. To its patient toil and admirable discipline I am indebted for all the success which has attended this perilous undertaking. The men are much jaded and somewhat destitute, but cheerful and confident, without a murmur."

These honeyed words were doubtless intended to take the edge off the bitter dislike which, he well knew, so many of his men held for him— but there is nothing in the record to indicate that they worked.

The whole Confederacy was of course tremendously elated by this success following on the heels of Kirby Smith's smashing victory at Richmond. All confidently expected that Bragg, now possessed of the initiative and being directly in the enemy's rear, would turn on Buell and administer a stinging defeat. His own officers expected it. Bragg himself appears to have had some such fleeting intention at first. He arrayed his army in a strong position south of Green River in the captured works, presumably with the idea of giving battle. In his telegram to General Cooper he had said that Kirby Smith would join him (he didn't) and that Buell could not possibly escape. But something—some innate timidity, some doubt or fear, some lack of confidence—stayed his wavering hand. The stage was perfectly set for a battle—but there was no battle.

It is hard to divine the reason for this sudden cooling off of Bragg's avowed combativeness. His original plans were essentially offensive. His communications while he was at Chattanooga and after he started on the march breathed a fiercely belligerent spirit. "By rapid movements and vigorous blows we may beat him in detail, or by gaining his rear very much increase his demoralization and break him up," he had said. But now he had gained Buell's rear, and he took no steps to " break him up."

There was nothing the matter with Bragg's plan of campaign. It was well conceived, and well carried out—up to the critical point of actual combat. From this he seemed to shrink. He stated that his concentration at Glasgow was for the purpose of "striking a blow at Bowling Green," but he struck no blow at Bowling Green. Even when Buell pushed out his way with a challenging gesture he did not take the dare. Granting that circumstances might have rendered it inexpedient to give battle there and then, one finds his continued timidity even after the capture of Munfordville hard to explain. It would be difficult to conceive of more favorable conditions. After an admirably devised and executed movement of more than 600 miles, he had placed his army exactly where he wanted it—squarely across the enemy's line of communication. His soldiers were inspired by the capture of Wilder's garrison and might well expect to find Buell's men correspondingly depressed. There was every sound reason why Bragg should fight Buell at once, and there is some evidence that he thought of it. But he did not fight. "Here," General Basil W. Duke says, "was the first exhibition of that vacillation, that fatal irresolution, which was to wither the bright hopes his promises and his previous action had aroused." Duke sadly speaks again of "the strange contrast exhibited by the nerve and purpose of his plan and the timidity and vacillation of his conduct."[20]

One excuse advanced for him is the disparity in strength. Bragg at this time had close to 30,000 men and Buell was supposed to have 38,000. But this was by no means an overwhelming difference. Confederate armies could rarely fight on a basis of superiority or even equality of numbers, and in this case Bragg's advantage of position would have offset his shortage. Furthermore, it was his own fault that there was any difference at all. Kirby Smith writes: "All my movements [after Bragg's arrival at Glasgow] were made under orders from General Bragg and in strict accordance with his instructions."[21] But Bragg did not instruct him to join up. Instead he ordered him to hold on at Lexington and watch the Federal General Morgan—an unprofitable occupation for a confident and enthusiastic force which could so easily have moved either to Glasgow or Munfordville, joined Bragg and helped him smash Buell.

In his official report Bragg lamely explained his unwillingness to fight.

"Reduced at the end of four days to three days' rations, and in a hostile country, utterly destitute of supplies, a serious engagement brought on anywhere in that direction could not fail (whatever its results) to materially cripple me. The loss of a battle would be eminently disastrous." This labored justification provides a good index to his character. It simply will not hold water; it is an excuse—a feeble excuse—and nothing else.

In the first place, three days' rations were enough to carry the army through any ordinary battle, leaving the question of further supplies to be considered after the battle was fought and won, or even lost. If he won, there were ample stores at Bowling Green; if he lost, it was not impossible to arrange for subsistence. Bragg had not considered the country "destitute of supplies" a few days before when, from Carthage, he wrote to Polk that although the greatest need of the army was food, "we shall be in a plentiful country at Glasgow and beyond."[22] This country was not hostile in the sense that the people were hostile; on the contrary, Southern sympathizers predominated. It was a rich country which had not been subjected to the ravages of the armies of either side. Even if it had been, supplies could have been obtained promptly from Kirby Smith —in fact, a supply train from Kirby Smith did reach Bragg on the nineteenth. Aside from all this, he must have known that an invading army such as his should expect to live largely off the country and more or less take its chances. He was faced with no emergency that an ordinarily prudent commander might not have foreseen.

The conclusion is inescapable that Bragg was simply unequal spiritually to the responsibility of precipitating a battle—the first battle of his independent command—and, as an afterthought, he invented the scarcity of supplies as a cloak for timidity.

In a negative way, General Bragg's failure to fight at Munfordville was one of the great crises of the whole war—probably its greatest moral crisis.

"It can be demonstrated, I think," says General Duke, "that upon no effort which the Confederacy made during its brief existence of constant struggle did more depend than on the success or failure of this well conceived but futile attempt to transfer the combat to fields where victories might be of some value and give hope of final triumph. Much has been said and written about the possibly different result of the war had an effort to improve the victory of the First Manassas been made by the Confederate commanders, had Albert Sidney Johnston lived to complete the first day's work of Shiloh, or if Lee had won Gettysburg. But the promise of a substantial and permanent benefit to the Southern cause which a successful consummation of this campaign in Kentucky offered was larger and more certain, I am persuaded, than on any of these occasions."[23]

Granting the importance of the campaign—a campaign involving more territory and more hazards to both armies than any other of the war—one would not overstate Bragg's failure here by calling it a major disaster of the conflict. He had skillfully and enterprisingly created the opportunity he sought for a damaging blow—and then he let the opportunity slip between his fingers. When a final appraisal of his generalship is made by history, his inadequacy in this crisis should weigh more heavily against him than some of his more conspicuous failures elsewhere.

The night of the seventeenth he called a council of his generals. At this conference it was proposed that they draw aside from Buell's front, double back quickly to Nashville, overpower its garrison and reoccupy that important point—important for sentimental and political as well as strategical reasons.[24] Bragg seemed to favor this and it was thought the next day that he would go ahead with it. But on the morning of the nineteenth he surprisingly announced his determination to march on to Bardstown without further contesting Buell's advance to Louisville. "This campaign must be won by marching, not fighting," he said to Colonel Urquhart—an aphorism of questionable soundness.

Wheeler's cavalry was left behind to delay Buell's passage of Green River, which it did effectively until the twenty-second. By that time Bragg was well along to Bardstown; and Buell, his way undisputed, marched happily on to Louisville, harassed but not seriously impeded by Wheeler. During this march Buell's right flank was, of course, dangerously exposed to attack, but Bragg made no effort to seize the occasion.

2. ON THE CORINTH FRONT

The success of Bragg's plans depended, to a great extent, on the co-operation of Van Dorn and Price in Mississippi, but, to his disappointment, their expected help had been totally lacking. When Bragg started for East Tennessee he had left behind him in Mississippi some 16,000 men at Vicksburg under Van Dorn[25] and about the same number under Price at Tupelo. Owing to the fatally complex system of organization, the two generals were independent of each other and, worse still, both were independent of Bragg. Soon afterward Van Dorn had so successfully defended Vicksburg as to insure at least a temporary cessation of the Federal attack there, and he was enabled to rejoin Price and resume command of the army which they had brought across the Mississippi a few months before.

By this time the big Federal force of Halleck had been pretty well scattered, but Van Dorn and Price were still faced with about 42,000 men under Grant. When Halleck went to Washington, he had lifted the ban from Grant and restored him to the command of his old troops, with headquarters at Corinth. Grant had established an attenuated line stretching across northern Mississippi and Western Tennessee. The left wing, in the neighborhood of Iuka and Corinth, was commanded by General W. S. Rosecrans; General Ord commanded the center; and General Sherman at Memphis commanded the right, the troops being dispersed in detachments all that way from Iuka to Memphis. Grant built fortifications around Corinth to protect it against a possible recapture and apprehensively prepared to defend himself if the Confederates left in Mississippi attacked him. He felt keenly his difficult position in a hostile country, and in his *Memoirs* describes this as, for him, "the most anxious period of the war."[26]

On August 11 Bragg had written to Van Dorn impressing on him the need for activity in Mississippi to help his own campaign, and the next day he wrote Price to the same effect. "If you hold them in check we are sure of success here," Bragg said confidently, pointing out that if the Federals in that quarter weakened themselves by sending reinforcements to Buell, Van Dorn might occupy West Tennessee and might even cross over onto Buell's rear. Before leaving Chattanooga, Bragg had telegraphed Price explaining his plans and concluding: "Sherman and Rosecrans we leave to you and Van Dorn, satisfied that you can dispose of them, and we shall confidently expect to meet you on the Ohio and there open the way to Missouri"[27]—a diplomatic hint that Price might realize his dream of going back to his home state.

Meanwhile Van Dorn, as visionary as he was courageous, had established himself at Holly Springs where he was hatching a grandiose scheme to move against Paducah or "wherever circumstances might dictate" in that locality. Price was honestly striving to make a move against Rosecrans at Iuka, as instructed by Bragg, and he called on Van Dorn for aid. But Van Dorn was too preoccupied with his own notion. He wanted Price to furnish him with men and guns. Price declined; Van Dorn appealed to President Davis for full control over Price; and Davis, apparently unfamiliar with Bragg's plans, or forgetting them, granted his request.

While all this dillydallying was going on, Rosecrans sent three divisions to Buell, remaining himself between Iuka and Corinth with two divisions amounting to 9,000 men. Price promptly moved in and occupied Iuka without a contest, capturing all its Federal stores. There he received instructions from Bragg to march on Nashville, where the garrison was supposed to be sufficiently reduced to justify an attack. In view of Van Dorn's plans, Price hesitated, and while he hesitated he received the orders placing him under Van Dorn's command. So the projected Nashville campaign was automatically abandoned.

On the afternoon of September 19 Price was attacked at Iuka by Rosecrans, the battle continuing until dark. Ord had been directed to advance as soon as he heard the sounds of battle at Iuka. But he did not move. He said that he did not hear this fighting. Neither did Grant. Price did not consider the outcome of the afternoon battle a defeat and was inclined to hold his ground and renew the engagement in the morning, but, heeding the counsel of his subordinate officers, he consented to withdraw during the night and march to join Van Dorn.

Grant meanwhile was planning to recapture Iuka—and probably to capture Price. General Ord with about 10,000 men was moved from Corinth to Burnsville, seven miles west of Iuka, and then marched to the north of Iuka where he occupied the road out of town. Rosecrans was to close in from the south and west, and Price would be trapped. Grant stayed at Burnsville to direct the battle by remote control.

This was just a few days before Bragg's arrival at Bardstown. When he got there, on September 28, he wired Van Dorn to "push your columns to our support." Nashville, he told him, was defended only by a weak garrison and Bowling Green only by a regiment. "Sweep them off and push up to the Ohio. Secure the heavy guns at these places and we will secure the Tennessee and Cumberland Rivers. All depends on rapid movements." His enthusiasm and hope were running high when he penned that message. The crisis was passed and almost forgotten two months later when Van Dorn returned the telegram with this endorsement: "The above dispatch was this day [November 28th] received and forwarded. I can not account for the delay in transmission."

He had been fully occupied, though not along the lines Bragg suggested. Joined by Price, after the latter's misadventure at Iuka, Van Dorn—whose projected attack on Paducah had been abandoned—now launched a movement he had been contemplating for some time—an attack on Corinth. He had been told that the defenses of Corinth to the northwest were the weakest, and he swung around to approach it from

Hd. 2d Army of Kentucky
Lexington, Ky. Sept. 18th 1862

General,

I have the honor to acknowledge this morning, the receipt of your communication of the 15th instant.

Gens. Smith's and Cleburne's Brigades will be at Shelbyville the 22d; they will there receive orders from you, and can effect a junction with your columns.

The enemy have been largely reinforced at Cincinnati especially by troops from Louisville — They have fortified Covington, but have taken no steps toward strengthening Louisville, — the Stores & Supplies, have been crossed to the Indiana Side, and everything indicates an intention to evacuate the latter place, on the approach of our troops.

I will withdraw the remainder of my command to Paris, Georgetown & Frankfort, it can then readily be concentrated in either direction.

Marshall should advance to Mount Sterling, but I fear he will not come. His position there is the more important, as my spies from Cumberland Gap, say every preparation was made to evacuate on the 16th; their movements indicate Manchester, Booneville and Mt. Sterling as their probable line of retreat. I shall be on the lookout for them.

Original letter from General Kirby Smith to General Bragg, regarding disposition of troops during invasion of Kentucky. (carried over to next page)

I do not anticipate any immediate advance from Covington, they will await the movements of Buell on the arrival of old troops from the Mississippi.

I have still some 10.000 Stand of Arms, the trophies of the Richmond battles.

The Kentuckians are slow and backward in rallying to our Standard — their hearts are evidently with us, but their blue-grass and fat cattle are against us — Several Regiments are in process of organization, and if we remain long enough, recruits will be found for all the disposable arms in our possession.

It is to be regretted that Breckenridge could not have moved into this portion of the State; his Regiments would have been filled up immediately, and his personal influence would have forwarded the organization of new levies.

Some steps should be taken towards the organization of a Provisional Government — Where is Gov. Hawes?

I am Sir Respectfully
Your obt Servt

E Kirby Smith
Maj. General

To
General
Braxton Bragg
Comdg Dept No 2.

"The Kentuckians are slow and backward in rallying to our standard — their hearts are evidently with us but their blue grass and fat cattle are against us."

that direction, with his men massed in the angle between the two intersecting railroads. He attacked with great vigor on the morning of October
4 and had no difficulty passing through the outer line of works, which
were weakly held, and even penetrated into the town itself. But the inner
works, which Grant recently had built, afforded the defending forces
under Rosecrans too strong a position to be forced. Van Dorn was compelled to withdraw.

Grant had ordered reinforcements to Corinth—a brigade under Mc-
Pherson from Jackson, Tennessee, and 4,000 under Ord and Hurlbut
from Bolivar. Neither detachment arrived in time to take part in the battle, although McPherson came just as it was over and gave Rosecrans the
moral effect of reinforcement. Ord's force encountered Van Dorn's
retreating army at the bridge crossing the Hatchie River ten miles out of
Corinth. There was a sharp but indecisive clash, the only effect of which
was to force Van Dorn to cross elsewhere. Rosecrans made no effort to
pursue him until the day after the battle—and then took the wrong
road, subjecting himself to considerable censure from Grant, who had
not been present. The Battle of Corinth was brief but intense and
bloody. The Federal loss was 355 killed; 1,841 wounded and 324 missing;
the Confederate, 473 killed; 1,997 wounded and 1,763 missing.

Press and public castigated General Van Dorn for the Corinth defeat.
It was said that his attack was ill-advised, improperly organized and poorly
conducted; that his soldiers, particularly his wounded, were neglected;
that he was drunk on duty; that he did not even have a proper map of the
country roundabout. He demanded and was given a court of inquiry, held
in Abbeville on November 15, 1862. He was unanimously cleared by the
court, which found that the charges against him "are not only not proved,
but they are disproved."

Shortly after, General Pemberton was transferred to the Department
of Mississippi and North Louisiana, and Van Dorn was made commander
of the cavalry division under Pemberton. His successful raid on Holly
Springs gave wide publicity to his prowess as a cavalry leader. As soon as
Grant, determined on his river campaign, abandoned his advance down
the line of the Mississippi Central, Van Dorn was ordered to transfer the
scene of his operation to Middle Tennessee south of Nashville. He
took command of the cavalry there, supporting General Bragg at
Tullahoma. He was a major general and he had serving under him the
brigades commanded by Bedford Forrest, W. H. Jackson and Frank C.
Armstrong. His headquarters were at Spring Hill, about thirty-five miles
south of Nashville. Here he directed a number of slashing cavalry raids

on the garrisons in the neighborhood, and here, on May 7, 1863, he met his end—not on the battlefield but at the hands of a private citizen.[28]

3. PERRYVILLE

While Van Dorn and Price were sparring with Grant in Mississippi, the opposing armies of Bragg and Buell were approaching the climax in Kentucky. Buell had his entire force in Louisville by September 27. He reached there in time to avert an incipient panic growing out of the threatening presence of Bragg's army at near-by Bardstown. Louisville was defended by an aggregation of untrained recruits, commanded by General Nelson. So indefensible was it considered that Buell telegraphed Nelson not to attempt to hold it if Bragg attacked. But Bragg obliged them by refraining, and Nelson sent an ecstatic telegram to General H. G. Wright at Cincinnati: "Louisville is safe. . . . God and Liberty!"[29]

Kentucky was within the military jurisdiction of General Wright who, from his headquarters at Cincinnati or in the field, commanded the Department of the Ohio. When Buell got to Louisville he found Wright in active charge of the assembled troops. A stickler for military etiquette, Buell submitted the question of precedence to Halleck, who immediately issued an order placing under his command all the troops in that vicinity. But he was not popular with the Washington bigwigs, and on September 29 he was relieved of his command by President Lincoln, and Thomas ordered to take his place. Thomas declined the proffered advancement on the score that Buell had just perfected all his arrangements to move immediately against the enemy and that he was not familiar enough with these plans to undertake the campaign. At his request the order was revoked, Buell was restored, and Thomas was named second in command.

After merging his army with the half-raw force at Louisville, Buell proceeded with preparations for aggressive action. On October 1 he moved out of Louisville to offer Bragg battle at Bardstown. His army was organized into three corps, commanded respectively by McCook on the left, Crittenden in the center and Gilbert on the right. His plan of campaign against Bragg, as he explains it, was "to force the enemy's left back and compel him to concentrate as far as possible from any convenient line of retreat, while at the same time making a strong demonstration against his right, so as to mislead him as to the real point of attack and prevent him from moving upon my left flank and rear."[30] With that object, General Sill, commanding a division in McCook's corps, was ordered to march boldly toward Frankfort through Shelbyville, followed temporarily by the division of raw troops under Dumont which had been organized as a guard for Louisville. McCook with his two remaining divisions moved upon Taylorsville, where he halted the second night in a position that pointed to either flank. The other two corps moved respectively through Shepherdsville and Mount Washington to converge upon Bardstown, and halted the second night at Salt River.

General Bragg was not at Bardstown when Buell started. He had other things on his mind. On the twenty-eighth he had gone to Lexington, and on October 2 he ordered Kirby Smith to concentrate his army at Frankfort, where it was planned to stage elaborate ceremonies inaugurating Richard Hawes as Provisional Governor of the state under the Confederate government. Johnson, who had been elected governor when the provisional government was set up at Russellville in 1861, had been killed at Shiloh, and Hawes, who had been chosen lieutenant governor, succeeded him. He had joined the army in Kentucky, and much political importance was attached to his actual seating in the Governor's chair in the capitol. Kentucky had been formally and officially accepted as one of the Confederate States of America; it had representatives in the Confederate Congress, and it had a star in the Confederate flag. Its theoretical and technical allegiance to the Confederacy was, however, but a mockery so long as a state government of Northern sympathies occupied Frankfort. If Hawes could set up a *de facto* government of Confederate allegiance it would change the whole political picture. Granting its influence on public opinion, one may still think that Bragg gave this matter too much attention, to the point of preoccupation, at a time when his army was face to face with the enemy and he should have been on hand.

Apparently he was carried away with the political implications of his presence in Kentucky. To supplement the sword with the pen, he sent to Mobile for John Forsyth, the famous newspaper editor. Forsyth joined the army in Kentucky and wrote a resounding proclamation addressed "To the People of the Northwest," which Bragg published in his own name at Bardstown on September 26.[31] In it he sought to impress on the Northwesterners that there was a bond of political and economic sympathy between them and the South. "It is from the meddlesome, grasping and fanatical disposition of the East," he told them, "which has imposed upon you and us alike those protective tariff, internal improvement and fishery bounty laws, whereby we have been taxed for their aggrandizement, that both upper and lower [Mississippi] Valley people should free themselves." Through this ghost-writer Bragg urged the West to consider the possibility of an alliance with the South as the only possible escape from the burden of the enormous war debt that was being built up and which they, as the only producers left in the Union, would have to pay. Forsyth also penned, in Bragg's name, an eloquent plea to the people of Kentucky to ally themselves with the Confederacy. But for all the results attained by his literary efforts, he might as well have stayed in Mobile.

General Buckner on September 24 issued an individual, personal proclamation "To the Freemen of Kentucky," calling their attention to the fact that the armies of Kirby Smith and Bragg were in Kentucky, "come to relieve you of the tyranny with which the North has so long oppressed you." Saying, "We have arms for all who will join us," he urged every Kentuckian to "utter a shout of defiance against the Northern tyranny and proclaim that, under the guidance of Heaven, Kentucky shall prove worthy of her ancient fame."[32] But the people of Kentucky were unmoved by his stirring appeals also and showed a distressing apathy to the political tenets of the occupant of the Governor's office at Frankfort.

Kirby Smith says he begged Bragg to give up the inauguration and concentrate the two armies at once so that they could fall on Buell while he was marching in divided columns. According to him, Buckner added his voice to this prayer. "For God's sake, General, let us fight Buell here."[33] Bragg retorted that his army could handle Buell alone, and went on his way. The inaugural ceremonies were broken up, however, by the approach of Sill's threatening column. Hawes, interrupted in the midst of his address by the sound of Federal shells bursting in the city, hustled back to the army along with Bragg and the other generals who were taking part in the proceedings. Kentucky's experience as a political unit of the Confederate States was spirited but brief.

Buell's avowed purpose to mislead his antagonist by the feint on the right was eminently successful. Bragg gullibly accepted it at full face value, and thought Buell's whole army was about to fall on Kirby Smith at Frankfort. When he had gone off to Frankfort on his political errand, he had left the army at Bardstown in Polk's charge with instructions, if attacked in force, to fall back in the direction of Bryantsville, where he had piled up the supplies captured in Kentucky and which he was using as a temporary base. On September 30 he wrote Polk a letter, which he got the next day, changing the instructions and ordering him to advance toward Louisville and occupy Taylorsville, Shepherdsville, Mount Washington and Elizabethtown.[34] Before Polk could start, however, his cavalry brought him word that Buell was moving out from Louisville. This Polk reported to Bragg, commenting pointedly: "It seems to me we are too much scattered."[35]

On October 2 Bragg again revised his directions to Polk, based on the theory that the main Federal objective was Frankfort. Now he ordered him to move on Frankfort by way of Bloomfield to strike Buell's flank and rear while Kirby Smith attacked in front.[36] The theory was entirely erroneous.[37] Polk, fortunately for the safety of the army, took the liberty of disobeying orders. He felt himself pressed so closely on his own front that it was out of the question for him to do anything except fall back slowly before the superior force, in line with the original instructions. He called a council of his wing and division commanders, who were unanimous in supporting his view, and he notified Bragg respectfully that compliance was "not only eminently inexpedient but impracticable."[38]

On October 3 Bragg wrote Polk that the movement on Frankfort was evidently a feint, and directed him to "act accordingly."[39] But he showed continued ignorance of the enemy's whereabouts by telling him to "place one flank at Taylorsville" which was already within Buell's lines. On the fourth Bragg ordered Polk to concentrate "in front of Harrodsburg."[40] He intended to give battle to Buell "just as soon as we can concentrate. We can and must defeat them." But he was still apparently under the impression that the main attack was directed at Frankfort, and further weakened Polk by ordering him to send Withers' division from his own corps to Kirby Smith's support. On the seventh, realizing that the opposing armies were on the point of contact, he issued a "Confidential Circular"[41] to his generals outlining plans in preparation for an engagement which he evidently thought would take place somewhere between Frankfort and Harrodsburg, probably at Versailles. This order[42] called for the following disposition of the troops:

"Cheatham's division will move forward tonight to Withers' position, and both divisions of the right wing [Withers' and Cheatham's] will move tomorrow to Lawrenceburg, thence to Versailles, and to follow General E. Kirby Smith's command.

"General E. Kirby Smith's command will move forward tomorrow to Versailles, throwing a division toward Frankfort. Allston's Cavalry, now at Salvisa, will cover Cheatham's movement, reporting to Major General Cheatham.

"Major General Hardee, commanding left wing, Army of Mississippi, will follow these movements as circumstances allow, notifying these headquarters of his move. Colonel Wade's infantry will join the guard at the

depot at Bryantsville, reporting to the commanding officer there, and his
cavalry will report to Colonel Wheeler, commanding cavalry of Hardee's
wing."

There it was, all nicely worked out on paper. Everybody was told just
exactly what to do. But battles have a disconcerting way of not working
out according to the commanding general's blueprint. While Bragg was
so carefully laying his plans for an engagement in the neighborhood of
Versailles, the Fates were making other arrangements. He was quite
right in thinking a battle imminent; he merely misjudged the location by
about twenty miles.

Hardee with his corps had reached the inconspicuous village of Perryville, ten miles from Harrodsburg, by the evening of the seventh, closely
followed by Gilbert's corps of the Federal army, which was now in the
center of Buell's advance. Throughout the day Gilbert's progress had
been stubbornly contested by Wheeler's cavalry, acting as Hardee's rear
guard. By the time Gilbert arrived in sight of Perryville he found Hardee
strongly fixed on a ridge beyond Doctor's Creek, a tributary of Chaplin's
Fork of Salt River. This section of Kentucky had been afflicted by a
severe drought for several weeks and most of the springs and creeks were
dry, but in the bed of Doctor's Creek were still standing some precious
pools of water, sorely needed by Gilbert's parched men and horses. He
launched out vigorously to seize those water pools. The fight went on far
into the night by the light of a full moon. The Confederates held on to
Doctor's Creek, and Gilbert's tired and thirsty men were forced to make
a dry camp.

Buell was now concentrating his whole army in front of Perryville.
Although Hardee did not have any accurate idea of the magnitude of the
force confronting him, he sensed that it was more than he could handle
with his single corps and appealed to Bragg for reinforcements. In response, Bragg late in the afternoon of the seventh directed Polk to divide
his corps and move with Cheatham's division to Hardee's relief, while
Withers' division continued on its way to Versailles. Bragg instructed
Polk to "give the enemy battle immediately" at Perryville, concluding
airily: "Rout him and then move to our support at Versailles"[43]—still
under the delusion that the main action would be at or near Versailles.

Bragg's misguided dissipation of the Confederate forces was so manifestly unwise and hazardous that Hardee, a seasoned and expert tactician,
was deeply disturbed, so disturbed that he adopted the unusual pro-

cedure of addressing, on the night of the seventh, a friendly, informal but pointed protest to his superior officer.

"Permit me, from the friendly relations so long existing between us, to write you plainly. Don't scatter your forces. There is one rule in our profession that should never be forgotten—it is to throw the masses of your troops on the fractions of the enemy. The movement last proposed will divide your army and each may be defeated, whereas by keeping them united success is certain. If it be your policy to strike the enemy at Versailles, take your whole force with you and make the blow effective. If, on the contrary, you should decide to strike the army in front of me first, let that be done with a force which will make success certain. Strike with your whole strength; first to the right, then to the left. I could not sleep quietly to-night without giving expression to these views." He added a postscript: "If you wish my opinion, it is that in view of the position of your depots, you ought to strike this force first."[44]

Hardee, his soldierly sense of duty satisfied, dispatched his admonitory letter to Bragg and turned in for the night. There is nothing in the record to indicate that Bragg had any inclination to heed his subordinate's lesson in elementary tactics, but, even if he had, he did not get the chance. While his men were marching in scattered detachments hither and yon— some under Hardee, some under Polk, some under Withers, some under Kirby Smith—a battle was just about to be forced upon him in a quarter where he least expected it. As Basil Duke caustically says, he "kept more than two-thirds of the force under his command idly maneuvering in a quarter where nothing could possibly be accomplished, and permitted less than twenty thousand men to become engaged upon a field where more than forty-five thousand could have been hurled upon them."[45]

Seldom in the annals of warfare have the commanders of two contending armies been so completely befuddled as to the location and plans of the other. Buell had been informed that Bragg's main force was at Perryville, and he was bending every energy to gather his full strength there. On the other hand, Bragg, up to the very last minute, was convinced that Sill's column was Buell's main army, marching to strike him through Frankfort, and he was intent on massing eventually in that quarter to meet the suppositious threat. The result was that he left Polk with 16,000 men to fight 58,000,[46] while he took 36,000 to meet Sill's 12,000.

During the night of the seventh the main body of Buell's army was closing in on Perryville. Gilbert in the center was already in position along the Springfield pike, only a few miles out from town; McCook was coming up on the left wing, and Crittenden was approaching on the right. Thomas, second in command of the entire army, accompanied Crittenden and was temporarily in charge of his corps. Gilbert was farther advanced by several miles than McCook and Thomas, and these two commanders were ordered to move up at 3 A.M. on the morning of the eighth until they were in line with him, and to report to Buell as soon as they were in position. Buell expected this alignment to be accomplished by 7 A.M. He planned to order an attack immediately thereafter.

Polk, now in command of the Confederate force at Perryville, had taken a good position on a ridge along the east side of Chaplin Fork, slightly in advance of the town, with his three divisions arrayed from right to left under Buckner, Patton Anderson and Cheatham, respectively. The Confederate left, resting on the town, did not extend beyond the Federal center, and was dangerously open to a flank movement if the Federal right should operate with any enterprise.

Across Chaplin's Fork from Polk's position was another range of hills. Beyond them was Doctor's Creek, which flowed into Chaplin's Fork two miles below town. It was on the high ground on both sides of Doctor's Creek that the battle was fought.[47]

Buell's arrangements did not work as smoothly as he had thought for. Neither Thomas nor McCook reached the field at anything like the time specified. Thomas, delayed during the night by a detour while he looked for a camping ground supplied with water, did not get to the position assigned him until about 11 A.M. on the eighth. Even then, he was so faultily aligned, and so harassed by Wheeler's cavalry, that only a small part of his force got into action.[48] McCook's corps did not arrive until nearly noon, when they were placed on Gilbert's left, his line formed along the crest of the hills to the west of Doctor's Creek. His right was separated from Gilbert's left by a ravine through which the creek ran, the interval between the two corps being nearly half a mile.

Early in the morning, before daybreak, a brigade of Gilbert's corps had made a spirited sortie that resulted in the capture of the precious pools of water in Doctor's Creek for which they had battled so furiously and unsuccessfully the night before. The Confederates made a half-hearted and futile attempt to recover possession of the creek bed but showed no signs of attempting a general advance. The early morning hours passed in some skirmishing along the center and a listless exchange of artillery fire—a form of noisy but ineffective gunnery exercise which was known to the soldiers as "shelling the woods."

Polk, kept informed of the enemy's movements by the alert Wheeler, was beginning to realize what a large army was in process of gathering before him. He had his explicit orders to "give battle immediately," and Wheeler got the impression that he meant to attack at daylight—but he did not. On the contrary, he called a council of his general officers about daybreak at which it was decided, he says in his official report, "to adopt the 'defensive-offensive'; to await the movements of the enemy and to be guided by events as they were developed." Polk wrote afterward:

"I did not regard the letter of instructions as a peremptory order to attack at all hazards, but that . . . I should carry the instructions into execution as judiciously and promptly as a willing mind and sound discretion would allow."[49]

Meanwhile Bragg had changed his mind again. He had come to the belated conclusion that perhaps there was more of a Federal force at Perryville than he had suspected. He waited at Harrodsburg, expecting to hear the sounds of battle there early in the morning of the eighth, but Polk's only activity then was to send Wheeler out skirmishing briskly on his left flank, while Liddell's brigade was thrown forward in the center to occupy and check Gilbert's aggressive advance brigade. The sound of the skirmish firing and the desultory "shelling the woods" for some reason was not heard by Bragg. If it had been, it would have been easily distinguished by his practiced ear from the steady roar of a real engagement. So at length, hearing nothing, Bragg made up his mind to go to Perryville in person. He arrived about 10 A.M. to find Polk had been reconnoitering the high ground between Chaplin's Fork and Doctor's Creek and was just about to advance to occupy it. This he approved. Polk had observed signs of activity on the Federal left, and to strengthen against possible pressure from that side he switched Cheatham from his left to his right. Here Cheatham's brigades were massed under cover of the hills overlooking the confluence of the two streams, the new Confederate right overlapping the Federal left and extended farther by Wharton's cavalry.

About one o'clock the whole Confederate force moved forward in general attack, the first shock falling on McCook's corps on the Federal left. It was Bragg's good fortune that this assault came at the most inopportune time for the Federal left wing. McCook, after placing his corps in position a few hours earlier, had gone to the rear. In his absence an overzealous subordinate, General Rousseau, lured by the much-desired water supply in Chaplin Fork, decided to take the creek bed. He was in the very act of forming four of his brigades for this purpose when the Confederate attack burst upon them, and the whole corps was quickly thrown into confusion. The deploying brigades, caught unawares, had difficulty in re-forming for defense. Another of the divisions, composed of raw recruits, dissolved quickly and fled. By the time McCook himself had been notified and reached the front he found his command in a state bordering on demoralization.

Those who stood their ground fought ferociously, and some of the most desperate hand-to-hand fighting of the whole war took place on this front.[50] But the Federals were driven back steadily, though slowly, for a distance of a mile or more. The Confederate infantry fire and bayonet charges were effectively supported by the skillful marksmanship of the artillerists who blasted the enemy out of successive places of refuge behind stone walls and fences as they retired. McCook appealed to Sheridan for assistance, but Sheridan had his own hands full and was unable to help. Most of Hardee's army had closed in on McCook's exposed right flank, taking advantage of the gap between him and Gilbert, but Patton Anderson with two brigades moved directly on Sheridan's division in the center of Gilbert's corps and occupied him so vigorously that he was completely deceived as to the force in front of him and did not venture to assume the offensive, as he might well have done. Late in the afternoon Mitchell's division of Gilbert's corps moved up and outflanked Anderson, driving him back on the town. But by this time the battle was over.

Owing to some unusual atmospheric and topographical conditions, the sound of this battle did not carry any great distance. As we have seen, Bragg at Harrodsburg had heard nothing of the morning firing, and Buell at his headquarters a few miles in the rear of his front lines[51] did not detect the furious musketry fire and sharp cannonading throughout the early afternoon. It was not until four o'clock that the receding tide of battle came close enough for him to hear the steady roar of the artillery that notified him of the serious nature of the engagement. "That is something more than 'shelling the woods'; it sounds like a fight," he exclaimed to General Gilbert, who was then at his headquarters, and he hastily sent Gilbert to find out what was going on. Gilbert soon met one of McCook's staff bearing a belated report of his desperate plight and appealing for aid. This was the first intimation Buell had that his army was fighting a battle in his immediate front. One of Gilbert's brigades under Colonel Gooding was finally sent to McCook's rescue, but it too was driven back and Gooding himself was captured.[52]

At the close of day there was no doubt in anybody's mind about the outcome of the immediate engagement. It was a complete victory for the Confederates.[53] They had had everything their way: the battlefield was in their possession; the Federals had been driven back a mile or more, broken and disorganized. Two Union generals—James S. Jackson and William R. Terrill—had been killed, and a large number of officers had been wounded. The Confederates had lost none of their general officers, but one of them—General Polk himself—had had a very narrow escape.

On the Federal left the battle had been savagely contested, with close hand-to-hand fighting clear to nightfall. Late in the evening Polk almost stumbled into a tragic accident like Zollicoffer's at Fishing Creek. The Bishop-General told the story to Colonel Freemantle of the Coldstream Guards.

"It was almost dark when Liddell's brigade came into action. Shortly after its arrival I observed a body of men, whom I believed to be Confederates, standing at an angle to this brigade, and firing obliquely at the newly arrived troops. I said, 'Dear me, this is very sad and must be stopped'; so I turned around, but could find none of my young men, who were absent on different messages; so I determined to ride myself and settle the matter. Having cantered up to the colonel of the regiment which was firing, I asked him in angry tones what he meant by shooting his own friends, and I desired him to cease doing so at once. He answered with surprise, 'I don't think there can be any mistake about it; I am sure they are the enemy.' 'Enemy!' I said; 'Why I have only just left them myself. Cease firing, sir; what is your name, sir?' 'My name is Colonel Blank, of the . . . Indiana; and, pray sir, who are you?' Then for the first time I saw, to my astonishment, that he was a Yankee and that I was in rear of a regiment of Yankees. Well, I saw there was no hope but to brazen it out; my dark blouse and the increasing obscurity befriended me, so I approached quite close to him and shook my fist in his face, saying, 'I'll soon show you who I am, sir; cease firing, sir, at once.' I then turned my horse and cantered slowly down the line, shouting in an authoritative manner to the Yankees to cease firing; and at the same time I experienced a disagreeable sensation, like screwing up my back, and calculating how many bullets would be between my shoulders every moment. I was afraid to increase my pace until I got to a small copse, when I put the spurs in and galloped back to my men."[54]

The battle had been viciously fierce. The Federal loss was 845 killed; 2,851 wounded; 515 captured or missing. The Confederates lost 510 killed; 2,635 wounded; 251 missing. General Buell predicted that the battle would "stand conspicuous for its severity in the history of the rebellion." General Bragg said in his official report that "for the time engaged, it was the severest and most desperately contested engagement within my knowledge." In this report, written two days after the battle, Bragg generously gave to Generals Polk, Hardee, Cheatham, Buckner and Anderson credit for "the brilliant achievement·on this memorable field. Nobler troops were never more gallantly led." In a subsequent report, written May 20, 1863, he attempted to saddle the onus for the failure of the Kentucky campaign onto Polk, and even sought to have him court-martialed, but the Richmond government suppressed the report and inferentially absolved Polk. The government seemingly agreed with Hardee, who wrote Polk: "If you choose to rip up the Kentucky campaign, you can tear Bragg into tatters."[55]

Encouraged by their decisive victory, the soldiers expected to renew the fighting the next morning, confident of continuing to drive Buell's forces before them and wanting no more of those fruitless successes that had become distressingly frequent. But Bragg decided otherwise. He got it through his head at last that Buell's main force was confronting him here, and he ordered a prompt junction with Kirby Smith at Harrodsburg. At midnight the troops were told to go back to their position of the preceding morning, and early on the ninth they started toward Harrodsburg. Bragg went ahead to hurry up the movement of Kirby Smith, leaving Polk in command. Polk stopped and formed a line of battle on the Harrodsburg road about eight miles from Perryville to await Buell's advance—if Buell decided to advance—and posted his cavalry in Perryville and on the surrounding roads to watch the enemy's movements. Buell's pickets reconnoitered cautiously the next morning. About ten o'clock General Joe Wheeler, watching on the edge of Perryville, saw a blue skirmish line inching forward. But it did not venture beyond the town. The Confederate army no longer stood before Buell, and he seemed for the time content to have things so.

Polk, as ordered by Bragg, continued his march to Harrodsburg,[56] where he finally made the belated conjunction with Kirby Smith. Here at last, on October 10, Bragg was able to present a battle front made up of his greatest available force. Buell was not at all sure of the total strength of the Confederates. He waited at Perryville until he was joined by Sill's division, and then went on toward Harrodsburg.

On the night of October 11 the two armies faced each other in battle array on the outskirts of that town, and in both armies everyone considered it certain that the decisive conflict for the control of Kentucky would be fought the next day. Kirby Smith, as soon as he joined Bragg, urged that with their combined commands they drive at the enemy. "For

God's sake, General, let us fight Buell here," he quotes himself as saying.

Bragg replied, "I will do it, sir."[57]

But again Bragg's resolution failed him. Again he did not fight—and there are many who believe that here again he lost a great opportunity.

"Had battle been joined at Harrodsburg," says General Basil W. Duke, "it would have been the only great field of the war—east or west—on which the Confederate forces were numerically the stronger; and every other conceivable factor was in their favor. Never was the morale of an army better than that of General Bragg's on the eve of that anticipated conflict. The men seemed to realize what was at stake and to fear nothing but retreat, which should carry back war and invasion to their homes and people. . . . General Bragg ought to have fought then and there, and must have won. But the gloomy and hostile destiny which seemed to pursue the Confederacy, and became manifest whenever victory was about to visit her banners . . . smote our commander at Harrodsburg with a consternation which no man in his ardent and undaunted ranks shared then or can understand now."[58]

Nor is this a mere might-have-been growing out of the rancor of final defeat. A similar view is expressed by General C. C. Gilbert, who commanded the Third Corps of Buell's army.

"It was a piece of very good fortune for the Union side that the Confederates did not return to renew the battle, for they would have had such an advantage in numbers and in the character of their troops that the Army of the Ohio would have been placed in great peril."

After explaining that McCook's raw brigades had been knocked out and that Crittenden's and his own corps together mustered only about 36,000 men after the fighting, Gilbert continues:

"In not returning to Perryville and resuming the battle, he [Bragg] lost for the Confederacy perhaps the only opportunity it ever had of fighting a great battle with a decisive preponderance in numbers and the character of its troops."[59]

Bragg, to quote another critic, "could not make up his mind to assume the offensive, evincing in fact a perplexity and vacillation which had now become simply appalling to Smith, to Hardee and to Polk."[60] After much cogitation and deliberation he decided to fall back to Bryantsville, and the movement began on the night of the tenth. The next morning when Buell saw that Bragg was gone from his front he found it difficult to believe that Bragg was actually retreating, considering it more likely that he was merely maneuvering for a more favorable position in which to fight the battle which Buell confidently expected would be fought. He therefore deployed his troops cautiously, following Bragg warily and watching for signs of his making a stand. Bragg did make a halt after crossing Dick's River, in the neighborhood of Camp Dick Robinson, but his position here was so strong that Buell did not dare precipitate an engagement. Bragg stood on the defensive for a day; then, when Buell moved to turn his position, he apparently gave up all idea of making any stand in Kentucky. On October 13 he began his active withdrawal from the state.

In a letter to his wife, Bragg attributes his retreat principally to the fact that the Kentuckians had shown too little inclination to enlist under his standard.

"Why," he asked, "should I stay with my handful of brave Southern men to fight for cowards who skulked about in the dark to say to us 'We are with you. Only whip these fellows out of our country and let us see you can protect us, and we will join you'? . . . In the midst of this comes the news of Van Dorn's defeat in Mississippi. With the whole Southwest thus in the enemy's possession, my crime would have been unpardonable had I kept my noble little army to be ice-bound in a Northern clime, without tents or shoes, and obliged to forage daily for bread, etc."[61]

The retreat from Kentucky was a dismal but picturesque affair. A brigade of cavalry led the way, followed by great herds of beef cattle, sheep and hogs, driven along the road by shouting cowboys and herders recruited from the ranks of the Texas cavalry regiments. There was a long caravan of refugees and their families with carriages, stagecoaches, omnibuses and farm wagons piled with household furniture strung out down the road for miles. Trains of army wagons, heavily loaded down with captured provisions, firearms, ammunition and merchandise, creaked along. Conspicuous among them were the 4,000 shiny new wagons, with the U. S. brands on their canvas, which Kirby Smith had captured from Nelson.

Following the trains came the army—the corps of Polk and Hardee, followed by Kirby Smith's. Straining horses and groaning oxen dragged captured cannon over the rough, flinty highways. The soldiers trudged through the dust, inexpressibly dispirited by this sad anticlimax to their invasion. Some of the Kentucky troops were shedding tears, open and unashamed, as they turned their backs on home. But nearly every man was loaded down with his share of the spoils of war—a bolt of goods or a sack of meal or a succulent Kentucky ham carried aloft on his bayoneted rifle.

All the while Wheeler's cavalry fanned out in a protective cloud along the caravan's flanks and rear. Again and again the Federals snapped at their heels. Again and again the gallant horsemen drove them off. They fought no less than twenty-six separate engagements in five days and nights. But at last the hacking attacks abated, and the retreating army settled down to its march with no greater obstacles than rocky roads (mighty hard on barefoot soldiers whose shoes had been marched into shreds), deep fords and steep mountain passes.

The route was by way of Crab Orchard, London and Barboursville to Cumberland Gap, then on to Morristown and Knoxville in East Tennessee. Buell kept up the semblance of a pursuit until they reached London, but there abandoned the chase and took steps to transfer his army back to Nashville in anticipation of Bragg's ultimate move against that city.

When the Confederates got back to East Tennessee, General Kirby Smith, now once more in his own department, resumed command of his force—glad to be released from subordination to Bragg, whose ability he had come to regard very lightly. Bragg marched his men back to Knoxville, and here on October 23 he received a message calling him to Richmond to make an oral report of the Kentucky expedition to President Davis. He put the army under the command of General Polk, with orders to take it by rail to Chattanooga and then on to Murfreesboro, which Polk did.

The small force—mostly cavalry—which had been left at Murfreesboro to menace Nashville while Bragg marched into Kentucky had been under the command of Forrest, but Forrest had recently been joined by Breckinridge with his 6,000 men, and Breckinridge was now in general charge. While he was collecting his forces at Knoxville early in October a group of Confederate Congressmen had petitioned President Davis to send him directly from Knoxville to capture Nashville. This suggestion was disregarded and he was ordered to join Bragg.[62] Bragg had already started his retreat when he heard of it. He promptly told Breckinridge[63] to return to Knoxville and then go on to Murfreesboro, with the idea of taking steps "for the defense of Middle Tennessee or an attack on Nashville." Breckinridge got to Murfreesboro on October 28, where he was joined in a short while by Bragg's army under Polk.

Bragg's men had marched a thousand miles, had fought a bloody battle, and were back about where they had started two months before. The campaign had extended over more territory than any other of the war, but the results were just exactly nothing—except that the tarnish on Bragg's prestige was a little more pronounced.

CHAPTER XI

MURFREESBORO

THE ostensible purpose of Bragg's visit to Richmond after the Kentucky campaign was to report to President Davis and also to make plans for his army. As subsequent events indicated, however, he improved this opportunity to rid himself of all blame for the misadventure by fastening it to General Polk. Davis generally accepted at face value anything Bragg told him, but Polk too was a favorite of his, and he was not willing to condemn him without hearing his side. So Polk also was summoned to Richmond, and he obeyed with alacrity.

Subjected to something very like a cross-examination, he gave blunt answers to his old schoolmate's blunt questions. He generously accorded Bragg all proper credit for skill as organizer and disciplinarian, but in his candid opinion Bragg was "wanting in the higher elements of generalship."[1] Polk said flatly that the Kentucky campaign had been a failure, that both Kirby Smith and Hardee thought so, that Bragg had lost the confidence of his generals. In response to an inquiry of the President, he suggested that the command be given to Joseph E. Johnston if Bragg were displaced. This was not particularly diplomatic. If Bragg were a special pet of Davis', Johnston was already becoming the object of his festering antipathy. Making complimentary remarks about Joe Johnston was no way to ingratiate oneself with Jefferson Davis.

That Bragg's criticism had not undermined Polk in the President's esteem was demonstrated by his promotion to lieutenant general—the highest rank in the Confederate Army short of full general. Similar promotions were given Hardee and Kirby Smith. Kirby Smith, upon his return to Tennessee, had asked President Davis to relieve him of any further service in which he would be subject to Bragg's orders,[2] but Davis appealed to his patriotism and urged him to retain his command. It was obvious, however, that he was unhappy in his job. So in January 1863 he was called to Richmond to assist in the reorganization of the Confederate armies, and in February was designated to command the department west of the Mississippi. This transfer to the remote fastnesses of the Trans-Mississippi he did not welcome. "Am I then to be sent into exile?"[3] he lamented to Davis. Well, at any rate, the new assignment would remove him from the range of Bragg's authority! Like a good soldier he obeyed orders and left at once for Alexandria, Louisiana, where he relieved the bumbling and insubordinate General Theophilus H. Holmes.

General Buell's conduct of the Kentucky campaign had been unsatisfactory to the Federal authorities; the last gun at Perryville had hardly been fired before he was being bombarded with inquiries and criticisms from Washington. He had the misfortune to be at loggerheads with Andrew Johnson and with Abraham Lincoln too. It was little surprise to him when, as he was moving his army back to Nashville, he received, on October 30, an order from Washington to turn his command over to General W. S. Rosecrans.

For a while a similar fate seemed about to overtake Bragg, but President Davis was stubbornly reluctant to believe him as incompetent as his many critics claimed. Davis adopted the halfway remedial measure of appointing General Joseph E. Johnston department commander, with supervision over the commands of Bragg and Kirby Smith, and also over General Pemberton in Mississippi.

Joseph Eggleston Johnston was a Virginian, at this time fifty-five years old—the same age as Robert E. Lee, whose friend and classmate he had been at West Point. Another schoolmate had been Jefferson Davis—but not a particularly friendly one. In fact, it was said that during their Academy days they had had a fist fight over a girl's affections, and some trace their enmity to this early beginning. After leaving West Point Johnston had served with distinction in the Indian wars and the Mexican War and in 1860 had risen to quartermaster general of the United States Army, with the rank of brigadier. He resigned when Virginia seceded, and when her troops were turned over to the Confederacy he was made a full general in the Confederate Army. In the rating of the generals, however, he was ranked by Samuel Cooper, Albert Sidney Johnston and Robert E. Lee. He did not like that at all. It left a bad taste in his mouth for the duration of the war. He shared with Beauregard the leadership of the victorious forces at First Manassas in July 1861, but it was nearly a year later before his troops again engaged in a battle—at Seven Pines in the very suburbs of Richmond. Here he was seriously wounded and superseded by Lee, and when he recovered found himself without a command. Davis, despite his personal dislike, knew that he was too valuable a man to be standing idle in Richmond. He probably felt that he was making a judicious use of his available personnel when he appointed Joe Johnston to super-command in the West.

Bragg, having established his headquarters at Murfreesboro upon his return from Richmond, announced his determination to "occupy Middle Tennessee in force, and if possible to hold for the coming winter the country between the Cumberland and Tennessee Rivers."[4] Johnston made his temporary headquarters at Chattanooga, but went to Murfreesboro on November 26 to spend several days inspecting the army of about 40,000 which Bragg had assembled and which Johnston now officially called the Army of Tennessee—the name which it was to make lustrous.

He had hardly got back to Chattanooga before he was in a clash with Davis—his first, but not his last, in his new position. A telegram from General Cooper pointed out the necessity for strengthening Pemberton in Mississippi and quoted the President as wishing Johnston to send "a sufficient force from General Bragg's command" to his relief. Johnston was not unaware of Pemberton's need; he had already twice suggested that he be reinforced by General Holmes' army from Arkansas. Now he repeated this proposal; Bragg could not send reinforcements to Mississippi "without exposing himself to inevitable defeat."[5]

Davis was not pleased. On December 10, accompanied by his aide, General G. W. C. Lee (Robert E. Lee's son), he showed up in Murfreesboro to size up General Bragg's army for himself. After three days there, he went on to Chattanooga and instructed Johnston to order Bragg to send General C. L. Stevenson with his division of 10,000 men to help Pemberton out. This Johnston obediently but reluctantly did. So Bragg was shorn of the balance of strength he was to need so sorely in his struggle with Rosecrans.

Bragg strenuously opposed this weakening of his army. He told Davis that the Federals' threatened advance into Mississippi could be broken up by Forrest's raids on Grant's rear in Tennessee before Stevenson could meet Grant in front—which proved to be true. The President, however, was inflexible. He insisted that Stevenson must go and said to Bragg: "Fight if you can, and fall back beyond the Tennessee."[6]

Having ruined Bragg's chances of success, Davis then proceeded to Mississippi, taking Johnston with him to investigate conditions on that front. It did not take Johnston long to see into what an impossible position he was being maneuvered, and he frankly said as much to Davis. The two armies in Tennessee and Mississippi, he pointed out, were too far apart to be managed effectively by one man; their objectives and their opposing forces were different, making it impossible to combine them, and there was really nothing for him to do unless he should take personal command of one or the other—which he did not think necessary or desirable. Davis replied that because both armies were so far away from Richmond he wanted a high officer on the ground who could transfer troops from one to the other at need. But each army, Johnston said, was already too weak to operate effectively and neither should be called on to strengthen the other. He predicted boldly that the system adopted for holding Mississippi and Tennessee would probably result in the loss of both, and he was particularly exercised over the possibility of losing Tennessee, which he aptly described as "the shield of the South."

When first notified in Richmond of his appointment to the department in the West Johnston had suggested to Secretary of War George W. Randolph that Pemberton's army in Mississippi be brought to Bragg and the combined forces, approximately 100,000 men, drive Rosecrans out of Tennessee. He felt that a successful outcome would make it necessary for Grant to abandon effort to penetrate Mississippi. To hold Grant at bay, he had made for the first time his suggestion about transferring to Mississippi the army of General Holmes, 30,000 men who were doing nothing in Arkansas. Randolph had told him that he had already ordered Holmes across the Mississippi, but when Holmes objected the President had countermanded the order—which, by the way, led to Randolph's early resignation from office.

Johnston now recounted to Davis his views as to the proper disposition of the troops in the West, but Davis shook off all his proposals and objections and went back to Richmond, leaving Johnston in a very unhappy frame of mind.

The newly christened Army of Tennessee was fanned out in a sort of wide semicircle southeast of Nashville, so disposed that they could watch the enemy and still be easily concentrated whenever and wherever necessary. Bragg himself was at Murfreesboro, thirty miles from Nashville, with his center under General Polk; his left at Triune and Eagleville, twenty miles west of Murfreesboro, under General Hardee; and his right at Readyville, twelve miles east of Murfreesboro, under General McCown, who had been returned from Kirby Smith.

In reorganization Bragg had rewarded Wheeler's good work in the Kentucky campaign by promoting to the rank of brigadier general and putting him over all the cavalry. This placed both Forrest and Morgan under Wheeler, a boyish-looking, slender young man of twenty-six, who had only recently graduated from West Point. Neither Forrest nor Morgan showed any dissatisfaction with their subordination and kept at their work with undiminished energy. The cavalry serving directly under Wheeler was now attached to Hardee's corps, with Wharton's mounted forces assigned to Polk. The Confederate pickets extended to within two miles of the Federal lines at Nashville, and the cavalry constantly patrolled all the intervening country.

Bragg made good use of his cavalry while encamped on the Murfrees-boro line, keeping them on spectacular raids on the enemy's communications and interfering seriously with his plans. Morgan on December 7 with 1,300 men made a brilliant swoop on Hartsville, Tennessee, fifty miles north of Nashville, where a Federal brigade was encamped. His attack was cloaked by an advance of two of Cheatham's infantry brigades against Lavergne on the Nashville road, and a similar move by Hanson's brigade toward Lebanon. Morgan surprised the Hartsville camp and after a sharp engagement overwhelmed it. The Federals lost 1,834 captured, in addition to 58 killed and 204 wounded. Morgan lost only 139 in all.

A few days later, on December 11, Forrest started from Columbia on the raid into West Tennessee which was to check Grant's advance into Mississippi. His brigade consisted of four depleted regiments and a four-gun battery of artillery. His men were armed principally with shotguns and flintlock rifles—and he did not have even a sufficient supply of flints for the rifles or caps for the shotguns. He had been promised modern guns, but they were never furnished him, and he had been ordered to ride into the enemy's country west of the Tennessee River armed just as he was.

By the fifteenth the mobile force had managed to cross the river at Clifton, and on the seventeenth they attacked and captured Lexington. Here Forrest took 150 prisoners, including Colonel Robert G. Ingersoll, who was in command, and, of even greater importance, he captured 300 Sharp's rifles and a supply of ammunition. Included in the spoils were two three-inch rifled steel Rodman guns, which were the pride of Forrest's artillery for the rest of the war. He swept on from Lexington and attacked Jackson, but was driven off. Then he dashed north and took Trenton, Humboldt and Union City, tearing up miles and miles of railroad track and cutting off Grant's communication with the North. Circling through West Tennessee, he soon found himself hotly pursued by such a large force of Federals that it seemed inevitable he must be surrounded and captured, but at Parker's Cross Roads, near Huntingdon, he made a stand and fought off his pursuers. He retreated through Lexington, and by January 3 had crossed the river again and was back in Middle Tennessee. In a little more than two weeks he had killed or captured 2,500 of the enemy, had taken 10 guns, 10,000 rifles and 1,000,000 cartridges, and, most important of all, had completely destroyed the usefulness of the Mobile & Ohio Railroad, burning up fifty trestles and wrecking no end of track.

Before Forrest got back, Morgan was off on another raid into Kentucky, his favorite stamping ground. He left Alexandria on December 21, struck directly north through Glasgow as far as Bardstown, then swung back through Campbellsville and Burkesville, and arrived at Smithville in Tennessee on January 5. He demolished the Louisville & Nashville Railroad from Munfordville to within eighteen miles of Louisville, took 1,887 prisoners, destroyed $2,000,000 worth of enemy property, and suffered a loss of only two killed and 24 wounded.

During the army's stay in the environs of Murfreesboro the social life of the little town burgeoned. A notable occasion was the visit of President Davis, who was lavishly fêted. He dined in state with the general officers at Bragg's headquarters, and on the last day of his stay reviewed Polk's corps, which he pronounced "the best appointed troops he had seen—well appointed and well clad."[7]

Another high spot was General Morgan's marriage to Miss Mattie Ready, a belle of the Murfreesboro section. Mrs. Chesnut in her *Diary* tells how Miss Ready, long before she had ever seen Morgan, took umbrage when Federal officers made slighting remarks about him in her presence. So spirited was her defense that one of the Yankees asked her name. "It's Mattie Ready now," she replied, "but by the grace of God one day I hope to call myself the wife of John Morgan." Morgan heard the story and when he got near Murfreesboro made it a special order of business to look up his spunky champion. He found her "as pretty as she was patriotic," he made a whirlwind courtship, and so—by the grace of God—she became Mrs. John Hunt Morgan. This was a military wedding in the most complete sense of the word. The ceremony was performed by General Polk, who donned his vestments over his uniform, the general's stars on his gray coat collar eclipsed by the sign of the cross. The bride's home was the scene of the wedding, and General Bragg and his staff and a few of Morgan's close friends were there to see the knot tied— and a few days later he was off raiding again.

As Christmas approached, the social life among both officers and men approached a climax. Christmas Day was featured by horse racing, card-playing and other gay doings traditional to Christmas celebrations in the South. It is easy to understand the lament of one of Wheeler's young cavalry captains: "The morning after Christmas Day . . . I felt feeble;

but, being anxious to be with my men, reported for duty."[8] Invitations were out for a big ball to be held the day after Christmas—but the day after Christmas Rosecrans started out from Nashville, and all festivities were forgotten in the Confederate camp.

The news of the departure of Stevenson's division for Mississippi had soon leaked through the Federal lines to Nashville and is supposed to have been one of the deciding factors in Rosecrans' determination to advance against his weakened foe. This resolve was encouraged also by the knowledge that Forrest and Morgan had been sent away on raids.[9] Rosecrans' movement began early on the morning of December 26, word of it being promptly carried to Bragg by his scouts. The Confederate cavalry was so superior to the Federal at this time that Rosecrans had been able to get very little accurate information about the exact location and extent of Bragg's forces, and he was uncertain where the Confederates might decide to make a stand. Consequently he marched his columns along different roads in such manner that they could support one another if necessary. His army, now totaling 46,940, was composed of three corps, commanded by Generals A. M. McCook, T. L. Crittenden and George H. Thomas.[10]

Crittenden's corps went direct along the Murfreesboro pike. General Thomas marched out the Franklin pike to Brentwood, thence by the Wilson pike to Nolensville, and thence by cross roads to the Murfreesboro pike about twenty miles out from Nashville. McCook's corps followed the Nolensville pike through Nolensville to a dirt road along which they proceeded to the outskirts of Murfreesboro.

The Federal advance was smartly and continuously contested by the Confederate cavalry, General Wheeler having assured Bragg that he could hold it off for four days while Bragg was pulling his scattered detachments into line of battle at Murfreesboro.[11] Wheeler made good. His was purely a delaying action. One of his officers says: "General Bragg sent us word not to fight them too much, but to let them come on."[12] It was not until the thirtieth that Rosecrans had his full force arrayed before Murfreesboro, with McCook on the right, Thomas in the center and Crittenden on the left.

Rosecrans had thought it likely that Bragg would take his stand at Stewart's Creek, some miles north of the town, a stream with steep banks that would afford natural defensive advantages. Bragg, however, elected to receive him on a line just outside Murfreesboro, about two miles to the north, the only benefit being that this line covered the roads. Hardee

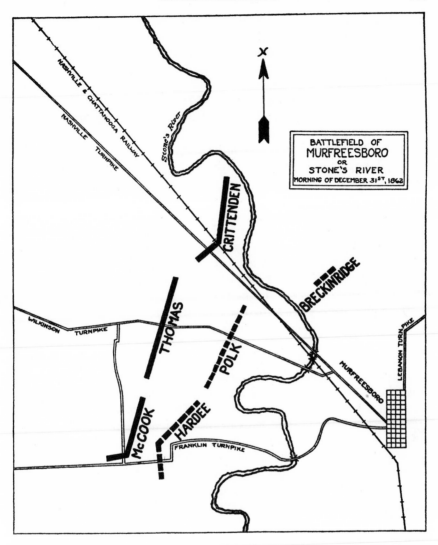

said frankly in his report: "The field of battle offered no peculiar advantages for defense. . . . The country on every side was entirely open and accessible to the enemy." The terrain was, in fact, peculiarly unsuited to fighting. The ground was rough and uneven, interspersed with outcroppings of limestone ledges broken by deep crevices, and strewn with huge boulders behind which men could take refuge from rifle fire. The country was wooded to a great extent, though broken by open farm lands and cotton fields with rail fences. The forests were mostly of the indigenous Tennessee red cedar, which grew in dense brakes or "glades," with limbs to the ground, providing exceptionally difficult obstacles in the way of cavalry maneuvering or artillery fire.

Bragg's whole force amounted to 37,719, including 3,873 cavalry. On his left he had Polk's corps, with Withers' division in the front line and Cheatham's about five hundred yards back. His right under Hardee had Breckinridge in front, with Cleburne some eight hundred yards behind and Jackson's brigade in reserve. McCown's division was in reserve near the center behind the river. The cavalry was placed in position with Wheeler on the right and Wharton on the left to cover the flanks, and Pegram in the rear as a reserve.

Stone's River, by which name the battle was known in the North, meandered across the chosen battlefield, and Bragg's line was divided by it—Polk with the river in his rear separating him from the town, and Hardee to the right and east on the same side of the river as Murfreesboro. The field was intersected also by the railroad and the turnpike to Nashville. These were vertical to the line of battle, and generally parallel north and south, but crossed each other in an acute angle to the right of Polk near the Confederate center, a few hundred yards from the river. In an east-and-west direction the field was crossed on Polk's front by what was then known as the Wilkinson turnpike and by the parallel road from Murfreesboro to Triune and Franklin. From the other side of town a road led out to Lebanon, and this was covered by the cavalry guarding the extreme right flank of the Confederate position.

On December 30 General Wheeler led several regiments of this cavalry on a daring raid completely around the flank and rear of the whole Federal army. Under way about midnight of the twenty-ninth, they rode out the Lebanon pike about five miles, then whirled around to the north to Jefferson where they captured and burned a train of twenty army wagons. By noon they had got as far as the village of Lavergne, halfway to Nashville. Here they captured and burned McCook's immense train of 300 wagons loaded with army stores (valued at close to $1,000,000) and took and paroled 800 prisoners. The next morning one of Thomas' brigades passed through Lavergne on its way up, and an officer has left a description of the scene:

"The turnpike as far as the eye could reach was filled with burning wagons. The country was overspread with disarmed men, broken-down horses and mules. The streets were covered with empty valises, trunks, knapsacks, broken guns and all the indescribable debris of a captured and rifled army train."[13]

From Lavergne Wheeler galloped on across country to Nolensville, and there fell on another Federal wagon train of ammunition and medicines which he burned, and captured more prisoners whom he paroled. Early on the thirty-first, before the battle started, Wheeler showed up on Bragg's left flank. In his circuit of Rosecrans' force, he had left a trail of devastation in his wake, brought off enough captured guns to arm a brigade, and remounted all of his men who needed fresh horses.

Throughout the thirtieth, the two armies had spent their time getting into position and endeavoring by active skirmishing and artillery fire to spot the opposing lines. By nightfall these lines had been pretty definitely located. For most of the way they were so close together that bugle calls could be heard across the intervening space. Both armies were equipped with the usual military bands. Just before tattoo they began to play their favorite tunes. The music carried clearly on the still, wintry air. While the strains of *Yankee Doodle* and *Hail Columbia* drifted through the cedars from the Northern camps, the Confederate bands answered with *Dixie* and *The Bonnie Blue Flag*. After this exchange of musical bombardments had continued for a time, one of the bands struck up the air that was known and loved by all the soldiers, regardless of the color of their uniforms—*Home Sweet Home*. At once, as though by prearrangement, the tune was taken up by all the bands on both sides, and soon across the rocky cedar glades for miles the simple melody rose in a great combined volume as Federals and Confederates joined in. The familiar and beloved words sprang to the lips of the soldiers, and the chorus of thousands of homesick voices almost drowned out the brassy blare of the instruments. The music swelled and died away, but that haunting last line—"There's no place like home"—choked in the throats of bluecoat Yankees and butternut-clad Rebels alike as they huddled, shivering in their blankets, and waited for the morning and its bloody work.

It was a queer feature, an unusual coincidence, of the Battle of Murfreesboro that both the opposing commanders determined to take the offensive on the morning of the same day and both planned to pursue identical tactics—an assault in force by the left wing against the enemy right. Rosecrans, to cover his proposed attack, kept up an especially vigorous skirmishing with the Confederate left throughout the thirtieth, which deceived Bragg all too well for Rosecrans' own comfort on the morrow. Making the same error of diagnosis he had made in Kentucky, Bragg mistook the feint for the main movement. He called Polk and Hardee to his headquarters the night of the thirtieth and told them he was convinced that Rosecrans was massing his troops for an assault on his left flank.[14] He would forestall this by attacking the Federal right before their advance could get under way. To that end he ordered McCown's division to the left in extension of Withers' front line and transferred Cleburne from the extreme right to the extreme left in support of McCown, Hardee being assigned to the command of these two divisions. This left Breckinridge's lone division on the east side of the river, where he would have been an easy prey to Rosecrans' planned attack; but Rosecrans was forced into the defensive before he could assume the offensive, and Breckinridge was not attacked the whole day.

Bragg's orders called for the execution of a right wheel, with the pivot on Chalmers' brigade at Polk's extreme right near the Nashville pike and the brigades attacking in succession from the left to the right until the Federals were driven back.

Rosecrans had ordered his attack to be delivered at 7 A.M., as soon as the men had had their breakfast. But Bragg had ordered his at daybreak, and so he gained the initiative and entirely disrupted Rosecrans' arrangements.

The first streaks of daylight were just beginning to break through the December clouds when the brigades of Rains and Ector and McNair stealthily left their positions on McCown's extreme left and moved in the half-light across the Triune pike toward the camp of McCook's corps on the Federal right. The full force of the initial assault fell on the brigades of Kirk and Willich of Johnson's division of that corps. Kirk's outposts had discerned the advancing gray masses, and he was ready for them. But Willich was not. He had gone to division headquarters for orders, and his men were caught in the act of cooking and eating their breakfast, their arms stacked.[15] They formed quickly and fought bravely but could not match the élan of the Confederate onset. McCook's brigades yielded ground until McCown's men had exhausted their ammunition. While they replenished their cartridge boxes, Cleburne's division moved up and continued the assault.

Meanwhile the front brigades of Polk's left were plunging to the attack on the right of Cleburne and McCown, and Wharton's cavalry had swung around the Federal right and was viciously hacking at right and rear. As one of the Federal commanding officers said in his official report: "With cavalry on their right, infantry assailing their left, and heavy masses rushing to the assault in the front, these regiments were directed to retire as the only escape from annihilation or capture." Fleeing through the cedars in panic, they cried out, "We are sold again! We are sold again!"—testifying to the almost inexplicable belief of some of the private soldiers that Buell had "sold out" to Bragg at Perryville—a strange hallucination.[16]

The left division of McCook's corps was commanded by Phil Sheridan, who put up a more stubborn defense than Johnson's brigades which had received the first shock of the Confederates' surprise attack. Facing Polk's left front, Sheridan was stoutly posted behind the scattered boulders and in the impenetrable cedar thickets which tangled this part of the field, and he threw off three successive attacks delivered by the brigades of Withers and Cheatham from Polk's left. But at length, as Cleburne pressed on Withers' left, Sheridan was overpowered by the envelopment and the enfilading artillery fire and was forced to give way toward the Nashville pike. Left among the dead on the battlefield was the body of one of his gallant brigade commanders, General Sill. Rousseau's division had been sent to Sheridan's support, but there was no stopping the fury of the Confederate assault, and Rousseau was swept back along with Sheridan.

The next forward movement of the Confederate line was by Patton Anderson's brigade of Withers' division against the division of General Negley on Thomas' right. Negley was in a dense cedar glade, with his right resting on the Wilkinson pike, his artillery raking the old cotton field across which Anderson had to go. The first charge was repulsed, but A. P. Stewart's brigade was brought up to his support. The Confederates charged again and now they succeeded. The Federals fell back through the cedars, abandoning the twelve guns which had played such havoc.

So swift and relentless was the Confederate follow-up that by ten o'clock in the morning they had put McCook's entire corps to flight in a wide sweep of four or five miles to the Nashville pike, and by noon Bragg's first objective had been attained: the Federal line had been doubled back like a jack-knife blade until its right wing was at right angles with the original line of battle. The divisions of Van Cleve and Wood numbering 12,000 fresh men had come to bulwark that wing and, backed up against the Nashville pike, were making a desperate stand to hold communication with the rear. Cleburne's and McCown's elated but exhausted divisions, now facing to the east, confronted them. One more push, it seemed, and the rout of the right wing would be complete. If Stevenson's absent division could have been thrown into action at this juncture it would probably have pulverized the Federal defense—a wishful thought that flashed through many Confederate minds that day. But Stevenson was off on his futile trip to Mississippi.

Bragg felt keenly his lack of reserves. He knew well that additional pressure would probably result in the repulse of the whole Federal army. To supply that pressure he called on the only available source of help, Breckinridge on his right. Quickly he ordered Breckinridge to send two brigades to Hardee's support, but an unusual combination of circumstances prevented the execution of the order. Following his original plan, Rosecrans had sent Van Cleve's division across the river early in the morning to lead the assault on the Confederate right and Wood was in readiness to follow him. When Bragg seized the initiative and hurled his own attack at the Federal right, Rosecrans immediately recalled Van Cleve's men. They waded the river and, together with Wood's division, took up the position along the Nashville pike where they were so effective in rallying the disorganized and flying forces of McCook.

Pegram's cavalry on the Confederate right flank had observed Van Cleve's original movement across the river and reported it promptly to Breckinridge—but the cavalry did not see or report Van Cleve's withdrawal. So when Breckinridge received Bragg's call for two brigades to be sent to Hardee he replied that he could not weaken his lone and unsupported division—the enemy was crossing the river in heavy force and even then coming straight on him; he needed reinforcements himself. Thus Rosecrans had the good fortune to hold Breckinridge's four brigades inactive most of the day by simply moving a division across the river and immediately withdrawing it. Bragg could not throw in reinforcements in the morning to push his successes against the Federal lines west of the river, and the coup de grace was impossible. Breckinridge later discovered that he was unopposed, but by then the opportunity had passed.

The new doubled-back position of the Federal line as established late in the morning created a sharp salient at the center, where Rousseau's division of Thomas' left joined Palmer's division of Crittenden's right. Within this angle, on a slight elevation just to the east of the Nashville pike and on both sides of the railroad track, was a thick clump of trees covering about four acres which the officers in their reports referred to as

the "Round Forest," but which the soldiers inelegantly called "Hell's
Half-Acre." Here Rosecrans assembled every available brigade not already
in action and buttressed them with field artillery massed on the high
ground back of the forest. This stronghold was maintained against the
successive waves of attacking Confederates through the rest of the day.
The Federal positions to the right continued to be driven and doubled
back, but the Round Forest salient held stoutly.

The brigade commanded by General Chalmers was the first Confederate force to impale itself on this blazing spearhead. It was the farther-
most brigade on the right of Withers' line, and therefore the last of the
front line to move into action. Chalmers' position was on a rise of ground
in an open field, in full view of the enemy and within easy range of their
guns. He had dug a shallow rifle pit to protect his men, who had
been forbidden to build fires lest they betray their location; so for forty-
eight hours they had crouched, shivering, in their narrow ditch, so
cramped and uncomfortable that when, shortly after noon, they got the
order to charge, it was a welcome relief.

Their charge was bravely made across the open field, supported by
Breckinridge's artillery from across the river. But they were swept by a
devastating fire of musketry and guns from the Round Forest. They were
literally mowed down, some regiments losing as many as six or eight color-
bearers. At length a shell fragment wounded General Chalmers; the
brigade faltered, and some of its regiments fell back. Quickly General
Donelson's Tennessee brigade was rushed up. It became separated and
disorganized as its advance was hampered by having to pass around the
Cowan house—a burned brick house to the west of the Nashville pike—
with its fences and outbuildings. Despite this temporary confusion and
the tornado of fire it faced, the brigade attacked with what one of its opponents called "indescribable gallantry"[17] and captured eleven guns and a
thousand prisoners. The success was against the lines to the right of the
Round Forest; the Forest itself still held strongly, and Donelson finally
was forced to fall back into the cedars west of the Cowan house toward
the Wilkinson pike. The ferocious determination of the Confederate
attack is attested by their own terrific losses—the 8th Tennessee lost 306
men and officers, including its colonel, out of 425 who went into action;
the 16th Tennessee lost 207 out of its total strength of 402. Other regiments in the brigade suffered similarly. There was no lack of valor and
persistence—but the knockout punch was lacking.

Meanwhile Bragg had finally learned that the supposed threat against

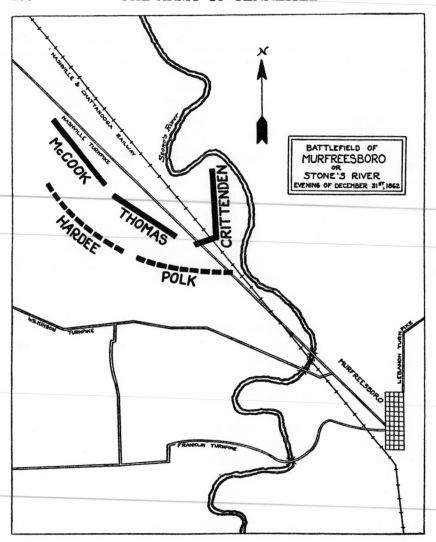

BATTLEFIELD OF
MURFREESBORO
OR
STONE'S RIVER
EVENING OF DECEMBER 31ST, 1862

Breckinridge was entirely imaginary; so eventually, late in the afternoon, he ordered Breckinridge to send the brigades of Adams, Jackson, Preston and Palmer to the west side of the river to aid the attacks on the Round Forest salient. They came across the stream in detachments. Two hours after Donelson's attack, the brigades of Adams and Jackson arrived. An hour later Breckinridge came in person, accompanying the brigades of

Preston and Palmer—Palmer's now being commanded by General Gideon J. Pillow, back in active service after the temporary eclipse that followed his abdication at Fort Donelson.

Bragg threw the four brigades into action piecemeal as they reached the field and thus lost the possibly decisive effect of an onslaught by the whole fresh force. Adams and Jackson assailed the salient with energy and gallantry, but they too had trouble getting around the Cowan house. Also, the Round Forest had been strengthened and the Federals had had time to pull themselves together after Donelson's savage onset. Adams' charge was described by a Federal commentator as "without doubt the most daring, courageous and best-executed attack which the Confederates made on our line between pike and river."[18] He lost a third of his whole brigade in killed and wounded. But it was all in vain; the survivors had to fall back into the protecting cedars. Preston and Pillow fared no better—they charged with splendid spirit but the defenders of the Round Forest· met them with a hail of fire and threw them back. It was now late in the evening. The red winter sun had set behind the cedars. Darkness shut in on the brief twilight and put an end to fighting—to the great relief of both exhausted and crippled armies.

The Battle of Murfreesboro was really two battles in one, its action divided into two distinct engagements separated by a day of inaction. In the fight on the thirty-first the Confederate victory was complete and overwhelming. The Federals were driven from their positions on their right for a distance of four or five miles, and the Confederates held the field at the close of day. True, Bragg's army had suffered terrific losses, but so had Rosecrans, and the result Bragg had gained seemed worth the price—Rosecrans was badly whipped. Bragg was a little premature, but not entirely inaccurate, when he telegraphed Richmond, "The enemy has yielded his strong position and is falling back. We occupy the whole field and shall follow him. . . . God has granted us a happy New Year."[19]

He thought it likely that Rosecrans would retreat during the night. When his scouts brought him news of long wagon trains rumbling on the pike toward Nashville he was sure of it. A cavalry reconnaissance developed, however, that they were merely carrying the wounded and that Rosecrans was still encamped on the field.

As a matter of fact, Rosecrans did come close to retreating. After the battle he called his corps commanders to headquarters to confer on the course to be pursued. "Do you deem it advisable to fight out this battle on the ground we now occupy?" he bluntly asked them. Crittenden and

Thomas were noncommittal. The question was "grave and vital," they said; it must be decided by Rosecrans himself: they would stand by him, whatever he did. McCook advised a retreat to Nashville, in which he was supported by General Stanley.[20] Rosecrans himself seemed to favor retreat. In fact, he went so far as to ask McCook to accompany him on a ride to the rear (instructing the others to wait for his return) in order to locate a position beyond Overall's Creek to which the army might fall back during the night. As they approached the creek they observed a number of mounted men with torches riding up and down. Rosecrans exclaimed to McCook: "They have got entirely in our rear and are forming a line of battle by torchlight." With retreat apparently shut off, he went back to headquarters and grimly told the assembled generals to "prepare to fight or die."[21] Not until next morning was it discovered that the moving torches they had seen were brands to light the campfires of the Federal cavalry along the creek.

Neither commander showed a disposition to renew the fight New Year's morning. Rosecrans seemed satisfied with the respite from attack with no thought of counterattack. During the night of the thirty-first he had re-formed and consolidated his lines, withdrawing from the advanced salient of the Round Forest. When Polk observed this new alignment the next morning, he stepped into the position vacated by the Federals—the position before which so many of his men had fruitlessly sacrificed their lives. Otherwise there was no activity on either side that whole day. Bragg seemed to have no definite plans and to be making no preparations. He had thought Rosecrans would certainly fall back after his drubbing, and when he did not Bragg seemed at a loss what to do himself. His army held the field and he set detachments to work gathering up the discarded arms, burying the dead and succoring the wounded, but he attempted no military action.

A serious oversight on his part was his failure during this interlude to push forward his right wing to seize the unoccupied high ground across the river. Rosecrans, on the other hand, did not overlook the opportunity. Van Cleve's division—now under Colonel Beatty, since the wounding of its commander the day before—was again crossed to the east bank. Reinforced by the brigades of Grose and Hazen, it occupied a ridge about a mile in advance of Breckinridge who had re-crossed the river and was back in his original position.

On the morning of the second Bragg engaged in a brief exploratory artillery duel with Rosecrans on his center, near the Round Forest, which developed the fact that though they were out of the advanced salient, the Federals were still there in force. Bragg considered their presence a menace to Polk, and he hit upon the idea of trying to drive them out by a cross fire of artillery from beyond the river. Accordingly he sent his adjutant general and an artillery officer to examine the ground in front of Breckinridge and discover the best location for guns to enfilade the Federal line. These officers reported that the ridge Beatty had seized was what Bragg was looking for. So he decided that Breckinridge must take it from Beatty.

He sent posthaste for Breckinridge to come to his headquarters beside the Nashville pike near where it crosses Stone's River. There, as they stood together beneath a big sycamore tree, he outlined his plan to his surprised corps commander. Breckinridge was emphatic in saying he did not like it. He insisted that it was bound to prove disastrous; the high ground held by the Federals to the west of the river completely commanded the ridge he was ordered to take, and they could rake it with their guns. With a stick he drew in the earth a rough map of the situation.[22] But Bragg's mind was curiously inflexible. His orders given, he galloped down the road to Polk's headquarters where he would have a better view of the ground on the other side. This was Polk's first intimation of what was up. At once he volunteered his advice against it—the position sought was not essential to his protection.[23] But Bragg valued Polk's opinion no more highly than Breckinridge's, and he did nothing to stop the futile, fatal charge.

Breckinridge felt that he had been asked to do "an impossible thing," but, consumed with dejection, he returned to his command to attempt it. Before ordering the advance, he rode over to General Preston and said:

"General, this attack is made against my judgment and by special orders of General Bragg. Of course we all must try to do our duty and fight the best we can; but if it should result in disaster and I be among the killed, I want you to do justice to my memory and tell the people that I believed this attack to be very unwise and tried to prevent it."[24]

He advanced with 4,500 men at 4 P.M., the time being set for this late hour on Bragg's theory that after Breckinridge had driven Beatty from the ridge it would be about nightfall and too dark for the Federals to counterattack; then Breckinridge could entrench himself during the night. But Bragg seemed to forget that Rosecrans had artillery—plenty of guns, wellmanned, and a station from which to use them tellingly.

It happened that General Crittenden, accompanied by his chief of artillery, Major John Mendenhall, was riding along the Nashville pike on the other side of the river and observed Breckinridge as he was forming to unleash his attack on Beatty. Mendenhall straightway began to get together all the available guns in reach. In a few minutes he had massed fifty-eight on an eminence on the west bank at McFadden's Ford, a bristling array that completely covered the field on the other side where Breckinridge was now grappling with Beatty and the supporting brigades of Grose and Hazen.

All went well for Breckinridge at first. The charge overpowered Beatty's brigades, drove them down toward the river and across the ford to the other bank. But as the pursuing Confederates swarmed over the ridge and into the range of Mendenhall's guns they were greeted with a blast that stopped them with tremendous slaughter. The fifty-eight guns belched out their volleys at a rate of not less than a hundred shots a minute. Supporting Federal infantry and cavalry were rushed across the river, Beatty's fleeing regiments were rallied, and within a few minutes Breckinridge's men—all that were left alive—were in full flight. They reformed when they reached the line from which they had started, where they had the support of their own ten guns. For their part, the Federals were content to reoccupy the position from which they had been driven a few minutes before, without pushing their counterstroke. Both armies bivouacked where they had started—but Breckinridge had suffered a loss of 1,700, including the mortally wounded General Hanson.

This day's battle was confined to the sector east of the river, and the action lasted only an hour and twenty minutes in the dusk of a winter evening. But those eighty minutes proved decisive. No ground was lost or won on either side, but the futility of the engagement and the bad judgment that prompted it proved the last straw in breaking down the confidence of Bragg's officers and men.

As soon as he observed Breckinridge's tragic failure and his great losses, Bragg sent Anderson's brigade across the river to help cover his retreat. Hardee with Cleburne's division followed hard after, and McCown was sent over shortly after dark. This left only the divisions of Cheatham and Withers west of the river to oppose the whole Federal army there. Cheatham had suffered the staggering loss of 36 per cent during the battle of the thirty-first and Withers 28 per cent, and there remained a total of only about 7,000 effectives between them. The disparity was to become even more painfully pronounced during the night of the third. The river, which during the course of the fighting had been at a low stage and easily forded on foot, began to rise rapidly when a steady rain started on the evening of the second. As the river rose it became clear there would soon be no easy fording, and Rosecrans drew west of the river all the troops from the east side, finally concentrating his whole army in front of the depleted divisions of Cheatham and Withers.

Those generals did not know of the increasing concentration before them, but they did know that they were unsupported on their side of the river—and, above all, they were convinced that their commanding general was unequal to handling the army as things stood. So, after the Breckinridge debacle, they held a long and earnest consultation that lasted far into the night. Their good sense told them that the army was in serious plight—decimated by losses, confidence in its leader at lowest ebb, rumors flying that Bragg planned to renew battle next day.

After midnight, Cheatham and Withers composed and signed their names to an unusual document—a letter addressed to General Bragg expressing the view that "this army should be promptly put in retreat. . . . You have but three divisions that are at all reliable, and even some of these are more or less demoralized from having some brigade commanders who do not possess the confidence of their commands." They expressed a fear of "great disaster from the condition of things now existing" unless the army were withdrawn.

This letter was sent to Bragg through Polk, who forwarded it with an endorsement: "After seeing the effect of the operations of to-day, added to that produced upon the troops by the battle of the 31st, I very greatly fear the consequences of another engagement at this place on the ensuing day." He did not in so many words advise a retreat but said: "We could now, perhaps, get off with some safety and with some credit if the affair was well managed. Should we fail in the meditated attack, the consequences might be very disastrous."

General Polk's aide reached Bragg's headquarters with the message at 2 A.M. Roused from sleep, the commander sat up in bed and started to read it, but as soon as he sensed its purport, he snapped out: "Say to the general we shall maintain our position at every hazard," dismissed the messenger and went back to sleep. Polk told Hardee about this. "I think the decision of the general unwise in a high degree."[25]

The next morning, the third, at ten o'clock, Polk and Hardee were called to Bragg's headquarters, where they found him in a different frame of mind. Rosecrans, he told them, had a stronger force than he had thought—General McCook's papers had been captured and they showed it was close to 70,000.[26] Furthermore, he said, Rosecrans was receiving additional reinforcements (which he was not).[27] On the whole, after thinking the matter over, he felt they had better retreat. Polk and Hardee gave their ready concurrence, and preparations proceeded through the day for the withdrawal that night.[28]

Bragg himself went to Winchester, fifty miles southeast in the direction of Chattanooga, planning on the establishment of a new line for his army along Elk River. Hardee's corps marched to Tullahoma, thirty miles off, by way of Manchester, and Polk fell back to Shelbyville, twenty miles from Murfreesboro. The weather was intensely cold. The plodding men were alternately drenched with rain and pelted with sleet. They were physically miserable and spiritually depressed. They had met the enemy in fair combat and had given him a good beating—and now they were retreating! It was the same old Bragg technique—fight, win and fall back. What was the use of winning a battle if Bragg didn't know what to do with it? Where were they going now, and what for? When would rations be issued? Why couldn't they stop and build fires and get dry and warm? With numb feet and hands, the grumbling soldiers stumbled along, bent under their sodden packs.

Rosecrans was as surprised as he was delighted when he woke up on the morning of the fourth and discovered that the Confederate army was gone. Like Sherman at Shiloh, he had had quite enough of them. He made no move to follow. Polk stopped at Shelbyville and let Bragg know that Rosecrans was not pursuing as had been expected. He was told to stay where he was. Hardee's corps was ordered to encamp at Wartrace, on the Nashville & Chattanooga Railroad a few miles before Tullahoma, where Bragg now made his headquarters, with the new line of the army along Duck River and its rich valley.

CHAPTER XII

MISSISSIPPI INTERLUDE

THE story of the Army of Tennessee may not be told without some account of the related Vicksburg campaign. To make it understandable and carry it to completion one must begin this account in the preceding year and go forward beyond the present point in the main narrative.

The defeat of Van Dorn at Corinth on October 4, 1862, apparently opened the way for Grant to move forward through Mississippi to Vicksburg, the surviving Confederate stronghold on the river. Rosecrans, flushed with victory at Corinth, asked that he be permitted to advance and take it. Grant, on October 25, was placed in command of what was styled the "Department of the Tennessee," including northern Mississippi, all of Tennessee and Kentucky west of the Tennessee River and Cairo, Illinois. Despite his enlarged authority, he was wary about seeming to disregard the now-supreme Halleck, so he referred Rosecrans' request to Washington. Halleck told Grant to use his discretion. For some reason, never quite clear, Grant did not order the advance. A little later, on October 26, Grant wrote Halleck: "With small reinforcements I think I would be able to move down the Mississippi Central Railroad and cause the evacuation of Vicksburg." Halleck encouraged this, and on November 4 Grant started out from Grand Junction, Tennessee, with about 30,000 men.

His immediate objective was the Confederate army along the Tallahatchie River. It was now commanded by General John C. Pemberton, who on October 14 had been put in charge of the Confederate "Department of Mississippi and Eastern Louisiana," with headquarters at Jackson.

Pemberton's life as a Confederate general had been, and continued to be, an unpleasant one. His Northern birth engendered suspicion and his personality was not ingratiating. He was "wanting in polish," Colonel Roman says, "and was too positive and domineering in manner to suit the sensitive and polite people among whom he had been thrown."[1] In his first command in Charleston he had got off on the wrong foot by declaring martial law; the people there never liked him. He was not unpopular with civilians only, but also with his brother officers, who viewed with mistrust and jealousy his rapid rise in rank—a rise hard to understand as, until Vicksburg, he had not been engaged in any battles. He rushed up the ladder of rank from colonel to lieutenant general "over the heads," Roman says, "of many Confederate officers who had already distinguished themselves and given unquestioned evidence of capacity, efficiency and other soldierly qualities." Placing Pemberton in command in Mississippi must rank as one of Jefferson Davis' major mistakes.

Grant had hardly started on his proposed advance down through Mississippi to Vicksburg before he was held up by an unexpected development in his political rear. General McClernand (one of the so-called "political generals" and one whom Grant did not like) had conceived a plan for opening the Mississippi and gone straight to Washington to lay it before President Lincoln in person. In the pre-war days McClernand and Lincoln had both practiced law in Springfield. The President was impressed with McClernand's intellectual powers, even though he was not a professional soldier. He liked McClernand's scheme and told him to consult Halleck. Halleck disapproved it, but Lincoln, like Jefferson Davis, fancied himself as a military expert. He overruled Halleck and instructed the Secretary of War to authorize McClernand to go ahead. So McClernand went to Springfield to recruit and organize his private expedition to capture Vicksburg. Grant was officially in charge of this department, and might have expected to be officially advised. The first he heard of it was when he read about it in the newspapers.

He felt deeply perturbed, really incensed, by this exercise of executive power in creating an independent command within his own, and he checked his advance while he investigated. "Two commanders on one field are always one too many," he said,[2] and, besides, he thought McClernand inexperienced and otherwise unqualified for the duty assigned him. At length, however, Grant was informed by Halleck that any troops sent to his department would be under his command. Thus reassured, after ordering Sherman with two divisions to move out from Memphis and reinforce him, he pushed on into Mississippi and by October 29 had reached the Tallahatchie. Pemberton promptly retreated to Grenada on the Yalobusha, and Grant at Oxford again telegraphed Halleck for instructions: "How far south would you like me to go?"

His indecision was soon resolved by the Confederates themselves. Forrest in West Tennessee suddenly broke out in that slashing raid on his communications which put the Mobile & Ohio out of operation there. Simultaneously Van Dorn, late in December, moved east out of Grenada,

started ostentatiously in the direction of New Albany, then swept around
Grant's rear and dashed down on Holly Springs in one of the most brilliant and materially successful cavalry raids of the war. Grant had stocked
at Holly Springs an immense store of supplies to back his expedition, and
Van Dorn captured the town and everything and everybody in it—the
entire garrison and its commander and Mrs. Grant (who, much flustered,
was courteously sent inside the Federal lines), as well as the stores, valued
at several million dollars, which were burned for want of means to
bring them off.

These destructive raids behind him made Grant's progress into Mississippi impracticable. He withdrew his army to Holly Springs and
camped it there, while he went to Memphis to see what was happening on
the Mississippi. In a desire to anticipate and frustrate McClernand, he
had been quietly organizing a river expedition of his own. On December
8 he had sent Sherman back to Memphis from Oxford to transport an
army down to the mouth of the Yazoo just above Vicksburg, there to
make a landing and, if possible, capture the town. His movement was to
be supported by Grant's own along the Mississippi Central, but when
Grant was forced to give it up he did not attempt to hold back Sherman,
who proceeded downriver, unaided on land. One of Grant's Northern
critics said that he appeared to be operating more actively against McClernand than against Pemberton, so anxious was he to get Sherman down the
Mississippi before McClernand could complete plans for his expedition.
At any rate, Sherman did get away from Memphis with 30,000 men,
picked up 12,000 more at Helena, on the twenty-seventh of December
landed on the south bank of the Yazoo about eight miles above Vicksburg, and marched overland on the town through the low ground bordering Chickasaw Bayou.

As soon as Pemberton heard what Sherman was up to, he transferred
the greater part of his army from Grenada to Vicksburg and arrayed about
25,000 men on the Chickasaw Bluffs in a strong defense. Strong as it was,
Sherman ordered its assault, saying callously that it would eventually cost
at least 5,000 men to take Vicksburg, "and we may as well lose them here
as anywhere else."[3] The attack was "as valiant as it was hopeless," according to one of the Federal generals.[4] It was directed at General Stephen D. Lee's brigade, and the energetic and skillful manner in which he
conducted his defense here first attracted attention to a man who was
later to rise to the rank of corps commander in the Army of Tennessee.
Sherman's attack was so roundly repulsed that he did not try to renew it.
He did not lose 5,000 men—only 1,776; the Confederate loss was 207.

This was but the first of a number of vain attempts[5] to take Vicksburg by frontal assaults. At length, after months of futile efforts, Grant (who was now on the Vicksburg front in personal charge) changed his tactics completely and decided to approach the city by a circuitous route. Early in April Pemberton came to the conclusion that Grant must be thinking of a march through Mississippi from the north. To thwart this he began to assemble a force at Jackson. But Grant had abandoned any such idea and was preparing a daring move. He moved his men across to the west bank of the Mississippi and southward, loaded them on transports, and on April 30 landed them on the east bank at Bruinsburg, sixty miles below. From this point he planned a march of 35,000 men up through Mississippi that would result in the capture of Jackson and then permit him to envelop Vicksburg from the rear, while he held the railroad between the two cities.

Pemberton heard of Grant's movement downriver almost as soon as it started. On April 29 he sent a call for assistance to General Joseph E. Johnston, then sick in bed at Tullahoma. Johnston telegraphed back that if Grant was on the east bank the safety of Vicksburg demanded that he be defeated, and he ordered Pemberton to unite all his strength to do it. He forwarded to Richmond Pemberton's plea for help, with an endorsement that reinforcements could not be sent him from Bragg's army "without giving up Tennessee."

On the evening of May 9 Johnston got a wire from the War Department to go at once to Mississippi and take chief command. Though still unfit for active duty, he obediently took the first train for Jackson. Pemberton telegraphed him that Grant was moving on Edwards—midway between Vicksburg and Jackson—and he expected to lead his army out and fight him there. Johnston had hardly arrived at Jackson, exhausted by his four-days' journey, before a Confederate brigade under General Gregg quick-stepped into town. It had been driven in from Raymond by the Federals. Gregg reported that Pemberton was at Edwards and 25,000 of Grant's army had reached Clinton, only ten miles away, between Jackson and Edwards. Johnston made a quick survey of the situation and on the evening of the thirteenth telegraphed Secretary Seddon: "The enemy is in force between here and Vicksburg. Communication is cut off. I am too late."

The Confederate authorities were now making frantic efforts to assemble reinforcements at Jackson, and Johnston realized that the only hope of success was to unite these troops with Pemberton's. On the evening of the thirteenth, he ordered Pemberton to move on the advance corps of Federals at Clinton while he attacked them from the Jackson side, hoping that thus they might establish communication between them.[6]

Here occurred one of those breakdowns in co-operation which so frequently bedeviled Confederate efforts. General Pemberton answered that he was moving at once with all his men—but, instead, he thought it over and called a council of war. To his assembled generals he read Johnston's orders, expressing his own opinion that they should not be obeyed in the circumstances. A majority voted to march on Clinton as commanded; a minority recommended a swing around to the north on Grant's communications in an effort to force Grant to the attack. Pemberton did not agree with either majority or minority, but he adopted the minority plan and, as Johnston witheringly expressed it, "determined to execute a measure which he disapproved, which his council of war opposed, and which was in violation of the orders of his commander."[7] Pemberton's inability or unwillingness to attack promptly as ordered made Johnston's stay in Jackson impossible. He removed all the stores to safety and on the afternoon of the fourteenth withdrew toward Canton, permitting Sherman to occupy Jackson unopposed except for Gregg's perfunctory rear-guard action.

Pemberton stood stock-still for another twenty-four hours and got under way so late on the fifteenth that he could march only four miles that day. The next morning he received another order from Johnston to march on Clinton, so that their forces might be joined, and again he answered that he would obey at once. Still he did nothing for several hours. And while he was waiting Grant brought up six divisions and lost no time in attacking him in his position on Baker's Creek, an engagement known to history as the Battle of Champion's Hill. His force was defeated and retreated hastily to the Big Black River where it camped for the night near the bridge. Attacked here again on the seventeenth, Pemberton was once more driven back and this time retired within the Vicksburg defenses.

Johnston saw at once that Pemberton had placed himself in a trap. He wrote Pemberton that if he permitted himself to be besieged in Vicksburg he must eventually surrender. Johnston pointed out, soundly, that it was better to lose the town than to lose both the town and the army. He ordered Pemberton to pull out immediately and march northeast. In another council of war, Pemberton decided to disobey orders again and stay where he was. Vicksburg was completely invested by Grant's army on the nineteenth, and Pemberton's doom was sealed.

His perplexity, as explained by his chief engineer, Colonel S. H. Lockett, grew out of the contradictory nature of the dispatches he received from General Johnston and from President Davis.

"Neither those of Mr. Davis nor those of General Johnston exactly comported with General Pemberton's views. He then made the capital mistake of trying to harmonize instructions from his superiors diametrically opposed to each other, and at the same time to bring them into accord with his own judgment, which was averse to the plans of both. Mr. Davis's idea was to hold Vicksburg at all hazards, and not to endanger it by getting too far away from it. Johnston's plan was to cut loose from Vicksburg altogether, maneuver so as to avoid a general engagement with Grant until the Confederate forces could be concentrated, and then beat him. Pemberton wished to take a strong position on the Big Black and wait for an attack, believing that it would be successfully resisted, and that then the tables could be turned upon Grant in a very bad position, without any base of supplies, and without a well-protected line of retreat. . . . None of these plans was carried out, but a sort of compromise or compound of all these attempted, resulting in the unfortunate battle of Baker's Creek or Champion's Hill, and the disgraceful stampede of Big Black bridge."[8]

Pemberton was immensely distressed by the failure of his effort to hold off Grant's army from investing Vicksburg. As he rode along with his army, retreating from the Big Black, he said disconsolately to a companion: "Just thirty years ago I began my military career by receiving my appointment to a cadetship at the U. S. Military Academy, and to-day—the same date—that career is ended in disaster and disgrace."[9] He was a little premature, but disaster and disgrace were truly on their way. A full measure of both were to be his in a few weeks.

He drew up his infantry within the works of Vicksburg, bristling with such a formidable array of big guns that he waited for the Federals' approach in renewed confidence. The town was strongly fortified both by nature and by the engineers, and it was justly regarded as well-nigh impregnable to direct attack.

Grant's army appeared on the eighteenth and on the following day delivered the first of a series of attacks, which was easily repulsed. Then the Federals took two days to complete their line about the city. On the twenty-second, assisted by a bombardment from the gunboats, they made another assault, this one violent and carried out with such vigor and determination that at times they appeared to have success within their grasp. But at last they were thrown off, leaving some 3,500 dead and wounded before the breastworks. There were other attacks, and from the river the gunboats kept up a continuous fire, but by the first of June Grant seems to have decided that Vicksburg could not be taken in this way and he must settle down to siege operations.

Meanwhile Johnston was hovering anxiously but ineffectually between Jackson and Vicksburg, eager to rescue Pemberton but uncertain how to go about it. He had moved twice to effect a junction, and each time Pemberton had failed him. On May 19, when he learned of Pemberton's determination to hold Vicksburg, he wrote him: "I am trying to gather a force which may attempt to relieve you. Hold out."[10] He did succeed in getting together about 15,000, but that was still only one-third the strength of Grant's army and it was short of ammunition and almost entirely without artillery and field transportation. The two Confederate generals kept up an interchange of communications—most of which were read by Grant in transit, thanks to a treacherous courier. Johnston urged Pemberton to state his plans and suggest how they might co-operate. Pemberton proposed that Johnston advance on the north side of the railroad while he tried to get out. But it was not until the latter part of June that Johnston could assemble enough wagons and artillery to take the field—and by that time it was almost too late to do anything at all.

Johnston tried also to arrange for a relief expedition from the Trans-Mississippi Department, which would approach Vicksburg from the west bank, but he got nowhere with this. He thought Pemberton might save his army by transporting it across the river and temporarily joining it with the Trans-Mississippi forces, but nothing came of that either.

Striving desperately to work out some plan Johnston kept in touch with the President and Secretary of War at Richmond. He told them Grant had 60,000 men against which he had only 23,000, and appealed for reinforcements. Davis held out no hope. Johnston, he said, must be mistaken; according to the Secretary of War his force amounted to 34,000 instead of the 23,000 he reported. This led to bickering between Seddon and Johnston in which Seddon stubbornly insisted on the accuracy of his figures and finally shut off discussion by telling Johnston flatly he could get no more troops—"You must rely on what you have." On the heels of this, Seddon wired urging him to attack, despite his inferior numbers. Johnston replied that this was impracticable—that Grant's position was naturally strong and well entrenched, protected by artillery and the obstructed roads, with the Big Black River serving to defend him while cutting off Johnston's retreat if he should move up and be defeated.

From his office in Richmond, Seddon read Johnston a telegraphic lecture on his duties in this emergency: "The eyes of the whole Confederacy are upon you . . . with the sentiment that it is better to fail nobly daring than, through prudence even, to be inactive." Johnston explained that "there has been no voluntary inaction," and patiently set forth his material deficiencies, especially in field transportation.

On the twenty-ninth of June, having finally got the necessary supplies and wagons, Johnston moved his army toward the Big Black River in the hope of discovering some way of breaking Grant's lines. "This expedition," Johnston explains, "was not undertaken in the wild spirit that dictated the dispatches from the War Department of the 16th and 21st of June. I did not indulge in the sentiment that it was better for me to waste the lives and blood of brave soldiers 'than, through prudence even,' to spare them."[11] He reconnoitered on July 2, 3 and 4 north of the railroad and convinced himself that no attack was possible from that quarter. He planned to march on the morning of the fifth south of the railroad and create a diversion which might enable Pemberton to cut his way out. He sent a note to Pemberton about it, but the courier had hardly left camp before news came that it was all over.

Around Vicksburg the Federal investment had been drawing closer and closer since the siege began in late May. Grant's army, like an army of moles, was burrowing its way nearer and nearer the Confederate works by a series of entrenched approaches. Tunnels were driven underneath the Confederate lines and an occasional mine exploded, but without serious effect. The Confederates built and exploded countermines, also without doing much damage. The bombardment from the siege guns in the Federal works and from the gunboats on the river continued day and night. Most of the citizens took refuge in caves dug out of the hillsides and cliffs where old men, women and children led a life of terror and privation. The supply of food grew gradually lower until it was exhausted. Mule meat became a standard item on Vicksburg menus. The army suffered not only for food but for ammunition. Failing relief from outside there could be but one outcome of the siege.

The beleaguered troops, inspired by patriotic devotion, stood all these hardships with remarkable patience and courage, but as the food supply dwindled away, their fortitude began to yield to something like despair. Their feeling is reflected in a remarkable communication—anonymous but moving—which was sent to Pemberton during those trying days of late June. Signed "Many Soldiers," it recounted the hardships endured by the army until now the daily issue of rations had almost reached the vanishing point—"one biscuit and a small bit of bacon per day. The emergency of the case demands prompt and decided action on your part. If you can't feed us, you had better surrender us—horrible as the idea is. . . . This army is now ripe for mutiny unless it can be fed."[12]

At last, on the night of July 2, Pemberton called a council of war to consider what they should do. All his officers but two, Generals Lee and Baldwin, voted to surrender. Pemberton accepted the vote as decisive and began to make his plans to get the best terms possible from Grant for a surrender on July 4. Some of the Confederates objected to humiliation on the national holiday, but Pemberton had a queer idea about this. "I am a Northern man; I know my people," he said. "I know their peculiar weaknesses and their national vanity; I know we can get better terms from them on the Fourth of July than any other day of the year. We must sacrifice our pride to these considerations."[13]

His application to Grant for an armistice to discuss peace was met by a demand for unconditional surrender. At a parley held between the lines, the Confederate commander proposed to give up the city with the right reserved for his troops to march out with the honors of war, taking their arms, colors and field batteries. Grant scornfully rejected any such qualified capitulation, and the parley broke up. Then ensued a correspondence between the generals which soon resulted in the surrender of the city and the defending force, the men being paroled instead of sent north to prison camps, as they had so greatly feared they might be.

Pemberton's signal corps had succeeded in deciphering the Federal code system used in wigwagging messages from the land forces to the gunboats. They decoded all the Federal messages sent from the signal tower to the boats and vice versa. So, while the surrender negotiations were on, they eavesdropped on an exchange of messages and discovered that Admiral Porter of the fleet objected to the use of his transports to convey Confederate prisoners to the North, as Grant desired, wishing to use them instead for dispatching Federal troops farther down the river. Strengthened by this knowledge, Pemberton held out for the parole and got his way.

In capitulating at Vicksburg, Pemberton surrendered 31,600 men, 172 cannon and 60,000 muskets. At Port Hudson, a short distance below Vicksburg and dependent on it, General Gardner on July 9 surrendered 6,300 men, 51 guns and 7,500 small arms. At the close of the siege Grant had a force of 75,000 men. In the campaign leading up to the surrender he had suffered a total loss of 9,362—1,514 killed, 7,395 wounded and 453 missing.[14]

As soon as Johnston received the bad news, he fell back to Jackson, arriving there on the afternoon of July 7 and taking position in the field works which had been thrown up by Pemberton. Early on the ninth General Sherman, commanding three corps of the Federal Army, appeared before these works, but instead of attacking, as was expected, he laid siege. There was active skirmishing and some cannonading throughout the next two days, and on the twelfth there was an assault on a part of the line, which was driven off without much trouble. But because Sherman outnumbered Johnston, a defense of the city against either siege or determined assault did not seem possible, so on the night of the sixteenth Johnston evacuated it and retreated eastward to Morton. Sherman did not pursue him, but burned Jackson and on the twenty-third returned to Vicksburg. On the same day a telegram from General Cooper at Richmond relieved Johnston of command of the Department of Tennessee—which was construed as a rebuke, although he was later given formal instruction to assume immediate charge of the army in Mississippi.

Davis, himself a Mississippian, was deluged with communications from prominent citizens of the state expressing keen dissatisfaction with the turn of affairs there. The President was inclined to lay all the blame on Johnston, and Johnston, for his part, did not vouchsafe any explanation of what he had done or what he was planning to do. "General Johnston is retreating on the east side of Pearl River," Davis wrote Robert E. Lee on July 21, "and I can only learn from him of such vague purposes as were unfolded when he held his army before Petersburg."[15] On the twenty-eighth he wrote Lee again: "General Johnston, after evacuating Jackson, retreated to the east to the pine woods of Mississippi, and if he has any other plan than that of watching the enemy it has not been communicated."[16]

Soon after Johnston established his army at Morton he received a letter in which President Davis strongly censured much of his recent military conduct. He made a long and spirited answer, defending himself against the accusations. The whole wrangle finally got before the Confederate Congress, where it was acrimoniously debated—none of which improved the relations between President and General or served the Confederate cause.

The disposition of Pemberton's army of paroled prisoners soon became a serious problem. Johnston had recommended furloughing them until they could be relieved of their paroles by exchange and again made eligible for active service. The President, however, wanted to hold them together intact while negotiating the exchange, and he ordered Pemberton to establish them in a camp at Demopolis, Alabama. The tedium and inaction of a parole camp did not appeal to the men, already depressed by the siege and surrender at Vicksburg, and, denied furloughs, many of them began to absent themselves without leave and go home. A system of furloughs was then belatedly instituted, but, between furloughs and desertions, the army rapidly dwindled away. There was grave question whether it could ever be reassembled as a fighting force, at least under its old commander.

The soldiers and the people of the South felt for Pemberton at this time the most intense hostility and contempt, well expressed in a letter to Jefferson Davis from a friend in Mississippi, E. Barksdale.

"I will not endeavor to pronounce judgment upon his merit as an officer; but it is due to truth and the common cause to say that he has entirely lost the confidence of the country and the army he has commanded and that his capacity for usefulness, however great it otherwise might be, is utterly destroyed. I have made diligent inquiry, and my conclusion is that he can not hold in a state of organization, much less efficiency and discipline, the army he has commanded."

These views were echoed in every quarter, until at last the President realized that some action must be taken. To meet the immediate emergency, he detached General Hardee from Bragg's army at Chattanooga and sent him to the Mississippi front to gather up the stragglers and remold them into a real fighting unit. Hardee was a good organizer and exceptionally well qualified to handle this task, but it seems a misuse of talent to have deprived Bragg of one of his two experienced corps commanders at what was a critical time in the affairs of the Army of Tennessee.

The surrender of Vicksburg was a shattering blow to the Confederate cause. Aside from the loss in troops and material, serious enough, it opened up the Mississippi River to the Federals and cut the Confederacy in two. But the moral effect was even greater than the physical results. Coming almost simultaneously with the news of Gettysburg, it reinspired the drooping spirit of the North and correspondingly depressed the South. It was the turning point of the war.

CHAPTER XIII

THE RETREAT FROM TENNESSEE

BRAGG's withdrawal from Murfreesboro, after what had been so widely hailed as a great victory, aroused an uproar. The Confederate newspapers were filled with unrestrained censure which accurately reflected the feelings of the people. First Perryville and now Murfreesboro—victory and then retreat. It was more than they could understand. What was the matter with Bragg, anyhow?

Even if he did not read the newpapers, Bragg could not escape knowledge of the low esteem in which he was generally held. Expressions of it were on every tongue. One day while riding on the road near Tullahoma he met a countryman, dressed in nondescript jeans, of whom he asked the way. Then, not being sure whether or not the man was in uniform—the Army of Tennessee was not always clothed in the regulation Confederate gray—the general asked if he belonged to Bragg's army. "Bragg's army?" repeated the countryman. "Bragg's got no army. He shot half of them himself in Kentucky, and the Yankees killed the other half of them up at Murfreesboro."

Gradually all these barbed comments, written and spoken, got under Bragg's skin. Smarting from the continued attacks, especially over his retreat from Murfreesboro, and relying on that letter from Cheatham and Withers with its endorsement by Polk, he committed the sad error of making an issue of it. "It becomes necessary for me to save my fair name, if I can not stop the deluge of abuse which will destroy my usefulness and demoralize this army," he said in a letter which on January 11 he addressed to his corps and division commanders.[1] He asked them to acquit him of the published allegation that he had insisted on the retreat against the advice of his officers. He made the not altogether accurate statement that the retreat "was resisted by me for some time after advised by my corps and division commanders." He continued: "Unanimous as you were in council in verbally advising a retrograde movement, I can not doubt that you will cheerfully attest the same in writing."

If he had stopped right there he would have been on fairly safe ground, but he went on: "I desire that you will consult your subordinate

222

commanders and be candid with me. . . . General Smith has been called to Richmond—it is supposed with a view to supersede me. I shall retire without a regret if I find I have lost the good opinion of my generals, upon whom I have ever relied as upon a foundation of rock."

Seldom has a correspondent received more wholehearted co-operation than Bragg got in his request for "candid" comment. All exonerated him from responsibility for originating the idea of the retreat. But his statement that he would retire without a regret if he found he had lost the good opinion of his generals gave them just the opportunity they had been looking for. They embraced it with enthusiasm.

Polk was on leave of absence, visiting his refugee family in North Carolina. In his absence, Cheatham and Withers considered themselves obligated to refrain from detailed reply, although Cheatham wrote Bragg a brief note acknowledging manfully that he was one of the first to suggest the retreat.[2]

Hardee took pains in his answer to point out that neither he nor his division commanders had made any proposal to retreat, although he had concurred in Bragg's decision to retire when it was announced to him on the morning of the third. Then he said that he had consulted his general officers, as requested in Bragg's letter, and they "are unanimous in their opinion that a change in the command of this army is necessary. In this opinion I concur." He sugar-coated this stinging statement with assurances of "the highest respect for the purity of your motives, your energy and your personal character," but he insisted firmly that "the peril of the country is superior to all personal considerations."[3]

Cleburne was equally obliging with his "candid" views. "I have consulted with all my brigade commanders," he said, ". . . and they unite with me in personal regard for yourself, in a high appreciation of your patriotism and gallantry, and in a conviction of your great capacity for organization; but at the same time they see, with regret, and it has also met my observation, that you do not possess the confidence of the army in other respects in that degree necessary to secure success."[4]

Breckinridge[5] was just as frank. "Acting with the candor you invoke," he wrote, "they [his brigade commanders] request me to say that in their opinion the conduct of the military operations in front of Murfreesboro made it necessary and proper for our army to retire. They also request me to say that while they entertain the highest respect for your patriotism, it is their opinion that you do not possess the confidence of the army to an extent which will enable you to be useful as its commander. In this opinion I feel bound to state that I concur."[6]

When he got back on January 30 Polk tried to escape the necessity of voicing his opinion on Bragg's fitness for command. The chieftain's letter of inquiry, he wrote on January 30,[7] seemed to present two points: First, whether the corps and division commanders were willing to give a written statement on the responsibility for the retreat; and, second, whether Bragg had lost the confidence of his officers as a military commander. "To avoid being placed in a false position," he asked Bragg to advise him whether he was correct in this interpretation. Not being particularly anxious for any more "candid" statements, Bragg grasped at the straw. He replied the same day that his letter contained only one point of inquiry—that about the retreat. "The paragraph relating to my supersedure," he said, "was only an expression of the feeling with which I should receive your replies, should they prove I had been misled in my construction of your opinion and advice."[8] This gave the bishop-general his loophole for not wounding Bragg's feelings. He answered simply that the original letter written by Cheatham and Withers, with Polk's endorsement, showed plainly enough their support of the retreat.[9]

Two days later he learned that Hardee and his officers felt he had evaded the real issue—the question of confidence in Bragg as commander of the army. They thought his action had left them in the attitude of insubordinate malcontents. Polk, though concerned not to do his brother officers an injustice, did not see how, in the light of Bragg's explanatory letter, he could express to the man himself a judgment of his capacity. So he chose the course of writing a letter to President Davis, attaching all the correspondence. To him it would seem natural for Bragg to have wanted to know the opinions of all, "as he had been forced to know those of half of his subordinates of the highest grade, but it was declined." Then he said:

"Had I and my division commanders been asked to answer, our replies would have coincided with those of the officers of the other corps. . . . My opinion is he had better be transferred. . . . I think too that the best thing to be done in supplying his place would be to give his command to General Joseph E. Johnston. He will cure all discontent and inspire the army with new life and confidence. He is here on the spot, and I am sure will be content to take it."[10]

Johnston was indeed "on the spot," both literally and in the now currently accepted meaning of that expressive phrase. While inspecting the works at Mobile on January 22, he had been ordered by President

Davis to Murfreesboro to investigate the disaffection and dissatisfaction with Bragg's leadership which was so widely reported, and to ascertain whether he had so far lost the confidence of the army as to necessitate his removal. Davis informed Johnston of Bragg's "candid" correspondence with his subordinates, commenting: "Why General Bragg should have selected that tribunal and have invited its judgments upon him is to me unexplained. It manifests, however, a condition of things which seems to me to require your presence. . . . Although my confidence in General Bragg is unshaken, it can not be doubted that, if he is distrusted by his officers and troops, a disaster may result."[11]

Johnston devoted three weeks to the investigation, but he was in a peculiarly delicate position—particularly in view of his none too cordial relations with the President. To report adversely on Bragg's capacity might easily be construed by Davis as a bid for command of the Army of Tennessee. So Johnston leaned backward. Davis has been blamed for obstinately holding onto Bragg in the face of such criticism, but his correspondence with Johnston indicates that he was inclined to relieve Bragg but was dissuaded by the tenor of Johnston's reports. Johnston wrote on February 3 definitely advising against Bragg's removal because, he said, the field officers had represented to him "that the men were in high spirits and as ready as ever to fight, such a condition seeming to be incompatible with the alleged lack of confidence in their general's ability."[12] His own faith had been confirmed by Bragg's recent operations which "evince great vigor and skill." He closed by making the pointed suggestion that "should it appear to you necessary to remove General Bragg, no one in this army or engaged in this investigation ought to be his successor."[13]

A few days later, on February 12, Johnston wrote the President again. Now, he said, he had inspected the whole army; the men were "well clothed, healthy and in good spirits," giving "positive evidence of General Bragg's capacity to command. . . . The operations of this army in Middle Tennessee have been conducted admirably. I can find no record of more effective fighting in modern battles than that of this army in December, evincing skill in the commander and courage in the troops." Polk and Hardee had told him that they had advised his being put in Bragg's place, but the part he had taken in the investigation "would render it inconsistent with my personal honor to occupy that position." Furthermore, he said, he did not believe Bragg should be removed at all.[14]

Davis expressed gratification at this commendation of the general under attack, but still seemed to fear that the disaffection of the officers might communicate itself to the men in the ranks. Though he deprecated Johnston's unwillingness to serve in Bragg's stead, he said: "You shall not be urged by me to any course which would wound your sensibility or views of professional propriety,"[15] while at the same time he pointed out "how small is the field of selection if a new man is to be sought whose rank is superior to that of the lieutenant generals now in Tennessee."[16]

Supposing things settled, Johnston went back to Mobile to continue his tour of inspection. But apparently the reassuring tone of his letters had not after all entirely convinced the President. On March 9 he was ordered by Secretary Seddon to direct General Bragg to report to the War Department at Richmond, and to go himself to Tullahoma and assume command of the army. He went as directed but when he got there he found General Bragg so very much concerned over the critical illness of his wife, supposed to be at the point of death, that he considerately refrained from mentioning the War Department's order. He temporarily assumed command while Bragg devoted himself to the restoration of his wife's health. By the time Mrs. Bragg had recovered, Johnston was himself so ill that he had to take to his bed under a doctor's care. On April 10 he declared he was unable to serve actively in the field. Bragg was automatically restored by default, so to say.

General Polk, holding to his strong conviction of Bragg's incapacity for active leadership, wrote another insistently frank letter to President Davis on March 30.[17] He urged again that Johnston be put at the head of the army and Bragg transferred to "another field where his peculiar talent—that of organization and discipline—could find a more ample scope." He suggested that Bragg could be of service to all the Confederate armies if he were kicked upstairs by assignment to the office of Inspector General at Richmond; the duties would be sufficient to keep him employed, and he would provide welcome help for General Cooper.

Jefferson Davis had a deeply rooted aversion to advice. There was no immediate indication that Polk's suggestion had registered. The action to be taken at Dalton a few months later may have grown out of his March letter, but for the present there was no result. General Johnston continued ill in Tullahoma for another month. Bragg forgot his emphatically announced willingness to "retire without regret" if he had lost his generals' good opinion. They had all spoken out with a frankness unparalleled in military history. To the average commander, the very suggestion, the barest hint of such want of confidence would furnish compelling reason for resignation, but Bragg—sometimes so supersensitive—seemed suddenly to have developed a skin of elephantine toughness. He held on, and the unhappy Army of Tennessee continued to function under the impossible condition of command by a man whose ability was openly and unreservedly distrusted by his subordinates. It is a monument to the mettle of the army's personnel that it was able to function at all in such distressing circumstances. Clearly it knew its own strength and looked forward to the day when it would get the leadership its qualities deserved.

While Johnston was inspecting Bragg's forces a further complication had arisen in Richmond. The Confederate Senate held up action on a resolution which the House had passed thanking Bragg and the Army of Tennessee for their conduct at the Murfreesboro battles. A friend of Bragg's wrote him that Senator Burnett of Kentucky was the obstructionist and it was suspected he was animated by the supposed reflection on Breckinridge in Bragg's Murfreesboro report. There was a seething undercover battle between the pro-Bragg and the anti-Bragg Congressmen. Senator Burnett threatened to demand a Congressional investigation of the ill-fated Kentucky campaign. Bragg's friends cunningly counterthreatened to challenge the right of Kentucky's Senators and Representatives to hold seats in the Confederate Congress at all. And after that nothing more was heard from Mr. Burnett.

Bragg's reaction to the threat of investigation was typically ill-advised and truculent. Instead of trying to quiet things down, he adopted the provocative course of addressing a circular letter to all his generals (except Polk), in which he reopened the question of Polk's alleged failure to comply with his orders before the battle at Perryville. He asked each of them to advise him "to what extent you sustained the general in his acknowledged disobedience."[18] Hardee put Polk on guard by sending him a copy of Bragg's letter, and replied stiffly to Bragg that he did not consider it proper to answer such a communication.[19] Cheatham also declined to answer.[20] Anderson wrote that he thought Polk had done right.[21] Stewart said he did not take part in the council.[22] Buckner wisely advised Bragg to refrain from further agitating the matter but to try to iron it out by personal consultation.[23] This cooled Bragg off to some degree, but not before Polk had become highly incensed and permanently antagonized.

While the relations between Bragg and his generals naturally remained strained, they all accepted conditions as they existed, without sulking or recrimination, and the army showed no falling off in its efficiency and morale during its six months' encampment at Tullahoma and

Shelbyville. Bragg was at his best in such circumstances, where there was no need for the maneuvering of troops in offensive or defensive movements against the enemy. Here, during these months of inactivity, he had an opportunity to exercise those talents for organization which everybody admitted he possessed, and there was not in the whole Confederacy at that time a more excellently drilled and disciplined body of soldiers than the Army of Tennessee.

Bragg knew how to train and condition an army, and he knew how to organize an efficient staff. Incidentally he seems to have had also a knack for attracting odd and outlandish characters to his entourage. There was, for instance, Colonel Hypolite Oladowski, his chief ordnance officer. This native of Poland and professional soldier was serving as an ordnance sergeant at the United States arsenal at Baton Rouge when the war broke out in 1861, and it was facetiously said by the soldiers that Bragg had captured him along with the other ordnance stores. His difficulties with the English language made him the butt of many a joke, and his penurious attitude in doling out ammunition often excited criticism. But he was devoted to Bragg and to the ordnance branch and he did serve faithfully and efficiently to keep the army in ammunition—which was his job.

Then there was that flaming, that almost legendary, figure, George St. Leger Grenfell—a sixty-year-old retired officer of the British Army, veteran of the Crimean War and numerous other wars, who scented the battle from afar and ran the blockade into the South to join the Confederate Army just for the zest of it. Stumbling upon General Morgan early in 1862, he was charmed by the unorthodox, wild-and-woolly style of that commander, and attached himself to his force. Bragg was attracted by Grenfell's technical knowledge of the military art and his skill and made him inspector general of his cavalry early in 1863. But, "while all admired his splendid courage, few really liked the man because of his savage temper and strict discipline."[24] Finally, wishing to get a taste of army life in Virginia, Grenfell transferred to that field just before the retreat from Tullahoma. His subsequent adventures carried him to a tragic death in the stormy waters that lash the rocky shores of the Dry Tortugas.

A distinguished and attractive young soldier who spent some time in the Confederate camp was Lieutenant Colonel Arthur Fremantle of the Coldstream Guards. He had made his way into Texas from Mexico and then set out on a tour of the South, which included a short stay with the Army of Northern Virginia and presence at the Battle of Gettysburg. When he got back to England he set down his observations in an interesting, well-written little book entitled *Three Months in the Confederate States*, from which we get most charmingly intimate sidelights on Confederate leaders, as well as fresh and unspoiled views of army and civilian life.

A prominent—albeit an unwilling—visitor was the Hon. Clement L. Vallandigham of Ohio,[25] who had been branded a "copperhead" and who by order of President Lincoln had been sentenced to banishment from the United States and conducted within the Confederate lines under a flag of truce. Because of the political implications involved, General Bragg refused to receive him officially but agreed to treat him as a "distressed wayfarer" after he had been set down on the roadside by his Federal guards in the no-man's-land between Murfreesboro and Wartrace. Said Vallandigham: "I am a citizen of Ohio and of the United States, still claiming and owing allegiance to both. I am within your lines against my will and by military compulsion, and therefore surrender myself a prisoner of war." He did not tarry long at Bragg's headquarters. As quickly as possible he was given transportation to Wilmington, where he ran the blockade and went to Canada.

President Davis' aide, Colonel William Preston Johnston, who visited the camp in late March, was very complimentary in his comments on the appearance of the troops. For his benefit Hardee staged a review of his whole corps at Tullahoma on the thirtieth, and a few days later Polk turned out his at Shelbyville. Even Colonel Fremantle, accustomed to the precision of the Coldstream Guards, admitted that "they drilled tolerably well, and an advance in line was remarkably good." There is a shudder discernible between the lines as Fremantle tells how some of the soldiers, on account of the heat, had taken off their coats and marched past the general in shirt-sleeves. He mentions that "General Liddell had invented several dodges of his own, for which he was reproved by General Hardee." Fremantle relates also that most of the men were now armed with Enfield rifles, captured from the enemy, but that many had thrown away their bayonets, "as they assert that they have never met any Yankee who would wait for that weapon." He expressed a desire to see them form in square (a favorite drill maneuver of the British Army for defense against cavalry charges), but he was told that they had not been taught this, since "the country did not admit of cavalry charges, even if the Yankee cavalry had stomach to attempt it." If a bit dismayed by some of the military gaucheries, Fremantle remarked admiringly that "the discipline in this army is the strictest in the Confederacy."[26]

These reviews were gala affairs, taking on aspects of a carnival or fiesta. Hardee, described by Polk as "the beau of the army," invited all the women from the neighboring small towns, as "nothing pleases him so much as to have a bevy of ladies around him."[27] Colonel Fremantle made note of Hardee's gallantries. "He is a widower and has the character of being a great admirer of the fair sex." The young British officer relates that "during the Kentucky campaign last year he was in the habit of availing himself of the privilege of his rank and years, and insisted upon kissing the wives and daughters of all the Kentucky farmers. And although he is supposed to have converted many of the ladies to the Southern cause, yet in many instances their male relatives remained either neutral or undecided. On one occasion General Hardee had conferred the 'accolade' upon a very pretty Kentuckian, to their mutual satisfaction, when, to his intense disgust, the proprietor produced two very ugly old females, saying 'Now, general, if you kiss any you must kiss them all around,' which the discomfited general was forced to do, to the great amusement of his officers."[28]

After Hardee's review, he staged a tournament (an old-fashioned Southern display of horsemanship) and a horse race. Polk wrote his wife about all the festivities; he was planning to "reciprocate the civility" the following week when Bragg came to Shelbyville for inspection—although he was careful to explain that the horse-racing part would be turned over to General Cheatham. Bragg was well pleased with what he found, Polk wrote afterward. "Our transportation is in fine condition; horses and mules all fat, and battery horses and batteries in fine condition. The troops have plenty of clothes and are well shod. We have plenty of food also, and as far as the fields before us are any indication, there never was such a wheat harvest."[29]

The spiritual needs of the soldiers were not overlooked. The Confederate authorities made an effort to supply chaplains of various faiths so that the men might worship according to their sect or denomination. Polk, bishop and general, of course gave this arrangement his hearty approval.

"On the judicious application of the means of imparting religious instructions to the army very much depends the future condition of our people when it shall please God to relieve us from the pressure of this scourging war and restore us to peace.... If we should allow our troops to give vent to their natural feeling and passions in retaliating on the enemy, we should train them up in a condition of mind totally unfitting them to fall into a well-disciplined and chastened civilization when the war shall have closed."[30]

Bragg set an example for his men by being baptized in an impressive ceremony administered by Bishop Elliot. The influence was felt, and a revival spirit developed in the camps. There were church services and prayer meetings and baptizings—but there were also cockfighting and keno games and whisky drinking among the unregenerate.

Concealing their asperities, Bragg and his generals fraternized freely in all these activities, military and social, during the army's long sojourn at Tullahoma. There were no more open clashes. Deep down in his heart, however, Bragg still felt the jagged wound to his pride left by the barbed words of his subordinates, while they, for their part, looked forward with dread to the time when this interlude should pass and Bragg must once again face the task of handling troops in combat.

No other Confederate army, in any theater of operations or at any stage of the war, enjoyed such a protracted period of inaction as the Army of Tennessee spent in its camps along the Duck River line during the first half of 1863. For six whole months it lay encamped with its left wing under Polk at Shelbyville and its right at Wartrace under Hardee. The cavalry extended the line on the left to Columbia and on the right to McMinnville. Immediately before Polk's and Hardee's camps a strong system of breastworks had been thrown up, protected by an abatis for a space of six hundred yards. Tullahoma, where Bragg maintained his headquarters, was in the rear of Wartrace on the main line of the Nashville & Chattanooga. This railroad served as his line of supply to the south; north of Murfreesboro, it was Rosecrans' life line to his depot at Nashville. With its connection at Chattanooga, the state-owned Western & Atlantic, it was in fact the principal facility that made possible the advance of Rosecrans and Sherman into the South. The various engagements of the opposing forces between Nashville and Atlanta were along it or in sight of it.

The total strength of the Army of Tennessee at this time came close to 44,000 men. Breckinridge's division, along with some other detachments, had been sent to Mississippi to help Johnston. But there had been accessions, and by June Bragg had about 36,000 infantry and artillery and 8,000 cavalry. Further accessions were earnestly sought to offset the heavy reinforcements Rosecrans was understood to be getting. Appeals were published urging the "absent without leave" to return to the colors. Conscription efforts were pushed, and General Pillow was placed in charge of organizing conscription boards to bring out the fullest possible man power. Pillow was still somewhat under a cloud in public esteem because of his abandonment of Fort Donelson, but Bragg, remembering his services in Mexico, endeavored to make use of his experience and ability. He had been in temporary charge of a brigade in Breckinridge's division at Murfreesboro, serving in this relatively lowly capacity in spite of his former status. He entered into the discharge of his new duties with alacrity and vigor, working to build up the army through a rigid application of the conscription laws.

Beauregard, though shelved and side-tracked in Charleston, still kept up a lively interest in Tennessee. After the Battle of Chancellorsville in which Lee dealt the Federals under Hooker such a crushing blow, Beauregard considered the time propitious for striking the enemy in the West. On May 15 he wrote to General Johnston at Jackson (sending a copy of his letter to Bragg at Tullahoma) suggesting an elaborate plan for a general offensive in Tennessee and Kentucky as the best way to relieve the state of Mississippi and the Mississippi River. To expedite such a move, he suggested, all the other Confederate armies should be held on the defensive and all possible reinforcements from them should be added to the forces under Johnston and Bragg. If these augmented forces, led by Johnston, should suddenly attack Rosecrans in overwhelming strength, he thought Rosecrans must surely be routed and driven to the Ohio River. Then it would become feasible for Johnston with the bulk of the army to turn and strike directly at the Mississippi River, and seize Fort Pillow and Columbus again. Grant, with his communications thus cut, would find himself "compelled to fight his way through a victorious army equal to his own in strength, on its own selected battlefield . . . and the result could not be doubtful for an instant."[31]

This plan may have struck Johnston as too visionary. Perhaps it was too daring for his conservative nature. At any rate, he did nothing with it. Bragg told Beauregard later that he thought well of it,[32] but he was subordinate to Johnston and could do nothing about it without orders. President Davis, if he ever had it brought to his attention, evidently did not favor it, for his idea of the proper procedure, as soon developed, was Lee's ill-fated invasion of Pennsylvania, and the West was left to shift for itself.

Bragg's health, never robust, was very poor at this time. He wrote Johnston in June that he had been suffering from a siege of boils which culminated in "a general break-down." He said he had recovered, but, in truth, was so visibly enfeebled that in a few weeks Hardee confidentially expressed to Polk his fear that the commanding general was in no condition "either to examine and determine his line of battle or to take command on the field." Colonel Fremantle noticed how weak he looked.

"This officer is in appearance the least prepossessing of the Confederate generals. He is very thin; he stoops; and has a sickly, cadaverous, haggard appearance; rather plain features, bushy black eye-brows which unite in a tuft on the top of his nose, and a stubby, iron-gray beard; but his eyes are bright and piercing. He has the reputation of being a rigid disciplinarian, and of shooting freely for insubordination. I understand he is rather unpopular on this account, and also by reason of his occasional acerbity of manner."[33]

Defense was all Bragg seemed to think about at Tullahoma. There was some talk of another invasion of Kentucky, but the only thing done was disastrous—Morgan's famous raid into Indiana and Ohio. About the middle of June Morgan represented to Wheeler that Louisville was defended by only about 300 men. He asked permission to make a dash on the city and destroy the public works. Wheeler authorized him to take 2,000 men, urging him to ride with such speed that he might be on his way back to Tennessee before Rosecrans could learn of his absence and take advantage of it. Afterward Morgan intimated that Bragg and Wheeler knew of his intention to cross the Ohio River, but they claimed that they did not, and it seems improbable that Bragg, or even Wheeler, would have sponsored such an escapade when Rosecrans was momentarily expected to advance. At any rate, Morgan took 2,480 mounted men and two pieces of artillery and started out. On the very day Rosecrans was moving around Bragg's right flank—when Bragg so sorely needed cavalry— Morgan was gaily crossing the Cumberland River at Burkesville and striking for the Ohio. General Burnside was in Cincinnati, but Morgan felt a justified contempt for his ability to act with celerity enough to interfere. By the eighth the Rebel raiders were on the banks of the Ohio at Brandenburg below Louisville, ready to cross into Indiana.

The raid north of the Ohio was a showy affair and struck terror into Hoosier and Buckeye communities, but it was without military significance or possibilities. The outcome was almost inevitable. The troopers dashed wildly across southern Indiana and Ohio until they reached the Ohio near Parkersburg. A great hue and cry was raised; the countryside boiled with pursuing militia and United States regulars. Before the month was over Morgan and practically all his men had been captured and were locked up in various Northern prisons—Morgan himself and most of his officers in the Ohio State Penitentiary at Columbus. He escaped from prison in late November and made his way back to the Confederacy, but his days of usefulness to the Army of Tennessee were over.

On Bragg's left wing, however, the cavalry of Forrest and Van Dorn was constantly and brilliantly astir. On March 4 the Federals sent out a column on a reconnaissance from Franklin under Colonel John Coburn. It encountered Van Dorn's cavalry at Thompson's Station, between Franklin and Spring Hill, and after a spirited engagement Coburn surrendered with 1,300 men. In late April and early May Forrest carried out one of the most spectacular exploits of the war—his pursuit of a party of Federal cavalry under Colonel Streight who were on a daring foray across northern Alabama eastward, aimed at Rome, Georgia, in Bragg's rear. Nearly 2,000 Federals landed from transports at Eastport on the Tennessee River on April 19 and by the twenty-fifth reached Tuscumbia. As soon as Forrest heard of the raiders behind him, he set out from Columbia with less than 500 and caught up with Streight at Decatur on the twenty-eighth. Five days and nights ensued of steady fighting and marching, in which the untiring Forrest somehow managed to keep his own force going and gave his opponents no time to rest or sleep. Finally, on May 3, between Gadsden and Rome, he captured Streight and his whole command—now about 1,800 men—with their mounts, rifles, guns and supplies. Outnumbered four to one, Forrest tricked Streight by the moth-eaten stratagem of marching his small body of men around a little rise of ground. Streight did not realize that he was seeing the same men over and over, thought the little band a considerable force.

For intelligence Bragg did not depend only on his cavalry and his scouts. He kept up with what the Federals were doing by the simple expedient of reading the Northern dailies which, entirely uncensored, gave all available information as to troop movements and military plans. He subscribed to several in the name of a Confederate sympathizer in Elizabethtown, Kentucky, and a line of scouts in relays conveyed the precious bundles to his headquarters every day.[34]

While he remained passive at Tullahoma, Rosecrans was just as passive at Murfreesboro—and got sharp criticism for his lassitude. Grant in Mississippi repeatedly urged Halleck to order Rosecrans to advance on Bragg. Halleck did so, not once but several times. There was a cross fire of caustic telegrams[35]—but Rosecrans stayed where he was. His later explanation was that by his inaction he held Bragg in Tennessee and so helped Grant by preventing Bragg from going into Mississippi to reinforce Johnston. Finally, as he tells it, he got news that Vicksburg could not hold out more than two or three weeks; so, on June 24, he began his "movements to dislodge Bragg from his entrenched camp."[36] He had been steadily recruiting his force and now had about 70,000 men. Of these 10,000 were cavalry, a branch in which the Federals had been lamentably weak, but which he had built up.

His campaign was a masterpiece of offensive strategy. He maneuvered the Confederate army entirely out of Tennessee almost without firing a shot, except in the preliminary cavalry brushes as he unexpectedly pressed through the thinly held mountain passes. Bragg, placing too much reliance on the strong defenses in his front and taking it for granted that Rosecrans would obligingly advance that way,[37] did not realize what was happening to him on his right flank until it was too late to do anything about it. Though he had been in position for six months, he seems never to have thought of the possibility of flank attack, and in the early stages of the turning movement he showed a fumbling in decision and action that filled his corps commanders with dismay.

The two armies were separated by a range of foothills almost mountainous in height, through which passed roads connecting Murfreesboro and Tullahoma. These roads crossed the hills at three defiles—Hoover's, Guy's and Liberty Gaps. Through Hoover's and Liberty Rosecrans' main force struck at Hardee's right and rear while a heavy demonstration was staged against Polk at Shelbyville. Stanley's cavalry advanced on Shelbyville with an ostentation intended to indicate a movement in force. At night they kindled campfires through the country from Polk's left to the Shelbyville road to give the impression of a big infantry advance in that direction. This was enough to hold Polk at Shelbyville for two days. Meanwhile the main Federal force moved on Bragg's right in such strength that by the morning of the twenty-seventh they had swept the scanty Confederate patrols out of the gaps and reached Manchester, twelve miles behind it. Following up this vital thrust, Rosecrans on the twenty-eighth hurried a detachment across country to destroy the railroad in Bragg's rear, and the Confederate commander found himself in a most perilous predicament.

Bragg was not aware of this thrust until it had been accomplished. He had gone along on his comfortable theory that Rosecrans was making a simple advance on his front. On the morning of the twenty-sixth he ordered Polk to march through Guy's Gap and the next morning attack the Federal force that was pressing Hardee at Liberty. Polk made so bold as to advise against this movement of his corps—it would be just what the enemy wanted. Bragg insisted, and Polk prepared to do as directed. Later in the day Bragg woke to find the Federals at Manchester on his right flank. So Hardee and Polk were both ordered to fall back and concentrate at Tullahoma.

The entire campaign was carried out under conditions extremely difficult for both sides, as extraordinarily heavy rains fell day after day for
more than two weeks and the ground anywhere off the few macadamized
roads was reduced to a spongy mire that hampered the movement of men,
horses and guns. Though Polk marched out of his elaborate works at
Shelbyville early on the twenty-seventh, he did not reach Tullahoma,
eighteen miles away, until late the next afternoon. Hardee had a shorter
distance to get his corps down the railroad. On the morning of the
twenty-ninth Bragg's whole army was in the Tullahoma works.

He had now made up his mind to give battle there. He said as much
when Polk went to headquarters for orders that morning. During the
day his resolution seemed to weaken. At 3 P.M. he called a conference
which was attended by Polk, Hardee, Mackall, and Colonel Urquhart, his
military secretary. Bragg asked Polk first for his advice. Disturbed by the
cutting of the railroad at Decherd, Polk said the first job was to re-establish communications. Bragg answered that this had already been done;
he had recovered possession of the railroad during the day and expected
to hold it with his cavalry. Polk thought there was not enough cavalry
for this and warned Bragg that if Rosecrans got the railroad they would be
so hemmed in the only course would be to cut loose and march south
into northern Alabama—and Rosecrans could advance unopposed
through Chattanooga into north Georgia, the Carolinas or wherever he
might wish to go. "Then," said General Bragg challengingly, "you propose that we shall retreat?" To which Polk replied firmly: "I do, and that
is my counsel."[38] Hardee was unwilling to advise retreat and suggested
that an infantry force be sent back along the railroad to support the cavalry. But there was no definite decision, and the council of war adjourned.

Bragg did nothing further until the night of the thirtieth, when, finding that the whole Federal army was now in force at Manchester, he fell
back to the south side of Elk River near Decherd and Winchester—presumably to make a stand on the river. On the evening of July 1 he addressed to Polk and Hardee this request for advice: "The question to be
decided instantly: shall we fight on the Elk or take post at foot of mountain at Cowan?" Polk favored Cowan. Hardee was more explicit: "Let us
fight at the mountain."

Hardee was greatly perturbed over Bragg's wavering. Earlier in the
day he had written Polk:

"What shall we do? What is best to be done to save this army and
its honor? I think we ought to counsel together. Where is Buckner?[39] . . .

I do not desire that any but Buckner and yourself should know my anxiety."[40]

But Rosecrans halted. The immediate crisis was passed. The Confederate army fell back to Cowan on the second and established a line of battle with both flanks resting on the mountain. Then, Rosecrans still showing no disposition to force the issue, Bragg was content to continue his retreat on across Sewanee Mountain[41] to Chattanooga.

To the ever-vigilant Forrest was assigned the task of holding the pass near Cowan and guarding the rear. After the infantry had safely made its way over the mountain, a strong force of Federal cavalry fell upon the rear guard, who retreated rapidly through the village of Cowan before the superior attacking force. One of the patriotic women of the town, distressed at the flight of the gray troopers, rushed into the street and began reviling them. Singling out Forrest himself for particular attack, with no idea of his identity, she shrilled at him: "You great big cowardly rascal, why don't you turn and fight like a man instead of running like a cur? I wish old Forrest was here; he'd make you fight!" "Old Forrest" enjoyed the joke and joined in the troopers' laugh at his expense—but he kept on running. Later he told the story on himself, and said he would rather have faced a Yankee battery than that fiery female.[42]

Jefferson Davis tries to gloss over Bragg's ignominious retreat before the flanking strategy.

"In June," he writes, "some movements were made by General Rosecrans which were followed by the withdrawal of our forces from Middle Tennessee and a return to the occupation of Chattanooga."[43]

But Bragg himself yielded to no self-delusion. Bishop Quintard relates that on the morning of July 3 he came upon him at Cowan, and he seemed "thoroughly out-done." The bishop spoke of it. Bragg replied: "Yes, I am utterly broken down." Then, leaning from his saddle, he whispered sadly to the bishop: "This is a great disaster."[44]

Whether because of his physical exhaustion or his distress of mind, Bragg failed to do one thing that might have saved grave eventualities. Just beyond Cowan the Nashville & Chattanooga Railroad runs through a long tunnel under the mountain. It should have been a simple matter to damage it so that the railroad could not be used for several months at least. This would have checked the Northern advance pending its repair. It might even have been feasible to block the tunnel permanently. That would have made Sherman's march into Georgia difficult if not impossible.

But Bragg was not thinking about the tunnel. He himself proceeded from Cowan to Chattanooga by rail, pausing at Bridgeport long enough on July 3 to dispatch to the government a report of his withdrawal. On the same day Sheridan's division occupied the former Confederate camp at Tullahoma. Bragg's message was received in Richmond the next day—July the Fourth—a Glorious Fourth indeed for the North, but a sad, bleak day for the Confederacy. In the East that day Lee was getting ready to fall back from Gettysburg. In the West the prediction of Johnston was fulfilled—Pemberton was surrendering Vicksburg to Grant, and with it the control of the Mississippi River. Bragg was giving up Tennessee without a battle. Gloom rested over the Executive Mansion and the War Department office in Richmond. The wave of the Confederate cause had reached and passed its crest. From then on it was all ebb tide.

CHAPTER XIV

CHICKAMAUGA

BRAGG, encamped with his army at Chattanooga during the summer of 1863, was deeply enmeshed in perplexed indecision. Rosecrans was still on the other side of the Cumberland mountain range. Bragg could not fathom his intentions, and as he felt that his own movements must depend largely on what Rosecrans might do, he was in a haze. Reaching about for some positive course, he wrote General Johnston on July 17 stressing the importance of holding Mississippi, and suggesting that he might take his army west to join with Johnston's for a quick blow at Grant. "I do not think the enemy can advance here in force for six weeks," he said. "Our success can only result from concentration"— which was patent. Johnston did not react favorably. He dismissed the idea with the terse comment: "It was too late. Such a combination might have been advantageous before or during the siege of Vicksburg, but not after its disastrous termination."[1] Bragg did not push it.

The President and the War Department had been engrossed with Vicksburg and Lee's invasion of Pennsylvania, and seemed to have no time for the Army of Tennessee. Bragg, in a letter to Beauregard on July 21,[2] deploring his own inaction, said that he had asked for orders three times since July 1 and got no response from Richmond. "Yet Johnston, within five days of me," he said fretfully, "is falling back day by day, yielding ground we can not recover, and without which we can not survive. By this time this whole army could have been in Mississippi and a victory won. As it is, we may be expected to be defeated in detail."

With Vicksburg lost and Lee pushed south of the Potomac, Richmond again remembered the Army of Tennessee. General Cooper came to life. On August 1 he wrote Bragg: "If we can spare most of Johnston's army temporarily and reinforce you, can you attack the enemy?" Bragg thought he could "if a fight can be had on equal terms," but mentioned the geographical difficulty of reaching the enemy's position. After mulling it over, his caution assumed the ascendancy. On second thought, he wrote Cooper four days later, he felt "it would be unsafe to seek the enemy," even if his force were combined with Johnston's and Buckner's.

239

To Johnston he privately reviewed all the things that stood in the way of an advance, and said: "The defensive seems to be our only alternative, and that is a sad one."[3]

Cooper was not at all satisfied. He referred the letter to President Davis, asking if Bragg should not be peremptorily ordered to advance and fight. Davis retorted that a commanding general could not be given an order, only a suggestion to fight a battle, and opined it was unwise to insist on fighting when the commander predicted failure.

So the Army of Tennessee lay idly at Chattanooga as the summer drifted by, waiting for something to turn up. The men were in fairly good health and spirits, but, as was not unusual under Bragg's command, provisions were scanty and they grumbled much about that.[4] But principally they grumbled at their idleness. They wanted to fight; they were weary of camp life and marching—particularly of so much retreating. But all they did was wait and wait.

While they waited important changes in organization and in the scope of Bragg's authority occurred that were to make a decided difference in their campaigning. Hardee's transfer to Mississippi left a vacancy at the head of his corps. To fill it with the right man was a gravely serious matter. Instead of advancing some major general in the Army of Tennessee, President Davis promoted General D. H. Hill to the rank of lieutenant general and sent him to Chattanooga.

Hill was a trained soldier, a graduate of West Point, but a sort of stormy petrel and for some reason a misfit officer. He never seemed able to find exactly the right niche for his individual talents. Douglas Freeman describes him as "a most tenacious fighter" and says that "few division commanders could get more from a given number of men." This is true, but he was always in some sort of dispute with somebody about something. He had shown talent and bravery at Bethel, at South Mountain and at Sharpsburg, but he was jealous and sensitive and regarded as "peculiar." He and Stonewall Jackson had married sisters, and he was an enthusiastic admirer of Jackson's military genius; also he was properly and thoroughly impressed with the competent way Robert E. Lee managed the affairs of the Army of Northern Virginia, and on coming to the Army of Tennessee he was struck by the great contrast between Lee's smooth, soldier proficiency and Bragg's awkwardness. He was a native of South Carolina, and up to this time his service had been entirely in the East.

He was a complete stranger to the troops he was now to command and to the country in which he was to operate, but he was no stranger to Bragg. George H. Thomas, John F. Reynolds and D. H. Hill had been lieutenants in Bragg's battery of artillery in the old army back in the forties. As Hill traveled from Virginia to Tennessee to take over his new command his thoughts went back to the days in Mexico and on the Texas frontier when the celebrated Captain Bragg had the three of them as messmates. Now Reynolds was dead, killed at Gettysburg a few days before, and "Old Tom" Thomas was commanding a corps in the Federal army confronting Bragg at Chattanooga. Hill looked forward to pleasant service under his old captain, but he was to be sadly disappointed. Bragg's worries, he found, had weighed heavily on him; he was nervous and distraught and, to Hill's eyes, prematurely old. "He was silent and reserved and seemed gloomy and despondent," Hill wrote later.[5] And that first chill presaged a rift between the old friends which was soon to widen into a chasm of hostility and recrimination. Hill assumed command of his corps, consisting of the divisions of Pat Cleburne and A. P. Stewart, and took up position at Tyner's Station on the Knoxville Railroad a few miles east of Chattanooga. General Polk's corps, consisting of Hindman's and Cheatham's divisions, was quartered in and around the little city—with the exception of one detached brigade which was stationed in observation at Bridgeport.

There were other changes. Johnston had been finally relieved of responsibility for Bragg's department, and the scope of Bragg's own authority was enlarged to include jurisdiction over the Department of East Tennessee.

General Buckner had been in charge of it at Knoxville since May. But he had no particular ambition for office and had readily accepted, in fact had suggested, the creation of the new "Department of Tennessee" which on July 25 was set up and put under Bragg. However, General Cooper's letter to Bragg announcing the change said: "General Buckner will continue to correspond directly with this office." On August 6, when Bragg officially took charge and proclaimed that the troops in East Tennessee would thenceforward constitute the Third Corps of the Army of Tennessee and be known officially as "Buckner's Corps," he specified that the administration of the Department of East Tennessee was to remain a part of Buckner's duties.[6] This created an anomalous and well-nigh impossible state of affairs. Buckner quite understandably protested to Cooper that if he was not to have the status of a department commander he did not wish to be saddled with the duties and responsibilities; he would rather give his whole time to his troops.[7] Cooper took no action, and before this technical matter of jurisdiction could be settled, Buckner was confronted with a pressing military emergency.

The fall of Vicksburg had released Burnside's corps which had been sent to reinforce Grant. Late in August, after insistent urging from Washington, Burnside began a threatening movement with about 20,000 men out of Lexington, Kentucky, toward East Tennessee. The Confederates held Cumberland Gap strongly so Burnside went south through Big Creek Gap and in the latter part of the month was drawing near to Knoxville. Buckner, with only 6,000 men, called on Bragg for help. Bragg could not send help to anybody. He had troubles of his own.

Rosecrans, after several weeks spent in preparation, perfecting his lines of communication and insuring his source of supplies, was now ready to start against the Confederates at Chattanooga. He had of necessity moved slowly. The campaign he was undertaking would have been beset with complexities under the best of conditions. The Federal army, with its line stretching from Winchester to McMinnville, was separated from Bragg's army by several towering mountain ranges as well as by a deep, wide river. The mountains were rugged and precipitous, passable only by rough and winding roads at widely separated gaps. The river presented a formidable barrier especially because the retreating Confederates had burned the only bridge at Bridgeport. Rosecrans had two courses of advance available to him. The more direct was by his left from McMinnville across the Sequatchie Valley and Walden's Ridge, approaching Chattanooga from the north. But this route he found impracticable, since he had established his base of supplies at Stevenson, the junction of the Nashville & Chattanooga[8] and the Memphis & Charleston Railroads, near the Tennessee River at Bridgeport. To keep in touch with his base and with the railroad, he elected to cross the river below Chattanooga, and move over the mountains of northwestern Georgia into the country south of the town where operations against Bragg and his line of supply would be feasible.

This country was so exceptionally rugged that Bragg seems to have minimized the probability of an approach from that direction. It did indeed seem to offer almost insurmountable obstacles. Chattanooga is located in southeastern Tennessee on the Tennessee River, only a few miles north of the Georgia state line. The river, flowing from northeast to southwest, from its headwaters in East Tennessee into the northeastern corner of Alabama, is flanked immediately to the east in northwestern Georgia by a rocky bulwark. Sand Mountain is not a solitary peak, but really a great ridge fifty or sixty miles long and several miles wide, with sheer walls rising at some places a thousand feet, and ending at the north in Raccoon Mountain, which fills one of the bends of the river below Chattanooga. Eastward from this imposing rampart the country is crumpled with ridges or mountains. Across Lookout Creek and its narrow valley towers the formidable bulk of Lookout Mountain—nearly a hundred miles long and some 3,000 feet above sea level at its highest point. At its northern extremity Lookout juts out in the bold and familiar promontory that overlooks Chattanooga and the river where it sweeps around Moccasin Bend. A few miles south of Chattanooga, Missionary Ridge[9] spurs off from Lookout Mountain to the eastward, with Chattanooga Creek flowing between them in a narrow valley that widens as it reaches the river at the city. Forty-five miles south of Chattanooga Lookout Mountain throws out from its eastern side another spur or range, called Pigeon Mountain, crescent-shaped, with the west branch of Chickamauga Creek flowing in the valley between it and Lookout. As this valley narrows to the southward, where the mountains join, it forms a natural triangular cul-de-sac called McLemore's Cove, some six miles wide. Fertile farm lands lie in the bed of McLemore's Cove, but the sheer mountain walls rise around it, passable only by widely separated, rough, narrow and circuitous roads. Dougherty's Gap is at its southernmost extremity. Pigeon Mountain is crossed by Catlett's, Dug and Bluebird Gaps. Lookout is crossed at Stevens' and Cooper's Gaps. It would be hard for an army to get into McLemore's Cove through those holes— but it might be harder to get out. Farther eastward from Pigeon Mountain there is another, lower range called Taylor's Ridge. Still farther east are the so-called Chattanooga Mountains, and east of them the Western & Atlantic Railroad runs in a southerly direction to Atlanta, passing through the towns of Ringgold, Dalton and Resaca in northern Georgia, respectively eighteen, forty and sixty miles south of Chattanooga.

Apparently it was Rosecrans' general idea to strike across these natural barriers toward Dalton in Bragg's rear, cutting his communications to the southward—a bold and hazardous project.

For the avowed purpose of confusing and befuddling Bragg—mostly a waste of effort—Rosecrans spread out his advancing army over an astonishingly wide area. In the presence of an alert and enterprising antagonist with skillfully employed cavalry he would have been exposing himself to very grave danger. But Bragg again was guilty of unpardonable sloth. He let his enemy go ahead practically without molestation. Hill was horrified at this supine attitude, especially at the ignorance of the enemy's whereabouts and movements. He contrasted it with the minute knowledge General Lee always had of what his opponents were doing. "I was most painfully impressed," he says, "with the feeling that it was to be a hap-hazard campaign on our part."[10]

The force under Rosecrans, officially known as the "Army of the Cumberland," consisted of three army corps: the Fourteenth, of four divisions, under General Thomas; the Twentieth, of three divisions, under General McCook; and the Twenty-first, of three divisions, under General T. L. Crittenden. Thomas and McCook had been concentrated around Winchester, with one division advanced to the depot at Stevenson. Crittenden and his corps were at McMinnville. There were a reserve corps under General Gordon Granger, and two divisions of cavalry, temporarily commanded by General Mitchell. The total was about 60,000 men, with 200 guns.

The Federal army started on August 16. Crittenden marched eastward across the Cumberland plateau to the Sequatchie Valley. Van Cleve's division reached Pikeville at the northern head of the valley. Thomas' corps, constituting the center, moved to Jasper at the foot of the Sequatchie Valley and then on to Shell Mound, crossing the mountains by way of Sewanee, now the site of the University of the South. McCook's corps followed the railroad line to Stevenson and Bridgeport. A brigade of cavalry under Colonel Minty covered the left flank as far north as Sparta, and three brigades of mounted men under General Mitchell protected the right to Fayetteville, Tennessee, and Athens, Alabama. Not counting the far-flung cavalry, the three corps were now spread out in motion over a front of more than fifty miles. Still Bragg seemed only vaguely aware of what was doing and gave no sign of other plan than merely marking time until the crisis should be right on top of him.

He did have enough appreciation of his peril to take steps to augment his force. On August 21 he appealed to Johnston for aid—an appeal that resulted in the dispatch of two divisions, amounting to 9,000 men, under Generals Breckinridge and W. H. T. Walker. As he could not reinforce Buckner, he instructed him to evacuate Knoxville and fall back to the Hiwassee River, about thirty miles north of Chattanooga. Buckner occupied this position after burning the bridge over the Tennessee at Loudon.

The authorities at Richmond were now belatedly aroused to the importance of strengthening Bragg's army and reached at length the momentous decision to do it with Longstreet's corps from the Army of Northern Virginia. It is not certain with whom the idea originated. Longstreet says he himself suggested it as early as May 1863, and urged it upon Secretary Seddon again in August when the Army of Northern Virginia was lying idle on the Rapidan.[11] That others had the same thought about the same time is indicated in a letter written to President Davis late that month by Senator G. A. Henry of Tennessee.

"We want some fighting generals in the Army of Tennessee," he said. "I think Bragg exhausts himself in organizing his army, and that Buckner has not developed that dogged resolution that wins victories. As sure as you are born, that army is better than its commanders, and you will see my statement verified if men of more nerve are put in its command. Can't Longstreet be sent there? The fate of Virginia depends upon the defense of East Tennessee."[12]

Whether or not he thought of it first, the idea seems to have obsessed Longstreet. His critics attribute his enthusiasm to personal ambition. Whatever his motive, he pushed it for all he was worth. He took it up with General Lee; the interests of the Confederacy, he represented, could best be served by placing Lee's army on the defensive with its two remaining corps while he took his off to help Bragg strike Rosecrans a knockout blow. "Our best opportunity for great results is in Tennessee,"[13] he wrote Lee on September 15. As alternative he ventured the remarkable suggestion that, in view of Bragg's unpopularity with his troops, it might be advisable for them to exchange places—Bragg to assume command of Longstreet's corps in Lee's army and Longstreet to take over the Army of Tennessee. This was quite too drastic for Lee to stomach, but he did approve of sending Longstreet to Bragg's assistance. He went to Richmond to lay the matter before President Davis. On his recommendation it was decided that Longstreet should go with Hood's and McLaws' divisions as soon as possible.

The movement was to be by rail. It was not until September 9 that transportation was provided and the first trainload of troops left Orange Courthouse. By that time Buckner had abandoned Knoxville, and on that very day the garrison left at Cumberland Gap surrendered, the Confederates thereby losing permanent control of the direct railroad connection to Chattanooga through East Tennessee. The only rail route now open was by way of Wilmington and Charlotte to Augusta, and thence by a single track through Atlanta, so that Hood's division, the first to entrain, did not reach Bragg until the eighteenth. By modern standards that seems a long time for the distance involved, but, considering the pitifully run-down condition of the lines in the Confederacy, it was really a great tribute to Quartermaster General Lawton that it was possible to do it at all.

"Never before," says General Moxley Sorrel, "were so many troops moved over such worn-out railways. . . . Never before were such crazy cars—passenger, baggage, mail, coal, box, platform, all and every sort, wabbling on the jumping strap-iron—used for hauling good soldiers. But we got there, nevertheless."[14]

The barren victories of the Army of Tennessee had become notorious in Virginia. Lee advocated the separation of Longstreet from his command only on the assurance that "vigorous pursuit, even to the Ohio River, should follow success."[15] Longstreet relates that before leaving Virginia he went to Lee's tent to say good-by. Lee walked out to his horse with him and said impressively: "Now, general, you must beat those people out in the West." Longstreet goes on: "I promised: 'If I live—but I would not give a single man of my command for a fruitless victory.' He . . . said that arrangements had been made that any success we had should be followed; that orders to that effect had been given!"[16] So Longstreet went off to the West, his heart filled with hope.

Meanwhile affairs were developing rapidly on Bragg's immediate front. Rosecrans had all his preparatory movements completed by late in August and the actual crossing of the Tennessee began. Hazen's brigade of Crittenden's corps, consisting of about 7,000 men, had been detached to make a demonstration opposite to and above Chattanooga in order to give Bragg the idea that the Federals would attempt to cross there. On the twenty-first an Indiana battery unlimbered on the north side of the river and threw shells into the town. This happened to be a day set aside by President Davis for fasting and prayer in the Confederacy, and religious services were in progress when the shelling began. General Hill dryly remarks that there was "a perceptible diminution" of the congregations.[17] Fasting and prayer were all right, but "watch and pray" would have been a better motto for Bragg in this crisis—with the emphasis on the "watch."

Under cover of this misleading racket, Rosecrans went ahead with the actual crossing of Thomas' and McCook's men—some crossing at Caperton's Ferry near Stevenson, some by the rebuilt railroad bridge at Bridgeport, others by pontoons, boats and rafts. It began on August 29, and the last detachments were over by September 4. Two days later Thomas and McCook were respectively in the neighborhood of Trenton and Valley Head in Lookout Valley. Thomas' van had reached Johnson's Crook, about twenty-five miles from Chattanooga, where the road from Trenton to LaFayette leads up Lookout Mountain and crosses into McLemore's Cove. His whole corps was directed to move by this road into the Cove and thence across Pigeon Mountain to LaFayette. Meanwhile McCook was to cross Lookout at Winston's Gap, twenty miles farther

GENERAL BRAXTON BRAGG

A Federal position at Chickamauga

south, and occupy Alpine which was on the eastern side of the mountain.

Once the Federals were actually across, Bragg had a fairly good idea what was happening. With a flash of aggressive spirit, he wrote to D. H. Hill, who was still stationed above Chattanooga:

"There is no doubt of the enemy's position now: One corps opposite you, and two this side of the river from Shell Mound by Bridgeport to Caperton's. . . . If you can cross the river, now is our time to crush the corps opposite. What say you? . . . We must do something and that soon. . . . The crushing of this corps would give us a great victory and redeem Tennessee. . . . Consult Cleburne. He is cool, full of resources and ever alive to a success."[18]

Hill forwarded the note to Cleburne, who approved. But before anything could be done, General Bragg changed his mind again.

Those two enemy corps east of the river on his left and rear worried him, especially as the barrier of Lookout Mountain screened their movements. "Mountains hide your foe from you," he had said querulously to General Hill, "while they are full of gaps through which he can pounce on you at any time. A mountain is like the wall of a house full of rat-holes. The rat lies hidden at his hole, ready to pop out when no one is watching. Who can tell what lies hidden behind that wall?"[19] The obvious answer, of course, is that an up-and-coming commander would have made it his business to know what was there. He would not have waited for the rat to pop out of his chosen hole at his own convenience. He would have got the facts on the rat—and might have set a trap to catch him before there was any popping out.

Bragg was now deeply apprehensive about the broad strategic situation—and not without reason. If Burnside should move to a junction with Rosecrans, he would find himself greatly outnumbered, even with the addition of Buckner's army. If he let Rosecrans move across north Georgia onto his line of communication with his base at Atlanta, he faced being hemmed up in Chattanooga and starved into submission, a fate like Pemberton's at Vicksburg. Tactically it was not feasible for him to move now on Rosecrans' rear. The only course open was to throw his army before the mountain gorges and meet the Federal columns as they emerged.

That, of course, involved the evacuation of Chattanooga. Students of military science all agree, however, that the true objective of any commander is the opposing army—a mere geographical point is of no particular importance except as a base, a means to an end. Bragg's objective was Rosecrans' army, and he had no intention of letting the occupation of Chattanooga interfere with its pursuit. As early as August 23 he had written to President Davis: "We can not hold this town," and Davis, a military man, raised no protest. Orders for evacuation were issued on September 6. Though there was great popular clamor against Bragg when it got around that he had given Chattanooga up without a fight, the movement was sound.

Rosecrans, after he had fought and lost the Battle of Chickamauga, tried to put over the theory that the city had been the object of his campaign, that "Chickamauga was the price of Chattanooga"—a contention made somewhat ridiculous by the fact that Chattanooga could easily have been (and was, in fact) occupied by him without a fight. It was left abandoned and undefended on September 8, when the Army of Tennessee took up its march south for LaFayette. The Federals were quickly apprised. The next morning Crittenden's corps moved in and took possession without firing a shot. If possession of Chattanooga had been Rosecrans' goal it would have been a simple matter that day to march the corps of Thomas and McCook down the wide-open Lookout Valley in Crittenden's wake and establish the whole army there. In fact, by Rosecrans' false criterion, the campaign was over on September 9 when Crittenden was in the town and thereby accomplished what Rosecrans later claimed was his whole object. This was really just a face-saving afterthought. Rosecrans was not after Chattanooga; he was after the Army of Tennessee, and he was taking the proper steps to bring it to battle.

From the standpoint of correct military science, Bragg's plan of seeking out Rosecrans' army and attacking it seems beyond reproach. It was entirely right, but, as was all too often true of Bragg's operations, the execution was not so good as the conception. He made exceptionally good use of propaganda spread by carefully coached "deserters,"[20] who sifted into the Federal lines with high-colored cock-and-bull stories about the whole Confederate army being in wild retreat to Rome or Dalton or somewhere. So well did these butternut Thespians act their parts that their yarn was swallowed, hook, line and sinker. Rosecrans, thoroughly deceived, wrote Halleck on the ninth:

"The army has retreated to Rome. If we pursue vigorously they will not stop short of Atlanta. Troops badly demoralized; all feel that they are whipped; one seventh of the troops mostly naked; the rations for three days would make one good meal."[21]

Bragg speaks rather gloatingly in his report of the way he made Rosecrans believe the Confederates were in full flight, "when in reality we had
concentrated opposite his center," so that "the enemy pressed on his
columns to intercept us, and exposed himself in detail." Rosecrans did
that very thing with a carelessness probably unexcelled. And with a sluggishness equally unprecedented Bragg failed to improve any of his numerous chances—chances that a Lee or a Stonewall Jackson would have converted quickly into stunning victories.

Rosecrans' orders reveal his complete ignorance of Bragg's purposes.
At first he seems to have accepted the theory that the whole Confederate
army was running to Rome. Then he figured that the main body must
have retired by way of Ringgold and Dalton down the Western & Atlantic. He ordered Crittenden to leave one of his brigades at Chattanooga and with the others pursue the phantom army that way. He sent
Thomas on the ninth across the mountains to LaFayette to strike it on
the flank. McCook was dispatched to Alpine, farther south, and was to
extend his cavalry to Resaca on the tracks south of Dalton.

"Seldom in the annals of warfare," says General John B. Turchin, who
commanded a brigade in Thomas' corps, "has such a magnificent opportunity been presented to completely defeat the opposing force in detail
as that which was now offered to the rebel General Bragg. In his report
Bragg says that at this juncture his effective force, including reinforcements from Mississippi, and without counting his cavalry, consisted of
35,000 men, all concentrated north and northeast of Lafayette; while of
our army, Thomas's stood opposite him; McCook's was twenty-five miles
to the right of Thomas in a bee-line, but by the roads which he had to
take to join Thomas the distance amounted to over forty miles, with a
very wild tract of country stretched between them; and Crittenden was at
Ringgold, twenty-five miles to the left of Thomas."[22]

Rosecrans opened wide the door, but Bragg did not walk in. Why?
General Hill attempts an explanation.

"The trouble with him was: first, lack of knowledge of the situation;
second, lack of personal supervision of the execution of his orders. No
general ever won a permanent fame who was wanting in these grand
elements of success: knowledge of his own and his enemy's condition, and
personal superintendence of operations on the field. . . . The truth is,
General Bragg was bewildered by 'the popping out of the rats from so
many holes.' The wide dispersion of the Federal forces, and their con-

frontal of him at so many points, perplexed him instead of being a source of congratulation that such grand opportunities were offered for crushing them one by one. He seems to have had no well-organized system of independent scouts such as Lee had. . . . So General Bragg only learned that he was encircled by foes, without knowing who they were, what was their strength and what were their plans.

"The nightmare upon Bragg for the next three days was due, doubtless, to his uncertainty about the movements of his enemy and to the certainty that there was not that mutual confidence between him and some of his subordinates that there ought to be between a chief and his officers to insure victory. Bragg's want of definite and precise information had led him more than once to issue 'impossible' orders, and therefore those entrusted with their execution got in the way of disregarding them. Another more serious trouble with him was the disposition to find a scapegoat for every failure and disaster. This made his officers cautious about striking a blow when an opportunity presented itself, unless they were protected by a positive order."[23]

D. H. Hill has put his finger on it. In truth, the officers were convinced by now that Bragg often did not know what he was doing, that it was an even chance whether or not the enemy was where Bragg thought he was. So they were reluctant to carry out his commands unless their own information justified the action.

It was directly due to this, and to another great fault of his—the loose ambiguity of his orders—that the first great chance to smash Rosecrans slipped through his fingers. Till now there had been no flaw in his conception of the campaign. He had brought the bulk of his army into approximate concentration just across Pigeon Mountain from Thomas' lone corps. Polk was at Lee and Gordon's Mill on the Chattanooga-LaFayette highway. Hill's corps, now consisting of the divisions of Breckinridge and Cleburne, was posted at LaFayette, with Breckinridge in charge of the reserve artillery and wagon trains and Cleburne holding the three gaps in Pigeon Mountain—Catlett's on the north, Dug in the center and Bluebird to the south. All three had been obstructed with felled trees. Thomas, obeying orders, was crossing into McLemore's Cove, on his way across the mountains to LaFayette, with Negley's division leading and Baird's close behind.

As soon as Bragg, on the evening of the ninth, heard that Negley had reached the Cove and was alone there, he detached Hindman from Polk's corps to march as fast as he could to Davis' Crossroads in the Cove and attack the enemy "reported to be about 4,000 or 5,000 strong."[24] At the same time, he ordered Hill to lead or send Cleburne's division across Pigeon Mountain and unite with Hindman.

Hindman moved at 1 A.M. on the tenth. Shortly after sunrise he halted at Morgan's, four miles from Davis', waiting to hear from Hill. But Hill did not get his orders until that morning. When he got them he sent Bragg word that they could not be complied with for a variety of reasons—Cleburne was sick abed, four of Cleburne's best regiments were absent on other duty, the roads through the gaps had been rendered impassable, etc. He wrote Hindman that he could not support him, offering the gratuitous comment that Negley's advance was probably "sent out as a bait to draw us off from below," and that Negley, if pressed, "will fall back in the gap and there the matter will end." A few weeks had been enough for Hill to catch the infection of doubting the accuracy of his commander's information and the wisdom of his orders.

Bragg, on receiving Hill's dispatch, ordered Buckner to go to Hindman's help, and Buckner went about it smartly, joining up at 4:45 P.M. Meanwhile Cleburne had been able to cut out the obstructing timber and advance through Dug Gap and was ready to debouch into the Cove by daylight of the eleventh. He kept Hindman advised of his movements. But a message from Bragg late on the tenth told Hindman that Crittenden was rapidly advancing from Chattanooga and urged him to finish up in the Cove as quickly as possible. Hindman, who possessed no visible qualifications for his important independent command, seems to have become confused by all the messages flying around. The mention of Crittenden introduced a new element in his uncertainty. Instead of attacking Negley promptly on the morning of the eleventh as ordered, he called a council of officers that same night. They determined, to quote from his own report, that "they ought not to advance without more definite information." He so advised Bragg, volunteering a suggestion that the attack on Negley be abandoned and that the Confederate turn and attack Crittenden.

To add to poor Hindman's befuddlement, Bragg at midnight sent him from LaFayette still another message—received at 4:20 A.M.—again mentioning Crittenden's advance and ordering him to "attack and force your way through the enemy to this point at the earliest hour that you can see him in the morning." Hindman did not understand this exactly, but eventually concluded he had better move. He started at 7 A.M. but marched with such deliberation, not to say timidity, that it took him the whole morning to go less than four miles, and he did not establish communication with Bragg—now at Hill's headquarters at Dug Gap—until afternoon. The first message had given Hindman an exaggerated idea of the force before him. He stopped and decided to retreat. Then, reassured by new reports from his scouts, he decided to go on again. Then there was some misunderstanding as to whether Hindman or Hill should attack first, with the result that neither attacked, though Hindman had a slight skirmish at the Crossroads late in the day with Negley's vanguard which had been joined by Baird's division. In the face of the superior Confederate force the two divisions withdrew to the safety of Stevens' Gap, from which they had just emerged, and thus evaded probable destruction. Hill united with Hindman at the Crossroads about dark, but no effort was made to pursue the enemy or to hold the position.

Hindman says: "As soon as I reported to the general commanding he remarked 'We can't stay here,' and ordered the command marched that night and with the least possible delay to LaFayette." He adds: "It is due the officers and men to say that they evinced the utmost anxiety to meet the enemy and an admirable alacrity in obeying all orders"—but, no matter how eager an army may be to fight, what can they do when the general commanding says "We can't stay here"? Wyeth in his biography of Forrest is biting. "Any student of the art of war, desiring to learn how badly a bit of strategy may be spoiled, is referred to the official records of this affair."[25]

Opportunity had knocked at Bragg's door in McLemore's Cove, and her summons had not been answered; but, contrary to the proverb, she straightway knocked again—and again went unheeded. Despite the bungling and the relinquishment of the attack on Thomas, Bragg's army was still in an ideally strong strategic position, squarely between Thomas and Crittenden—with McCook out of the picture in his remote corner at Alpine.

Thomas' prudent withdrawal from the Cove to the inaccessible top of the Lookout Mountain range made it impossible to get at him, but Crittenden offered a wide-open mark. He had been moving slowly and uncertainly, feeling for contact with that Confederate army which was supposed to be fleeing before him toward Dalton. Finding no signs of it, he continued deliberately with two of his divisions to Ringgold, where they halted. The other division he sent off exploring to Lee and Gordon's Mill. Later, acting under orders from Rosecrans, he got his three divisions together again at the mill on the west bank of Chickamauga Creek. But for two days his corps was thoroughly in the air and vulnerable to an attack that might well have resulted in its destruction or capture.

But Bragg was still beset by indecision. McCook's presence at Alpine worried him, made him fear an assault from that quarter; whereas, in truth, McCook was completely insulated and was himself so bewildered and so ignorant of the whereabouts both of the Confederates and of the other two Federal corps that he stood still, afraid to go either forward or back. As late as the evening of the twelfth he was sending messages to Rosecrans expressing the belief that the Confederates had abandoned LaFayette and were probably concentrating at Resaca.

After giving up the attack on Thomas, Bragg had marched his army to LaFayette, to concentrate there against McCook. So he wasted precious time that might have been used to smash Crittenden. Crittenden had completed his concentration at Lee and Gordon's by the night of the twelfth.[26] Now no longer could the Confederates wipe out the division that had been there alone the day before or strike the two divisions marching in from Ringgold. It took till the night of the eleventh for Bragg to become convinced of McCook's harmlessness and give his attention to Crittenden. Then he ordered Polk to move Cheatham's division to Rock Springs Church, eight miles from LaFayette and five from Lee and Gordon's. During the afternoon of the twelfth Walker's division was sent to reinforce him, and on the morning of the thirteenth Hindman's division rejoined him.

Bragg wrote Polk on the evening of the twelfth ordering him to attack Crittenden at Peavine Church on the Graysville road. He thought Crittenden's divisions still separated. He placed Crittenden at Peavine on the way from Ringgold. Of course he was all wrong. He said fatuously to Polk: "This division crushed and the others are yours. We can then turn again on the force in the Cove." Polk himself was in doubt where the enemy might be. The reports of his cavalry led him to believe that Crittenden's entire corps, together with Wilder's cavalry brigade, was concentrating to the east of his position toward Peavine. He passed this on to Bragg, asking for reinforcements. He said he expected the enemy would attack the next morning, but "if I find he is not going to attack me, I will attack him without delay."

Polk's cavalry moved out on the Graysville road to develop the enemy —but there was no enemy there, the demonstration in that quarter the previous day having been for the sole purpose of covering Crittenden's concentration across the Chickamauga at Lee and Gordon's. It was not until noon of the thirteenth that the Confederates definitely located Crittenden with his whole corps in its new position. Still it was not too late to fall on him in force before he could be joined by either of the other two Federal corps. But Bragg was worried about McCook again.

Instead of proceeding immediately against Crittenden with the troops on the ground, he returned to LaFayette, taking back with him Buckner's corps which had been brought up to reinforce Polk. Polk also was withdrawn to LaFayette, and there the Confederate army lay in a paralysis of inaction for four days.

After the event, Bragg sharply reproached Polk for not moving quickly and spiritedly against Crittenden, but the blame, if any, belongs as much at Bragg's door as at Polk's. There was no reason why Bragg should not have gone to Rock Springs Church and taken personal command of the desired action. There was nothing of importance to hold him at La-Fayette. And there was no other body of the enemy within striking distance in any other quarter. If, as he claims, he had cause to doubt Polk's willingness to obey orders, that was all the more cause for not leaving the attack in Polk's hands. The basic flaw in the planned action against Crittenden was that Bragg on the evening of the twelfth issued one of those "impossible" orders, instructing Polk to attack Crittenden at Peavine Church when, in fact, Crittenden was not there at all but at Lee and Gordon's Mill. Aside from this fatal error in timing, Bragg's idea of crushing Crittenden in detail was entirely sound. The execution of the idea was woefully feeble. It was the old story over again.

General Turchin says with justifiable bluntness:

"It is impossible to ascribe this frittering away of the opportunity that chance at that time presented to Bragg to anything else than his individual indecision of character and the lack of that indomitable energy and cool daring which, allied with accurate planning, makes perfect generalship. Those three memorable days of September, 1863, which would have made a talented general famous, manifested Bragg's mediocrity and low-grade generalship, above which he never rose subsequently."[27]

Even after this failure against Crittenden, the Federal army was widely scattered, but Bragg seemed uncertain what to do—and wound up by doing nothing until the golden opportunity had evaporated.

On the thirteenth Rosecrans at last became aware of the actual state of affairs, realized that the "disorderly retreat" of the Confederate army was mythical, and thought he would concentrate for battle himself. Crittenden he retired slightly to the foot of Missionary Ridge near Lee and Gordon's; McCook he ordered to join Thomas at Stevens' Gap as quickly as possible; and abandoning his personal headquarters in Chattanooga, where he had been since the ninth, he attached himself to

Thomas' corps. Granger with the reserve corps he moved up from Bridgeport to Rossville. McCook, who seems to have had a highly developed talent for blundering, did not approach Thomas by the direct route through Dougherty's Gap at the head of McLemore's Cove, but took the long way round across the mountain. He marched fifty-seven miles in four days over the most terrifically difficult roads. By the seventeenth the three corps were in supporting distance of one another, their left at Lee and Gordon's and their line extending through McLemore's Cove to the top of Lookout Mountain at Stevens' Gap.

The night of the seventeenth Bragg moved up from LaFayette and placed his army in position on the east side of Chickamauga Creek confronting the Federals, his left at the Cove, his center opposite Lee and Gordon's, and his right at Reed's Bridge over the creek.

Rosecrans saw that his left flank was overlapped by Bragg's right, and grew fearful that he might be enveloped and cut off from Chattanooga. Therefore that same night he began to slide his line to the left, northward, extending Crittenden beyond Lee and Gordon's to cover the Chattanooga-LaFayette road, moving Thomas down to Crawfish Spring, and McCook up to Pond Spring to take the position Thomas had vacated.

At this juncture General Polk advised Bragg to make a quick swing around the Federal left to occupy Rossville and shut Rosecrans off in some such fashion as he feared. Bragg had a more ambitious plan, a masterpiece of strategy which, if successful, would have driven the whole Federal army into McLemore's Cove, and never could they have scaled those precipitate walls in time to escape butchery or capture. That this was Bragg's purpose appears from a study of his order for battle issued on the eighteenth: Bushrod Johnson's division, starting from Ringgold early in the morning, was to cross the creek at Reed's Bridge and "sweep up the Chickamauga toward Lee and Gordon's Mill," where Crittenden had been located on the left of the Federal line.[28] Polk was to demonstrate in front of Lee and Gordon's, cross the creek and attack if practicable. Walker was to cross at Alexander's Bridge and join Johnson's advance. Buckner was to cross at Dalton's Ford. These movements, if happily carried out, would force the Federal left back onto the center in the Cove, and pen the whole army in that mountainous impasse.

If one overlooks the fact that Rosecrans had changed the position of his army from where Bragg thought it was, one can again find no fault with Bragg's basic strategy. It was admirable. But there does seem room again to criticize his timing. While the Federal corps were separated, time was the essential factor. Swift and unhesitating action was demanded. This occasion having passed, and Rosecrans having well-nigh concentrated, it would have been wiser for Bragg to wait another day or two until he might receive the reinforcements under Longstreet and so could throw his full effective force against his adversary. He did not act when it was time to act—and he did not wait when it was time to wait.

Rosecrans was by now thoroughly alarmed over the dangerous position in which he found himself. He bombarded Halleck and Burnside with urgent pleas for assistance.

"It is of the utmost importance that you close down this way to cover our right flank," he wired Burnside. "I want all help we can get promptly. . . . The enemy, reenforced by Johnston and Longstreet from Virginia, doubtless intend to do us all the mischief in their power."[29]

All appeals to Burnside were in vain. That pompous general was too thoroughly enjoying the role of savior of the loyal Unionists of East Tennessee; he had no idea of leaving Knoxville, where he was in supreme command, and going off to a battle in Georgia where he would be under another. Halleck saw Rosecrans' peril, but his appeals to Burnside were useless, and there was no chance for quick aid from anywhere else.

Rosecrans' reference to Bragg's reinforcements was based on rumor, but was approximately correct—more nearly correct than the excited dispatch sent to Secretary Stanton by Charles A. Dana,[30] Assistant Secretary of War, from Crawfish Spring on the eighteenth in which he stated that "Johnston is with Bragg, with a large portion of his force," and that reinforcements had arrived also from Virginia. Johnston was not with Bragg, though he had sent him two divisions, and the reinforcements from Virginia under Longstreet did not begin to arrive until that day— and the artillery and several of the infantry brigades did not get there until the battle was over.

Also that day the movement of the Confederate columns started as outlined in the battle order, with Bushrod Johnson's division taking the lead. His advance, supported by Forrest, was disputed sternly by Minty's cavalry. Similarly Walker's force was checked by Wilder's mounted infantry and compelled to cross at Lambert's Ford instead of Alexander's Bridge.

There was a stir on the Confederate side when, about four in the afternoon, General John B. Hood of Longstreet's corps came up with three of his brigades and joined Johnson's column, Hood taking command by virtue of his seniority. He had been badly wounded in the arm at Gettysburg and was on sick leave in Virginia when his division was ordered to Georgia. Though the bad arm was out of commission, he could not bear to have his men go into action without him; when he heard of their transfer he boarded the first train and started after them. Seeing him for the first time since Gettysburg, his soldiers gave him a rousing welcome as he rode onto the battlefield with his arm in a sling.[31] Hood was a fighter, and he plunged into action. Driving the enemy steadily before him, he crossed the creek at Reed's Bridge, and when he bivouacked for the night he had thrust the Federals back for six or seven miles. Walker too encamped on the west side of the creek that night as planned. The other Confederate forces were still on the east side: Buckner at Thedford's Ford, Polk opposite Lee and Gordon's, and Hill on the extreme left opposite Glass's Mill. But during the night Bragg continued to move his men over, and by morning all the infantry were across except the divisions of Cleburne, Breckinridge and Hindman.

Rosecrans, still nervous about that left flank of his, lengthened his line farther during the day and night of the eighteenth till it covered the roads to Reed's and Alexander's Bridges. Now his left overlapped the Confederate right considerably. Bragg did not know it. He thought his adversary's left still at Lee and Gordon's. He expected to open the battle there with a turning movement on the nineteenth.[32] As Hill put it in his official report: "While our troops had been moving up the Chickamauga, the Yankees had been moving down, and thus outflanked us."

The field on which the battle was fought on the nineteenth and twentieth lay largely between Chickamauga Creek on the east and the foothills of Missionary Ridge to the west. The road from Chattanooga to LaFayette ran through it in almost a straight line from Rossville, where it crossed Missionary Ridge, on the north, to Lee and Gordon's Mill on the south, where it crossed the creek. Chickamauga Creek, so deep as to be hardly crossable except at bridges and fords, wound along the eastern edge of the terrain in a generally northeastern direction. Like Shiloh, much of the country was heavily wooded, with thick underbrush, though there were open fields and pastures interspersed, and a few small farmhouses.

On the first morning the opposing lines were each five or six miles long and at their closest point less than a mile apart. Still neither commander seemed to have exact knowledge of his adversary's location. Bragg did not mean to precipitate a general engagement at once, but expected to spend the day marshaling his forces west of the creek. The action began early, however, when Thomas ordered Brannan on the extreme Federal left to reconnoiter toward the stream. This brought him in contact with Forrest's cavalry—dismounted and fighting as infantry—which was guarding the Confederate right flank and which had started out at dawn on a prowl, feeling for the Federal line. Forrest fell back, after skirmishing briskly, but Walker's infantry division moved quickly into action and struck Brannan with terrific force. Brannan was reinforced by Baird's division, but they were unable to withstand the ferocity of Walker's attack. Baird and Brannan, thoroughly beaten up, fell back and were practically out of action for the rest of the day.

The tables were promptly turned on Walker when Johnson's division of McCook's corps, sent to aid Thomas, fell on his flank and drove it in with heavy loss until it was rescued from disaster by Cheatham and Stewart. There ensued a regular dogfight along this front, with each side feeding in divisions and brigades and even regiments as the struggle waxed and waned. In the course of the afternoon Stewart managed to pierce the Federal line and momentarily gained possession of the LaFayette road, but reinforcements repulsed him. On the Confederate left, Hood pushed the Federals back for a mile.[33] But at nightfall, though withdrawn from his original position, Rosecrans still held the road, his left flank battered but intact.

There had been no general advance of the Confederate line—only a piecemeal, desultory sort of fighting that spread gradually from right to left. "It was the sparring of the amateur boxer, and not the crushing blows of the trained pugilist," says General Hill. "From daylight on the 19th until mid-day there was a gap of two miles between Crittenden and Thomas into which the Confederates could have poured, turning to right or left and attacking in flank whichever commander was least prepared for the assault." He points out also that the veteran divisions of Breckinridge and Cleburne, which he commanded on the extreme left, stood practically idle all day, when they might have been utilized to turn the Federal right, weakened as it was by Rosecrans' massing of strength on his left. But, he concludes, "Bragg had other plans."[34]

Bragg did indeed cling tenaciously to his original plan of caging Rosecrans in McLemore's Cove. The only use he made of Cleburne was to shift him to support his right late in the afternoon. Cleburne got into position after sundown and moved to the attack immediately. He drove the enemy back a mile and captured prisoners and artillery. The fighting went on into the night until all either side could see of the other was the flash of their guns.

As compiled from the *Official Records*, the Federals fighting on the nineteenth numbered over 45,000. There were nearly 34,000 Confederates on the field, but Bragg got into action only the 22,000 men under Polk on the right and the 8,400 that Hood carried with him in his attack on the left. The Confederates' élan led Rosecrans to overestimate their strength. In his official report he speaks of being "opposed to superior numbers of the enemy." His conviction that "we were greatly outnumbered" is a tribute to the energy of those men of Bragg once they were given a chance to meet the foe face to face. D. H. Hill paid his tribute to the spirit of the Army of Tennessee:

"I witnessed some of the heaviest fighting on the afternoon of the 19th, and never saw so little straggling on the field. I saw but one deserter from Hood's ranks, and not one from Cleburne's."[85]

General Longstreet with the remainder of his corps arrived now, and during the night of the nineteenth the regiments from Virginia were placed in their positions and given a chance to get acquainted with their new companions in arms. "The personal appearance of Bragg's army was, of course, a matter of interest to us," writes General Sorrel.[86] "The men were a fine-looking lot—strong, lean, long-bodied fighters." But he adds: "The tone of the army among the higher officers toward the commander was the worst conceivable. Bragg was the subject of hatred and contempt and it was almost openly so expressed." That feeling must have been almost electric, to have been sensed so quickly by a strange officer arriving in the night.

Longstreet himself reached headquarters at 11 P.M.[87] Bragg was roused from slumber in his ambulance for an hour's conference. In the middle of the night and in the midst of the battle, he undertook the perilous experiment of reorganizing his army into two new grand divisions—Longstreet to command the left and Polk the right wing. The former was given a copy of the general orders of the eighteenth and the new instructions for action on the twentieth, together with a map of the surrounding country. The map was particularly welcome; he was quite unfamiliar with this district.

By the new alignment of the forces, Longstreet's left wing comprised Buckner's corps, consisting of Stewart's and Preston's divisions; the divisions under Bushrod R. Johnson and Hindman; three of Hood's brigades, to which were added the two brigades of McLaws' division—Kershaw's and Humphreys'—which had come with Longstreet. These mixed Virginia brigades were commanded by Hood. McLaws himself, with two of his brigades, two of Hood's and all of Alexander's artillery, was still en route from Virginia and did not reach the field until after the battle.

The right wing under Polk consisted of the corps commanded by Hill, comprising Breckinridge's and Cleburne's divisions, together with Walker's corps of his own and Liddell's divisions acting as a reserve, and the division of General Cheatham. Previously Hill had been stationed on the extreme left. It was necessary therefore for Breckinridge to move his command from one end of the line to the other so that Hill would have his complete corps in position in the morning. Wheeler's cavalry was on the left flank, Forrest's on the right.

At a headquarters conference Bragg had told Polk of his plan to open the attack at daylight, the division on the far right—Hill's position—to hit first and the others to follow from right to left. The objective remained the same: "To turn the enemy's left and by direct attack force him into McLemore's Cove."[38]

Attack by successive divisions was a favorite device of Bragg's, who preferred it to a simultaneous assault all along the line. It had one fatal defect: no division could come into action until the division on which it waited had started fighting. The battle could never get going at all if the outside division failed to start the ball rolling at the appointed time. That was exactly what happened on this fateful morning.

Polk, on reaching his headquarters near Alexander's Bridge shortly before midnight after the conference with Bragg, sent written orders to Hill, Cheatham and Walker to begin the attack at dawn. He asked Hill to come meet him in personal conference. Cheatham and Walker were ready to go into action as soon as they heard Hill's guns—but the sun rose in the heavens and General Hill's corps showed no signs of life. About 5 A.M., the courier who had been dispatched to Hill returned to Polk's headquarters with the disconcerting report that he could not find him anywhere. Then Polk sent orders directly to Hill's division commanders to "move upon and attack the enemy as soon as you are in position." The courier with this message found Hill, Cleburne and Breckinridge in consultation at Cleburne's headquarters. Bragg himself came up at about the same time, seeking the cause of delay. Hill said he could not get into action yet a while; he was just starting to issue the breakfast rations and would not be ready to move "for an hour or more."

Bragg was infuriated. He placed the blame on Polk's shoulders, though including Hill in his condemnation. Defending himself, Hill says that after the fight on the nineteenth he rode from the battlefield to the point designated by Bragg in his battle order as the place where he could be found; neither Bragg nor Polk was there and he heard nothing of the proposed daylight attack till next morning "some time after sunrise" when he was giving his men their breakfast.[39]

Minimizing the importance of his failure to receive Polk's orders, Hill contends that the Confederate army was not ready at daybreak to go into action, anyhow. Breckinridge's division, which was expected to fire the first shot, was not yet in line, was still transferring from the left flank. Bragg had neglected making "the essential preparations for battle" during the night.

"The position of the enemy had not been reconnoitered," Hill says. "Our line of battle had not been adjusted, and part of it was at right angles with the rest. There was no cavalry on our flanks, and no order had fixed the strength or position of the reserves. My corps had been aligned north and south to be parallel to the position of the enemy. Cheatham's division was at right angle to my line, and when adjusted was found to be exactly behind Stewart's and therefore had to be taken out after the battle was begun and placed in reserve."[40]

There seems merit in this. Certainly considerable readjustment of the Confederate line had to be made during the morning hours before the attack was finally opened. Longstreet, at break of day, proceeded to the front to get acquainted with his new command[41] and its position. He soon discerned the necessity for closing to the right to occupy a half-mile or more of vacant ground between the two wings and to make room for Hood's column in the front line. When Stewart was thus extended to the right he was found to be in front of Cheatham; so Stewart had to be shifted again and Cheatham placed in the reserve along with Walker.

Rosecrans too had been busy, his anxiety edged by his gullible acceptance of Bragg's rumored reinforcements. As a matter of fact, Longstreet had brought not more than 5,000 men from Virginia, but Rosecrans, still tricked by the tall tales of the "deserters," believed them from 15,000 to 20,000. His fears multiplied the whole Confederate force until he thought himself confronted by no less than 120,000.

To meet the advance of this imaginary host he labored through the night hours to gain as strong a defensive position as possible. He took up a line in the rear of the ground over which the battle had been fought the day before. The Federal troops were now all north of Lee and Gordon's Mill. The new line stretched diagonally from northeast to southwest along the foothills at the eastern base of Missionary Ridge. Its left was east of the Chattanooga road and its right to the west of the road, so ex-

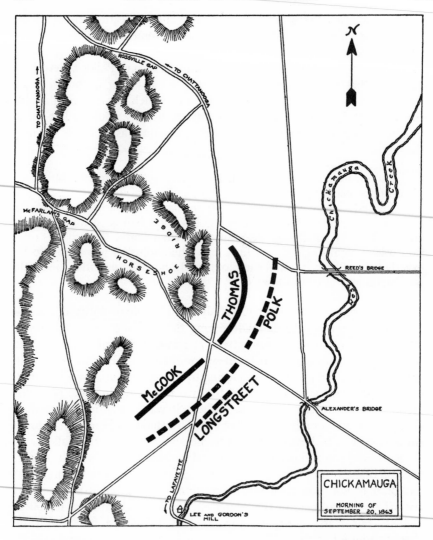

tended as to cover not only the road to Chattanooga through Rossville Gap but also the Dry Valley road to Chattanooga through McFarland's Gap. Thomas was in command on the left, McCook on the right. Crittenden's corps was held in reserve on the right. Granger's reserve corps was at McAfee's Church, near Rossville Gap, guarding the left and the gap road, while at the same time threatening the Confederate right from which it was only four miles distant.

Thomas' position was on a crest of wooded ground east of the road. He arrayed his forces in a crescent, strongly protected by log breastworks, bending back to the road at each end. Rosecrans had no suspicion of Bragg's intent to pen him in McLemore's Cove. He still thought Bragg was just trying to get between him and Chattanooga—something Bragg might have done at any time in the past ten days, but Rosecrans in guarding against this supposed strategy effectually frustrated Bragg's real plan. To protect his flank he was determined to hold his left at all hazards. Thomas had crowded into his position no less than four divisions—those of Baird and Reynolds of his own corps, along with Johnson of McCook's and Palmer of Crittenden's corps—and these were reinforced during the morning. Rosecrans placed his headquarters in the rear of his right wing, at the Widow Glenn's house.

The Confederate attack against Thomas' left was finally launched at 9:30 A.M. by Breckinridge, supported by some of Forrest's men. Cleburne got into action a few minutes later. Forrest's cavalry, again fighting dismounted, was still on the extreme right flank. It swept well around the Federal left. General Hill asked: "What infantry is that?"[42] and was astonished when told it was not infantry at all. He had heard of Forrest in Virginia and asked to meet him. As Forrest approached, Hill took off his hat. "General Forrest, I wish to congratulate you and those brave men moving across that field like veteran infantry upon their magnificent behavior. In Virginia I made myself extremely unpopular with the cavalry because I said that so far I had not seen a dead man with spurs on; but no one can speak disparagingly of such troops as yours."[43] He had only to see him in action to become Forrest's warm admirer. In his official report he refers to "that ever-watchful officer, General Forrest. . . . I would ask no better fortune, if again placed on a flank, than to have such a vigilant, gallant and accomplished officer guarding its approaches."

Hill's overlapping assault was delivered with such vim, threatening the extreme Federal left and rear, that Thomas immediately began to cry for more reinforcements—a cry repeated at intervals throughout the day. Although enthusiastically launched and vigorously pushed, this initial attack of two Confederate divisions against four Federal divisions behind breastworks was thrown back with heavy losses.[44] The Federals attempted no countercharge, quite willing to remain behind their protection while the discomfited men of Breckinridge and Cleburne fell back and pulled themselves together.

The heavy reinforcement on his left enabled Rosecrans to hold it—which he considered vital—but it so weakened his right as to lead to eventual defeat. The confused shifting of troops on his right gave the Confederates a famous opening. A hole was created when Wood—acting on ambiguous orders—drew his division out of the line at the point where it crossed the road and moved it to the left to support Reynolds. Just at this juncture the Confederate left wing went into action—late in the morning. Things had been delayed not only by the awkward relation of Stewart's and Cheatham's positions, but also by the battle order's clear injunction that the left wing should wait on the right. About eleven o'clock, however, Bragg himself ordered Stewart to advance. He was thrown back, but Longstreet then hurled Hood forward. By good luck Hood drove into the hole with his eight brigades arrayed in three lines. It was by pure chance that the spearhead of Longstreet's attacking column thrust itself into this opening in the Federal position, but it was by exercise of his own soldierly instincts and talents that he capitalized the opportunity. Seizing the chance for a break-through of major and decisive proportions, he disregarded the orders of the day to bear to the left. Instead he wheeled his main force to the right and took the enemy in reverse. To the west and rear he pursued the demoralized brigades of the Federal right wing. In this charge General Hood was severely wounded. His leg had to be amputated on the field of battle—and he had one arm out of use.

The rush of Longstreet's exultant men was irresistible. They pounded through the Federal line with a power that swept everything before it. Five of McCook's brigades and two of Crittenden's were thrown into wild disorder. As the drive continued it reached and captured Rosecrans' headquarters. The general himself was running with the rest down the Dry Valley road through McFarland's Gap to Chattanooga.

Charles A. Dana, who was with Rosecrans that day, says: "Bull Run had nothing more terrible than the rout and flight of these veteran soldiers."[45] Even gallant Phil Sheridan was overcome by the contagion of the panic. He galloped away with his demoralized brigades to the environs of the city before shame overcame fear and he belatedly resolved to re-form and go back—though indeed he moved by the safer road through Rossville and never got near the battlefield again.

The break-through is graphically described by a Federal eye-witness, General Gates P. Thruston:

"All became confusion. No order could be heard above the tempest of battle. With a wild yell the Confederates swept on far to their left. They seemed everywhere victorious. Rosecrans was borne back in the retreat. Fugitives, wounded, caissons, escort, ambulances, thronged the narrow pathways. He concluded that the whole line had given way, that the day was lost, that the next stand must be made at Chattanooga. McCook and Crittenden, caught in the same tide of retreat, seeing only rout everywhere, shared the opinion of Rosecrans."[46]

John Fiske writes: "About four o'clock Rosecrans rode up to the door of the adjutant general's office in Chattanooga faint and ill. . . . The officers who helped him into the house did not soon forget the terrible look of the brave man, stunned by sudden calamity. . . . In later years I used occasionally to meet Rosecrans, and always felt that I could see the shadow of Chickamauga upon his noble face."[47]

That the breach did not utterly destroy the Federal army then and there was due to the skill and vigilance with which General Thomas met the crisis—the only superior officer left on the field. Anxious about the reinforcements he had been calling for, he had ridden to the right to hurry them up and so saw with his own eyes the wheel of the Confederates, the collapse of the Federal wing. His flank was exposed. Instantly recognizing the gravity of the catastrophe, he moved swiftly to stave off complete disaster. Fortunately for him, the rugged terrain lent itself to quick improvisation of a strong defense along the crest of a spur of Missionary Ridge called Horseshoe Ridge. It was made up of a series of high, steep hills. He formed a line running along its southern face east-and-west, approximately at right angles to the breastworks-defended crescent on the east side of the Chattanooga road which he had so strongly held all morning. Into this new line he hurried Brannan's and Wood's divisions, with two of Negley's brigades and what was left of the shattered corps of McCook and Crittenden. So he stood his ground until Granger's corps reinforced him. Granger had marched without orders, "guided simply by the din of battle and his common sense."[48]

The elated Longstreet had paused to eat a hasty lunch at 2:30 P.M.,[49] when he received word the commanding general wanted to see him. He reached Bragg's tent about three and had an interview that opened the eyes of the fighting man from the well-managed Army of Northern Virginia. Longstreet sketched a swift and happy picture of the situation— the Federal line broken, two of the corps in flight, more than forty field-pieces, quantities of small arms and many prisoners captured. To follow up he suggested that the Confederate right wing temporarily assume a defensive position while detachments from it join him in pursuit. This would not only harass the brigades flying to Chattanooga, but would at the same time throw the Confederates behind Thomas. The whole Federal army might be demolished.

But Bragg was in no mood for suggestions. He was disappointed because the battle had not worked out the way he had planned. Now the scheme to cage Rosecrans in McLemore's Cove was impossible. He was temperamentally unfitted for quick shifting of plans. Longstreet's proposal to detach forces from the right elicited merely the surly response, "There is not a man in the right wing who has any fight left in him."[50] That was a cruelly unjust indictment of Polk's men. They had proved there was plenty of fight in them when they could fight on anything like equal terms. They belied this slander that very day when they moved gallantly to a frontal charge on General Thomas' breastworks just before sunset.

Longstreet was amazed. He knew Bragg's reputation for vacillation, but he could hardly take in this defeatist attitude when the battle was at full tide and at least partially won, with obvious odds for pressing it to complete and crushing victory. "It is my opinion that Bragg thought at 3 P.M., that the battle was lost," Longstreet wrote later.[51] At any rate, Bragg showed a haughty disinclination to discuss it further with the commander of his right wing. "General," he said coldly, "if anything happens, communicate with me at Reed's Bridge," and turned on his heel and walked off.

From then on, Bragg was out of touch with the battle's progress and had little or no part in its direction. He did not show himself at all on Polk's line after the morning's repulse, and Longstreet saw him no more before next day. Thus was presented the strange spectacle of a major conflict fought to its decisive close, one commander having fled the field, the other sulking in his tent.

Crestfallen and perturbed, Longstreet returned to his troops confronting Thomas' newly established right flank and began to examine it in the hope of finding some vulnerable spot. To do this under fire was no easy task, especially as he was so unfamiliar with the ground and as the enemy lines had been constantly changing to meet the exigencies of the engagement.

The Federal position consisted in reality of two separate lines at right angles to each other, and the action against them constituted two practically independent battles. East of the Chattanooga road, with flanks curved back across the road, Thomas' force still retained intact the original barricade that had been the impregnable Federal left wing of the morning. And in front of it Polk's right wing of the Confederate army still stood, licking its wounds after its rough treatment. Perpendicular to the barricade was the other Federal line, facing south, with its left salient on the eastern hill of Horseshoe Ridge. Opposite it was Longstreet's force—Bushrod Johnson on the left, then Hood's command, then Stewart's.

Unknown to anyone on the Confederate side, the two Federal lines were not continuously joined at their angle. On the contrary there was a gap at least half a mile wide. General Turchin,[52] who commanded the brigade on the exposed right flank of the left wing, is caustic with Longstreet for not finding this hole and leaping into it.

"The key to the mastership of the field," he says, "was right there in the open half-mile space between the wings. This was the key to our last position, the key to our final destruction. If Longstreet, instead of ordering Preston to attack Horseshoe Ridge, had supported him by Stewart and, say, by Cheatham . . . and wedged those three divisions into this space between our two wings, while the other rebel troops took the offensive at the same time all along the lines, it is frightful to contemplate what would have become of our decimated army."[53]

General Turchin is unfair. For one thing, Cheatham was not under Longstreet's command. More to the point, Longstreet was hardly censurable for failing to see during the melee of pitched battle an opening which, though painfully obvious to Turchin who was immediately affected by it, could not be quite so apparent to an opponent separated by several hundred yards of woodland. Had Bragg been an alert commander, with a first-class scouting system, he might have developed this weakness—but Bragg was not that kind of commander.

When Longstreet got back from his baffling conference with Bragg he found that his brigades had been making desperate but disconnected charges. Kershaw, who, just a few weeks before, had charged the heights at Gettysburg, had stormed up the steep slopes of Horseshoe Ridge only to be hurled back. Anderson's brigade of Hindman's division had joined in the struggle, and then Bushrod Johnson on the extreme left. Hindman had won a momentary foothold near the western end of the ridge, but just at this critical moment Steedman's division of Granger's reserve came on the scene—bringing not only 4,500 fresh men but a precious supply of 95,000 rounds of ammunition. It was Thomas' intention to throw the first available men into that gaping hole between his left and his right. When Steedman came he was started there. Then the Confederate success at the western end made that the immediately vital spot. So Steedman was thrown onto the Confederates who had gained the crest there and drove them down the southern slope. In a few minutes the line on

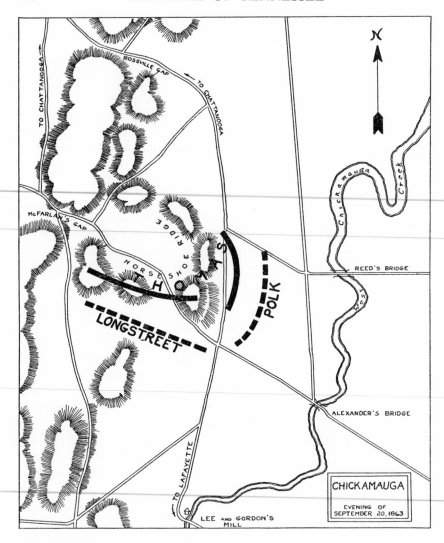

the ridge was further strengthened by 1,200 men under Vanderveer, shifted from the left front, and they were quickly placed in position to help stem the Confederate countercharge. But Kershaw and Johnson and Hindman had not been daunted by repulse. Again and again they had charged. Still the boys in blue had held with desperate firmness. Hindman in his report says he "had never seen Confederate troops fight better" but he "had never seen Federal troops fight as well."

Longstreet returned in time to see Kershaw's last desperate charge repelled, after it had clung for a time near the top of the ridge. He brought up Preston's division of Buckner's corps from its place in reserve on Chickamauga Creek and threw the brigades of Gracie and Kelly against the eastern end of the ridge, sometimes called Snodgrass Hill, but actually some distance south of that smaller hill on which the Snodgrass house stood. At the same time he opened an artillery fire that enfiladed the Federal line before Polk and was of material assistance in forcing its retreat when Polk attacked.

Preston's assault did not at once make head. It was valiantly resisted by a blue line that stood its ground, using bayonet and clubbed muskets when ammunition was exhausted. But finally Gracie, and Kelly after him, gained and held the hill, and then Buckner came on with his reserve artillery and Stewart's division which had been for some time idle. Preston's final charge was so determined it swept up three whole Federal regiments, the 21st and 89th Ohio and the 23rd Michigan being captured where they stood.[54]

The advance by Buckner and Stewart was, quite by accident, in the direction of that gap between Thomas' two positions which had been open for hours, though by this time it had been partially closed by the shifting of Hazen's brigade—the same brigade that had held the Round Forest at Murfreesboro. Now this was of minor importance, for the whole Federal line had begun to crumble under the steady pressure from left to right, and a general collapse impended.

Before five o'clock the dash of their charge had carried Longstreet's men to the Snodgrass house, across the ridge and behind Thomas' left.

Polk had given the order to advance as early as half past three, but Hill was slow and it was not until four that he got going. Once under way, he relates, "the men sprang to their arms with the utmost alacrity ... and showed by their cheerfulness that there was plenty of 'fight in them.' "[55] The advance was general: Breckinridge swung around to the right. Cleburne, always ready for a scrap, led his division gleefully into the contest, running his artillery up close to the opposing lines. The leading brigade was commanded by General Polk's nephew Lucius, who carried the northwestern angle of the works and took in succession three lines of breastworks. Cheatham's men drove powerfully through the opposing ranks.[56] Soon the entire Federal left was in retreat, and the Confederate right wing had reached the west side of the Chattanooga road, where they almost collided with the advance of their own left wing.

Hill writes:[57]

"As we passed into the woods west of the road, it was reported to me that a line was advancing at right angles to ours. I rode to the left to ascertain whether they were foes or friends, and soon recognized General Buckner. The cheers that went up when the two wings met were such as I never heard before and shall never hear again."[58]

Buckner says:

"We encountered in our advance the right wing of our army, which ... was moving in a direction perpendicular to our line of march. ... The battery was about to fire on a body of men, rapidly moving westward across the road. But I directed Williams to withhold his fire, saying: 'Those men are not beaten, they are cheering'; and galloping forward I found them to be the 'Orphan Brigade' of Kentucky Confederates. It was here that I soon afterwards met General D. H. Hill. ... The continued cheers of the army announced at dark that every point of the field had been gained."[59]

Indeed, by sunset (6 P.M.)[60] the whole Federal army was in precipitate retreat through McFarland's Gap, and did not pause until they got to Rossville on the outskirts of Chattanooga. Such demoralization attended their flight that, according to Bragg's official report, the Confederates captured 8,000 prisoners, 15,000 stand of small arms, 51 pieces of artillery, and large quantities of stores, ammunition, wagons, teams, ambulances, etc. Rosecrans had sent his chief of staff, General James A. Garfield, back from Chattanooga to the battlefield with orders for Thomas to withdraw to Rossville. So Thomas bivouacked there.

It is no belittlement of Thomas' magnificent stand that day to discount some of the extravagant claims made by too-ardent admirers. Typical is the comment of the eminent historian, John Fiske: "Night found Thomas still master of the Rossville road and the Union army saved from destruction."[61] This is just not so. Thomas was not master of the Rossville road at the close of the day's fighting, and he retreated to Chattanooga not by the Rossville road but through McFarland's Gap. Nor did he hold his ground until night, as has been so widely claimed, and then retire at his leisure. Valiant as his defense had been, he was driven from his position by the combined assaults of Longstreet and Polk, and, by his own report, his "withdrawal" began by 5:30 P.M.[62]—which was not nightfall by a long shot. An examination of all the official reports, as so minutely analyzed by Mr. Archibald Gracie,[63] shows conclusively that the retrograde movement began much earlier than Thomas states, at some time between four and four-thirty, when Reynolds' division started to the rear out of the breastworks on the left, followed by the other bodies of Federal troops.[64] The whole left wing was off the field by five-thirty. Thomas himself left his headquarters behind the ridge about four-thirty and in an hour was several miles back arranging for the withdrawal to Rossville.

Fiske is wrong too when he talks about a great opportunity which the Confederates lost in the afternoon, quite different from the one discussed by General Turchin.

"The key of the position," he says, "was the Rossville road, which Thomas had been holding like a vise since yesterday morning. If the enemy were to gain that road and interpose between Thomas and Missionary Ridge they could force him to surrender on the spot. The Army of the Cumberland would be annihilated."[65]

This is a loose and highly misleading statement for a professional historian. The "Rossville road"—that is, the road from LaFayette to Chattanooga by way of Rossville and Rossville Gap—had indeed been held like a vise, but it was not "the key of the position." The inviting opportunity which it offered to turn the Federal left was by no means overlooked. In fact, it was in some measure accomplished. Thomas' tight grip on the road was broken and he was shoved back, but this did not result in his annihilation. He merely made his retreat through McFarland's Gap instead of Rossville Gap. Hill had seen the possibilities of a turning movement on this flank early in the morning, as soon as he looked over the ground. He had urged a corresponding change in tactics, but Bragg had insisted on carrying out his favorite tactical plan, frontal attack by successive division charges. In the afternoon, when the Federal force was so obviously weakened as to be ready for a knockout blow, Bragg was not on the ground to order a wheel by the whole right wing in a devastating nutcracker envelopment. Forrest's dismounted cavalry did at one time sweep around the Federal left, across the road as far as Cloud's house and to the ridge road at the head of McFarland's Gap, but his meager force was thrust aside when Granger's divisions had pushed over to reinforce Thomas on Horseshoe Ridge. When the Federal line on the left did finally collapse and withdraw, it was by reason of the frontal attack rather than by any flank movement.

Left largely to their own independent resources, Longstreet and Polk had fought the two separate battles against the two separated Federal positions. These had culminated in the headlong rout of the enemy during the fading hours. But there was not, as there should have been, a single guiding hand in control, and consequently no follow-up of the great success gained at such heavy cost.

When the day was done the Army of Tennessee held the ground over which they had fought for three days, their enemy disrupted[66] and flying, if not annihilated, having left the dead and wounded behind. But then the palsying touch of incompetent and timorous leadership again fell upon them. Buckner relates that at the close of the battle, "at sunset," when "the enemy was retreating hastily from all parts of the field," he was with General Longstreet at the end of Horseshoe Ridge. A report came from General Preston who, flushed with his triumphant charge, asked leave to pursue the foe by moonlight.[67] Buckner, in the presence of his superior, had no authority to act. Longstreet did not order the pursuit.

In his official report Longstreet has this to say: "As it was almost dark, I ordered my line to remain as it was, ammunition boxes to be filled, stragglers to be collected, and everything in readiness for the pursuit in the morning." In a letter he writes: "It did not occur to me on the night of the 20th to send Bragg word of our complete success. . . . Every one in his army was supposed to know on the night of the battle that we had won a complete victory. . . . I know that I had been laying a plan by which we might overhaul the enemy at Chattanooga or between that point and Nashville."[68] But he goes on to say that Bragg had not realized that a victory was won!

Polk, after his wing's complete success in the late afternoon, established headquarters on the Chattanooga road within the former Federal works and sent out scouts to locate the enemy. The scouts reported the enemy gone. Polk then dispatched a staff officer to notify Bragg that the Federals were in full retreat. Bragg called him to headquarters for consultation. Polk's aide, Colonel Gale, gives a vivid picture of the victorious wing commander's call on his confused superior.

"General Bragg had gone to bed, but got up to listen to his report of the day's work of his forces. General Polk urged upon him the fact that the enemy was routed and flying precipitately from the field, and that then was the opportunity to finish the work by the capture or destruction of the army by prompt pursuit, before he had time to reorganize and throw up defenses at Chattanooga. General Bragg could not be induced to look at it in that light, and refused to believe that we had won a victory."[69]

A victory not recognized is almost as profitless as a victory not gained. The Battle of Chickamauga was a frightfully bloody affair, the losses

Flag of the 17th Tennessee regiment of Cleburne's division. This unique "Silver Moon" flag was designed by General Hardee, and was carried by all the regiments of his (later Cleburne's) division. The crossed cannon are a complimentary decoration, granted in honor of the capture by this regiment of a Federal battery.

The shoulder of Lookout Mountain, upon which the battle was fought.

in proportion to the numbers engaged being shockingly high. General Hill says he had never seen dead soldiers so thick on the ground since the day of the sunken road at Fredericksburg. The perils and terrors of the battle were accentuated when the dry leaves caught fire that littered the slopes up which the Confederates had repeatedly charged and which were strewn with their dead and wounded.[70] Estimates of the numbers on both sides differ widely. General Joe Wheeler places Bragg's "entire strength" at 46,000 and Rosecrans' at 72,603 "actually engaged." On the other hand, Livermore gives the Federal strength as 58,222 and the Confederate as 66,326. Livermore's figures seem to be far too low for Rosecrans who reported 67,692 "present for duty, equipped" on September 10, and his estimate of Bragg's strength is certainly too high, as Bragg never had any such army as that and probably had fewer than 50,000 at Chickamauga. The total Confederate losses are estimated at 17,800, the Federal at 16,550. Longstreet says he lost 44 per cent of his strength in two hours' fighting on the afternoon of the twentieth, and of the forces opposed to him on Horseshoe Ridge, Steedman's and Brannan's brigades lost respectively 49 per cent and 38 per cent in less than four hours, some individual regiments suffering even more heavily. Among the Confederate regiments the percentages of loss ran amazingly high—for example: 10th Tennessee, 68 per cent; 5th Georgia, 61 per cent; 2nd Tennessee, 60 per cent; 15th and 37th Tennessee, 60 per cent; 16th Alabama, 59 per cent; 6th and 9th Tennessee, 58 per cent—and so on, down the line. Chickamauga is said to mean "River of Death" in the Indian tongue. It was a river of death indeed that hot September day.

In writing General Cooper, Bragg took pains to eulogize the spirit of the men—in contrast to what he had said about Polk's soldiers.

"The conduct of the troops was admirable. Though often repulsed, they never failed to respond when called on, and finally carried all before them. For two weeks most of them had been without shelter, on short rations, in a country parched by drought, where drinking water was difficult to obtain; yet no murmur was heard, and all was glee and cheerfulness whenever the enemy was found."

This admiration he expressed also in an Address to the Army issued on September 22. "Your patient endurance under privations, your fortitude and your valor, displayed at all times and under all trials, have been meetly rewarded." The last words of the Address were: "But our task is not ended. . . . Much has been accomplished—more remains to be done."

The Confederate victory at Chickamauga was a strong tonic for Southern hopes that had drooped since Gettysburg and Vicksburg. War Clerk Jones at Richmond wrote in his *Diary:*

"The effects of this great victory will be electrical. The whole South will be filled again with patriotic fervor, and in the North there will be a corresponding depression. . . . Surely the Government of the United States must now see the impossibility of subjugating the Southern people, spread over such a vast extent of territory; and the European governments ought now to interpose and put an end to this cruel waste of blood and treasure."[71]

But when the first flush of this enthusiasm wore off, the people of the South gradually came to realize that it was a hollow victory, that it was, as General Alexander says, "but another story of excellent fighting made vain by inefficient handling of an army hastily brought together, poorly organized and badly commanded." Bragg was not the man to do what remained to be done.

CHAPTER XV

THE CHATTANOOGA CAMPAIGN

When General Bragg wrote his report of the Battle of Shiloh, in which he made such a proud record as a corps commander, he was not content with a mere factual account but injected a short lecture on military principles. In the result of the battle, he said, "We have a valuable lesson by which we should profit—never on a battlefield to lose a moment's time; but, leaving the killed, wounded and spoils to those whose special business it is to care for them, to press on with every available man, giving a panic-stricken and retreating foe no time to rally, and reaping all the benefits of a success never complete until every enemy is killed, wounded or captured."

It was indeed a salient lesson—but, unfortunately for his own fame and for the fortune of the Confederacy, Bragg after the Battle of Chickamauga gave no evidence of having learned it. Perhaps, as both Polk and Longstreet surmised, he did not realize on the evening of the twentieth that he had won a great victory. Anyhow, he made no effort to reap the harvest, and he gave "a panic-stricken and retreating foe" all the time needed to rally.

Three months later, when he wrote his official report of the battle from Warm Springs, Georgia, where he was recuperating, he sought to exculpate his sluggish inaction by saying that "any immediate pursuit by our infantry and artillery would have been fruitless, as it was not deemed practicable with our weak and exhausted force to assail the enemy, now more than double our numbers, behind his entrenchments." This is unconvincing and misleading. The entrenchments, as he well knew (having built them himself), were not of a formidable nature,—at least, not until Rosecrans was given time to make them so. Bragg's force was no more weak and exhausted than Rosecrans' which, in addition, was suffering from the semipanic of defeat while the Confederates were inspired by the jubilance of triumph. Furthermore, immediately after the battle, Rosecrans' strength was by no means double that of Bragg.

Moreover, his comment on the condition of the army is directly contradicted by General Polk who, in a rigidly just letter to President Davis on October 6, said:

"The troops at the close of the fight were in the very highest spirits, ready for any service; and the moon, by whose guidance the enemy fled from the field, was as bright to guide us in pursuit as the enemy in flight. Besides, if the commander-in-chief thought the troops were fatigued, and chose to put off pursuit until the morning, why did he not attempt it then? . . . General Bragg did not know what had happened. He let down as usual, and allowed the fruits of the great but sanguinary victory to pass from him by the most criminal negligence, or rather incapacity; for there are positions in which 'weakness is wickedness.' By that victory, and its heavy expenditure of the life-blood of the Confederacy, we bought and paid for the whole of the state of Tennessee to the Mississippi River at the very least; and all that was wanted was to have gone forward and taken possession of it."[1]

Two days after the battle, on September 22, General Bragg wrote his wife an account of the engagement. He told her that on the evening of the twentieth "night put a stop to our progress" and that next morning "the enemy had entirely disappeared from our front," but, he added, "We shall follow as soon as we can get provisions." In his preliminary report to General Cooper at Richmond, under date of September 24, he said that "a vigorous pursuit followed [the enemy's] rear-guard into Chattanooga, where we found him strongly intrenched"—which was not an exactly accurate statement of fact.

The only thing resembling a "vigorous pursuit" was supplied by General Forrest who, with 400 troopers, came upon a rear guard of Federal cavalry near Rossville, charged them and drove them into Chattanooga. General Armstrong, who was a member of the party, tells a dramatic story of how during the pursuit General Forrest's horse was fatally wounded with a Minié ball which severed an artery in the neck. As soon as he saw the blood spurting from the wound, Forrest leaned over, thrust his forefinger into the bullet hole and staunched the flow of blood so that the horse stood up until the pursuit was ended on a spur of Missionary Ridge. The brave charger fell dying to the ground when Forrest removed his finger and dismounted.[2]

Forrest's approach had been so rapid that he personally captured a Federal officer who was perched in a tall tree on top of the ridge as a lookout. Forrest took his field glasses from the prisoner, climbed the tree himself to a point of vantage from which he could see all Chattanooga, Lookout Mountain, Chattanooga Valley and the river. A full panorama of the Federal army spread out before him.[3] From the tree top he dictated a dispatch to General Polk to his aide on horseback below him. "The enemy's trains are leaving, going around the point of Lookout Mountain. The prisoners captured report two pontoons thrown across for the purpose of retreating. I think they are evacuating as hard as they can go. They are cutting timber down to obstruct our passage. I think we ought to press forward as rapidly as possible." He asked Polk to forward this message to Bragg,[4] and Polk did so.

According to a story the old soldiers tell, Bragg heard that night of Rosecrans' disorderly retreat from another eye-witness—a Confederate soldier who had been captured and carried to Chattanooga but had escaped and made his way back to his command. When he told his captain that he had seen the demoralization of the enemy and evidences of intent to retreat, he was taken directly to Bragg, to whom he repeated his story. Skeptical of the soldier's capacity for accurate observation, Bragg asked him sharply: "Do you know what a retreat looks like?" And the soldier, nettled by his commander's skepticism, answered: "I ought to know, General; I've been with you during your whole campaign."

Forrest had accurately appraised the signs he saw of panic, the Federals' apparent expectation to withdraw from Chattanooga if pressed. Rosecrans was in a funk. On the evening of the twentieth he wired Halleck: "We have met with a serious disaster; extent not yet ascertained. . . . [The] enemy overwhelmed us."[5] The next morning he sent a telegram to Lincoln from Chattanooga, officially breaking the news and saying sadly that "after two days of the severest fighting I ever witnessed, our left and center were beaten. The left held its position until sunset. . . . Our loss is heavy and our troops worn down. . . . We have no certainty of holding our position here."[6] Greatly alarmed, Lincoln that same day impressed on Halleck the importance of holding Chattanooga; he did not consider any advance from there necessary, Rosecrans in a defensive position would so embarrass the Confederates that "the rebellion can only eke out a short and feeble existence, as an animal sometimes may with a thorn in his vitals."[7] This, however, was predicated on the assumption that Rosecrans could hold even a defensive position at Chattanooga, which was by no means certain. Two days later Lincoln telegraphed Rosecrans for more information, pleading: "Please relieve my anxiety as to the position and condition of your army up to the latest moment,"[8] to which Rosecrans replied, none too reassuringly: "We are about 30,000 brave and determined men; but our fate is in the hands of God, in whom I hope."[9]

That Rosecrans apprehended he would have to retreat farther is seen in his telegram to General James D. Morgan at Bridgeport on the afternoon of the twentieth—the first telegram he sent after he arrived breathless in Chattanooga. "We have suffered a serious disaster," he said, and warned Morgan: "You must secure the bridges at Bridgeport and Battle Creek at all hazards." The only possible need for the bridges would be in a retreat. The same evening he wired Burnside: "We have met with a severe disaster," and urged Burnside to join him at once.[10] Halleck followed this up the next morning. "The extent of our defeat and loss is not known here," his wire ran, but he knew that the Confederates had driven Rosecrans back to Chattanooga and he told Burnside that if he did not go there immediately Rosecrans would be "compelled to move down the north side of the Tennessee River."

It soon appeared that Burnside, in spite of such urgent and repeated appeals, had still no intention of joining Rosecrans "immediately" or otherwise. But it also became apparent that there was to be no pursuit by the Confederates. So the panic subsided in the Federal headquarters in Chattanooga and in Halleck's office in Washington. A few weeks later, on November 5, Halleck with egregious audacity and mendacity was officially proclaiming an account of the battle in which he unblushingly stated: "At nightfall the enemy fell back beyond the range of our artillery, leaving Thomas victorious on his hard-fought field."[11] This may have fooled some of the Northern people, but Grant, who was a stern realist, says frankly: "Rosecrans was badly defeated."[12]

Longstreet took it for granted that Rosecrans would be pursued. That was the promise he had had from General Lee before he left Virginia— "vigorous pursuit, even to the Ohio River" in the event of a successful battle. He probably had that promise in mind when about sunrise on the twenty-first he told Bragg he was ready to take up the chase. But Lee's resolution had not been transmitted to Bragg's soul. To Longstreet's surprise and dismay, Bragg hemmed and hawed—mentioned the defensive works at Chattanooga, asked Longstreet what course he would recommend. Longstreet knew the country only from the maps, but he felt very keenly that the occasion demanded some sort of aggressive action. Since Bragg's reference to the defensive works indicated that a direct assault on the city would not be favored, Longstreet on the spur of the moment brought up the possibility of a movement across the Tennessee north of Chattanooga to Rosecrans' rear. This, he thought, would force him to retreat, in which event they could either chase him back to Nashville or else turn on the army under Burnside in East Tennessee and put it out of business.

Longstreet says unequivocally: "[Bragg] stated that he would follow that course" and ordered the right [Polk's] wing to march and the left

[Longstreet's] wing to follow as soon as Polk was out of the way, Longstreet to care for the dead and wounded during the wait.[13] Longstreet was greatly pleased at this evidence of an offense, but his pleasure was short-lived, for when his wing got under way on the twenty-second Bragg ordered him to direct his march toward Chattanooga. Taken aback, Longstreet asked if Bragg had given up the original plan. Bragg replied that the people would be greatly gratified to know that his army was marching through the streets of Chattanooga with bands playing and citizens cheering. He seems to have imagined that Rosecrans was in full retreat from the city and all he would have to do was march in and take possession.

"I thought," said Longstreet, "and did not fail to say, that it would give them greater pleasure to know that he had passed the Tennessee River, turned the enemy out of Chattanooga in eager flight to save his rearward lines, whilst we marched hammering against the broken flanks of his columns. . . . The praise of the inhabitants of a city so recently abandoned to the enemy, and a parade through its streets with bands of music and flaunting banners, were more alluring to a spirit eager for applause than was the tedious march for fruition of our heavy labors."

In later years Longstreet expressed the opinion that Bragg's plans were altered by the message from Forrest which said that the Federal army was retreating from the city.

"It was that dispatch which fixed the fate of the Confederacy," he wrote. "General Bragg had decided to march around Rosecrans, leaving him in Chattanooga, when the dispatch was received which caused Bragg to think that the place would be abandoned on the night of the 22nd, when he decided to turn back and march through Chattanooga."[14]

Possibly Longstreet does not exaggerate the magnitude of the crisis. Perhaps the move around Rosecrans' flank would have changed the course of the war. It would be ironic indeed if Forrest's zeal and enterprise bore such unhappy fruit.

Bragg, however, never admitted that he had agreed to, or even considered, this turning movement. In his official report he takes cognizance of the course suggested by Longstreet, without mentioning that general's name, but dismisses it contemptuously as "utterly impossible. . . . It is hardly necessary to say that the proposition was not even entertained."

After halting his retreating columns at Rossville for bivouac the night

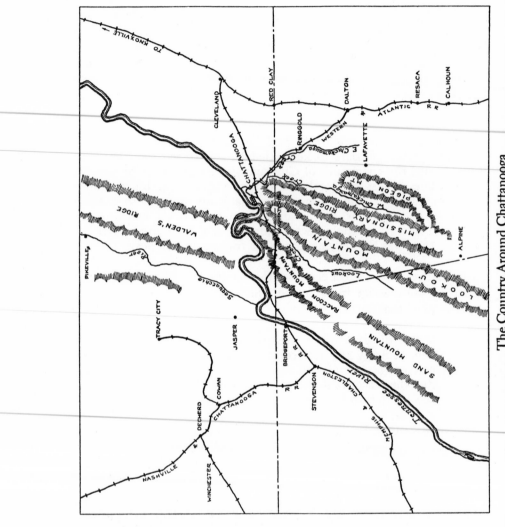

The Country Around Chattanooga

of the twentieth, Thomas had hurried on to Chattanooga. By October 22 the whole Federal command was in. The redoubts which Bragg had left unfinished were hastily occupied. They were connected by rifle pits before noon on the twenty-second, and within two days had been converted into what are described on the *Official Records* maps as "formidable earthworks." Rosecrans and his officers and men felt cheered when they realized they were not to be pursued. They gave over thought of retreat and were now determined to hold the city strongly. Reorganization succeeded demoralization.

Bragg, now that Chattanooga could not be occupied without a contest, could think of nothing more enterprising than to establish his army in a position of quasi-investment, spread out in a semicircle some six miles long. His left reached to the foot of Lookout Mountain, where the railroad from Chattanooga to Bridgeport squeezed between the mountain and the river, and cut Rosecrans off from rail connection with his base at Nashville. The Confederate line extended eastward across Chattanooga Creek to Missionary Ridge, and along the north face of the ridge to Chickamauga Creek about two miles from its confluence with the Tennessee above the city.

General Polk wrote to his wife on September 27 venting his keen disappointment at Bragg's failure to make more out of the Chickamauga victory and deploring the delay. "The troops are in fine spirits," he concluded. "We shall make a forward movement in a few days, I think, without doubt."[15] On the same day, by a coincidence, General Robert E. Lee in a letter to his son Custis[16] said he hoped Bragg would advance across the Tennessee River and force Rosecrans to battle.[17] But there was no forward movement—then or for many long months afterward—for the luckless Army of Tennessee. Bragg was not thinking of forward movements, but of a sort of siege of Chattanooga, by a vague trial-and-error system. Longstreet's artillery under Alexander had come up, after its long and devious railroad ride from Virginia. It was posted on the crest of Lookout Mountain with the idea of shelling the Federals out of their works—but the range was too great and only an occasional shell reached the lines.

The heart of Bragg's strategy was to starve the Federal force into submission, an aim by no means impracticable. His control of the rail and wagon roads on the south bank of the river made it necessary for Rosecrans to bring supplies from Bridgeport by wagon trains over the roads on the north side. The shortest way to Chattanooga was by the road skirting the north bank, but Longstreet established a long line of artillery and sharpshooters along Raccoon Mountain that soon made it untenable. The Federal supplies were then hauled up through Jasper across the Sequatchie Valley and Walden's Ridge, a roundabout way of sixty miles. This route became increasingly difficult as the fall rains set in and mud grew deep. Food began to get scarce in Chattanooga. For that matter, food for a while was scarce in the Confederate camp too. One Confederate private writes:

"In all the history of the war, I can not remember of more privation and hardships than we went through at Missionary Ridge. . . . The soldiers were starved and almost naked, and covered all over with lice and camp itch and filth and dirt. The men looked sick, hollow-eyed and heart-broken, living principally upon parched corn which had been picked up out of the mud and dirt under the feet of officers' horses. We thought of nothing but starvation."[18]

Any shortage of food in the Confederate army at this time, it should be said, must have been due to a faulty system of transportation and distribution, as there was plenty of produce in the South. When, later on, the army retreated from Missionary Ridge, it burned large quantities of foodstuffs at the Chickamauga depot.

Bragg's most ambitious attempt to hit the Federal supply line was an expedition by Wheeler with 4,000 cavalry. It started off October 1 on what turned out to be a long and destructive operation in the Federal rear. Wheeler forded the river below Chattanooga, swept up the Sequatchie Valley, encountered and captured a long train of 800 wagons and 4,000 mules. He burned the wagons and killed the mules, pushed on to McMinnville, captured it and burned its stores. Then he fought a running, day-by-day battle with various bodies of Federal cavalry on a wide swooping raid which carried him on to Murfreesboro and nearly to Nashville, then down through Middle Tennessee to Pulaski and finally on the eighth across the Tennessee River near Decatur. He had done no end of damage, but his own force was now so disorganized and exhausted by its hard riding and fighting that it was some time before he could get it back on a normal basis.

Bragg, meanwhile, according to his unhappy custom, was looking for somebody on whom to unload the burden of his own mismanagement of the Battle of Chickamauga. To make assurance triply sure, he put the stigma not on one victim but on three, Polk, Hill and Hindman.

Polk got a hint of the rod in pickle for him when on September 22 he received a stern note from Bragg asking why he had delayed the attack on the morning of the twentieth. Occupied with the movement to Missionary Ridge, Polk did not reply promptly. After a sharp reminder, he wrote Bragg on the thirtieth, stating the plain facts, that he had sent the orders to Hill the night of the nineteenth, but his courier had been unable to find him. Bragg haughtily pronounced this "unsatisfactory." The next day Polk was relieved of his command and ordered to Atlanta. Hindman also was sacked and sent along with Polk, his offense being his failure to attack in McLemore's Cove on the tenth as ordered. Many thought his gallant conduct at Chickamauga had been enough to outweigh his dereliction and confusion in McLemore's Cove, but Bragg was inexorable and out he went. Later Bragg relented and restored him, but Hindman never forgave or forgot.

Polk bitterly resented Bragg's attempt to hold him up to public disgrace. He laid his case before President Davis in a personal letter. To his wife he described Bragg's action as "a part of that long-cherished purpose to avenge himself on me for the relief and support I have given him in the past. . . . The truth is, General Bragg has made a failure, notwithstanding the success of the battle, and he wants a scapegoat. But the flimsiness of the accusation is transparent to all."[19] He said to his daughter: "I certainly feel a lofty contempt for his puny effort to inflict injury upon a man who has dry-nursed him for the whole period of his connection with him and has kept him from ruining the cause of the country by the sacrifice of its armies."[20]

President Davis diplomatically suggested that Bragg countermand the order in Polk's case, mildly reminding him, "You will not fail to perceive how readily others predisposed to censure you will connect the present action with former estrangement said to have followed an expression of opinion by your generals in answer to interrogatories pronounced by you."[21] Bragg was in no humor to be placated and went so far as to prefer formal charges against Polk. The War Department dismissed them, and Polk's urgent request for a court of inquiry was denied by Davis as quite unnecessary. Polk was ordered restored to his command but he refused to serve under Bragg any longer. The President showed his continued confidence by telling him he thought Bragg's action "a great blunder"[22] and by transferring him to Missisippi, where he changed places with Hardee.

Bragg's animosity toward Polk was hardly greater than his antipathy for Hill. He refers to his former messmate's "critical, captious and dictatorial manner" and his "general deportment" by which he had "greatly demoralized the troops he commanded, and sacrificed thousands at Chick-

amauga."[23] He asked that Hill be suspended, and this was done. Breckinridge was placed in temporary charge of Hill's corps, with the understanding that Hood would take this place when he recovered from his
Chickamauga wound.

Hill indignantly demanded that reasons be assigned for his dismissal.
When they were not forthcoming he asked for a court of inquiry, but
this was denied. He then went home to stay until the latter days of the
war.

In his letter to President Davis on October 11 applying for Hill's suspension, Bragg made inefficiency the sole and sufficient reason.

"Possessing some high qualifications as a commander, he still fails to
such an extent in others more essential that he weakens the morale and
military tone of his command. A want of prompt conformity to orders
of great importance is the immediate cause of this application."[24]

When Bragg wrote to Davis on the subject again, some eight months
later, he evidently forgot these high grounds and disclosed that personal
pique was a determining factor.

"Having taken active steps to procure my removal in a manner both
unmilitary and un-officerlike, in which he failed after a full personal investigation by yourself, he was, at my request, transferred from the army
as a necessary consequence of the line of conduct he had pursued."[25]

This allusion to Hill's "unmilitary and un-officerlike" conduct had
reference to a strange episode in the history of the Army of Tennessee in
which both he and Polk had figured. Feeling increased alarm at Bragg's
sluggishness after the Chickamauga victory, they had met with Longstreet on September 26 to discuss his "palpable weakness and mismanagement manifested in the conduct of the military operations of this
army."[26] They thought the state of affairs so serious they should lay it
before the authorities at Richmond. Longstreet would write to Secretary
Seddon and to General Lee, and Polk to President Davis, calling their
attention to the deplorable collapse of the army's confidence in its leader
and recommending his removal.

Longstreet's letter to the Secretary of War was a straightforward recital
of events since he had come west. Summing up, he said:

"Our chief has done but one thing that he ought to have done since I
joined his army—that was to order the attack upon the 20th. All other

things that he has done he ought not to have done. I am convinced that nothing but the hand of God can save us or help us as long as we have our present commander."[27]

As a remedy he advocated the radical step of replacing Bragg with Robert E. Lee. The Army of Northern Virginia, he said, could operate on the defensive during Lee's absence, while under Lee the Army of Tennessee could assume the offensive with prospect of great results, including the recovery of Tennessee. "We need some such mind as General Lee's (nothing more) to accomplish this," he concluded. Longstreet wrote Lee along the same lines, and Polk urged Lee to come and "give us the benefit of your skill and judgment and experience at this most important crisis."[28] Polk frankly declared his distrust of Bragg's ability to reap the benefits of the great victory just won at Chickamauga. "We must have a change before any permanent success can be had in this region."

It would be interesting to speculate on what the Army of Tennessee might have accomplished under the guidance of Lee's genius. But this is a factual account. Lee replied to both Longstreet[29] and Polk, modestly disclaiming any special capacity for leading it out of its difficulties. Furthermore, he said, his physical infirmities made it impossible for him to consider any change; in his recent operations against Meade he had been so crippled with rheumatism that he had to be hauled about from place to place in a wagon. "The President, being on the ground," Lee wrote to Polk, "I hope will do all that can be done."

President Davis was indeed on the ground. He had decided to make a personal effort to allay the seething discontent with Bragg's leadership which was threatening to disrupt the discipline of the army, and of which there was such growing evidence it could not longer be ignored. Close on the heels of the conference among Longstreet, Hill and Polk on the twenty-sixth a similar indignation meeting had been held on October 4 which practically all the superior officers attended. This session drafted and dispatched to President Davis a remarkable "round robin" petition which rehearsed the woes of the army in restrained but convincing terms.

"Two weeks ago," it stated, "this army, elated by a great victory which promised to prove the most fruitful of the war, was in readiness to pursue its defeated enemy. That enemy, driven in confusion from the field, was fleeing in disorder and panic-stricken across the Tennessee River. To-day, after having been twelve days in line of battle in that enemy's front, within cannon range of his position, the Army of Tennessee has seen a new

Sebastopol rise steadily before its view. . . . Whatever may have been accomplished heretofore, it is certain that the fruits of the victory of the Chickamauga have now escaped our grasp." With prophetic foresight the petition went on: "The Army of Tennessee, stricken with a complete paralysis, will in a few days' time be thrown strictly on the defensive, and may deem itself fortunate if it escapes from its present position without disaster."[30]

To remedy this critical plight, the removal of Bragg was recommended on the considerate score that "the condition of his health unfits him for the command of an army in the field."

This astonishing document was carefully phrased in respectful terms. Admitting that "the proceeding is unusual among military men," the officers firmly insisted that "the extraordinary condition of affairs in this army, the magnitude of the interests at stake, and a sense of the responsibilities under which they rest to Your Excellency and to the Republic, render this proceeding, in their judgment, a matter of solemn duty from which, as patriots, they can not shrink." They ended: "Your petitioners can not withhold from Your Excellency the expression of the fact that under the command, as it now exists, they can render you no assurance of the success which Your Excellency may reasonably expect."

There was, and still is, some question as to the authorship of the petition. Longstreet says, "It was written by General D. H. Hill (as he informed me since the war)."[31] Bragg evidently believed Hill wrote it. Hill, however, in a letter written to Jefferson Davis in 1886, disclaims the authorship and says: "I had nothing to do with the petition . . . save that I signed it willingly. General Polk got it up and it was written by General Buckner."[32] The *Official Records* state that it was "supposed to have been written by Buckner."[33] They do not give a complete list of the signers, merely mentioning "Hill, Brown, Preston and others."

Some officers who approved its sentiments hesitated to sign because those who made their opposition to Bragg known at Tullahoma had since been noticeably overlooked in the passing out of promotions. General Preston, it is related, when asked if the officers in his division were signing, said cryptically: "We all over our way have very bad colds."[34] Elucidating, he told the fable of the wolf, sovereign of the beasts, who was rumored to have a foul breath. When this rumor reached the wolf, he summoned all the animals, his subjects, to verify or disprove the report. Opening his jaws, he called upon the rabbit to stick his head in and take a whiff. The simple rabbit complied, announced he detected a bad smell, and promptly had his head snapped off. Several other animals suffered a like fate. But when the wily fox was called on, he thrust in his head and, quickly withdrawing it, said: "Your Majesty, I have a bad cold and cannot smell a thing."

It is clear that a preponderance of the officers believed in the sense of the petition whether or not they had head colds.

The round robin, reaching Richmond on the heels of the letters from Polk and Longstreet, could not be disregarded. Davis determined to go and pour oil on the troubled waters. When he reached Bragg's head-quarters on October 9,[35] the oil of peace was almost ignited into a blaze of revolt because it was found that Davis had brought General Pemberton and his staff with him and meant to put Pemberton at the head of Polk's corps. This was an appointment approved by Davis and Bragg, but by nobody else. Both President and commander must have been poor psychologists. Neither seems to have had any appreciation of the low esteem in which Pemberton was held by the public and the soldiers in the ranks alike. There was a perfect uproar of protest when Polk's corps heard the "hero" of Vicksburg was to be put over it. The Army of Tennessee was not far from open mutiny that day. Pemberton seems to have been just as dense about his unpopularity. General Mackall, Bragg's chief of staff, broke it to him. "I told him that there was not a division in this army that would be willing to receive him; that I was sorry to be obliged to tell him so unpleasant a truth, but so it was."[36]

Rather sulkily Davis and Bragg bowed to the prevailing opinion, and Pemberton and his staff were sent sadly on their disappointed way. This matter disposed of, the President applied himself to the Herculean task of smoothing the ruffled relations between Bragg and his subordinates. With all the finesse of a surgeon performing a brain operation with meat ax and handsaw, he called Longstreet, Buckner, Hill and Cheatham (in temporary charge of Polk's corps) to meet him in Bragg's headquarters, and there, in Bragg's presence, he required them to give their personal views of Bragg's fitness to command.

Longstreet makes the plain and unequivocal statement that the President "made known the object of the call, and asked the generals, in turn, their opinion of their commanding officer, beginning with myself." When he attempted to evade the question and "turn the channel of thought" the President "would not be satisfied, and got back to the question."[37] Could he have made this up? Hardly. All the testimony of those present bears him out. But President Davis a few weeks later tried to make it appear that the subordinate generals' animadversions had been entirely voluntary with them. After Longstreet and Buckner were sent to

East Tennessee and Hill was relieved and sent home, General Cheatham, alone of those involved in the conference, was left under Bragg's command. He felt that his free expressions about Bragg and before Bragg had placed him in an intolerably compromising position. He prevailed on a mutual friend, Andrew Ewing of Tennessee, to write to Davis on his behalf.

"He says," Ewing's letter ran, "that when you visited the army you desired him (with others) to state in the presence of General Bragg his views as to the propriety of retaining General Bragg as commander of this army. He complied with your request and did frankly but respectfully urge the considerations that induced the belief in his mind that General Bragg was incompetent."[38]

Cheatham thought after that either he would be transferred or Bragg would be removed. When neither was done he asked to be relieved; he could not "without humiliation and mortification" remain subject to his orders.

On the back of this letter from Ewing, President Davis wrote:

"Have read with surprise the statement of General Cheatham that I 'desired him with others to state in the presence of General Bragg his views as to the propriety of retaining General Bragg as commander of this army.' In the conference I held with General Bragg and his four highest generals I desired them to give their views on their military condition and future operations. After a discussion of various programmes, mingled with retrospective remarks on the events attending and succeeding the battle of Chickamauga, I inquired whether there were any other suggestions which either of them would make. General Longstreet then, unexpectedly to me, said in substance that he thought a change of commander desirable, and he was sustained in this by the others, to what extent by General Cheatham I do not recollect. . . . If he chose to follow others and publicly to express his disapprobation of General Bragg, it was not because I would not have heard him in private."

This seems to raise a sharp issue of veracity as to who brought up the subject of Bragg's capabilities. Longstreet, Cheatham, Buckner and Hill have all written that it was Davis himself. Whoever did, the subject once opened was certainly discussed without gloves. Embarrassing to the generals, it must have been an excruciatingly painful and humiliating session for Bragg. There he sat and heard his generals, one after the other, say, as Longstreet politely puts it, "that our commander could be of greater service elsewhere than at the head of the Army of Tennessee." There he sat stoically mute, not offering to withdraw and not flinching.

At the end of the session the President gave no indication what action, if any, he would take.

On the morrow he had an all-day conference with Longstreet, in which, Longstreet says, he offered him the command of the army. Longstreet promptly declined. He nominated Joseph E. Johnston for Bragg's place, but "the suggestion of that name only seemed to increase his [Davis'] displeasure, and his severe rebuke."39 The interview was "exciting, at times warm." Longstreet grew so irritated that he tendered his resignation "to make place for some one who could better meet his [Davis'] ideas." At the close of the day, however, they parted on outwardly good terms, as the President took the general's hand "in his usual warm grasp and dismissed me with his gracious smile."40

The next day, says Longstreet, the President got the subordinate generals together again to consider how the army might best be employed. Bragg proposed that they march upriver, cross over and force Rosecrans out of Chattanooga by threatening his rear—a plan he had but recently rejected as "utterly impossible." Longstreet advocated a change of base to Rome, Georgia, and a movement on the Federal right against the railroad bridge at Bridgeport; Davis seemed to approve and, according to Longstreet, before he left ordered the change of base.

In after years it came out that Bragg's plan was presented at second hand. General Beauregard was the real author. Still taking that proprietary interest in the Army of Tennessee, Beauregard wrote Bragg on October 7 summarizing the whole military situation and reaching the conclusion that the most promising opportunity for Southern arms lay in the West. The armies in Virginia, he thought, should act on the defensive and send all possible reinforcements to Bragg, who should get 5,000 or 10,000 more men from Polk. This, he said, "would enable you to take the offensive forthwith and cross the Tennessee to crush Rosecrans before he can be reinforced. Then you could attack and defeat the enemy's reinforcements in detail." Because he felt the President and the Secretary of War would be prejudiced against anything he might advance, he suggested that, if Bragg approved the scheme, he submit it to the War Department as his own. "What I desire is our success. I care not who gets the credit for it."41

Beauregard sent his brother, Armand, to Missionary Ridge to back up his letter with oral argument. He arrived the same day as President Davis but avoided a meeting. Bragg assured him that he would handle the matter as General Beauregard requested.[42] Promptly Armand reported to his brother.

"[Bragg] submitted your last document, in his name, to the President, urging its importance. . . . The President admitted its worth and was inclined to adopt it, only he could not reduce General Lee's army . . . but reinforcements from all other quarters would be hurried up as soon as possible . . . and General Bragg entertained every hope of having under his command a very large army, able to undertake a successful campaign on a large scale."[43]

In a few days the rains began to descend. Bragg made the muddy roads excuse for not moving against the Federal right as ordered by the President[44]—which he did not want to do anyhow. The Army of Tennessee settled down to the investment of Chattanooga with all ranks distressed and perturbed. Polk was gone, Hill was gone, Hindman was gone. Mackall on October 13 wrote to Joseph E. Johnston (whom he addressed as "Dear Joe"):

"Mr. Davis has decided to retain Bragg, though he must have been fully satisfied of his unpopularity and the decided opposition of the mass of the generals." He predicted that Buckner would succeed to Polk's place, and that this would increase "the discontent of the Army of Tennessee."[45]

The President's visit not only failed to still the clamorous discontent but before he departed it broke out in a new place—an open breach over what Forrest considered Bragg's prejudice and persecution. While Bragg was entrenching himself on Missionary Ridge just after Chickamauga, he sent Forrest and his troopers up into East Tennessee to operate against Burnside's flank. But suddenly on September 28 Forrest received an unexplained order to turn over his troops to General Wheeler. Its purpose was to strengthen Wheeler for his raid on the Federal rear, but Forrest was not told that and he was infuriated. Without waiting to cool off, he sent Bragg a violent letter of protest in which he charged him "in plain straight language with duplicity and lying"; he would come to headquarters and repeat to his face what he had said in writing.[46] "Bragg never before got such a letter as that from a brigadier," Forrest chortled in savage glee as his courier rode away.

True to his word, he galloped to headquarters, accompanied by his chief surgeon, Dr. J. B. Cowan, who has left a vivid account of the stormy interview. Forrest confronted his commander, refused to take his proffered hand, and burst out: "I am not here to pass civilities or compliments with you, but on other business. You commenced your cowardly and contemptible persecution of me soon after the battle of Shiloh, and you have kept it up ever since. You did it because I reported to Richmond facts, while you reported damned lies." In a tirade bristling with abusive epithets, he worked up to this: "You have played the part of a damned scoundrel, and are a coward, and if you were any part of a man I would slap your jaws and force you to resent it. You may as well not issue any more orders to me, for I will not obey them." With that he turned his back on Bragg, mounted his horse and rode off.

Forrest went straight from Bragg to President Davis and told him his troubles. By this time Davis had come to appreciate his rugged genius, and though probably deploring his insubordination, sought to placate him with praise and soft words. As a result of their interview, Forrest was soon afterward transferred to an independent cavalry command in West Tennessee, "to raise and organize as many troops for the Confederate service as he finds practicable." In his new field he won new laurels for himself and his men, but more than a year would elapse before the Army of Tennessee would again have his dashing assistance.

On his arrival the President had issued a fulsome address to the army. With one breath he congratulated them on their "glorious victory on the field of Chickamauga," and with the next gave them a thinly veiled admonishment for the way they regarded their chief.

"Obedience and cordial co-operation are essentially necessary. To zeal you have added gallantry; to gallantry, energy; to energy, fortitude. Crown these with harmony, due subordination and cheerful support to lawful authority, that the measure of your duty may be full."[47]

Strangely enough, though so strongly recommending harmony to the rank and file, the President held that "cordial co-operation" was not "essentially necessary" from the officers! By this cool assumption he tried to brush aside a situation that had become intolerable. In a long letter to Bragg, written from Atlanta on October 29, he said soothingly:

"My recollections of my military life do not enable me to regard as necessary that there should be kind personal relations between officers to secure their effective co-operation. . . . Relying upon the self-sacrificing spirit which you have so often exhibited, I must leave you to combat the difficulties arising from the disappointment or the discontent of officers by such gentle means as may turn them aside."[48]

Thus deftly dodging the responsibility that rested so squarely on his executive shoulders, he went away to Richmond and left unsolved the problem which sicklied o'er the native hue of resolution for the Army of Tennessee and turned awry its enterprises of great pitch and moment. His hope that the discontent of the officers might be quieted by gentle means—or any other means short of Bragg's removal—was fond and vain. On the contrary, their animosity was intensified by a new controversy—this time between Bragg and Buckner, acrid and long drawn out. It sprang from that impossible conflict of authority created when Buckner's army was put under Bragg's control but Buckner still left to administer affairs in his old Department of East Tennessee. Mutual dislike did not make it less bitter—though Bragg was capable on occasion of putting patriotism and justice above personal feeling. When Buckner, at the conference with President Davis, voiced his mistrust of Bragg's ability, Davis blurted out: "Why, General Buckner, General Bragg recommended you for promotion in the recent action." Buckner replied stiffly: "Mr. President, I certainly would not be deserving of it if I did not frankly tell you my opinion when you demand it."[49] The ill-natured argument, the sour exchange of lengthy letters went on till part of Buckner's troops were sent off with Longstreet to Knoxville in November, when Buckner was absent on sick leave.

While all this destructive dissension was boiling among the Confederate leaders, there was a similar stir of dissatisfaction on the Northern side—with the important difference that the Federals ended their bickering quickly in positive action. Rosecrans preferred charges against Crittenden, McCook and Negley—all of whom were cleared after an exhaustive court-of-inquiry hearing at Nashville. The Washington authorities had gradually become aware that Rosecrans was not up to his job. On October 19 he was removed and supplanted by Thomas. Then Grant, whose star was in the ascendancy, was put over all operations east of the Mississippi and south of the Ohio as commander of the newly created Military Department of the Mississippi.

He moved to Chattanooga and assumed active charge of operations. Immediately Sherman with his Army of the Tennessee was brought up from Mississippi. Other reinforcements had already been provided by Secretary Stanton—two corps from the Army of the Potomac in Virginia under General Joseph Hooker, the famous "Fighting Joe,"[50] who had come off second best at the Battle of Chancellorsville. They had traveled by railroad, through Louisville and Nashville to Bridgeport, where they were early in October. Grant ordered Hooker to come right on to Chattanooga, and Hooker marched down the Lookout Valley, west of Lookout Mountain.

Through his signal service in observation of Bridgeport, Longstreet was notified of the activities of large bodies of enemy troops. He forwarded these reports to Bragg who discredited them with curious obstinacy. Unless he saw them with his own eyes, Bragg was not going to believe that enemy troops were where he did not want them to be. It was not long before his eyes would be surprised.

His grip on their bread line had brought a threat of starvation to the Federal army in Chattanooga. Rosecrans thought he might break it by floating pontoons and flatboats quietly down the river at night and establishing a force at Brown's Ferry, on the south bank, several miles below the mouth of Lookout Creek. This was successfully carried out on the night of October 26. When Bragg heard of it next day he perceived its seriousness and asked Longstreet to meet him on top of Lookout Mountain the morning of the twenty-eighth to discuss what to do about it.

At the rendezvous he began at once to rebuke Longstreet again for "sending up false alarms" about movements out of Bridgeport. But at that very moment one of Longstreet's dispatch riders came dashing up through the woods to report the advance of a large body of enemy infantry and artillery from Bridgeport along the western base of Lookout. Bragg, still unwilling to credit unwelcome truth, reproved the messenger for going sensational. The soldier said: "General, if you will ride to a point on the west side of the mountain I will show them to you."[51] The three of them rode there, looked down the broad sweep of Lookout Valley and saw the men of Hooker's command marching peacefully along toward Brown's Ferry.

Though late, it was still not too late to take effective steps. But Bragg could be trusted to bungle. He promised to send Longstreet two divisions to operate against Hooker's rear guard, which was commanded by General Geary. Instead, he sent only one—Hood's, temporarily under General Jenkins—and did not notify Longstreet of the change. Longstreet posted Jenkins, in the expectation that McLaws was coming up to join in. With culpable carelessness he did not verify it and Jenkins was left to fight Geary's division alone.[52] The result was foreordained. Jenkins' attack—unwisely delivered at midnight—was a failure. The Confederates were driven off in a spirited engagement which some historians have dignified with the title of the "Battle of Wauhatchie."

Thus the Federal grasp on the river at Brown's Ferry was firmly established, together with control of the road across Raccoon Mountain to

Kelly's Ferry. A steamboat line was established from Bridgeport to the Ferry, affording direct and uninterrupted communication between the Federal army and its base of supplies, and the threat of starvation was removed. The situation in Chattanooga had been really serious. Now Grant telegraphed Halleck: "If the rebels give me one week more time I think all danger of losing territory now held by us will have passed away and preparations may commence for offensive operations."

He had no cause to worry over "the rebels" not giving him plenty of time. Bragg had nothing in mind but to follow the line of least resistance and maintain the *status quo* as long as possible, while he waited to see what the Yankees would do now.

While he waited, and while the Federals were so actively recruiting their force in Chattanooga, Bragg was incredibly doing the opposite—dividing his strength by sending Longstreet on a wild-goose chase after Burnside. This foolhardy project seems to have occurred first to President Davis himself before he went back to Richmond. In a letter to Bragg from Atlanta he expressed regret that the general could not carry out "the projected operations upon your left flank"—the change of base to Rome, and offered this alternative: "You might advantageously assign General Longstreet with his two divisions to the task of expelling Burnside."[53] General Grant thought Davis took this step to separate two incompatible commanders. He remarks: "Mr. Davis had an exalted opinion of his own military genius. . . . On several occasions during the war he came to the relief of the Union army by means of his *superior military genius!*"[54]

Longstreet says he first heard of it through camp rumors. When he was ultimately called to Bragg's headquarters—along with Hardee and Breckinridge—to be formally advised, he was ready with a counterproposal. Seeing the almost certainly fatal result to the army of detaching so large a part of its strength, he suggested that if Bragg would withdraw his whole force to a strong defensive concentration behind Chickamauga Creek, it might then be feasible to make a quick dash with a strong column against Burnside, erase him, and return to the Chickamauga before any further reinforcements could reach Grant. Bragg saw no merit in this. He ordered Longstreet to proceed against Knoxville with his two divisions, Alexander's artillery and Wheeler's cavalry. Longstreet was afraid his force might not be sufficient for the task assigned, but with "a sardonic smile" Bragg "intimated that further talk was out of order."[55] Could a seasoned soldier like Bragg fail to realize the folly of dividing his force in the face of an ever stronger enemy? Was he willing to do almost anything to get rid of Longstreet? "The Virginia troops will move in the direction indicated as soon as practicable," Bragg wrote Davis on October 31. "This will be a great relief to me."[56]

So Longstreet marched off on his hapless enterprise in East Tennessee and eventually back to the Army of Northern Virginia. So ended the brief sojourn of the doughty old "war horse," as Lee described him, with the Army of Tennessee. If it was a relief to Bragg to be free of him, it was an even greater relief to Longstreet to serve again with Lee whose genius he was the better able to appreciate—by contrast.

Grant did not leave Bragg long in doubt of his intentions. He was essentially a man of action. Now that there was no need to worry about his line of supply, he made things hum for a forward move against the Confederate force that lay so close to the city. Bragg was right there before him, in full sight. His instinct told him that there was only one thing to do—march out, fight him and try to drive him away. President Lincoln had diagnosed this opportunity. He had wired Thomas that he might go out and test his strength with Bragg without extending his line of supply; he could fight a battle and still "board at home." Thomas had been held up because the scarcity of feed had weakened his horses. The horses were getting plenty now through Bridgeport. As soon as they were strong enough to pull the guns, Grant would be on his way.

So close were the opposing lines during the siege of Chattanooga that the music of the bands could be plainly heard across the intervening space. At one point on narrow Chattanooga Creek the Union and Confederate picket lines were just across from each other. Bragg's headquarters on Missionary Ridge were in plain sight from the Federal position. And the whole Federal camp, spread out in its natural amphitheater, was in full view of the Confederates on the ridge and on Lookout Mountain. No need for either side to spar or feel about for the enemy's position! There they were, glowering at each other. It remained only to see which would make the first move. And Grant would answer that.

His plan of operation was simple but practical, and awaited only the arrival of Sherman. Sherman's van reached Bridgeport on November 14. He came on ahead of his troops and spent a day with Grant looking over the ground and familiarizing himself with his assigned role. By the twentieth he was at Brown's Ferry at the head of his column which had marched up through Lookout Valley. Now Grant was ready.

From the fact that the Confederates could so clearly see the Federal menace to their left and center along Missionary Ridge, Grant assumed that Bragg would feel a false security for his right flank on the northern end of the ridge. His scheme therefore was to have Sherman cross at the ferry, march around behind the hills and back across the river above the town, then fall on that flank in a surprise attack. Hooker, reinforced with one of Sherman's divisions, was to go over the point of Lookout Mountain and across Chattanooga Creek to Rossville, threatening Bragg's left and rear. Thomas was to attack in the center when the flanks were engaged.

His many scouts had kept Bragg fully informed of the heavy forces come from Mississippi to Grant's assistance.[57] Generals Chalmers and Stephen D. Lee had been slashing away at Sherman all across northern Mississippi and Alabama. Yet Bragg seemed blissfully unaware that all this aggregation meant anything dangerous, that the enemy might be about to strike. He went on blindly, unaccountably dissipating his already slim force. Longstreet was gone, and on November 22, the very day Grant's arrangements were completed, Bragg sent Buckner to reinforce Longstreet. On the twenty-third, when the Federal advance was actually launched, Cleburne's division also was entraining at Chickamauga to join Longstreet. News of the attack was dispatched to him just in time for part of his division to return with him and take its position on the right flank, where it was to perform prodigies of valor. The only reinforcements received by Bragg were two brigades sent him by Johnston. Two brigades did not amount to much of an offset for the great Federal accessions—or for the detachments Bragg was sending away.

His army was now reduced to two corps—one commanded by Hardee, the other for the time being by Breckinridge. The main part of the army was arrayed on the crest of Missionary Ridge, with Hardee on the right and Breckinridge on the left. General Walker's division was posted in the Chattanooga Valley, between Missionary Ridge and Lookout Mountain. Across Chattanooga Creek the line extended on the left to Lookout Mountain, and was under the immediate command of General C. L. Stevenson. Lookout Mountain, now recognized by both sides as of relatively minor importance, was lightly held by the three brigades of Walthall, Moore and Jackson, with a small force under Pettus on the summit together with some artillery and sharpshooters.

It may have possessed no particular tactical value but as a scene for a battle nature made Lookout Mountain of unsurpassed grandeur. At its northernmost tip it abuts on the Tennessee River in a declivity so abrupt that rights of way for the railroad and the highroad had to be blasted out of its perpendicular face. The promontory rises almost vertically from the river, but about midway between the water level and the mountaintop the steep ascent is interrupted by a slope or bench, a rugged sort of plateau, upon which in the wartime days were a farm and farmhouse occupied by the Cravens family. Above this bench the cliff rises vertically again to its famous peak, where countless tourists have stood and gazed at the imposing panorama spread out below them.

Grant opened up on the morning of the twenty-third by advancing Thomas' Army of the Cumberland out of its place in the lines at Fort Wood, but it was not till afternoon that they made contact with the Confederate skirmish lines. These they drove in before nightfall and captured the fortified outpost on Orchard Knob, where they promptly mounted a battery, trained on the ridge. By evening Sherman's men had completed all their secretive marching on the other side of the river. Next morning they crossed a pontoon bridge and by 1 P.M. were ready for the assault on the right flank of Missionary Ridge. Their first go was something of a ludicrous anticlimax, after all their elaborate preliminaries. Unfamiliarity with the ground led Sherman into the error of attacking a hill off the end of Missionary Ridge which was occupied by only a few skirmishers and was quite detached from the ridge proper on which the Confederate army was posted. Undaunted by this faux pas, the men held their ground for the night, ready to charge down the hill the next morning and across the valley against Hardee's true position. Grant says: "Thomas, having done on the 23rd what was expected of him on the 24th, there was nothing for him to do this day, except to strengthen his position."

On the right, Hooker with his 10,000 crossed Lookout Creek on the morning of the twenty-fourth and moved on Lookout Mountain. By ten o'clock, marching up the zigzag wagon road and scrambling over the rocky ground, they had encountered Walthall's brigade. The 1,500 men of this brigade were spread out in a thin line for a mile up Lookout Creek, and then up the rocky slope of the mountain's base to the bench, with their right near the Cravens house, behind which Moore's brigade was posted. Jackson's brigade was at the foot of the mountain on the eastern side. Walthall had been ordered, if attacked, to "fall back fighting over the rocks," and this he did as Hooker's overwhelming force struck him front and flank. The Confederate guns on top the mountain, with their trails raised, fired on the advancing Federals as long as the muzzles could be depressed enough to keep them in range, but they were useless when the men fighting on the bench far below got closer to the cliffs.

The engagement took place in a dense fog rising from the Tennessee River. This gave it the doubly misleading label of the "Battle above the Clouds." "There were no clouds to fight above," as the New York *Tribune* said, "—only a heavy mist." Blunt General Grant writes: "The battle of Lookout Mountain is one of the romances of the war. There was no such battle and no action even worthy to be called a battle on Lookout Mountain. It is all poetry."[58] So there was neither battle nor cloud in the "Battle above the Clouds."

Hooker's army and Walthall's outnumbered brigade fought desperately over that rugged mountain bench throughout the morning. Both were hampered by the thickness of the fog, but the Confederates were gradually forced back. When they reached the Cravens house and Moore's brigade came to Walthall's support they tried to establish a line and make a stand, but the Federal artillery posted on Moccasin Point across the river played heavily on them, exposed as they were on the ground around the house. So in the afternoon they had to fall back to another line behind the house, which they held until night put a term to the fighting.

At midnight General Stevenson ordered the battered survivors to withdraw and join the forces on Missionary Ridge, where it was now evident the main Federal attack was to be centered. Hooker woke up in the morning to find that he was in complete possession of the mountain—an achievement which he celebrated by sending a detachment to plant the Stars and Stripes on the mountain's peak, while the army cheered. From then on he did not do so well. His orders for the twenty-fifth were to march across the narrow Chattanooga Valley to Rossville Gap, which he was to carry and then operate on the Confederate left and rear. He was to notify Thomas as soon as he had accomplished this; whereupon Thomas was to attack the Confederate center on the ridge. Since the bridge across the creek had been destroyed by the retreating Confederates, Hooker had difficulty getting over. Its windings bewildered him, he lost his way and did not arrive on the battlefield till the fighting was just about over.

Bragg's whole force was now concentrated on Missionary Ridge—a position extremely strong tactically, with its steep slopes, but perilous strategically, with both flanks open to attack and with the deep stream of Chickamauga Creek between him and his depot of supplies at Chickamauga. It might have been wiser for him to withdraw during the night to the other side of the creek and refuse the gage of battle which Grant had thrown down. But he believed the position impregnable, and there he was determined to fight it out.

General Pat Cleburne, who could never be suspected of undue timidity, felt so sure Bragg would not attempt to fight Grant's superior army on Missionary Ridge that, when he returned from the railroad station on the twenty-third in response to Bragg's hurried call, he left his artillery and ordnance train on the other side of the creek. Grant had been strengthened by the accession of the forces of Sherman and Hooker;

Bragg had been weakened by the detachment of Longstreet and Buckner, and his left flank had been exposed when Lookout Mountain was abandoned. To Cleburne all the logic of the situation pointed to a withdrawal. He sent a staff officer to General Hardee, his corps commander, to learn Bragg's plans. Hardee met Cleburne's aide just after leaving Bragg's headquarters at midnight. "Tell Cleburne that we are to fight; that his division will undoubtedly be heavily attacked and that he must do his very best." The aide relates proudly: "I replied that the division had never yet failed to clear its front, and would do so again."[59] As soon as he got Hardee's message, Cleburne ordered up his guns, and he spent the rest of the night putting his men and his artillery in position. Hardee, who came over to help him, commented on the thinness of the Confederate center, so spread out in single rank the men could not touch each other with outstretched arms. But the main attack was expected on the right wing, and Breckinridge in the center had vowed a fierce determination to "get even with them"—which promised that the assailants would have a hot reception.[60]

Sherman attacked the Confederate right at daylight of the twenty-fifth, as per order, throwing his entire force against Cleburne's division at the end of the ridge. Between then and 3 P.M. his six divisions were hurled back repeatedly by Cleburne's stubborn defense of a stout position. As on Lookout Mountain the slope of the ridge was so sharp the guns could not be trained down on the charging bluecoats. But Cleburne's resourceful men made up for this by tumbling heavy boulders down on their heads, and the artillerists lighted the fuses of their shells and bowled them down the hill by hand. As the contending infantry lines made contact on the face of the ridge, there was a fierce man-to-man, musket-to-musket, bayonet-to-bayonet combat of a savagery unexcelled in the war's annals. Sherman's boldly charging divisions learned to respect that day the valor of the men who fought under Cleburne's unique blue flag.[61]

General Sherman had been told, he says in his *Memoirs*, that his attack would be supported by a simultaneous assault by Thomas "early in the morning." He was disappointed and puzzled when this support did not develop, but he kept plugging away. About the middle of the afternoon he won a lodgment on the ridgeside at Tunnel Hill (where the railroad tunnel passes through), but the Confederates charged downhill and drove him off. He was out of action for the rest of the day. Grant's elaborate plan to open the battle by turning Bragg's right had been frustrated by Cleburne's valiant resistance. The way the Confederates used the tunnel gave novelty to this phase of the battle. A detachment swarmed through it in a startling dash from the other side of the ridge and, taking the Federals in reverse, captured a large number.

Grant had taken up headquarters with Thomas on Orchard Knob, from which, as the day was clear, he had a full view of the entire battle-field, including Bragg's headquarters on top of the ridge. He was im-mensely disconcerted by the repeated failures of Sherman's attacks and their ultimate cessation. He was perturbed also not to see Hooker emerge on the ridge from the valley of Chattanooga Creek—poor Hooker was still confounded by the creek's meanderings. At about 3:30 P.M., therefore, Grant ordered Thomas with his force of 20,000 to advance on the center, but he distinctly ordered that they carry only the first line of advanced rifle pits at the base of the ridge, then halt and await orders.

The Confederates, through some faulty engineering which is unex-plained, had established three lines of rifle pits—one at the base, one halfway up the side and one at the top of the ridge, which here was 200 feet high, its steep sides broken with ravines and swales. Moreover, the engineers had located the top line on the "natural" rather than the "military" crest, which made it harder to defend; there were many places where an assault column could get within a short distance of the top without receiving any fire at all from the defenders.

Whether due to these technical reasons, or to something else, the defense of the Confederate center was not strongly maintained—certainly not with the unconquerable pertinacity shown by Cleburne against Sherman. Thomas' men had no difficulty carrying the skirmish line of Confederates in the first rifle pits, and there, in obedience to orders, they halted briefly. Briefly—because they were exposed to a galling fire from the upper Confederate works that was unendurable. They took the bit in their teeth and without orders[62] went surging up the ridgeside hard after the skirmishers—across the second line, and on up toward the top.

Perhaps the defenders on the summit could not fire effectively on the climbing Federals for fear of hitting their own men. Perhaps the attack-ing force took good advantage of the cover of those ravines and swales. Perhaps the line was too thin to stand against a superior number. Possi-bly sudden panic gripped it—a sort of contagion of fear. Bragg, after he had given up his command, wrote President Davis: "Breckinridge was totally unfit for any duty from the 23rd to the 27th—during all our trials—from drunkenness." And incidentally: "The same cause prevented our complete success at Murfreesboro."[63]

Whatever the reason, the center of the Confederate line within an hour after the charge began—almost before anyone realized what was

(Courtesy of U. S. Army Signal Corps)

The slope of Missionary Ridge, up which Thomas' men charged to victory.

The northern end of Missionary Ridge, where Cleburne held Sherman at bay.

happening—had broken into headlong flight. The break was so quick, so utterly unexpected, it swept over Bragg's headquarters. Bragg and Breckinridge narrowly missed capture by the onrushing bluecoats. One who was there tells how Bragg tried to check the Confederate retreat by rushing among the soldiers crying, "Here is your commander!" But the soldiers gave him back the Confederates' pet gag, "Here's your mule!"[64] and kept running. Bragg had joined the church at Tullahoma, but this soldier comments: "He had backslid at Missionary Ridge. He was cursing like a sailor" as he labored to stem the rout.[65]

In his report Bragg says:

"A panic which I had never before witnessed seemed to have seized upon officers and men, and each appeared to be struggling for his personal safety, regardless of his duty and his character. . . . In all the panic on the left, Bate's division alone held firm, and to it was assigned the duty of covering the retreat of Breckinridge's command."

Hardee was completely surprised by this disaster. When he had driven off Sherman's last charge late in the afternoon, he had rectified his lines and, with his right secure, had gone to the far left to learn the situation there. To his astonishment, he found that the left center had been swept away and that Federal infantry were driving down the ridge upon his flank. One of Cheatham's regiments hastily changed front and held the position till dark. Then Hardee withdrew, with Cleburne's division covering the retreat. Bragg's orders were for concentration of the Confederate force on the farther side of the Chickamauga, where the depot of supplies had been established at Chickamauga Station on the Western & Atlantic. In his official report General Cleburne says:

"By 9 P.M. everything was across, except the dead and a few stragglers lingering here and there under the shadow of the trees for the purpose of being captured: faint-hearted patriots succumbing to the hardships of the war and the imagined hopelessness of the hour."

Bragg's army at the Battle of Missionary Ridge amounted to about 37,000, and he suffered a loss of 361 killed, 2,180 wounded and 4,146 captured or missing. Grant's estimated effective strength is given as close to 80,000, and his loss, 752 killed, 4,713 wounded and 350 captured or missing.

The next day was Thanksgiving. There was pious rejoicing in the Federal camp, but Bragg had mighty little to be thankful for. After sizing things up he determined to retreat to Dalton on the Western & Atlantic—or, as his report expressed it in the circumlocution generally used: "It was decided to put the army in motion for a point further removed from a powerful and victorious army, that we might have some little time to replenish and recuperate for another struggle." As Cleburne had given such signal evidence of steadfastness and fighting quality, to his division was assigned the honor of holding off any possible pursuit until the rest of the army could be concentrated somewhere to the rear. Bragg said to the officer bearing the order: "Tell General Cleburne to hold his position at all hazards and keep back the enemy until the artillery and transportation of the army is secure, the salvation of which depends on him," and as he said this Bragg "exhibited more excitement than I supposed possible for him. He had evidently not rested during the night."[66] Bragg had good cause for worry. He was indeed hard pressed. He privately expressed the fear that the wagon trains and artillery would probably be lost. But he did not realize Cleburne's mettle for resistance in an emergency.

On the way from Chattanooga to Dalton, just east of Ringgold, the railroad, a wagon road and a creek all crowd their way through a narrow gorge in Taylor's Ridge. Cleburne, on receiving his orders in the early hours of the twenty-seventh, roused his 4,000 men from sleep, waded them through the icy waters of the creek, and took up position in this gap. They were there in time to meet the first advance of Hooker's pursuing army of 16,000. Hooker's skirmishers, driving the Confederate cavalry through the gorge, were followed by the solid column of the infantry, marching by fours down the railroad track. A volley from Cleburne's massed infantry and artillery checked them. They recoiled, renewed the assault, and Cleburne deployed his thin brigades on the top of the ridge to meet them as they tried to cross. Ensued a desperate struggle that lasted for several hours. On a smaller scale it was like the fierce combat on Missionary Ridge. The hard pressed Confederates again resorted to the use of rocks, clubbed muskets—any weapon that could be grabbed for hand-to-hand fighting.[67] Shortly after noon Bragg sent Cleburne word the wagon trains were safe and he might withdraw at pleasure—welcome news to the battle-weary! They fell back behind the ridge and formed in line, ready to fight again if necessary. But the Federal pursuit had spent its force. Hooker turned back to Chattanooga, and Cleburne's battered division went on next day in the wake of the retreating army.

The engagement at Ringgold was, comparatively speaking, a small affair, but it meant much to the Army of Tennessee in a time of great peril. Cleburne's service there was officially recognized by a joint resolution of thanks from the Confederate Congress, which credited him with saving the wagon train and artillery.

The outcome of the Battle of Missionary Ridge was not only a serious reverse to the Confederate arms, it was an almost irremediable blow to Bragg's personal pride and prestige. Here, John Fiske writes exultantly, "were arrayed portions of our three great armies of the Potomac, the Cumberland and the Tennessee, thus for the first time brought together under one leader; and, of all the battles of the war, this was the only one in which our four most famous Union generals—Grant, Sherman, Thomas and Sheridan—happened all to be engaged. No wonder there was so little left of Braxton Bragg!"[68] Bragg was not the man to admit that he had been outmatched in generalship, nor to assume any share of the responsibility for defeat. Robert E. Lee, after Gettysburg, said generously—too generously—"It is all my fault." Braxton Bragg was no Robert E. Lee. "It was all the soldiers' fault" was the burden of his official report of the battle.

"No satisfactory excuse can possibly be given," he said, "for the shameful conduct of the troops on the left in allowing their line to be penetrated. The position was one which ought to have been held by a line of skirmishers against any assaulting column, and wherever resistance was made the enemy fled in disorder after suffering heavy loss. Those who reached the ridge did so in a condition of exhaustion from the great physical exertion in climbing which rendered them powerless and the slightest effort would have destroyed them. . . . But one possible reason presents itself to my mind in explanation of this bad conduct in veteran troops who had never before failed in any duty assigned them, however difficult and hazardous. They had for two days confronted the enemy, marshalling his immense forces in plain view and exhibiting to their sight such a superiority of numbers as may have intimidated weak-minded and untried soldiers; but our veterans had so often encountered similar hosts when the strength of position was against us, and with perfect success, that not a doubt crossed my mind."

His effort to shift the blame fell on deaf ears. The Southern people were not disposed to excuse or extenuate his defeat. All they knew was that he had been whipped and had retreated again—a sickeningly familiar story. War Clerk Jones in his Diary relates that a witty countryman brought a gamecock into the War Department just after news of the

disastrous battle had reached Richmond and offered "to send its left wing
to Bragg." Of more serious import, he noted on the same day: "There
are rumors of a break in the Cabinet, a majority it is said having been in
favor of Bragg's removal."[69] But there was no need now for a Cabinet
split over this long-standing controversy. Bragg had fought his last battle
for the Confederacy, had ordered his last retreat.

CHAPTER XVI

"OLD JOE" JOHNSTON RETREATS

His army safely encamped at Dalton, behind Rocky Face Ridge, Braxton Bragg on the night of November 28 sat down, as he had done so many times before, to draft a routine telegram to General Cooper reporting his whereabouts and his condition. The familiar phrases of military communication sprang readily to his pen—"Our advance last night . . . We hope to maintain this position . . . Heavy loss in artillery . . . We may have to cross the Oostenaula . . . Longstreet . . . My first estimate of our disaster was not too large . . . All possible aid . . ." And then, before setting down that signature he had signed so many times—"Braxton Bragg, General Commanding"—there came a final sentence which it must have seared his heart to write: "I deem it due to the cause and to myself to ask relief from command."[1]

Cooper replied on November 30 that the President had acceded to his request, and notified him to transfer the command of the army to the officer next in rank and present for duty, General Hardee. On December 1 Bragg formally stepped down. On the same day he sent his aide, Colonel Urquhart, to Richmond with what Bragg described in an accompanying letter to President Davis as "a plain, unvarnished report of the operations at Chattanooga, resulting in my shameful discomfiture."[2] The disaster at Missionary Ridge, he said, "admits of no palliation and is justly disparaging to me as a commander. I trust, however, you may find upon full investigation that the fault is not entirely mine. . . . I fear we both erred in the conclusion for me to retain command here after the clamor raised against me. The warfare has been carried on successfully, and the fruits are bitter. You must make other changes here or our success is hopeless." He then mentioned the alleged drunkenness of Breckinridge, and, commenting that "Cheatham is equally dangerous," said: "I can bear to be sacrificed myself, but not to see my country and my friends ruined by the vices of a few profligate men who happen to have an undue popularity."

The next day he wrote Davis in a somewhat different tone; he reverted to the defeat of his army at Missionary Ridge "by sheer force of numbers" and went on:

"No one estimates the disaster more seriously than I do, and the whole responsibility rests on my humble head. But we can redeem the past. Let us concentrate all our available men, unite them with this gallant little army, still full of zeal and burning to redeem its lost character and prestige, and with our greatest and best leader at its head, yourself if practicable, hurl the whole upon the enemy and crush him in his power and his glory. I believe it practicable, and trust that I may be allowed to participate in the struggle which may restore to us the character, the prestige and the country we have just lost."[3]

Was Bragg merely indulging in a little harmless flattery? Was he playing the part of sycophant? Or was he really sincere in suggesting that Davis himself filled the requirements of "our greatest and best leader"? At any rate, Davis ignored this part of the letter. Likewise he disregarded Bragg's offer to stay and "participate."

Just what to do with an officer of Bragg's high rank, a full general, was a considerable problem. To the surprise of most Confederates—and to the dismay of many—the President solved it by kicking him upstairs to the post of military adviser to the President, where he acted as a sort of chief of staff or ex officio commander in chief. The official description of his new duties specified that "under the direction of the President" he was "charged with the conduct of military operations in the armies of the Confederacy." War Clerk Jones was among those unpleasantly surprised. Admitting that "no doubt Bragg can give the President valuable counsel," he opined that undoubtedly Davis "enjoys a secret satisfaction in triumphing thus over popular sentiment, which just at this time is much averse to General Bragg."[4] And then he uses a discerning word: "The President is naturally a little oppugnant"—a trait that had not gone entirely unnoticed by others.

The appointment was a particularly bitter pill to E. A. Pollard, the anti-Administration editor of the Richmond Examiner who in an editorial just the day before had sharply questioned Bragg's military ability and emphatically opposed his appointment "to any prominent position." The news stung him to vitriolic irony.

"The judicious and opportune appointment of General Bragg to the post of Commander-in-chief of the Confederate armies will be appreciated as an illustration of that strong common sense which forms the basis of the President's character. . . . Johnston, Lee and Beauregard learn with grateful emotions that the conqueror of Kentucky and Tennessee has been elevated to a position which his superiority deserves. . . . This happy announcement should enliven the confidence and enthusiasm reviving among the people like a bucket of water on a newly kindled grate."

No doubt it did dampen the ardor of the people, but there is nothing to indicate that it was distasteful to either Lee or Beauregard, both of whom were on friendly terms with Bragg. On the other hand, Johnston, though he had always been a friend while he was Bragg's superior, was not of a temperament to react favorably when the positions were reversed and he had to take orders from Bragg—as was to happen for the next few months.

Then there was the problem of selecting Bragg's successor. Hardee was next in command, but when directed to take over he had replied that he appreciated this "expression of the President's confidence, but, feeling my inability to serve the country successfully in this new sphere of duty, I respectfully decline the command, if designed to be permanent."[5] This was displeasing to Davis, who, according to Seddon, "thought such distrust of himself must render his [permanent] selection hazardous and unwise."[6]

Robert E. Lee recommended to President Davis the appointment of Beauregard and the immediate reinforcement of the Army of Tennessee to as great an extent as possible from other departments. He was anxious over the state of affairs in Tennessee and Georgia, and every effort should be made, he thought, to concentrate all the troops they could there "under the best commander" to insure the discomfiture of the Federals. His military genius made plain to him the vast importance of the Western front. "Upon the defense of the country threatened by General Grant," he said, "depends the safety of the points now held by us on the Atlantic"; his own position in Virginia was in as great danger from the successful advance of Grant against the Army of Tennessee as it was from the immediate attacks of Meade.[7]

Davis' response was to inquire if Lee could go to Dalton himself. He could go if desired, Lee replied, but, "unless it is intended that I should take permanent command, I can see no good that will result, even if in that event any could be accomplished." He was afraid he would not receive cordial co-operation. There was also the question of a suitable commander for the Army of Northern Virginia if he should leave it. He concluded: "I have not that confidence either in my strength or ability as would lead me of my own option to undertake the command in question."[8] So Lee was not sent to Dalton—but neither was Beauregard.

General Polk wrote President Davis he thought the command should go to General Joe Johnston. Polk knew how Davis felt about Johnston, but as an old personal friend he could speak freely.

"When," he said, "there is so general a desire on the part of the army and the country as there is to have General Johnston placed in that command, a part of your duty seems to your friend to be to yield to this general desire, that those whose all is staked upon the issue may have something to say as to the hand in which it shall be saved or lost."[9]

Secretary Seddon also recommended Johnston but found a majority of the Cabinet opposed. Benjamin in particular had grown while Secretary of War to be distrustful of Johnston's "tendencies to defensive strategy and lack of knowledge of the environment." Seddon admitted he had not been showing much aggressiveness in Mississippi, but excused this on the ground of his inferior force; if he were placed in command of the Army of Tennessee "his military sagacity would not fail to recognize the exigencies of the time and position, and to direct all his thoughts and skill to an offensive campaign." Davis wondered if Johnston could overcome his natural inclination for the defensive. As one name after another was brought up and debated, it gradually became the opinion of a Cabinet majority that Johnston was the best man available—and Davis concurred, though Seddon says he manifested "doubt and misgiving to the end."

Under such dubious and inauspicious circumstances, Joseph E. Johnston was elevated to the command of the Army of Tennessee. A wire to Bolton, Mississippi, on December 18 brought him the news. He was to turn over the Department of Mississippi to General Polk and go to Dalton where he would find additional instructions awaiting him. He arrived at Dalton on the twenty-seventh, took over from Hardee, and issued a simple announcement to the troops: "By order of His Excellency, the President, I have the honor to assume command of this army." His appointment was popular with the soldiers. One of them writes: "At every bivouac on the field, at every fireside in the rear, the joyous dawn of day seemed to have risen from the night. . . . Thousands who had continued the flight from Missionary Ridge to their homes returned"[10] —a polite way of saying that a great many deserters and "absent without leave" returned to the colors.

The "instructions" which Johnston found awaiting him consisted of a rambling sort of letter from the Secretary of War. "It is apprehended the army may have been, by recent events, somewhat disheartened"—a superb example of understatement. The Secretary hoped that Johnston's presence would "re-establish hope and inspire confidence"—which it did. "It is desired that your early and vigorous efforts be directed to restoring the discipline, prestige and confidence of the army, and to increasing its numbers; and that at the same time you leave no means unspared to restore and supply its deficiencies in ordnance, munitions and transportation"—but he need expect no reinforcements. All of which was so elementary that it irritated Johnston and put him in bad humor from the outset. The only thing like military instructions was this:

"The movements of the enemy give no indications of a purpose to attack your army . . . and, as soon as the condition of your forces will allow, it is hoped that you will be able to assume the offensive. . . . While, however, these suggestions are ventured, your own experience and judgment are relied on to form and act on your plans of military operations."[11]

Johnston answered that in the short time he had been there he had been unable to learn much of the Federals' strength and position, though they were reported to have 80,000 men, but that heavy rains had made the country unfit for operations and things were at a standstill anyhow. With a shade of the ironic he assured Seddon: "The duties of military administration you point out to me shall be attended to with diligence." But it was no easy matter to procure supplies of food, and "this army is now far from being in condition to 'resume the offensive.' "[12]

To add to Johnston's irritation,[13] the President himself wrote blandly that the information he had received about the condition of the Army of Tennessee was encouraging and "induces me to the hope that you will soon be able to commence active operations against the enemy." Davis had sent one of his aides, Colonel Ives, to inspect the army after Missionary Ridge, and he quoted Ives's report as presenting "a not unfavorable view of the material of the command." In contrast with Seddon's opinion that the army was "somewhat disheartened," the President expressed the view, gained from Colonel Ives, that it was in good spirits, its morale unshaken. He concluded: "Of the immediate measures to be adopted . . . you must be the best judge," but "it is my desire that you should communicate fully and freely with me concerning your proposed plan of action."[14]

These letters seem to reflect nothing more than a genuinely helpful and sympathetic attitude, a desire to co-operate in putting the army back into good fighting condition. Yet somehow they aroused that fretful streak so conspicuous in Johnston's character, and particularly offended his sense of official dignity—of which he had perhaps too much. It irked him for the President to think he could be told anything about the army out of the relayed, second-hand observations of Colonel Ives, "who had never seen military service."[15] Davis' letter did, in fact, reveal an astonishing ignorance of the actual status of the Army of Tennessee. It is hard to see how he could have really believed this absurdity: "The morning report exhibited an effective total that, added to the two brigades last sent from Mississippi, and the cavalry sent back by Longstreet, would furnish a force exceeding in number that actually engaged in any battle on the Confederate side during the present war." No wonder Johnston was nettled. Even if the premises had been correct the conclusion would not have been true. Johnston knew, and the President should have known, that with all these supposititious accessions the Army of Tennessee would still have far less strength than it had once had, far less than various other Confederate armies. Furthermore, Longstreet had not returned the cavalry, and the two brigades from Mississippi were to be ordered back there by the President himself within two weeks.

Johnston replied to the President at some length. He coldly gave him the facts about the army's numbers, discipline and spirit. He agreed as to the importance of recovering the territory lost, but there were difficulties in the way—difficulties which he detailed. He granted the desirability of an offensive movement, if it were possible, but, he said, "I can see no other mode of taking the offensive here than to beat the enemy when he advances and then move forward. But, to make victory probable, the army must be strengthened."[16]

The irrepressible Beauregard, off in Charleston, regarded an offensive campaign as the best means of keeping the Federal army from penetrating Georgia. Writing to Pierre Soule in early December he set forth his views. All other Confederate forces should be robbed of a portion of their troops and assume the defensive while an army of 100,000 was assembled at Dalton and hurled on Grant. The outcome would certainly be the rout of Grant's army, and the only problem whether to pursue it to the banks of the Ohio or to return the reinforcements to the armies from which they were drawn.[17]

After Johnston got to Dalton Beauregard wrote him in similar vein. Johnston replied that the principles laid down were incontrovertible, but—— There was always a but when Johnston agreed to an aggressive action, even in principle. The country intervening between Dalton and Sherman's communications in Tennessee was "a rugged desert," and for a march over that rugged desert he did not have sufficient wagons, forage, etc. It might be possible to march on Nashville by way of Huntsville, but that route would be too long. The direct route could not be taken without the siege and reduction of Chattanooga, "now a fortress." He gave Beauregard an outline of the only plan he ever suggested for a forward movement—the abandonment of the Georgia line, and an advance into Tennessee from Mississippi. But he finally got around to his basic idea, that the one practicable thing to do was to wait for the enemy to advance and attack, and "be ready, if we defeat them to press on into Tennessee." He cordially assured Beauregard that "it is as interesting to me now to receive your military opinions as it was when we were side by side in Virginia."[18]

The encampment at Dalton had not been dictated by any military factors; it was simply the place where the army had stopped to rest when it retreated from Missionary Ridge and where Bragg left it when he resigned the command. Dalton is at the junction of the Western & Atlantic and the railroad to East Tennessee, and lies to the east of Rocky Face Ridge which runs for about twenty-five miles in a north-and-south direction. About three miles north, the Western & Atlantic passes through the ridge at Mill Creek Gap, and about a mile north of the gap the railroad passes through a tunnel. Wheeler's cavalry was posted at Tunnel Hill. So was Cleburne's division of infantry, on the crest of the ridge, covering the wagon road from Dalton to Ringgold which passes around the northern end of the ridge some three miles north of the gap at Mill Creek. Near the southern end of the ridge is Snake Creek Gap, but this was left unguarded by Johnston, who evidently looked for no trouble that far in the rear.

The position, as Johnston says, "had little to recommend it as a defensive one. It had neither intrinsic strength nor strategic advantage."[19] In such circumstances, his first impulse was to withdraw to Calhoun, farther south beyond the Oostenaula River, where sounder defensive arrangements might be made, but, apprehensive of the detrimental effect of another backward movement on the spirit of the people and the soldiers, he determined to stay where he was and make the best of it. The enemy showed no signs of aggression and the army settled down to the prospect of a winter of inactivity.

When he had time to make a complete inspection, Johnston found his new command in even worse condition than he had expected. The Commissary Department was inefficient, the supply of food irregular.

The men were suffering from want of enough blankets. He remarks that "it was painful to see the number of bare feet in every regiment." Many of the brigades were without shoes, in no shape to march. There was a deficiency of rifles. The artillery was well-nigh out of commission by reason of the run-down condition of the horses due to lack of proper forage. As late as February Johnston was writing President Davis that his artillery horses were still so feeble that the guns could not be maneuvered in case of battle or saved in the event of a reverse; and a large part of the men were still barefooted.[20]

But Johnston attacked these problems with vigor, and before the winter was over he had worked wonders both in physical condition of the army and in its morale. When the blockade runner Giraffe sailed in from Nassau with 100,000 pairs of shoes, he heard about it and saw to it that the Army of Tennessee got their share. The food shortage he soon solved by diplomatic handling of touchy Governor Joe Brown. The Western & Atlantic from Chattanooga to Atlanta was owned by the state of Georgia, and Bragg had been in constant controversy with Brown over the use of its equipment for handling his supplies. Johnston quickly established amicable relations with Brown, and the provision trains started running regularly again. New supplies of clothing were requisitioned. Early in April one of the young officers in the army wrote home to his wife:

"I doubt whether a volunteer army could be more perfect in its organization than the Army of Tennessee. General Johnston seems to have infused a new spirit into the whole mass, and out of chaos brought order and beauty. Our men are better clothed than at any previous time, while their food is better than one would have anticipated two months ago."[21]

As the winter progressed the strength of the army was increased by the return of several thousand absentees—stragglers and quasi-deserters. Johnston had proclaimed a general amnesty for all who returned to the ranks, and this brought back many who had gone home in a revulsion of depair after Missionary Ridge but whose patriotic fervor was rekindled now that they had a commander whom they trusted. He instituted also a system of furloughs by which the entire army, in detachments, was able to visit home on leave of absence, and this vastly improved the morale. The soldiers became possessed of a strong belief in his great military genius. They grew to regard him with a veneration and affection approaching that of the Army of Northern Virginia for Robert E. Lee.

When he first came to Dalton a body of troops, with a band, marched to his headquarters to serenade him and called loudly for him to come out and show himself. He came to the front door, accompanied by the well-loved General Cheatham, who introduced him by patting him affectionately on his bald head and saying: "Boys, this is Old Joe." And "Old Joe" he was to the Army of Tennessee forever after.

The return of the absentees helped some, but it was obvious to everyone that the principal weakness of the army was its numerical inferiority. Among the officers a common topic of conversation was the great disparity between the Federal and the Confederate forces, and there was much speculation over how this great difference might be offset. Out of this discussion grew one of the most breath-taking proposals that were made on the Confederate side during the whole war— but one of such revolutionary character that it was quickly hushed up as something shameful and unholy, and it did not come to light till long after.

Though General Pat Cleburne had lived for some years in the South, he had been born in Ireland and grown up in the British Isles. He had none of the Southerner's inborn feeling about the institution of slavery and its accompanying problems. Without this inhibiting native background, it seemed to him a perfectly natural thing to suggest that the Confederate Army might be increased by recruiting the negroes as soldiers. Recognizing that it would be impractical to have an army half slave and half free, he thought it logical to remove this obstacle by the simple expedient of emancipating the slaves. These ideas he set down in a written document which he read to a meeting in General Johnston's headquarters attended by the commander and the other general officers. It created a sensation. There were strong expressions of dissent, and none present favored it. Johnston refused to transmit it to President Davis, declaring it to be political rather than military, but General Walker considered the paper of such an "incendiary" character that it ought to be brought to the President's attention; so he made it his business to get a copy of it and send it to Richmond. In the executive office it created another flurry. Secretary Seddon wrote Johnston that "while no doubt or mistrust was for a moment entertained of the patriotic intents of the gallant author," the President thought that the "promulgation or dissemination" of the paper would produce "discouragement, destruction and dissension," and asked that it be suppressed. Johnston replied that none of the officers to whom it was read had approved it, and that Cleburne in deference to their views had voluntarily withdrawn it. So effectually was it "suppressed" that nothing more was heard of this extraordinary proposal until 1896 when a copy turned up in the files of a deceased member of Cleburne's staff, and it was published in the *Official Records*.[22]

One of his officers had strongly advised him in the first place to keep his ideas to himself lest they so prejudice the higher authorities as to preclude his promotion to the command of a corps, for which his distinguished record as a division commander had put him directly in line. It may not have been a factor which worked against him, but the fact remains that Cleburne, in spite of his widely recognized ability, and his nickname of the "Stonewall Jackson of the West," was never advanced in grade after the day he read his emancipation proposal to the astonished generals.

Promotion or lack of promotion did not seem to bother Cleburne especially. He was genuinely and intensely devoted to the Confederate cause, and his main object was to keep his command at the highest possible level of efficiency. He had served in the British Army and was convinced of the practical value of military training. While at Wartrace in the spring of 1863 he had conducted a school in rifle shooting, with a class made up of selected officers from his several regiments. Some of them were a little reluctant to spend time dissecting the army rifle and submitting to quizzes on the technique of rifle construction and firing. But Cleburne was a driver and he kept them at the dull work till his division was probably the best-schooled of the whole army in the basic art. His ideas about the value of intensive training he carried further at Dalton, where he built a log cabin and conducted in it a daily school of instruction in the art of war for the benefit of the brigade commanders. They in turn instructed their regimental officers, and these the company commanders. With such thorough work, no wonder Cleburne's command gained such a reputation for soldierly qualities. They knew what to do and how to do it—and they did it.

General Wheeler was of the same stripe. He put his men through a rigorous course of training while they were in camp at Dalton, drilling them and their horses in the art of charging an infantry line. To give an air of reality, he had dummies made of old clothes stuffed with straw, which he ranged like infantry in a line a hundred yards long. Behind the line of dummies he put a line of men on foot, with guns loaded with blank cartridges. The cavalrymen would charge the dummies at full speed. The men behind the line would fire their blank cartridges and run. The horses would rear and snort and the troopers would slash at the dummies with their sabers. It was fatiguing work for the men, and often they would be unhorsed by stumbling over the dummies. At times somebody would be wounded by a gun that had a ball in it instead of a blank. But it made tough and seasoned troopers of Wheeler's men, and though they grumbled at the rigor of his training, they gained new confidence and respect for the "War Child," as they called their slender, youthful general.[23]

The winter days get cold in north Georgia, and this was an exceptionally cold winter, the thermometer going to three degrees below zero in January. Late in March came a heavy fall of snow—a novel sight to many of the Southern boys and hugely enjoyed. The young soldiers began throwing snowballs at one another. One of the regiments started a snowballing contest with the regiment in the adjoining camp. The frolicking was contagious, and before long a huge, formal snowball battle was under way between the divisions of Cheatham's Tennesseans and Walker's Georgians, with generals, colonels and other officers directing the movements. It was without doubt the most prodigious snowball fight in the world's history. The line of battle extended for more than a mile, at least five thousand men took part, and the furious fun lasted for three or four hours. According to Cheatham's men, the Georgians were finally driven back through their camp in great confusion—but perhaps Walker's veterans told a different story.

That winter at Dalton was not given over entirely to sham battles and skylarking. There was a flurry of excitement early in February when Johnston was informed by Polk in Mississippi that Sherman[24] was advancing eastward from Vicksburg with an army of 35,000 men and had crossed the river at Jackson, presumably headed for Meridian and then Mobile. A similar warning was sent by Polk to Richmond. President Davis wired Johnston to send Polk reinforcements or else join him with whatever force he himself could lead to Mississippi. Here ensued one of the earliest of those unfortunate clashes between the President and the new commander of the Army of Tennessee. Johnston telegraphed that he could not send troops in time to intercept Sherman before he reached Mobile, and asked further instructions. Apparently Davis did not receive this message. On the thirteenth he wired again to know what Johnston could do to strike Sherman while in motion. Johnston replied that it would take two-thirds of his men and would mean the abandonment of his position in Georgia. On the sixteenth Richmond ordered that "unless immediately threatened" he must send enough infantry to Polk to beat Sherman. Johnston doggedly answered that it would be too late to accomplish anything. The next day the President peremptorily ordered him to send General Hardee to Polk's relief with the divisions of Cheatham, Cleburne and Walker.[25] This order was obeyed—but meanwhile Sherman's expedition had gone on the rocks. His infantry advance was to be supported by the movement of General W. Sooy Smith from Memphis with 7,500 cavalry, but Smith en route had the ill luck to encounter Forrest with 3,500 men, and Smith beat a hasty retreat to Memphis with Forrest at his heels. Disgusted at the upset of this feature of his plans, Sherman burned Meridian and then turned and marched back to Vicksburg. Hardee and his detachment, the first of whom had just reached Demopolis, Alabama, were immediately returned to the Army of Tennessee at Dalton. Sherman laid all the blame on Sooy Smith for the failure of his expedition. He wrote his wife that if Smith had joined him, he would have captured Polk's whole army. Even as it was, he boasted, he had "scared the bishop out of his senses."

It had not escaped Grant that the Confederates would probably try to send reinforcements to Polk. On the thirteenth he had instructed General Thomas to go from Chattanooga with all the troops he could spare to co-operate with Burnside in "driving Longstreet from East Tennessee." But he countermanded these orders the next day and Thomas was instructed to march into Georgia "to gain possession of Dalton and as far south of that as possible." By the evening of the twenty-second Thomas' slow advance had reached Ringgold. On the following night he camped at Tunnel Hill, from which Cleburne's division had been withdrawn to go to Mississippi and which was defended now only by Wheeler's cavalry. On the twenty-fourth the Federal army moved in three columns against Mill Creek Gap, and for a while the Confederates were hard pressed. It happened, however, that at just the critical moment Granbury's brigade of Hardee's corps returned from its excursion to Demopolis. Thrown in, it was the balance of power which decided Thomas to retreat to Chattanooga.

In the midst of the alarm prior to Thomas' advance, General Hood reported at Dalton to take command of the corps assigned him. He had been convalescing from his wounds in Richmond, where he enjoyed the friendly confidence of President Davis.[26] He came back to the army imbued with the enthusiasm for a forward movement which he had absorbed from Davis, Bragg and Lee,[27] all of whom, he says, "were desirous that the offensive be assumed and an attempt made to drive the Federals to the Ohio River."[28]

Hood was still a young man, thirty-two years old, but already had made a reputation in the Army of Northern Virginia as a brigade and division commander of energy, ability and conspicuous bravery. He was a native of Kentucky, but had moved to Texas and called Texas his home. At the Military Academy he had been in the class of 1853 with McPherson, Sheridan and Schofield of the Federal Army. He was a captain in the 2nd U. S. Cavalry when Texas seceded and he resigned. He entered the Confederate service as a captain of cavalry, was rapidly promoted for courage and for efficiency in drill and discipline, was successively colonel of the 4th Texas infantry and a brigadier in charge of the famous Texas Brigade. During the summer of 1862 he and his brigade distinguished themselves in the fighting around Richmond, and he was made a division commander with the rank of major general—though his name still clung to "Hood's Texas Brigade." He commanded his division at the Battle of Gettysburg, where he got that bad wound which permamently deprived him of the use of his left arm. This and the amputation of his leg at Chickamauga might well have retired an older and less determined man, but Hood was young and vigorous and exceedingly active. As soon as his stump had healed he returned to service though still on crutches and so crippled he could not sit on his horse unless strapped into the saddle. His wounds had not chilled his martial ardor. He came to the Army of Tennessee surcharged with burning aggressiveness—almost the exact opposite of the cool and cautious Johnston. The fire of battle was in his eye.

Hood's enthusiasm was somewhat checked when he arrived at Dalton and found that Johnston, in contemplation of Thomas' advance, thought of falling back. Thomas' retreat to Chattanooga removed any necessity to retire just then, but Hood's first interview was not encouraging to the Richmond dream of driving the enemy to the Ohio River. He outlined to Johnston the plan that had been discussed there—to reinforce the army with all or part of Polk's men, march around Chattanooga to the east, effect a junction with Longstreet[29] between Chattanooga and Knoxville, and force the Federal army either into retreat or into probable defeat if they elected to fight. He not only voiced his own approval of this idea, but cited what he rightfully thought should be a clinching argument, that "General Lee favored the projected campaign."[30]

But he found no responsive chord in Johnston. That commander, who seemed allergic to any offensive program, was quick to point out, along with other real or supposed difficulties, his own unfamiliarity with the country where the campaign would be waged. He was quite willing to have Polk's and Longstreet's armies sent to him at Dalton—and then he could decide what movement, if any, to make.[31]

Hood's exact status at this time is somewhat hard to determine. Officially he was a corps commander under Johnston, like Hardee, but he seems to have been also a sort of private observer for Bragg and Davis, with whom he had been so intimately associated in Richmond for the past several months. At any rate, he wrote to Davis on March 7, giving him a report of affairs as he had found them and apologizing for not having written sooner—which indicates that Davis expected him to write. He found the "troops anxious for battle," Hood said. "I am exceedingly anxious, as I expressed to you before leaving Richmond, to have this army strengthened, so as to enable us to move to the rear of the enemy and with a certainty of success. . . . I feel that a move from this position, in sufficient strength, will relieve our entire country. . . . I am eager for us to take the initiative, but fear we will not be able to do so unless our army is increased."[32] He spoke of the possibility of uniting with Longstreet, of sending Polk to support Johnston, but said nothing of having discussed these matters with his chief. On the same day he wrote Bragg along similar lines.[33]

In thus communicating directly with Davis and Bragg about the proper strategy for the army Hood seems to have behaved in a fashion that borders close on insubordination. Certainly he was officious in the extreme, and it is hard to believe that he would have escaped rebuke if he had not been acting under instructions. If Davis and Bragg objected, they said nothing to indicate it. As for Johnston, he apparently did not know his subordinate was going over his head to plan his strategy for him.

After his conversation with Hood, but making no reference to it, Johnston had written to Bragg on February 27 about President Davis' desire to regain possession of Middle Tennessee. If this undertaking were intended for the spring, he said, it was none too early to be making preparations for it in arranging for additional troops, more field transportation, subsistence stores and forage, fresh artillery horses, etc. He should be reinforced from the departments of Beauregard and Polk, he thought, and Longstreet also should lend a hand.

On March 18 Colonel Sale, one of Bragg's aides, reached Dalton with a letter setting forth the details of what was contemplated.[34] The plan was to try to draw the forces in Knoxville and Chattanooga out of their fortified positions and force them to battle in the field, and, failing this, to operate on their lines of communication. The Army of Tennessee was to be interposed between Knoxville and Chattanooga, and then to destroy the railroad between Chattanooga and Nashville. Specifically, Johnston was to move his forces to Kingston on the Tennessee River below Knoxville, there effect a junction with Longstreet and then march across the mountains to Sparta where the army could be self-sustaining. This campaign, Bragg thought, "would necessitate the withdrawal of the enemy to the line of the Cumberland." It was explained that while Johnston was advancing, a "heavy column of cavalry" would be thrown into West Tennessee as a diversion. It was hoped that he might move on Nashville and capture that city before the Federals could fall back in time to defend it. Even if this attempt were foiled, Bragg believed it would be possible to get in the rear of the city across the Cumberland "and compel a retrograde movement of the enemy's main force." In enumerating the troops that would be available, Bragg listed Johnston's present command at 41,000, to be strengthened by Longstreet's 16,000, 10,000 from Beauregard, 5,000 from Polk, and an additional 3,000 of cavalry: a grand total of 75,000—on paper. The reinforcements were ready to be put in motion as soon as needed, Bragg assured Johnston. There was an abundance of ammunition on hand, and subsistence could be be arranged without trouble.

This, it will be remembered, was much the same plan that Bragg himself had dubbed "impossible" when he had been in command and Longstreet had proposed it. Although it does seem that something of the sort offered alluring prospects of a fortunate issue, it did not appeal to Johnston, whose inclination tended so decidedly toward defense. He promptly telegraphed Bragg a list of all his reasons for not doing what Bragg suggested.[35] Grant was at Nashville and Sherman at Memphis; surely they were not in Tennessee to stand on the defensive; undoubtedly they would advance on him at Dalton. The best procedure for him to follow was to meet that attack, defeat it, and then follow the retreating Federals. But to do this, he urged, it would be necessary for him to have the suggested reinforcements at Dalton at once; then they would be on hand, ready for the defensive, or for the offensive if the Federals did not advance as expected. In a follow-up letter he expressed the view that the proposed junction with Longstreet[36] at Kingston was impracticable (a view which Longstreet shared);[37] it would be easy for the enemy with his united forces to attack either of the advancing Confederate armies as they thus exposed themselves on the flank.

Bragg's reaction was distinctly antagonistic. In a telegram of March 21 he said:

"Your dispatch of the 19th does not indicate an acceptance of the plan proposed. The troops can only be drawn from other points for an advance. Upon your decision of that point further action must depend."

Johnston hastily replied by wire:

"In my dispatch of the 18th I expressly accept the offensive. Only differ with you as to details. I assume that the enemy will be prepared to advance before we are, and will make it to our advantage. Therefore I propose as necessary both for the offensive and defensive to assemble our troops here immediately. Other preparations for advance are going on."[38]

But, Johnston says tersely, "No notice was taken of this explanation."[39]

When he received no reply from Bragg he became apprehensive lest President Davis might not fully understand his position. So on April 8 he sent his adjutant general, Colonel B. S. Ewell, to Richmond to explain in person that he "had not declined to assume the offensive, as General Bragg had charged, but on the contrary was eager to move forward."[40] He qualified his avowed eagerness, however, by the proviso that he would move forward "whenever the relative forces of the opposing armies should justify me in such a measure"—and Davis and Bragg knew enough about his defensive-mindedness to guess what that meant.

On the way Colonel Ewell passed General W. N. Pendleton, who had been sent to acquaint Johnston with the President's wishes and to get a categorical answer to the question: Are you ready and willing to assume the offensive? Johnston told Pendleton that Ewell would deliver the explanation of his attitude, but he explained it himself to Pendleton and apparently convinced him of its soundness, judging from Pendleton's letter to Bragg on April 16. General Johnston, he wrote, "cordially approved of an aggressive movement," but opposed the proposed advance into East Tennessee on account of its "hazard of ruin." He mentioned that the Federals had a force of 103,000 to oppose Johnston's 39,000, and that because of this and other facts he "did not feel justified in pertinaciously advocating the particular movement into Tennessee, and could not but admit that the mode of attack preferred by General Johnston might, on the whole, prove most proper."[41]

Unknown to Johnston, Bragg had evidently written privately to ask Hood to use his influence on Johnston, for Hood was saying on April 13: "I received your letter, and am sorry to inform you that I have done all in my power to induce General Johnston to accept the proposition you made to move forward" but he would not consent, as he desired the troops to be sent to him at Dalton and the decision as to their use left in his hands. "I regret this exceedingly, as my heart was fixed upon going to the front and regaining Kentucky and Tennessee. . . . To regain Tennessee would be of more value to us than half a dozen victories in Virginia"—a conviction that may have guided his own strategy a year later. Hood quoted a letter he had had from General Lee saying, "You can assist me by giving me more troops or by driving the enemy in your front to the Ohio River," and he recommended to Bragg that Polk's army be transferred to Dalton, where it could be used to help Johnston or sent to reinforce Lee if that became necessary.[42]

The net result of all this correspondence and discussion was that the forward movement was dropped. Polk was shortly after moved up to join Johnston, following the shift of the Federal army from his front in Mississippi, but Longstreet was recalled to the Army of Northern Virginia in April, and the opportunity to throw 90,000 Confederate troops— even paper troops—into Tennessee never again presented itself.

An entertaining sideshow to the negotiations between Johnston and the Richmond authorities was Longstreet's attempt to organize some sort of advance into Kentucky from his station in East Tennessee. First he flirted with the harebrained idea of mounting his entire infantry command on horses and mules and galloping across the mountains into central Kentucky and on to Louisville. When he finally became convinced that he could not gather up 16,000 mounts, he had another grandiose brainstorm—Beauregard to march 300 miles from South Carolina through the mountains and join him at Abingdon, Virginia, for the Kentucky invasion. He wrote about it to Davis, to Beauregard, to Johnston, to Lee. He even went to Richmond to talk it over with Lee. In his letter to Johnston he indicated that Lee approved the scheme (which seems highly doubtful). In writing Davis he waxed expansive—let Johnston's and Polk's armies be joined to his and Beauregard's, and all be put under Beauregard's command. To Lee he suggested that Lee himself lead the combined armies into Kentucky. "My great hope is in you," he wrote, "and I know that this is the feeling of the army, and I believe it to be of the country."[43] (This was before Longstreet convinced himself—after Lee's death—that he was Lee's mastermind.) But pretty soon Beauregard's troops began to be drawn to Virginia. And Lee, though willing for Longstreet to join Johnston on the offensive, was not willing for him to idle away his time dreaming vain dreams in his East Tennessee camp. On April 7 Longstreet was ordered to Charlottesville, Virginia, to resume his place under Lee.

Meanwhile a most important change had been made in the Federal military organization. On March 3 General Ulysses S. Grant had been called to Washington from Nashville and placed in supreme command of all the armies in the field, with the revived rank of "Lieutenant General of the Army." He made his headquarters with Meade's Army of the Potomac, then in camp at Culpeper, but began at once to develop a program of co-operative action for all the armed forces—"to work all parts of the army together," as he expressed it. One of his chief contributions to the ultimate success of the Union cause was the institution of this unity of purpose and the correlation of activities. Within thirty days after assuming command he had evolved plans for a simultaneous advance in the spring of the troops in Virginia and Georgia, with other supporting movements. On April 4 he sent an outline of his plans to Sherman, who had succeeded him as commander of the "Military Division of the Mississippi" and who was now in active charge of all the Federals at Chattanooga. Sherman had brought back with him from Mississippi the 25,000 men in his Army of the Tennessee now under direct command of General James B. McPherson, and these were added to the 60,000 in the Army of the Cumberland under General Thomas. General John M. Schofield had succeeded Burnside at the head of the Army of the Ohio in East Tennessee, and it also was ready to be transferred to Sherman's aggregation when Longstreet went back to Virginia. All these, together with his cavalry of 10,000, gave him a total of more than 100,000 men.

Grant told Sherman he wanted him "to move against Johnston's army, break it up, and to get into the interior of the enemy's country as far as you can, inflicting all the damage you can." Sherman said he understood thoroughly what was expected of him, paraphrasing it: "I am to knock Joe Johnston and do as much damage to the resources of the enemy as possible."

Sherman put his forces in motion on May 4 as planned—the same day that Meade and Grant crossed the Rapidan and ran afoul of Robert E. Lee in the Wilderness. By the seventh he had reached the western side of Rocky Face Ridge and was ready to make his first effort to "knock Joe Johnston." Johnston had his troops in position along the ridge, with his right bent down the mountain to the east. Hardee commanded the left wing, Hood the right, with Wheeler's cavalry covering the right flank, which was otherwise in the air.

Sherman, writing of his Georgia campaign, emphasizes that the Confederates had "the most decided advantage of operating in their own difficult country of mountain, forest, ravine and river, affording admirable opportunities for defense." If he really wanted to come to prompt grips with Johnston, it is hard to understand why he deliberately chose the route which interposed the barrier of Rocky Face Ridge between them, when it would have been a simple matter to approach by the Chattanooga-Dalton highway which passes around the northern end of the ridge three miles from Dalton. This would have brought him face to face with Johnston's army on a broad plain ideally adapted to maneuvering or fighting, and would also have simplified the junction with Schofield who had moved down the railroad from Knoxville. With more than twice as many men as Johnston's 45,000, why should he not have been eager to bring Johnston to decisive battle? At any rate he chose another and more complicated course. Thomas and Schofield were to demonstrate heavily against the Confederates along the northern end of the ridge near Mill Creek Gap, while McPherson with his army of 25,000 was to slip through the unguarded Snake Creek Gap ten miles south. Then McPherson was to dash across and break the railroad at Resaca, fall back to the Gap and lie in wait for a flank attack on Johnston who, it was thought, would have to retreat as soon as the rail line was cut.

For an operation of tactics rather than combat, this was well thought out. Resaca commanded the railroad bridge over the Oostenaula River and was vital to Johnston's communications with his Atlanta base. Also, at this particular time the railroad was the only link between Johnston and the reinforcements coming up from Polk. To break it was to break his life line. But McPherson had difficulty getting across the rugged country between the gap and the railway (the roads all ran the wrong way, he complained), and when his van finally did reach the neighborhood of Resaca it encountered unexpected opposition in Canty's division of Polk's army which had just got there from Mississippi. Canty had only 4,000 men—but that was 4,000 more than McPherson expected, and the spirited defense made it impossible for him to seize or damage the track before dark. So at nightfall he fell back to bivouac at Snake Creek Gap without having accomplished anything. Sherman was furious, disposed to be harshly critical of McPherson for this miscarriage. A movement to Johnston's left flank and rear still appealed to him as the most promising tactic, and so he decided to bring his entire army down and through Snake Creek Gap and suddenly appear at Resaca astride Johnston's line of supply.

The wily and wary Johnston, however, was not to be so easily caught napping. Wheeler's cavalry, on the evening of the eleventh, had been sent around the north end of Rocky Face Ridge to find out what Sherman was up to. He returned with the interesting information that the whole Federal army was in motion on the other side of the ridge headed, ac-

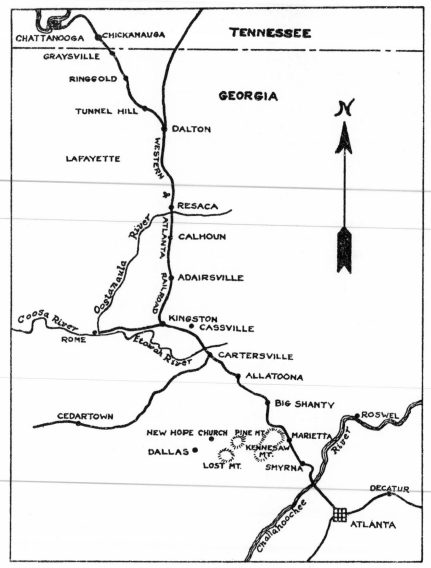

cording to report, for Resaca. Johnston ordered an immediate withdrawal to Resaca; and when Sherman emerged from Snake Creek Gap on May 13, he found Johnston waiting for him behind breastworks. What's more, Johnston at Resaca was much stronger than he had been at Dalton. At the critical moment Polk had come from Mississippi with 14,000 men—a lifesaving accretion. At the first signs of Sherman's advance, Johnston had wired Polk for aid, and had appealed to Bragg to have Polk help him. Bragg ordered Loring's division from Polk's army to reinforce Johnston, and at the same time, without consulting Bragg, President Davis independently instructed Polk to go himself with Loring and take along all the troops he could spare. So Polk left with 10,000 infantry and 4,000 cavalry, and arrived at Resaca the evening of the eleventh. He was met by General Hood, who conducted him to Dalton to report to Johnston.[44] Johnston shook him warmly by the hand. "How can I thank you? I asked for a division, but you have come yourself and brought me your army." Bragg, ignorant of Davis' order, telegraphed Polk—his old enemy—demanding why he took so many men. There was a sharp exchange of wires before Bragg understood.

Johnston's army was arrayed west of the town, facing west, with Polk on the left, his outer edge resting on the river, Hardee in the center, and Hood on the right. Hood's line faced northwest across the railroad north of the town. After some skirmishing on the thirteenth and the next morning, Hood late in the afternoon of the fourteenth attacked the Federal left and thrust it back till nightfall stopped the fighting. On the Confederate left, Polk was attacked by McPherson and had to retire from his advanced skirmish line, but Johnston's general position was maintained.

About noon next day, Hood and Hooker, both pushing forward simultaneously, met in an indecisive clash that lasted through the afternoon. After dark Johnston got news that the Federal army had effected a crossing of the Oostenaula several miles to his left and rear, near Calhoun. So he gave up all idea of a general engagement and the army at midnight crossed at Resaca and fell back toward Calhoun, burning the railroad bridge behind them.

One of Sherman's Northern critics says:

"It is well known among those who participated in it that the prominent officers of the three [Federal] armies which began the Altanta campaign considered its opening moves at Dalton and Resaca as grave and needless failures. The feeling was that Sherman with his 100,000 should have brought Johnston's 45,000 to decisive battle in front of Resaca."[45]

It is quite true that Sherman did miss a great opportunity when the odds were all in his favor. On the other hand, by not precipitating a general engagement he frustrated any plans Johnston might have been laying for counterattack. The upshot was that Johnston was maneuvered out of an exceedingly strong position and forced to retreat.

This was the beginning of the game of strategy and tactics as played by the two opposing commanders during the summer of 1864 between Dalton and Atlanta, which resulted in Johnston's gradual and steady surrender of ground without a single pitched battle. His Fabian policy created a rising tide of bellicose protest from the Richmond officials and a large part of the Southern populace, and as its adoption had so great an influence on the final fate of the Confederate arms, it is well to hear and consider Johnston's own explanation of it as given some time later:

"The disposition of the Confederate army about Dalton [he writes] was predicated on the belief that the Federal general would attack it there with his whole force. . . . I supposed, from General Sherman's great superiority of numbers, that he intended to decide the contest by a battle, and that he would make that battle as near his own and as far from our base as possible—that is to say, at Dalton. On general principles, that was his true policy. It is evident that he did not so act because he thought, as I did, that in the event of his assailing us the chances would have been very strong in our favor. My own operations, then and subsequently, were determined by the relative forces of the armies, and a higher estimate of the Northern soldiers than our Southern editors and politicians were accustomed to express, or even the Administration seemed to entertain. This opinion had been formed in much service with them. . . . It was not to be supposed that such troops, under a sagacious and resolute leader, and covered by intrenchments, were to be beaten by greatly inferior numbers. I therefore thought it our policy to stand on the defensive, to spare the blood of our soldiers by fighting under cover habitually, and to attack only when bad position or division of the enemy's forces might give us advantages counterbalancing that of superior numbers. . . . A material reduction of the Federal army might also reasonably be expected before the end of June, by the expiration of the terms of service of the regiments that had not re-enlisted. I was confident, too, that the Administration would see the expediency of employing Forrest and his cavalry to break the enemy's railroad communications, by which he could have been defeated."[46]

As a statement of proper military policy in the existing circumstances, this outline seems sound. General Grant says: "Johnston's tactics were right. Anything that could have prolonged the war a year beyond the time it did finally close would probably have exhausted the North to such an extent that they might have abandoned the contest and agreed to a separation."[47] Sherman also pays a tribute to Johnston's tactics. "No officer or soldier who ever served under me will question the generalship of Joseph E. Johnston. His retreats were timely, and he left nothing behind."[48] Granted that Johnston was right, he made a great mistake to wait ten years before explaining himself so clearly. If he had written as frankly to President Davis and to General Bragg while he was at Dalton he might have saved himself much anguish—and he might have won a greater measure of support than they accorded him while he gave lip service to their avowed policy of offense but in his heart opposed it. At any rate, Johnston from the early days of May was definitely embarked on a campaign of movement which did not contemplate any more actual fighting than was necessary—and if Richmond had known it, his life as commander might have been very short indeed.

The next clash was at Cassville, and what happened in between demonstrates the false moves into which a general may be misled by preconceived ideas and imperfect information. Seldom have two large armies been in such close proximity with each so ignorant of the other's whereabouts, and seldom has chance played so large a part in the outcome.

The railroad below Resaca proceeds almost directly southward through Calhoun and Adairsville to Kingston on the Etowah River. At Kingston the railroad turns sharply southeast by east to Allatoona, passing by Cassville which is a short distance off the line to the east of Kingston. Sherman looked at the map and took it for granted that Johnston would continue his retreat along the track and probably make a stand at Kingston. He acted confidently on this wrong assumption, marching his three armies southward in roughly parallel columns, with the idea of converging at Kingston—McPherson on the right, Thomas in the center and Schofield, accompanied by Hooker, on the left. The roads they took were far apart and they were to a great extent independent of one another, with faulty intercommunication, laying them wide open to attack.

Now Johnston, unable to find a position that suited him for a stand at either Calhoun or Adairsville, after some skirmishing with Sherman's vanguard, ordered his army on southward, with Cassville for destination. To mislead the enemy, Hardee's corps started toward Kingston, but Hardee, and Polk too, by-passed that town entirely and took the short cut across country. On May 18 when Sherman was trying to bring his scattered columns together in front of Kingston to overwhelm Johnston, Johnston was not there at all. He was at Cassville. He saw the chance this gave him to fall on Sherman's unsuspecting left flank—but he in turn neglected to find out just where the troops on that flank were actually located.

That day Johnston issued one of his few general orders.

"Soldiers of the Army of Tennessee, you have displayed the highest qualities of the soldier—firmness in combat, patience under toil. By your courage and skill you have repulsed every assault of the enemy. By marches by day and marches by night, you have defeated every attempt upon your communications. Your communications are secure. You will now turn and march to meet his advancing columns. Fully confiding in the conduct of the officers, the courage of the soldiers, I lead you to battle. We may confidently trust that the Almighty Father will still reward the patriot's toils and bless the patriot's banners. Cheered by the success of our brothers in Virginia and beyond the Mississippi,[49] our efforts will equal theirs. Strengthened by His support, these efforts will be crowned with like glories."

This order, read at the head of each regiment on the morning of the nineteenth, had the right martial ring. The men were thrilled. When Johnston rode along the lines, they cheered him lustily. He had promised to lead them into battle. But was that what he meant? Instead of marching forth to meet those advancing columns of the foe, they were put to throwing up breastworks and lined up behind them.

Hardee, astride the railroad, was on the left, Polk in the center, and Hood on the right, his line somewhat obliqued from Polk's. Hood discerned signs of the enemy ahead of him, and asked and was granted leave to advance against them. As he was first moving up to straighten his line with Polk's, he was suddenly surprised to see blue-clad infantry with artillery approaching his right flank and rear. He sent Johnston word and, quickly readjusting his line to the right, was soon briskly engaged. Johnston just could not believe enemy troops were there; even as late as 1874 when he wrote his Narrative he said: "The report upon which General Hood acted was manifestly untrue"[50]—well, as a matter of fact these enemy troops did not mean to be there. They were a wandering fragment of Hooker's corps who had lost their way and, nearly ten miles east of where they should have been, had blundered into the right wing of the whole Confederate army—and thus unconsciously and accidentally upset whatever plans Johnston may have had for a general advance.

For Johnston, strangely enough, while so skeptical about the existence of these Federals with whom Hood was engaged, decided nevertheless that Hood had better fall back at once. So the Confederate line was withdrawn during the afternoon to a ridge below Cassville. In this new position both Polk and Hood were soon exposed to the enfilading fire of the artillery which the Federals brought up. Both told Johnston that they must attack or move elsewhere. By now he must have forsworn any notion of attacking. He ordered another retreat and the army next day retired to camp a few miles south of the Etowah at Allatoona.[51] Here there is a spur of high hills, traversed by Allatoona Pass, a deep and narrow gorge through which the railroad runs—constituting a natural stronghold where Johnston threw up breastworks and waited, with his new base at Marietta on the railroad south of Kennesaw Mountain.

Sherman had some knowledge of the strength of Allatoona from personal observations made in 1844, and he had no desire to tackle it. He determined to give up, at least temporarily, his plan to "knock Joe Johnston." He would place his base at Kingston, rest his army there a few days, and then strike out directly across country southward for Atlanta. Atlanta, it seems, and not Johnston's army, began to appeal to him as the true objective.

Johnston stayed in his Allatoona camp while Wheeler's cavalry kept Sherman's army under close watch and reported his movements. When it was ascertained that Sherman had cut loose from the railroad and was apparently driving for the Chattahoochee River, Johnston effected a quick slide of his whole force to the left. On the twenty-fifth when Sherman got near Dallas and New Hope Church, he found the Army of Tennessee again in battle array between him and his objective point. The Confederate line extended from New Hope Church on the right to Dallas on the left, Hardee again on the left, Polk in the center and Hood on the right, in a well selected line on a series of ridges strengthened wherever possible with hastily prepared breastworks of logs and fence rails. Here the two armies locked horns in a desultory but violent four days' battle of disconnected skirmishes, charges and countercharges in which each side lost about 3,000 men.

The first clash was early in the morning of the twenty-fifth when Hood on the right made contact with the enemy in sharp but indecisive skirmishing. Late that afternoon, Hooker's corps in solid formation of three lines of division front attacked Hood's center. Its concentrated impetus fell on Stewart's division in a powerful assault that lasted nearly three hours but was finally repulsed. Johnston relates that, before the attack, Stewart rode along the line on his old roan horse "to instruct his officers and encourage the men," but "he soon found the latter to be superfluous, from the confident tone in which he was addressed by his soldiers and urged by them to lay aside all anxiety and trust for success to their courage. Such pledges were well redeemed."[52]

This engagement was one of the most spectacular of the whole war. In the midst of it a severe thunderstorm came on with blinding downpour of rain. Through the waning hours of the day the booming thunder kept pace with the roar of the artillery and the lightning vied with flashes of the guns as the rain pelted down on the men struggling in the thick underbrush. "No more persistent attack or determined resistance was anywhere made," says Stewart in his official report, and Hooker's men showed what they thought of it by spontaneously dubbing the spot the "Hell Hole."[53] Hooker reported his loss at 1,665 dead and wounded, though the Confederates estimated it at a much higher figure and were probably right. General Howard said that Wood's division alone lost 1,400. The Confederate loss was much less. Hooker, being the attacker, was exposed to the devastating fire of Stewart's well-served artillery; also two of Stewart's brigades had had time to throw up makeshift log breastworks which protected them while they delivered a withering play of rifle fire on Hooker's men. In the course of the desperate fighting Johnston sent to Stewart to ask if he needed reinforcements. Stewart answered calmly: "My own troops will hold the position."

The next morning it was discovered that Sherman during the night had extended his left to the east, so that he considerably overlapped the Confederate right. Polk was transferred from the center to Hood's right to meet this situation. Aside from cavalry clashes and a constant skirmishing along the whole line, there was no fighting that day. Sherman again took advantage of the night to extend his line leftward and again on the morning of the twenty-seventh Johnston shifted accordingly. Now the Confederate right, and the Federal left, reached to Little Pumpkin-vine Creek. Sherman made a determined effort to turn Johnston's right flank with his Fourth Corps late in the afternoon, but was repulsed in an engagement that lasted till after the sun went down and cost the attacking force 1,500 men. Cleburne's division once more distinguished itself. On the twenty-eighth Johnston made a costly sortie against the Federal right flank with Bate's division of Hardee's corps and planned an attack on the Federal left for the next morning—but the Federal position was not found to be as expected and this was abandoned. There was no other general engagement in the neighborhood of New Hope Church—instead the Federal forces began a general and gradual shift toward the Western & Atlantic on the east, with Johnston moving in the same direction to keep constantly before Sherman.

One significant outcome of this fighting was to convince both armies of the advantage of having breastworks, and during the remainder of the Dalton-Atlanta campaign both followed the practice of throwing up entrenchments wherever they stopped long enough. The Confederates grew so adept at it that the Federal troops said, "The Rebels must carry their breastworks with them." But so well did they emulate this example that the Confederate soldiers too had a saying, "Sherman's men march with a rifle in one hand and a spade in the other." The customary procedure was to select the line, cut down trees to provide logs to form a revetment, hastily dig a ditch behind it, and throw the dirt up on the logs. At the top of the revetment would be a head log, resting on skids or poles that extended across the ditch to prevent it from falling on the men if hit by a shell. At the same time the poles under the head log provided an open space, an elongated horizontal loophole for rifle fire. If time were available, an abatis was formed by cutting down any trees in front of the line so that their tops fell toward the enemy—an entanglement that would slow down the most determined charge. The adoption of this style of fighting changed the entire character of the campaign. It was an admitted fact that a force behind breastworks was equal to triple or quadruple its strength in the open, and attacks had to made with great caution.

When it became definitely established that the Federal march was to the railroad line, Johnston on June 4 moved—in a downpour of rain—to a position previously selected by his engineers. It threw his right across the railroad north of Kennesaw Mountain and placed his left at Lost Mountain, with a salient in the center on Pine Mountain.

After the usual cavalry sparring it developed four days later that the main body of Sherman's army was at Acworth on the railroad. Then Johnston shortened his line in a new position to the rear which interposed his force to cover not only the railroad but also the wagon roads between Acworth and Atlanta. He was strongly placed on the mountain spurs before Marietta—Hood's right behind Noonday Creek, extending to the base of Brush Mountain, Hardee in the center, and Polk on the left, with a salient still on Pine Mountain.

Pine Mountain is really hardly more than an overgrown hill, with a sharp face which affords a full view to the north. The main Confederate line ran south of this so-called mountain, but it was held as an outpost by Bate's brigade, and on its crest were two batteries of the Washington Artillery from New Orleans, one of them commanded by General Beauregard's son. Johnston, apprehensive over the proper location of the line in this sector, invited Polk and Hardee to accompany him on a visit of inspection on the morning of the fourteenth. When the generals and their staffs climbed to the top of the hill they were warned by the artillery officers that a Federal battery of Parrott rifled guns about a half mile to the front had been firing at anyone who exposed himself on the parapet, and had the range with most dangerous accuracy. Disregarding the warning, Johnston and his party mounted the parapet and were immediately greeted with a bursting shell. Johnston instantly ordered the group to disperse and seek protection behind the crest. A second shell flew over their heads. General Polk turned and walked off slowly by himself, his hands clasped behind his back, and just then a third shell hit him squarely in the side, entering his left arm, passed through his body and his right arm, and exploded only when it struck a tree.[54] As his son poignantly expresses it: "A cannon shot crashed through his breast and, opening a wide door, let free that indomitable spirit."[55]

Johnston was moved to quick tears as he turned to view the mangled corpse of his friend and corps commander. He issued a touching address to the soldiers:

"You are called to mourn your first captain, your oldest companion in arms. Lieutenant General Polk fell to-day at the outpost of this army— the army he raised and commanded, in all of whose trials he shared, to all of whose victories he contributed. In this distinguished leader we have lost the most courteous of gentlemen, the most gallant of soldiers. The Christian, patriot, soldier has neither lived nor died in vain. His example is before you; his mantle rests with you."

Polk had been associated with the Army of Tennessee since its organization. He had helped to gather together its original constituents in the first days of the war. At one time or another he had commanded practically all the troops in the army; they respected him as a leader and loved him as a man. It must be admitted, in all truth, that this high regard was not shared by all of his associates. Bragg, of course, detested him, and some of the Confederate officers felt that his actual military experience had not been sufficient to justify the important commands entrusted to him. General French said: "Thus died a gentleman and a high Church dignitary. As a soldier, he was more theoretical than practical."[56] Jefferson Davis, who was not given to overpraise, called his death "an irreparable loss" and said that the country had sustained no heavier blow since Stonewall Jackson was killed.[57]

After Polk's tragic end his corps was commanded for a few days by

General Loring but was then assigned to General Alexander P. Stewart, whose conduct at New Hope Church had centered attention on a brave, stanch and reliable leader.

On the fourteenth Sherman advanced cautiously on his right close up to and partially beyond the Confederate salient on Pine Mountain, which proved untenable and was abandoned that night. The Confederate left was then placed in entrenchments south of the mountain, which were the logical prolongation of the line. Hooker started against them the fifteenth, but found them too strong and had to fall back. Pressure on this flank was increased the next day, and Johnston was forced to bring his left back still farther, bending it to the southward. This left a sharp angle which could not be defended, and so the engineers prepared another line farther to the rear before Marietta. It had as its key the impregnable summit of Kennesaw Mountain, which was promptly and thoroughly fortified with massive breastworks. This was an extremely powerful position—but, after all, there was no disguising the fact that its occupation represented another step backward, another retreat for the Army of Tennessee under Sherman's relentless push.

Curiously enough, during all this withdrawal which had carried them so far from their starting point, the army lost no faith in General Johnston. Bragg's retreats had brought grumbling and protest, but the soldiers all felt Old Joe Johnston knew what he was doing, they were ready to follow him blindly. Every time he fell back their hearts told them it was only to prepare to deal the enemy a heavy blow, and when there was no battle and another order to retreat was given they somehow felt it was all right, the fight would come the next day—or the next.

This prevalent attitude is reflected in the letters General Polk had been writing to his wife. They all emphasize the high morale; all mention the constant retrogression, but all express belief that Johnston will soon turn and whip Sherman. Just before his death he wrote her from Kennesaw: "Our army is in fine condition and in excellent spirits. . . . The troops and the country appear to have undiminished confidence in the ability and skill of General Johnston, and he seems to be managing things very prudently."[58]

Kennesaw Mountain stands, a long steep bastion, four miles in front of Marietta. It is about two and a half miles in length, and at its highest point rises seven hundred feet above the surrounding country. As the railroad approaches from the north it turns sharply eastward and goes through a pass between Kennesaw and Brush Mountain to the northeast.

Kennesaw's steep sides made it wonderful for defense, and its elevation gave magnificent means for observing the movements of the approaching enemy. That it was truly impregnable to direct assault Sherman was to discover. The mountain proper—both Big and Little Kennesaw—was occupied by Polk's old corps under Loring, with Hood still on the right across the railroad to the foot of Brush Mountain. Hardee was southeast on the left with his line curved back across the road which ran from Marietta by Lost Mountain. The whole line was strongly fortified with thick breastworks, protected by the familiar abatis.

Sherman began a cautious feeling-out of Johnston's new situation on June 19. For two or three days there was extensive skirmishing along the whole front until the strong Confederate line on the mountaintop was fully developed. Hesitant about attempting to storm such a formidable position, Sherman continued his turning tactics by applying pressure on Johnston's thinly stretched-out left. This pressure soon became too insistent for Hardee to hold it; so during the night of the twenty-first Johnston transferred Hood's whole corps from the right to the left and filled up the weakened right by extending Loring's line down the railroad side of Kennesaw, supported by Wheeler's dismounted cavalry.

No sooner had Hood arrived on the left near Zion Church and Culp's Farm than he lashed out on Hooker. He staged this attack, it seems, on his own responsibility, without orders, believing he outflanked the Federal right and might be able by a quick stroke to do a lot of damage. It happened, however, that Sherman had been extending his own lines on this front, strengthening Hooker with Schofield, and Hood's charge met with a stout and valorous defense which finally threw him back with losses that Johnston estimated as "about a thousand men." Though repulsed, the power of Hood's blow is indicated by the fact that Hooker reported excitedly to Sherman he had been attacked by all three corps of the Confederate army. This exaggeration so alarmed Sherman that he rushed over to investigate. Hooker got a biting rebuke and an estrangement grew between them which before long resulted in his resignation.

Sherman now found himself more or less checkmated. He felt confident that with his great superiority of numbers, he ought to be able to break that Confederate line, but just how to do it was another matter. His final decision was based on the supposed weight of the unexpected. The Confederates, he reasoned, must naturally look for him to continue his attacks on their flanks, considering the strong works in their center as providing immunity. Feeling thus secure, they might well have weakened the center to bulwark the wings, and a bold and sudden attack might catch them napping. It took Sherman three or four days to work this out in detail, but at last he fixed on the morning of the twenty-seventh as the time for it. Schofield on the extreme right was to threaten the Confederate left flank; McPherson was to move vigorously against the face of the so-called "Little Kennesaw" on his front, and the main attack was to be delivered by Thomas directly against the right of Hardee's position. Reading between the lines of the official dispatches and reports, one surmises that Thomas had no great enthusiasm for his job, but he was a good soldier and obeyed orders. Perhaps he—and Sherman too—remembered a similar charge by his men against the supposedly impregnable face of Missionary Ridge. But Kennesaw Mountain was not Missionary Ridge, and the soldiers were fighting under Joe Johnston with a different spirit from that they had shown under Braxton Bragg.

The attack was preceded by heavy artillery fire along the whole front of ten miles to soften up the defenses. Then Logan's corps of McPherson's army marched straight forward against Little Kennesaw, while Thomas directed his attack at Cheatham's and Cleburne's divisions of Hardee's corps. A Confederate skirmish line out a few hundred yards was quickly drawn into the main works as the Federals advanced. Then a devastating fire of small arms and cannister was poured into the solid ranks of the Federal columns as they pressed forward with a courage that elicited the admiration of friend and foe alike. During the first part of their advance the charging columns were to some extent protected by the intervening forest and the slope of the ground, but when they emerged into the area covered by the fallen timber they began to receive the full force of a terrific fire. Bravely they pressed on across the rocky soil until they almost reached the parapets. "At several points," says Johnston admiringly, "the characteristic fortitude of the Northwestern soldiers held them under a close and destructive fire long after reasonable hope of success was gone."[59] He was not alone in this praise of the enemy's valor; all the Confederate commanders and men testify to the tenacious gallantry, the refusal to admit defeat.

Perhaps the most violent fighting of all that violent day was at the sharp angle in the line where the 1st and 27th Tennessee regiments of Maney's brigade, Cheatham's division, were stationed. Here Thomas' principal attack was concentrated, and here the slaughter was so great that it was dubbed the "Dead Angle" by the bluecoated soldiers who bravely breasted the solid sheets of rifle fire spurting out in a murderous stream from beneath the head logs. Here, too, the Federal attack reached high tide as the Stars and Stripes were planted on the crest of the Confederate works by a color-bearer who, miraculously advancing through the tornado of bullets, jumped upon the parapet and stood there for a brave moment, defiantly waving his flag until a shower of rifle balls struck him down. One of the Tennessee infantrymen, in the midst of the tumult, yelled out: "Hell has broke loose in Georgia, sho' 'nough"—and nobody disputed it.

To add to the terrors of the battle, the woods caught fire and some of the Federal wounded were burned horribly as they lay helplessly exposed to the twin dangers of incineration and death from the cross fire of the opposing armies. Colonel W. H. Martin of the 1st Arkansas, Cleburne's division, appalled at their ghastly plight, tied his handkerchief to a ramrod and, leaping to the parapet, offered a truce. "We won't fire a gun until you get them away," he yelled to the foemen huddled behind the protecting rocks and fallen trees only a few yards away, "but be quick." The Federals, of course, gladly accepted the chance to save their wounded from the fire, and before the truce was ended a Federal major, in appreciation of Colonel Martin's generous gesture, presented him with his brace of fine pistols.

The Federal soldiers had done a bit of grumbling during the continuous rains of the preceding weeks; they thought the "Sunny South" a painful misnomer. But on that day the name was deserved. The sun beat down from a brassy sky, sending the mercury to 110 degrees in the shade,[60] as the solid Federal masses pressed persistently against the Confederate works and the defending force just as persistently fought to throw them back.

"The Yankees seemed very obstinate," writes one participant on the Confederate side of the Dead Angle, "and in no hurry to get away from our front, and we had to keep up the firing and shooting them in self-defense. They seemed to walk up and take death as coolly as if they were automatic or wooden men. . . . It was verily a life and death grapple. We could not be reinforced on account of our position, and we had to stand up to the rack, fodder or no fodder. When the Yankees fell back and the firing ceased, I never saw so many broken down and exhausted men in my life. I was as sick as a horse, and as wet with blood and sweat as I could be; and many of our men were vomiting with excessive fatigue, over-exhaustion and sunstroke.[61] Our tongues were parched and cracked for water, and our faces blackened with powder and smoke; and our dead and wounded were piled indiscriminately in the trenches."[62]

Outside the trenches there were literally piles of Federal dead, mute and bloody monuments to the gallantry of the assault. But all this furious valor was wasted—what had been asked of them was impossible. By

Federal breastworks before Kennesaw Mountain (in background showing effect of Confederate artillery fire).

(Courtesy of U. S. Army Signal Corps)

Confederate works at Atlanta.

eleven-thirty the attack was over, the attempt abandoned and the men withdrawn to their original positions. "They retired—unsuccessful," says General Johnston, "because they had encountered intrenched infantry unsurpassed by that of Napoleon's Old Guard or that which followed Wellington into France out of Spain."[63] The onslaught "lasted for forty-five minutes, and there were more dead men in front of Cheatham and Cleburne than there were in front of Jackson at the celebrated battle of New Orleans." General Howard, whose division stood the brunt of the Confederate fire, says: "Our losses in this assault were heavy indeed, and our gain was nothing. We realized now, as never before, the futility of direct assaults upon intrenched lines already well prepared and well manned."[64]

Sherman in his account of his Georgia campaign written after the war refers rather lightly to the sterile and suicidal attempt on Kennesaw Mountain: "I ordered a general assault, with the full co-operation of my great lieutenants, Thomas, McPherson and Schofield, as good and true men as ever lived or died for their country's cause; but we failed, losing 3,000 men to the Confederate loss of 630."[65] In his report he elaborates somewhat. It was not without its good results, he says, as it taught his men they sometimes had to attack fortified lines, and also showed the Confederates that sometimes he "would assault, and that boldly."

Some of his critics do not view the Kennesaw Mountain episode quite so complacently. One of them characterizes it as "an utterly needless move, and so an inexcusable slaughter"; evacuation of Kennesaw might be forced without a battle, as was shown a few days later.[66] Many in the North felt that way about it, and there was much murmuring, but the ultimately successful outcome of Sherman's Georgia campaign overshadowed any regret that too many eggs were broken in the making of the omelet.

Although Sherman wasted no vain repining over the loss of a few thousand men, he was at sea over what to do next, and so he sat down for some days in front of Kennesaw Mountain while he cogitated. He had now advanced 120 miles into the enemy country, dependent on one single-track railroad for supplies for his 100,000 men and 23,000 horses.[67] He could not stand and wait; he had to act. His conclusion was to push once more against Johnston's left in a strong feeler movement that might develop along any one of several lines. Perhaps he could strike back at the railroad south of Marietta, or possibly go directly south, cross the Chattahoochee and march on against Atlanta. In any event, this would make it hard for Johnston to cling to Kennesaw Mountain. So, on July 2, McPherson's army was swung around from Sherman's left to the extreme right and the flank movement started.

Johnston was on the alert for it. He saw at once that he would have to give up the mountain and Marietta. Anticipating Sherman's tactics, he had instructed his engineers to fortify two positions between Marietta and the Chattahoochee for use in just such an emergency, and also to improve the fortifications of Atlanta. By the morning of the third he had his army in motion for its first prepared line, along a ridge behind Nickajack Creek which crossed the railroad at Smyrna about six miles south of Marietta. Here Hood was on the left, Hardee in the center and Loring on the right, with Wheeler's and Jackson's cavalry protecting the two flanks. On the left with Hood, Johnston stationed a recent accession to his ranks, a division of some 3,000 Georgia state militia under General G. W. Smith— those unique Confederate soldiers who, by the dictum of Governor Joe Brown, were permitted to fight only when an enemy had actually crossed the state line to invade the sovereign soil of Georgia, and only subject to his own whimsical and capricious orders, as their legal commander in chief. They were mostly young boys under seventeen, or elderly men, outside the age limits of the Confederate conscription. As soldiers, they were better than nothing—but not much better.

As soon as Johnston evacuated Kennesaw Mountain and Marietta, Sherman pressed Thomas straight forward along the railroad through Marietta to Smyrna, with constant skirmishing which, according to one Federal observer, "had nearly the weight of a line of battle." Johnston was soon forced back to his second line, five or six miles of entrenchments on the bank of the Chattahoochee, and prepared to make there his final stand north of the river. Sherman still bore down on him powerfully with his superior masses, but the strength and extent of that new position baffled Sherman for a time. He describes it as "one of the strongest pieces of field fortification I ever saw," and he telegraphed Halleck that he would have to "study the case a little" before he could decide how to proceed.[68] While he studied he made his headquarters at Vining's Station on the railroad where, from a near-by hill, he could see in the distance the promised land—the city of Atlanta, now the objective of his campaign and almost within his grasp.

So the armies paused there, looking back with varied emotions on the month of hard, incessant struggle since they had crossed the Etowah. There had been rain and mud—and lately excessive heat. There had been exhausting marches, night and day, punctuated by the never-ending skirmishing. There had been the steady outthrust of skirmish lines and extension of flank movements by the Federals, the matching adjustments rearward by Johnston. During that month both sides had suffered heavy casualties. Johnston places the Confederate loss in the campaign while under his command at 9,972 killed and wounded, not including the cavalry. Very few were taken prisoners, for the Confederates were generally protected by breastworks and not exposed to capture, and there was little or no straggling on the retreats. Johnston estimates the Federal loss in killed and wounded as "six times as great as ours."[69] The development of the new technique of fighting behind breastworks had led also to a new style of skirmish line, entrenched until almost as strong as the main line, and the roar of the skirmish fire, Hardee says, "was sometimes hardly distinguishable from the sound of a general engagement." All month long Johnston's army had been subjected to an almost continuous cannonading, which it could answer only fitfully, as the supply of artillery ammunition was running low and the guns could be used only to repel direct assaults.

As they lay there in this fortified position, with the Chattahochee behind them, the soldiers of the Army of Tennessee realized their peril. They knew that they had been pushed dangerously deep into their own country, that their backs were to the wall—but they still felt that Old Joe would get them out of their plight somehow. And he knew how they felt.

"The troops themselves," he says, "who had been seventy-four days in the immediate presence of the enemy—laboring and fighting daily; enduring toil and encountering danger with equal cheerfulness; were more confident and high-spirited even than when the Federal army presented itself before them at Dalton; and, though I say it, full of devotion to him who had commanded them and belief of ultimate success in the campaign—were then inferior to none who ever served the Confederacy or fought on this continent."[70]

The Federals, on the other hand, though recognizing the dangers inherent in being so far from their base of supplies, were sustained by the élan of a victorious advance.

Sherman's "study of the case" brought him to the same solution he had found so useful all the way from Dalton—a turning operation by the flank. Though his preliminary movements south of Marietta had still been directed at Johnston's left, with a lively threat to cross the Chattahoochee far on that flank, when he finally undertook the crossing it was by his own left and so far above Johnston's right that it seems to have been beyond the scope of that usually careful commander's expectations.

While Thomas and McPherson kept up an unremitting attack on the entrenchments, Schofield, early on the eighth, swung around out of sight to Sherman's rear and left and crossed at the mouth of Soap Creek ten miles above the Confederates. Before Johnston knew what was happening, the 23rd Corps of the Federal army had effected a lodgment on the south bank of the Chattahoochee, far on his right flank, with nothing between them and Atlanta, only a few miles away. In this emergency, Johnston on the night of the ninth fell back again, to the south side of the river near the mouth of Peachtree Creek, where he waited while Sherman arranged the transfer of his entire army over the Chattahoochee, finally effected eight days later. As Sherman approached Atlanta from the north and east, Johnston shifted to an entrenched line on a rise of ground to the south of Peachtree Creek, only six miles from the city limits, and again waited.

Sherman censures Johnston for lying in entrenchments on the river "comparatively idle while we got control of both sides of the river above him,"[71] and this stricture seems fully justified. The point where Schofield crossed was guarded only by a light patrol, hardly more than a picket, and his maneuver appears to have gone quite unobserved until it threatened Johnston's rear.

The presence of Sherman's army south of the Chattahoochee roused great alarm in Atlanta—but even greater alarm in Richmond, as was not at all unnatural. Through the latter stages of the retreat increasing apprehension and dismay had struck the President and the Cabinet, not allayed by Johnston's taciturn reception of their many and urgent messages and inquiries. On the fifteenth at his headquarters in Atlanta, he had a surprise visit from General Bragg—a visit which, Bragg assured him, was entirely unofficial. Bragg said he was on his way from Richmond to Mississippi to see if it were possible for General Stephen D. Lee to send any reinforcements, or if they might be had from Kirby Smith across the Mississippi—all of which was only half-truth. There was no hint of any official dissatisfaction with Johnston's activities, and he accepted Bragg's reassurances at face value.

He was entirely unprepared for the telegram he received on the morning of July 17:

"Lieutenant General J. B. Hood has been commissioned to the temporary rank of General, under the late law of Congress. I am directed by the Secretary of War to inform you that, as you have failed to arrest the advance of the enemy to the vicinity of Atlanta, far in the interior of Georgia, and express no confidence that you can defeat or repel him, you are hereby relieved from the command of the Army and Department of Tennessee, which you will immediately turn over to General Hood."

CHAPTER XVII

HOOD TAKES COMMAND—ATLANTA FALLS

To JOSEPH E. JOHNSTON it may have seemed a lightning flash that struck the baton from his hand after he had borne it only four months. But to others it was no bolt from the blue sky. There had been plenty of premonitory rumblings. Jefferson Davis says that the "clamor for his removal" began as soon as his retreat from Dalton was known and that this "clamor gathered volume with each remove toward Atlanta."[1] According to him, when the army finally reached the actual environs of Atlanta, the apprehension as to Johnston's intentions mounted. The people belatedly sensed the city's tremendous importance, with its vital railroad communications, its vast stores of supplies and ammunition, its rolling mill and foundries and munitions plants. Atlanta was the workshop of the Confederacy. As Sherman began to draw his strangling noose about it the people grew justifiably excited. Then, Davis says, he began to receive "delegations, petitions and letters" urging Johnston's removal, emanating from many sources, "including such as had most urged his assignment."[2] He resisted all this pressure till he became convinced that Johnston meant to give up Atlanta without a battle, and then he felt that his removal was imperative.

Meanwhile, he had sent General Bragg on his emergency visit to Johnston's headquarters to see what could be done—unquestionably an official visit, whatever Bragg may have told Johnston.

Bragg wired Davis on July 15 that Johnston had received him "courteously and kindly," but, as far as he could see, had no more plans for the future than he had had in the past.[3] In a letter of the same day he went into greater detail: Sherman was in the very act of crossing the Chattahoochee and Johnston would merely await his approach and be governed by developments. "Position, numbers and morale are now with the enemy," Bragg admitted. Despite its obvious disadvantages, "offensive action" was the only remedy for the army's plight. Reinforcements should be brought quickly from Mississippi and the Trans-Mississippi to put up a life-and-death effort near Atlanta. General Hood, ever since joining the army at Dalton, had been in favor of taking the offensive,[4] Polk had been

341

for it and now Stewart was, since his promotion. On the other hand, Hardee "generally favored the retiring policy" and Johnston himself "has ever been opposed to seeking battle." However, Bragg urged against a change in leadership, pointing out that Hardee, the second in command, was not only of the same school of thought but did not have the confidence of the army. "If any change is made, Lieutenant General Hood would give unlimited satisfaction." And then he summed up Hood's limited qualifications with admirable terseness: "Do not understand me as proposing him as a man of genius, or a great general, but as far better in the present emergency than any one we have available." In short, Hood, in Bragg's estimation, was "the best of a bad lot."

President Davis was confronted with a crisis—perhaps the most serious crisis in all the military history of the Confederacy. He did not act precipitately. The opinion has long prevailed that he summarily and arbitrarily removed Johnston out of personal dislike. The records do not bear this out.

When the subject became a matter of sharp controversy in the years just after the war, Secretary Seddon revealed that "the whole Cabinet concurred in advising and even urging" a change and that Davis arrived at a conviction of its necessity "slowly and not without much hesitation, misgiving and, even to the last, reluctance."[5] Seddon himself was in an embarrassing position, since he had been so strong for Johnston's replacing Bragg in the face of decided Cabinet opposition. Now he had had a complete change of heart about Johnston's ability. He says: "I felt myself from previous responsibility the more bound to recommend and urge a change of commander and the immediate adoption of vigorous offensive operations."

Judah P. Benjamin was another Cabinet member who was a strong anti-Johnston man. He wrote Davis[6] after the war that he not only concurred in Johnston's removal before Atlanta but had favored it at a much earlier date, because the general had abandoned one position after another "without any serious attempt at defense." The Cabinet decided, Benjamin says, only after it looked as though Johnston would give up Atlanta without a fight. While expressing greatest admiration for Johnston's personal gallantry, he says, in a shrewd analysis: "From a close observation of his career I became persuaded that his nervous dread of losing a battle would prevent at all times his ability to cope with an enemy of nearly equal strength, and that opportunities would thus constantly be lost which under other commanders would open a plain path to victory."

When it became open gossip in Richmond that Johnston's dismissal was under Cabinet discussion, there was great concern among his friends in Congress. They resorted to the extreme measure of selecting a committee to go to Georgia and urge him to take aggressive action before executive patience was exhausted. George C. Vest, later a member of the United States Senate, was in this delegation. He relates that Johnston became highly indignant when told of the feeling in Richmond.

"You may tell Mr. Davis that it would be folly for me under the circumstances to risk a decisive engagement. My plan is to draw Sherman further and further from his base in the hope of weakening him and by cutting his army in two. That is my only hope of defeating him."

Vest insisted that Davis expected him to hand Sherman "a crushing blow" without further delay, and made the tactless error of quoting the President as saying: "If I were in his place I could whip Sherman now."

Johnston replied heatedly: "Yes, I know Mr. Davis thinks that he can do a great many things that other men would hesitate to attempt. For instance, he tried to do what God had failed to do. He tried to make a soldier of Braxton Bragg, and you know the result. It couldn't be done." While they were in conference a courier arrived with news that part of Sherman's army had crossed the Chattahoochee. Johnston immediately declared the time had come to strike Sherman and "whip him in detail"— but the order relieving him from his command arrived before he could put his plans into operation.[7]

One thing that crystallized the fears of the President and the Cabinet was Johnston's telegram to the War Department suggesting the removal of the prisoners from the prison camp at Andersonville—125 miles south of Atlanta. Johnston must be looking beyond Atlanta for the scene of his future operations. They would have had stronger reason to fear it if they had known then what Hood later asserted, that during the latter days of May while they were at New Hope Church Johnston had suggested to the corps commanders that Macon (ninety miles south of Atlanta) was "the place to fall back upon."[8] In all fairness, neither his actions nor his words indicated any purpose other than to continue retiring.

President Davis asked the advice of General Robert E. Lee, telegraphing him at Petersburg on July 12: "General Johnston has failed and there are strong indications that he will abandon Atlanta. . . . It seems necessary to relieve him at once. Who should succeed him?" Then, mindful no doubt of Bragg's idea, "What think you of Hood for the position?"[9]

Lee replied by wire. He regretted the news for it was a bad time to relieve the commander of an army situated like the Army of Tennessee. "We may lose Atlanta and the army too." As to Hood, he was guarded. "Hood is a bold fighter. I am doubtful as to other qualities necessary."[10]

Later in the day he wrote Davis at greater length, reiterating his distress at the prospect of changing commanders but saying reluctantly: "Still, if necessary, it ought to be done. I know nothing of the necessity. . . . We must risk much" to save the threatened territory. He proposed the concentration of all the cavalry in Mississippi and Tennessee on Sherman's communications. He went more into detail about Hood. "He is a good fighter; very industrious on the battlefield, careless off; and I have had no opportunity of judging of his action when the whole responsibility rested upon him. I have a high opinion of his gallantry, earnestness and zeal." He added, significantly: "General Hardee has more experience in managing an army."[11]

General Lee's idea of throwing Morgan and Forrest on Sherman's service of supply seems to have appealed to the imaginations of a great many people.[12] Howell Cobb on July 1 had written to Secretary Seddon from Athens, Georgia, advocating that some movement be made "by Forrest (if possible) or some other cavalry" on Sherman's line—if his communications could be cut for ten days his army would be destroyed.[13] Senator Henry of Tennessee also urged this. Governor Brown insistently wrote Davis, pressing it on him.[14] Johnston himself was among those who favored it, in fact, according to Senator B. H. Hill, considered it, after the Battle of Kennesaw Mountain, as the only means of defeating Sherman. The day after that fight Johnston sent for Hill and asked him to use his influence with the President to put it through. Hill writes that he was himself so convinced of its urgent importance he went at once to Richmond.[15] The President explained that Morgan, then located at Abingdon, Virginia, had already attempted to operate on Sherman's rear by making a roundabout swing through Kentucky and Tennessee. It had resulted in his defeat and retreat to Abingdon without doing any damage. All the cavalry in Mississippi, including Forrest's and Roddey's, was currently needed there to oppose an expedition under General A. J. Smith which was expected to set out from Memphis through Mississippi. Hill despairingly telegraphed Johnston on the fourteenth: "You must do the work with your present force. For God's sake do it."[16]

The President's alarm for Atlanta was brought to a head by the retreat across the Chattahoochee. On the sixteenth he sent Johnston a final telegram. He spoke of his apprehension and said crisply: "I wish to hear from you as to present situation and your plan of operations so specifically as will enable me to anticipate events."[17]

Johnston, who could not have realized how thin Davis' patience had been worn, still stubbornly refused to take him into his confidence. He replied vaguely: "As the enemy has double our numbers we must be on the defensive. My plan of operations must, therefore, depend upon that of the enemy. It is mainly to watch for an opportunity to fight to advantage."[18] To this evasive dispatch he attached his official signature—and thereby signed his warrant of dismissal. The order for it followed the next day.

General Bragg's statement to Davis that Hood's appointment would give "unlimited satisfaction" seems to have been based on a very inaccurate understanding of the sentiment of the troops. One man in the ranks wrote after the war that "the most terrible and disastrous blow that the South ever received was when Hon. Jefferson Davis placed General Hood in command of the Army of Tennessee. I saw thousands of men cry like babies. . . . The private soldiers of the Army of Tennessee looked upon Hood as an overrated general."[19] To support this, he relates that a whole picket guard of five men on the Chattahoochee deserted the night they heard the news. Another private writes that the change was "a death knell to the Army of Tennessee. . . . With bowed heads and sorrowful hearts the Army . . . yielded to the mandate of fate. . . . As Sherman said, this was giving to him twenty thousand men."[20] And still another says: "Great stalwart sun-burnt soldiers by the thousands could be seen falling out of line, squatting down by a tree or in a fence corner, weeping like children. This act of the War Department threw a damper over this army from which it never recovered."[21]

Nor was this feeling confined to the privates. General A. P. Stewart writes: "My conviction is that the removal of Johnston was the final coup de grace to the Confederate cause."[22] General Hardee did not mince words. To him Hood was incompetent to command. He was so incensed that he at once applied to be relieved of duty. Bragg talked to both of them and reported to Davis on July 27 that they agreed Hardee should be transferred elsewhere. Hardee himself wrote the President on August 3[23] asking that the change be made "to relieve me from an unpleasant situation." Davis tried to assuage him—his attitude when proffered the command at Dalton had indicated he would not object to Hood's being given the position instead of him. Hardee answered irritably that nothing he had ever written was intended to convey the impression "that the appointment of a junior to command me would be satisfactory." He insisted on being relieved from a situation "personally humiliating."[24] In a letter a few days later to his friend General Mackall he said: "The President is endeavoring to create the impression that in declining the command at Dalton I declined it for all future time."[25] Davis appealed to Hardee's patriotism and his duty as an old soldier to support the public defense, and this persuaded Hardee to carry on, but his relations with Hood were openly and notoriously hostile.

Hardee's low estimate of Hood was heartily reciprocated. "Whilst General Hardee had," Hood says, "perhaps no superior as a corps commander during retreat in the presence of an enemy, or in defensive operations, he was wanting in that boldness requisite for offensive warfare. . . . Long and gallant service had, however, endeared him to his troops, and because of further demoralization which I feared might ensue in the event of his removal, I decided to retain him in command."[26]

One man to whom the change in commanders did indeed give "unlimited satisfaction" was General William Tecumseh Sherman. "At this critical moment the Confederate Government rendered us a most valuable service. . . . The character of a leader is a large factor in the game of war, and I confess I was pleased."[27] Sherman inquired of McPherson and Schofield, Hood's classmates at West Point, about the characteristics of the new Confederate commander. They agreed, he says, that now they would have to be "unusually cautious, and prepared at all times for sallies and for hard fighting, because Hood, though not deemed much of a scholar, or of great mental capacity, was undoubtedly a brave, determined and rash man."[28] Sherman was shrewd enough to observe that the change in commanders at this juncture very clearly reflected an official displeasure with Johnston's defensive tactics.

Hood, too, saw this as clearly as anybody. Johnston had been displaced because he had not been willing to march out and provoke a fight. Hood had been chosen to replace him because he had the name of being a fighter. If anything was written in bold characters, plain for all to see, it was that he was expected to throw down the gage of battle without further delay—a course far from distasteful to one of his natural combativeness.

He felt no doubt or hesitation about attacking the enemy, but, thrust suddenly into the command, he lacked accurate information of the exact location of the enemy troops—or, for that matter, of his own. Johnston states that he transferred the command to General Hood "immediately," that "General Hood came to my quarters early in the morning of the 18th and remained there during the day" and that "I explained my plans to him."[29] Hood's account presents quite a different picture. He denies that Johnston explained his plans.[30] He makes the more serious charge that Johnston "deserted" him right after turning over the command and after promising "with tears of emotion gathering in his eyes" to stay with him and give him the advantage of his advice and counsel while he was assuming his new duties.[31]

"Deserted" is an ugly word to use about a soldier, but Hood felt very keenly that Johnston did not show a proper spirit of co-operation in the difficult situation that confronted him. He represents his predecessor as hurrying off and leaving him imperfectly prepared for his impending engagement—an unattractive picture of a retiring commander, even with due allowance for natural chagrin. Many of Johnston's friends and Hood's enemies have professed to believe that Hood came to the Army of Tennessee with the deliberate purpose of undermining Johnston and replacing him, but Hood declares in his memoirs that the order to assume the command "so astounded me and overwhelmed me with a sense of the responsibility attached that I remained in deep thought throughout the night."[32] Before daybreak of the eighteenth, he says, he started for Johnston's headquarters and on the way met General A. P. Stewart, who suggested that Hood join with him and Hardee in persuading Johnston to "pocket" the President's order and retain command of the army "until the impending battle should have been fought."[33] Hood readily concurring, as Stewart notes, they went to headquarters together. Hood inquired the reason for the order and Johnston replied simply that he did not know—the President had seen fit to relieve him.

Then Hood says he insisted that Johnston should temporarily disregard the President's dispatch, leave Hood in command of his corps "and fight the battle of Atlanta," in the extraordinary emergency created by the imminence of Sherman's descent on the city. Johnston rejected any such irregular procedure; whereupon Hood, Stewart and Hardee sent a wire to President Davis urging him to defer the change at least until the fate of Atlanta was decided and pointing out the extreme hazard it might involve at such a critical juncture.[34] Davis replied stiffly that "a change of commanders under existing circumstances was regarded as so objectionable that I only accepted it as the alternative of continuing a policy which has proven disastrous" and that, the order having been issued, he could not then suspend it without making matters worse.[35]

When he got this message Hood says he returned to Johnston's room alone and again begged him "for the good of the country" to put the correspondence in his pocket and fight for Atlanta. Again Johnston declined. Hood emphasized his own embarrassing position. Faced with the probability of immediate battle, he did not even know where the other two corps of the army were stationed. He pleaded with Johnston, even if he would not retain the command, to stay with him and give him his counsel while he fought the fight. This earnestness must have made an impression, for then it was that, with the tears in his eyes, Johnston promised that after riding into Atlanta he would return to headquarters and assist him. But Johnston "not only failed to comply with his promise, but, without a word of explanation or apology, left that evening for Macon, Georgia."[36]

In taking his departure Johnston issued a simple, touching farewell to his troops:

"I can not leave this noble army without expressing my admiration of the high military qualities it has displayed. A long and arduous campaign has made conspicuous every soldierly virtue—endurance of toil, obedience to orders, brilliant courage. The enemy has never attacked but to be repulsed and severely punished. You, soldiers, have never argued but from your courage, and never counted your foes. No longer your leader, I will still watch your career, and will rejoice in your victories."[37]

Of the defense of Atlanta Johnston wrote later on that he had intended to engage the enemy "on terms of advantage" while they were divided in crossing Peachtree Creek. If unsuccessful, he planned to man the works on the side toward Peachtree Creek with the state militia, "and leisurely fall back with the Confederate troops into the town and, when the Federal army approached, march out with the three corps against one of its flanks." If he were successful in this, "the enemy would be driven against the Chattahoochee . . . ; if unsuccessful, the Confederate army had a near and secure place of refuge in Atlanta, which it could hold forever, and so win the campaign, of which that place was the object."[38]

If only he had said as much to President Davis and Secretary Seddon! The declaration that he could hold Atlanta "forever" evinces so much more confidence than any message he sent to Richmond. There is strong suspicion that the plans of which he wrote so confidently in 1874 were the product of reflection after the event. But, granting that he did actually intend to follow such a course, what assurance is there that the tactics would have worked as well as he seemed to think? Foremost among their most obviously faulty features is the assumption that the militia could hold off Sherman's overwhelming army while he was moving the main army out in a "leisurely" flank movement. Hard to believe that 100,000 could have been stayed by a handful of poorly armed boys and old men! General Smith, the commander of the militia, in a letter written to Hood after Johnston's book was published, says that it would not have worked; he could not possibly have mustered more than 5,000 and they would have been "entirely inadequate" to hold off Sherman. If the plan had been followed, he says, "Atlanta would, in all probability, have been taken by the enemy within twenty-four hours."[39]

Johnston's exaggerated faith in the Georgia militia is not easy to understand. Certainly it is at variance with the prevalent opinion of this remarkable body of troops—popularly known as "Joe Brown's Pets" because of the Governor's evident determination to protect them from the perils of combat. Brown was a rugged individualist of most individualistic traits, a queer combination of patriot and political quack. He carried his belief in states' rights to a degree extremely annoying and embarrassing to the Richmond authorities. In its first burst of patriotism, the state had sent off to the battle fronts, largely in Virginia, no less than fifty regiments of Confederate troops, but of late Brown had adopted a policy of keeping all Georgia's troops at home. When Sherman started his invasion of the state in May, Brown had issued a stirring appeal to his people to "hasten to the field." In response some 2,500 militiamen eventually assembled in Atlanta, who were sent to Johnston's aid as he fell back from Dalton. Brown promised him 10,000 more—but they never materialized.

The veterans of the Army of Tennessee had supreme contempt for these state troops, and a soldier's description of the militia perhaps does not present a fair picture. For what it is worth, however, it is interesting to read how a private in Hood's army thought of "Joe Brown's Pets":

"It was the richest picture of an army I ever saw. It beat Forepaugh's double-ringed circus. Every one was dressed in citizen's clothes, and the best they had. A few had double-barreled shot-guns, but the majority had unbrellas and walking sticks; and nearly every one had on a duster, a flat-bosomed 'biled' shirt and a plug hat; and, to make the thing more ridiculous, the dwarf and the giant were marching side by side; the knock-kneed by the side of the bow-legged; the driven-in by the side of the drawn-out; the pale and sallow dyspeptic . . . was placed by the three hundred pounder."[40]

Admit that this is derisive exaggeration, admire the patriotic zeal that prompted these unprepared and unarmed civilians to rush out, in defense of their homes, give all credit to their ardor and their good intent—still, could Sherman's 100,000 hardened veterans have been held off from Atlanta even if there had been 10,000 such amateur soldiers?

Indeed, on that morning of July 19, when Hood took active command, it seemed doubtful whether anything could keep Sherman's host out of the city. Hood was manifestly and justifiably appalled by the magnitude of the task,[41] and none too sure of his ability to extricate the army from its perilous position; yet with the energy and determination characteristic of him he had worked through the night before and he worked that morning preparing a cohesive line of battle to meet the Federal advance. Though he knew the fine basic quality of the men who composed the army, he felt that the retreat across the Chattahoochee had been almost a final straw to the load of frustration they had been carrying on their backs, and he says he found them "downcast, dispirited and demoralized."[42] His adjectives are perhaps too strong, but undoubtedly the crossing marked for most of them the end of their hopes that Johnston planned—some time, somewhere—to turn and give battle. And, though Hood may not have been able to recognize the fact or willing to admit it, no little of this depression grew out of his appointment. It was a good army, but its spirit was at a low ebb.

Johnston had left it in a well-chosen and fairly good position behind Peachtree Creek. The Chattahoochee north of Atlanta flows generally southwestward. Peachtree Creek flows almost due west, joining the river just north of the railroad bridge. The Confederate line to the south of the creek had its left on the railroad north of the city about two miles from the Chattahoochee, and extended six miles east to the confluence of Peachtree and Peavine Creeks. There it turned south along Peavine until it intersected the Georgia Railroad—which led to Augusta—between Atlanta and Decatur. Stewart's corps was on the left, nearest the river, Hardee in the center and Cheatham—now temporarily in command of Hood's old corps—was on the right. Cheatham's part of the line was "strengthened" by the Georgia militia under General Smith—now increased to about 5,000—and its flank was protected by Wheeler's cavalry.

In moving his army across the river toward Atlanta Sherman had brought Schofield forward straight from his point of crossing in the direction of Decatur. McPherson was swinging around to Schofield's left, with his cavalry operating to destroy the railroad between Decatur and Stone Mountain, while Thomas, whose corps numbered about 50,000, crossed directly over the river near the mouth of Peachtree Creek with his left near Buckhead and his right capable of being stretched to

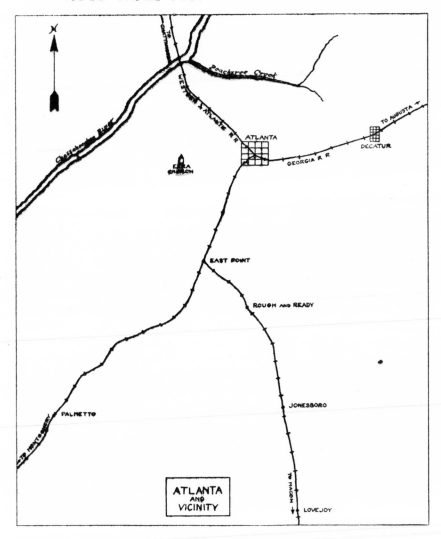

ATLANTA
AND
VICINITY

cover the railroad. Sherman's separating his armies so widely was open to grave criticism from a military standpoint, but he considered Thomas strong enough to withstand any attack, and it did not seem likely that the Confederates could do much harm to the wide-sweeping columns of Schofield and McPherson.

Whether or not Johnston told Hood of his plan to attack the columns in detail as they crossed Peachtree Creek, this was the course Hood decided to follow—perhaps because it was so plainly the proper course. An inviting opportunity was presented on the nineteenth when Hood discovered that Thomas' army was in the act of crossing with a part of his force already on the south side. That night Hood assembled his corps commanders, announced to them his decision to attack next day, and explained in detail his plan of action: Hardee and Stewart to fall on Thomas astride the creek at 1 p.m. and attempt to crush him; Cheatham, assisted by Smith, to hold Schofield and McPherson at bay as they moved slowly forward from the direction of Decatur, McPherson along the railroad and Schofield on the highway more than a mile to the north. The immediate object of the engagement, as Hood explained it, was to drive Thomas back in confusion into the narrow space between the creek and the river, and then all three corps could turn on Schofield and McPherson and finish them off.

In this, his first battle as an independent commander, Hood took extreme precautions to assure himself that each of the corps commanders was familiar with his expected part. He emphasizes in his official report that he gave specific instructions that "everything on our side of the creek was to be taken at all hazards." But the best laid plans for battle have an unhappy way of going agley. The human equation cannot be eliminated, and the enemy often does not perform just exactly as counted on. At one o'clock, the time Hood set for loosing the attack on Thomas, it suddenly became necessary to take emergency defensive steps on his other wing. McPherson with 25,000 men, opposed only by Wheeler's 2,500 cavalry, was pushing straight for Atlanta along the railroad and showing more than anticipated power. He had driven Wheeler back onto a rise of ground called the "bald hill" in the accounts of the battle. Hood ordered Wheeler to hold on there at all hazards. Wheeler feared the swiftly moving McPherson was about to outflank him, so Cheatham was ordered to bring his whole corps to the right by the length of a division. This made it necessary for Hardee and Stewart to shift to their right correspondingly, and it was therefore nearer four o'clock than one when Stewart and Hardee finally got under way against Thomas.

This delay of three hours, it developed, was just what Thomas needed to finish crossing the creek. By 4 p.m. he had all his men on the south side and partially entrenched. The attack struck him, however, just as his left under Howard was moving to connect with Schofield's right, and there was still a gap of at least two miles between them.

The attack did not prove as destructive and decisive as Hood had looked for. He blames this on Hardee. He warmly praises Stewart who, he says, "carried out his instructions to the letter,"[43] but berates Hardee, whose corps "although composed of the best troops in the army, virtually accomplished nothing" and "did nothing more than skirmish with the enemy."[44] Hood relates he learned afterward from Cleburne that before going into action Hardee had ridden along the line and warned his men that they must move cautiously and be on the lookout for breastworks, which Hood construed as an evidence of undue timidity and as inconsistent with his order that the position must be carried at all risk.[45]

But there seems merit in Cox's comment that Hood's reflections on Hardee are "neither quite just nor generous."[46] As a matter of fact, Hardee seems to have done all that could have been expected of him in the circumstances. He had formed his men with Bate's division on the right, Walker's in the center, Maney's on the left, Cleburne in reserve, the attack to be made by the divisions from right to left. Whatever may have been their commander's warning and whatever may have been his feeling of the need for caution, Hardee's men showed no hesitation as they came surging out of their lines against the Federal position. Sherman described it as "a furious sally."[47] It was indeed so furious it hurtled part of Thomas' force out of the breastworks, and quickly turned the exposed left flank. Bate's division poured into this opening and around to the enemy left and rear but was thrown back when Thomas brought up his reserve brigades. Walker's division struck the strongest point in the entrenched Federal line and, though it persistently attacked, it was ultimately repulsed, badly punished. Stewart's corps soon came into action on the Confederate left, and there was violent fighting along the whole front. One account reports that the Confederates were "fearfully slaughtered. . . . Few battefields of the war have been strewn so thickly with dead and wounded."[48] After their first repulse on Thomas' exposed left, the Confederates formed again and renewed the attack, but Thomas was now in personal charge of the field. He brought up his reserve artillery and blasted Hardee's men back with great loss.

Still Hardee had no intention of abandoning the attack. He was in the act of placing Cleburne's division in Walker's place in the line to carry it on when an order came from Hood to rush a division to the sorely pressed right where McPherson was pushing so hard. So he sent Cleburne's fresh division to Wheeler's aid, and Cleburne moved in to occupy the bald hill south of the railroad and held it until nightfall. Before Hardee could pull his depleted corps together for another try, it had grown too dark. But one could not fairly say that he "did nothing more than skirmish."

No exact figures are available as to the losses in this battle on Peachtree Creek, but it appears that Hood's loss, including prisoners, must have been close to 5,000, with the Federals probably losing no more than half as many.

Hood, though much disappointed at the failure of his effort to smash Thomas on Peachtree Creek, was resourceful as well as aggressive. He at once began to lay other stratagems for the enemy's discomfiture. During the evening of the twentieth his cavalry brought him detailed information of the completely exposed condition of the Federal flank—McPherson's line, running north and south, lay quite open on its left about three miles southeast of Atlanta and five miles southwest of Decatur. With reminiscent visions of Stonewall Jackson at Chancellorsville and Second Manassas, Hood quickly determined to capitalize this situation by swinging around against McPherson with a crushing force, while the other two corps of Sherman's army were held off before Atlanta.

Regardless of its outcome, the plan was brilliant in its conception. The conventional movement against the enemy's flank was supplemented and covered by the apparent retreat of the whole army from its line in front of the city. There seems no doubt that the maneuver completely befuddled Sherman. Hood during the twenty-first had his engineers stake out a new line of inner defenses to guard Atlanta on its northern and eastern sides, and, withdrawing his whole army, he occupied this new line with the troops of Stewart, Cheatham and Smith. Hardee's corps was selected for the turning movement because, Hood untruthfully and maliciously comments, they were "comparatively fresh, as they had taken but little part in the attack of the previous day."[49] In truth, Cleburne's division was the only one that had not been vigorously engaged. It made up for lost time on the twenty-first when it defended the bald hill against impetuous attack till dark in what Cleburne describes as "the bitterest fighting"[50] of his life. The day was intensely hot, and the Federal loss of 250 killed and wounded was swelled by heat prostrations; three staff officers of one brigade suffered sunstroke as they charged up the hill under the blistering Georgia sun.

Hood's flank movement looked to have every promise of success. If the Confederate forces, after their shifting, could be brought into sharp, united action, some such shattering blow as befell Hooker at Chancellorsville or Pope at Second Manassas might well result—except that Sherman would not have the advantage of a near-by refuge. Hood was not just indulging in wishful dreams when he designed a destructive attack. The stage was all set. In detail, the plan called for Hardee to start his corps soon after nightfall on a wide swing around to the right which would throw him onto the rear of McPherson's left flank, with Wheeler's cavalry joining in when the attack was delivered. Cheatham, on the right of the new line protecting Atlanta, was to take up the assault with his right as soon as Hardee had forced back the Federal left and to assist in driving the enemy back to Peachtree and down the creek. Smith in turn was to take up Cheatham's charge at the proper time, and Stewart was to confront Thomas, hold him from assisting Schofield and McPherson, and actively attack him if the engagement became general. Hood remained on the front line near Cheatham's right: The men under Cheatham, Stewart and Smith toiled through the night hours to fortify themselves.

Hardee's movement was delayed, awaiting an opportunity for the withdrawal of Cleburne's division, and it was after midnight before the last of Hardee's men marched out of Atlanta to the south, then across to the east, and then back northeast through the woods toward the Georgia railroad. Aside from that unavoidable delay in his start, he seems to have moved with all possible celerity, considering that the whole force had to march along one road in pitch-black darkness in an unfamiliar country, and was improperly guided through the woods. Again Hardee appears to have done everything that it was fair to ask for. Certainly his sudden appearance was a complete surprise to the Federal left and the entire movement of Hood's army was a complete surprise to Sherman. He not only did not suspect Hardee's flank attack, but on the morning of the twenty-second was under the delusion that the Confederate army was in retreat, resolved to give up Atlanta without further contest. So convinced of it was he that he "announced the occupation of Atlanta by Schofield, and ordered pursuit by Thomas and McPherson."[51] But as a telegraph operator chaffed in a dispatch to the War Department: "Vigorous pursuit was made, and the enemy found in the fortifications of Atlanta and not Schofield."

But what Hood hoped for was far from accomplished. In after years, when he wrote his book, he again blamed Hardee for what happened, expressing unrestrained dissatisfaction with the execution of the movement entrusted to him.[52] In the first place, he says, Hardee did not start the attack at daybreak—got into action only "about ten or eleven o'clock"—though as a matter of fact it was nearer noon. Then Hardee did not swing far enough around to get into McPherson's unprotected rear, but moved only such a short distance that when at last he came to grips, with his line roughly at right angles to Cheatham's, his left was "within gunshot" of the main Confederate line before the city. Finally, he says, the attack was not vigorously pushed, because Hardee had absorbed too much of Johnston's "timid defensive" attitude.[53]

Hood made similar reflections in his official report of the battle, which drew from Hardee an indignant letter to General Cooper denying any deviation from orders. The two generals, however, do not agree what his orders were. Hardee admits that "the original plan" was to send his corps to Decatur to approach by the rear and turn the enemy, but says that after some discussion this scheme was abandoned and "General Hood decided to strike the enemy in flank." Moreover, when Hood got his dispatch announcing his readiness to attack, Hood exclaimed to General Mackall, with his finger on the map: "Hardee is just where I wanted him."[54]

Hardee's foes are more friendly than his chief in their remarks on his generalship. General Cox says the facts are against Hood. The precision of the operation he describes as "marvelous, . . . the movement of blocks upon a map could hardly be more exact"; that Hardee could not have wished for a change in his position if he had known in advance exactly where the Federal line was located. Cox says the attack was made as early as was feasible, was energetic and persistent, and that Hardee's handling of his assignment, "viewed as a piece of military maneuvering, will excite more admiration among students of the art the more it is examined."[55]

Hardee did in fact move his command to the point Hood wished, but the consummation was prevented by the discovery that McPherson's left was not in the rear, and at that particular moment he did not have any rear. General Blair's Seventeenth Corps occupied the extreme left of McPherson's line. During the night it had been refused and entrenched at right angles to the main line, with the angle at the bald hill. General Dodge's Sixteenth Corps had been ordered to march to that wing and extend Blair's left. On their march, Dodge's men had halted behind Blair's on the morning of the twenty-second, waiting for orders to proceed to the place selected. Here they stood in position under arms as Hardee's force came bursting through the underbrush in the surprise assault which, but for the fortuitous presence of Dodge's divisions, would have taken McPherson in his rear and curled up Blair's left, just as originally designed. Hardee's advance—which was entirely unobserved—was made with Cleburne on his left, then Maney, Bate and Walker. He came forward at an angle of about forty-five degrees to McPherson's line, with Cleburne and Maney striking the entrenched refusal of its extreme southern end. Bate and Walker, expecting to strike the rear of McPherson's works, encountered instead the fresh Sixteenth Corps. They were headed back, but at the other end the entrenchments were forced and McPherson's line recoiled for several hundred yards, despite savage resistance.

All the Federal commentators agree on the vigor and determination of Hardee's attack—contrary to Hood's opinion of it. The colonel of an Ohio regiment in Dodge's corps gives his praise:

"Nor can I restrain a tribute to the bravery of the enemy. Their assaults were repulsed, only to be fearlessly renewed, until the sight of the dead and wounded lying in their way, as they charged again and again to break our lines, must have appalled the stoutest hearts. So persistent were their onslaughts that numbers were made prisoners by rushing directly into our lines."[56]

General Blair writes:

"The attack upon us was renewed again and again. . . . The movement of General Hood was a very bold and a very brilliant one, and was very near being successful. . . . The position taken up accidentally by the Sixteenth Corps prevented the full force of the blow from falling where it was intended to fall. If my command had been driven from its position at the time that the Fifteenth Corps was forced back from its entrenchments, there must have been a general rout of all the troops of the army commanded by General McPherson."[57]

Upon such hairs do history's crises hang.

When Hood observed that Hardee had driven Blair's left back so far they were pushing up the bald hill from the south, he ordered Cheatham to attack Logan's corps on McPherson's right to the north of the hill. There was bad timing and lack of correlation, and Cheatham did not get going till Hardee's drive had spent its initial force. The troops that had been withdrawn from Cheatham's front to oppose Hardee were now turned around and hurried back to defend their own post. Cheatham's drive smashed a big hole in the opposing line and carried him to the capture of a Federal battery. This brought him to the rear of the line fighting Cleburne. That line had to reverse quickly and turn to face their new aggressors. Sherman was observing the action through field glasses from his headquarters at the Howard house. He ordered Schofield to mass his artillery and concentrate its fire on Cheatham's onrushing men. This tornado of gunfire, in conjunction with the countercharge of Logan's infantry, forced the Confederates back to their original position, badly punished. By this time night was approaching, and there was no renewal of the fighting.

Though his attack was a disappointment to Hood, Hardee had dealt the Federals a heavy blow. He had taken 2,000 prisoners, eight guns and thirteen stands of colors. A Confederate private who took part in the charge relates rather sheepishly that he was advanced to the rank of fourth corporal for his "bravery," after he had turned in a captured flag—a banner he had picked up out of curiosity when he saw it lying on the ground. "I have never seen so many battleflags left indiscriminately upon any battlefield," he says. "I ran over twenty in the charge, and could have picked them up everywhere."[58]

Sherman has been subjected to criticism by some military experts for leaving Thomas and 50,000 men idle during this bitter battle in which he admits that "the slaughter done to our enemy was at sad cost to ourselves." He justifies this handling by the amazing assertion that he did it deliberately; he was afraid that if he sent them any assistance McPherson's army "would be jealous."[59] This sounds puerile. Why would they not have welcomed succor from any source while battling for their lives against a two-sided attack?

He was quite correct when he said the Federal repulse of the attack had been costly, for besides the heavy loss in killed and wounded in the ranks, their commanding officer, General McPherson, was killed. McPherson had been with Sherman at the latter's headquarters when the sound of firing on his extreme left and rear notified him of the assault in that quarter. He galloped across country to assume active command of his army and ran squarely into the spearhead of Hardee's drive behind his lines. Surrounded by the advancing Confederates, he refused their order to surrender and attempted to force his way out, but was shot and instantly killed. He was an exceptionally able and attractive young officer, and his tragic end was a great sorrow not only among his men and throughout the North but also among his friends on the Confederate side.

Hood writes feelingly of the death of McPherson, his schoolmate and boyhood friend.

"Although in the same class, I was several years his junior and, unlike him, was more wedded to boyish sports than to books. Often, when we were cadets, have I left barracks at night to participate in some merrymaking, and early the next morning have had recourse to him to help me over the difficult portions of my study for the day. . . . Neither the lapse of years nor the difference of sentiment which led us to range ourselves on opposite sides in the war had lessened my friendship. . . . His acts were ever characterized by those gentlemanly qualities which distinguished him as a boy. No soldier fell in the enemy's ranks whose death caused me equal regret."[60]

Hood too suffered a loss, both personal and military, in the death of General W. H. T. Walker, who fell at the head of his division in the violent fighting on McPherson's flank. He was a veteran of the Mexican War and Hood's warm friend. On the eve of the battle, before Hardee's corps marched off, he stopped by the chief's headquarters to assure him of an understanding of his problems and responsibilities and a desire to support him and co-operate with him.

Neither Hood nor Hardee gives any estimate of the casualties suffered in the engagement on the twenty-second, commonly referred to as the Battle of Atlanta, though Hardee reckons it "one of the most desperate and bloody of the campaign." Cox places the Confederate loss at 10,000, of whom 2,500 were killed. The Federal loss he counts at 3,521.[61]

If the bigwigs at Richmond wanted aggression, Hood had certainly given them what they asked for. Within four days of taking command he had fought two bloody battles. Sherman's men knew they were now opposed to a fighting man—a rash and reckless man, perhaps, but one who would not rest in his works and wait for things to happen. His attacks of the twentieth and twenty-second had been expensive, but they had developed a new psychology on both sides. Everyone knew the character of the campaign had changed.

Sherman, however, felt that the repulse on the twenty-second would discourage Hood for a while, and so he seized on this as a good time to entend his lines around the city to the westward with the idea of gaining control of the railroads leading to the south and west. The railroads to Macon and Montgomery ran on the same track to the suburban station of East Point, where they branched. If they could be seriously damaged it would cut off the Eastern part of the Confederacy from the Gulf states and make it impossible for Hood to hold Atlanta.

The city itself was now being subjected to steady bombardment. Sherman had started to shell it as soon as his lines approached close enough. The guns were elevated so that the shells went screaming over the Confederate lines and fell on the unprotected business houses and private residences. The citizens, of course, were jeopardized, but they were not demoralized and soon learned to take refuge in underground bombproof shelters. There was great destruction of property. The night sky was regularly illuminated with the light of the fires set by the falling shells, but the spirit of the people of Atlanta was never broken. In testimony of their stoic courage, Hood records that he never heard "one word from their lips expressive of dissatisfaction or willingness to surrender."

Sherman, in accordance with his newest idea, moved McPherson's army, now under the command of General O. O. Howard,[62] around the rear of Schofield and Thomas to occupy ground west of the city, the new line to face east, with its right reaching out toward the railroads at East Point. The march started on the morning of July 27. Sherman was with Howard as the army got near Ezra Church and was moving into its works the next day. There was the sound of active firing in front. Howard thought it was more than mere skirmishing, saying with positive conviction: "Hood will attack me here." Sherman was skeptical; Hood couldn't have caught his breath yet. But, Howard writes, "I said that I had known Hood at West Point and he was indomitable."[63]

Howard was right. "Indomitable" was the word for Hood. He had noted the Federals' march. He was determined to prevent their establishing themselves to the west of Atlanta if he possibly could. He must keep them away from the railroad lines. So he turned again to his favored device of a flank movement—this time with a complex variation. On the morning of the twenty-eighth, General Stephen D. Lee, now in charge of Hood's old corps, was ordered to march straight through Atlanta and westward on the Lick Skillet Road, there to take a stand that would stop the extension of the Federal right that way. Then, as Hood planned it, on the morning of the twenty-ninth Stewart was to march out of the city in a wide sweep to the south of Lee and come in on the Federal rear for a whacking blow. Hood was still dreaming of Stonewall Jackson.

Lee was out on the Lick Skillet Road promptly on the twenty-eighth and early in the afternoon collided with the Federal forces near Ezra Church before they had got themselves well-fixed in their newly built breastworks. His charging men were met with a savage fire. The engagement grew swiftly to battle proportions. Hood threw over his original plan of delayed flank attack and sent Stewart to Lee's immediate aid, but even with this help the Confederates' attack could not force out the Federals. They advanced again and again, but Howard's men busily strengthened their works between charges, and, as Cox writes, "each attack was less vigorous and had less chance than the one before it."[64] In late afternoon Hood resorted to the unusual expedient of ordering

Hardee to leave his own corps—still on the other side of Atlanta—and go to Ezra Church to take command of the two corps engaged there. But by the time he arrived the day had ended, and so had the battle. Hardee did not get into the fight, but the fact Hood had trusted him with this great responsibility provided an almost unanswerable argument when Hood attempted to belittle his ability.

Hood's memoirs say little about the Battle of Ezra Church, but it was really a severe encounter. The failure to achieve the objective was very disappointing. Hardee says: "No action of the campaign probably did so much to demoralize and dishearten the troops engaged in it."[65] Hood, assuming an attitude that will forever remain a smirch on his record, attempts to explain away his lack of success here, as well as on subsequent occasions, by unwarranted reflections on the courage of his men. During the retreat through Georgia, he quoted General Stephen D. Lee as saying, they had been so imbued with their inability to carry even temporary breastworks that "when orders were given to attack and there was a probability of encountering works, they regarded it as reckless in the extreme . . . and did not generally move to the attack with that spirit which nearly always ensures success."[66] Specifically about the action at Ezra Church, he uses Lee as an authority for the difficulty of getting united action and comments that "the lack of spirit manifested in this instance will convey a just idea of the state of the Army at this period."[67]

His failure as an army commander saddened and embittered Hood's life. All through his book is a manifest inclination to evade the responsibility and place the blame elsewhere—on his officers or on his soldiers. This is not only bad sportsmanship; it is grossly unfair to their reputation for bravery under fire and tenacious determination; it is basest ingratitude to an army that loyally fought his battles for him long after it had lost all faith in his competence. It is preposterous for him to allege that the men were unwilling to charge breastworks. The belying fact is that they did charge breastworks wherever and whenever he called on them. They had charged breastworks on Peachtree Creek. They had charged them in the battle on the twenty-second. They charged them at Ezra Church. And at all these places, not once but time after time. A few weeks later, on the suicidal field of Franklin, they gave perhaps the greatest exhibition of cold-blooded, mass courage ever seen on a battlefield when, without preparation or support, they hurled themselves against the Federal works after a long charge across an open field and clung there in a death grapple which was almost their destruction.

It is perhaps true that at Ezra Church they did not display until the last minute of the day the unquenchable aggressiveness of fresh troops. But it was not a matter of the spirit. The spirit, indeed, was willing, but the flesh was weak. These men had absorbed a terrific amount of punishment during the days on the other side of Atlanta. They were tired out and worn down—yes, and discouraged. But they moved forward when ordered up the slope against the works at Ezra Church, and even their enemy bears witness that "they advanced with their usual bravery," and that they returned to the attack again and again.[68] Men who were afraid to charge breastworks would not have done that. And if toward the close of day they moved with dragging feet, it was not moral but physical strength that they lacked.

It is an old army story that in the banter between pickets during the long contest around the outskirts of Atlanta a bluecoat yelled out: "Well, Johnny, how many of you are left?" and the Johnny replied: "Oh, about enough for another killing." It is not unlikely that after three sanguinary and unsuccessful sorties the men were beginning to question the wisdom of Hood's headlong tactics as compared with the "safety first" defensive policy of "Old Joe." But there is no flaw in the spirit of an army that can look death in the eye and meet it with a jest. They wouldn't charge breastworks? Why, it was a soldiers' saying that the Army of Tennessee "would charge Hell with a cornstalk." Better for the memory of General Hood if in his pursuit of extenuation he had left that unworthy thing unsaid.

Under cover of the march to Ezra Church and the fighting there on the twenty-eighth, Sherman had sent out large bodies of cavalry from two directions in a sort of pincers movement against the Macon Railroad. Stoneman raided around the Confederate right aiming not only at the railroad but also at the release of the Federal prisoners confined in Macon and at Andersonville. Simultaneously McCook rode down the western side of the Chattahoochee and, crossing the river at Campbelltown, succeeded in reaching Lovejoy's on the Macon Railroad twenty-five miles south of Atlanta, where his men destroyed a mile and a half of track and burned a wagon train—but 950 were captured in trying to get back. Stoneman's movement, more ambitious in scope, got to the river opposite Macon, which he shelled, but his plan to release the prisoners came to an ironically inglorious end when he was captured along with 500 of his troopers and ended up in the Macon prison himself. Sherman concluded, from the outcome of this elaborate effort, that he could not put much dependence in his cavalry to make a lodgment on the railroad below Atlanta, "and that nothing would suffice but for us to reach it with the main army."[69]

Hood too was so impressed with the inadequacy of the Federal cavalry that he felt he could safely use his own mounted force in an offensive against Sherman's life-giving line of supply, the railroad. He laid plans for Wheeler to go out against the Western & Atlantic between Atlanta and Chattanooga, hoping this might force Sherman's retreat. The plans were submitted to President Davis, who telegraphed his approval, suggesting that Wheeler's success might "compel the enemy to attack you in position or retreat." Then, probably with visions of those three bloody affrays around Atlanta, he added: "The loss consequent upon attacking him in his entrenchments requires you to avoid that if possible."[70]

So Wheeler early in August with 4,500 men, about half of all the cavalry, moved to his appointed task, and within a few days had destroyed about thirty-five miles of track near Marietta, Dalton and Resaca and burned the bridge over the Etowah. He demonstrated against Dalton and Chattanooga; then, on some wild impulse, he rode on through East Tennessee as far as Strawberry Plains, north of Knoxville. Thence he turned southward against the Nashville & Chattanooga and broke it in several places, getting within a few miles of Nashville. Forrest also had been after the railroad in Tennessee and had done considerable damage. The superior man power and resources of the Federals were here strikingly manifested. Troops were quickly sent from Atlanta, Chattanooga and Nashville against the cavalry raiders, and both Forrest and Wheeler were forced off into north Alabama, south of the Tennessee River. Hood deduced from this experience that the defensive facilities of the Federals were so vast "no sufficiently effective number of cavalry could be assembled in the Confederacy to interrupt the enemy's line of supplies to an extent to compel him to retreat."[71] So faded that dream.

Sherman, of course, learned soon of the absence of Wheeler's cavalry, and took advantage of it to make another attempt by his own mounted men on the Macon Railroad. On August 19 General Kilpatrick swept around the Confederate flank and seized the line at Jonesboro, where he burned the station and tore up track. Jackson's cavalry drove him out, the railroad was repaired in a few days, and Sherman writes that when he saw trains from the South coming into Atlanta on the twenty-third he "became more than ever convinced that cavalry could not or would not work hard enough to damage a railroad properly, and therefore resolved at once to proceed to the execution of my original plan."[72]

All this time, while keeping up the bombardment of Atlanta, he had been steadily inching his right southward, working always behind entrenched lines, with Hood maneuvering correspondingly to keep before him. By August 25 the southern extremities of the two lines were in the vicinity of East Point, with Hardee now on this left wing of the Confederate line, Lee's corps on his right and Stewart's corps in Atlanta. On the twenty-sixth Sherman launched a determined advance in force to his own right. Hardee says that when he started it Hood was completely deceived. Hood knew that Wheeler had cut the railroad north of Marietta, and when he saw the Federals starting out of their breastworks he thought they were retreating—his fond hopes running away with his judgment. So far was he deluded that he ordered Jackson's horse to harass their rear as they withdrew. Jackson did his best to persuade him that they were not retreating, but it was hard to make Hood believe something he did not want to believe; and so the whole Federal army, during the five days it was on the move southwestward, was spared from attack on its open flank.

Hood was confirmed in his error when someone brought to his headquarters an old woman who lived in the neighborhood. She had applied to some of the Confederate soldiers for food; inside Schofield's lines she had been refused because the men said they did not have enough for themselves.[73] On this slender evidence, Hood had hardened his conviction that Sherman, his supplies cut off, was retreating across the Chattahoochee.

On the morning of the twenty-eighth scouts reported that the Federals were in force at Fairburn on the Montgomery railroad, and Hood began to suspect that maybe they were not withdrawing after all. He wasn't sure. While Sherman stopped to tear up the railroad track—tearing up railroad tracks had become an obsession with Sherman—Hood began to take precautions. All surplus stores and property in Atlanta were ordered to the rear, and five brigades were sent to Jonesboro twenty miles south of Atlanta. By the twenty-ninth the Federals had reached across the Montgomery railroad and were advancing toward Jonesboro on the Macon line. Hardee moved to his left, to the neighborhood of Rough and Ready, a station on the Macon road, and Lee slid down to occupy Hardee's former position near East Point. On the thirtieth it became clear that Jonesboro was Sherman's objective. Not till then was Hardee able to convince Hood of the enemy's concentration in that quarter and even then, he says, Hood had an erroneous idea of the force there.[74] The corps of Hardee and Lee were sent to Jonesboro, under Hardee's command, with Cleburne temporarily in charge of Hardee's corps. Hood stayed in Atlanta with Stewart and his corps.

Hood's instructions for the ensuing operations were "explicit": Hardee was to attack with his entire force on the morning of the thirty-first and drive the enemy "at all hazards" into the Flint River in their rear. In the event of success, Lee's corps was to be withdrawn that night to Rough and Ready, where he was to be joined by Stewart and Smith, and the whole force was to advance the next morning to "attack the enemy in flank, and drive him down Flint River and the West Point Railroad."[75]

Cleburne met with difficulties in his advance and did not get to Jonesboro until about 9 A.M. on the thirty-first, and the last of Lee's brigades did not get there until the early part of the afternoon. This delay gave the Federals plenty of time to entrench themselves. Hardee says he wired the situation to Hood and urged him to come and take command. "Communication with Atlanta by rail was then still open, but he did not come."[76] Hood, on the other hand, complains that he heard nothing from Hardee throughout the day, and that early the next morning, fearing the attack had not been made, he sent a courier—the wires having then been cut—to Hardee to order Lee's corps returned to Rough and Ready. His message was prompted principally by the fact that Schofield's army, pressing forward, had slashed the railroad at Rough and Ready, and Hood when he learned of it grew sure that Atlanta was about to be attacked in force from the south and west.

Meanwhile, Hardee, despite his fears of the consequences of delay, made his attack on the Federal lines at two in the afternoon, Cleburne opening on the left. Cleburne succeeded in taking a portion of the Federal works and capturing some artillery. But Lee, on the right, was unable to force the breastworks and fell back in what Hardee terms "a demoralized condition."[77] Late in the evening Hardee withdrew a division from Cleburne to strengthen Lee, but by this time the daylight had faded and without more fighting he went into his breastworks and determined to act on the defensive. During the night he got the order to return Lee's corps—not to Rough and Ready, as Hood states, but to Atlanta. It specified also that Hardee was to stay at Jonesboro with his corps and protect Macon by disposing his men as best he could.

On the morning of September 1 he started Lee's corps back northward along the railroad, while he remained with his lone corps at Jonesboro to face the concentration of six corps of Sherman's force, almost his entire army. Sherman was making elaborate movements to envelop Jonesboro, with Schofield crossing over and approaching from the east, Thomas from the north and Howard from the west. But they moved

slowly and uncertainly, much to Sherman's exasperation, and Lee somehow managed to slip between their columns and march on toward
Atlanta. Slocum's corps, the sole Federal force near Atlanta, was north
of the city and was gradually feeling its way forward to see if the Confederates were still there.[78]

Hood's report says the feebleness of Hardee's attack at Jonesboro
may be gathered from the casualties—"only 1,400 were killed and
wounded out of two corps engaged," and in a telegram to Bragg he styled
it "a disgraceful effort." In a letter to Cooper Hardee contends that
"troops which for two months had been hurled against breastworks, only
to be repulsed or to gain dear-bought and fruitless victories" might be
pardoned if they now moved against such works "with reluctance and
distrust." But for the developments which made it necessary for him to
assume the defensive he would have renewed the attack, "which would
probably have resulted bloodily enough to have satisfied even the sanguinary expectations of the Commanding General."[79]

Left with his lone corps to stand off the concentration of the Federal
armies, Hardee spread out his men west of the railroad, with the northern
end of the line hooked back across the road north of Jonesboro. It was
against this northern angle that the main Federal onset was directed the
afternoon of the first. Hardee's whole right wing was soon enveloped by
the powerful attack from both front and flank and General Govan was
captured with much of his brigade and his artillery. The angle was
quickly strengthened, the rest of the line held firm through the day, and
by night Hardee was able to withdraw to Lovejoy's, six or eight miles
south of Jonesboro, where he quickly threw up a strong line of works.

Hood, at last awake to what was up, decided on a concentration. Lee's
northward march was stopped just outside the city. He was ordered to
stand guard and then follow on as Stewart and Smith were sent out of
Atlanta for a juncture with Hardee at Lovejoy's. Atlanta was deserted
without further struggle. Large supplies of provisions and six railroad
trains of ordnance stores and ammunition were burned to avoid their
falling into the hands of the enemy. On the morning of the second the
Army of Tennessee was massed at Lovejoy's, and Slocum was sending a
joyous message to Sherman at Jonesboro that he had marched his corps
into the city and received its formal surrender from the mayor.

Hood had no other idea than that Sherman would continue the active
offensive, and on the third he telegraphed Bragg that if the country was
not to be overrun the army would have to be reinforced.[80] He apprehended that the cry for reinforcements had become a too familiar sound

in Richmond and backed up his plea by having Hardee send a personal message to President Davis. Davis replied that no resources for reinforcement remained; the best he could do was recommend that "the means in hand be used with energy proportionate to the country's needs."

Sherman, however, as soon as he received news of the fall of Atlanta, appears to have lost all immediate interest in Hood's army, and while it stood in its entrenchments at Lovejoy's, doubtless with marked misgiving as it faced that overwhelming force, Sherman treated them to a novel experience. He pressed them no further. On the sixth he retired his entire army to Atlanta for, as he put it, "a short period of rest and to think well over the next step required in the progress of events."[81] It is hard to square this with his gloating over the state of complete submission into which he had whipped Hood's army. If he had dealt it such crashing blows, and if he were himself so lightly touched by Hood's assaults, why did he not press his advantage and give the coup de grâce?

Sherman had started out with the militarily correct idea that the Confederate army was his objective. Now, with that army huddled before him in inferior force, he deliberately turned his back on the supposed goal and marched off thirty miles in the other direction. Had Atlanta, somewhere along the way, substituted itself in his mind as his objective, or was he simply carried away by the temptation to bask in the glory that would come from occupying the city and sending President Lincoln the soul-satisfying message, "Atlanta is ours, and fairly won"? Atlanta would have been his just as much if he had left it for a while behind him to push Hood to a conclusive battle at Lovejoy's. There was no sound military reason for pulling his army from Hood's front backward into the city and permitting Hood to pursue unmolested whatever plans he might have to rest and recruit.

As a matter of fact, neither Hood nor Sherman had much to boast about in the handling of their armies during the latter days of the Atlanta campaign. Hood had apparently been completely bewildered by Sherman after August 25. He thought in the first place that Sherman was retreating when he was making a flank movement. He evidently did not know where Sherman was during the last two or three days of the month. He thought Sherman was advancing northward on Atlanta when he was advancing southward on Jonesboro. In his bewilderment he overlooked one chance after another to smash Sherman's columns in their vulnerable flank and even in their rear. Sherman, on the other hand, after he had gained a position astride Hood's railroad line, with his troops interposed between segments of Hood's carelessly scattered army, made no effectual use of his commanding position and permitted Hood to bring those divided segments together right under his nose. The only attack he made at this time was against Hardee's fortified corps on the second, while Hood's other two corps marched by his rear unscathed. The next day Sherman's elated men, in overpowering numbers, faced Hood's dispirited and battered forces—and they turned around, marched off and left them.

Hood, to be sure, was glad to see Sherman go. The Army of Tennessee, as well as Sherman's army, was in need of rest, for it had been through a grueling experience in the six weeks it had campaigned around Atlanta. It had been almost constantly engaged in combat for forty-five days—from July 20 to September 6—and it had suffered heavy losses. At the same time, it had inflicted even heavier losses on the enemy, and although Sherman and his generals have shown an inclination to belittle Hood as a mere headlong, impetuous fighter of no particular skill, his rapid hammer blows had served to slow down their aggressiveness and make them move with greater caution. In one of his dispatches Sherman grumbled that he could not get his men to move a hundred yards without entrenching—proof enough of wholesome respect for their bellicose antagonist.

There is some dispute as to the casualties suffered during the Atlanta campaign. Hood estimates that Johnston turned over to him on July 28 48,000 to 50,000 men, and that between then and September 20 he suffered a total loss from all causes of 9,124.[82] Sherman's loss is not definitely known, but he gives his aggregate force on July 1 as 106,070, on August 1 as 91,675 and on September 1 as 81,758, which would indicate a loss of about 24,000 during the two months.[83]

CHAPTER XVIII

HOOD'S NEW STRATEGY—TENNESSEE HO!

SHERMAN had hardly established his headquarters in Atlanta before he took the extraordinary step of decreeing the expulsion of all civilians. He was resolved, he said, "to make Atlanta a pure military garrison or depot, with no civil population to influence military measures."[1] He said he needed all the houses for the army's use. Also, if the people stayed some might have to be fed. And a civilian population "absorbs the attention of officers in listening to everlasting complaints and special grievances that are not military."[2] He had become such a thoroughgoing soldier that he couldn't be bothered with noncombatants and their petty nonmilitary affairs. "If the people raise a howl against my barbarity and cruelty," he wrote Halleck, "I will answer that war is war and not popularity seeking."

That is, in fact, just about the answer he made when the Mayor of Atlanta appealed to him to rescind his order because it would involve "consequences appalling and heart-rending. . . . Suffer this unfortunate people to remain at home." Sherman replied sharply that his orders "were not designed to meet the humanities of the case" but to facilitate his conduct of the war. "War is cruelty, and you can not refine it."[3] He administered a stern admonition to "go, and take with you the old and feeble," whose prospective sufferings the Mayor had so feelingly pictured.

He anounced the exile order to Hood in a formal letter on the seventh. He was willing, he said, to transport as far as Rough and Ready all of the citizens who desired to go south within the Confederate lines. He proposed a truce in that neighborhood so Hood might meet the refugees and convey them to Lovejoy's, the railroad being out of service between these two stations. Out of necessity, Hood agreed to it and consented to co-operate in assisting the refugees on their way, but he added: "Permit me to say that the unprecedented measure you propose transcends in studied and ingenious cruelty all acts ever before brought to my attention in the dark history of war. In the name of God and humanity, I protest."

Followed an acrimonious exchange of letters in which Sherman attempted to defend the expulsion and Hood persisted in denouncing it. And while it was going on, the victims streamed southward. The Georgia roads were crowded with the pitiful pageant of rickety wagons and buggies and carriages, loaded with trunks and household goods. Fugitive women and children and old men trudged sadly through the dust, hoping to find shelter somewhere. Hood's soldiers assisted them all they could, the army wagons helped haul them and their household gear, but, for all this aid, the exiles suffered cruelly, and the vocabulary of vituperation was exhausted in reviling Sherman's name.

During this unpleasant episode, Hood did not forget that his pressing problem was military, and that he was in a dangerous situation. He wrote Davis from Lovejoy's on the sixth that the prisoners should be removed from Andersonville, so he might be free to maneuver without the need of keeping his army between Sherman and the prison.[4] If they were put somewhere else, he said, he could move on Sherman's communications, which seemed the best strategy to follow. At the same time he suggested that it would be a good idea if Davis or Bragg could visit the army—and he mentioned incidentally the soldiers had not been paid for ten months and something ought to be done about it.[5]

His little army was reduced still further when, on the tenth, Governor Brown recalled the state militia, so they might return to their homes to look after their personal interests, gather their crops, et cetera. This talk about the crops was generally recognized as just a subterfuge for withdrawing the troops from the Confederate service. Sherman wired Halleck that he believed Governor Brown and Alexander S. Stephens, Vice President of the Confederacy, wanted to come to see him—presumably with the intent of making a separate peace for the sovereign state of Georgia.[6] When Lincoln heard of it, he telegraphed Sherman that he was deeply interested. Sherman replied on the seventeenth that he was negotiating with Brown, seeking the withdrawal of Georgia from the Confederacy and her assistance in expelling Hood from the state, in return for which he would refrain from "desolating the land." He thought "it would be a magnificent stroke of policy if we could . . . arouse the latent enmity of Georgia against Davis."[7] Brown's enmity to Davis could not have carried him quite so far as Sherman wished, for nothing came of Sherman's adventure into appeasement diplomacy. But Brown's co-operation with the Confederacy was thereafter of an increasingly passive nature.

Sherman's military plans were uncertain. He had vaguely hoped that by the time he reached Atlanta he could establish a line of communication to Mobile. Admiral Farragut had gained entrance to Mobile Bay by his "damn-the-torpedoes" daring, and General Canby, in charge of the Federal land forces, was expected to advance on Mobile and probably capture it. But just at this time there was an outburst of hostilities in a surprising quarter—in Missouri, where Sterling Price had returned and organized a formidable aggregation. Canby was compelled to give this his attention to the neglect of the Mobile enterprise. In fact, the Missouri situation grew so serious that Sherman himself finally had to send out there two divisions of his Sixteenth Corps under General A. J. Smith before Price could be quieted down. Other changes in organization were made, and Sherman's force at Atlanta dwindled as officers were transferred and troops' terms of enlistment began to expire. Schofield was sent back to Knoxville to look after administrative duties in his department, the command of his army with Sherman being transferred to General J. D. Cox. Thomas was sent to Chattanooga, accompanied by two of his divisions, General D. S. Stanley succeeding him. General Dodge had been wounded; his Sixteenth Corps was broken up and its divisions scattered among the other corps. Logan and Blair, whom Sherman contemptuously called "political soldiers," had gone home to take part in the elections.

On September 21, the prisoners having been shifted from Andersonville to Florida, Hood moved across from Lovejoy's to Palmetto on the Montgomery Railroad, about twenty-five miles west of Atlanta, and here he sought to reorganize and reinspire the army, whose morale had been sadly damaged by the loss of the city.[8] Faith in him was beginning to show distinct signs of raveling out. He was a gallant soldier, "a clever fellow," a daring strategist—but he had lost a lot of lives without gaining any advantage. Even the men who had been grumbling about the steady falling back from Dalton to the Chattahoochee began to wonder if they hadn't made a bad trade when they exchanged "Old Joe" for Hood. Their confidence corroded under an aching depression of spirit.

That there was considerable distrust of Hood among his officers is revealed in a letter written to President Davis on September 14 from Lovejoy's by General S. G. French—a letter reminiscent of the famous "round robin" document after Chickamauga. "Several officers," said French, had asked him to write to the President "in regard to a feeling of depression more or less apparent in parts of this army." Adopting a strange indirection, he declared that he had declined to write such a letter and then he proceeded to convey the very impression they sought. He suggested that Davis "send one or two intelligent officers here to visit the different divisions and brigades to ascertain if that spirit of confidence so necessary for success has or has not been impaired within the past month or two. They might further inquire into the cause, if they find in this army any want of enthusiasm."[9]

Hood may have sensed something of the undercurrent, for the day after French wrote his letter he mentioned in a dispatch to Bragg that he was much gratified at the feeling among the officers and took a left-handed slap at them by saying they were "all mortified at their feeble efforts on the 31st [at Jonesboro]. . . . I think we will make a better fight the next time than we could have done at any time since we left Resaca."[10]

This cheery optimism found no echo in Richmond, where the fall of Atlanta had created a wave of despair among the high Confederate officials. Could nothing be done to stop the Yankee juggernaut as it rolled so relentlessly through Georgia? President Davis decided to go to the scene, investigate the exact state of affairs and make a desperate effort to strengthen and reinvigorate the battered Army of Tennessee.

Davis, accompanied by two of his aides, arrived at Palmetto on September 25, and, for the supposedly good political effect, General Howell Cobb of Georgia and Governor Harris of Tennessee visited the army at the same time. There were speeches galore by all the statesmen, but the soldiers in the ranks knew that the time had passed for speeches, and they were little affected. President Davis, accompanied by Hood, rode along the lines for an informal review of the troops—an event which was marred by some uncouth cries from the ranks of "Give us back General Johnston." This made no visible impression on Davis, but it must have been painful, if not surprising, to Hood.

Hood says he reminded the President that he had accepted the assignment with reluctance, he was aware of the "outcry" against him through the press and was willing to be relieved entirely or would command a corps or division "under a more competent leader than myself."[11] Davis held long conferences with Lee and Stewart, and with Hardee. A contemporary newspaper correspondent wrote that they told him some other commander would "better serve to satisfy the wishes of the men, conciliate existing differences between officers, and inspire greater confidence throughout the army."[12] When he asked their ideas about a new commander, they said, "J. E. Johnston and Beauregard were the great favorites"—which must have been gall and wormwood to Davis,[13] who loathed both of them.

The President, however, could not be blind and deaf to the popular dissatisfaction with Hood or ignore the dangerous destruction of man power incident to his type of fighting. His tour of inspection decided him to place operations under some more seasoned and experienced head, without making any actual change in the commander of the army. To restore Johnston was for him unthinkable. But in the emergency he could lay aside personal feeling so far as to call on the talents of General Beauregard—then at Petersburg, Virginia, serving in a relatively minor capacity under General Lee.

Because their relations were so strained he delegated to Lee the delicate task of ascertaining whether Beauregard would assent to a transfer to the West again. Lee wrote from Petersburg on September 19 that he had discussed the Georgia situation fully with Beauregard and found him willing to "obey with alacrity" any order to go there. "Should you deem, therefore, a change in the commander of the army in Georgia advantageous," Lee said, "and select General Beauregard for that position, I think you may feel assured that he understands the general condition of affairs, the difficulties with which they are surrounded, and the importance of exerting all his energies for their improvement."[14] This paved the way for a personal conference between Davis and Beauregard at Augusta on October 3. The President regaled him with praise of Hood and censure of Johnston who, he said, would have retreated to the Gulf of Mexico if Sherman had followed him that far. Beauregard agreed that the proper move for Hood was now against Sherman's line of communications—everybody seemed to agree on that—and when the President found that they saw eye to eye, he spoke of his wish to place him at the head of a new "Military Division of the West," embracing the departments of Hood and General Richard Taylor.[15]

The President had already notified Hood that he was contemplating something of the sort, "so as to secure the fullest co-operation of the troops, without relieving either of you of the responsibilities and powers of your special commands, except so far as would be due the superior rank and the above assignment of General Beauregard." He invited Hood's views, but Hood raised no objection to the awkward arrangement, and so it came to pass.

Perhaps as a measure of solace to Hood, the President at the same time instructed him to relieve General Hardee from duty with the Army of Tennessee. Hardee was to proceed to Charleston to assume command of that department. In their personal relations Hood and Hardee had maintained a sort of armed truce during the active fighting around Atlanta. As soon as it was over Hood begged Bragg to have General

Richard Taylor appointed in Hardee's place. Nothing was done about this, and after a few days he wired Davis: "It is of the utmost importance that Hardee be relieved at once. He commands the best troops of this army. I must have another commander."[16] Hardee was as anxious to get away as Hood was to see him leave, and he wasted no time in departing for Charleston. Cheatham was advanced to the command of Hardee's corps, Hood's three corps now being commanded by Cheatham, Lee and Stewart.

On his visit to the army, Davis made a number of speeches. There is considerable variation between his account of what he said and what others reported. At Columbia and at Macon, where he stopped on his way to Palmetto, he expressed great concern over the loss of Atlanta, and openly denounced General Johnston and Governor Brown as responsible for Sherman's success.[17] This was also the tenor of the address he made the soldiers at Palmetto, but there, according to the testimony of those who heard him, he also gave very broad hints of an impending campaign into Tennessee. Forrest was already in Middle Tennessee, he was reported as saying, and Hood's men would soon be there; the soldiers from Tennessee he bade to be of good cheer, as their feet would soon tread again the soil of their native state. An Augusta paper quoted him: "We must march into Tennessee and push the enemy back to the banks of the Ohio."[18]

Sherman says these speeches were reported in the papers and also repeated to him by spies, and his subsequent strategy was guided by the knowledge. "He made no concealment of these vainglorious boasts," Sherman writes, "and thus gave me the full key to his future designs. To be fore-warned was to be fore-armed."[19] Sherman was so impressed with the importance of the information in Davis' speeches, that when he got a copy of one of them from a Macon newspaper he forwarded it by wire to Washington.[20]

In the face of all this, Davis denies not only that he gave any hint of the strategy of the Army of Tennessee, but even that he planned, discussed or considered any such strategy while he was in Georgia.

Just who did originate the idea of Hood's campaign into Tennessee is difficult to discover. Beauregard says Hood told him, when broaching the plan to him in Gadsden, that it had General Bragg's sanction—a thing he found easy to believe, since it was substantially the same plan Davis had discussed with him at Augusta and presumably the same one the President had discussed with Hood also.[21] But Davis categorically and emphatically denies the responsibility. His story is that he left the army at

Palmetto with the understanding that if Sherman started toward the sea Hood's army was to follow him; when he met Beauregard at Augusta he explained his "policy and hopes"; Beauregard "cordially accepted them" but then went on and "joined the army, changed his program to an advance into Tennessee, left the army, and the execution of the plan devolved on Hood, who has avowed himself the author of the movement and taken so far as he could the whole responsibility for it."[22]

Davis goes into details. He says he proposed to Hood that he move the army to some point on the Western & Atlantic in Sherman's rear and entrench. Sherman, he reasoned, would then turn and attack, and Hood was expected, "if he should not find the spirit of his army such as to justify him in offering battle," to fall back to Gadsden, in Alabama near the Georgia line, and there make a firm stand "and fight a conclusive battle." If Sherman refused to fight, Hood would go to Augusta to prevent Sherman's advancing in that direction. In preparation for this plan of campaign, Davis says, he went to Montgomery and arranged for the sending of Alabama militia to Gadsden, and then to Augusta to provide for strengthening the defenses of that important point.[23]

Regardless of the long-run strategy, the best immediate step for Hood, all agreed, was to transfer his army north of the Chattahoochee and operate on the railroad in Sherman's rear. This he proceeded to do with a minimum of delay. On October 2 he was able to notify General Bragg that he was in line of battle a few miles west of Marietta, with his left at Lost Mountain threatening the railroad, and, as expected, this caused Sherman to bestir himself. Leaving one corps under Slocum in Atlanta to hold the depopulated city, on the third and fourth he crossed the Chattahoochee with the other five, numbering about 65,000 men.

Hood got to work on the railroad promptly. On the fourth Stewart's corps captured the garrisons at Acworth and Big Shanty and tore up about fifteen miles of track. The next day General French was sent with his division to Allatoona, the next station farther north, where Sherman had established a sort of sub-base, with a large store of supplies. Hood says he ordered French to "capture the garrison, if possible, and gain possession of the supplies."[24] French, on the other hand, quotes his orders as merely directing him to obstruct the railroad cut at Allatoona and saying nothing about a garrison or depot of supplies there; he knew nothing of either until he heard about them from some citizens in the neighborhood.[25]

The Allatoona episode affords an excellent example of the manner in which popularly accepted history is written, and, for that reason, it is worth examining in some detail. Allatoona, it will be recalled, was a strong natural position—so strong Sherman had declined to attack it on his way south. The Federals had now made it still stronger by erecting three redoubts, and their garrison had just been reinforced by a brigade under General Corse hurried up by rail from Rome. French succeeded in capturing the blockhouse at the railroad bridge with its defending force, but his demand on Corse for the surrender of the main defenses was contemptuously refused. Thereupon French attacked, and an engagement followed which has been called the Battle of Allatoona, though it was hardly enough of a fight to deserve the name. French carried two of the redoubts and had the garrison crowded into the third, when he got a message from General Armstrong that enemy infantry was moving up the railroad and entering Big Shanty in his rear. Fearing this force would cut him off from Hood's main column, he withdrew. He said after the war that he seized and held the depot of supplies and could have destroyed it during the fight, except that he expected to capture the place and wanted to preserve the stores for the Confederates' use. When he decided to retire and attempted to burn them he found there were only three matches in his party and none of them would ignite.[26]

The engagement at Allatoona would probably have attracted no more attention than many other small brushes, except that out of it grew one of the popular legends and bywords of the war. When Allatoona was invested, Sherman was himself only thirteen miles away on top of Kennesaw Mountain, where wigwag signals were being sent to Corse and received from him. "General Sherman says hold fast; we are coming" was the encouraging message sent Allatoona on the evening of the fourth, and throughout the morning of the fifth similarly inspiriting exhortations and promises sped across the ozone.[27] Corse, who had been nicked in the side of the face by a Minié ball, caught the theatrical spirit of the thing, and climaxed the exchange, after French had withdrawn, by signaling back: "I am short a cheekbone and an ear, but am able to whip all hell yet."[28]

His declared ability to "whip all hell" was not put to the test, but he did outlast French, which was all that was just then required of him. The interesting feature of the incident, however, is that he did it without the promised aid from Sherman—aid that was never sent. Sherman's much publicized assistance was no more than a cheerleader's at a football game. His official report claims he made French withdraw by moving Cox's corps "due west" onto his rear; in fact Cox did not reach Kennesaw until the evening of October 5, was not ordered to move until the sixth, and no infantry at all went out from Sherman's army toward Allatoona.[29] It is not clear where Armstrong got his information—entirely false—of an infantry approach through Big Shanty, for no Federal infantry was there that day. Perhaps a cavalry patrol might have been sighted by some excitable scout; possibly Armstrong read Sherman's wigwag. At any rate, French retreated because of an entirely imaginary hazard, and Sherman emerged, clothed in glory based on an utterly ficticious demonstration of valor. Sherman's comforting message to Corse was freely translated by current journalism into: "Hold the fort; I am coming!" And the phrase so caught the popular fancy that it inflated him overnight into a hero. The episode inspired the revival hymn *Hold the Fort*—and so the pages of history were embellished with another indelible myth.

But after all, Sherman could not really have given much thought on top of Kennesaw Mountain to getting himself embalmed in the amber of legend. He had something more important to think about. He was not quite sure where Hood was or what he was doing. On the seventh he warned Slocum at Atlanta that Hood might be moving back in his direction, as he had "gone off south."[30] Actually he was moving north. In a letter to Corse Sherman grumbled that Hood was so eccentric "I can not guess his movements as I could those of Johnston, who was a sensible man and only did sensible things."[31] It was raining on the eighth, so Sherman did nothing that day, but on the ninth he arrived with his advance guard at Allatoona, and discovered then that Hood was going northward in the tangled country above Dallas and New Hope Church where there had been so much hard fighting in June. Sherman considered it impracticable to attack there, and, without knowing Hood's intentions, he did not quite know how to formulate his own. From Allatoona, however, he telegraphed Grant that he could not protect his railroad connections now that "Hood, Forrest, Wheeler and the whole batch of devils" were loose, and as Hood would probably move into Alabama he was of a mind to destroy the railroad south of Chattanooga and start a march with his wagons for Milledgeville and Savannah—the first suggestion of his famous March to the Sea. "I can make this march and make Georgia howl!" he told Grant.[32]

Hood, however, was not yet through with his work in Georgia. He telegraphed Bragg on the eighth that he planned another dash at the railroad, to destroy as much of its track as he could between Kingston and Tunnel Hill. This, he thought, would force Sherman to fall back to Chattanooga or else abandon the railroad and march south. In the latter event, he said, he would move on his rear, but if Sherman returned to Tennessee he would move to the Tennessee River. To provide for this contingency, he asked that the Memphis & Charleston Railroad be repaired to Decatur. The first part of this telegram indicates that he was faithfully adhering to the original plan of campaign which Davis says he outlined for him, but the latter part discloses that he was at least considering the possibility of going into Tennessee—whether on his own responsibility or as an alternative authorized by Davis will never be known.[33]

He crossed the Coosa River west of Rome on the tenth. When Sherman heard the news he shook himself out of his lethargy and started energetically to bring his whole army in the direction of Rome, which he considered the probable object of Hood's attack—although he commented irritably, in a letter to one of his corps commanders, that Hood's "whole movement is inexplicable to any common-sense theory."[34] On the hypothesis that Hood might possibly be aiming at Tennessee, he ordered Thomas to protect the Tennessee River west of Chattanooga "and be prepared for anything."[35] Thomas began the accumulation of a large force there.

Sherman had his army at Kingston by the eleventh—but Hood had flanked Rome and swung around eastward toward the railroad, which he struck at Resaca on the twelfth. The demand for the surrender of the Resaca blockhouse was refused. Hood did not attack, but moved on to Dalton which surrendered the next day with its garrison of 1,000 men. The railroad was torn up from Resaca to Tunnel Hill, nearly twenty miles, and then the army marched swiftly west again, obstructing Snake Creek Gap behind them with felled trees. Sherman and his army got to Resaca on the thirteenth, but by the time they discovered which way Hood had gone and forced their way across Rocky Face Ridge, Hood had his men encamped in the valley a few miles south of LaFayette—not far from where the army had maneuvered before the battle of Chickamauga more than a year ago.

Sherman was now right back where he had started in May, and was still in the dark over Hood's designs. For that matter, Hood did not seem to know them much better, himself. He says his first thought was to take a stand here and await Sherman's approach—Sherman was pursuing him and declaring, "I will follow Hood wherever he may go!"[36]—and stake everything on a pitched battle. Hood's explanation for not doing so is unconvincing. Through his personal investigation and an inquiry by his staff officers, he says, he found that "although the Army had much improved in spirit, it was not in a position to risk battle against the numbers reported by General Wheeler."[37] It was then that he made the decision—for want of something better to do, apparently—to march into Tennessee "with a hope to establish our line eventually in Kentucky."

He thus recounts his plans for the invasion of Tennessee:

"I decided to make provision for twenty days' supply of rations in the haversacks and wagons; to order a heavy reserve of artillery to accompany the army, in order to overcome any serious opposition by the Federal gunboats; to cross the Tennessee at or near Guntersville, and again destroy Sherman's communications at Stevenson and Bridgeport; to move upon Thomas and Schofield, and to attempt to rout and capture their army before it could reach Nashville. I intended to march upon that city, where I would supply the army and reinforce it, if possible, by accessions from Tennessee."

This accomplished, he planned to march on into Kentucky and take a position near Richmond where he could threaten Cincinnati. If Sherman followed him, by that time he would be strong enough to whip him, and he could then send reinforcements to Lee in Virginia, or might march his whole army across the mountains and attack Grant in the rear. If Sherman did not follow him north, but marched on through Georgia and thence up to Virginia to join Grant, Hood thought he could get to Virginia before Sherman did, and could attack Grant in conjunction with Lee. This, he believed, "would defeat Grant and allow General Lee in command of our combined armies to march upon Washington, or turn upon and annihilate Sherman."[38] It was an entrancing dream—and it was by no means impossible.

In pursuit of his new plan, Hood put his army in motion on the morning of the seventeenth and marched directly to Gadsden. At Gadsden he was joined by Beauregard, and both generals assert that Beauregard first learned of the Tennessee campaign then and there. They sat up most of the night talking it over, with their maps spread out before them. After deliberating for two days, during which he interviewed many of the officers as to the morale of the army personnel, Beauregard authorized what Hood proposed. The only condition he imposed was that Wheeler and his cavalry must be left south of the Tennessee, but to take Wheeler's place he offered Forrest.

It appears from Beauregard's account of the interview that he consented with some reluctance, as he doubted Hood's capacity for managing such a campaign in all its details. "The plan was a good one in itself," Beauregard says, "but success depended upon the manner in which it should be carried out."[39] Among the soldiers there were no misgivings. The announcement of the impending march into Tennessee recharged them with their old-time enthusiasm. Hood records that when they heard the news, from the encampments arose "that genuine Confederate shout so familiar to every Southern soldier—the famous 'Rebel yell.' "[40]

Without further parley, on October 22 he marched the army from Gadsden to Guntersville. Beauregard stayed behind to get off dispatches to the War Department notifying them of the movement and to take the necessary steps for the change of the army's base to Tuscumbia, but he meant to catch up and accompany them until after they crossed the river.

The ambitious Tennessee campaign had not been under way twenty-four hours before it struck a snag—possibly a fatal one. The first night out from Gadsden Hood says he got word that Forrest was at Jackson, in West Tennessee, and could not cross the Tennessee River into the central part of the state as planned, because the river was too high. Without Forrest, Hood was unwilling to cross at Guntersville—he could hardly operate north of the river without cavalry—so he decided to march westward over northern Alabama on the south side of the river, effect a junction with Forrest, and then cross at Florence.[41] Beauregard got a different account from Hood: he had heard the crossing at Guntersville was too strongly guarded by Federals and so marched to Decatur, expecting to take it and cross there.

Beauregard did not get this word until he overtook Hood and the army on the twenty-sixth just before they reached Decatur. He was upset because the crossing would be made so far west of Stevenson, the first objective, and he rebuked Hood for not telling him sooner. His irritation was sharpened when Decatur was found too strongly garrisoned by General Granger's division to be taken by storm; there was not time to besiege it; so they would have to keep on going west to Courtland. At Courtland on the thirtieth, it developed that a crossing could be made only with great difficulty. Hood chose this juncture to tell the unhappy Beauregard he did not have sufficient provisions to go on into Tennessee; many of his men were without shoes, and, everything considered, he thought it best to march on to Tuscumbia, twenty miles still further west.[42] There was a good crossing at Tuscumbia, and it was only ten miles from Cherokee (then the terminus of the Memphis & Charleston) which would facilitate his getting shoes and other supplies.

Beauregard reports himself full of chagrin at all this; but there was nothing for him to do but swallow it. He incited Hood to use the greatest possible speed and make up for lost time. Now that they were so far to the west, he represented that they might as well give up the notion of doubling back to attack Stevenson and Bridgeport, but instead go straight into Middle Tennessee and try to capture Nashville with its garrison and great depot while the cavalry operated on the railroad between Nashville and Chattanooga. Hood agreed. So they marched on to Tuscumbia.

Sherman had followed Hood through LaFayette and Alpine out of Georgia as far as Gaylesville in Alabama, about twenty-five miles northeast of Gadsden. He tarried at Gaylesville from the twenty-first to the twenty-eighth, in a quandary over Hood's intentions—and equally uncertain what he should do himself, though the idea of marching to the sea was constantly growing in his mind. One thing appears certain, if inexplicable: he was not anxious to engage Hood in a decisive trial at arms. When he started out from Atlanta northward he acted again on the sound theory that the Army of Tennessee was his proper objective, and Grant reminded him of this pointedly. He had belligerently declared he would follow Hood "wherever he goes," but when Hood stopped, Sherman stopped—at a safe distance—and showed no aggressiveness.

Sherman, dozing at Gaylesville, did not learn of Hood's march from Gadsden until October 26, and by then Hood was at Decatur. This knowledge decided his own plans. He made up his mind at once to leave Hood to Thomas, with such force as could be concentrated at Nashville, while he took his main army and marched off southward through Georgia to the seacoast. Thus was created a situation unique in military history: two opposing armies, theoretically campaigning to destroy each other, deliberately marching in opposite directions. Sherman returned direct to Atlanta and, after burning the city, set forth, on the morning of November 16, on his famous March to the Sea. On the outskirts of the city he paused to look back gloatingly. He writes: "Behind us lay Atlanta, smouldering and in ruins, the black smoke rising high in air, and hanging like a pall over the ruined city."[43] The March to the Sea is in itself an epic of warfare at its destructive worst, but it has no place in the story of the Army of Tennessee. Sherman was riding out of that great story, not to enter it again until the ragged remnants flared up in a last defiant gesture against him six months later in North Carolina.

Thomas, to whose attention Sherman consigned General Hood, had an ample force at his command to handle the situation, if he could get it all together at the proper time and place. In Nashville he had some 8,000 or 10,000 troops under arms, not to mention about as many more employees in the quartermaster's department who were available to man the fortifications in case of attack. There were various detachments scattered about—Steedman with 5,000 men at Chattanooga; Rousseau's 5,000 at Murfreesboro; Granger with 4,000 at Decatur; and a number of other smaller garrisons. The two divisions under General A. J. Smith, numbering about 14,000, were ordered to return from Missouri and report to Thomas, and before Sherman started on his march he detached the Fourth Corps under Stanley, numbering 12,000, and the Twenty-third under Schofield, amounting to 10,000, and ordered them to Tennessee. Including the cavalry force of about 10,000 which Wilson[44] was assembling at Nashville, Thomas had about 70,000 men at his call.

The delays endured by Hood at Tuscumbia were multitudinous and maddening. For example, in spite of his request, weeks before, that the railroad from Corinth be repaired, nothing had been done when he got there and a gap of ten miles existed from Tuscumbia to Cherokee. This thwarted his expectation of picking up supplies and getting promptly across the river. With one harassing difficulty after another, he spent three valuable and fateful weeks, chafing at the delay but unable to do anything about it. The fall rains had set in, and the work of repairing the railroad crept slowly along. A pontoon bridge had been completed on the second, but the continuous rainfall made the Tennessee rise, and after part of Lee's corps had got across and gone into camp at Florence the bridge was partly submerged, the approaching roads were impassable, and the crossing had to be suspended. Word came from Forrest on the third that he was still west of the river at Johnsonville, where he had destroyed vast stores accumulated for the supply of Thomas and Sherman. At Johnsonville his cavalry had accomplished a miraculous thing: the capture and destruction of two gunboats and five army transports. Even Sherman spoke of this as "a feat of arms which, I confess, excited my admiration," but Hood, while pleased to hear of the damage done the enemy, was growing impatient for Forrest to join up.

Faced with all this dismaying delay, Hood and Beauregard reviewed the proposed campaign at length, and gave consideration to the possibility of abandoning it and going back to Georgia to harass Sherman. But while they realized that Sherman, without Hood's army to resist him, might continue the penetration of Georgia to the coast, there were various reasons which Beauregard detailed to President Davis, why it was not feasible for Hood to take up the pursuit.[45] Moreover, when Beauregard passed through Georgia in October Governor Brown and Howell Cobb had assured him that a makeshift army of 30,000 men could be gathered together in the state to dispute Sherman's southward movement if he attempted it—an excessively optimistic prediction that Beauregard ought to have been wise enough to discount.

Evidently his misgivings over the Tennessee expedition lingered on, but he could not quite bring himself to the point of forbidding it—which he had the power to do. His lack of faith was, however, sufficient to prompt him to dissociate himself from its actual performance—and this reflects no great credit on him. He tries to explain his actions by saying that he was reluctant to interfere with Hood, who was sensitive to supervision,[46] but he was Hood's superior, and he should either have forbidden the expedition or stayed with Hood and helped make it victorious.

If Beauregard had such doubts, they certainly did not impress Hood. On November 6 he telegraphed President Davis that he hoped to march for Middle Tennessee by the eighth or ninth and that "General Beauregard agrees with me as to my plan of operation." Davis' reply advocated that he endeavor to beat Sherman in detail "and subsequently, without serious obstruction or danger in your rear, advance to the Ohio River."[47] To this Hood responded that he had been delayed by the rains, lack of supplies and Forrest's failure to join him, but he said: "You may rely upon my striking the enemy whenever a suitable opportunity presents itself, and that I will spare no effort to make that opportunity."

The friction between Hood and Beauregard must have become exacerbated because, on the thirteenth, Hood crossed over to make his headquarters at Florence, where he was out of personal contact with his superior officer and written communication could take the place of oral discussion. Though Forrest and his command reported for duty the next day, and the day after that the remainder of Lee's corps crossed the Tennessee, a renewal of the rains held up Stewart and Cheatham and it was a week before the Army of Tennessee finally got into motion north of the river, bound for Middle Tennessee.

Misfortune continued to dog Hood at the inception of his active campaign. His marching columns set out in the midst of a prematurely early blast of sleet and snow and rain, accompanied by freezing temperatures, and soon the roads were churned up into quagmires which alternately froze into hard ruts and thawed into tenacious mudholes. The three corps, aggregating about 30,000 men, moved forward along separate roads, all in a generally northern direction, the immediate goal being Columbia to the northeast—forty-four miles south of Nashville. Leaving Florence, Cheatham's corps was on the left (west) on the road to Waynesboro, Stewart on the right on the Lawrenceburg road, Lee on the country roads between the two main highways. Forrest's cavalry, to the number of about 8,000, operated in front of the infantry, having left Florence two days ahead, and Hood relates that Forrest had no trouble in driving the enemy cavalry, under Hatch and Croxton, "from one position to another."[48]

In aiming for Columbia Hood's purpose was to interpose himself between Thomas at Nashville and Schofield at Pulaski, which is thirty miles south of Columbia and twenty miles east of Lawrenceburg. Schofield had drawn Stanley with the Fourth Corps into Pulaski, making a total force there of 23,000. He learned of Hood's advance on the twenty-second, when the head of the Confederate column reached Lawrenceburg, and, justifiably alarmed, he turned at once to join Thomas and began a rapid march by way of Columbia. The two armies were now therefore in a race for Columbia, a race which Schofield won because he was a few miles nearer and because of the tireless vigilance with which he forced his men forward day and night. As it was, he got there, on the twenty-fourth, barely in the nick of time to prevent Forrest's fast-moving cavalry from seizing the Duck River bridge and cutting off his line of retreat—but he got there, and he had thrown up a stout line of breastworks around south of the town when Hood got his complete force up on the twenty-seventh. Hood made no effort to storm those rather formidable works, but contented himself with putting his three corps in line of battle while he figured out what to do.

Here again, as so often in the past, he had recourse to his pet scheme of a flank movement—if he kept on trying it, surely it must prevail some time. In this instance it was well conceived, and there was every reason to think it would work. His strategy was based on the correct guess that Schofield, as soon as he saw he was not to be attacked, would cross to the north side of Duck River—which Hood permitted him to do undisturbed the night of the twenty-eighth. Hood then meant to leave Lee with Clayton's and Stevenson's divisions, together with all his artillery, on the south side of the river to demonstrate heavily in Schofield's front, while he led his main force in a secret crossing of the river above the town and moved by country roads to bring it behind Schofield, eleven miles north of Columbia at Spring Hill. Here the Columbia-Nashville turnpike was intersected by several other roads, and a Confederate force in control would have Schofield in a trap from which he would not easily extricate himself.

The situation of the two armies at Columbia, Hood writes, "presented an occasion for one of those interesting and beautiful moves upon the

chess-board of war, to perform which I had often desired an opportunity.
. . . I had beheld with admiration the noble deeds and grand results
achieved by the immortal Jackson in similar maneuvres; I had seen his
corps made equal to ten times its number by a sudden attack on the
enemy's rear, and I hoped in this instance to be able to profit by the
teaching of my illustrious countryman."[49]

Hood moved with great care to perfect his plans. During the night of
the twenty-eighth his engineers laid pontoon bridges at Davis' Ford, five
miles above Columbia, whence a good county road led to Spring Hill.
Forrest's mounted men were over the river before the bridges were ready.
Their part was to drive and keep the enemy cavalry, now under General
Wilson, out of the way. Forrest did his job with customary thoroughness.
He forced Wilson off so quickly and so far northeast that Wilson had to
tell Schofield the next morning that he would not attempt to join him
but would go on to Franklin. Forrest left one of his brigades to keep him
occupied while he took the bulk of his riders back to Spring Hill.

Impressed by Forrest's vigor, during the night of the twenty-eighth,
Wilson sent word to Schofield that the Confederates were probably cross-
ing the Duck in force, and advised him to fall back to Spring Hill at once.
Later that night Thomas gave Schofield direct orders to retreat to Franklin. Next morning he started his wagon trains and artillery along the
turnpike northward, accompanied by the two divisions of Wagner and
Kimball under the command of General Stanley. Kimball's division was
left at Rutherford's Creek, halfway between Columbia and Spring Hill,
Stanley going on with Wagner's. Just before they reached Spring Hill,
Stanley had word that the Confederate cavalry was approaching from the
east; so he double-quicked Wagner's men into the town just in time to
get them in position and drive off Buford's division of Forrest's force. He
parked the wagon trains and artillery in an open space between the railroad station and the town on the pike, and deployed Wagner's three
brigades in a thin line around the village—Opdyke to the north across
the pike, protecting the wagons and guns, Lane and Bradley to the east
and southeast, shielded by makeshift breastworks hastily built of fence
rails.

Meanwhile, at dawn on the twenty-ninth, Hood in person at the head
of Cleburne's division had led the Confederate advance across Davis'
Ford, and at the same time Lee's divisions moved up to the river and
began a feint on Schofield with a great uproar of artillery. Hood's heart
was filled with high hopes as he rode along toward Spring Hill that morning. The weather had cleared and it was a fine fall day; the men were

full of enthusiasm; his crossing had been unopposed, perhaps unobserved; surely he was at last to accomplish one of those Jacksonesque coups of which he had dreamed so long. A few enemy cavalrymen appeared on the hills to his left, but these were ignored, and the troops pressed on without interruption. Everything was going smoothly; nothing, it seemed, could save Schofield from destruction or capture.

What happened from then on is a subject of controversy. The principals directly contradict each other. The outstanding and undisputed fact is that Schofield, apparently caught in a trap, in some unexplained fashion escaped and got away. That there was some sort of tragic bungling in the handling of the Confederate forces is inescapable. "Hood let the whole Yankee army march by him during the night at Spring Hill" is a statement that has become firmly embedded in the might-have-been folk-lore of the Confederacy. Whose fault it was is a question upon which there has never been agreement, but that it was the greatest of all the "lost opportunities" of the Confederate armies is almost universally conceded. The peculiarity of the situation and the transcendant importance of the unexpected outcome are such as to justify a detailed consideration of the events of that fateful afternoon and night.

In his book Hood writes:

"Thus I led the main body of the army to within about two miles and in full view of the pike from Columbia to Spring Hill and Franklin. I here halted about 3 P.M. and requested General Cheatham, commanding the leading corps, and Major General Cleburne to advance to the spot where, sitting upon my horse, I had in sight the enemy's wagons and men passing at double-quick along the Franklin pike."

'He says he pointed out the enemy, marching along with their wagons in plain view, instructed Cheatham to "go with your corps, take possession of and hold that pike at or near Spring Hill," and told Cleburne to "go with General Cheatham and assist him in every way you can and do as he directs." Stewart with his corps was "near at hand" and would double-quick his men to the front. That is Hood's account of the first act in the Spring Hill drama.[50]

In commenting on this, Cheatham says: "There is not a bit of truth in this entire paragraph." At 3 P.M., says Cheatham, there was no movement of wagons and men on the road at or near Spring Hill, and if there had been Hood could not have seen it except in "a mirage," as at that hour he was at the crossing of Rutherford's Creek, two and a half miles from Spring Hill.[51]

From reading Hood's account and Cheatham's account of the same events, it is clear that they both cannot be right. Either one of them misrepresents the facts, or one or both had a hazy recollection. And though it is a serious matter to challenge a commanding general's veracity, the weight of evidence favors Cheatham. It is a physical fact that from the point where the Davis' Ford road crosses Rutherford's Creek one cannot see the turnpike road. And it is a historical fact that by 3 P.M. the Federal wagon trains were parked at Spring Hill near the railroad station, with Wagner's infantry drawn up before them—and these were the only men and wagons who could have been on the turnpike there, as the rest of Schofield's army was back near Duck River. Moreover, it was extremely loose use of language to say that Stewart was "near at hand," and Stewart was at no time ordered to double-quick to the front.

Continuing Cheatham's account: Hood's oral orders to him at the crossing of Rutherford's Creek were to send Cleburne forward to Spring Hill (which he did) to get in touch with Forrest there and attack the enemy as soon as their position could be ascertained. He was to stay at the creek and move up with Bate's division to Cleburne's support as soon as it came along. Hood said he would push forward Cheatham's third division, under General John C. Brown, when it arrived at the creek.

Cleburne did move forward, as ordered, and about 4 P.M. formed on the Rally Hill road and filed off westward across the fields toward the Nashville pike, with Bell's brigade of Forrest's cavalry on his right. His advancing line struck Bradley obliquely, while Bell's dismounted men encountered Lane's force. The attack was partially successful, despite the awkward position of the lines (and despite Hood's description of it as "feeble"), and Bradley and Lane were driven back until they were in front of the town to the south, across the pike, supported by an array of eighteen pieces of artillery. Cheatham in his official report says that Cleburne was "compelled to fall back," but this is an improper use of words. Cleburne's line was disarranged by the attack, and Bell's men were withdrawn on account of the exhaustion of their ammunition. This made it necessary for Cleburne to re-form, but he had done this and was ready to advance again when, according to his adjutant general, he received orders to engage in no further action that night.[52]

Meanwhile Bate having come up with his brigade, General Hood personally directed him to move straight to the pike, on Cleburne's left, and to swing down it toward Columbia. He reached the turnpike just north of the home of Major Nat F. Cheairs, and there encountered a Federal regiment on guard, which he drove off toward the town. Just at this moment the head of Schofield's column appeared on the pike, marching to Spring Hill, and Bate opened fire on them; but this action had hardly begun before he received peremptory orders from Cheatham to change direction to his right and form on Cleburne's left, confronting Bradley and Lane. Cheatham, it is to be assumed, did not realize that Bate was in actual contact with the enemy when he issued this order, but if it had not been issued, Bate might have stopped the movement of Schofield's force along the pike at least until morning.

Brown's division did not get up until about 5 P.M. He was ordered at once to Cleburne's right, both divisions to attack as soon as he got in posi- tion—Brown first, then Cleburne. But when he arrived in his designated place Brown found that he was flanked on his right and "must meet with inevitable disaster" if he advanced.[53] As to the next development, there is also dispute. Brown says he was ordered to wait until Stewart came up, and hold himself in readiness for further orders then. Cheatham says he ordered Brown to throw back his threatened right flank and attack any- how, and Cleburne to take up the attack when he heard Brown's guns. But Brown's guns were never fired. Presumably he misunderstood his orders, but that is only conjecture. The only certain things about this phase of the confused afternoon are that Brown did not attack and there- fore Cleburne did not attack, that Cheatham was eventually told by Hood "he had concluded to wait until the morning, and directed me to hold my command in readiness to attack at daylight";[54] and that Schofield was molested no further that day.

According to Hood's story, he exclaimed to Cheatham when he rode up at "twilight": "General, why in the name of God have you not at- tacked the enemy and taken possession of that pike?" Cheatham remon- strated that the line should be extended to the right. Hood says he then made an effort to get Stewart into position on Cheatham's right, which would bring the line across the turnpike, but it could not be done in the darkness, and Stewart "at about eleven or twelve o'clock" went into bivouac on Cheatham's right, "near but not across the pike."[55] Cheatham caustically denies that there was any such dramatic scene or conversation, says it "only occurred in the imagination of General Hood."[56]

Stewart's corps, it appears from all accounts, was utilized in a particu- larly inept manner on a day when ineptitude was being bountifully dis- played. When he arrived at Rutherford's Creek early in the afternoon he was stopped and ordered by Hood to go into line of battle on the south side of the creek—for what purpose is not clear. Not until sunset did Hood order him forward "to place his right beyond Spring Hill." The road he was marching on intersected the turnpike north of Spring Hill and would have carried him to his destination, but he was halted on the way with the order from Hood to form on Cheatham's right, and finished up by merely camping by the wayside without having been in action all day.

General Edward Johnson's lone division of Lee's corps was behind Stewart. When Johnson finally came up he was ordered to take position on the road near Cheatham's left, and at nightfall he camped about in the position originally occupied by Bate near the Cheairs house.

Soon the Confederate campfires twinkled along the sloping hillsides. The Army of Tennessee was in bivouac for the night—and the road from Columbia to Nashville was still wide open.

General Schofield at Duck River had not been entirely unaware what was going on. At least he knew he was in peril. At first he seemed to think that Hood's crossing Duck River was the beginning of an effort to strike his flank somewhere near Columbia, and it was to protect against this that he had stationed Kimball's division at Rutherford's Creek in the morning. Later Kimball was joined by Wood's division, and Ruger was advanced on the pike to a place near the creek, leaving only Cox's division at Duck River. Schofield stayed with Cox until late in the day, when he ordered a general movement to Spring Hill, with Ruger's division leading. It was Ruger's column that was waylaid by Bate near the Cheairs place about dusk. Schofield, who was with Ruger, breathed a relieved sigh when Bate's attack was called off and they could proceed on peacefully to Spring Hill. Cox followed behind Ruger, with Kimball and Wood bringing up the rear, and the whole army was safely concentrated in Spring Hill by the early morning hours.

The Confederate generals' muddling during the afternoon provided a perfect example of how not to handle troops, but even the conspicuous failure to attack Wagner's sole and unsupported division with overwhelming power might have been offset if the soldiers had been deployed at nightfall so as to intercept the rest of Schofield's army. Colonel Henry Stone of Thomas' staff says: "A single Confederate brigade . . . planted squarely across the pike, either north or south of Spring Hill, would have effectually prevented Schofield's retreat, and daylight would have found his whole force cut off from every avenue of escape by more than twice its numbers, to assault whom would have been madness and to avoid whom would have been impossible."[57] But no obstacle was placed in Schofield's way although Hood was not uninformed of the opportunity.

A straggling, barefooted Confederate private sought Hood out at his headquarters at the Thompson place during the night and excitedly told him the news. Hood says, after "eleven or twelve o'clock" it was reported to him "that the enemy was marching along the road, almost under the light of the campfires of the main body of the army. I sent anew to General Cheatham to know if at least a line of skirmishers could not be advanced, in order to throw the Federals in confusion, to delay the march and allow us a chance to attack in the morning. Nothing was done. The Federals, with immense wagon trains, were permitted to march by us the remainder of the night, within gunshot of our lines. I could not succeed in arousing the troops to action. . . . General Forrest gallantly opposed the enemy further down to our right to the full extent of his power; beyond this effort, nothing was done, although never was a grander opportunity offered to utterly rout and destroy the Federal Army."[58]

No one denies or disputes that a grand opportunity was frittered away. There is, however, considerable dispute among the Confederate leaders over what took place. According to Cheatham,[59] one of his staff officers, Major Bostick, returned to his headquarters after placing General Edward Johnson's division in position near the pike, with the story that he had heard "straggling troops passing northward" on the pike. They were discussing this "about midnight" when a note came by courier from Major A. P. Mason, Hood's assistant adjutant general, saying the commander had just learned of the "stragglers" and "You had better order your picket line to fire on them." He sent Bostick to tell Johnson to take a brigade or his whole division "and go on to the pike and cut off anything that might be passing." After a while Bostick came back to say that he and Johnson had ridden "close up to the pike, where they found everything quiet and no one passing"; and so Johnson's division was not moved.

This seems a straightforward, circumstantial account. But in one salient detail it is directly at variance with another story.

Observe this item: Cheatham says he received the warning note from Major Mason about the stragglers and acted on it. The next day, however, after Hood had angrily told Governor Harris that he blamed Cheatham for "his failure to make the night attack," Mason drew Harris aside and made the astounding confession: "General Cheatham is not to blame for that. I never sent him the order . . . I fell asleep again before writing it."[60] Harris told Mason that he should inform Hood of this, and Mason promised to, but no evidence appears that he ever did so.

There is tantalizing mystery about all this. Major Mason remorsefully confesses that he did not send the order, but General Cheatham tells what he did when he got the order that was not sent. Did Mason send it and forget that he had sent it? Or did Cheatham just imagine that he had received it? The investigator finds himself in a blind alley.

The actions and statements of Hood and Cheatham in this complex controversy are difficult of analysis and appraisal. Certainly they do not square with each other. It is known that Hood originally blamed Cheatham for the failure at Spring Hill. This is indicated not only by Harris' statement but also by the fact that on December 7 Hood wired Secretary Seddon recalling his recommendation of Cheatham for promotion and followed it with another telegram the same day urging that "a good lieutenant general" be sent at once to take command of Cheatham's corps. Harris, carrying Mason's guilty secret, was disturbed by the sending of these messages. He was reluctant to tell Hood of Mason's strange dereliction, but he did go so far as to say he knew Cheatham had not received the order. So the next day Hood wired Seddon once more—he was now convinced that Cheatham's failure "will be a lesson to him," and he withdrew his previous messages. On December 11 he wrote Seddon in explanation that Cheatham "has frankly confessed the great error of which he was guilty, and attaches much blame to himself. . . . In consideration of this, and of his previous conduct, I think that it is best that he should retain for the present the command he now holds." Hood tells all this in his book,[61] and also that Cheatham "with candor and nobility" came to his headquarters outside Nashville before the battle there a few days later and "standing in my presence, spoke an honest avowal of his error . . . and that he was greatly to blame."

Again an account that sounds positive and convincing. But Cheatham[62] says even more positively and convincingly that Hood's recital of his alleged responsibility is "a statement for which there was not the slightest foundation"; that Hood had previously, on December 3rd, volunteered in a note to him: "I do not censure you for the failure at Spring Hill. I am satisfied you are not responsible for it," etc.; and this was his first intimation that he had been suspected of responsibility. Governor Harris recounts that Hood made a "graceful and ample" oral apology to Cheatham "in the presence of his whole staff"—but Cheatham does not mention this.

In 1887 Governor Harris wrote a letter[63] to Governor James D. Porter of Tennessee in which he undertook to explain what happened at Spring Hill that critical night. Perhaps he reveals more than he intends. At any rate, between the lines of this letter we seem to catch a glimmer of light as to the capacity to command which Hood and his staff possessed then.

"General Hood, his Adjutant General Major Mason, and myself," writes Governor Harris, "occupied the same room at the residence of Captain Thompson, near the village. Late at night [In his statement to Major Brown he places the time at 3 A.M.] we were aroused by a private soldier, who reported to General Hood that, on reaching the camp near Spring Hill, he found himself within the Federal lines; that the troops were in great confusion, a part of them marching in the direction of Franklin, others had turned toward Columbia, and that the road was blocked with baggage-wagons and gun-carriages, rendering it impossible to move in order in either direction. Upon the receipt of this report, General Hood directed Major Mason to order General Cheatham to move down on the road immediately and attack the enemy. General Hood and myself remained in bed. I went to sleep, and I suppose that General Hood did the same. At daylight on the following morning we learned that the Federal army had left Spring Hill and was being concentrated at Franklin."

Governor Harris then relates how Major Mason the next day confessed to him that he had not sent the order to General Cheatham.

General Hood was asleep. Governor Harris was asleep. Major Mason was asleep. But General Schofield was not asleep. With his heart in his throat, he was quick-stepping his army silently down the turnpike, within sight of the camp-fires of the slumbering Army of Tennessee.

Old soldiers and old residenters around Spring Hill explain all that night's fumbling in blunt terms: "Hood was drunk." That is a grave charge. It can not now be proved or disproved. It is mentioned because the local tradition is so strong. Hood did not claim to be a total abstainer. Robert E. Lee, in guarded words, called his conduct off the field "careless." It must be borne in mind that he was a badly maimed man. He must have suffered almost constant pain from that withered arm and that barely healed stump of a leg. Other sufferers have sought stimulation and comfort in the anodyne of the bottle. The befuddlement of intoxication might account for the otherwise inexplicable confusion and paralysis at Spring Hill.

Schofield, after arriving safely in Spring Hill, reconnoitered personally as far as Thompson's Station in the direction of Franklin, and, when he found that the road was not obstructed, ordered the whole command forward to Franklin. The only opposition he encountered on the way was from Forrest's cavalry—and even concerning Forrest's activities there is conflict of testimony.

General Bate relates[64] that "between ten and twelve o'clock" that night he went to Hood's headquarters, where he found his chief in consultation with Forrest. When Forrest had departed, Bate told Hood about his brush with the passing enemy on the turnpike earlier in the evening and how his fight had been interrupted by orders from Cheatham.

"General Hood replied, in substance," Bate goes on, " 'It makes no difference now' or 'It is all right anyhow, for General Forrest as you see has just left and informed me that he holds the turnpike with a portion of his force at Spring Hill and will stop the enemy if he tries to pass toward Franklin; and so in the morning we will have a surrender without a fight.' He further said, in a congratulatory manner, 'We can sleep quiet to-night.' "

Forrest's biographers, Jordan and Pryor, tell quite a different story.[65] According to them, Hood asked Forrest if he could throw his cavalry across the turnpike in time to check the Federal retreat. Forrest replied that Chalmers' and Buford's divisions were entirely out of ammunition and therefore helpless, but Jackson's division had captured some during the afternoon and he would "do the best he could in the circumstances." Hood offered to have ammunition furnished Chalmers and Buford, but it developed that neither Cheatham nor Stewart could supply any. Jackson, who had only 2,000 men, had been driven back off the turnpike north of Spring Hill earlier in the evening, but when Forrest laid the emergency before him after he got back from Hood's headquarters, Jackson undertook to interpose his force at Thompson's Station and hold Schofield in check as long as possible.

But one brigade was no match for Schofield's whole army. Jackson was easily brushed aside and Schofield marched rapidly on to Franklin, where the head of the column arrived about dawn and the last of it was in about noon. The men were placed in strong earthworks on the southern outskirts, and there Schofield's men waited while he sent Thomas panicky cries for help.

CHAPTER XIX

THE BEGINNING OF THE END

1. FRANKLIN

GENERAL HOOD was almost beside himself with rage and chagrin when he woke up the next morning and discovered that Schofield had eluded him while he slept. General Brown says[1] he was "wrathy as a rattlesnake." Indeed, everyone's temper was short. Most of the generals ate breakfast at the home of Major Nat Cheairs, and stories have come down of a violent quarrel at that breakfast table. There were angry accusations of neglect, followed by flashing swords and demands for apology, as the edgy commanders stewed in impotent exasperation. In his blind anger, Hood lashed out viciously at his subordinates, placing the blame everywhere but where it belonged—on himself.

Worst of all, and most unfairly and unjustifiably, he blamed the soldiers. He experienced "grave concern," he writes,[2] at "the discovery that the Army, after a forward march of 180 miles, was still seemingly unwilling to accept battle unless under the protection of breastworks"—the breastworks blather again—though there was not a jot of evidence that the fiasco had been due to any faltering of the troops. "In my inmost heart," Hood writes, "I questioned whether or not I would ever succeed in eradicating this evil." In his inmost heart he might better have questioned whether he could ever succeed in eradicating his own strongly developed unwillingness to take responsibility for his own errors.

Hood was quite correct in saying:[3] "The best move in my career as a soldier, I was thus destined to behold come to naught." It was indeed a brilliant conception of strategy, frustrated by amazingly poor tactical work. Whose work? Whose fault? After all is said and done, he was in command, he was present on the field. Whatever was done, or was left undone, was his responsibility.

But that sad morning all such considerations had become mere historical speculations. He had a new and pressing problem—how to retrieve his lost advantage. The chance to get between Schofield and Thomas had been irretrievably lost. Schofield at Franklin was only

eighteen miles from Nashville—too short a distance for effective inter-
position. There were other tactical possibilities, but Hood was in no
mood for finesse. He was in a humor to come to grips with Schofield and
punish him, and so he arrived at the desperate resolve "to make that same
afternoon another and final effort to overtake and rout him, and drive
him in the Big Harpeth River at Franklin."[4]

So the troops were roused and pressed forward from Spring Hill "at
early dawn," their van not far behind Schofield's rear guard which, according to Colonel Stone, did not leave the village "till it was fairly daylight."
Stewart's corps was first, then Cheatham's. Lee, following the last of
Schofield's men as they retreated from Duck River, reached Spring Hill
at about nine o'clock on the morning of the thirtieth with Clayton's and
Stevenson's divisions of his corps, and they marched on behind Cheatham.

It is doubtful if an army ever marched to battle in such a temper as
pervaded the Army of Tennessee plodding along the dusty road from
Spring Hill to Franklin, fifteen miles away. Its commander was disappointed and angry; his subordinates were in equally bad humor; and the
feeling of frustration had permeated the ranks and engendered in the men
as well as the officers a resolution to overtake and whip the enemy who
had slipped through their fingers the night before. If Hood had been an
expert psychologist he could have sensed something electric in this martial spirit. He was to learn before the day was over that the Army of Tennessee need not be behind breastworks to fight, was not afraid to charge
an enemy in his entrenchments.

Early in the afternoon, about three miles from Franklin, the vanguard
came up with Schofield's rear arrayed where the turnpike crosses Winstead Hill. No direct attack was made, but Stewart swung down Henpeck
Lane in a flank movement around the right, and the Federals marched
on toward the town. Stewart's swing brought him to the Lewisburg turnpike, by which he approached Franklin. Cheatham continued along the
Columbia pike, and at about three in the afternoon the head of his advancing column came over the crest of Winstead Hill and saw spread out
before them, across undulating Harpeth Valley, the little town where
their quarry had turned on them and stood at bay. The scene from the
top of Winstead Hill looking toward Franklin is one of great pastoral
beauty. The soldiers say that a roar of cheering broke spontaneously from
the throats of Cheatham's Tennesseeans as they looked out on that
peaceful land where in a few hours so many were to give their lives.

Franklin is situated on the south side of the Harpeth River, on elevated ground enclosed within a bend of that stream. From the south it is

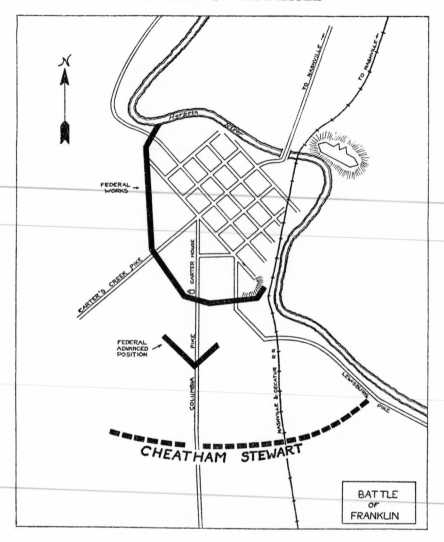

BATTLE
OF
FRANKLIN

approached by three turnpikes and by the Nashville & Decatur Railroad. Chief of these turnpikes is the road from Columbia, running about due north and south, with the railroad almost parallel a half mile to the east. East of the railroad is the Lewisburg pike. From the southwest the town is approached by the Carter's Creek pike. Going northward the railroad and the highway cross the river on bridges close together, but at this time the highway bridge had been destroyed.

The crossing of the Harpeth was commanded by a stout post called Fort Granger and by other batteries along the banks on the north side of the river. The line of works south of Franklin which Schofield occupied had been built by the Federals when they were here before and were now strengthened by him. They made a wide crescent, stretching from a strong position on the extreme left where the railroad passed through a cut near the river, westward across the Columbia pike, bending back across the Carter's Creek pike to the west of the town, with outworks extending to the river on the other side. The center was where it crossed the Columbia pike, and here the works were the strongest. Just inside the line on the pike was a one-story brick dwelling house occupied by the Carter family.[5] A brick smokehouse stood between this house and the entrenchments, and just across the road was a cotton gin. The gin and the Carter house were to become historic landmarks in the bloody battle.

Between the gin and the river on the left was a hedge of Osage orange, and there was a small grove of locusts west of the Columbia pike just outside the line. These trees were cut down to form a rude abatis. Otherwise there were no obstructions in front of the line—"not so much as a mullein-stalk," one of the soldiers said—as the ground fell away in a gentle slope of rolling, unfenced fields and pasture land. The breastworks were interrupted at the Columbia pike to keep it open for the wagon trains and artillery as they came in, but this gap was protected by a barricade across the road a short distance back from the opening, all well guarded by a heavy battery of artillery at the Carter house. There were other guns sprinkled plentifully along the whole line, and across the river from the left end of the works was a well-placed battery which murderously commanded the approach.

On a slight rise of ground about a half-mile in front of the main Federal works, Schofield had entrenched two of Wagner's brigades astride the pike to serve as an advanced skirmish line, with instructions to remain there in observation until Hood showed a disposition to advance in force, whereupon they were to retire. Schofield himself, during the early afternoon, had taken up his headquarters in Fort Granger across the river, leaving Cox in charge of the line, and Schofield was not present on the battlefield at any time during the action.

Those well-constructed and well-manned works must have impressed General Hood as he stood under a linn tree on the side of Winstead Hill and examined the situation through his field glasses. His subordinates were by his side and breathlessly waited his decision. At length he turned and, as he snapped shut the case of his glasses, announced crisply: "We will make the fight." This decision was against the judgment and the advice of those of his generals who were bold enough to volunteer opinions. Cheatham, after studying the lay of the ground for himself, told Hood emphatically: "I do not like the looks of this fight." The enemy, he thought, occupied an excellent, well-fortified position.[6] Hood replied brusquely that he would prefer to fight them there, where they had had only a few hours to get ready, than at Nashville, "where they have been strengthening themselves for three years"—a conclusion neither accurate nor logical. Forrest also advised against a direct frontal assault. He thought they should try to flank Schofield by crossing the Harpeth River to the right. He is said to have offered to attempt this himself, if given one brigade of infantry to support his cavalry. Hood says in his report, however, that "the nature of the position was such as to render it inexpedient to attempt any further flanking movement," that it was essential to attack Schofield "before he could make himself strong." But Schofield had already made himself strong in his works, and if Hood could have restrained his headlong assault that evening, he would have found in the morning that the enemy was out of his way. Even while he scanned the entrenchments through his glasses the Federal wagon trains were being rushed across the Harpeth toward Nashville on planking laid on the crossties of the railroad bridge, and instructions had been issued for the troops to follow the wagons at six o'clock if there had been no attack by that time.

Hood was consumed with a burning impetuosity. He could not wait even long enough to make proper preparations. It was growing late in the day, and if he was going to fight he must act forthwith. He could not wait for Lee to come up with his divisions. He could not wait for the artillery to arrive. Lee's force would have been of great help in bolstering the thin Confederate line. A blast of preliminary artillery fire might have softened up that tough Federal line. But Hood was too impatient to wait. Stewart and Cheatham were up; he would attack with them immediately, as soon as they could get in line. He explains that the artillery was not used on account of "the danger to which women and children in the village would be exposed,"[7] but there is a suspicion that this compunction is an afterthought. The fact is that one battery of guns was brought up with each corps, and they were used in the attack. The other guns were not used because they were not there.

Stewart's corps was ordered up along the Lewisburg pike and the Nashville & Decatur Railroad, and aligned in the grove behind the John M. McGavock place, with Walthall in the center, Loring on the right and

French on the left. Cheatham went directly forward along the Columbia turnpike with the divisions of Cleburne and Brown, respectively to the right and left of the road. Bate's division was marched by the left flank around behind Merill's Hill, toward Carter's Creek pike, to come in on Brown's left as they neared the works. Johnson's division of Lee's corps, which had moved with Cheatham, was held in reserve. Forrest was ordered to divide his cavalry between the two flanks; he assigned Chalmers and Biffle to Bate's left, with Buford and Jackson on Stewart's right, east of the Lewisburg pike toward the river.

Cleburne, according to Hood, asked and received special permission to form his division in three lines of assault. Hood, who has a dramatic penchant for direct quotations in his narrative, reports this conversation:

Cleburne: "General, I am ready, and have more faith in the final success of our cause than I have had at any time since the first gun was fired."

Hood: "God grant it!"[8]

This alleged confidence on Cleburne's part is strangely at variance with his emotions as reported by his fellow-Arkansan, General Govan, who rode with him from Spring Hill to Franklin and who says he had never seen him so despondent.[9] General Brown also says that Cleburne "was quite angry"; he had heard that Hood blamed him for the Spring Hill fiasco, which he deeply resented, and he meant to call for an investigation.[10] It is hard to imagine his exchanging unnecessary amenities with Hood just before the curtain rose on the battle; harder still to suppose him confident in the circumstances. All the contemporary evidence depicts him as moody and melancholy during those last days. On passing the Episcopal Church at Ashwood near Columbia—Bishop-General Polk's church—he had admired its vine-clad Gothic beauty and had remarked to his aide that it was "almost worth dying to be buried in such a beautiful spot."[11]

As soon as Stewart and Cheatham announced that their lines had been formed and adjusted to each other, Hood ordered the assault, and at four o'clock they went forward under the declining autumn sun, their bayonets flashing, their tattered battle flags flying in the November breeze. In the whole history of the war there was never such an imposing military spectacle as was here presented—eighteeen brigades of infantry, with their cavalry support, marching in a straight line across an open field, in full view of their commanding general and of the entrenched enemy. As they swept on, the watchers from the Federal works could see before them a long line of rabbits, roused from their coverts in the fields and scampering in fright from the menace of the long line of men. Coveys of quail by the thousands were flushed and whirred up out of the grass to circle about, then settle back, then whirr into the air again as the gray-clad line came on. As soon as the line got within range of the guns, it was greeted with a rain of cannister and shrapnel, but as the shells burst and wounded men dropped to the ground, the ranks closed up and moved on forward.

"It was a grand sight," writes a Federal officer who was in the works near the cotton gin, "such as would make a lifelong impression on the mind of any man who could see such a resistless, well-conducted charge. For the moment we were spell-bound with admiration, although they were our hated foes; and we knew that in a few brief moments, as soon as they reached firing distance, all that orderly grandeur would be changed to bleeding, writhing confusion, and that thousands of those valorous men of the South, with their chivalric officers, would pour out their life's blood on the fair fields in front of us."[12]

The divisions of Cleburne and Brown were the first to come into action as, advancing on both sides of the turnpike, they clashed with the outpost held by Wagner's brigades. Wagner, with an excess of courage and in disobedience of his orders, told his men to hold onto their position as long as they could, and they received the Confederates with a sharp burst of rifle fire. But their small force was hopelessly overmatched, and in a few minutes they were running headlong for the main works, closely pursued.

Indeed they were so panic-stricken that they continued their flight on through the town and across the river. Their terror could hardly fail to impress itself on the men within those breastworks, who stood there and witnessed it, unable to fire themselves until these flying men had gained protection and were out of range. Cheatham's panting, weary men were within a hundred yards of the entrenchments before the defending force could open fire, but, though exhausted by their long run up the slope, they were so animated by success that their drive carried them up and over the main works and well behind the Federal center. Here they seized the battery and won a foothold that seemed to threaten the whole Federal position. For several sanguinary minutes a desperate man-to-man struggle raged in the yard and garden of the Carter house, along the road and across the pike in the field around the gin.

But the penetration of the Federal line by that hard-driven spearhead of Cleburne and Brown was short-lived. Quickly the reserve brigade of Opdyke, massed to the rear of the Carter house, was brought into action, with several other reserve regiments. They rushed fiercely to the counter-

GENERAL JOHN B. HOOD

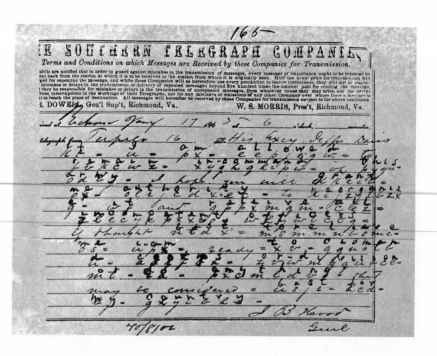

Original of cipher telegram received by President Davis from General Hood, January 17, 1865, following his disastrous rout at Nashville and retreat at Tupelo. "If thought best to relieve me, I am ready to command a corps or division or do anything that may be considered best for my country."

attack, and the tired Confederates were slowly forced back to the works and beyond them, bitterly contesting every inch of the way.

Cleburne's men, east of the pike in front of the gin, were in a particularly bad plight. On their right Stewart had been thrown back and the forces facing Stewart could turn attention on them and pour into them a decimating storm of cross fire. "I never saw men put in such a terrible position as Cleburne's division was for a few minutes," says a Federal veteran of the battle. "The wonder is that any of them escaped death or capture." A pathetically large number of them did not escape—foremost among them the gallant Pat Cleburne himself. Early in the charge his favorite mount, "Red Pepper," was shot from under him; his second horse was killed; and then, sword in hand, he led his men on foot until the fatal bullet laid him low, just outside the works. General Adams, commanding one of his brigades, was killed as his horse was leaping the Federal works, and when his body was found in the trench, his dead horse still stood with forefeet over the palisade.

West of the turnpike Brown's division had rushed past the Carter house with a wild élan and one of the brigade commanders, General Gordon, swept so far through to the rear that he was captured. This division was also pushed back by the reserves, but gave ground grudgingly, and when finally thrust to the breastworks over which they had stormed, they settled down and refused to yield another foot. They held that stand throughout the battle and compelled the Federals to throw up a barricade across the Carter garden. Neither side could advance in the face of the withering fire. The Confederates clung to their precarious foothold though devastation rained on them from three sides. On their right, the Federals from their regained works poured a steady stream of musketry, and their left too was open because Bate had never made connection. Brown's loss was terrific—he himself was wounded and he lost all four of his brigade commanders: Gist and Strahl killed outright in the ditch, Carter mortally wounded, and Gordon taken prisoner.

On the left Bate had farther to move than Hood had estimated and did not get up in time to take part in the grand charge. When he did reach the front, it was to discover that the Federal line angled away to the north, and when H. R. Jackson's brigade on his right was in contact with it the brigades on his left were still far away. In consequence Bate never got into effective co-operation with the other Confederate forces, but Jackson maintained his position at the works.

On the right, things had gone badly. The cavalry had started off well. Buford and W. H. Jackson drove Wilson's force beyond the McGavock house and east from the pike across the river at McGavock's Ford, Jackson's division following and threatening Schofield's line of retreat. The infantry of Loring and Walthall, almost as soon as the forward movement started, struck an unexpected obstacle in the railroad cut. They were forced to change front and move by the left flank, subjected to a massed fire from the Federal batteries across the river. French came into action before the cotton gin and carried some of the breastworks, but was soon forced back. Walthall's and Loring's divisions had charged through the Osage orange abatis, and struck the line where it was defended by Casement's division armed with the new repeating rifles. It has been said that never before in the history of warfare had a command the size of Casement's killed and wounded so many in so short a time. The quick-firing repeaters seemed to blaze out a continuous sheet of destruction. This, and the enfilading fire of the artillery, were more than Stewart's men could stand. They fell back. The savagery of the fighting and the frightful loss of life among the officers in this charge are indicated by Walthall's report that in Quarles's brigade the highest ranking officer left was a captain.

Just one repulse was not enough to check the Army of Tennessee that day. Cheatham's and Stewart's men re-formed for another assault, with the attack concentrated along the center before the cotton gin. Again they were thrown back, again they re-formed and once more they charged. Time after time, in the teeth of the blinding storm of musketry and the devastating volleys of the guns, they forced their way up to those bloody breastworks and hung on in a hand-to-hand struggle with the defenders, battling man to man across the parapet.

"It is impossible," writes Colonel Stone, "to exaggerate the fierce energy with which the Confederate soldiers, that short November afternoon, threw themselves against the works, fighting with what seemed the very madness of despair. . . . Assault after assault was made, some of the Union officers declaring in their reports that their lines received as many as thirteen distinct attacks."[13]

About seven o'clock the reserve division under General Edward Johnson was thrown in to Brown's left. They charged the line with desperation, stumbling over the dead and wounded in the darkness, but their onset was repelled, Brigadier General Maningault being wounded in this final conflict.

The annals of war may long be searched for a parallel to the desperate valor of the charge of the Army of Tennessee at Franklin, a charge which has been called "the greatest drama in American history." Perhaps its only rival for macabre distinction would be Pickett's charge at Gettysburg. A comparison of the two may be of interest. Pickett's total loss at Gettysburg was 1,354; at Franklin the Army of Tennessee lost over 6,000 dead and wounded. Pickett's charge was made after a volcanic artillery preparation of two hours had battered the defending line. Hood's army charged without any preparation. Picket's charge was across an open space of perhaps a mile. The advance at Franklin was for two miles in the open, in full view of the enemy's works, and exposed to their fire. The defenders at Gettysburg were protected only by a stone wall. Schofield's men at Franklin had carefully constructed works, with trench and parapet. Pickett's charge was totally repulsed. The charge of Brown and Cleburne penetrated deep into the breastworks, to part of which they clung until the enemy retired. Pickett, once repelled, retired from the field. The Army of Tennessee renewed their charge, time after time. Pickett survived his charge unscathed. Cleburne was killed, and eleven other general officers were killed, wounded or captured.

"Pickett's charge at Gettysburg" has come to be a synonym for unflinching courage in the raw. The slaughter-pen at Franklin even more deserves the gory honor.

General Strahl said just before the battle: "Boys, this will be short but desperate."[14] That is just what it was. The principal action was confined to the last two hours of the day, but in that short interval the combat was waged with a maniacal desperation witnessed on no other field of the war. "Never," said Hood in his official report, "did troops fight more gallantly." He speaks admiringly of their advance into "a concentrated roar of musketry which recalled to me some of the deadliest struggles in Virginia."

Schofield's casualties were 2,326, of which about 1,000 were prisoners. Hood officially places his loss at 4,500, but this seems much too low. Livermore gives it at 6,202. His effective strength after the battle Hood reckons at 23,053, which would show a total loss from all causes of 7,547 since leaving Florence, and most of this must have been suffered at Franklin.

A staggering feature was the loss in general officers. In no other battle were so many generals killed. Generals P. R. Cleburne, S. R. Gist, H. B. Granbury, John Adams and O. F. Strahl were killed outright, and General John C. Carter fatally wounded. General George W. Gordon was captured, and Generals John C. Brown, A. M. Manigault, William A. Quarles, F. M. Cockrell and T. M. Scott were wounded. That morning five of these generals had sat down to breakfast at the hospitable table of

Major Nat Cheairs at Spring Hill. The next day the dead bodies of all five of them lay on the long back gallery of the McGavock house near Franklin. Pat Cleburne, that valiant fighter, was to be brought to his long rest in the lovely church at Ashwood.

The fury of the fighting was such that it did not end with darkness, but went on fitfully as late as 9 P.M. The still indomitable Hood, when his artillery came up late at night, ordered that the guns should fire a hundred rounds each into the Federal works early the next morning and the troops would charge again. The guns did fire a few volleys, but there was no reply. The works were deserted. Schofield had given the order to retire at 11 P.M., and as soon as the men could be moved out of the breastworks they had so valorously defended, they filed over the Harpeth and along the highway to Nashville.

The forces engaged in the Battle of Franklin were about even, according to Colonel Livermore, but his figures may be subject to some correction. He gives Hood's total as 26,897, including the cavalry and Lee's divisions which were not engaged. Actually, he had only about 20,000 infantry in action, against Schofield's 22,000 in the works.

In his dispatches and in his report Schofield refers to the battle as a "victory," but that seems to be stretching things too far. The actual outcome was that just as soon as he possibly could, he retreated with all haste, leaving the field, and his dead and wounded, in the possession of the enemy. True, that enemy had failed in his effort to storm the works, but Thomas wanted Schofield to hold Hood at Franklin for three days— and Schofield held him hardly three hours. Hood, of course, could scarcely claim a victory, in view of his repulse and his crippling casualties. Accurately it should be classified as a drawn battle, a heartbreaking, murderous, unnecessary battle that settled nothing—unless it settled in Hood's mind the question whether the Army of Tennessee would charge breastworks.

2. NASHVILLE

It was a ghastly scene that met General Hood's eyes when December 1 dawned and he viewed that bloody field, strewn with the wreckage of his army. The survivors had bivouacked where night had overtaken them. Before break of day, as soon as it was definitely known that Schofield was gone, search parties were out with torches to succor the wounded, and soon the field hospitals, the neighboring farmhouses and the village homes were crowded with the maimed and mangled. The ferocity of the attack was proved by the horrible plenitude of dead and wounded right in front of the entrenchments. At that portion of the line which Brown's men had seized and held, the bodies were piled in heaps as many as seven deep, the trench so glutted that many a gray-clad corpse was found stark upright, having no space in which to fall.

But the army could not pause to ponder. The wounded were removed; the pitifully blasted and contorted corpses were raked into long shallow trenches and buried—the blue and the gray in separate ditches. Then Hood, apparently oblivious to the condition of his men, again gave his favorite command: "Forward!"

He had faced a momentous decision—what to do next? The obvious course was to own that he had been out-maneuvered, that his Tennessee campaign was a failure—and to retreat to the Duck River or the Tennessee. With Schofield safely on the way to join Thomas and a superior force massed at Nashville, with his own army depleted and so many competent officers gone, the whole picture had changed. The relative conditions were not as they had been when he started his march from Gadsden, or even when he crossed the river at Florence. He was now at great disadvantage, strategically and numerically. Prudence said to fall back. But Hood was not noted for prudence. To retreat, as long as he had even remote chance for success, was unthinkable to his temperament.

With retreat rejected, alternatives of aggression remained. He might undertake to cross the Cumberland River somewhere above Nashville and move into Kentucky in Thomas' rear. Grant in Virginia—apparently misinformed of the relative strength of Hood and Thomas—was considerably afraid Hood would follow this course, that he might strike to Louisville or even to Chicago.[15] Hood's advisers suggested it but his report says that "in the absence of the prestige of complete victory" he did not view it with favor.

Another possibility was to advance on Nashville and make a direct assault on its fortifications—but even the audacious Hood recognized the folly and certain disaster of that.

Hood compromised on a sort of offensive-defensive step—to take his army to the hills just south of Nashville, entrench and maintain it in a threatening attitude and wait for General Thomas to make the next move. His theory was that Thomas would eventually march out of the fortifications and attack him, and that he could repulse the attack and carry his victorious army into Nashville on the heels of the retreating Federals. It was a pretty dream, but it is hard to see how even one of Hood's sanguine imagination could envision anything like that happening. He knew of the overpowering numbers being gathered in Nashville; he knew the shattered and battered condition of his own army; he knew that the careful Thomas would never come out till he felt reasonably sure he could crush him. All that could be accomplished by marching and taking a stand in the outskirts was to give Thomas the comfortable assurance that Hood would be conveniently at hand when he was ready to smash him. Seldom has an inferior military force so obligingly waited near by while the adversary completed preparations to demolish it.

Wise or unwise, that was the course Hood pursued. By late afternoon of December 1 he had his men started on the way. By the morning of the third he had them in line on the hills, and there he sat down to wait. Justifying his foolhardy step, Hood has said that he hoped to receive reinforcements from the Trans-Mississippi Department, but this was a forlorn hope of the most forlorn variety, a slender thread indeed on which to hang confidence.

As soon as Beauregard heard of the battle at Franklin he realized something must be done to replace the men lost in it if Hood's campaign was to be sustained. The Confederacy had been bled of its recruitable material, and most of the armies in the field were so hard pressed that there was no possibility of borrowing from one to bolster the other. Longstreet could not be shuttled out to the West and then back to Virginia, as in 1863; Lee was fighting for his life at Petersburg. The other organized bodies of troops east of the Mississippi were of negligible size. At his wits' end for some place to turn, Beauregard in Montgomery bethought himself of Kirby Smith, out in the Trans-Mississippi Department, and in a moving letter asked him to lend aid. "The fate of the country may depend on the result of Hood's campaign in Tennessee," he wrote. Would Kirby Smith send "two or more divisions" or else start an offensive against Missouri that would prevent assistance being sent from there to Thomas?[16] Beauregard sent his letter by one of his staff officers, as there was no mail service to the Trans-Mississippi, and sent a copy to President Davis with a plea for his personal influence. Secretary Seddon approved, but expressed doubts of Kirby Smith's willingness to aid—"no plans should be based on his compliance." Beauregard wrote Kirby Smith again on the thirteenth, and Seddon backed him up with a message direct. But Seddon's fears were well-founded. On January 6, 1865, Kirby Smith replied, explaining at great length why he could do nothing to help Hood—which was just as well, as Hood was then beyond the need of help.

As General Hood must have known, for he had spies sifting freely into and out of it, Nashville was perhaps the most thoroughly and skillfully fortified city on the American continent. In August of 1862, soon after the Federals came in, Captain James St. Clair Morton of the Engineers' Corps had been ordered to Nashville to plan its defenses. He laid out a series of three major fortifications, of which Fort Negley[17] was the key, with various minor works. He built parapets and stockades of earth around the capitol, with breastworks of cotton bales,[18] and manned them with a regiment of infantry and fifteen guns. The streets were barricaded at strategic points. The work dragged along on a large but slow scale until November, 1864, when Hood's march into Tennessee raised alarm for the safety of the city. To General Z. B. Tower was assigned the duty of perfecting the defenses in a hurry. He pushed on to completion the forts begun by Captain Morton, started feverishly on a number of other forts, and connected them with two strong lines of breastworks entirely around the city on its exposed sides, from the river above to the river below.

There was an inner line, close to the edge of town, seven miles long and supported by twenty batteries, which completely enclosed the hospitals and stores. A longer outer line rested on a range of hills running through what is now the residential portion of the city, with its main salient on a high point south of town just east of the Hillsboro pike. In this outer line the troops under Thomas were placed, while the men of the quartermaster's corps were given the job of defending the inner works in case of battle.

General Hood's numbers were not sufficient to match that long outer Federal defense, and his entrenchments, hastily constructed under adverse weather conditions, were too short to constitute any sort of besieging threat. His right wing rested on a deep railroad cut between the Nolensville and Murfreesboro turnpikes, with a small lunette across the tracks occupied by the 300 survivors of the brigade of General Granbury, killed at Franklin. The line crossed to the west of the Nolensville pike to the principal stronghold of the right flank on top of Rains's Hill, a commanding elevation. Two detached batteries, with a handful of infantry, extended southeastward, parallel to and east of the pike, and gave this flank an unusual T-shaped formation.

To the west, the line ran through the grounds of Melrose, the old home of Aaron V. Brown, across the Franklin pike at about the point where a monument now stands commemorating the battle. Thence it ranged on westward beyond the Granny White pike to its main salient on the left, just to the east of the Hillsboro pike, which was known as Redoubt No. 1. Here it was refused at almost a right angle southward to Redoubt No. 2, a short distance away, then diagonally across the pike to

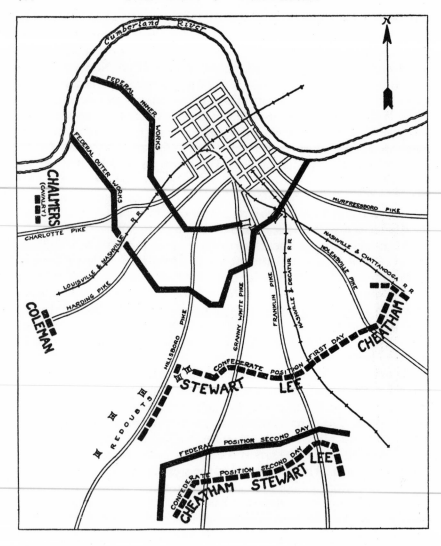

Redoubt No. 3. Hood planned to support his left by two more detached works west of the Hillsboro road, Redoubts Nos. 4 and 5, at intervals to the south, but these had not been completed at the time of the battle, though each was manned with a battery of artillery and about a hundred infantrymen. A stone wall ran south along the east side of the Hillsboro pike for a mile or so, behind which infantry was placed. Hood's engineers had located a skirmish line before the western front of the main line, stretching over the top of Montgomery Hill, just east of the Hillsboro pike, and facing the chief Federal salient.

West of the Hillsboro pike, except for the three isolated and incomplete redoubts close to it, Hood had practically nothing between his exposed left flank and the Cumberland River some four or five miles to the northwest. What was left of Ector's infantry brigade, now commanded by Colonel David Coleman, was on picket on the Harding pike in the neighborhood of the Belle Meade plantation, home of General W. G. Harding. It had suffered heavily at Franklin, was reduced to 700 men and made but a thin thread. This handful was supported by a part of the cavalry under General Chalmers, which undertook to patrol the country between the Harding pike and the river.

In the main Confederate works, Cheatham was on the right with his corps extended to a point a little east of the Franklin pike. Lee's corps was in the center, from Cheatham's left nearly to the Granny White pike. Stewart was on the extreme left. The Confederate line was spread far too thin. Stewart, for instance, in the mile-long works between the Granny White and Hillsboro pikes, had only a single division under Loring, made up of the depleted brigades of Featherston, Scott and Adams. A brigade under Sears took all the space from Redoubt No. 1 to Redoubt No. 3, and Walthall's division, made up of the brigades of Quarles, Shelley and Reynolds, was stretched out behind the rock wall along the Hillsboro pike. Loring's and Walthall's were the only two complete divisions left in Stewart's corps. General French's eyesight had failed on the eve of the battle and he had retired from active service. Cockrell's brigade of his division had been sent off to the mouth of Duck River; Ector's was stationed on the Harding pike, and the other brigade, under Sears, was attached to Walthall's division temporarily and sandwiched in between his right and Loring's left.

Reduced as he was by the losses at Franklin, Hood still did not have all his available force in line at Nashville. Bate's division had been detached from Cheatham's corps and sent off to Murfreesboro to operate on the railroad from Nashville and to menace the 8,000-odd Federals stationed there. Jackson's and Buford's divisions of cavalry, under Forrest's personal command, had been originally assigned to protect Cheatham's right, but on December 4 Forrest had been ordered to move on Murfreesboro, destroying the railroad blockhouses as he went. On December 6 he joined Bate a few miles south of Lavergne, and they advanced on Murfreesboro together, with Forrest in command. Reinforced by Sears' and Palmer's brigades, Forrest fought a little "Battle of Murfreesboro" with General Milroy, Stonewall Jackson's early victim in Virginia. The engagement took place along Overall's Creek, south of the site of the battle between Bragg and Rosecrans. Milroy was finally driven back into the town, and the brigades under Sears and Bate returned to the works at Nashville, but Forrest and his cavalry remained near Murfreesboro, and were not available for the Nashville battle. Hood made many errors in the handling of his troops, but he probably never made a more serious blunder than when he decided he did not need Forrest's help to repel Thomas.

The first week of December was treacherously fair and mild. The Confederates spent it digging their breastworks and trying to finish the five vital redoubts upon which their vulnerable left wing depended. On the night of the eighth the weather suddenly changed. One of those storms came on, with rapidly falling temperature, which sometimes feature this climate in December, and the next morning the ground was covered with sleet and snow. Then for a week there was rain and more sleet, and the whole country around Nashville was covered with ice, the ground so slippery that movement of troops was practically impossible and the temperature so low that work was extremely difficult.

This sudden change was a tremendous handicap to the entrenching Confederates, but a source of even greater disturbance to the Federals. Since Hood's arrival before Nashville, the authorities at Washington had been clamoring for Thomas to attack him immediately. As soon as they heard of the Confederate advance from Franklin, on December 2, President Lincoln and Secretary Stanton told Grant to telegraph Thomas to go out and go after the enemy. Thomas considered his cavalry inadequate, due to a shortage of mounts, and he took the responsibility of delaying until it could be remounted. He wired Grant why, and fixed his efforts on impressing every available horse in and about the city—carriage horses, plow horses, even the trained horses of a wandering circus. As the days passed, Lincoln and Stanton became more and more importunate. Stanton referred sneeringly to Thomas' "do nothing" strategy. Telegrams flew back and forth between the painstaking Thomas and the jittery Grant. At length on the sixth Grant sent a point-blank order to forget the remounts and attack at once. Thomas did not obey. On the eighth he wired apologetically that he had not been able to concentrate his troops and get their transportation in order. Thereupon Grant, his scanty patience exhausted, asked Halleck to relieve Thomas and succeed him with Schofield. An order to this effect was drawn up in the War Department on the ninth, but before sending it Halleck wired Thomas that Grant was much dissatisfied at his delay. Thomas replied that "a terrible storm of freezing rain" had just come on, rendering an attack impossible; but he was willing to "submit without a murmur" if it were decided to relieve him.[19] Grant then asked Halleck to suspend the order relieving Thomas. On the eleventh he begged Thomas once more to avoid "the mortifying spectacle" of "a rebel army moving for the Ohio. . . . Delay no longer, for weather or reinforcements."[20] But this seeming to make no impression on the Rock of Chickamauga, on the thirteenth General John A. Logan was dispatched to Nashville to take over. Then, still fretting, Grant decided to go himself. He left headquarters at City Point in Virginia on the fifteenth, and was in Washington on his way to Nashville when he got news of the battle. The news caught up with Logan at Louisville.

Meanwhile Thomas had called a meeting of his corps commanders, who sustained him in his opinion that it was impossible to fight a battle under the existing conditions, so he bided his time—willing to be deprived of his command if necessary, but unwilling to move against his judgment. A plan of attack was carefully prepared during the period of waiting, and as early as December 6 the troops were told to be ready to move on short notice. From the eighth to the fourteenth it was definitely understood that they would go out the minute the ice was off the ground, and when a warm rain began falling on the fourteenth it was an open secret that the waiting was at an end.

On the evening of the fourteenth General Thomas dictated a telegram to General Halleck in Washington: "The ice having melted away to-day, the enemy will be attacked to-morrow morning."[21] Then he called his corps commanders together, delivered to each a written order containing a detailed plan of the battle, and discussed it with them thoroughly. Hood's information service must have been of the best; he seems to have learned of Thomas' designs about as soon as Thomas' generals, and he told his own corps commanders that night to look for an attack the next morning.

Thomas' original arrangement of his forces in the Nashville works had Schofield on the left, Wood in the center and A. J. Smith on the right. Wilson's cavalry was back of Smith's line, and Steedman was a short distance in front of the Federal left, with Brown's Creek before him. The plan of battle envisaged a strong feint by Steedman against the Confederate right, to be followed by a grand wheel by the entire right wing on Wood's corps as a pivot, with Smith's corps, supported by Wilson's cavalry, making the outside sweep. Schofield's corps was pulled out of the front lines on the left and held in reserve near the center, with the idea of using it to support the right wing when the movement got under way.

Reveille sounded in the Federal camps at four o'clock and by six o'clock everything was in readiness. The calm and matter-of-fact Thomas checked out of his room at the St. Cloud Hotel, paid his bill, handed his packed valise to his orderly, and, accompanied by his staff, rode out to the battle front. The rain had stopped and the weather had turned decidedly warmer, but there was a dense fog, which did not disappear until about nine.

General Steedman took the first step in the day's fighting, advancing about six o'clock on the lunette east of the railroad which formed the extreme right of the Confederate line. His division, composed largely of negro troops, did not turn the Confederate right, but it kept Cheatham pretty well occupied all day long, and so accomplished its purpose.

Preparatory to the main drive against the Confederate left, Wood's men had been drawn out of the breastworks and deployed in the open diagonally across the Hillsboro pike, obliquely facing Hood's chief left salient and the exposed left of his skirmish line. A leading part in the attack was taken by the cavalry, which had just now reached its peak of capacity and power under the leadership of General Wilson; his reinforced corps now consisted of 12,000 well-mounted men, under Generals Croxton, Hatch, Johnson and Knipe. Some confusion was experienced in bringing the cavalry and Smith's infantry into position, but the delay was but slight and action was opened. Smith's whole corps, supported by artillery and part of Wilson's cavalry, assailed Ector's brigade on the Harding pike. Johnson's division of mounted Federals fell on Rucker's cavalry out at the extreme Confederate left beyond the Charlotte pike. Coleman, in command of Ector's brigade, had thrown out a picket line across the Harding pike near Richland Creek. He ordered it to hold off the enemy as long as possible while, with the rest of his men, he wheeled and made off hastily across country toward the Hillsboro pike.

The Confederate forces in this sector were altogether insufficient to meet the powerful blow. Both cavalry and infantry were soon overwhelmed and forced to retreat. Rucker's horsemen put up a surprisingly dogged resistance. They drove Johnson off and, crossing southward to the Harding pike, stationed themselves along Richland Creek and held their ground until late afternoon. The valiant defense of Rucker's little force did not serve to check the Federal road-roller, and the sweeping movement went on as scheduled. Smith's corps wheeled and swung through the section between the Harding and Hillsboro pikes, until his left joined with Wood's right. The remaining divisions of Wilson's cavalry plunged up the cross-lanes in the Belle Meade neighborhood to Smith's right with the object of turning the extreme Confederate left along the Hillsboro road.

As soon as Smith's corps was up in position facing the Confederate works, Wood led an advance against the skirmish line on Montgomery Hill and carried the outpost after a desperate resistance. But the Federals could not shake Loring's division in the main line. The salient it held seemed impregnable—as indeed it was, to direct attack.

Hood's Achilles' heel turned out to be the uncompleted and detached works on his left, west of the Hillsboro pike. Redoubt No. 4, for instance, between the Abbott road and Hobb's Lane, was held only by Captain Lumsden's battery of four 12-pound smoothbore Napoleon guns (fairly accurate at 600 or 800 yards) with 48 artillerymen, supported by 100 infantrymen of the 29th Alabama under Captain Foster, in shallow breastworks. This handful, with their pitifully weak armament, had been placed at this important point on December 9 and ordered by Hood to hold "at all hazards."[22] In spite of snow and sleet and bitter cold weather, they went at the frozen ground with spade and mattock and by the fourteenth had got up breastworks seven feet high, with embrasures for the guns, and scratched out infantry trenches two feet deep. The battle reached them late in the morning. About 11 A.M. Ector's retreating brigade started streaming by. Lumsden called to the officers to rally and help him hold the redoubt. "It can't be done," they cried; "there's a whole army in your front," and away they went. Some of Ector's men did take refuge in Redoubt No. 5 farther out the pike, but most of them went on across the road, and Lumsden's 148 with their four Napoleon guns were left to stem the tidal wave if they could.

McArthur's division of 4,000 came surging across country on Ector's heels. Taking no chances, they stopped on a ridge 600 yards away and three batteries of twenty-four rifled guns opened fire on the little redoubt. Lumsden sent General Stewart word of his peril—a charge would carry them away at any moment—but the best Stewart could do was to say, "Hold on as long as you can." By a miracle of valor, they held on more than two hours. About one o'clock they were enfiladed by another battery from their left. Then twelve regiments of infantry and four of dismounted cavalry armed with Spencer rifles charged them front and rear. There was no halting this avalanche. Still they held on to the last minute and manned the guns till the charging Federals were literally within arm's reach. Only then Lumsden gave the order for every man to

look out for himself, and what was left of them scampered across the
Hillsboro pike and took refuge behind the stone wall.

Similarly Redoubts No. 3 and No. 5 were overwhelmed and occupied.
The captured guns were turned on the Confederate infantry across the
pike. Hood's left wing was in extreme jeopardy. Too late he started reinforcing it from his inactive center. First Manigault's brigade from Edward Johnson's division was double-quicked to the scene of impending
disaster and placed behind the wall across the pike from Redoubt No. 4
before it fell. Then Deas's brigade from the same division came up, filled
in the gap between Manigault's right and Walthall's left, gave added
length to the thin gray line clinging precariously to the eastern edge of
the pike. But by then the redoubts were lost. The irresistible blue flood
swept on to the pike, and the two reinforcing brigades broke from their
cover and fled.

With nothing to impede their progress, Smith's corps crossed the pike
and marched to the east a full half-mile. They turned the flank and
gained the rear of both Walthall and Loring, who had stalwartly opposed
all frontal attacks. Now these two divisions, finding their positions untenable, had to withdraw, but they retired in good order and took up a
new station along the Granny White pike, facing west. There they
stopped the turning force and ended the fighting on the left wing as night
came on.

Meanwhile Schofield, ordered up to Smith's support, had sent Couch's
division on a sweep to Smith's right. It gained the hills east of the Hillsboro pike across from Redoubt No. 5. Wilson's cavalry galloped far out
and around to cross this road two miles beyond the scene of the infantry
fighting. They had almost reached the Granny White pike in the Confederate rear when the day was over.

With the collapse of the left wing, the Confederate center and right
necessarily fell back, and the early winter twilight found the whole army
in retreat. As the reeling soldiery streaked along the muddy Granny
White pike, a patriotic Southern girl, Mary Bradford, rushed out from her
home and, taking her stand in the middle of the road, begged them tear-
fully to turn and fight. It was no use. They ran on. When, some months
later, General Hood sat down to write his report of the battle, he remembered Mary Bradford and gave her brave but futile gesture his official
recognition.

General Thomas was well-pleased. Before dark he saw Hood's whole
left crushed like an eggshell, the soldiers flying from the field. He came
to the hasty conclusion that the battle was over, that Hood would seek

safety. He sent orders to Schofield to press the retreating enemy the next morning, mounted his horse and rode back to headquarters in Nashville, satisfied with the day's work. Schofield, however, had known Hood at the Military Academy. He knew his bulldog determination; he did not believe Hood was retreating, and he rode into town to tell Thomas so. "You don't know Hood," he said to his superior. "He'll be right there, ready to fight, in the morning."[23] Thomas was reluctant to believe it but played safe and made ready to renew the assault if Hood chose to remain and fight again.

Hood was there, all right. During the night the Confederate engineers located a new and shorter line on the Overton Hills about two miles behind the former position. When morning came the Army of Tennessee was waiting in hastily scraped-out breastworks. There was a new arrangement of the forces. Lee, whose corps had not been actively engaged and was in good condition, simply fell back out the Franklin pike to the high ground on the Overton place, and became the right wing. Stewart's corps, so roughly handled, was brought over into the center. And Cheatham's corps was switched from the right and put on the left flank.

The right of the new Confederate line, east of the Franklin pike, bent sharply back to the south toward the Overton home place, Travelers' Rest. The hill on which Lee's men took their stand is designated on the war maps as Overton Hill, but the Overton family called it Peach Orchard Hill. Crossing the pike westward, the line ran through the Lea place, and on beyond the Granny White pike to the short high range east of the Hillsboro road. The main salient on the left wing was on the northernmost of these hills, now known as Shy's Hill,[24] and was refused southward along them.

Just what malign influence made Hood stand and invite another attack it is impossible to uncover. He must have been apprehensive of the outcome. He showed it by ordering the wagons to the Harpeth River early in the morning, and instructing that in the event of defeat Lee's corps should hold the Franklin pike to insure a safe withdrawal. These preparations for disaster, not lost on the men, hardly served to revive their waning spirits, but like the true soldiers they were they took their appointed places and waited for the enemy to come on again.

On the Federal right the men who had pushed across the Hillsboro pike near Redoubt No. 5 the previous evening were already close to Hood's new left—closer than he had any idea. Elsewhere, particularly on the right center, the Federals were in considerable confusion, with some of the troops at right angles to others, and it took most of the morning to get them properly aligned. Thomas' strategy for the sixteenth was virtually a repetition of yesterday's program—an attack on the Confederate right, and a turning movement in force against the left. This time, however, the assault on the right, delivered about 9 A.M., was no mere feint; it was an attack in earnest to seize the Franklin pike. Lee's divisions put up a valiant defense, and time after time threw back the waves of negro[25] and white troops. They say the Federal dead were so thick that the slopes of Peach Orchard Hill looked blue—and they died in vain, for Lee's corps would not budge.

On the Confederate left affairs were not going so well. Early in the morning the Federals brought up artillery and placed it on the high ground commanding that flank. Through the day it was subjected to a merciless rain of shell and cannister, as Smith and Schofield kept up a deadly cross fire on the angle at Shy's Hill. Shortly after noon McArthur located a battery in the woods on the Confederate front which fired point-blank into the Shy's Hill works, and later more artillery still on a hill that took a part of the line in reverse.

The pressure on Hood's left was overwhelmingly powerful, so strong the Federals finally encircled his flank and got astride the Granny White pike behind Cheatham. So far did they overlap him that he had to bring up reinforcing brigades and bend his extreme left backward like a fishhook, until he had one line firing south and the other firing north, only a few hundred yards apart.

Such conditions could not last. With the enemy in the rear and with the angle at Shy's Hill pounded to pieces by the enfilading gunfire, it was only a question how soon the left must crumble. About four o'clock McArthur reported the Confederate parapets on Shy's Hill leveled and the position open to infantry attack. The attack was launched and succeeded handsomely. The troops on the hill held on gamely for a few minutes, but soon the summit was swarming with bluecoats and the overpowered Confederates were fleeing across the muddy fields toward the Granny White pike and the hills to the south.

As on the day before, when the left wing gave the center also fell back. Lee's corps found itself holding the right wing across the Franklin pike without support. It was his assigned task to save this avenue of retreat to the last ditch, and most gallantly Lee lived up to the assignment. When he saw the left and the center break and his own division begin to falter, he seized a flag from a color-bearer and rallied the men about him. The rally enabled Clayton's division to form a new battle line near the

Overton house, a little back of their old position. They held it till all
Hood's retreating army had streamed over the wooded hills and crowded
into the pike at Brentwood behind Clayton.

There was something akin to panic in Cheatham's and Stewart's ranks
that dismal, rainy December evening as they fled through the deep mud
of the fields on up and across the hills. Hardly recovered from the
ghastly nightmare of Franklin, they had taken a terrific pummeling yesterday on the outskirts of Nashville, and today they were getting more of
the same. It was simply too much for weary, mortal men to stand. They
were used to fighting against odds, but these odds were too long. They
were whipped and they knew it, and they wanted to get away from there.
"I doubt," says General Schofield admiringly, "if any soldiers in the world
ever needed so much cumulative evidence to convince them that they
were beaten."[26] But now they were convinced—and they wanted to live
to fight another day.

General Schofield understates the truth when he says: "The comparatively feeble resistance offered by the Confederate troops at Nashville
was due not so much, perhaps, to any lack of valor as to their comparatively small numbers." Just how much Thomas outnumbered Hood is
impossible to say exactly. The total effective Confederate force at Nashville, according to Hood's official report, was 23,053, though the ordnance
officer of the army stated that there were only 15,000 men actually under
arms. Livermore places the Confederate strength at 23,207, actual number engaged, including cavalry. Thomas had 70,272 "present for duty,
equipped," of whom about 55,000 took active part in the battle.

In Hood's official report he says that at Nashville "our loss in killed
and wounded was small"—there is no way of telling just how "small," as
no detailed figures are given. Thomas reports that he captured 4,462, and
it is probable that Hood's killed and wounded did not exceed 1,500 for
the two days. Thomas gives his own loss at 387 killed, 2,562 wounded, 112
missing. The light loss in killed and wounded is due to the fact that the
battle was primarily a contest of maneuver; on both days the Confederate
line was broken and driven into retreat by an enveloping movement which
so encircled the left wing as to make it untenable. Hood's men, fighting
from behind works, naturally suffered less than the attackers; the Confederate casualties could hardly have been more than half Thomas' reported
total of about 3,000. More general officers were lost: Major General Edward Johnson was captured again (he had only recently been exchanged
after capture at Spottsylvania Courthouse). Brigadier Generals H. R.
Jackson (called by his soldiers "Mud-fence Jackson") and T. B. Smith

also fell into Federal hands in the darkness and confusion of the second evening. Hood suffered an astonishing loss of artillery, leaving no less than fifty-four guns on the field. He explains this by saying that, expecting his line to hold, he had sent the horses to the rear to protect them from fire, and the break in the line came so suddenly it was impossible to bring them up in time to haul off the guns.

A wounded private of Cheatham's corps relates that as he passed by army headquarters at Brentwood the rainy night of the sixteenth he stopped to get a certificate of disability because of his wound and blundered into the tent of General Hood. There sat the commander, his useless left arm limp at his side, running the fingers of his right hand nervously through his hair as tears of disappointment and despair trickled down onto his bearded cheeks. The cold December rain drummed down noisily on the tent, but not noisily enough to shut out the confused babble of an army in retreat. They were in retreat, but the spirit of the Army of Tennessee could not be downed. If the heartbroken commander had listened he might actually have heard them singing as they splashed barefoot along the muddy road. The tune they sang was that old favorite, *The Yellow Rose of Texas*, but the words they used had been improvised by some camp wit, words that would have seared the wounded heart of Hood:

"So now I'm marching southward;
My heart is full of woe.
I'm going back to Georgia
To see my Uncle Joe.
You may talk about your Beauregard
And sing of General Lee,
But the gallant Hood of Texas
Played hell in Tennessee."

CHAPTER XX

THE END

THOMAS had completely outmatched Hood in the two days' fighting around Nashville, but in the days that followed Hood displayed considerably more skill in retreat than Thomas in pursuit.

The successful withdrawal of the routed army was made possible in the closing hours of the sixteenth, when Chalmers' mounted men fought Wilson's cavalry to a standstill on the Granny White pike. If Wilson's apparently irresistible drive across the Overton Hills had continued it would have carried him through to the Franklin pike and right into the midst of Hood's demoralized infantry crowding along that lone channel of escape. Chalmers, it is true, was eventually forced to give up the Granny White pike and retire to the Franklin pike, but Wilson's men were fought out. On this cold, dark, rainy night Thomas' whole army seemed willing to content itself with the day's victory and to leave pursuit for the morrow.

In the meantime the mass of the Confederate army crowded down the Franklin pike in a hodgepodge of infantry, cavalry, artillery and wagons. The road was clogged with broken-down guns and wagons, exhausted and abandoned horses, worn-out, bewildered men. At Brentwood, three miles back, they were brought into some sort of formation; then they passed on southward, gradually finding their organizations and moving in something like military order. Stephen D. Lee encamped near Brentwood with the brigades of Pettus and Stovall, and next morning, supported by Chalmer's cavalry, he took up the duty of guarding the rear.

The Federal pursuit was led by Wood's corps of infantry with Wilson's cavalry. Their initial assault drove Chalmers in. At Hollow Tree Gap, four miles north of Franklin, Lee and Chalmers made a determined stand and held the enemy off till they found they were outflanked on both sides; then they fell back again. They burned the bridge at Franklin as they crossed the Harpeth but went right on through the town. They made another stand across the pike at the range of hills a little way south. Here they fought through the afternoon and until dark. General Lee was wounded, but he stayed on the job till the pursuers had been repulsed and four or five hours of valuable time had been gained for the retreating army.

The next day Hood had his army pretty well under control and concentrated near Columbia, with Cheatham in the rear camped on Rutherford's Creek. The pursuit was slowed down by the continued heavy rains and the swollen streams. It was not until late on the nineteenth that some of Wilson's cavalry got across the creek. Thereupon Cheatham fell back across Duck River. As soon as he realized that he was whipped at Nashville, Hood had sent a message to Forrest at Murfreesboro to retire through Shelbyville to Pulaski, but Forrest, sensing the army's plight and its need for his help, struck out through the country and joined up at Columbia on the nineteenth—and never was anyone more welcome!

Hood asserts in his official report that he had planned to establish a line on Duck River and remain in Tennessee, but after taking stock of his army and its condition he thought it best to get across to the south side of the Tennessee without delay. Forrest counseled this course and volunteered to protect the rear if given the assistance of some infantry. A body of 1,900 men (400 of them barefoot) under Walthall were assigned him. With these and his 3,000 cavalry under Chalmers, Buford and W. H. Jackson, Forrest shouldered the backbreaking task of holding off the pursuit while the army retreated on through Pulaski to recross the Tennessee at Bainbridge, Alabama, near Florence.

The Federals were right behind them. The next ten days and nights were an almost unbroken nightmare of battling and falling back, battling and falling back. Forrest destroyed the Duck River bridges, and the Federal crossing was delayed also because, by some queer error, the pontoons had been sent to Murfreesboro instead of Columbia. When they finally got across on the twenty-fourth, Forrest and Walthall met them on Richland Creek between Columbia and Pulaski and gave them a lively set-to till outflanked by Wilson's mounted men. Here the infantry relinquished the pursuit, and from here on Wilson's pressure diminished steadily. The weather continued severe, forage was almost unobtainable, and men and horses on both sides verged on utter exhaustion.

Hood's main army crossed the river on the twenty-fifth and twenty-sixth—a dismal way to celebrate Christmas. Forrest's cavalry followed on the twenty-eighth, and on the twenty-ninth Walthall's infantry got over. The crossing was assisted by the providential aid of some enemy pontoons which had floated downriver after being captured and cut loose at Decatur by Roddey's cavalry. This was a lifesaver, as Hood's own pontoons had been held up by the bad roads, and did not get to the river until part

of the troops were on the other side. In the midst of the passage two of
the much-feared Yankee gunboats came upriver and threatened trouble,
but Stewart opened on them with a battery from the river bank and drove
them away. Hood marched on to Tuscumbia, then through Iuka to Corinth and thence to Tupelo, where he went into camp on January 10.
Within six weeks he had marched nearly five hundred miles, had fought
two battles—and had all but wrecked his army.

Heaped on all his other difficulties, Hood had had the misfortune to
fight his campaign in an abominable spell of weather. It was the earliest
and the coldest winter that Tennessee had known for years. The hardships and suffering of the men were perhaps worse than any American
army had faced since the days of Valley Forge. Most of the soldiers had
no tents, many had not even hats, and when a tired soldier tries to bivouac
in the open, a ragged blanket is mighty little protection from freezing
rain. Probably half the men were without shoes; the hard-frozen ruts in
the roads cruelly gashed their bare feet as they plodded through the snow
and slush. "Bloody footprints in the road" is a familiar figure of speech;
the Army of Tennessee literally stained the snow and the mud of the
roads with the blood of its lacerated feet. The resourceful Forrest allevi-
ated the suffering of the barefoot infantrymen in the rear guard by dump-
ing out the contents of some army wagons and using them for convey-
ances. When the rear guard went into action, the barefoot would pile
out and form in line of battle; the action over, they would jump back in
and ride on. But the rank and file of the army enjoyed no such luxury.
They trudged the whole long, weary way on foot.

All this while Beauregard was off in the Southeast, busy with the defenses of Savannah and Charleston before Sherman's onrush of destruction and pillage. The army of 30,000 so hopefully envisioned by Howell
Cobb and Governor Brown had not materialized, and Sherman and his
"bummers" swept through Georgia almost unopposed. Engrossed as he
was, Beauregard was disturbed by persistent rumors that Hood had suffered disaster in Tennessee, though he was still without official information. Eventually, when both Savannah and Charleston had to be evacuated and efforts to hold them no longer occupied him, he turned over the
active command of operations in Georgia and South Carolina to General
Hardee and on the last day of the year set out for Montgomery to give
his personal attention to these rumors. When he reached Macon on
January 3, he received his first direct word from Hood, a telegram from
Corinth[1] that must go down in history as a masterpiece of misleading
understatement: "The army has re-crossed the Tennessee River without

material loss since the battle of Franklin. It will be assembled in a few days in the vicinity of Tupelo to be supplied with shoes and clothing and to obtain forage for the animals." Nothing of the shocking losses at Franklin; nothing of the disaster at Nashville. Indeed, the terms of the message are so mild no wonder Beauregard extracted from it "a gleam of comfort"[2] and concluded that the alarming reports he had been hearing were exaggerations.

He hastened on to Tupelo. There on the fifteenth he saw for himself what was left of the army which at Tuscumbia such a short while before he had last seen hopefully preparing for the Tennessee campaign. Sixteen of its generals and thousands of its enlisted men were dead or in Northern prisons. He shuddered when he gazed on its ragged, bleeding survivors. "If not, in the strict sense of the word a disorganized mob," he says, "it was no longer an army."[3]

General Bragg's old Mobile friend, John Forsyth, wrote to him on January 17 describing it as "a shattered debris of an army." Forsyth was urging Johnston's reinstatement and was disposed to exaggerate the consequences if Hood was left in charge. "Hood's army is not worth the value of a regiment if that officer is retained in its command."[4]

But he need not have worried on that score. Hood realized all too well that he had shot his bolt. On the thirteenth he sent a short telegram to Secretary Seddon: "I request to be relieved from the command of this army."[5] This request was promptly granted, and Beauregard was instructed to place General Richard Taylor in command. Beauregard himself was to return to Georgia and South Carolina "with such troops as may be spared." He had already consulted Hood on the possibility of sending troops to Hardee at once, and proceeded to act promptly.

General Taylor wired President Davis on the fifteenth: "An attempt to move Hood's army at this time would complete its destruction."[6] But he, and its other detractors, underestimated the unquenchable spirit of the Army of Tennessee. Its demoralization was great. There can be no denying that. And who can say that it had not had enough to cause demoralization? Long marching, exposure, disappointment, suffering, defeat—they would have been supermen if they had not been shaken by such soul-trying experiences. But the fact remains that within a few days of their return to Tupelo they had pulled themselves together—what there was left of them—and were off to the wars again.

How many of them were there? It is hard to say exactly. The Official Return on January 20 showed an "effective total" of 17,709 infantry and artillery. Of these 4,000 were sent to Mobile to aid its defense. At about this time 3,500 were furloughed—some before and some after the date of the Official Return. Beyond any question, there were a large number of deserters, as there were from all the Confederate armies during its last, gasping months. Joseph E. Johnston says that only 5,000 finally reached North Carolina out of the army he had turned over to Hood at Atlanta— but Johnston is not always strictly accurate in statements relating to Hood.

Whatever their exact numbers, they went promptly to the Carolinas, with a minimum of preparation and delay. Lee's corps, now commanded by Stevenson, was apparently the least damaged of any; they left for Augusta at once. Cheatham's corps got off on the twenty-fifth, and Stewart's on the thirtieth. With the facilities at hand, it was no small physical task to transport an army corps—even the skeleton of an army corps—from Tupelo to South Carolina. The railroads were in frightful dilapidation; the highways were almost hopelessly ruined by the constant passage of troops, guns and wagon trains. An idea of the circuitous routing involved may be gathered from the itinerary of Cheatham's corps. On January 25 they left Tupelo on foot and marched to West Point, Mississippi, where they arrived on the twenty-eighth. From there they rode on the railroad cars to Meridian, and thence to Selma, Alabama, through Demopolis. From Selma they went by steamboat to Montgomery, and from there by train to Columbus, Georgia. From Columbus they marched to Macon, to Milledgeville, to Mayfield, where they again took the cars for Augusta. Then they marched to Newberry, South Carolina, and at last joined Stevenson's corps, who had gone on ahead.

It was not until the twenty-third that Hood surrendered command. He issued a farewell address thanking the troops for their patient endurance of hardship in the Tennessee campaign, of which he said manfully: "I am alone responsible for its conception, and strived hard to do my duty in its execution." General Taylor immediately assumed command— but there was not much left to command. Stevenson had already gone, Cheatham was under orders to go, and within a week Taylor advised Beauregard that Stewart was ready to travel. So ended General Dick Taylor's brief career as head of the Army of Tennessee.

While waiting at Tupelo, Hood had conceived the visionary scheme of going to Texas where, he fondly believed, he could raise 30,000 new troops and bring them to Lee's relief in Virginia. He went to Richmond and prevailed on President Davis to authorize his undertaking it. On the way north he stopped to visit friends in Chester, South Carolina. So Mrs. Chesnut, the diarist, met him again in circumstances very different from the last time she had seen him in Richmond, when he was the toast of the town. Now he was crestfallen and dejected, but "he made no excuses, he had nobody to blame but himself," she records.[7] Though his old friends loyally tried to cheer him up, he sat gazing into the fireplace, his face etched with agony, the little drops of perspiration popping out on his forehead as he saw again "the panic at Nashville, and the dead on the battlefield at Franklin." It was a horrid nightmare that clung to him.

Hood passed on to Richmond, and soon—in late March—Mrs. Chesnut recorded that she had just seen the corps of Stephen D. Lee march down Chester's main street, and, amazingly, they were singing!

"There they go," she wrote sadly in her *Diary*, "the gay and gallant few, doomed, the last gathering of the flowers of Southern pride, to be killed, or worse, to a prison. They continue to prance by, light and jaunty. They march with as airy a tread as if they still believed the world was all on their side, and that there were no Yankee bullets for the unwary. What will Joe Johnston do with them now?"[8]

For it was "Old Joe" Johnston to whose leadership they were marching now. Perhaps that was why they were so light and jaunty, why they sang. Now that the affairs of the Southern Confederacy were at last-ditch desperation, a step had been taken which, useless now, might have been decisive earlier in the war. Robert E. Lee was made general-in-chief of all the forces in the field, and one of his first steps was to recall Joseph E. Johnston to active service—a bitter blow to the pride of Jefferson Davis. An imposing array of generals was now in the Carolinas. Bragg was there to take charge of the defense at Wilmington. Hardee was moving up from the coast with the garrisons of abandoned towns. Beauregard was back from Mississippi. Even D. H. Hill had been recalled from retirement. No lack of generals—but such a pitiful paucity of men! Frantic efforts were made to gather a force that might halt Sherman as he swept northward from the sea.

When Johnston got to Charlotte on February 24 and took command, he found the available troops badly scattered. General Wade Hampton says: "It would scarcely have been possible to disperse a force more effectually."[9] Hardee was near Fayetteville. Bragg, who had abandoned Wilmington, was approaching Goldsboro. The three corps of the Army of Tennessee were moving in the general direction of Charlotte, but they were widely separated.

By early March Sherman had entered North Carolina and with his corps marching on different routes, was going toward Goldsboro, aiming

Head Qrs Army Tenn.
Tupelo, Miss.
January 23, 1865

Soldiers:

At my request, I have this day been relieved from the command of this Army. In taking leave of you, accept my thanks for the patience with which you have endured your many hardships during the recent campaign. I am alone responsible for its conception, and strived hard to do my duty in its execution. I urge upon you the importance of giving your entire support to the distinguished soldier who now assumes command, and I shall look with deep interest upon all your future operations, and rejoice at your successes.

J B Hood
General.

Genl G T Beauregard
Cõ dg. so.

General Hood's farewell address to the Army of Tennessee. This is the copy of the address, signed by Hood, which was sent to General Beauregard, commander of the department.

Head. Quarters
Greensboro No. Ca. C.S.A.
April 19th 1865.

Virginia   Richmond.   289 Men.
North Carolina.   Raleigh   2.645 ,
Tennessee.   Nashville 1.312 "
                             4,246
South Carolina.   Spartanburg 4.885 ,
Georgia.   Macon   5.626 ,
Florida. } Macon Tallahassee 351 "
Alabama   Montgomery 2.578 "
Mississippi   Macon.   2.187 ,
Lousiana.   Baton Rouge .104 "
Arkansas   Little Rock 741 "
Texas.   Austin   529 "
                             Total Prest 20,640

A.A.G.

Total Present - not Effective

Memorandum, from Beauregard's files, of the troops surrendered to
Sherman, written in ink by General Otey with Beauregard's notations
in pencil referring (presumably) to the original hope that each state's
troops might be returned to the state capital for parole and dispersal.

at a junction with Grant before Petersburg. To check him, Johnston finally managed to scrape together nearly 15,000 men at Smithfield, about fifteen miles south of Raleigh. One component of his force was Stewart's corps of the Army of Tennessee, and Stevenson and Cheatham were coming on as fast as they could.

Johnston's strategy was to fall on Sherman's left column before it could join the other wing at Goldsboro. He stationed his little army near the town of Bentonville, south of Smithfield. There on the morning of March 19 they waited, Stewart's corps on the right, with Bragg on the left, directly across the Fayetteville-Goldsboro highway.

The Battle of Bentonville was brought on by advancing Hampton's cavalry against Slocum's column, under orders to fall back through Bragg's corps and let the infantry take up the contest. The plan was carried out and soon Bragg's line was struck by Slocum. Slocum was thrown back, and an attack against Stewart's wing was also repulsed. Early in the afternoon the Confederates made a strong countercharge, led by General Hardee himself, supported by Stewart. Johnston's report says: "The Federals were routed in a few minutes, our brave fellows dashing successively over two lines of temporary breastworks." The Fourteenth Corps, after being pushed back for a mile, rallied on the Twentieth Corps in a strong position, where they made a stand. The Confederate drive was slowed down, and by nightfall the fighting stopped. Johnston concludes his report: "After burying our dead and bringing off our own and many of the Federal wounded, and three pieces of artillery, we returned to our first position." The Battle of Bentonville was a victory—the last victory for the Confederate arms—but the loss was heavy, and they needed all their man power now.

Stunned by the ferocity and surprise of the Confederate attack, the Federals spent the twentieth concentrating, strengthening their position and feeling for the location of Johnston's force. That day Johnston was cheered by the arrival of Cheatham's corps, but Lee's did not get up until all the action was over. The twenty-first was passed in skirmishes, winding up in a spirited cavalry encounter, where Hardee again led in person.[10] Sherman's whole army, now brought into play, outnumbered Johnston more than four to one, and was deployed so that he was almost surrounded, with a deep creek at his back. From this hazardous situation he retreated to Smithfield on the night of the twenty-first—and the fighting days of the Army of Tennessee were over. Johnston, advising Beauregard of the outcome at Bentonville, commented on the bravery and dash of Stewart's and Cheatham's men and, alluding to Hood's report, said:

"The troops of the Tennessee army have fully disproved the slander that has been published against them."

When Sherman reached Goldsboro on March 23 and joined his army to Schofield's, which had been transferred from Tennessee by rail to Virginia and thence by coastwise vessel, he had a total of more than 90,000. But the presence of Johnston in the field still troubled him; he was afraid Johnston, if pressed, might break his army up and resort to a long-drawn-out guerrilla warfare. Leaving Schofield in charge, he went to Grant's headquarters in Virginia to confer with the President and the high command. Admiral Porter, who was present at the interview, says Lincoln "wanted peace on almost any terms." When Sherman asked about conditions for Johnston's surrender, if and when it came to that point, Lincoln said that "all he wanted of us was to defeat the opposing armies and to get the men composing the Confederate armies back to their homes, at work on their farms and in their shops." Sherman was sure he could force Johnston to a surrender on his own terms, but Lincoln rejoined that it must be obtained "on almost any terms."[11]

Hardly had Sherman got back to Goldsboro before the Confederate house of cards started tumbling down. On April 6 he had word that Richmond had fallen on the second and that Lee's army had left presumably to try for a junction with Johnston. So he began to press Johnston, and on the tenth moved straight on Raleigh by way of Smithfield. As he approached, Johnston retreated through Raleigh, to Chapel Hill, to Salem and then toward Greensboro, burning the bridges behind him.

On April 9, the very day when Lee surrendered at Appomattox, Johnston effected a final formal reorganization of the remnants of the Army of Tennessee. In that roster were listed for the last time names forever associated with the history of the Confederacy. Johnston and Beauregard had been together, four years before, on the field of First Manassas. There Johnston had been in command, and Beauregard second, and so their names appear in the final line-up. The army was now organized into the familiar three corps, commanded by the equally familiar figures of Hardee, Stewart and Stephen D. Lee. Some familiar names were missing —Cleburne and all too many others—but among the division and brigade commanders many still shone there whose brilliance and devotion illumined the fields over which the Army of Tennessee had fought. There was stouthearted Frank Cheatham, commanding a division now. There were Loring and Walthall and John C. Brown and Patton Anderson and Stevenson and D. H. Hill—but the list is too long to repeat. It is an imposing array of names, and an impressive organization—on paper. In actuality, it was hardly more than the shadow of an army, a cadre, the ranks left bare by death, wounds, capture—yes, and by desertions. Companies and regiments had been consolidated, brigades were scarcely as large as normal regiments. The 19th Tennessee, for example, was down to 64 men from its original 1,297. But they still held their heads high, their flags still fluttered defiantly, as they marched to their camping place near Greensboro. Old Joe Johnston knew what he was doing; whatever he did was right.

Old Joe realized, sadly but inescapably, that the end was at hand. As he retreated from Raleigh he heard of Lee's surrender and knew a similar fate awaited him. Davis and three members of his Cabinet—Benjamin, Mallory and Reagan—fleeing from Richmond, reached Greensboro on April 12 and called Johnston and Beauregard to conference. Davis startled the group by expressing the fatuous belief they might still raise large levies of new Confederate troops and carry on the war. The sycophant Benjamin thought so too. All the others disagreed. Next day John C. Breckinridge, Secretary of War,[12] joined them, bringing official confirmation that the Confederacy was virtually at an end, that its government had collapsed. When Davis still seemed annoyed at the suggestion that Johnston's surrender was in order, Johnston insisted on the hopelessness of struggling with 21,000 against Sherman's 110,000—and Grant's now unoccupied 180,000 in the offing. It would be, he said, "the greatest of human crimes"[13] to attempt it.

At last Davis yielded. On April 14 Johnston sent a courier through the lines under a flag of truce with a request for a truce during negotiations. With Breckinridge he met Sherman at the Bennett farmhouse near Durham between the lines—Breckinridge there in his capacity as major general rather than as Secretary of War, out of deference to Sherman's political sensibilities. A newspaper story published a few years ago tells how a bottle was produced when the three old acquaintances got together for the parley, and how Breckinridge, his eloquence stimulated, discussed the terms in most persuasive manner. At length he proposed another round of drinks, but Sherman protested. "Hold on, Breckinridge. If you get one more drink inside of you, you'll talk me into surrendering to Johnston."

Whatever influenced them, the conditions as first agreed on were considered too liberal when they were sent to Grant for his approval. He came down to Sherman's headquarters to insist on the same terms as Lee's surrender to him. The result was another meeting at the Bennett house on the twenty-sixth, and then the final provisions were settled by which the activities of the Army of Tennessee came to a close. Officers were to retain their side arms and their private horses and baggage. The men in the ranks also were to keep their horses and private property and have the use of the army wagons and horses "for their march to their homes and in subsequent industrial pursuits." Each returning body of soldiers might hold a number of rifles, equal to one-seventh of their numerical strength, for protection and hunting on the way.

And so the Army of Tennessee was paroled and dispersed. On foot, or astride the bony army horses, or piled in the patched-up, creaking army wagons, they started home over the mountains. They had fought a good fight, they had finished their course, they had kept the faith.

It was grey and dirty weather,
And I heard a drum go rolling,
Rub-a-dubbing in the distance,
Awful dour-like and defiant.

Some had shoes, but all had rifles,
Them that wasn't bald was beardless,
And the drum was rolling "Dixie,"
And they stepped to it like men, sir!

Rags and tatters, belts and bayonets,
On they swung, the drum a-rolling,
Mum and sour. It looked like fighting,
And they meant it too, by thunder!

FINIS

NOTES

FOREWORD

[1]William M. Polk, *Leonidas Polk, Bishop and General*, II, 83.

[2]*The War of the Rebellion: A Compilation of the Official Records of the Union and Confederate Armies*, published by the United States Government; for convenience referred to in the text as the *Official Records* and in the footnotes as *O. R.*

CHAPTER I

[1]R. U. Johnson and C. C. Buel (Editors), *Battles and Leaders of the Civil War*, I, 273. Hereafter this will be referred to as *Battles and Leaders*.

[2]John Fiske, *The Mississippi Valley in the Civil War*, p. 217.

[3]*Memphis Appeal*, May 19, 1861.

[4]Jefferson Davis, *The Rise and Fall of the Confederate Government*, I, 417.

[5]James Peckham, *General Nathaniel Lyon and Missouri in 1861*, p. 222.

[6]*Ibid.*, p. 251.

[7]*The Land We Love*, I:5, 367.

[8]*Battles and Leaders*, I, 267.

[9]Fort Smith *Times & Herald*, July 12, 1861.

[10]*Battles and Leaders*, I, 269.

[11]*Ibid.*, p. 270.

[12]*Ibid.*, p. 270.

[13]William Watson, *Life in the Confederate Army*, p. 198.

[14]General Frémont, when he established his headquarters at St. Louis surrounded himself with an elaborate staff and a generally regal air which aroused the amusement and resentment of many, including some of even the staunchest Unionists. His extensive staff was composed largely of previously unknown personages, many of them with unfamiliar foreign names, such as General Asboth, Colonel DeAlma, Majors Kappner and Blome, Captains Emavic, Meizarras, Kalamaneuzze, Zagonyi, Van Stein, Kiste, Sacche and Geister, and Lieutenants Napoleon Westerburg, Addone, Kroger, etc. Perusing this staggering list of patronyms, even the taciturn General Albert Sidney Johnston was moved to comment smilingly: "There is too much tail to that kite."—William Preston Johnston, *Life of General Albert Sidney Johnston*, p. 326.

¹⁵Peckham, *General Nathaniel Lyon*, p. 292.
¹⁶*The Republic*, July 25, 1861.
¹⁷*Memphis Appeal*, July 25, 1861.
¹⁸*Battles and Leaders*, I, 279.
¹⁹*Memphis Appeal*, July 23, 1861.
²⁰O. R., III, 612.
²¹*Battles and Leaders*, I, 278.
²²O. R., III, 616.
²³*Ibid.*, p. 617.
²⁴*Battles and Leaders*, I, 285.
²⁵*The Southern Bivouac*, I:9, 550.
²⁶*Battles and Leaders*, I, 271.
²⁷*The Southern Bivouac*, I:10, 678.
²⁸*Ibid.*, p. 679.
²⁹*Ibid.*, p. 679.
³⁰*Ibid.*, II, 47.
³¹*Ibid.*, p. 13.
³²O. R., III, 184-185.
³³*The Southern Bivouac*, II, 47.
³⁴General M. Jeff Thompson of the Missouri forces gained widespread fame throughout the South for his defiant proclamation in answer to Frémont in which he promised that "For every member of the Missouri State Guard, or soldier of our allies the Confederate States, who shall be put to death in pursuance of said order of Gen. Frémont, I will Hang, Draw and Quarter a minion of said Abraham Lincoln. . . . I intend to exceed General Frémont in his excesses. . . . I will retaliate ten-fold, so help me God!" *Memphis Appeal*, September 12, 1861.
³⁵Dunbar Rowland (Editor), *Jefferson Davis, Constitutionalist; His Letters, Papers and Speeches*, V, 184. Hereafter this will be referred to as *Jefferson Davis, Constitutionalist*.
³⁶J. B. Jones, *A Rebel War Clerk's Diary*, I, 18.
³⁷The *Star of the West* was the target of the first gun actually fired in the conflict between the North and the South. She was sent with provisions to Fort Sumter soon after South Carolina seceded, before the Confederate States government was set up. When she arrived in Charleston harbor on January 9 she was driven away by the fire of the guns from the Charleston fortifications. After being captured at Galveston by Van Dorn, she was sent to New Orleans, where she was used for a while as a receiving ship by the Confederates. Later, when Grant was attempting to reach Vicksburg by the back-door route of the Yazoo Pass, the *Star of the West* was taken up into the Tallahatchie River (a tributary of the Yazoo), the rivers being in flood, and there sunk in the channel, effectually blocking the navigation of that stream.
³⁸Quantrill claimed to be a Confederate and even professed to have a

commission in the Confederate Army. It appears from a careful study of his record, however, that he had no fixed political principles and that he was at heart a desperado who took advantage of the war to carry on his outrageous excesses.

[39]The participation of the Indians in the War Between the States constitutes one of the least known but one of the most interesting chapters of the war's history.

Hardly had the Confederate States' government been established than President Davis named Albert Pike as "Commissioner to the Five Civilized Tribes" (the Cherokees, Chickasaws, Choctaws, Creeks and Seminoles) and hurried him off to the Indian Territory to make a treaty with the red men.

The Indians at this time had reached a high degree of civilization and education, were large landowners and slaveowners. The sympathies of a majority were with the Confederates, not only as a matter of political principle, but because the United States government was delinquent in its 1861 annuities. On the other hand, there was a very strong pro-Union sentiment among the Indians, and Pike's task required diplomacy and tact. He finally succeeded in October, 1861, in making the desired treaties of alliance with the ruling chiefs of all five of the tribes involved.

While these negotiations were pending, some of the young braves had slipped across the Arkansas line and joined the Confederate forces under McCulloch; others had organized "Home Guards" in the Indian Territory. After making his treaties, Pike mustered these Home Guards into the Confederate service, making up three all-Indian regiments. Under Pike's command they fought in the battle of Pea Ridge.

One of these Indian regiments was commanded by the able young Cherokee chieftain, Stand Watie. He showed a talent for military operations and eventually reached the rank of brigadier general in the Confederate Army, having shown considerable bravery and skill in the battle at Pea Ridge.

After the Pea Ridge affair, the Indian regiments returned to the Territory, and shortly thereafter the United States Government sent an expedition of 5,000 men under Colonel William Weer to drive them out. Weer's troops out-fought the Confederate Indians at Locust Grove on July 2, 1862, and on the sixteenth captured Tahlequah, the Cherokee capital, following it up with the capture of Fort Gibson. The Confederate Indians now being driven south of the Arkansas River, the Union Indians were organized into three regiments, making up a brigade under Colonel William A. Phillips, which took part in a number of minor engagements.

The Confederate Indians were subjected to many hardships during the war, suffering frequently from the raids of marauding Jayhawkers and bands of hostile pro-Union Indians. Yet, for the most part, they steadfastly maintained their loyalty to the Southern cause. A wing of the

Cherokee tribe held a meeting in 1863 and repudiated their treaty of 1861 with Albert Pike, but Stand Watie remained tenaciously loyal to the Confederacy and kept his little army of redskin Rebels intact. Throughout 1864 he was constantly active, although forced back into the Choctaw country in the southern part of the Territory. When the plight of the Confederacy, and of the Cherokees, grew increasingly desperate, he never lost heart. Even after Lee and Johnston had surrendered in 1865 he stubbornly fought on. When Kirby Smith finally surrendered the whole Trans-Mississippi Department on May 26, 1865, Stand Watie still did not give up. It was June 23 before he finally agreed upon a cessation of hostilities, his being the last organized Confederate military force to surrender.

[40]*Battles and Leaders*, I, 277.

[41]Johnston, *Life of General Albert Sidney Johnston*, p. 299.

[42]General Nelson was killed in Louisville in 1862 by General Jefferson C. Davis of the Federal Army as the result of a private quarrel growing out of what Davis considered Nelson's insulting manner. Davis was never prosecuted for the murder.

[43]John G. Nicolay, *The Outbreak of Rebellion*, p. 131.

[44]Nashville *Union and American*, August 29, 1861.

[45]*Ibid.*, September 13, 1861.

[46]O. R., III, 612-18.

[47]Nashville *Patriot*, September 9, 1861.

[48]The Board was composed of Andrew Ewing, John Marshall, William K. Bowling and Edward S. Cheatham.

[49]Nashville *Patriot*, September 12, 1861.

[50]Polk, *Leonidas Polk, Bishop and General*, II, 21.

[51]James D. Richardson (Ed.), *Messages and Papers of the Confederacy*, p. 137.

[52]The *Franklin Yeoman*, September 9, 1861.

CHAPTER II

[1]Memphis *Appeal*, April 14, 1861.

[2]In this crisis Tennessee lived up to her old sobriquet of the "Volunteer State." By the middle of June, 24 regiments of infantry had been organized and were in the field, along with cavalry, artillery and engineers in lesser numbers. She furnished to the Confederate Army during the war a total of just over 136,000 troops—more than was supplied by any other Confederate state. She sent also about 31,000 soldiers to the Union armies, making a grand total of 167,000 Tennesseans taking part in the war on both sides. Another interesting statistical fact is that a total of 454 battles and skirmishes were fought on Tennessee soil during the course of the war—a record exceeded only by Virginia.

[3]Gideon J. Pillow and Samuel R. Anderson were given commissions as major generals; Felix K. Zollicoffer, B. F. Cheatham, Robert C. Foster, John L. T. Snead and W. R. Caswell were made brigadier generals, and Daniel S. Donelson, adjutant general.

[4]The board consisted of Neill S. Brown (a former governor), James E. Bailey and William G. Harding.

[5]Memphis *Appeal*, July 7, 1861.

[6]Johnston, *Life of General Albert Sidney Johnston*, p. 321.

[7]"General Polk was well aware that he had been assigned to the most important military post in the Confederacy. He felt sure that the Southern States could withstand any force that might be brought against them from other directions; but he knew that their strength would be taxed to the utmost if the invading forces should advance from the Northwest by way of the Mississippi. That the invasion would ultimately, if not immediately, be made on that line he was fully persuaded, because, as the event proved, it was the line which good military judgment would select, and also because the people of the Northwest were already crying out against the closing of the Mississippi, which obstructed their commerce and depressed their industries, as well as offended their pride. He was not insensible to the honor which had been done him by the government in assigning him to the command of that department; but, while he appreciated the confidence reposed in his judgment and capacity, he would have preferred that the Department of the Mississippi should be committed to General Albert Sidney Johnston or to General Lee."—Polk, *Leonidas Polk, Bishop and General*, II, 2.

[8]Strangely enough, lack of military training was not at that time regarded by the general run of Southern people as a shortcoming, but rather as something of which to be proud. There was a vague sort of blind faith in the mysteriously and inherently superior merits of the volunteer soldiers—officers as well as privates—and West Point graduates were in particularly ill repute in the popular mind. When it was proposed to send General Henry Heth to Arkansas early in the war, the suggestion was opposed on the sole ground that Heth was "a West Pointer." The laughable extreme to which this prejudice was carried is shown by the indignation with which the dastardly slander was refuted when it was reported that General Sterling Price was a West Point graduate. "A correspondent of the New Orleans *Crescent*," said the Memphis *Appeal* on January 3, 1862, "noticing that General Price is set down by some of the papers as a West Pointer, says he owes his success to practical good sense and hard fighting. He never attended a military school in his life—is a *natural soldier*, possessing the unbounded confidence of every Missourian," etc.

[9]Polk, *Leonidas Polk, Bishop and General*, II, 5.

[10]*Ibid.*, p. 17.

[11]*Ibid.*, p. 14.

[12]Johnston, *Life of General Albert Sidney Johnston*, p. 324.

[13]The rank of general was given by the Confederate government in 1861 to five men: Samuel Cooper (who was made adjutant general and automatically headed the list), followed in order of rating by Albert Sidney Johnston, Robert E. Lee, Joseph E. Johnston and P. G. T. Beauregard. Later in the war this high rank was given also to Braxton Bragg and, temporarily, to John B. Hood. Under the Confederate system of Army organization, a full general commanded an army; an army was divided into corps, each of which was commanded by a lieutenant general; major generals commanded divisions and brigadier generals brigades. A somewhat different system prevailed in the Federal Army.

[14]*Jefferson Davis, Constitutionalist*, VIII, 232.

[15]*Ibid.*, p. 232.

[16]General Grant seldom had a good word for the commanders opposing him; for what it is worth, it may be interesting to read his comment on Johnston: "He was a man of high character and ability. His contemporaries at West Point, and officers generally who came to know him later and who remained on our side, expected him to prove the most formidable man to meet that the Confederacy would produce. I once wrote that nothing occurred in his brief command of an army to prove or disprove the high estimate that had been placed upon his military ability; but, after studying the orders and despatches of Johnston, I am compelled to materially modify my views of that officer's qualifications as a soldier. My judgment now is that he was vacillating and undecided in his actions. . . . I do not question the personal courage of General Johnston or his ability. But he did not win the distinction predicted for him by many of his friends. He did prove that as a general he was over-estimated."—Grant, *Personal Memoirs*, pp. 213-214.

[17]Johnston, *Life of General Albert Sidney Johnston*, p. 186.

[18]*Ibid.*, p. 267. Fitz-John Porter says that early in April, after a conference with Secretary Cameron in Washington, he sent a message to Johnston in California, by telegraph to St. Louis and thence by pony express, reading: "I take the greatest pleasure in assuring you, for the Secretary of War, that he has the utmost confidence in you and will give you the most important command and trust on your arrival here." Johnston replied, thanking him, but saying: "I have resigned, and am resolved to follow the fortunes of my state."—*Battles and Leaders*, II, 541.

[19]*Memphis Appeal*, September 4, 1861.

CHAPTER III

[1]Zollicoffer formally notified Governor Magoffin of Kentucky that, "the safety of Tennessee requiring," he was occupying Cumberland Gap

and the adjacent mountains, but he was careful to say that "Tennessee feels and has ever felt towards Kentucky as a twin sister; their people are as one people in kindred sympathy, valor and patriotism; we have felt and still feel a religious respect for Kentucky's neutrality. We will respect it as long as our safety will permit. If the Federal forces will now withdraw from their menacing position, the force under my command shall be immediately withdrawn."

[2]Buckner had previously been offered a commission in the United States Army by General Scott; also President Lincoln on August 17 had ordered Secretary Cameron to issue a brigadier general's commission for him. Many men at the outbreak of the war were confronted with the problem of deciding between loyalty to the North or South, but few decided for less selfish considerations than Buckner. His material interests would have been vastly better served had he accepted either of the two commissions offered him in the Union Army, as all his property lay in Kentucky and in the North. Going with the South, he had nothing to expect, in case of a Northern victory, but impoverishment. Following his decision he was persecuted in every conceivable way. He was vilified in the press, led by the serpent-tongued George D. Prentice who even gloated over his plight when he was locked in prison. His property in Louisville was confiscated. And (what is unusual in military annals) he was sued for $62,000 by the Louisville & Nashville Railroad, and a judgment obtained against him in the Louisville courts, for damages he had done to the railroad property while acting as an officer in the Confederate Army.—Arndt M. Stickles, *Simon Bolivar Buckner*, p. 86.

[3]Buckner, announcing his resignation as head of the Kentucky state militia, appealed to the people of Kentucky, in a proclamation on September 12, to "join with me in expelling from our firesides the armies which an insane despotism sends amongst us to subjugate us to the iron rule of puritanical New England." When he occupied Bowling Green at the head of the Confederate troops less than a week later, he issued another proclamation in the course of which he said: "I return among you, citizens of Kentucky, at the head of a force, the advance of which is composed entirely of Kentuckians," and assured them that "the Confederate States occupy Bowling Green as a defensive position."

[4]Breckinridge went to Richmond, where President Davis gladly welcomed him, made him a brigadier general and sent him to General Johnston, who assigned him to the command of the Kentucky Brigade in his army. Later by the demonstration of his native merit he rose to the rank of a corps commander, and during the last days of the Confederacy he served in the Cabinet as the last Secretary of War.

[5]Johnston, *Life of General Albert Sidney Johnston*, p. 306.

[6]*Ibid.*, p. 306.

[7]Memphis *Appeal*, September 12, 1861.

[8]Memphis *Appeal*, dispatch from Columbus, September 22, 1861.

[9]Johnston, *Life of General Albert Sidney Johnston*, p. 328.

[10]*Ibid.*, p. 314.

[11]*Battles and Leaders*, I, 542.

[12]O. R., I:4, 596.

[13]Johnston, *Life of General Albert Sidney Johnston*, p. 329.

[14]*Ibid.*, p. 334.

[15]*Ibid.*, p. 342.

[16]Edward A. Pollard, *Southern History of the War*, I, 210.

[17]Johnston, *Life of General Albert Sidney Johnston*, p. 346.

[18]Colonel Liddell has left an interesting, detailed account of this fruitless mission in an article, "Liddell's Record of the Civil War," in *The Southern Bivouac*, I, 417.

[19]Colonel Liddell says of the conditions in Johnston's army at this time: "The waste of life from lack of proper care and means was frightful; and this, too, at a time when the services of every man were required in support of the cause. I think at one time there could have been hardly less than 16,000 sick and absent out of a total of less than 40,000 men." He places the number of deaths from disease at 3,000.—*Ibid.*

[20]Morgan was already beginning to show evidences of that dashing daring which distinguished him later in the war. While attached to the forces at Bowling Green he took thirteen of his daredevils and rode all around Buell's command, returning with thirty-three prisoners—but there was no John Esten Cooke with the Western Army, and the episode went unnoticed and uncelebrated.

[21]Memphis *Appeal*, September 25, 1861.

[22]Sherman's *Memoirs*, p. 228.

CHAPTER IV

[1]Grant, *Personal Memoirs*, p. 151.

[2]*Ibid.*, p. 161.

[3]*Ibid.*, p. 163.

[4]This gun, one of four from England which had recently run the blockade into Charleston, was the pride of the Confederate camp, and was called the "Lady Polk" in compliment to the commanding general's wife. The day after the battle it exploded, killing eleven men and severely injuring General Polk himself.

[5]"While on the truce-boat [after the battle] I mentioned to an officer, whom I had known both at West Point and in the Mexican War, that I was in the corn-field near their troops when they passed; that I had been on horseback and had worn a soldier's overcoat at the time. This officer was on General Polk's staff. He said both he and the general had seen me and that Polk had said to his men: 'There is a Yankee; you may try your

marksmanship on him if you wish'; but nobody fired at me.

"The corn-field in front of our transports terminated at the edge of a dense forest. Before I got back the enemy had entered this forest and had opened a brisk fire upon the boats. Our men, with the exception of details that had gone to the front after the wounded, were now either aboard the transports or very near them. Those who were not aboard soon got there, and the boats pushed off. I was the only man of the National army between the rebels and our transports. The captain of a boat that had just pushed out, but had not started, recognized me, and ordered the engineer not to start the engine; he then had a plank run out for me. My horse seemed to take in the situation. There was no path down the bank, and everyone acquainted with the Mississippi River knows that its banks, in a natural state, do not vary at any great angle from the perpendicular. My horse put his fore feet over the bank without hesitation or urging and, with his hind feet well under him, slid down the bank, and trotted aboard the boat, twelve or fifteen feet away, over a single gang-plank."—Grant, *Personal Memoirs*, pp. 165-166.

[6]*Letters of Ulysses S. Grant*, p. 66.

[7]Grant, *Personal Memoirs*, p. 167.

[8]Johnston, *Life of General Albert Sidney Johnston*, p. 377.

[9]Nashville *Union and American*, September 19, 1861.

[10]General Marshall came of a distinguished family, being a grandson of Chief Justice John Marshall's cousin. He was a graduate of West Point and a veteran of the Mexican War, and was expected to play a prominent part in Confederate military activities—a hope which was never realized. He seemed always just on the verge of doing something which he never did. Meanwhile he occupied his own time and that of his associate and superior officers by writing extremely long and tedious letters of criticism and petulant complaint. Colonel William Preston Johnston's description of him is a masterpiece of damnation by faint praise. "He was a very vigorous and able lawyer, a shrewd politician and a man of wit, humor, acumen and judgment. . . . But he was not a man of action. Besides, his unwieldy size, weighing as he did some 300 or 350 pounds, unfitted him for the field." After other ineffective efforts as a commander, Marshall finally resigned his commission and became a member of the Confederate Congress.

[11]George B. Crittenden was a graduate of West Point and had been a lieutenant colonel in the old army. He was a native of Kentucky, a son of United States Senator John J. Crittenden and a brother of General Thomas L. Crittenden of the Union Army.

[12]Zollicoffer was the first Confederate general officer killed in the West. His death stirred the nation, the exultation of the North being exceeded only by the grief that swept the South. An extreme example of the Northern feeling is furnished by a war correspondent, who in the

Cincinnati *Commercial* of January 20 told gloatingly of seeing the dead Rebel's body: "He lay by the side of the road along which we all passed, and all had a fair view of what was once Zollicoffer. I saw the lifeless body as it lay in a fence-corner by the side of the road, but Zollicoffer himself is now in hell. Hell is a fitting abode for all such arch-traitors. May all the other chief conspirators in this rebellion soon share Zollicoffer's fate— shot dead through the instrumentality of an avenging God—their spirits sent straightway to hell and their lifeless bodies lie in a fence corner, their faces spattered with mud, and their garments divided up, and even the hair of their head cut off and pulled out by an unsympathizing soldiery of a conquering army." It should be added that General Thomas did not share this non-combatant's savage vindictiveness, but rescued the body from the indignities of the "unsympathizing soldiery," had it decently prepared for burial and sent it through the lines to Zollicoffer's family in Nashville.

On the other side of the picture, a fugitive newspaper poet of the South, Harry Flash, composed an elegy which was regarded as a minor classic in Southern homes for many years:

ZOLLICOFFER
by Harry Flash

First in the fight, and first in the arms
   Of the white-winged angel of glory,
With the heart of the South at the feet of God
   And his wounds to tell the story.

For the blood that flowed from his hero heart
   On the spot where he nobly perished
Was drunk by the earth as a sacrament
   In the holy cause he cherished.

In heaven a home with the brave and blest,
   And for his soul's sustaining
The apocalyptic smile of Christ—
   And nothing on earth remaining

But a handful of dust in the land of his choice
   And a name in song and story—
And Fame to shout with her brazen voice:
   "He died on the field of glory."

[13]Nashville *Gazette*, January 26, 1862.
[14]Memphis *Appeal*, February 5, 1862.

CHAPTER V

[1]*Jefferson Davis, Constitutionalist*, V, 179.

[2]Early in the following January the Cincinnati *Gazette*, commenting impatiently on the lack of progress made by the Federal forces in Kentucky, said: "Three months have elapsed. What has been done? Gen. Anderson was ill—and his nerves so shattered that he felt obliged to relinquish the command. Gen. Sherman, it is said, became crazy, but his friends deny it. It possibly will be well for Gen. S.'s reputation to avail himself of that excuse, for I am persuaded, and the country too, that if he had done his utmost he could hardly have done worse toward producing a disastrous result to the campaign in this state. Gen. Buell has scarcely had a full time for trial, but his probation can't last much longer."

[3]Jones, *A Rebel War Clerk's Diary*, I, 106.

[4]Roman, *The Military Operations of General Beauregard*, I, 212.

[5]Pryor, eager to persuade Beauregard, may have exceeded his authority in making these promises; it is hard to believe that he would have deliberately misled Beauregard. It developed, however, that his assurances were worth nothing. Johnston did not have 70,000 men or anywhere close to it, and he was not adequately reinforced as promised. Beauregard was never able to get the staff officers he wanted, nor was he ever restored to the command of his army in Virginia. To the day of his death he was consumed with the rankling conviction that he had been tricked into going to Tennessee as a means of shelving him.

[6]Johnston had 14,000 men at Bowling Green, 5,500 at Forts Henry and Donelson, 8,000 in Clarksville and its vicinity, and about 17,000 at Columbus under General Polk. General Halleck at St. Louis had at his command a total force of close to 125,000—about 75,000 under Buell in Johnston's immediate front, 20,000 under Grant at Cairo and 30,000 under Pope in Missouri.

[7]Roman, *The Military Operations of General Beauregard*, I, 214.

[8]*Ibid.*, pp. 215-16.

[9]The New York *Herald*, early in the fall of 1861, ran an editorial calling attention to the Cumberland as an inviting means of invading the South; and the Richmond *Enquirer* on October 23, 1861, in an editorial about the Tennessee and Cumberland Rivers, urged that "these routes should be strongly and vigilantly guarded."

[10]As early as May 17, 1861, F. G. Norman, president of the Military Commission of Alabama, wrote to Secretary of War L. P. Walker pointing out that the Tennessee River led directly from the Ohio into Alabama and suggesting its effective defense. (O. R., X, 1017.)

[11]*Thirteen Months in the Rebel Army*, by an Impressed New Yorker, p. 83.

[12]Bromfield L. Ridley, *Battles and Sketches of the Army of Tennessee*, p. 65.

[13]O. R., IV, 453.

[14]*Battles and Leaders*, I, 368.

[15]Johnston, *Life of General Albert Sidney Johnston*, p. 491.

[16]W. D. Pickett, *Sketch of the Military Career of William J. Hardee*, p. 6.

[17]Johnston, *Life of General Albert Sidney Johnston*, p. 6.

CHAPTER VI

[1]Johnston, *Life of General Albert Sidney Johnston*, p. 425.

[2]*Battles and Leaders*, I, 170.

[3]The *Essex* carried four guns; the *Tyler*, *Conestoga* and *Lexington* nine guns each; and the *Cincinnati*, *Carondelet* and *St. Louis* thirteen guns each.

[4]O. R., VII, 861.

[5]Grant in his *Memoirs* is brutally frank in his criticism of Johnston's handling of the Fort Donelson crisis. "Johnston made a fatal mistake in entrusting so important a command to Floyd, who he must have known was no soldier even if he possessed the elements of one. Pillow's presence as second was also a mistake. If these officers had been forced upon him and designated for that particular command, then he should have left Nashville with a small garrison under a trusty officer, and with the remainder of his force gone to Donelson himself. If he had been captured, the result could not have been worse than it was."—p. 192.

[6]Grant, *Personal Memoirs*, p. 173.

[7]General Smith was regarded as one of the most competent officers in the United States Army at the outbreak of the war. He had been commandant at West Point when Grant was a cadet there, and had served with distinction in the Mexican War. Although now subordinate to his former pupil, he served faithfully and efficiently, without murmuring.

[8]*Southern Historical Society Papers*, XIII, 165.

[9]Admiral Henry Walke, commander of the *Carondelet*, has left a graphic and interesting account of the effect of this hit: "A 128-pound solid shot at 11:30 struck the corner of our port broadside casemate, passed through it, and in its progress toward the center of our boilers glanced over the temporary barricade in front of the boilers. It then passed through the steam-drum, struck the beams of the upper deck, carried away the railing around the engine room and burst the steam-heater, and glancing back into the engine room, 'seemed to bound after the men,' as one of the engineers said, 'like a wild beast pursuing its prey.' I have preserved this ball as a souvenir of the fight at Fort Donelson. When it burst through the side of the Carondelet, it knocked down and wounded a

dozen men, seven of them severely. An immense quantity of splinters was blown through the vessel. Some of them, as fine as needles, shot through the clothes of the men like arrows. Some of the wounded were so much excited by the suddenness of the event and the sufferings of their comrades, that they were not aware that they themselves had been struck until they felt the blood running into their shoes. Upon receiving this shot we ceased firing for a while."

[10]Major Kelley, although of the clergy, had a fiery temper, and followers of Forrest said the high-tempered preacher was the only man he was afraid of. On one occasion, they tell, Major Kelley was changing the position of his men during a battle, when Forrest came upon him and demanded to know why he was running away. Thereupon Kelley whipped out his Colt and demanded, and received, an apology—and Forrest was not addicted to apologies.

[11]John Wyeth, Life of Gen. Nathan Bedford Forrest, p. 47.

[12]O. R., CX, 274-A.

[13]For some reason, the official reports of both Floyd and Pillow omit reference to this proposed sally. It is described fully, however, in the reports of Buckner, Forrest and other subordinate officers.

[14]The butternut-colored clothing of the Confederates provided them unconsciously and unintentionally with a crude sort of camouflage. Colonel Oglesby in his report tells how the Rebels "skulked behind every hiding place, and sought refuge in the oak leaves, between which and their uniforms there was so strong a resemblance our men were continually deceived by them."

[15]Grant's absence from the battlefield at this critical time remains something of a mystery, which has never been entirely cleared up. Grant himself explains by saying that "on the morning of the 15th, before it was yet broad day, a messenger from Flag Officer Foote handed me a note expressing a desire to see me on the flag-ship." He says further that "I had no idea that there would be any engagement on land unless I brought it on myself," so he proceeded to visit Foote on the St. Louis—after first instructing his division commanders to make no move without further orders from him. Pillow's attack on McClernand opened at five o'clock in the morning, and it seems strange that Grant, even if he were already on his way to Foote's flagship at that unlikely hour, did not hear the sound of the firing and retrace his way. Just why his conference with Foote should have occupied so many hours has never been revealed. It is almost incomprehensible that the commander of an army in the very midst of an important, major operation, would stay away from the field. That he would remain within sound of the firing for several hours and do nothing about it is as hard to understand. Grant's friendly biographer, Badeau, says he was back at his headquarters by 9 A.M.; but this is not borne out. The truth is that Grant did not arrive on the scene until

3 P.M., when McClernand and Wallace had been thoroughly whipped and Pillow had ordered his men back to the lines.

[16]*Battles and Leaders*, I, 420.

[17]Oddly enough, Grant in his official report stresses the unusually plentiful supply of food captured, but it may have come in on the steamboat that morning.

[18]Wyeth, *Life of Gen. Nathan Bedford Forrest*, p. 58.

[19]After Virginia seceded and Floyd went with his state, he was indicted in Washington for an alleged malfeasance while Secretary of War under President Buchanan, although he had been exonerated by a Congressional investigating committee.

[20]This account of the surrender is constructed from the official reports of those who took part in the final council.

[21]*Jefferson Davis, Constitutionalist*, VIII, 485.

[22]When Forrest took his men out by the road across Lick Creek, his progress was entirely undisputed by the enemy. Not a shot was fired, and the only difficulty encountered was the water, which for a distance of a hundred yards covered the road to a depth reaching to the saddle girths. Forrest himself looked into the supposed campfires which had carried so much weight in convincing Floyd that the roads were held by the enemy, and found that they were old campfires which had been started up again by wounded soldiers who had dragged themselves up for warmth.

[23]Stickles, *Simon Bolivar Buckner*, p. 168.

[24]Grant, *Personal Memoirs*, p. 184.

[25]John R. Porter, "A Blue and Gray Friendship," *Century Magazine*, April, 1897, p. 944.

[26]*Nashville Banner*, December 11, 1909.

[27]Basil W. Duke, *Reminiscences of General Basil W. Duke*, p. 346.

CHAPTER VII

[1]O. R., VII, 863.

[2]Johnston, *Life of General Albert Sidney Johnston*, p. 495.

[3]Basil W. Duke, *Morgan's Cavalry*, p. 113.

[4]Johnston, *Life of General Albert Sidney Johnston*, p. 496.

[5]Johnston's orders to Floyd were brief but clear: "I give you command of the city. You will remove the stores. My only restriction is: Do not fight a battle in the city."

[6]This was Nelson's division of Buell's army, which had been sent to reinforce Grant at Fort Donelson. When they arrived after the surrender, Grant sent them on up the river to Nashville.

[7]The flag first hoisted over the state capitol at Nashville was the regimental colors of the 6th Ohio regiment. It was later replaced, however, by the original "Old Glory" flag, the one to which this now familiar nick-

name was first given. It was the property of Captain William Driver, a resident of Nashville in 1862 and a strong Union man. He had come from New England, where he had been a ship captain in his earlier days, and he brought with him an American flag to which he had given the name "Old Glory" when in 1831 it was presented to him for use on his ship, the *Charles Daggett*. Retired from the sea and removed to Nashville, he laid his old flag away in a chest, where it remained hidden from Confederate eyes during the early days of the war. When Nashville was occupied by the Union troops, however, Captain Driver brought out his precious "Old Glory" and had the satisfaction of seeing it raised above the Tennessee capitol—the first statehouse in the South to be returned to the Stars and Stripes.

[8]January 18, 1862.

[9]*The Southern Bivouac*, I, 530.

[10]E. M. Bruce of Kentucky.

[11]Johnston, *Life of General Albert Sidney Johnston*, p. 512.

[12]*Ibid.*, p. 497.

[13]*Ibid.*, p. 551.

[14]*Ibid.*, p. 520.

[15]*Battles and Leaders*, II, 550.

[16]Johnston, *Life of General Albert Sidney Johnston*, p. 521.

[17]*Jefferson Davis, Constitutionalist*, p. 214.

[18]*O. R.*, VII, 213.

[19]*O. R.*, VII, 889.

[20]Beauregard makes much of the fact that Johnston had considered falling back to Stevenson, Alabama. Stevenson was the junction point of the Memphis & Charleston and the Nashville & Chattanooga Railroads, and Johnston could have transported his men there and then to Corinth by rail. A movement to Stevenson was not necessarily inconsistent with a concentration at Corinth.

[21]Johnston, *Life of General Albert Sidney Johnston*, p. 488.

[22]*Ibid.*, p. 503.

[23]*The Southern Bivouac*, I, 417.

[24]*Jefferson Davis, Constitutionalist*, IX, 570.

[25]At Burnsville the army received from the War Department at Richmond a shipment of Enfield rifles, which had just run the blockade from England. The Tennessee troops here laid aside their flintlocks, each man receiving one of the new rifles and 200 rounds of Enfield ammunition.

[26]Alfred Roman, *The Military Operations of General Beauregard*, I, 233.

[27]Beauregard's health was and had been extremely bad for several months. Before leaving Virginia he had had a serious operation on his throat from which he had not recovered when he came to Tennessee. He caught cold in Bowling Green and was confined to his bed several days

before the retreat from that point. His debility continuing, he was eventually forced to retire temporarily from active service.

[28]The command of the rivers and the possession of an ample supply of gunboats and transports gave to the Federal armies in the West a peculiarly valuable advantage. Troops in transports could be moved with a celerity which could not be matched by marching men, and the vigilance of the defending forces was sorely taxed.

[29]Capt. William P. Snow, *Lee and His Generals*, p. 250.

[30]*The Southern Bivouac*, II, 529.

[31]*Battles and Leaders*, III, 605.

[32]Grant, *Personal Memoirs*, p. 388.

[33]*Ibid.*

[34]Irving A. Buck, *Cleburne and His Command*, p. 209.

[35]Polk, *Leonidas Polk, Bishop and General*, II, 287.

[36]O. R., VIII, 12.

[37]Grant, *Personal Memoirs*, p. 194.

[38]O. R., VII, 22.

[39]W. T. Sherman, *Personal Memoirs*, I, 228.

[40]O. R., VIII, 27.

[41]Smith's division was now commanded by General W. H. L. Wallace. Smith was confined to his bed at Savannah, suffering from an infection from a shin skinned while he was getting into a skiff at Fort Henry. It caused his death at Savannah, April 25. When his condition became serious, Grant was relieved of his arrest on March 17 and ordered to Savannah to assume command of the forces there and at Pittsburg Landing.

[42]This division of the army into small corps was to facilitate handling by inexperienced commanders; also to give the enemy a false impression of strength, as ordinarily an army corps would consist of at least 20,000 men. That the latter purpose was accomplished is indicated by Grant's dispatches estimating the Confederate strength at from 80,000 to 100,000.

[43]On March 31 General Hardee, under Bragg's orders, went to Iuka and placed General Crittenden (with one of his brigadiers) under arrest, charged with drunkenness, neglect and incapacity. General Breckinridge was advanced to Crittenden's position.

[44]*Battles and Leaders*, II, 550.

[45]*Ibid.*, p. 578.

[46]Roman, *Military Operations of General Beauregard*, II, 266.

[47]After the war Jefferson Davis wrote: "In my opinion the only mistake of General Johnston in relation to the battle of Shiloh was in not personally making the order of march from Corinth toward Pittsburg Landing, for which his large experience in the movement of troops peculiarly qualified him, instead of entrusting that duty to General Beauregard, his second in command, who had seen comparatively little service with

troops in the field. If in this way, as appears from contemporaneous statements, a day was needlessly lost on the march, it was a mistake with serious consequences."—*Jefferson Davis, Constitutionalist*, IX, 537.

CHAPTER VIII

[1]T. Worthington, *Shiloh: The Only Correct Military History of U. S. Grant*, passim.

[2]Looking back on the event, in the light of all the facts known now and not then, one feels that the Confederate army launched its attack at almost exactly the time when it had least chance to succeed. If it had been made on the fourth or fifth it might have finished off Grant's destruction before Buell's reinforcements could possibly arrive. On the other hand, if it had been delayed a few days longer, especially if it had been delayed until the arrival of Van Dorn's army from Arkansas, it might have come at an even more propitious time. It is now known that Grant had arranged to station Buell's army at Hamburg, separated from Pittsburg Landing by Lick Creek. This fatal policy of separation would have afforded an opportunity for the advancing Confederate army to march directly on Hamburg and with its superior force quickly overcome Buell's isolated force and then move on to the attack of Grant. All this, however, is but another of the "if's" of Shiloh.

[3]*Battles and Leaders*, I, 555.

[4]While the men were drawn up in line of battle, General Johnston's first and last formal address was read at the head of each regiment: "I have put you in motion to offer battle to the invaders of your country. With the resolution, and discipline, and valor becoming men fighting, as you are, for all worth living or dying for, you can but march to a decisive victory over the agrarian mercenaries sent to subjugate and despoil you of your liberties, your property, your honor. Remember the precious stake involved. Remember the dependence of your mothers, your wives, your sisters, and your children on the result. Remember the fair, broad, abounding land, the happy homes that will be desolated by your defeat. The eyes and hopes of eight millions of people rest upon you. You are expected to show yourselves worthy of your lineage, worthy of the women of the South, whose noble devotion in this war has never been exceeded in any time. With such incentive to brave deeds, and with the trust that God is with us, your generals will lead you confidently to the combat, assured of success."—*O. R.*, X:2, 389.

[5]*Battles and Leaders*, I, 557.

[6]*Ibid.*, p. 558.

[7]Roman, *Military Operations of General Beauregard*, I, 282.

[8]*O. R.*, X:1, 330.

[9]*Autobiography of Henry M. Stanley*, pp. 188-189.

[10]Captain Smith was carrying out the instructions in the order of battle: "Field and company officers are especially enjoined to instruct their men, under all circumstances, to fire with deliberation at the feet of the enemy. They will thus avoid over-shooting and, besides, wounded men give more trouble to our adversary than dead, as they have to be taken from the field."—O. R., X:1, 392.

[11]Stanley's career in the Confederate Army was near an end when he made that first charge at Shiloh, as he was taken prisoner early in the second day's fighting. A native of England, he had been shamed into joining a Confederate company when one of the local girls sent him a package containing a petticoat—a more or less gentle hint that his place was in the army. Stanley says in his Autobiography: "I loved the South because I loved my Southern friends and had absorbed their spirit into every pore." He had no taste for soldiering, however, and even less for prison life, as he discovered when he was captured and hurried off to Camp Douglas at Chicago. Here the horrid squalor and privation soon undermined his health and weakened his vicarious loyalty to the South. Within a few weeks he succumbed to the wiles of the prison commander, took the oath of allegiance to the United States, enlisted in a Federal artillery regiment and was assigned to duty at Harper's Ferry. Here his health continued bad and he was soon discharged from the service. He drifted to New York and to the newspaper work which eventually led to his fame.

[12]That Johnston's reckless exposure of himself to danger may have been a reaction from the criticism to which he had been subjected is suggested by one participant in the battle, then serving on Breckinridge's staff, who reports hearing Johnston say to Breckinridge: "I will lead your brigade into the fight to-day; for I intend to show these Tennesseans and Kentuckians that I am no coward."—Thirteen Months in the Rebel Army, p. 151.

[13]Three days after the battle, when the army had returned to Corinth, Beauregard made official announcement of Johnston's death in a formal address: "Soldiers—Your late Commander-in-chief, A. S. Johnston, is dead. A fearless soldier, a sagacious captain, a reproachless man has fallen. One who in his devotion to our cause shrunk from no sacrifice; one who, animated by a sense of duty and sustained by a sublime courage, challenged danger and perished gallantly for his country while leading forward his brave columns to victory. His signal example of heroism and patriotism, if generally imitated, will make this army invincible. A grateful country will mourn his loss, revere his name, and cherish his many virtues."— O. R., X:2, 408.

[14]That General Beauregard was hors du combat in his ambulance when advised of Johnston's death is one of the most persistent popular beliefs in the South. The misunderstanding seems to have grown out of the fact that, in his advance from Corinth, he had lost track of his tent,

and on the night of the fifth, for want of a better place to rest his head, had slept in the bed in his ambulance. It is entirely probable that Beauregard may have told Johnston that if he wanted him during that night he would find him there. Governor Harris, however, said afterward that Beauregard made this statement to Johnston on the morning of the sixth. Colonel W. P. Johnston repeated it in his biography of his father, and Jefferson Davis gave it further publicity: "General Beauregard told General Johnston that morning as he rode off that if it should be necessary to communicate with him or for him to do anything he would be found in his ambulance in bed."—*Rise and Fall of the Confederate Government,* p. 67. After the publication of President Davis' book Beauregard in enraged indignation wrote a detailed, circumstantial account of his movements that day, which, checked with the recorded observations, seems to be undoubtedly true: "I had ridden with General Johnston from Monterey, on the preceding day (the fifth) to the field. I only slept in my ambulance that night as I had no tent, and did not see it again until my return to Corinth. I was again on horseback shortly after daybreak on the sixth— earlier, for that matter, than General Johnston, whom I found at his headquarters taking his coffee. . . . I was on horseback all that day, with very few intervals, until . . . about sundown, after my return from the front; and I was again on horseback all the next day from about seven o'clock, with few intervals, until my arrival at Corinth late that night."—Roman, *Military Operations of General Beauregard,* p. 349.

[15]Gen. Thos. Jordan and J. P. Pryor, *The Campaigns of Lieut. Gen. N. B. Forrest,* p. 151.

[16]*Rebellion Record,* IV, 413.

[17]O. R., X:1, 333.

[18]The confusion on the battlefield during the day almost defies belief. Like the Orleans Guard (See Note 28), Pond's brigade was mistaken for the enemy and fired upon by its own side. After the capture of the Hornets' Nest the flanking forces closing in from both directions found themselves face to face, perpendicular to the line of battle, and much time was lost in reforming them and facing them in the direction of Grant's new line in the rear. The mortality rate among officers was unusually high, and many companies, even regiments, floundered around aimlessly for lack of leadership.

[19]*Battles and Leaders,* I, 591.

[20]Roman, *Military Operations of General Beauregard,* is now generally regarded by historians as a palpable piece of "ghost-writing," with Roman's name appended to what is actually a none too modest autobiography .

[21]*Ibid.,* I, 305-6.

[22]*Ibid.,* p. 306.

[28]*Battles and Leaders,* I, 602.

[24]Jordan and Pryor, *Campaigns of Lieut. Gen. Forrest*, p. 137.

[25]*Battles and Leaders*, I, 603.

[26]Beauregard was no great admirer of Polk, but commenting on this charge in his report of the battle, he paid the bishop-general a notable tribute: "Dashing forward with drawn sword, at the head of Cheatham's fine division, he soon formed his line of battle at the point where his presence was so much needed and, with unsurpassed vigor, moved on against a force of at least double his own, making one of the most brilliant charges of infantry made on either day of the battle. He drove back the opposing column in confusion."

[27]When Beauregard resigned from the United States Army after Louisiana's secession and returned to New Orleans, he enlisted as a private in the Orleans Guard, and his name was carried on its rolls as long as the battalion remained in service. Even on the field at Shiloh his name was read out at roll-call, the color-sergeant answering: "Absent on duty."

[28]As the Orleans Guard, upon their arrival, moved into position on the Confederate right wing, their blue coats misled the Confederates into greeting them with a volley, which was returned with enthusiasm by the spirited Creoles. Informed by a horrified staff officer that they were firing on their own men, the commander of the Louisiana troops explained with unassailable logic: "I know it; but, damn it, we fire on everybody who fires on us!"

[29]*Battles and Leaders*, I, 603.

[30]Grant, *Personal Memoirs*, p. 209.

[31]Polk, *Leonidas Polk, Bishop and General*, II, 109.

[32]*Thirteen Months in the Rebel Army*, p. 170.

[33]Major D. W. Reed, *The Battle of Shiloh*, p. 23.

[34]O. R., X:1, 398.

[35]*Ibid.*, p. 112.

CHAPTER IX

[1]Roman, *Military Operations of General Beauregard*, I, 358.

[2]Sherman, *Personal Memoirs*, I, 278.

[3]The Federals followed a general policy of naming their armies for the rivers near which they operated; the Confederates named theirs from the states or regions in which they were active. Thus the Federals had an Army of the Tennessee—not to be confused with the Confederate Army of Tennessee.

[4]Pope, when transferred to Virginia a few months later to try his hand against Robert E. Lee, made himself an international laughing-stock by his vainglorious address to his new troops from his "Headquarters in the Saddle," followed so closely by his ignominious rout at Second Manassas.

[5]O. R., VIII, 784-785.

[6]Price in one sortie seized the enemy's telegraph office, and impudently wired his compliments to President Lincoln in Washington.

[7]Major Matthew F. Steele says that Halleck with his 120,000 men "ought to have moved promptly against the Confederate army with a view to capturing or destroying it. In not doing so he violated what von der Goltz considers the first principle of modern warfare: namely that 'the immediate objective' against which all our efforts must be directed is the hostile main army."—*American Campaigns*, I, 321.

[8]Colonel Northrup was the notoriously incompetent chief of the Commissary Department at Richmond, concerning whose administration of this vital arm of the service there was universal complaint throughout the war. Northrup, however, was an old crony of the President's, and Davis' stubborn loyalty to his personal friends kept him in place to the end.

[9]The issue of regular provisions proving unsatisfactory and irregular, Beauregard sent to Texas and Arkansas and bought a large herd of cattle, which were brought to Corinth in time to save the army from starvation. Other supplies, however, were scanty and of poor quality.

[10]"The General" was afterward used by General Bragg to haul ammunition trains to his army in Georgia. It is now on display in the station of the N. C. & St. L. Railroad at Chattanooga.

[11]Roman, *Military Operations of General Beauregard*, I, 578.

[12]*Ibid.*, p. 390.

[13]Characteristic of Beauregard's painstaking attention to detail was his order for the removal of all sign-posts on the roads leading out of Corinth, to bewilder and delay the pursuing army.

[14]The President's attitude toward Beauregard is well shown by a letter he wrote his wife about this time. Speaking of the presence of Federals on the Mississippi River, he said: "If Mississippi troops lying in camp (when not retreating with Beauregard) were at home, they would probably keep a section of the river free for our use and closed against Yankee transports." (*Jefferson Davis, Constitutionalist*, V, 266.) Again on June 21, 1862, commenting to her on McClellan's approach to Richmond, he wrote that after McClellan was defeated "we must make a desperate effort to regain what Beauregard has abandoned in the West." (*Ibid.*, p. 233.)

[15]O. R., X:1, 774.

[16]Upon Bragg's request for a specific designation of his territory, officially known as "Department No. 2," it was defined as covering that part of Louisiana east of the Mississippi, the entire states of Mississippi and Alabama, and the territory of Georgia and Florida west of the Chattahoochee and Apalachicola Rivers.

[17]Governor Pickens of South Carolina had been bombarding Davis with letters insisting on the removal of Pemberton, whom he described as

"confused and uncertain about everything." *Jefferson Davis, Constitutionalist*, V, 275.

[18]Watson, *Life in the Confederate Army*, p. 368.
[19]Samuel R. Watkins, Co. "Aytch"—*First Tennessee Regiment*, p. 40.
[20]Augustus W. Alexander, *Grant as a Soldier*, p. 89.
[21]Roman, *Military Operations of General Beauregard*, I, 593.
[22]*Ibid.*, p. 402.
[23]Forrest's work was officially commended by General Bragg, and on July 21 he received his commission as brigadier general.
[24]It was on this occasion that Forrest stopped at the "Hermitage," Andrew Jackson's old home near Nashville, and relaxed the discipline of cavalry campaigning behind the enemy's lines long enough to permit his men the privilege of an hour's inspection of Old Hickory's home. They encountered a group of young ladies of the neighborhood who were celebrating the anniversary of the battle of Manassas with a picnic on the grounds, and the war-worn cavalrymen enjoyed a pleasant interlude.
[25]Morgan himself captured the railroad station at Gallatin, representing himself to the station agent as a Federal officer looking for Morgan. The station agent, flourishing a large revolver, wished him good luck, breathing fierce maledictions on Morgan. "I wish I could meet the damned guerilla," he said; whereupon Morgan formally introduced himself and disarmed the astonished agent.

CHAPTER X

[1]O. R., XVI:2, 751: "I will make no movement that your judgment does not sanction;" and "I will not only cooperate with you, but will cheerfully place my command under you, subject to your order."—*Ibid.*, p. 734.
[2]O. R., XVI:2, 741.
[3]*Ibid.*, p. 741.
[4]General Morgan had been a classmate of General Kirby Smith at West Point.
[5]Arthur Howard Noll, *General Kirby Smith*, p. 205.
[6]O. R., XVI:2, 748.
[7]*The Annals of the Army of Tennessee*, I, 197.
[8]Cleburne escaped death by a hair's breadth. He was in the act of speaking to Colonel Lucius E. Polk, who was being carried to the rear wounded, when a rifle ball entered his left cheek, carried away his teeth on that side, and emerged through his open mouth. Cleburne's display of his ability at the Richmond fighting was recognized by the Confederate Congress, which passed a formal vote of thanks to him for "gallant and meritorious conduct."
[9]Nashville *Banner*, December 11, 1909.

[10]O. R., XVI:2, 995.

[11]*Ibid.*, p. 995.

[12]*Ibid.*, p. 995.

[13]Andrew Johnson had been made military governor of Tennessee when Nashville was occupied by the Federal troops.

[14]Noll, *General Kirby Smith*, p. 213.

[15]O. R., XVI:2, 822.

[16]Bragg's stern determination to protect the sanctity of property rights was carried to the extreme of a drum-head court martial and execution of a young soldier who had taken a few apples from an orchard outside Glasgow. The soldiers, though used to Bragg's iron rule, were shocked and indignant at the severity of the punishment for such a trivial offense, and the people of Glasgow, including the owner of the orchard, were horrified.—Don C. Seitz, *Braxton Bragg, General of the Confederacy*, p. 174.

[17]At the start of the Kentucky campaign, President Davis had instructed Bragg and Kirby Smith (and similarly General Lee, who was invading Maryland,) to address reassuring proclamations to the people of the invaded states "in accordance with established usage."

[18]*The Southern Bivouac*, IV, 300.

[19]*The Confederate Veteran*, XVII, 55.

[20]*The Southern Bivouac*, I, 167.

[21]Noll, *General Kirby Smith*, p. 216.

[22]O. R., XVI:2, 815.

[23]*The Southern Bivouac*, I, 161.

[24]This was such an obvious possibility that Andrew Johnson in Nashville was highly alarmed and telegraphed President Lincoln that Bragg's invasion of Kentucky was just a ruse to draw Buell out of Tennessee and that Bragg's real objective was Nashville.

[25]When it was found to be impossible for General Bragg to go to Vicksburg to replace General Lovell, General Van Dorn was ordered to that command, embracing the Department of South Mississippi and East Louisiana. Van Dorn turned over the command at Tupelo to General McCown, who held it until June 30, at which time he was superseded by General Sterling Price.

[26]Grant, *Personal Memoirs*, p. 234.

[27]O. R., XVL: 2, 782.

[28]General Van Dorn was shot and killed at his headquarters in the private residence of Mr. Martin Cheairs at Spring Hill under circumstances which were the subject of controversy. His assassin was a resident of the neighborhood, Dr. Peters, who stated in justification of his act that Van Dorn had "violated the sanctity of his home." Van Dorn's friends, on the other hand, indignantly deny there was any such reason. They say Van Dorn was shot in the back, in cold blood, and for political reasons.

[29]O. R., XVI:2, 540.

[30]*Battles and Leaders*, III, 47.

[31]O. R., XVI:2, 363.

[32]*Ibid.*, p. 358.

[33]Noll, *General Kirby Smith*, pp. 218-220.

[34]O. R., XVI:2, 891.

[35]*Ibid*, p. 898.

[36]*Ibid.*, p. 897.

[37]General Gilbert of Buell's army says: "An order more inapplicable to the situation could not very well have been penned."—*The Southern Bivouac*, IV, 340.

[38]O. R., XVI:2, 901.

[39]*Ibid.*, p. 903.

[40]*Ibid.*, p. 904.

[41]*Ibid.*, p. 1095.

[42]Forrest, who later came to be recognized as the greatest cavalry genius of the war, was not with Bragg's army now, when his talents might well have turned the balance. Bragg, who neither liked Forrest personally nor appreciated his ability, had sent him back to Murfreesboro with his staff and four companies, turning over the remainder of his brigade to Colonel Wharton of the Texas Rangers. He instructed Forrest to organize a new battalion at Murfreesboro and harass the Federal force in and around Nashville—but, though he gave this avowed purpose, it was the general opinion at the time that Bragg was really trying to sidetrack him.

[43]O. R., XVI:2, 1096.

[44]*Ibid.*, XVI:1, 1098.

[45]*Battles and Leaders*, III, 27.

[46]Gilbert had 23,000 men; McCook, 12,500; Crittenden, 22,500. Buell states that "the force actually engaged on the Union side was about 22,000, though more came into position for battle near the close.—*Battles and Leaders*, III, 48.

[47]The first Federal reports referred to the engagement as the "Battle of Chaplin Hills."

[48]In his official report General Buell says: "The corps of General Crittenden closed in, and Wagner's brigade of Wood's division, became engaged and did good service on the right of Mitchell's division (of Gilbert's corps); but, knowing nothing of the severity of the fight on the extreme left, the rest of the corps did not get into action."

[49]O. R., XVI:1, 1101.

[50]A conspicuous example of the indomitable bravery of the Federal defense is furnished by the behavior of Colonel Charles Carroll Parsons who commanded a battery of artillery at a point where the attack was fiercest. When nearly all his officers and men had been killed, he continued singlehanded to work one of the guns, and when the Confederate

infantry closed in on him he did not flee but drew his sword, stood at
"parade rest" and awaited the fire of the advancing force. His calm courage so impressed the Confederate colonel, however, that he ordered his
men to withhold their fire, and Colonel Parsons was permitted to walk
off the field. After the war he became a minister of the Episcopal Church,
and was rector of a parish in Memphis, Tennessee, of which Jefferson
Davis was a vestryman. He remained at his post during the yellow fever
epidemic of 1878, was stricken with the disease and died.—Arthur
Howard Noll (Ed.), *Bishop Quintard's Memoirs*, p. 57.

[51]Buell had been painfully injured early in the morning by a fractious
horse and was confined to his headquarters throughout the day.—*The
Southern Bivouac*, IV, 473.

[52]The circumstances surrounding Gooding's capture give a good idea
of the confusion of the battle. Gooding, seeking orders for the placing
of his brigade, rode up to General Polk—mistaking him for McCook—
and said: "I have come to your assistance with my brigade." Polk asked
the name of his command, and upon being told said: "There is some
mistake about this. You are my prisoner."—Polk, *Leonidas Polk, Bishop
and General*, II, 154.

[53]"I was badly whipped," General McCook testified before the Military Commission which investigated Buell's conduct of the battle.

[54]Lieut Col. Arthur Lyon Freemantle, *Three Months in the Southern
States*, pp. 165-166.

[55]Polk, *Leonidas Polk, Bishop and General*, II, 159.

[56]Polk the soldier, did not forget his *alter ego*, Polk the bishop. As
soon as he had placed his corps in position, Bishop Quintard tells in his
Memoirs, Polk went with him to a church in Harrodsburg, and there
Quintard donned his surplice and stole and entered the sanctuary. Polk
knelt at the altar, and as the bishop read the litany and pronounced the
benediction, Polk bowed his head upon the altar and, overcome with emotion, wept.

[57]Noll, *General Kirby Smith*, p. 219.

[58]*The Southern Bivouac*, I, 239.

[59]*Ibid.*, p. 551.

[60]Polk, *Leonidas Polk, Bishop and General*, II, 156.

[61]Seitz, *Braxton Bragg, General of the Confederacy*, p. 207.

[62]The failure to send Breckinridge's force to Bragg at the outset of the
campaign appears a grave error of judgment. Breckinridge's men, if they
had been joined to Bragg's force in Kentucky, might well have constituted
the needed balance of power. His personal popularity and prominence in
Kentucky would almost certainly have added to the Confederate prestige
and stimulated recruiting. Furthermore, Breckinridge's force investing
Nashville was not strong enough really to menace the strongly fortified

city—and Nashville would have fallen automatically into Confederate possession if Bragg had been able to deal Buell a decisive defeat in Kentucky.

[62]O. R., XVI:2, 999.

CHAPTER XI

[1]Polk, Leonidas Polk, Bishop and General, II, 158.

[2]Noll, General Kirby Smith, p. 223.

[3]Ibid., p. 225.

[4]O. R., LII:2, 382.

[5]Battles and Leaders, III, 474.

[6]Seitz, Braxton Bragg, General of the Confederacy, p. 255.

[7]Polk, Leonidas Polk, Bishop and General, II, 168.

[8]John Witherspoon DuBose, General Joseph Wheeler and the Army of Tennessee, p. 138.

[9]Rosecrans, Campaign with the Fourteenth Army Corps by "W.B.D.," p. 120.

[10]Thomas had been the first lieutenant in Bragg's battery of artillery in the regular U. S. Army, and Bragg had the greatest respect and admiration for his former lieutenant, to whom he referred affectionately as "Old Tom."

[11]DuBose, General Joseph Wheeler, p. 120.

[12]Ibid., p. 141.

[13]Battles and Leaders, III, 614.

[14]Ibid., p. 606.

[15]Bragg in his official report of the battle says: "A hot and inviting breakfast of coffee and other luxuries, to which our gallant and hardy men had long been strangers, was found upon the fire unserved, and was left while we pushed on to the enjoyment of a more inviting feast, that of captured artillery, fleeing battalions and hosts of craven prisoners."

[16]A. F. Stevenson, The Battle of Stone's River, p. 44.

[17]Battles and Leaders, III, 628.

[18]Stevenson, The Battle of Stone's River, p. 113.

[19]O. R., LII:2, 402.

[20]Stevenson, The Battle of Stone's River, p. 120.

[21]Battles and Leaders, III, 634.

[22]Stevenson, The Battle of Stone's River, p. 131.

[23]Polk, Leonidas Polk, Bishop and General, II, 186.

[24]Stevenson, The Battle of Stone's River, p. 132.

[25]Polk, Leonidas Polk, Bishop and General, II, 188.

[26]O. R., XX:1, 682.

[27]Bragg's delusion as to the reinforcements might possibly be explained by a passage from The Battle of Stone's River: "In order to deceive Gen-

eral Bragg, he [Rosecrans] organized a large number of men endowed with stentorian voices who were to represent the officers of companies, regiments and brigades, composing a division. As soon as these men were properly stationed, a loud voice could be heard calling out 'Fourteenth Division, Halt!' Immediately afterwards other voices could be heard commanding brigades and regiments to halt, followed by a number of company commands. A few minutes intervened and again these loud voices could be heard in the stillness of the night giving the necessary orders by which the imaginary regiments were to take their respective camping-grounds and companies to stack arms and break ranks. A short time after this had taken place General Rosecrans ordered the men to build camp-fires in front of these supposititious new reinforcements."— Stevenson, p. 144.

[28]In spite of the fact that they retreated, the Confederates classified Murfreesboro as a victory. In a speech in Richmond on the night of January 5, President Davis, after referring to Lee's bloody repulse of Burnside at Fredericksburg, said: "In the West, too, at Murfreesboro, you have gained a victory over hosts vastly superior to our own in numbers. You have achieved a result there as important, as brilliant as that which occurred on the soil of Virginia."—Richmond *Enquirer*, January 7, 1863.

CHAPTER XII

[1]Roman, *The Military Operations of General Beauregard*, II, 2.
[2]Grant, *Personal Memoirs*, p. 253.
[3]*Battles and Leaders*, III, 467.
[4]*Ibid.*, p. 468.
[5]After Grant abandoned his overland advance on Vicksburg in November, 1862, he conceived the idea of taking the city in the rear by sending a fleet of gunboats and transports through the Mississippi bottoms from the Mississippi River into Moon Lake, by way of Yazoo Pass, thence into the Tallahatchie River and down the Tallahatchie and the Yazoo to the rear of Vicksburg. The levee was cut at Yazoo Pass and the gunboats and transports passed into Moon Lake and on into the bayous leading into the Tallahatchie. The Confederates had obstructed the bayous with felled trees, but the Federals cleared them rapidly away. The gunboats and transports were stopped, however, when they got into the Tallahatchie, for here near Fort Pemberton (just above Greenwood) they had sunk the famous steamer, the *Star of the West*, swung squarely across the channel of the river.
[6]Grant, *Personal Memoirs*, p. 299; also *Battles and Leaders*, III, 545.
[7]Joseph E. Johnston, *Narrative of Military Operations*, p. 181.
[8]*Battles and Leaders*, III, 486.

[9]*Ibid.*, p. 487.

[10]O. R., XXIV:3, 892.

[11]Johnston, *Narrative of Military Operations*, p. 203.

[12]O. R., XXIV:4, 982.

[13]*Battles and Leaders*, III, 492.

[14]Among the unique casualties of the Vicksburg siege was the camel, called "Old Douglas," which belonged to Colonel William M. Moore of the 43rd Mississippi Regiment. The camel was officially assigned to the regimental band, and carried all their instruments and knapsacks. The soldiers soon grew used to the sight of Old Douglas plodding along in the wake of Colonel Moore's outfit, which came to be known as the "camel regiment." But the horses and mules of the wagon train were not so easily accustomed to the alien beast, and stampedes were not infrequent. Old Douglas was killed by a stray bullet during the Vicksburg siege, and was given a formal and affectionate burial by the men of the 43rd Mississippi.—*The Confederate Veteran*, XI, 494.

[15]*Jefferson Davis, Constitutionalist*, V, 574.

[16]*Ibid.*, p. 579.

CHAPTER XIII

[1]O. R., XX:1, 699.

[2]*Ibid.*, p. 684.

[3]*Ibid.*, p. 683.

[4]*Ibid.*, p. 684.

[5]Breckinridge enjoyed, probably more than any of the other officers, this opportunity to express his views frankly for the record. Bragg's official report of the Battle of Murfreesboro commented on the conduct of Breckinridge and his division in terms which his soldiers considered unbearably disparaging. Their indignation had been so great they had urged Breckinridge to challenge Bragg to a duel.

[6]O. R., XX:1, 682.

[7]*Ibid.*, p. 701.

[8]*Ibid.*

[9]*Ibid.*, p. 702.

[10]*Ibid.*, p. 698.

[11]*Ibid.*, XXIII:2, 613.

[12]Johnston, *Narrative of Military Operations*, p. 62.

[13]O. R., XXIII:2, 624.

[14]*Ibid.*, p. 632.

[15]*Ibid.*, p. 640.

[16]The only other full generals besides Bragg and Johnston were Beauregard and Robert E. Lee, both of whom were busily occupied where they were.

[17]O. R., XXIII:2, 729.
[18]*Ibid.*, XVI:1, 1098.
[19]*Ibid.*
[20]*Ibid.*, p. 1107.
[21]*Ibid.*, p. 1104.
[22]*Ibid.*
[23]*Ibid.*, p. 1105.
[24]*The Confederate Veteran*, XIII, 80.

[25]Clement L. Vallandigham was a prominent Democratic politician of Ohio, a former member of the House of Representatives, recently defeated by a narrow margin for re-election to the House. While in Congress he had made the most outspoken attacks on the Lincoln administration and its conduct of the war. This policy, of course, had hopelessly antagonized Lincoln and the Republican majority in Congress, but there was a strong anti-Administration feeling in the North, as evidenced by the fact that Lincoln was re-elected by a majority of only 400,000 over McClellan's 1,800,000 popular votes. Vallandigham had declared himself in 1860 as favoring a "Union of free will, not of arms" and opposed to coercion of the seceding states. He openly accused Lincoln of a "wicked and most desperate cunning" in provoking the war and of usurpation of power and violation of the Constitution in carrying it on. Naturally enough, he was branded a "copperhead," and when he continued to make speeches against the Administration, he was finally arrested at his home and taken to Cincinnati. Here he was tried by a military commission on the charge of "publicly expressing . . . sympathies for those in arms against the Government of the United States," etc., was found guilty and sentenced to confinement in prison for the duration of the war. President Lincoln changed his sentence to banishment from the United States and transportation within the Confederate lines. He was conveyed to Nashville and thence to Murfreesboro on a special train, arriving at Rosecrans' headquarters on the evening of May 24. Soon after midnight he was taken through the Federal lines and, under a flag of truce, to the Confederate outposts.

[26]Fremantle, *Three Months in the Southern States*, p. 156.
[27]Polk, *Leonidas Polk, Bishop and General*, II, 204.
[28]Fremantle, *Three Months in the Southern States*, p. 137.
[29]Polk, *Leonidas Polk, Bishop and General*, II, 205.
[30]*Ibid.*, p. 207.
[31]O. R., XXX:4, 745.
[32]Roman, *Military Operations of General Beauregard*, II, 84.
[33]Fremantle, *Three Months in the Southern States*, p. 145.
[34]*The Confederate Veteran*, V, 269.

[35]"Is it your intention to make an immediate movement forward?" Halleck finally telegraphed Rosecrans on June 16. "A definite answer,

yes or no, is required." To which Rosecrans replied: "If 'immediate' means to-night or to-morrow, No. If it means as soon as all things are ready, say five days, Yes."

[36]*Battles and Leaders*, III, 679.

[37]Colonel Johnston reported to President Davis in March that Bragg had considered the possibility of a movement of the enemy by way of Manchester, but felt that if they made it they would expose their flank "and could gain nothing by it." Even if the enemy reached his rear, Bragg thought, he "could afford to exchange bases."—O. R., XXIII: 2, 724.

On the other hand, Hardee in January had warned Bragg that their chosen position was a poor one defensively, and could be turned by way of Manchester and Decherd—as it was.—*Ibid.*, 617.

[38]Polk, *Leonidas Polk, Bishop and General*, II, 213.

[39]Buckner was in Knoxville, where on May 11 he had been put in command of the Department of East Tennessee. He had been co-operating closely with Bragg, and a few days before Hardee wrote this anxious letter to Polk he had been there with some reinforcements for Bragg, but had now returned to Knoxville.

[40]Polk, *Leonidas Polk, Bishop and General*, II, 215.

[41]The army paused for rest on top of the mountain—and General Polk found himself stirred with mingled emotions. In 1856, as Bishop of the Episcopal Church, he had recommended that the church establish an educational institution, and the next year the University of the South was formally organized and chartered by the state of Tennessee. A tract of some ten thousand acres of land was acquired on top of Sewanee Mountain, pledges for an endowment fund were obtained, and in 1860 the cornerstone of the main building was laid and the location formally christened "University Place." Then came the outbreak of war, and the progress of the University movement was stopped. Now, for the first time since the laying of the cornerstone, Polk was back at Sewanee, his episcopal vestments displaced by the gray coat of a Confederate general, and he was surrounded by the tired and ragged rank and file of his retreating army instead of by the college students with whom his mind's eye had fondly peopled the wooded domain. It was Polk's last visit to the site of the fulfillment of his dream, but after the war was over, the work was resumed under Bishop Quintard. The war had swept away the endowment fund; the soldiers of the Federal army had demolished the cornerstone, but the land was still there, and in 1866 work was resumed on building that great school, the University of the South, better known by the name of the mountain on which it stands.

[42]Wyeth, *Life of General Nathan Bedford Forrest*, p. 235.

[43]Davis, *The Rise and Fall of the Confederate Government*, II, 426.

[44]*Bishop Quintard's Memoirs of the War*, p. 86.

CHAPTER XIV

[1]Johnston, *Narrative of Military Operations*, p. 211.
[2]*O. R.*, XXIII:2, 920.
[3]*O. R.*, LII:2, 514.
[4]The dearth of provisions in the army and the frugal fare even of the officers are illustrated by an anecdote told by a member of the 1st Tennessee Infantry: "About this time my father paid me a visit. Rations were mighty scarce. I was mighty glad to see him, but ashamed to let him know how poorly off for something to eat we were. We were living on parched corn. I thought of a happy plan to get him a good dinner, so I asked him to let us go up to the colonel's tent. Says I, 'Colonel Field, I desire to introduce you to my father, and as rations are a little short in my mess, I thought you might have a little better, and could give him a good dinner.' 'Yes,' says Colonel Field, 'I am glad to make the acquaintance of your father, and will be glad to divide my rations with him. Also, I would like for you to stay and have dinner with me,' which I gladly accepted. About this time a young African came in with a frying-pan of parched corn and dumped it on an old oil-cloth and said, 'Master, dinner is ready.' That was all he had. He was living, like ourselves, on parched corn."—Watkins, Co. "Aytch."
[5]*Battles and Leaders*, III, 639.
[6]*O. R.*, XXIII:1, 954.
[7]*Ibid.*, p. 962.
[8]The Nashville & Chattanooga Railroad constituted Rosecrans' (and later Sherman's) life line. From Nashville there was a direct railroad connection with Louisville. Also the Nashville & Chattanooga itself, after Nashville was captured, had been extended westward to the Tennessee River at Johnsonville, where a great depot of supplies was established, fed by river steamboats from Louisville, Cincinnati and St. Louis. Without this line of track, the Federal army's operations would have been exceedingly difficult, perhaps impossible.
[9]So named because of the location on the ridge, several decades previously, of the Brainerd Mission to the Cherokee Indians.
[10]*Battles and Leaders*, III, 639.
[11]James Longstreet, *From Manassas to Appomattox*, p. 327.
[12]*O. R.*, XXX:4, 760.
[13]*Ibid.*, XXIX:2, 699.
[14]Gen. G. Moxley Sorrel, *Recollections of a Confederate Staff Officer*, p. 189.
[15]Longstreet, *From Manassas to Appomattox*, p. 436.
[16]*Ibid.*, p. 437.

[17]*Battles and Leaders*, III, 640.

[18]O. R., XXX:4, 595.

[19]*Battles and Leaders*, III, 641.

[20]Judge Albion W. Tourgee, in *A Story of a Thousand*, says: "The Confederate deserter was an institution which has received too little consideration. Taken altogether, he was of far greater value to the Southern cause than the best corps in the Confederate army. He was ubiquitous, willing and altogether inscrutable. Whether he told the truth or a lie, he was always equally sure to deceive. He was sometimes a real deserter and sometimes a mock deserter. In either case he was sure to be loaded."

[21]O. R., XXX:3, 481.

[22]John B. Turchin, *Chickamauga*, p. 34.

[23]*Battles and Leaders*, III, 641-646.

[24]O. R., XXX:1, 28.

[25]Wyeth, *Life of Gen. Nathan Bedford Forrest*, p. 242.

[26]O. R., XXX:1, 604.

[27]Turchin, *Chickamauga*, p. 47.

[28]O. R., XXX:2, 31.

[29]*Ibid.*, XXX:3, 601.

[30]Dana had been sent by Stanton to Georgia to follow Rosecrans, as a sort of personal spy, and make regular and frequent reports. His daily dispatches to his chief are interesting reading, but reflect not only the confusion prevailing in the Federal command and the gross inaccuracy of its information, but also the callow incapacity of the excitable young Mr. Dana.

[31]J. B. Hood, *Advance and Retreat*, p. 55 et seq.

[32]Polk, *Leonidas Polk, Bishop and General*, II, 234.

[33]Hood and his staff, during this action, encountered an unusual hazard on the battlefield—a nest of yellow-jackets. The officers' horses, attacked by the venomous insects, became so unmanageable as almost to destroy the effectiveness of the charge, and for a short while there was more immediate concern over the yellow-jackets than over the Minié balls and shells that filled the air.

[34]*Battles and Leaders*, III, 651.

[35]*Ibid.*, p. 652.

[36]Sorrel, *Recollections of a Confederate Staff Officer*, p. 199.

[37]General Longstreet came perilously close to being captured before he reached Bragg's headquarters. When he alighted from the train at Catoosa Station, near Ringgold, no guide awaited him, and his only direction was to "follow the main road." Totally unfamiliar with the country, he and his two aides rode squarely into the Federal lines, where they were challenged. Longstreet asked what troops these were, and when they gave the name of their division and brigade by number, instead of by the name of the commander as was the Confederate custom, he became aware of

his peril. But coolly he said: "Let us ride down a little way to find a better crossing," and before the Federal picket could object, they rode off into the shadow of the near-by trees.

[38]Polk, *Leonidas Polk, Bishop and General,* II, 243.

[39]*Jefferson Davis, Constitutionalist,* IX, 498.

[40]*Battles and Leaders,* III, 653.

[41]General Alexander P. Stewart, who commanded one of the divisions of this wing, was Longstreet's roommate at West Point, and they greeted each other warmly as they met again there in the Georgia woods, confronting the enemy.

[42]Hill, like most other newcomers to the Army of Tennessee, was surprised at the manner in which the cavalry, when in action, dismounted and fought as infantry. After they had ridden to their chosen position, every fourth man in the ranks would be assigned to the duty of holding his own and three other horses, remaining in the rear while his comrades moved up to attack on foot. The horse-holders were supposed to keep up with the movements of the dismounted men so that the horses would always be available for quick transportation when needed.

[43]Wyeth, *Life of Gen. Nathan Bedford Forrest,* p. 252.

[44]Breckinridge lost two of his brigadiers in this charge, Adams who was wounded and captured, and Helm who was killed. Helm and Abraham Lincoln had married half-sisters in Kentucky, and after he was killed Mrs. Helm made her way to Washington and visited Mrs. Lincoln, arousing a furore of Northern protest against "that Rebel woman in the White House."

[45]O. R., XXXI:1, 192.

[46]*Battles and Leaders,* III, 664.

[47]Fiske, *Mississippi Valley in the Civil War,* p. 277.

[48]*Ibid.,* p. 278.

[49]Longstreet, in his *Manassas to Appomattox,* tells how he and his staff were enjoying their lunch of bacon and sweet potatoes—sweet potatoes were considered a rare delicacy but were somewhat dry without anything to wash them down. While they were eating, a fragment of shell came screaming through the treetops, tore through a book in the hands of a courier who sat on his horse reading, and struck Longstreet's chief of ordnance, Col. P. T. Manning. Manning fell gasping in what was thought to be the struggle of death, but it was soon discovered that he was merely choking on a large bite of the sweet potato which he had just taken when the shell struck him. By quick first-aid treatment his throat was relieved of the obstructing potato, his breath was restored, and his wound found to be only slight.

[50]*Ibid.,* p. 452.

[51]*Battles and Leaders,* III, 659.

[52]Turchin, *Chickamauga,* p. 140.

[53]*Ibid.*, p. 140-142.

[54]Fiske, *Mississippi Valley in the Civil War*, p. 272.

[55]Colonel Carlton of the 89th Ohio had been a classmate of General Kelly at West Point. When he was brought a prisoner to Kelly's headquarters, his old schoolmate greeted him generously: "Carlton, I am glad to see you; but you have no cause to be ashamed of your work. Two-thirds of my brigade lie yonder dead, the result of those charges made on your command."

[56]*Battles and Leaders*, III, 661.

[57]Here occurred the incident so often told about in later years. Cheatham ordered his division into the fight, crying "Forward, boys, and give 'em hell!" Polk, the bishop-general, approved the idea, and he cried out to his men: "Give 'em what General Cheatham says, boys!"

[58]*Battles and Leaders*, III, 661.

[59]Longstreet, who was an old campaigner and had been in many battles, was also impressed by this extraordinary burst of cheering when the two wings of the victorious army came together. "The Army of Tennessee knew how to enjoy its first great victory," he writes. "The two lines, nearing as they advanced, joined their continuous shouts in increasing volume, not as the burstings from the cannon's mouth, but in a tremendous swell of heroic harmony that seemed almost to lift from their roots the great trees of the forest."

[60]Archibald Gracie, *The Truth About Chickamauga*, p. 443.

[61]In his *The Truth About Chickamauga*, Archibald Gracie has with painstaking care established, as nearly as is humanly possible, the exact time of the various movements. He quotes the meteorological records showing that the sun set on that day at exactly six seconds after six o'clock.

[62]Fiske, *Mississippi Valley in the Civil War*, p. 275.

[63]O. R., XXX:1, 253.

[64]Gracie, *The Truth About Chickamauga*, p. 80 *et seq.*

[65]*Battles and Leaders*, III, 659.

[66]Colonel Devol of the 36th Ohio of Reynolds' division, says they held their position in the breastworks "until 4 P.M., when the enemy had us surrounded" and "I heard General Reynolds remark that he thought he would have to surrender." They pulled out, however, faced to the rear, and on their way out drove off Liddell's brigade which had got around onto the Federal left and rear.

[67]"Disorganized" is the word used by Thomas in describing the condition of his army when he met Sheridan near Rossville late in the afternoon of the twentieth and explained to him that there was no hope then of stemming the army's flight from the field.

[68]Gracie, *The Truth About Chickamauga*, p. 37.

[69]Polk, *Leonidas Polk, Bishop and General*, II, 267.

⁷⁰An amusing incident is told in *The Truth About Chickamauga* of a lieutenant in the 14th Ohio who, "moved to compassion by the cries of the wounded Confederates who lined the slope in front of us (the dry leaves had caught fire), jumped over the barricade of rails and began sweeping the burning leaves away from them. He grew interested in his work and went on down the hill until he got in range of the enemy's skirmishers, when one banged away and shot him through the backsides. I was near when two of his men brought him to our line, and he was one of the angriest men I ever saw. With a volley of oaths he exclaimed, in substance: 'The idea of a man going through two days of battle without a scratch and then, while engaged in a work of mercy, getting shot so that when he goes home on furlough he can not tell the girls where he was shot."—Gracie, p. 444.

⁷¹Jones, *A Rebel War Clerk's Diary*, II, 50.

CHAPTER XV

¹O. R., XXX:2, 67-68.
²Wyeth, *Life of Gen. Nathan Bedford Forrest*, p. 259.
³*Ibid.*, p. 260.
⁴O. R., XXX:4, 681.
⁵*Ibid.*, XXX:1, 142.
⁶*Ibid.*, p. 149.
⁷*Ibid.*, p. 148.
⁸*Ibid.*, p. 161.
⁹*Ibid.*
¹⁰*Ibid.*, p. 142.
¹¹*Ibid.*, p. 39.
¹²*Battles and Leaders*, III, 681.
¹³Longstreet, *From Manassas to Appomattox*, p. 461.
¹⁴Wyeth, *Life of Gen. Nathan Bedford Forrest*, p. 260.
¹⁵Polk, II, 271.
¹⁶J. William Jones, *Life and Letters of Robert Edward Lee*, p. 284.
¹⁷O. R., XXIX:2, 709, 730, 742.
¹⁸Watkins, Co. "Aytch," p. 99.
¹⁹Polk, *Leonidas Polk, Bishop and General*, II, 283.
²⁰*Ibid.*, p. 284.
²¹O. R., LII:2, 535.
²²Polk, *Leonidas Polk, Bishop and General*, p. 284.
²³O. R., XXX:2, 138.
²⁴*Ibid.*, p. 138.
²⁵O. R., LII:2, 677.
²⁶Polk, *Leonidas Polk, Bishop and General*, p. 288.
²⁷O. R., XXX:4, 705.

[28]*Ibid.*, p. 708.

[29]*O. R.*, LII:2, 549.

[30]*Ibid.*, XXX:2, 65-66.

[31]Longstreet, *From Manassas to Appomattox*, p. 465.

[32]*Jefferson Davis, Constitutionalist*, IX, 498.

[33]*O. R.*, XXX:2, 66.

[34]Irving A. Buck, *Cleburne and His Command*, p. 157.

[35]When President Davis arrived at Chickamauga Station he was met by a crowd of soldiers who called on him for a speech as he mounted his horse to ride to Bragg's headquarters. Raising his hat, he said to them: "Man never spoke as you did on the field of Chickamauga, and in your presence I dare not speak. Yours is the voice that will win the independence of your country and strike terror to the heart of a ruthless foe."

[36]*O. R.*, XXX:4, 742.

[37]Longstreet, *From Manassas to Appomattox*, p. 465.

[38]In the collection of the author.

[39]Longstreet, *From Manassas to Appomattox*, p. 465.

[40]*Ibid.*, p. 466.

[41]Roman, *The Military Operations of General Beauregard*, II, 162.

[42]*O. R.*, XXX:4, 734.

[43]*Ibid.*, p. 745.

[44]Longstreet, *From Manassas to Appomattox*, p. 470.

[45]*O. R.*, XXX:4, 742.

[46]Wyeth, *Life of Gen. Nathan Bedford Forrest*, p. 264.

[47]*O. R.*, XXX:4, 744.

[48]*O. R.*, LII:2, 55.

[49]Stickles, *Simon Bolivar Buckner*, p. 236.

[50]Ex-Governor James D. Porter of Tennessee is authority for the statement that "Fighting Joe" Hooker was given this nickname in derision at West Point. He says that Hooker and E. Kirby Smith had an argument in the course of which Hooker made remarks that Kirby Smith considered personally offensive. Smith demanded an apology. Hooker refused and Smith "gave him a half dozen kicks in the seat of his pants, which was not resented." It was because of this that the cadets dubbed him "Fighting Joe," which name, Governor Porter adds, "he could not repudiate and dared not appropriate, and yet there are thousands on both sides of the line who believe that he honorably won it on the battlefield in the War between the States."—*The Confederate Veteran*, XII, 523.

[51]Longstreet, *From Manassas to Appomattox*, p. 474.

[52]Longstreet says in his book: "Under the impression that the other division commander [Jenkins] understood that the move had miscarried, I rode back to my headquarters, failing to give countermanding orders. . . . It was an oversight of mine not to give definite orders for the troops to return to their camps before leaving them."

⁵³*O. R.*, LII:2, 554.
⁵⁴Grant, *Personal Memoirs*, p. 388.
⁵⁵Longstreet, *From Manassas to Appomattox*, p. 474.
⁵⁶*O. R.*, LII:2, 557.

⁵⁷It was in connection with the development of this information that one of the most famous and dramatic episodes of the entire war occurred— the execution as a spy of Sam Davis, a scout for Bragg. This youth (he was only twenty-one years old) had been sent on a dangerous mission into Middle Tennessee as one of a detachment of scouts under Captain Coleman to learn the strength of the Federals and ascertain what movements were being made to reinforce Grant at Chattanooga. The scouts started on their foray behind the Federal lines early in November, and soon discovered the Sixth Army Corps under General G. M. Dodge near Pulaski, moving from Corinth, presumably to the relief of Chattanooga. Armed with this and other information, they started to make their way back into the Confederate lines at Decatur to inform General Bragg by means of a line of couriers maintained from that point, but several of them, including Davis, were captured and put in jail. When Davis was searched he was found to be carrying a miscellaneous and interesting array of baggage. In his saddlebags he had three cakes of soap and three toothbrushes he had obtained in Nashville and was sending to General Bragg—scarce articles in the Southern Confederacy. Concealed in his boot was a letter from his captain to Bragg giving complete details as to the movement and location of the Federal troops. In the seat of his saddle was a remarkably accurate map and description of the fortifications at Nashville. On the strength of this letter and map, Sam Davis was charged with being a spy, although he was in Confederate uniform and a regularly enlisted member of the 1st Tennessee regiment. After trial by a military commission he was sentenced to death by hanging. The accuracy of the map and description of the Nashville works was such that General Dodge felt sure that they emanated from someone near his headquarters or someone who had the confidence of the staff officers. He was extremely anxious to locate and stop this leak. Accordingly he called Davis to his headquarters and offered to spare his life if he would reveal the source of his information. The offer was refused and Dodge reluctantly ordered the execution to proceed. On the morning of November 27 Sam Davis was taken out of his cell and, seated on his coffin in a wagon, was driven to the hill on the outskirts of Pulaski where the gallows had been built. While they were waiting for the trap to be adjusted, one of General Dodge's staff officers galloped up with a dramatic, last-minute renewal of the conditioned offer to spare his life and set him free. It was a hard decision to make. Life looks very precious when a boy is twenty-one. But Sam Davis did not hesitate. In words that are now chiseled on his monument in Nashville, he refused to exchange his honor for his life: "If I had a thou-

sand lives, I would lose them all here before I would betray my friend or the confidence of my informer." Turning to the provost marshal, he said calmly: "I am ready"; then, stepping on the trap, he paid the required penalty.

No better epitaph could a soldier have than the sadly admiring comment of General Dodge, his captor and executioner: "He was too brave to die."

[58]John R. Young, *Around the World With General Grant*, p. 306.

[59]*Southern Historical Society Papers*, VIII, 466.

[60]Buck, *Cleburne and His Command*, p. 166.

[61]A writer in *The Confederate Veteran* says: "Among the many designs submitted to the War Department for battle flags, this one, the full-orbed silver moon in a blue field surrounded by a white border, was designed by Brigadier General W. J. Hardee, who organized and commanded the troops . . . known at the close of the war as Cleburne's Division, and it was by him adopted as the ensign of his chivalric troops, this right being a special grant by the authorities at Richmond for his Division only." (III, 245.) All of the regiments in Cleburne's Division carried this Silver Moon flag, and it was easy for the enemy to spot Cleburne's location in the Confederate lines by reason of his flag's unique design.

[62]General Joseph S. Fullerton relates: "As soon as this movement was seen from Orchard Knob, Grant quickly turned to Thomas who stood by his side and I heard him say angrily: 'Thomas, who ordered those men up the ridge?' Thomas replied, in his usual slow, quiet manner: 'I don't know. I did not.' Then, addressing General Gordon Granger, he said: 'Did you order them up, Granger?' 'No,' said Granger, 'they started up without orders. When those fellows get started, all hell can't stop them.' General Grant said something to the effect that somebody would suffer if it did not turn out well and then, turning, stoically watched the ridge. He gave no further orders."

General Fullerton says that Sheridan, standing at the foot of the ridge, after taking a swig from a brother officer's flask, waved it defiantly at a group of Confederate officers who were to be seen standing in front of Bragg's headquarters, "with the salutation, 'Here's at you!' The Confederates replied to this toast with a blast from two cannon which struck so close to Sheridan as to throw dirt all over him, whereupon he said 'Ah! That is ungenerous; I shall take those guns for that.' " Fullerton, on the authority of a Kansas colonel, quotes Granger as saying jovially to his troops after the battle: "I am going to have you all court-martialed! You were ordered to take the works at the foot of the hill, and you have taken those on top! You have disobeyed orders, all of you, and you know that you ought to be court-martialed!"—*Battles and Leaders*, III, 719.

[63]O. R., LII:2, 745.

[64]"Here's your mule" was one of those inanities, always good for a

laugh, which Confederate soldiers yelled at one another, or at visitors in camp—something on the order of the "Where's Elmer?" of the American Legion. It is said to have had its origin in the complaint of a peddler, during the early days of the war, who charged that his mule had been taken by the soldiers and who was invited to look through the camp to see if he could find it. As he made the search, there were cries of "Here's your mule" from all sides. The soldiers so hugely enjoyed the hapless peddler's dashing hither and yon that they adopted "Here's your mule" as their standing joke.

[65]Watkins, Co. "Aytch," p. 104.

[66]Buck, Cleburne and His Command, p. 191.

[67]General Cleburne's young brother, Christopher, was serving as a private in the ranks of one of his brigades. Captain Buck says he took a gleeful part in the hurling of stones down on the charging Yankees. General Cleburne was vastly amused when one of the bleeding prisoners, a burly Irishman, spied "Kit" and, shaking his fist at him, cried: "Ah, you are the little divil who smashed me jaw with a rock!"

[68]Fiske, The Mississippi Valley in the Civil War, p. 315.

[69]Jones, A Rebel War Clerk's Diary, p. 106.

CHAPTER XVI

[1]O. R., XXXI:2, 682.

[2]Ibid., LII:2, 745.

[3]Ibid., p. 567.

[4]Jones, A Rebel War Clerk's Diary, p. 157.

[5]O. R., XXXI:3, 765.

[6]Jefferson Davis, Constitutionalist, VIII, 351.

[7]O. R., XXI:3, 779.

[8]Ibid., p. 792.

[9]Ibid., p. 796.

[10]DuBose, General Joseph Wheeler, p. 265.

[11]O. R., XXXI:3, 842.

[12]Johnston, Narrative of Military Operations, p. 264.

[13]Johnston says in his Narrative that he could not understand how anybody supposed to be as busy as the President could find time to write so many long letters. This thought must occur to anybody who reads over Davis' voluminous correspondence.

[14]O. R., XXXI:3, 856.

[15]Johnston, Narrative of Military Operations, p. 269.

[16]O. R., XXXII:2, 510.

[17]Ibid., XXXI:3, 812.

[18]Ibid., LII:2, 597.

[19]Johnston, Narrative of Military Operations, p. 277.

[20]O. R., XXXII:2, 644.

[21]DuBose, General Joseph Wheeler, p. 274.

[22]O. R., LII:2, 586.

[23]DuBose, General Joseph Wheeler, p. 275.

[24]Sherman, after the battle of Missionary Ridge, had been sent back with his army to Mississippi, where he was in charge of the Federal forces until recalled to Chattanooga soon afterward to take charge of the advance into Georgia.

[25]O. R., LII:2, 621.

[26]Mary Boykin Chesnut, in her Diary from Dixie, that invaluable storehouse of intimate information about the Confederate great and near-great, makes many passing references to Hood during his stay in Richmond in the winter of 1863-4, while recovering from his amputation. She describes him as "tall, thin and shy; [he] has blue eyes and light hair; a tawny beard, and a vast amount of it, covering the lower part of his face—the face of an old Crusader—the whole appearance that of awkward strength." She speaks of "the light of battle in his eyes," and says: "The fierce light of Hood's eyes I can never forget." She reveals that for some obscure reason he was known as "Sam" to his intimates. The wounded hero of Chickamauga had a gay winter in Richmond, despite his crippled condition. A handsome young bachelor, he was showered with attentions by the patriotic ladies, who brought him oranges (which cost five dollars apiece) and other delicacies, and, as soon as he was able to be moved around, invited him to all the parties. But it is not of his social conquests that the historian reads with so much interest in Mrs. Chesnut's spicy comments; it is of those long rides he took with Jefferson Davis in the President's carriage. If we knew what they talked about during that long convalescence in Richmond, we might know more about the inner history of the Army of Tennessee.

[27]Those historians who censure Robert E. Lee for an alleged narrowness of view which confined his interest and attention to the operations in Virginia do so in disregard of ample evidence to the contrary afforded by a study of the written records. Officially, Lee's authority was limited to his Army of Northern Virginia, but that he was thoroughly alive to the importance of the operations of the Army of Tennessee is revealed by his many communications regarding its problems and their solution.

[28]Hood, Advance and Retreat, p. 89.

[29]Longstreet's attack on Burnside stationed within the fortifications of Knoxville had been unsuccessful, and Longstreet, after his repulse, had been wintering near Greeneville in East Tennessee.

[30]Hood, Advance and Retreat, p. 91.

[31]Ibid., p. 92.

[32]O. R., XXXII:3, 606.

[33]Ibid., p. 607.

[34]*Ibid.*, p. 614.

[35]*Ibid.*, p. 649.

[36]*Ibid.*, p. 653.

[37]Longstreet wrote to Johnston that such a movement might bring about a condition where "both armies (yours and mine) will be obliged to disperse in the mountains and many of us perish or surrender to the enemy without a fight. It may be that this would be sport to some people, but I confess that I should not enjoy it at all."—O. R., LII:2, 634.

[38]O. R., XXXII:3, 666.

[39]Johnston's *Narrative of Military Operations*, p. 299.

[40]O. R., XXXII:3, p. 839.

[41]Seitz, *Braxton Bragg, General of the Confederacy*, p. 428.

[42]O. R., XXXII:3, 781.

[43]*Ibid.*, p. 641.

[44]An unexpected by-product of Polk's journey from Resaca to Dalton in company with Hood was the latter's expression of a desire to be baptised and received into the church. It was after midnight before Polk and Johnston concluded their consultation. Then the fighting cleric went to Hood's headquarters, laid aside his sword, and with a tin wash-pan for a baptismal font, performed the rite on the big, bearded Texan as, with bowed head, he leaned on his crutches. A few days later, on the eighteenth, Polk was asked to perform a similar service for General Johnston, and the ceremony took place in Johnston's tent that night, after his usual conference with his corps commanders, the rite being administered in the presence of Hood and Hardee. Thus the bishop-general (his soldiers always called him "Bishop Polk") had the unique distinction of baptising two of the commanding officers of the Army of Tennessee—two who, despite the common bonds of Christian fellowship and service to the Confederacy, became the most unrelenting enemies.

[45]H. V. Boynton, *Sherman's Historical Raid*, p. 96.

[46]Johnston, *Narrative of Military Operations*, p. 317.

[47]Grant, *Personal Memoirs*, p. 435.

[48]*Battles and Leaders*, IV, 253.

[49]This has reference to Lee's resistance of Grant's advance in the Wilderness, and of Richard Taylor's activities on the Red River.

[50]Johnston, *Narrative of Military Operations*, p. 321.

[51]The accounts of this episode, as given by Hood and Johnston, are widely at variance. Johnston says in his *Narrative* (pp. 323-324) that Polk and Hood "expressed the opinion very positively that neither of their corps would be able to hold the position next day" and "on that account they urged me to abandon the ground immediately and cross the Etowah." He says nothing of a reservation to this recommendation, or of their suggesting an advance. Hood in his *Advance and Retreat* (p. 108) says: "I do at this day and hour, in the name of truth, honor and justice,

in the name of the departed soul of the Christian and noble Polk, and in the presence of my Creator, most solemnly deny that General Polk or I recommended General Johnston at Cassville to retreat when he intended to give battle, and affirm that the recommendation made by us to change his position was throughout the discussion coupled with the proviso: If he did not intend to force a pitched battle." This poses a question of personal veracity—or, at least, accuracy of recollection. After examination of all the available evidence, it appears that General Hood's account is correct. It is supported by the statement of General Polk's son and by Captain Walter Morris, chief engineer of Polk's corps, who was present at the interview between Johnston and his generals and who states unreservedly that both Hood and Polk urged Johnston to take the offensive.—*Advance and Retreat*, p. 114.

[52]Johnston, *Narrative of Military Operations*, 327.
[53]Sherman, *Personal Memoirs*, III, 44.
[54]Buck, *Cleburne and His Command*, p. 258.
[55]Polk, *Leonidas Polk, Bishop and General*, II, 349.
[56]Gen. S. G. French, *Two Wars—An Autobiography*, p. 202.
[57]Davis, *Rise and Fall of the Confederate Government*, II, 554.
[58]Polk, *Leonidas Polk, Bishop and General*, II, 338 et seq.
[59]Johnston, *Narrative of Military Operations*, p. 341.
[60]Watkins, *Co. "Aytch,"* p. 143.
[61]To protect themselves from the broiling rays of the Georgia sun, the men kept their blankets stretched on the poles across the trenches during the day, but this protection was hastily pulled down when the lines were attacked, and both sides fought fully exposed to the terrifically hot rays.
[62]Watkins, *Co. "Aytch,"* p. 145.
[63]Johnston, *Narrative of Military Operations*, p. 343.
[64]*Battles and Leaders*, IV, 311.
[65]*Ibid.*, p. 252.
[66]Boynton, *Sherman's Historical Raid*, p. 107.
[67]The speed and facility with which Sherman repaired the damage to the railroad was a source of amazement to the Confederates, and reflected great credit on the enterprise of his engineers. With an efficiency remindful of the advance of the German columns into the Low Countries in 1940, Sherman's repair crews rushed forward as fast as the line of battle advanced. They carried ample supplies of cross-ties, bridge timbers and rails, and they quickly replaced bridges and torn-up tracks and soon had the supply trains rolling forward again. They worked so rapidly that a legend grew up among the Confederates that Sherman carried with him duplicates of all the railroad bridges. A story is told of two Confederate soldiers, lolling in the shade of a tree on Kennesaw Mountain, discussing the campaign. "Well," said one, "the Yanks will have to git up and git now, for I heard General Johnston himself say that General Wheeler had

blown up the tunnel near Dalton, and that the Yanks would have to retreat because they could get no more rations." To which the other replied, "Oh, hell! Don't you know that old Sherman carries a duplicate
tunnel along with him?"

[68]Sherman, *Personal Memoirs*, II, 66.
[69]Johnston, *Narrative of Military Operations*, p. 357.
[70]*Ibid.*, p. 351.
[71]Sherman, *Personal Memoirs*, II, 70.

CHAPTER XVII

[1]Davis, *Rise and Fall of the Confederate Government*, p. 557.
[2]*Ibid.*, p. 556.
[3]O. R., XXXVIII:5, 881.
[4]Hardee, however, in a letter to General W. W. Mackall in August,
stated that Hood had been in favor of retreat all along, and that Johnston
would have crossed the Chattahoochee three weeks sooner if he had
listened to Hood.—O. R., XXXVIII:5, 988.
[5]*Jefferson Davis, Constitutionalist*, VIII, 349.
[6]*Ibid.*, p. 355.
[7]Seitz, *Braxton Bragg, General of the Confederacy*, p. 445.
[8]Hood, *Advance and Retreat*, p. 124.
[9]O. R., LII:2, 282.
[10]Douglas Southall Freeman (Ed.), *Lee's Dispatches*, p. 282.
[11]*Ibid.*, p. 283.
[12]Though it was generally agreed that Sherman could have been hopelessly crippled by the simple expedient of assigning to the cavalry the task
of cutting his railroad communications with Nashville, there is sound reason, in the light of present knowledge, for questioning whether this would
have been so easy to do. The lines of the Nashville & Chattanooga through
Tennessee, and the Western & Atlantic through Georgia, were protected
by an elaborate system of blockhouses—one at every bridge—and at every
railroad station from Nashville to Atlanta small bodies of infantry were
posted. By use of the railroad trains, effective fighting forces could be
quickly concentrated at any one point; any raiding party would have to
work fast and retreat rapidly. Furthermore, the Federals had ample
facilities for the quick repair of any damage done, and it seems doubtful
whether the Confederates could have amassed sufficient cavalry to wreck
the railroad beyond the Federals' capacity to restore it.
[13]O. R., XXXVII:5, 858.
[14]*Ibid.*, LII:2, 680.
[15]*Jefferson Davis, Constitutionalist*, p. 560.
[16]O. R., XXXVIII:5, p. 879.
[17]*Ibid.*, p. 882.

[18]*Ibid.*, p. 883.

[19]Watkins, Co. "Aytch," pp. 164-165.

[20]Dr. W. J. Worsham, *The Old Nineteenth Tennessee*, p. 125.

[21]W. J. McMurray, *History of the Twentieth Tennessee Regiment*, p. 319.

[22]Original letter in private collection of author.

[23]O. R., XXXVIII:5, 987.

[24]*Ibid.*, p. 988.

[25]*Ibid.*

[26]Hood, *Advance and Retreat*, p. 186.

[27]*Battles and Leaders*, IV, 253.

[28]Sherman, *Personal Memoirs*, II, 75.

[29]Johnston, *Narrative of Military Operations*, pp. 349-350.

[30]Hood, *Advance and Retreat*, p. 141.

[31]*Ibid.*, p. 128.

[32]*Ibid.*

[33]*Ibid.*, p. 127.

[34]O. R., LII:2, 708.

[35]O. R., XXXVIII:5, 888.

[36]Hood, *Advance and Retreat*, p. 128.

[37]O. R., XXXVIII:5, 887.

[38]Johnston, *Narrative of Military Operations*, p. 350.

[39]Hood, *Advance and Retreat*, p. 147.

[40]Watkins, Co. "Aytch," p. 184.

[41]Seddon telegraphed Hood on July 17: "You are charged with a great trust. . . . Be wary no less than bold. . . . God be with you."

[42]Hood, *Advance and Retreat*, p. 165.

[43]*Ibid.*, p. 168.

[44]*Ibid.*, p. 171.

[45]*Ibid.*, p. 185.

[46]Jacob D. Cox, *Atlanta*, p. 162.

[47]Sherman, *Personal Memoirs*, II, 72.

[48]Cox, *Atlanta*, p. 162.

[49]Hood, *Advance and Retreat*, p. 174.

[50]Buck, *Cleburne and His Command*, p. 272.

[51]Boynton, *Sherman's Historical Raid*, p. 125.

[52]Hood, *Advance and Retreat*, p. 179 et seq.

[53]Hood is borrowing Sherman's descriptive term. Sherman, *Personal Memoirs*, II, 53.

[54]*Southern Historical Society Papers*, III, 339.

[55]Cox, *Atlanta*, p. 176.

[56]*Battles and Leaders*, IV, 326.

[57]Hood, *Advance and Retreat*, p. 189.

[58]Watkins, Co. "Aytch," p. 170.

[59]Sherman, *Personal Memoirs*, II, 82.
[60]Hood, *Advance and Retreat*, p. 182.
[61]Cox, *Atlanta*, p. 175.
[62]Hooker was the senior corps commander and expected McPherson's post, but Sherman disliked him and never considered him for the place. Howard's appointment was particularly distasteful to Hooker as Hooker blamed Howard for his defeat at Chancellorsville. At Howard's promotion, Hooker resigned in indignation. Sherman made no effort to dissuade him and, in fact, was really pleased that an obnoxious associate was removed.
[63]*Battles and Leaders*, IV, 319.
[64]Cox, *Atlanta*, p. 185.
[65]*Southern Historical Society Papers*, VIII, 340.
[66]Hood, *Advance and Retreat*, p. 184.
[67]*Ibid.*, p. 195.
[68]Cox, *Atlanta*, p. 184.
[69]Sherman, *Personal Memoirs*, II, 98.
[70]O. R., XXXVIII:5, 946.
[71]Hood, *Advance and Retreat*, p. 200.
[72]Sherman, *Personal Memoirs*, II, 104.
[73]*Southern Historical Society Papers*, VIII, 341.
[74]Cox, *Atlanta*, p. 198.
[75]Hood, *Advance and Retreat*, p. 205.
[76]*Southern Historical Society Papers*, VIII, 342.
[77]*Ibid.*
[78]O. R., XXXVIII:5, 1021.
[79]*Southern Historical Society Papers*, VIII, 344.
[80]Hood, *Advance and Retreat*, p. 245.
[81]Sherman, *Personal Memoirs*, II, 110.
[82]Hood, *Advance and Retreat*, p. 225.
[83]Sherman, *Personal Memoirs*, II, 136.

CHAPTER XVIII

[1]Sherman, *Personal Memoirs*, II, 111.
[2]*Ibid.*, p. 118.
[3]This is as close as can be found in any of the written records to the popular saying attributed to Sherman: "War is Hell."
[4]O. R., XXXVIII:5, 1023.
[5]*Ibid.*, p. 1027.
[6]Sherman, *Personal Memoirs*, II, 138.
[7]*Ibid.*, p. 139.
[8]For all its long retreat, its successive defeats, and the fact that the soldiers had not been paid for nearly a year, the Army of Tennessee at this

time still maintained a surprisingly high standard of efficiency of administration. Colonel A. H. Cole, inspector general of field transportation of
all the Confederate armies, visited the army at Palmetto. He asked permission to take a six-mule team and army wagon to exhibit to the quartermaster of the Army of Northern Virginia as a sample of the transportation of the Western Army, "and by such an exhibition to arouse their
pride and induce them to put forth greater energies in behalf of their
respective departments."—O. R., XXXVIII:2, 865. Hood, however, put
his foot down. He needed all the mules and wagons he could get, without
sending any away for exhibition purposes. Colonel Cole went back to
Virginia disappointed.

[9]O. R., XXXVIII:5, 836.

[10]Ibid., p. 837.

[11]Hood, Advance and Retreat, p. 254.

[12]Augusta Chronicle, September 26, 1864.

[13]Accompanying President Davis on his visit to the Army of Tennessee
was General James Chesnut—husband of the famous diarist. General
Chesnut was so indiscreet as to remark to Davis that "every honest man
he saw" thought well of Joe Johnston. Mrs. Chesnut comments reprov-
ingly: "He knows that the President detests Joe Johnston for all the trouble he has given him, and General Joe returns the compliment with compound interest. His hatred of Jeff Davis amounts to a religion. With him
it colors all things."

[14]O. R., XXXIX:2, 846.

[15]Roman, The Military Operations of General Beauregard, II, 279.

[16]Hood, Advance and Retreat, p. 249.

[17]Sherman, Personal Memoirs, II, 141.

[18]Augusta Constitutionalist, October 4, 1864.

[19]Sherman, Personal Memoirs, II, 141.

[20]O. R., XXXIX:2, 488.

[21]Roman, The Military Operations of General Beauregard, II, 288.

[22]Jefferson Davis, Constitutionalist, VIII, 376.

[23]Ibid., p. 415.

[24]Hood, Advance and Retreat, p. 257.

[25]O. R., XXXIX, 814.

[26]The Annals of the Army of Tennessee, I, 315.

[27]O. R., XXXIX:3, 78.

[28]Ibid., p. 113.

[29]Ibid., p. 100.

[30]Ibid., p. 125.

[31]Ibid., p. 135.

[32]Ibid., p. 162.

[33]Ibid., p. 804.

[34]Ibid., p. 177.

[35]*Ibid.*, p. 191.

[36]Sherman, *Personal Memoirs*, II, 152.

[37]Hood, *Advance and Retreat*, p. 263.

[38]*Ibid.*, p. 266.

[39]Roman, *The Military Operations of General Beauregard*, II, 288.

[40]Hood, *Advance and Retreat*, p. 270.

[41]*Ibid.*

[42]The scarcity of provisions was indirectly confirmed from enemy sources. A dispatch sent from Decatur by General Granger to Sherman said that Hood was evidently out of supplies as "his men were all grumbling; the first thing the prisoners asked for was something to eat."

[43]Sherman, *Personal Memoirs*, II, 178.

[44]General Wilson had been sent out by Grant from the Army of the Potomac to take command of all Sherman's cavalry. Sherman decided to keep immediately with him a force of only 4,500 mounted men, under General Kilpatrick. He sent Wilson with all the rest to Nashville to reorganize the cavalry force and to act under Thomas in the defense of Tennessee. The cavalry of the Federal armies in the West had been notoriously inferior in organization and effectiveness, but Wilson worked a complete change. He and his cavalry were of great assistance to Thomas in the Battle of Nashville less than two months later.

[45]Roman, *The Military Operations of General Beauregard*, II, 304.

[46]*Ibid.*, p. 299.

[47]In his loyal zeal to exculpate Davis from responsibility for the disastrous expedition, Hood tortures this telegram into an indication of "the President's opposition to the campaign into Tennessee previous to a defeat of Sherman in battle," but it is difficult to read any such meaning into the message. Davis, at most, seems noncommittal, perhaps a leaning toward the campaign as indicated by his reference to an "advance to the Ohio river."

[48]Hood, *Advance and Retreat*, p. 282.

[49]*Ibid.*, p. 283.

[50]*Ibid.*, p. 284.

[51]*Southern Historical Society Papers*, IX, 529.

[52]*The Confederate Veteran*, XVI, p. 32.

[53]*Ibid.*, p. 34.

[54]*Southern Historical Society Papers*, IX, 526.

[55]Hood, *Advance and Retreat*, p. 286.

[56]*Southern Historical Society Papers*, IX, 530.

[57]*Battles and Leaders*, IV, 446.

[58]Hood, *Advance and Retreat*, p. 287.

[59]*Southern Historical Society Papers*, IX, 526.

[60]Unpublished manuscript account by Major Campbell Brown, Spring Hill, Tenn., of his conversation with Governor Harris, May 5, 1868.

[61]Hood, *Advance and Retreat*, p. 289.
[62]*Southern Historical Society Papers*, IX, 533.
[63]*The Annals of the Army of Tennessee*, I, 49.
[64]*Southern Historical Society Papers*, IX, 533.
[65]Jordan and Pryor, *Campaigns of Lieut. Gen. N. B. Forrest*, p. 623.

CHAPTER XIX

[1]*The Confederate Veteran*, XVI, 36.
[2]Hood, *Advance and Retreat*, p. 290.
[3]*Ibid.*
[4]*Ibid.*, p. 291.
[5]An example of the truth that is stranger than fiction is provided by the fatal wounding of Captain Theodoric ("Tod") Carter, during the course of the battle, as he charged the Federal breastworks in close proximity to the Carter House, his own home. The next morning he was found on the battlefield by his father and sisters and brought to the house to die.
[6]Buck, *Cleburne and His Command*, p. 327.
[7]Hood, *Advance and Retreat*, p. 293.
[8]*Ibid.*, p. 294.
[9]Buck, *Cleburne and His Command*, p. 339.
[10]*Southern Historical Society Papers*, IX, 539.
[11]Buck, *Cleburne and His Command*, p. 328.
[12]Levi T. Schofield, *The Retreat from Pulaski to Nashville*, p. 18.
[13]*Battles and Leaders*, IV, 453.
[14]Worsham, *The Old Nineteenth Tennessee*, p. 141.
[15]*Around the World With General Grant*, p. 294.
[16]O. R., XLV:2, 639.
[17]Fort Negley has been entirely reconstructed on its original foundations as a Federal WPA project, and is now maintained as a Nashville city park.
[18]George D. Prentice, the fire-breathing pro-Union editor of the Louisville *Courier*, was trying to turn an honest penny by speculating in cotton. He had just invested $5,000 in cotton in Nashville when his bales were seized and used in the fortifications. He wrote a plaintive letter to Governor Andrew Johnson, bewailing the fact that some less expensive material for the fortifications could not be found.
[19]O. R., XLV:2, 114.
[20]*Ibid.*, p. 143.
[21]*Ibid.*, p. 180.
[22]*The Confederate Veteran*, XII, 84.
[23]Schofield, *John*, p. 244.

[24]So named in honor of Colonel Wm. M. Shy of the 37th Georgia Regiment who was killed there on December 16.

[25]Steedman, in command of the Federal troops on this wing, had been an active Democratic politician before the war, and one of the delegates to the 1860 Convention which nominated Breckinridge for President. During his charge on Peach Orchard Hill he laughed and said: "I wonder what my Democratic friends over there would think if they knew I was fighting them with 'nigger' troops."

[26]Schofield, John, p. 248.

CHAPTER XX

[1]O. R., XLV:2, 757.

[2]Roman, The Military Operations of General Beauregard, II, 329.

[3]Ibid., II, 332.

[4]O. R., LII:2, 808.

[5]Ibid., XLV:2, 781.

[6]Ibid., XLV:2, 785.

[7]Chesnut, A Diary from Dixie, p. 342.

[8]Ibid., p. 371.

[9]Battles and Leaders, IV, 701.

[10]A sad feature of this charge was the loss of General Hardee's only son, Willie, a sixteen-year-old boy. He had arrived on the field and enlisted in a Texas cavalry regiment just two hours before it was led by his father in the charge in which he met his death.

[11]Sherman, Personal Memoirs, II, 324 et seq.

[12]Breckinridge, early in 1864, had been transferred from the Army of Tennessee to the Army of Northern Virginia. He took part in the battle at Cold Harbor, and later was second in command to Early in the Shenandoah Valley Campaign. In January, 1865, Seddon sent in his resignation as Secretary of War; and in February, 1865, Breckinridge succeeded to this portfolio and served the remaining few months of the year.

[13]Roman, The Military Operations of General Beauregard, II, 665.

BIBLIOGRAPHY

BIBLIOGRAPHY

The principal source of factual material regarding the Army of Tennessee (or any other army participating in the War Between the States) is to be found in the *Official Records*, published by the War Department at Washington. Aside from this vast and priceless store of documentary material, I am indebted chiefly to the published sources as listed below. Very little unpublished manuscript material has been discovered, aside from a few minor items in the author's collection of Confederate historical letters and documents.

Published Books

Alexander, Augustus W.: *Grant as a Soldier.* St. Louis, 1887.

Alexander, E. P.: *Military Memoirs of a Confederate.* Scribner's, New York, 1907.

Berry, Col. Thomas F.: *Four Years with Morgan and Forrest.* Oklahoma City, Okla., 1914.

Boynton, H. V.: *Sherman's Historical Raid.* Cincinnati, 1875.

Buck, Irving A.: *Cleburne and His Command.* Neale, New York, 1908.

Burne, Col. Alfred H.: *Lee, Grant and Sherman.* Scribner's, New York, 1939.

Connelley, William Elsey: *Quantrill and the Border Wars.* Cedar Rapids, Iowa, 1910.

Chesnut, Mary Boykin: *A Diary from Dixie.* Appleton, New York, 1905.

Cox, Jacob D.: *Atlanta.* Scribner's, New York, 1909.

———: *The March to the Sea—Franklin and Nashville.* Scribner's, New York, 1906.

Cumming, Kate: *A Journal of Hospital Life.* Louisville, 1866.

Davis, Jefferson: *The Rise and Fall of the Confederate Government,* 2 volumes. Appleton, New York, 1881.

Dinkins, James: *1861 to 1865—by an Old Johnnie.* Cincinnati, 1897.

DuBose, John Witherspoon: *General Joseph Wheeler and the Army of Tennessee.* Neale, New York, 1912.

Duke, Basil W.: *Morgan's Cavalry.* Neale, New York, 1906.

———: *Reminiscences of General Basil W. Duke.* Doubleday, Page, Garden City, N. Y., 1911.

Fiske, John: *The Mississippi Valley in the Civil War.* Houghton Mifflin, Boston, 1900.

483

Force, M. F.: *From Fort Henry to Corinth*. Scribner's, New York, 1908.

Freeman, Douglas Southall (Editor): *Lee's Dispatches*. Putnam's, New York, 1915.

Fremantle, Lieut. Col. Arthur Lyon: *Three Months in the Southern States*. New York, 1864.

French, Gen. S. G.: *Two Wars—An Autobiography*. Nashville, 1901.

Gracie, Archibald: *The Truth About Chickamauga*. Houghton Mifflin, 1911.

Grant, Ulysses S.: *Letters of Ulysses S. Grant*. Putnam's, New York, 1912.

———: *Personal Memoirs*, 2 volumes in 1. Webster, New York, 1894.

Hay, Thomas Robson: *Hood's Tennessee Campaign*. Neale, New York, 1929.

Head, Thomas A.: *Campaigns and Battles of the Sixteenth Regiment*. Nashville, 1885.

Hood, J. B.: *Advance and Retreat*. New Orleans, 1880.

Johnson, Robert Underwood, and Buel, Clarence Clough (Editors): *Battles and Leaders of the Civil War*, 4 volumes. Century, New York, 1887.

Johnston, Joseph E.: *Narrative of Military Operations*. Appleton, New York, 1874.

Johnston, William Preston: *Life of General Albert Sidney Johnston*. Appleton, New York, 1878.

Jones, J. B.: *A Rebel War Clerk's Diary*. Lippincott, Philadelphia, 1866.

Jones, J. William: *Life and Letters of Robert Edward Lee*. Neale, New York, 1906.

Jordan, Gen. Thomas, and Pryor, J. P.: *The Campaigns of Lieut. Gen. N. B. Forrest*. Blelock, New Orleans, 1868.

Livermore, Thomas L.: *Numbers and Losses in the Civil War*. Houghton Mifflin, Boston, 1900.

Longstreet, James: *From Manassas to Appomattox*. Lippincott, Philadelphia, 1896.

Marshall, Park: *A Life of William B. Bate*. Nashville, 1908.

Morgan, Mrs. Irby: *How It Was—Four Years Among the Rebels*. Nashville, 1892.

McMurray, W. J.: *History of the Twentieth Tennessee Regiment*. Nashville, 1904.

My Cave Life in Vicksburg, by a Lady. Appleton, New York, 1864.

Nash, Chas. E.: *Biographical Sketches of Gen. Pat Cleburne and Gen. T. C. Hindman*. Little Rock, 1898.

Nicolay, John G.: *The Outbreak of Rebellion*. Scribner's, New York, 1905.

Noll, Arthur Howard: *General Kirby Smith*. Sewanee, 1907.

———— (Editor): *Bishop Quintard's Memoirs of the War*. Sewanee, 1905.

Oates, William C.: *The War Between the States*. Neale, New York, 1905.

Pickett, W. D.: *Sketch of the Military Career of William J. Hardee*. Lexington, 1910.

Peckham, James: *General Nathaniel Lyon and Missouri in 1861*. New York, 1866.

Polk, Wm. M.: *Leonidas Polk, Bishop and General*, 2 volumes. Longmans, New York, 1893.

Pollard, Edward A.: *The Lost Cause*. New York, 1866.

————: *Southern History of the War*, 2 volumes. New York, 1866.

————: *Rebellion Record*, 5 volumes. G. P. Putnam, New York, 1863.

Reed, Major D. W.: *The Battle of Shiloh*. Washington, 1909.

Reed, Samuel Rockwell: *The Vicksburg Campaign*. Cincinnati, 1882.

Rich, Joseph W.: *The Battle of Shiloh*. Iowa City, Iowa, 1911.

Richardson, James D. (Editor): *Messages and Papers of the Confederacy*. Nashville, 1905.

Ridley, Bromfield L.: *Battles and Sketches of the Army of Tennessee*. Mexico, Missouri, 1906.

Roman, Alfred: *The Military Operations of General Beauregard*, 2 volumes. Harper, New York, 1884.

Rosecrans' Campaign With the Fourteenth Army Corps, by "W. D. B." Cincinnati, 1863.

Rowland, Dunbar (Editor): *Jefferson Davis, Constitutionalist; His Letters, Papers and Speeches*, 10 volumes. Jackson, Miss., 1923.

Schofield, Lieut. Gen. John M.: *Forty-Six Years in the Army*. Century, New York, 1897.

Schofield, Levi T.: *The Retreat From Pulaski to Nashville*. Cleveland, 1909.

Seitz, Don C.: *Braxton Bragg, General of the Confederacy*. Columbia, 1924.

Sherman, W. T.: *Home Letters of General Sherman*. Scribner's, New York, 1909.

————: *Personal Memoirs*, 2 volumes. Webster, New York, 1892.

Snow, Capt. William P.: *Lee and His Generals*. New York, 1867.

Sorrel, Gen. G. Moxley: *Recollections of a Confederate Staff Officer*. Neale, New York, 1905.

Stanley, Henry M.: *Autobiography of Henry M. Stanley*. Houghton, Mifflin, Boston, 1906.

Steele, Matthew Forney: *American Campaigns*, 2 volumes. Washington (War Dept.), 1909.

Stevenson, A. F.: *The Battle of Stone's River*. Osgood, Boston, 1884.

Stickles, Arndt M.: *Simon Bolivar Buckner*. Chapel Hill, 1940.

Taylor, Richard, *Destruction and Reconstruction*. Appleton, New York, 1879.

Thirteen Months in the Rebel Army, by an Impressed New Yorker. New York, 1862.

Turchin, John B.: *Chickamauga*. Chicago, 1888.

War of the Rebellion, Official Records of the Union and Confederate Armies, 128 volumes. Washington, 1881-1900.

Watkins, Samuel R.: *Co. "Aytch"—First Tennessee Regiment*. Nashville, 1882.

Watson, William: *Life in the Confederate Army*. New York, 1888.

Worsham, Dr. W. J.: *The Old Nineteenth Tennessee*. Knoxville, 1902.

Worthington, T.: *Shiloh: The Only Correct Military History of U. S. Grant*. Washington, 1872.

Wyeth, John Allan: *Life of Gen. Nathan Bedford Forrest*. Harper, New York, 1899.

Young, John R.: *Around the World with General Grant*. New York, 1879.

NEWSPAPERS AND PERIODICALS

I have consulted the files of contemporaneous Southern newspapers freely, principally for background information. References in the text are mostly from the *Patriot* and the *Union and American* of Nashville and the *Appeal* of Memphis, for the years 1861-1862.

Annals of the Army of Tennessee, The, Vol. I (All published). Nashville, 1878.

Century Magazine. April, 1897.

Confederate Veteran, The, 40 volumes. Nashville, 1893-1932.

The Franklin Yeoman, Franklin, Ky.

Land We Love, The, 6 volumes. Charlotte, 1866-1869.

Southern Bivouac, The, 6 volumes. Louisville, 1886-1887.

Southern Historical Society Papers, 49 volumes. Richmond, 1876.

MAPS

The maps used in illustrating the text were prepared by Frances Tucker Horn, to whom I am much indebted for her assistance.

ACKNOWLEDGMENTS

My research and study in the history of the Army of Tennessee have extended over so many years and have brought me into pleasant contact with so many people that it would be impossible for me to enumerate all those to whom I am under obligations for assistance, advice and information. Should I attempt a list of all those who have helped me it would, I fear, be far from complete. I therefore resort to the unsatisfactory expedient of here expressing my appreciation to all the many generous spirits—friends, acquaintances and strangers—who have assisted me in gathering together the raw material of this biography of an army. To them, as well as to those who have helped me in the preparation of the manuscript, I say: I thank you. To the following publishers grateful acknowledgment is made for their permission to reprint material as indicated:

Houghton Mifflin Company, Boston
    Autobiography of Henry M. Stanley
    The Mississippi Valley in the Civil War, by John Fiske
    Numbers and Losses in the Civil War, by Thos. L. Livermore

Charles Scribner's Sons, New York
    The Campaigns of the Civil War
    "Romance" from Poems, by W. E. Henley

Longmans, Green & Co., New York
    Leonidas Polk: Bishop and General, by Wm. M. Polk

The State Company, Columbia
    Braxton Bragg, by Don C. Seitz

G. P. Putnam's Sons, New York
    Lee's Dispatches, Douglas Southall Freeman, Editor

Harper & Bros., New York
    Life of Gen. Nathan Bedford Forrest, by John Allan Wyeth
    The Military Operations of General Beauregard, by Alfred Roman

Lippincott, Philadelphia
    From Manassas to Appomattox, by James Longstreet

University of North Carolina Press, Chapel Hill
    Simon Bolivar Buckner, by Arndt M. Stickles

Doubleday, Doran & Co., New York

Reminiscences of General Basil W. Duke, by Basil W. Duke, copyright, 1911.

Appleton-Century Co., New York
    Battles and Leaders of the Civil War
    A Diary From Dixie, Mrs. Mary Boykin Chesnut
    Forty-Six Years in the Army, Gen. John M. Schofield

S.F.H.

INDEX

INDEX

491